In the Wake of War

IN THE WAKE
OF WAR

The Reconstruction of German Cities after World War II

JEFFRY M. DIEFENDORF

New York   Oxford
Oxford University Press
1993

Oxford University Press

Oxford   New York   Toronto
Delhi   Bombay   Calcutta   Madras   Karachi
Kuala Lumpur   Singapore   Hong Kong   Tokyo
Nairobi   Dar es Salaam   Cape Town
Melbourne   Auckland   Madrid

and associated companies in
Berlin   Ibadan

Published by Oxford University Press, Inc.,
200 Madison Avenue, New York, New York 10016

Oxford is a registered trademark of Oxford University Press

Library of Congress Cataloging-in-Publication Data
Diefendorf, Jeffry M., 1945–
In the wake of war : the reconstruction of German cities after
World War II / Jeffry M. Diefendorf.
p.   cm.   Includes bibliographical references and index.
ISBN 0-19-507219-7
1. Urban renewal—Germany—History—20th century.
2. City planning—Germany—History—20th century.
3. Reconstruction (1945–1951)—Germany.
I. Title.   HT178.G4D54   1993   307.76′0943′09045—dc20   92-28145

2 4 6 8 9 7 5 3 1

Printed in the United States of America
on acid-free paper

For Barbara

Acknowledgments

This work, forged over many years, would not have been possible without strong financial support. I received fellowships or grants from the National Endowment for the Humanities, the National Science Foundation, the University of New Hampshire, the Hoover Institution at Stanford University, the Woodrow Wilson Center for International Scholars, and the Alexander von Humboldt Foundation. A travel grant from the German Academic Exchange Service (DAAD) made it possible to spend a summer collecting photographs in German archives. The generosity of these institutions has been greatly appreciated. I am also indebted to a great many Germans and Americans, more than I can acknowledge individually here, who provided valuable help and encouragement along the way. I offer my thanks to the many librarians and archivists in Germany and the United States who shared their expertise and advice. In particular I am grateful for the help rendered by my research assistants Dana Hollander (at the Wilson Center) and Rani Tudor (at New Hampshire). Friedrich-Wilhelm Henning, Hermann Wellenreuther, and Werner Durth kindly served as my sponsors and hosts during my stay in Germany as a Humboldt Fellow. Paul Müllejans and Klaus-Dieter Ebert, directors of the city building administrations in Aachen and Hamburg, went out of their way to provide access to materials not yet turned over to the public archives. My sincere thanks also to Niels Gutschow, Werner Durth, Karl Böttcher, and Hartmut Frank for sharing primary materials from their own collections and manuscripts of their work. The many scholars who commented on papers presented at different forums in Germany and the United States, and the anonymous readers of the manuscripts which subsequently appeared as journal articles helped clarify my thinking. While a fellow at the Woodrow Wilson Center, I benefitted greatly from the penetrating and stimulating comments on my work offered by other fellows and by those who participated in my colloquium there, including Dietrich Orlow, who was the main commentator. Diethelm Prove and Andrew Lees, who read this manuscript for Oxford, made useful suggestions for clarifying my arguments and helped me avoid some errors. Terri Winters of the University of New Hampshire assisted in preparing the graphs. I must also thank Elisabeth Nichols, who read the manuscript with great care, suggested many stylistic improvements, and pointed out problematic passages that required revisions.

Several architects and planners who had been active participants in postwar reconstruction were kind enough to grant me interviews. For this I wish to thank Karl Böttcher, Arthur Dähn, Hans von Hanffstengel, Rudolf Hillebrecht, Gunther Kühne, Helmut Prost, Theodor Schüler, and Hans Speck. Their observations sometimes provided answers to questions that still remained after my labors in the archives.

Luchterhand Literaturverlag of Hamburg kindly gave permission to quote two stanzas from Günter Grass's poem "Die große Trümmerfrau spricht." Chapman and Hall of London granted permission to reprint parts of my article "Reconstruction Law in Germany," which first appeared in *Planning Perspectives* in 1986. Similarly *Central European History* granted permission to reprint parts of "Konstanty Gutschow and the Reconstruction of Hamburg," which appeared in 1985, and Sage Publications granted permission to reprint parts of "Artery: Traffic Planning in Postwar Germany," which appeared in *The Journal of Urban History* in 1989. My thanks to all four of these publishers.

The following institutions generously granted permission to reproduce photographs: the Landesbildstelle Berlin; Bildstelle und Denkmalsarchiv, Nuremberg; Staatliche Landesbildstelle Hamburg; Landesbildstelle Württemberg; Presseamt der Landeshauptstadt Hannover; Verkehrsamt der Stadt Köln; Museum für Kunst und Kulturgeschichte der Hansestadt Lübeck; Rheinisches Bildarchiv, Cologne; and the Freie und Hansestadt Hamburg, Baubehörde-Lichtbildnerei. Michael Brix (Munich) and Christian Dalchow (Cologne) each granted permission to reproduce a photograph. Materal from the Gropius papers is cited by permission of the Houghton Library of Harvard University. Several publishers granted permission to reproduce tabular material, including: the Architekten- und Ingenieur-Verein Hamburg, Bund Deutscher Architekten, and Bertlesmann Fachzeitschriften.

During my research in Germany, several friends offered me extended hospitality, which made long hours in archives and libraries much easier to bear. For this my thanks to Hildegard and Claus Caspers, Evami and Aad Boonstoppel, Hermann-Josef Rupieper, Jim Shedel and Marilu Woods, Hilde and Robert Silberberger, and Elisabeth and Günther Marshall-Wagoner. Finally, as has been the case throughout my career, my thanks to two special persons, my aunt Elizabeth Rosenfield and my wife Barbara Diefendorf. With patience over the years they read pieces of the manuscript—sometimes several times—and offered well-considered, constructive criticism from which my thinking and my prose have always benefited.

Contents

Introduction, xi

1. Bombs and Rubble: The Air War and Its Consequences, 3
   The War from the Air, 4
   Cities of Rubble, 13

2. Work Amidst the Rubble, 18
   Rubble Clearance and the Repair of Utilities, 19
   Material for Rebuilding, 30
   Labor in the Construction Industry, 36
   Legal and Illegal Building, 38

3. The Face of Reconstruction: Architectural Style, 43
   The Bauhaus and Deutscher Werkbund, 45
   Heimatschutz and Traditional Architecture, 48
   Nazi Architecture and Neoclassicism, 50
   Postwar Architecture, 54

4. The Face of Reconstruction: The Role of Historic Preservation, 67
   Principles of Historic Preservation, 70
   Modernizing Cities, 74
   Determined Preservationism, 83
   Modernization and Preservation, 90
   Conclusion, 106

5. The Housing Problem, 108
   Cooperative Housing, 110
   Housing Policy under the National Socialists, 113
   Postwar Housing, 125

6. Town Planning to 1945, 151
    Planning Traditions before 1933, 152
    Urban Planning during the Third Reich, 158
        The Representative Cities Program, 160
        From Representative Cities to Reconstruction, 166
        Reconstruction Planning, 169

7. Planning and Planners after 1945, 181
    The Postwar Planners, 182
    Planning Models, 188
        The Extremes, 190
        Pragmatic Planning, 201
    Traffic Planning, 205
    Conclusion, 218

8. Reconstruction and Building Law, 221
    The Framework: Building Law and Proposals for Reform to 1945, 222
    The Postwar Debate: Defining the Scope of a New Building Law, 225
    Opposition to the New Laws: Property Rights and Politics 231
    The Struggle for a National Building Law, 235
    Politics, Democracy, and the Law, 240

9. Organizing Reconstruction, 243
    The Role of the Allied Occupation Governments, 244
    State and National Reconstruction Agencies, 251
    The National Associations and Their Affiliates, 253
    Organization at the Town Level, 255
        Traditional Practice, 255
        Extraordinary Agencies, 258
    Conclusion 273

10. Conclusion, 275

    Notes, 285
    Works Cited, 365
    Index, 393

Introduction

Writing a history of the rebuilding of Germany's cities after World War II has proven to be an intensely challenging and richly rewarding project. As my research progressed, new questions and material continually forced reconsideration of my research design and my hypotheses. Urban reconstruction is a complex and to many an emotionally charged subject replete with subtle intricacies and major implications for the conceptualization of the history of modern Germany. A sketch of the origins and evolution of this book will help explain its structure.

My interest in the subject began in the fall of 1977, when, as an "academic expert on Germany," I accompanied a University of New Hampshire alumni tour that began in Munich. On the bus ride from the airport, these tourists, some of whom had visited Germany right after the war, posed demanding questions. How could I explain the apparent harmony of the street scenes and the smooth flow of traffic in Munich? When we reached the Marienplatz, Munich's main square, I was asked to explain the disharmony between the old (the town hall) and the new (a Kaufhof department store). And even as they asked questions, these tourists offered their own answers: Munich was rebuilt through the generosity of American Marshall Plan aid and under the influence of American architectural values.

The tourists' provocative questions opened my eyes to scenes I had previously taken for granted. Though I taught modern German history, my general reading had never touched on the physical rebuilding of the bombed cities. The standard texts on postwar Germany dealt extensively with economic recovery, with the building of a new, democratic state and democratic political parties, with the Western orientation of West German foreign policy in the context of the Cold War, and to a lesser extent with the revival of literature and the arts, but they contained very little about how Germany met basic human needs, such as food, clothing, and in this case, shelter. Having to rebuild, brick by brick, a complex urban structure that had been reduced to rubble presented an extraordinary challenge, one that undoubtedly engaged the attention of most Germans in the years following the war, and yet almost nothing had been written on the subject by historians.

The Marienplatz represented a more complex blend of old and new than my group of tourists realized. The town hall they admired as historic was a neo-Gothic creation of the nineteenth century which had survived the bombing. They overlooked completely the older, smaller, Renaissance town hall, which had been destroyed and rebuilt. And the orderly pedestrian zone in the town center resulted not from postwar reconstruction planning but from planning and construction in the late 1960s and early 1970s in preparation for the Munich Olympic games.

Although unaware of such features, the tourists raised thought-provoking issues. I realized how often I had stood in one or another of Germany's churches—like the Marienkirche in Munich—and wondered at mounted photographs of the ruined building as it had stood in 1945. The roof was gone, the towers collapsed, the windows blown out, the interior filled with rubble, and the battered shell surrounded by other bombed and burned buildings. Yet now the church stood again, repaired and rebuilt, the new work blending discreetly with remains of the original building. Postwar repairs have acquired the patina of age. Were it not for pictures and the memories of those who experienced Germany during the war and the decade after, one would hardly realize the extent of the war's devastation. For me, and for the tourists, the photographs of the bombed cities held a certain fascination. Physical evidence of the bombing, broken bits of masonry, glass, and iron, had long since disappeared, and the images of the ruins seemed almost romantic and charming.

How had Munich been rebuilt? Who had been responsible? Why was one building restored in its historic form while others were replaced with modern buildings? What role had the Americans played, whether as representatives of the military occupation or as donors of Marshall aid? The rapidly multiplying questions resisted simple answers.

Reconstruction of the bombed cities had begun under extraordinarily difficult circumstances. Much of the infrastructure upon which cities normally depend had been completely disabled. Major transportation systems had suffered extensive damage, which exacerbated rubble removal and the flow of building materials, not to mention the supply of food and clothing for a dislocated population. Skilled labor was in short supply, with many able-bodied men incarcerated as prisoners of war. Commodity exchange, the letting of contracts, and financing were highly irregular in what became a virtual barter economy. Germany's unconditional surrender and the destruction of the Nazi state threw all law, including pre-Nazi law, into question, and basic decisions lay in the hands of the occupying forces or ad hoc local authorities. Those Germans not badly compromised by association with the Nazi regime cautiously laid plans for a new Germany while seeking to reach back into the past for acceptable cultural antecedents upon which to base a revival of public life. They were often frustrated by the fact that the Nazis had appropriated and therefore spoiled some of the most powerful symbols of a common past. In short, circumstances could hardly have been less auspicious and less promising for a rapid recovery of this highly industrial, urban society.

Moreover, the industrial revolution had brought with it a great many urban problems, such as pollution, overcrowding, poor housing, and inadequate transportation. In spite of the horrific conditions of 1945, Germany conceivably had the opportunity to correct or ameliorate these problems during postwar reconstruction and to build functional, livable urban centers. How did Germans balance the desire to reconstruct the past with the desire to build truly modern cities? Who made such decisions, and how? Where did financing come from, and who profited or lost in the process? What accounted for regional variations?

After some inquiries in American and German libraries, I initially proposed a comparative study of three cities: Cologne, Berlin, and Munich. Cologne was a city I knew quite well. Berlin, which I also knew to some extent, presented the additional challenging feature of being a divided city. Munich, according to the polls, was the favorite German city for natives and tourists alike. Cologne was in the British occupation zone, Munich in the American, and Berlin had been administered by all the powers. My interest was primarily in the rebuilding of the bombed centers of these cities, the historic cores which had determined the identity of each, and much less in building activity that took place on the fringes or in the suburbs.

At the time I began the research, I labored under several misconceptions. First, I felt that a comparison of the three cities would be sufficient to yield meaningful conclusions to the many questions that demanded attention. Second, I felt I could limit my study to the period from 1945 to 1955. It seemed obvious that rebuilding began after the bombing ceased, and German acquaintances who shared their memories of the postwar years insisted that nothing had been done about reconstruction during the war. A good, practical cutoff point appeared to be 1955, because German archival law sometimes made access to more recent documents impossible.

Gradually I found that a few other scholars in Germany had also begun to work on urban reconstruction. New and important work appeared on Münster and Würzburg, for example. This opened the possibility of basing my conclusions on more than just three cities. Furthermore, Germans were always saying: "Ah, but it was different in Düsseldorf," or Hamburg, or Stuttgart, or wherever, and I heard this refrain often enough to begin doubting my original research design. I therefore visited other cities to enlarge my perspective. Would it not be much more interesting to write about urban reconstruction in the whole Federal Republic? (I could leave what was then East Germany, the German Democratic Republic, aside with good conscience, since archival material was generally inaccessible there, and the task of understanding reconstruction in West Germany seemed formidable enough.) I continued to focus on the rebuilding of the cores of what Germans label *Großstädte*, cities which had populations of more than 100,000 in 1939.

While working in Hamburg, I contacted Niels Gutschow, who had just produced a two-volume study of reconstruction in Münster. This contact decisively influenced my project. Niels turned out to be the son of Konstanty Gutschow, an architect/city planner who in 1938 had been made responsible for redesigning Hamburg into a representative Nazi city. Although many of Konstanty Gutschow's official papers from the Nazi period rested in the Hamburg State Archives, his personal papers—a vast collection—remained in the hands of the family, and Niels generously granted me unlimited access to them. Moreover, this private archive contained correspondence, plans, drawings, and essays, published and unpublished, from the pens of dozens of planners and architects from 1938 into the 1950s and 1960s. Indeed, during the hours spent in the Gutschow home, I was both invigorated and exasperated by the richness of the material. No sooner had I tackled one set of documents than Niels appeared with another bulging binder of materials that veered off into still another direction. Here, for example, was an enormous amount of evidence indicating that systematic reconstruction planning began as early as 1943 within an organization in Albert Speer's ministry under the effective leadership of Konstanty Gutschow. Here too was evidence of frequent informal and formal exchanges of ideas between town planners from cities throughout Germany, which buttressed and confirmed my decision to go beyond a study of three supposedly isolated cases.

My starting date of 1945 also had to be abandoned. My topic now demanded study of the Nazi era, because I had to relate postwar reconstruction to the planning, architecture, and ideology of National Socialism. Nor was I alone. Niels Gutschow and Werner Durth, a historian of urban design at the University of Mainz, were already engaged in a study of the impact of wartime planning, based primarily on the Gutschow papers. I knew, however, that our perspectives would differ considerably. An American necessarily approaches a subject like fascist architecture and city planning and its legacy in modern urban life with less passion than a German either of my generation or of the generation that experienced the 1930s and 1940s. Niels Gutschow and Werner Durth had to struggle with the fact that their fathers and teachers had pursued careers during the Nazi period. Indeed, the Third Reich may be too immediate for Gutschow, Durth, and others of their generation; continuities between the Nazi and postwar periods take on far greater weight for them than continuities between the period before Hitler and the postwar period.

In any event, my exploration of the Gutschow papers and my discussions with Gutschow and Durth—and the reading of their published work—forced me to rethink my own conception of reconstruction.[1] Comparing the prewar appearance of German cities with their postwar appearance suggested fundamental, even radical change. No city was rebuilt as an exact copy of what had been destroyed. Most of the buildings date from the period after 1945, and newer buildings have been rebuilt behind historic facades. Upon examining the continuities between the Nazi and postwar periods, however, I became more convinced that, paradoxically, postwar rebuilding could be understood only in terms of continuities that reached back to the years before Hitler's 12-year Reich. Indeed, not only did these continuities exist, they informed Germany's surprisingly rapid reconstruction.

The impression conveyed in photographs of the ruins of Germany's cities in the spring of 1945 is one of complete and total devastation. Only a few buildings remained intact, and they stood alone amidst blocks of gutted buildings, walls without roofs and floors, mounds of twisted rubble. Contemporary observers clearly shared this impression. A group of senior American military officers toured several of the bombed cities by jeep between 17 and 22 April, just before the war ended. Of Nuremberg they reported: "This is the worst of all, hardly anything but dust. The medieval city center [is] obliterated, including parts of the old city walls. The Cathedral is shattered. A razed city, Biblical annihilation. No such destruction of a large city ever known." Of Cologne: "One gets a feeling of horror; nothing, nothing is left." And finally: "The implications of the destruction of Germany's industries and cities are beyond the reach of the war-bound imagination."[2]

To observers of this scene of "Biblical annihilation," it was logical that it would take a very long time to rebuild the German cities, if indeed they were worth rebuilding at all.[3] Hans Pieper, Lübeck's town planner from 1927 until his death in 1946, estimated that rebuilding would take 60 to 80 years.[4] Yet, as we know, the cities were rebuilt much faster than these predictions promised. Part of the explanation for this is that the impression that "nothing was left" exaggerated the extent of the destruction. In fact much remained: underground utilities, streets, foundations, structurally sound walls, and a great many intact or only moderately damaged buildings outside the areas where the bombs had fallen most thickly. But significant intangible legacies also made profound contributions to reconstruction. A complex heritage of urban planning concepts and practice only waited to be tapped; a 20-year-old discussion of building law could be promptly resumed; a strong tradition of public housing could be drawn upon; a longstanding debate about architectural styles and methods could define and shape new building; and finally, a rich human legacy of planners, architects, professionals, entrepreneurs, property owners, and citizens informed the reconstruction process. These people had contemplated rebuilding, weighed priorities, and evaluated resources, even as the bombs wreaked havoc in their cities.[5]

Because so much remained, reconstruction was not beyond the imaginative reach of many survivors of the devastating war. On the contrary, hundreds of Germans who were part of this architectural and planning legacy declared that the destruction should be viewed as an unprecedented opportunity to implement their ideas and plans, and they were eager to begin work. Thus Ludwig Neundörfer, postwar chairman of the Frankfurt group of the Deutscher Werkbund and director of the Socio-geographic Institute of the university, noted that "the bombing attacks have particularly affected the socially most unhealthy housing in the metropolis—the areas of slums and the overbuilt and too-densely inhabited old central city. From this there is now a unique chance for housing reform, for a liquidation of the fatal inheritance of the 19th century."[6] Hans Scharoun, Berlin's first postwar planner and an important proponent of modern architecture, observed that "the mechanical opening up [of Berlin] by the bombing and final battle gives us now the opportunity for a generous, organic, and functional renewal."[7] It is easy to find similar statements in the first postwar years in virtually every publication dealing with reconstruction.

However tempting it was and is to view 1945 as a great break in German urban history, a "zero hour" as some Germans call it, significant continuities linked the periods before and after 1945. Indeed, in terms of these intangible legacies, 1945 marks the midpoint rather than the beginning of an era. It is also crucial to recognize that in urban affairs the Nazi period is an intrinsic component of modern German history and not an aberration signaling a peculiar discontinuity. Many of the planning and building practices of the 1920s can be found throughout the 1930s, during the war, and after. I do not mean to detract from the horror of the Third Reich or the crime of Nazi persecutions when I point out that this era lasted only 12 years and that this fact made it easier for some Germans, themselves unaffected by the persecutions, to emerge from it desiring only to forget and rebuild, as if the Hitler years were some sort of natural disaster or, in the words of one commentator, "an industrial accident, whose consequences one can and must erase as quickly as possible through the restoration of former conditions."[8] Planners and architects vividly remembered discussions of architecture and planning following World War I, and many suppressed memories of the Third Reich in favor of resuming this older dialogue.

Of this suppression of memory, of the widespread desire to avoid coming to grips with the recent past, of the insistence on concentrating on the tasks at hand—of this there can be no doubt. I am not the only scholar to reject the existence of a complete zero hour in German urban history, but unlike many of my German colleagues, I do not want my denial of the zero hour myth to be construed as a means primarily of confronting the Nazi period.[9] Important connections with the pre-Nazi period existed, but similarities between reconstruction in Germany and in other countries also suggest that a single-minded fixation on the Nazi period would distort an analysis of reconstruction.[10]

What kind of periodization, then, is appropriate for a study of urban reconstruction? At least three possibilities presented themselves. First, if one conceives of the reconstruction of the bombed cities as a process that began with plans and models created in response to specific acts of destruction, then the beginning point is surely right after Germany's cities began to burn and crumble—that is, soon after the first great air raid against a major city, Lübeck, during the night of 28–29 March 1942. In cities like Hamburg, however, even those initial reconstruction plans reflected earlier grandiose schemes of the Nazis to redesign the metropolises into cities representative of the new National Socialist state. And if one continues to focus primarily on reconstruction plans and concepts, then the terminal point of 1950 chosen by Werner Durth and Niels Gutschow may well be appropriate. By that point, or very soon thereafter, most cities had approved their overall reconstruction plans.

Second, if one conceives of reconstruction not so much in terms of plans—many of which were truly dreams, as Durth and Gutschow call them—but rather in terms of real, practical activities, such as rubble removal, the repairs of damaged buildings, the manufacture of building materials, the decisions on priorities, financing, and the like, then the beginning point is early 1945, when the first occupation forces arrived on German soil. The terminal point for reconstruction in this sense, however, has not yet been reached. Cologne finished rebuilding its Romanesque churches only in 1985. West Berlin still has a large, unreconstructed area in the former diplomatic quarter near the Philharmonic, though this area will rapidly fill with buildings now that the Berlin Wall has disappeared. Indeed, virtually every West German city has building sites where real reconstruction has not yet taken place. Small, one-story shops in the middle of a block of five- or six-story buildings are usually buildings erected quickly after the war as "temporary" shops, with the expectation that larger, more permanent buildings would follow. And follow they do, as even current construction projects still seek to fulfill that mandate.

Third, one might also conceive of reconstruction primarily as part of a larger, long-term process of urban renewal, urban modernization, and urban expansion in the industrial twentieth century. For example, streets were widened during reconstruction in every German city in order to ease the congestion caused by the growing use of automobiles, but this happened in un-bombed cities as well, both inside and outside of Germany. Some of what happened during reconstruction thus might well have happened anyway, even in cities unscathed by the war. In this conceptualization, then, the reconstruction process is continuous and ongoing in all metropolitan centers.

The strategy I finally chose for this book draws on all three periodization schemes. Depending upon the topic, my discussion begins in the early twentieth century, during the war, or at the war's end. On the other hand, the terminal point in this book always falls between 1955 and 1960. Readers with memories of the 1950s may be puzzled by this, since it is true that many cities still boasted huge, empty, unreconstructed blocks even at the end of that decade. There are several reasons, however, for ending this story with the period between 1955 and 1960. In the bombed cities, planners and citizens shared a consciousness that the bombing had created a unique situation. Some viewed it as an opportunity to introduce needed changes; others viewed it as proof that change had to be resisted in favor of recapturing the special spirit of the vanished towns. I would argue that sometime between 1955 and 1960 this consciousness of *reconstructing* bombed cities faded away and was replaced by a conceptualization of urban change as part of a broader and more general process of growth and modernization.

Right after the war some planners rejected the term *Wiederaufbau*, or reconstruction, as misleading, and by the mid-1950s nearly all avoided talking of *Wiederaufbau* and spoke instead of *Aufbau* or *Neubau*, that is, building expansion or new building.[11] In his 1987 book on reconstruction, Klaus von Beyme argues that the first phase of rebuilding ended in 1960, when a wave of new criticism derided the principles underlying the first 15 years of rebuilding activity, particularly the attempts at functional decentralization and the lowering of urban densities in the central cities. Like Jane Jacobs in the United States, whose work was quickly read in Germany, German critics praised the vitality and urbanity of the densely populated, multifunctional neighborhoods in pre-war cities.[12] The fact that these criticisms appeared in 1960 indicates that what von Beyme calls the first phase had really already ended, and even he notes that the middle of the 1950s witnessed a widespread acceptance and even endorsement of social, economic, intellectual, and urban modernization.[13]

That a change in German thinking took place in the mid-1950s can also be seen in the shift from a self-consciously modest period of reconstruction to a period of new construction that was robust, self-congratulatory, and anticipating a modern future. Typical of the modest approach was Joseph Schlippe. In his plans for rebuilding Freiburg, he called for "a greater measure of the lost trait of humility" and rejected "brutal muscular gestures, whether derived from the Wilhelmine era or from the New Objectivity, whether Nazi or 'organic.' "[14] The "Economic Miracle," however, soon overwhelmed attempts at modest reconstruction. In many cities, still-standing facades of historic buildings were demolished to make way for new buildings. Indicative of the new-found confidence in modern building were the Thyssen company skyscraper in Düsseldorf and the residential towers of the Hansa Viertel in West Berlin, all planned and built in 1956–57.[15]

Finally, a wave of decisive developments between 1955 and 1960, which in themselves had nothing to do with the rebuilding of the cities, reinforced the public's awareness that a new age had truly begun. The Federal Republic joined the European Economic Community and NATO. The Economic Miracle bloomed brilliantly, generating record growth levels. By 1957, the work week had shrunk to 49 hours, the same as at the end of the 1930s.[16] Germany now financed its own economic growth as Marshall Plan aid had ceased. For West Germany, the postwar era of deprivation had finally ended; the echoes of exploding bombs resounded faintly if at all.

This history of reconstruction does not attempt to catalog developments in each individual city. Each experienced the process of reconstruction uniquely. Each city had boasted an individually identifiable physical structure before the war, experienced varying degrees and kinds of bomb damage, proposed widely divergent reconstruction plans, and so forth. Each city's reconstruction deserves a separate monograph.[17] This work draws selectively from research in more than two dozen public and private archives in Germany and the United States, from dozens of articles in German architectural journals of the postwar period, from published documents, and from archival studies by other scholars. All told, I have found excellent material on nearly half of the 44 cities lying within the borders of the Federal Republic (before the 1990 unification with the German Democratic Republic) that had had populations of over 100,000 in 1939 (the so-called Großstädte) and on two-thirds of the 17 cities with more than 250,000 inhabitants in that year. Throughout I try to achieve a suitable balance between general themes and empirical detail. To demonstrate the continued vitality of pre-1945 ideas and practices in architecture, planning, law, and the like, I trace important developments from the early twentieth century through the end of the Third Reich. The primary emphasis, however, always centers on West German reconstruction after World War II.

Now that Germany has been unified, the local and state archives of the former German Democratic Republic operate under the access rules of the

Federal Republic. A detailed study of urban reconstruction in East Germany is thus possible for the first time. However, because there is so much material on West German cities, because the nature of reconstruction was so different in centralized, state-dominated, communist East Germany, and because the manuscript for this book was nearly finished by the time the two German states became one, I decided against trying to include East German reconstruction, a task that would have necessitated an enormous new research effort.

This book was written with several audiences in mind. On the one hand, I hope that anyone—including my tourists from years back—who has already visited or plans to visit Germany's cities will be able to use this study to deepen his or her understanding of the rebuilt cities. On the other hand, historians and students of modern Germany, of planning and architecture, and of urban development should discover much relevant material in the following chapters. I also hope that the book will find readers among those interested in current urban affairs in Germany and elsewhere. With these different audiences in mind, I have tried to avoid burdening the reader with too many technical terms. For example, because there has always been a great diversity in governmental forms and structure in German cities, the titles of town planners varied from place to place. These titles included, among others, *Oberbaurat, Baudezernent, Baudirektor*, and *Leiter des Stadtplanungsamts*. Heads of subsidiary offices might also engage in planning, and individuals lacking official titles worked on planning on a contractual basis. For the sake of simplicity, I use the term "planner" for all of these. Similarly, the terms used for different stages of the planning process varied from place to place, but except when it is important to distinguish between those stages, I usually just call them "plans."

It seems appropriate to begin this book with the ruins of the cities, that is, with the destruction of the air war and the immediate German response to fields of rubble. Having begun with bricks and stones, I turn to reconstruction in its most direct sense, namely architecture. The primary purpose of this book is not merely to describe the way cities appeared before the war and after reconstruction (although some of the illustrations are indeed "before and after" comparisons) because appearances are often deceiving. People see architecture, but they seldom "see" urban planning. Moreover, sometimes buildings which today appear unattractive, such as certain housing projects with plain gray facades, in fact functioned and still function quite successfully in terms of their original purpose. Rebuilding also included finding solutions to many problems that went beyond surface appearances, such as redrawing property lines to make the best use of inner-city building lots. Thus the discussion moves from the physical level of buildings to the more abstract level of planning and finally to the pragmatic level of attempts to implement planning. The new availability of important primary material and recent publication of scholarly work in the area of urban planning dictate that this subject be discussed at considerable length. For the convenience of the reader, urban planning is considered in two chapters, with 1945 as the dividing point.

The approach in this book, then, is topical and analytical. The reader should not lose sight of the underlying unity of the various activities discussed. Housing construction, town planning, repairing of historic monuments, clearing rubble, restructuring government offices, and rewriting building law all happened simultaneously. The individuals who designed buildings, drew up town plans, and drafted building laws shared the same profession. They had essentially the same training, read the same professional journals, and belonged to the same associations. Consequently many individuals weave in and out of the chapters that follow.

As I generalize, I must apologize to the many Germans still living who experienced the destruction and rebuilding of their cities and also to those non-Germans, like some of my original group of tourists, who were in Germany after the war and witnessed the rebuilding process. To these people my account will doubtless lack the intense reality of their experiences. This is the inevitable consequence of my decision to enlarge the scope of this study to the whole Federal Republic, to cast it in an analytical framework, and to include as many dimensions of the rebuilding process as possible. Recounting the debates over building law or discussing statistics on housing or building materials will seem arid to those who were there, who saw the horrendous destruction and witnessed the determined and ultimately successful struggle, amidst very great suffering, of a people to rebuild. I have had to experience all of this secondhand, through the records and artifacts left behind, and I respect both the struggle and its achievements. At the same time, I am aware as a historian of the mythmaking capabilities of all peoples who experience great struggles. I know that memories of those who lived through this period are selective. The scenes of vast annihilation and deprivation remain vivid, as does the sense of heroic recovery. The specific paths this recovery took, the many steps and mundane processes through which it was achieved, have either slipped from view or were never entirely visible to the observer who stood within the framework of these events. My task as a historian is to help recall in all its complexity that which has faded from memory, at the same time helping to construct a more unified, if necessarily more distant view of the process by which the West German cities were rebuilt.

In the Wake of War

1

Bombs and Rubble: The Air War and Its Consequences

The fascination of a city in ruins is undeniable. Newsreels from war zones reveal buildings in flames, roofs caving in, and walls collapsing, while civilians—the terrified inhabitants of those buildings?—flee. Sometimes they run for their lives; sometimes they try to salvage a few possessions. After the fighting has ended and the damaged buildings have been rebuilt, someone mounts a display showing the "before-and-after" conditions. Visitors still find such displays in many of Europe's churches and public buildings, but they are also to be found here and there in private shop windows. West Germany boasts a series of books entitled "Hamburg (substitute any city name)—then and now." These books are photographic depictions of the prewar condition of streets, squares, and individual buildings; their ruined condition after the war; and their appearance at the time of publication, often from the same spot. (Similar pictures appear in this book.)

What lies behind this preoccupation with ruined urban landscapes? Naturally those responsible for reconstruction want to display their accomplishments, but sometimes there is also a morbid, even perverse interest in the ruins themselves. This is not new. The romantics of the early nineteenth century not only portrayed individuals amidst ruins but even constructed artificial ruins when none were at hand.[1] Ruins, whether in paintings, photographs, or in the form of monuments, remind viewers of the fragility of civilization. An American scholar recently suggested that people may need some form of devastation in order to develop a historical sense and begin a process of cultural renewal.[2] Adolf Hitler and his favorite architect, Albert Speer, envisioned their huge buildings as ruins even before they were built, though they expected "their" ruins to be monuments to the greatness of Nazi Germany. In his memoirs, Speer told of his "Theory of Ruin Value":

The idea was that buildings of modern construction were poorly suited to form that "bridge of tradition" to future generations which Hitler was calling for. It was hard to imagine that rusting heaps of rubble would communicate these heroic inspirations which Hitler admired in the monuments of the past. My "theory" was intended to deal with this dilemma. By using special materials and by applying certain principles of statics, we should be able to build structures which even in a state of decay, after hundreds or (such were our reckonings) thousands of years would more or less resemble Roman models. To illustrate my ideas I had a romantic drawing prepared. It showed what the reviewing stand on the Zeppelin Field would look like after generations of neglect, overgrown with ivy, its columns fallen, the walls crumbling here and there, but the outlines still clearly recognizable.[3]

The romance with ruins was not pure fantasy. In his diary, George Kennan described a visit to the old center of Berlin 15 years after the war:

All about us were the ruins of the great old buildings, semi-silhouetted against the bright sky. And what ruins! In their original state they had seemed slightly imitative and pretentious. Now they suddenly had a grandeur I had never seen even in Rome. . . . There was a stillness, a beauty, a sense of infinite, elegiac sadness and timelessness such as I have never experienced. Death, obviously, was near, and in the air: hushed, august, brooding Death— and nothing else.[4]

Hitler's dreams in fact transformed all of Germany into "rusting heaps of rubble," monuments to death, though little remains now to remind current and future generations of Germans of the consequences of war.

Sometimes an abstract, comforting feature emerges from pictures of war ruins. When one is distant from the actual experience of the bombing, war can become a mechanical process of physical destruction of solid objects, not the maiming, burning, and killing of humans.[5] For the reader, the historian, the viewer of photographs, that distance may be one of time. For the strategists of aerial warfare, the physical distance from the bombing targets helped make their planning an abstract, statistical exercise, cut off from the real damage and terror of the bombing campaign.

Volumes have been written about the bombing campaigns of World War II, and it would serve no great purpose to go over that ground in detail here. But the subject of the rebuilding of destroyed, bombed-out cities warrants a few words about how they got that way.

The War from the Air

The idea of bombing cities from airplanes did not originate in World War II. Early in the twentieth century there already had been fantasies about the possible destructiveness of bombing from the air. During World War I the Germans and British conducted air raids on each other's cities, and with similar goals. In part bombing was an act of revenge, a reprisal for attacks on one's own population; in part it was motivated by the belief that air raids could undermine the enemy's morale in a long war of attrition.[6] In the 1920s, theoreticians like Guilio Douhet of Italy, Basil H. Liddell Hart of England, and Billy Mitchell of the United States predicted that in future wars bombing would destroy the "nerve centers" of urban, industrial society, causing those societies to break down, possibly into Bolshevik-style revolutions.[7] In the early 1930s, the Americans developed the doctrine of precision bombing: accurate attacks on carefully chosen industrial targets that would destroy the enemy's military capacity in an efficient way. Should this fail, however, cities must be bombed.[8] Military analysts did not in fact carefully assess the actual results of bombing that occurred during the wars in Ethiopia, China, and Spain, where bombing campaigns failed to undermine morale or prove decisive in bringing victory. Typically, the actual results of the bombing—or the lack of them—did *not* lead the proponents of air power to revise their thinking.[9] Moreover, all studies agree that comparatively little thought was devoted to the ethical questions involved in making war on noncombatants. Cities, after all, were inhabited mostly by civilians, however much industry might be located within a town.[10]

Nevertheless, World War II witnessed the widespread bombardment of cities informed by the goals defined in previous decades: lowering the enemy's morale, gaining retribution for injuries suffered, and restricting the enemy's capacity to fight by destroying key industries. Expectations for the success of aerial warfare were very high, too high in fact, and the British and later American bomber commands always felt pressure to achieve something—anything—if only to justify the high expense of building an air force. Because predictions anticipated some sort of knock-out blow, no one thought about what to do if the war proved to be a long, drawn-out battle of attrition.

Which side first bombed cities? The question matters only if one attempts to justify such attacks as reprisals for enemy actions, but in fact revenge was the least important motive for military planners on both sides. The German bombing attack on Poland was ruthless from the beginning, and the Poles were not prepared to repulse German bombers or strike back at German cities. In any event, German bombers accidentally dropped bombs on a German town in May 1940, with the population assuming that it was the British who had attacked. The very next night a few British bombers did indeed try to hit industrial targets in the town of Mönchengladbach. The first instance of British "area" bombing—an attack on a generally defined urban area, rather than on specific targets like buildings or rail depots—was a raid on Mannheim in December 1940, but in October 1940 Air Vice-Marshal W. S. Douglas already had argued that the British bombers should target major towns if they were unable to deliver their loads on primary industrial targets.[11]

A report of the Chiefs of Staff on 7 January 1941 clearly defined British policy:

> The evidence at our disposal goes to show that the morale of the average
> German civilian will weaken quicker than that of a population such as our

own as a consequence of direct attack. The Germans have been under-nourished and subjected to a permanent strain equivalent to that of war conditions during almost the whole period of Hitler's regime, and for this reason also will be liable to crack before a nation of greater stamina.

It can be argued that concentrated attacks on the main centres of popula-tion in Germany, making the maximum use of damage by fire, combined with harassing action in the interval between the main attacks, might compara-tively quickly produce internal disruption in Germany. An incidental effect of this attack would be its repercussions on the morale of the German armed forces and on industrial production, and the stimulation of the morale of our own population.[12]

The British calculated that normally only 17% of dropped bombs would land within the target area, but Royal Air Force Marshal Lord Hugh Tranchard observed that even if all of the bombs missed their primary targets, bombs "all help to kill, damage, frighten or interfere with Germans."[13] In fact, strategists talked more about disrupting normal life in Germany by "de-housing" the population than by actually killing masses of German civilians. (The Germans, in turn, considered wartime programs to house the victims of the bombing as a "weapon" to combat the "housing blockade" being imposed by Allied bombers against German civilians.)[14] A report on the first "thou-sand bomber" raid on Cologne declared that the purpose of this "thousand-winged Pegasus" was the "complete neutralization of the densely populated central portion of Cologne proper."[15] Another memorandum of November 1942 estimated that bombing German cities would produce 6 million uninhab-itable dwellings and render 25 million Germans homeless (more than one-third of the population), while causing 900,000 civilian deaths and 1,000,000 seriously wounded civilians.[16]

Once they implemented the area bombing campaign, the British engaged in statistical exercises to try to calculate how much money and labor would be needed to repair the resulting damage. For example, a report of 19 October 1943 stated that Hamburg would require 1,525,300 "man-months" of labor to repair damage to housing and industrial plant. The calculations were based on estimates of repairs of bomb damage in Britain; they did not indicate to what extent the Germans would actually try to undertake repairs during the war.[17] Another report declared that intelligence gathered in Germany indicated a marked drop in morale after the Hamburg bombings. Masses of people were being evacuated from urban centers, creating "alarm verging on panic" and great tension between the evacuees and the residents of the areas into which they were being sent. "So far-reaching have been the consequences of evacua-tion and so complex the problem of housing, feeding and controlling the evacuated population, that a number of reports compare the low standard of living necessitated by evacuee conditions with Russian Communism." In addi-tion, "a by-product of the Hamburg raids was the diffusion of rumours on a scale and of a kind unparalleled in earlier periods. Lurid accounts of men and women with their clothes on fire running like living torches through the town seem to have gained immediate currency." Although the report goes on to note the large number of civilian deaths, especially in Hamburg, and gives the impression of a society nearing collapse, it concludes cautiously:

> Though the forces of repression, the hopes of a compromise with one or other of the belligerents, and the favorable climatic conditions of the past three months have so far prevented any general break in morale, it is not reasonable to infer that no such break in morale can occur, and we do not exclude the possibility that, in conjunction with further large-scale military reverses and with the advent of winter, air operations may exercise a decisive influence on conditions inside Germany.[18]

Air warfare strategy reflected not only the desire to strike at the German people in their cities but also the technological limitations of the Royal Air Force. Its bombers were neither heavily armed nor capable of flying at very high altitudes. Since precision bombing of specified industrial targets required daylight, the toll on British planes from German anti-aircraft fire and fighters was unacceptably high. Although safer for British fliers, night bombing permitted dropping the payload only on an area like a city, where the resulting fires would show other pilots where to drop their bombs. The technical argument in favor of night area bombing thus reinforced the tendency to carry the war to the mass of the German population and punish them for what Germany had begun.

The first large-scale area bombardment by the British was on the northern port city of Lübeck on the night of 28–29 March 1942. The attack fell on the historic center of medieval Lübeck—where there were no industrial targets at all. Supposedly a reprisal for a German attack on historic Coventry, the raid succeeded in destroying about 30% of the central area.[19] Attacks on more important cities followed, and even though German civilian morale did not break and industrial production remained high, the British saw no reason to revise their bombing strategy. More and more cities were reduced to rubble. The British Bomber Command enjoyed its greatest success in a series of four massive raids on Hamburg between 24 July and 3 August 1943. A variety of factors combined to produce this "ideal" raid, including excellent visibility for the pilots. The British weakened German fighter defenses by the use of foil chaff to confuse the radar and then dropped a high percentage of incendiary bombs, which ignited a large number of fires that were in turn fanned by the unusually hot and dry weather. High explosives and mines were dropped throughout the bombing deliberately to disrupt the efforts of Hamburg's fire department to fight the flames and impede the flight of those caught in the burning cauldron. The raids resulted in an uncontrollable firestorm that consumed almost everything and everyone in the target area.[20]

While the British went on to bomb almost every major and minor German city, improving the accuracy of their night bombing as time went on, the American Army Air Forces joined the air war with their campaign of precision daylight bombing of industrial targets. For a variety of reasons, however, the Americans soon joined their British ally in attacking cities.[21] Weather over

TABLE 1.1.   Tonnage of Bombs Dropped on Axis Europe

Year	Area Raids	Other Raids	Total	Percentage Area Raids
1940	1,453	12,094	13,547	11%
1941	14,475	22,631	37,106	39%
1942	39,044	11,412	50,456	77%
1943	131,668	74,520	206,188	64%
1944	324,965	876,569	1,201,534	27%
1945	96,428	384,721	481,149	20%
Total	608,033	1,281,947	1,989,980	31%

Source: United States Strategic Bombing Survey, *The Effects of Strategic Bombing on the German War Economy* (October, 1945), pp. 2–5, Tables 1–4.

Germany often proved a problem even during daylight hours; until February 1944 German flak and fighters continued to shoot down a large number of bombers, and it was difficult to achieve great bombing accuracy from high altitudes under fire. As a consequence, in October 1943 the American 8th Air Force conducted area bombing of the city of Münster in daylight, and a month later American pilots were authorized to undertake radar-guided attacks on cities when visibility precluded precision bombing of the primary designated industrial targets.[22]

Area bombing was downgraded somewhat during the spring of 1944, although the first massive daylight raids against Berlin took place in March of that year. In general, however, preparations for the invasion of Normandy dictated that the bombers be directed against the German transportation network and the oil supply system.[23] After the invasion, the war against the cities continued; some were bombed dozens of times and hit with more than 30,000 tons of bombs. (Table 1.1 indicates the shifting emphasis on area bombing.) The period between 1 August 1944 and 26 April 1945 saw 205 air raids on German cities, including 94 against Berlin, and witnessed the highest concentration of German cities crumbling under the onslaught of high explosives and incendiary bombs.[24] The most spectacular attack was the devastating raid on Dresden on 13–14 February 1945, a raid that served little clear military purpose beyond killing masses of civilians and obliterating a symbol of German culture.

Moreover, the use of area bombing undercut one of the more admirable features of American bombing policy: the attempt to prevent the destruction of great historic monuments. In the United States, pressure from a variety of private groups and individuals had led to the creation in August 1943 of the American Commission for the Protection and Salvage of Artistic and Historic Monuments in Europe.[25] Chaired by Supreme Court Justice Owen Roberts, the Roberts Commission, as it became known, provided the military with lists and maps of important works of art and historic or artistic architectural monuments. Although bombing strategic industrial and military targets and sparing cultural monuments theoretically complemented each other, in practice this neat separation of targets was seldom realized, especially in the German theater. Night bombing and radar-guided bombing simply lacked such precision, and commanders were not inclined to risk their flight crews or planes to protect buildings. It was accidental, therefore, that some monuments in city centers, like the Cologne cathedral, survived the bombardments.[26] One historian concluded that "despite the persistent efforts of the commission, there was no significant instance where the course of military operations was directly affected by regard for the cultural importance of sites or buildings."[27] German architecture that had endured for centuries was reduced to rubble.

The Allies incurred heavy losses in conducting their air war. One historian calculated that the Royal Air Force flew 297,663 sorties by night and 66,851 by day, with a loss of 8,000 bombers; 46,268 crew members died and 4,200 were wounded in combat, while another 8,090 died and 4,203 were wounded in noncombat flights. Only 24 of every 100 flyers would come through the campaign unharmed.[28] British casualties in the air war exceeded combat casualties after Normandy. One wartime study of a group of men in American 8th Air Force flying missions over Germany concluded that only 26.8% completed the full tour of 25 missions; more than half the men were killed and the rest either wounded or grounded for other reasons.[29] The monetary sums required to construct the British and American air forces were of course also enormous.

What did the bombing campaign achieve? The strategic bombing campaign did not fulfill its promise to end the war quickly and efficiently, that much is clear. The United States Strategic Bombing Survey was created in November 1944 to examine the effectiveness of the campaign. Entering Germany on the heels of the troops, it found—much to the discomfort of the air force strategists—that the bombing campaign had destroyed neither Germany's industrial capacity to make war nor German morale, the undermining of which was one of the justifications for air raids in a long war of attrition. The survey concluded that in terms of capital equipment, raw materials, and manpower (which was augmented by several million forced laborers from other countries), German industry remained strong in spite of the bombing.[30]

In his July 1945 interrogation, Armaments Minister Albert Speer stated: "We drew distinctions between morale and conduct. The morale following attacks upon towns was bad, the conduct of the civil population on the other hand was admirable." In terms of their value in decreasing armaments production, attacks on cities, in Speer's view, ranked fifth after attacks on basic industries or supplies, attacks on transport and communications, attacks on front-line positions, and attacks on the final stages of manufacture.[31] Concerted and repeated attacks in these other areas, rather than area bombing of cities, might well have had a greater impact on the German war effort. The Allies had mistakenly assumed that German industry always produced at full capacity, which was not the case until very late in the war. Thus even in the face of the bombing, production could be increased by gearing up under- or unutilized plants. The Allies also mistakenly equated destruction of housing with the urban depopulation. In fact, the elasticity of resources meant that inhabitants of bombed dwellings tended to remain in the city (and at their jobs) by moving into undamaged housing or doubling up with relatives or friends. Only later in the war, when the cumulative effects of repeated bombing destroyed a very high percentage of the housing stock, did large numbers of people abandon the cities.[32] Production did fall off and morale did begin to sag in the winter of 1944–45, but still the conquest of Germany needed to be on the ground. Most important was the disruption of rail transportation through the bombing of marshalling yards, which delayed the flow of coal, finished goods, and munitions.[33] Air power contributed to the victory, but the bombing campaign was not primarily responsible for it, and certainly the area raids on the cities contributed too little to justify the effort.[34]

Even if the bombing failed to force German capitulation, the impact of the bombing of the cities was incalculable—quite literally so, since compiling accurate statistical data often proved impossible, and since words were seldom adequate to describe the experience of living in the midst of falling bombs, explosions, fires, the collapse of homes, and the end to the comfort and security of normal life.[35] Naturally the intensity of the bombing varied from city to city, as did the efforts of local German officials to deal with what was happening. For example, Hamburg, one of the hardest hit cities, was also the best prepared to relieve the effects of the bombing. Responsible officials remained on duty during the air raids, rather than fleeing to safer ground, as apparently happened in some cities.[36]

In May 1941, a new Office for Activities Important to the War Effort (Amt für kriegswichtigen Einsatz, or AKE) was created to build air raid shelters and bunkers, organize crews to repair damaged buildings, and generally make Hamburg capable of withstanding anticipated air attacks. Several large, above-ground concrete bunkers were constructed in different parts of the city to provide protection from the bombs.[37] The AKE staff was dedicated and courageous, as was the city fire department, which by mid-1943 had grown to 9,300 men. Smaller raids were dealt with rather well, and the repair of damaged housing and construction of new housing had made up some of the losses in the air raids. Until mid-1943, the bombing had left 1,431 dead, 4,675 wounded, 24,375 homeless, and 50,701 relocated elsewhere; thus all together less than 5% of the city's population of over 1.6 million had been directly affected.[38] The great incendiary attacks of July and August 1943, however, simply overwhelmed the efforts to protect the population and contain the damage.

Fire bombs fell on densely populated blocks of apartment buildings, and "ideal" conditions produced the largest and most horrible firestorm to occur during the war in Europe. The fire department, augmented by the AKE units and self-help units, emerged from bomb shelters to find themselves without water and often surrounded by flames. Hurricane-force winds filled the air with burning debris, leading one observer to remark that "it rained fire, so to speak."[39] Furniture that residents had tried to salvage caught fire in the streets, and the winds caused burning buildings to collapse and block escape routes. For the first time the fire department was unable to extinguish all the fires during the night and day following a raid, and still-burning buildings served as beacons for the bombers the next night and helped the conflagration to grow. Within the area of the fire, people either burned to death or died of carbon monoxide poisoning. The police president wrote that the attack's

> horror is revealed in the howling and raging of the firestorms, the hellish noise of exploding bombs and the death cries of martyred human beings as well as in the big silence after the raids. Speech is impotent to portray the measure of the horror . . . . The streets were covered with hundreds of corpses. Mothers with their children, youths, old men, burnt, charred, untouched and clothed, naked with a waxen pallor like dummies in a shop window, they lay in every posture, quiet and peaceful or cramped, the death-struggle shown in the expression on their faces.[40]

What were the final statistics? The best estimate is that about 35,000 people died in the Hamburg raids (compared with 60,595 deaths in Great Britain from bombing during the entire war) and around 125,000 were wounded. In 1944 and 1945, an additional 6,200 individuals died when buildings collapsed on them, and some of these deaths must also be attributed to the great raids of 1943. Some 79.5% of the housing stock was damaged, 49.2% totally destroyed. The raids left more than half of the city's 1.6 million population homeless, and by the end of August 1943 the population had sunk to around 800,000 (though in fact many soon returned). Of 33 historic churches, 15 were damaged or destroyed, and 54 of the 70 major secular historic monuments were demolished.[41]

The only other German city to suffer such extensive human losses and property damage in such a short time was Dresden at the end of the war, but all of Germany experienced vast physical destruction. Many statistical assessments were made during and after the war, and while they differ, the outline is more or less clear. Somewhere between 400,000 and 600,000 civilians died in the air raids and between 650,000 and 850,000 were injured. Of the large cities with more than 100,000 inhabitants in 1939, on an average about 50% of their built-up areas were destroyed. In Würzburg the figure was 89%, in Remscheid and Bochum 83%, in Hamburg and Wuppertal 75%. Some 45% of the housing stock in the large cities was destroyed.[42] Casualties varied considerably, depending upon the effectiveness of local authorities in preparing the citizenry to cope with anticipated raids.[43] Either voluntarily or as part of an evacuation plan, a terrorized population moved back and forth, in and out of the cities, struggling to find shelter and safety. Over 200,000 people, mostly women and children, were evacuated from Munich by the end of the war.[44] The destruction was so great that in some cases authorities proposed abandoning the bombed cities entirely and building new cities, perhaps underground, to ensure protection from air raids. Other proposals advocated bulldozing the rubble, planting grass and shrubbery, and allowing a new natural landscape to emerge. A new city could then be built that would harmonize with that landscape. The first

Nuremberg, bomb damage on the Weißgerbergasse, October 1944. (Source: Stadt Nürnberg Hochbauamt, Bildstelle und Denkmalsarchiv, 4025/S, photo Hochbauamt.)

step in this process of course would be relocating the population of the old bombed city.[45] Such innovative proposals were never implemented. Instead, the bombed cities were rebuilt above ground on their original sites.

By the time the war finally ground to a halt, the cumulative effects of air raids, artillery fire, and street combat were staggering. Everyone collected statistics on Germany's bombed cities. Although fascinating, these numbers resist meaningful interpretation, for great quantities of data, like great quantities of ruined buildings, can be numbing, as they were to the Germans and allied soldiers who walked the streets and contemplated the magnitude of the destruction. The massive collection of data also resulted in great inconsistencies. Town planners, housing officials, local, state, and national statistical offices, the allied armies, scholars—everybody counted a little differently. Consequently, the totals vary and cannot easily be reconciled. From our standpoint, it is not so very important whether a given city contained 20 million or 22 million cubic meters of rubble, or whether a city's population on a given date was 450,000 or 480,000. Under the difficult circumstances, many of the figures collected were estimates rather than exact numbers. The data that appear in this book are accurate enough to frame the story, but the reader should keep in mind that the numbers are estimates and may not represent particular situations with statistical accuracy.

Cities of Rubble

What words would an American, or even a German, use today to describe the scene that existed in Germany's cities? After the war the Germans spoke of *Trümmer*, which translates as rubble. An age of rubble, life amidst the rubble, rubble literature, rubble mountains—these are phrases that ring with black humor and the grotesqueness of the situation, and they testify both to despair and to a subtle optimism with which, in spite of everything, some Germans viewed their world. Hans Werner Richter wrote in 1947:

> The sign of our times is the ruins. They surround our lives. They line the streets of our cities. They are our reality. In their burned-out facades there blooms not the blue flower of romanticism but the daemonic spirit of destruction, decay, and the apocalypse. They are the outer symbol of the inner insecurity of the people of our age. The ruins live in us as we in them. They are our new reality which is asking to be reshaped.[46]

For Richter, the ruins, which signified the death of bourgeois ideas of safety and security, forced Germans to look objectively at the true basis of their existence.

How much rubble was there in 1945? The amount varied from city to city, depending in part upon the type of bombs used and the character of the targeted city. For example, when a city like Hildesheim, consisting largely of medieval, half-timbered buildings, was hit with fire bombs, little remained of the old center. In Hamburg the great fire of 1842 had destroyed most wooden structures, and therefore most of the older parts of that city were of stone and brick. Hence, though Hamburg also suffered a great firestorm, the masonry walls were left standing while floors, roofs, and interiors burned. In Cologne, the initial fire bombing that had burned much of the city was followed late in the war by raids with high explosives and eventually by artillery bombardments. As a result, the standing walls of burned-out buildings finally collapsed as well.

The degree of damage and the amount of resulting rubble also depended upon how often a town was bombed. In general the cities in the northern and western parts of Germany—those most easily reached from the bases in Britain—suffered the most destruction. Finally, the amount of rubble also depended on the intensity or concentration of the bombing within a city. For example, one of Munich's eight central districts contained 4.3 times as much rubble as the least damaged of the eight.[47]

The Nazis placed very high priority on clearing the streets and bulldozed rubble into huge heaps on lots which now contained only the remnants of destroyed buildings. Toward the end of the war, of course, the Germans could

Hamburg, rubble in the Catharinenstraße canal. The city disposed of much of the rubble by filling in many canals, including this one. (Source: Staatliche Landesbildstelle Hamburg, 6564.)

not clear the rubble fast enough, and the earlier "progress" was undone. The Allies also sought to clear the streets and used some of their heavy machinery to push the rubble to one side. Basements were filled in, as were any available unused depressions in the land. Although all of this made it difficult to calculate accurately the amount of rubble that had to be cleared away, the 1949 statistical yearbook of the German towns included official estimates.

Table 1.2 gives statistics for the 10 cities in the new Federal Republic with the largest amounts of rubble. The figures for Berlin include all sectors of that city. Thirty-nine cities had more than 1 million cubic meters of rubble to clear, including Munich and Stuttgart, which had 5 million cubic meters each. (It was estimated that Dresden in the Soviet zone contained 25 million cubic meters and Leipzig about 8 million.)

These enormous sums are very hard to grasp. One attempt to come up with figures for total damages estimated that for cities with more than 250,000 prewar inhabitants, the damage ranged from 65% in Dortmund, to 54% in Hamburg, to 33% in Munich and Stuttgart, to only 22% in the western sectors of Berlin.[48] These estimates of total damage, however, fail to convey the appearance of utter devastation experienced by contemporaries. Hans Speier wrote that in his travels in Germany right after the war, he was overwhelmed by what seemed to be the total destruction of the cities. Upon seeing the statistics, in fact, he "was actually surprised at the 'low' figures,

TABLE 1.2.   Cities with the Largest Amounts of Rubble (in cubic meters)

Berlin	55,000,000	Frankfurt a.M.	11,700,000
Hamburg	35,800,000	Nuremberg	10,700,000
Cologne	24,100,000	Düsseldorf	10,000,000
Dortmund	16,777,100	Hannover	8,400,000
Essen	14,947,000	Bremen	7,920,000

Source: Dokumente deutscher Kriegsschäden, 1: 51.

because [his] visual impression in city after city was of a loss larger than the figures indicated."[49]

Let us try to visualize what these quantities of rubble meant. If Cologne's rubble were placed on a field 100 yards by 40 yards, the pile would be 4.48 miles high! If the surface area were enlarged to 1 square mile—and here the reader might try to imagine the inner square mile of some familiar city—the rubble would be over 30 feet high! If that same mass were used to build a wall 10 yards high and 2 yards thick, the wall would be about 895 miles in length! Contemporary Germans used this sort of conceptualization. Officials in Munich noted that their rubble mass of 5 million cubic meters was twice that contained in the Great Pyramid.[50] In Hamburg it was observed that if that city's rubble were to be loaded into normal freight railroad cars, the train would reach around the earth.[51]

Another way of looking at the rubble, also one invoked after the war, was to reduce it to cubic meters per inhabitant. Table 1.3 lists the eight cities from among Germany's cities with more than 250,000 prewar inhabitants that contained the most rubble on a per capita basis. For such calculations, 1939 population levels were always used, since urban populations in the early postwar years changed rapidly and dramatically. This approach made the amount of rubble to clear seem more manageable. Cologne's 31.2 cubic meters per inhabitant would form a cube 3.15 meters per side, or about 10 feet per side. One can well imagine an individual clearing such a mass one bit at a time, even without heavy machinery.

TABLE 1.3.   Rubble per Capita in Large
Cities (in cubic meters/inhabitant)

Cologne	31.2
Dortmund	30.9
Kassel	26.7
Nuremberg	23.5
Essen	22.4
Aachen	21.2
Frankfurt a.M.	21.1
Hamburg	20.9

Source: Dokumente deutscher Kriegsschäden, 1: 51.

This approach, however, was illusory. Nearly 775,000 people had lived in Cologne before the war, but in March 1945 only 40,000 people remained. The mass of rubble now equaled nearly 602 cubic meters per person (a cube 8.5 meters per side), and few of the inhabitants boasted sufficient energy and strength to move such quantities. On the other hand, by July 1945 the population expanded to between 250,000 and 300,000, and by year's end it had reached nearly 450,000.[52] In spite of a trickle of returning soldiers released from POW camps, however, most of the population still consisted of women, children, the elderly, and the infirm. They were poorly nourished, poorly clothed, and poorly housed, which limited their capacity for hard physical labor. Finally, even if every individual had indeed been physically able to clear 30 or 40 cubic meters of heavy debris, where would they have put it? Clearance required moving it some distance from the site of the ruin, making the magnitude of the task even greater.

Though the largest number of destroyed buildings were apartment houses, in every bombed city churches, schools, museums, and many other kinds of public buildings had been destroyed or damaged. The same was true for all kinds of commercial establishments—factories, warehouses, banks, retail establishments, restaurants, shops, and so forth. Total building losses in Munich for the retail trade were estimated at 30%, for the wholesale trade 10%, for crafts 25%, and for industry 30%.[53] In Darmstadt some 65% of the buildings with public functions and 63% of the commercial and industrial buildings were classified as badly damaged or totally ruined.[54] Table 1.4, which deals with damage in Hamburg, illustrates the kinds of losses a city could suffer in this regard. In addition, the allied forces confiscated for their own use many of the public buildings that remained in good repair, such as recreational and health facilities. In May 1945, of the 341 school buildings that were still usable to some degree, 217 were being used by German authorities for purposes other than schooling, and 64 billeted English troops. That left only 60 schools for instruction, at a time when a census based on identification and ration cards revealed that there were some 100,000 school-age children in the city, 12,000 more than in 1938.[55] Administrative buildings, such as the town halls, had been located in the inner cities, and, except in a city like Hamburg, where much of the central district escaped direct hits, these buildings also fell victim to the bombs. Since they contained the records, without which no government agency functions very well, the new German town administrations found it exceedingly difficult to get back to normal business operations. Services suffered accordingly.

Utilities particularly suffered directly from the bombing. The damage to water, gas, electric, telephone, and sewer lines depended upon the intensity and type of bombing but also on the placement of those lines. In his important 1951 study of the underground dimension of urban building, Ernst Randzio noted that electrical cables, typically located in front of buildings, endured far more damage than pipelines under buildings.[56] A city official reported that Stuttgart had an estimated 4,000 breaks in electrical lines, 1,000 breaks in gas lines, and 400 defects in water lines.[57] In April 1945, Münster had some 1,850

TABLE 1.4.   Damage to Public Buildings in Hamburg (excluding administration buildings)

Degree of damage	Religious Buildings	Medical Buildings	Schools	Cultural Buildings	Totals Number	Totals %
Undamaged	57	171	167	13	408	27.1%
Light	35	175	65	28	303	20.2%
Moderate	13	77	62	26	178	11.9%
Heavy	25	89	60	32	206	13.8%
Totally	75	192	97	38	402	27.0%
Totals	205	704	451	137	1,497	100%

Source: Arthur Dähn, "Die Zerstörung Hamburgs im Kriege 1939–1945," in *Hamburg und seine Bauten 1929–1953*, Architekten- und Ingenieur Verein Hamburg, ed. (Hamburg, 1953), p. 35.

breaks in water pipes, causing 70% of the water to be lost into the ground.[58] In Frankfurt 7,000 broken water mains reduced service more than 50%, while in Nuremberg it was noted that in addition to the damage to the mains, 32% of the city's water meters had been destroyed.[59] Hamburg reported 2,200 breaks in sewer lines.[60]

This was the condition in which the Germans found their cities in the spring of 1945. Masses of ruins required removal. Public services and public utilities had to be restored. Only then could actual rebuilding begin. The Germans quickly started to work.

2

Work Amidst
the Rubble

In addressing the problem of reconstruction, the Germans waited neither for the end of the war nor, after the defeat of 1945, for the creation of a new German state. Major wartime measures in the areas of planning and housing are discussed in later chapters. This chapter examines some of the practical attempts to deal with the immediate consequences of the air war.

As the war progressed, and as the damage to Germany's cities grew greater and greater, the Nazi regime anxiously sought to clear away the rubble left by the bombs. The failure to do so would imply that Germany was losing the war, and no one dared acknowledge the growing power of Germany's enemies. Streets were usually cleared after the raids, sometimes by "forced laborers" from other countries, by concentration camp inmates, or by prisoners of war.[1] Depending upon the availability of trucks, temporary "field" railroads, or existing streetcar lines, the debris was either carted off or simply piled onto the sites of demolished buildings. Utilities were repaired, and damaged buildings that threatened to collapse were torn down. For the cities of northern Germany, which suffered two years of repeated bombing, this was of course a labor of Sisyphus; each new air raid resulted in the same sort of damage requiring the same sort of labor. Since cities were not depopulated in proportion to their housing losses and casualties, clearly many individuals returned to their damaged homes and businesses and performed as many repairs as possible. They did so as best they could, given the shortage of building materials and construction workers, not only to preserve their property or even to obtain shelter, but also because they so strongly identified with their homes and their home towns.[2]

After February 1940, all new building projects were legally suspended except for those determined to be essential for the war effort.[3] Naturally, armaments plants and military installations were constructed throughout the war. Typically located either outside cities or on the outskirts, they need not be considered here, although it is perhaps worth noting that through 1943, at least three-fourths of the construction and repair projects under the control of Speer's Armaments Ministry could be completed, and only in 1944 did shortages of cement and construction steel really begin to affect essential building.[4] The accomplishments in terms of civilian construction during wartime were remarkable. Between the start of the war and the middle of 1943, around 400,000 dwellings were constructed, mostly for armaments workers.[5] In Hamburg, 1,200 new housing units were erected in 1942 and 3,500 units were repaired in the last six months of that year. Dwellings reinforced against air attack that had been completed since mid-1941 numbered 1,250; another 1,600 were under construction.[6] In March 1943, Rudolf Hillebrecht, the chief administrator of Hamburg's Office for Activities Important to the War Effort, reported on the efforts to clear rubble, repair housing, and build temporary housing in other cities. He noted that in Berlin, nearly 40% of the damage was usually cleared away without any official intervention by the property owners, who somehow managed to engage a supply of local laborers in spite of the labor shortage. On the other hand, in cities with less efficient self-help efforts and where authorities failed to organize effective clearance and repair programs, Hillebrecht discovered panic-stricken residents intent on fleeing the city.[7] Certainly Hamburg continued to function even after the great air raids and firestorm. Mail and telegraph services were restored almost immediately. Within two months, 170 miles of streets had been cleared and 7,668 ruined or partially ruined buildings demolished. Within five months, 80% of the city's industrial capacity was restored.[8] In Düsseldorf, some of the rubble was processed to manufacture new brick and to produce massive concrete roofing to repair bombed buildings. The new roofing would lessen fire damage in future raids as well as provide better thermal insulation[9] As the cities were bombed over and over again, much of the repair effort lasted only until the next raid, but the practical experience gained in making these repairs would be utilized more permanently and meaningfully after the war.

Rubble Clearance and the Repair of Utilities

In fact, though the damage was often extensive, disruptive, and dangerous to public health, a surprisingly large percentage of the underground capital investment in utilities survived the war. Munich reported damage to its electrical system at 6.58%, its gas system at 15.71%, its water system at 4.21%, its sewer system at 4%, and its telephone lines at 40–50%.[10] In Berlin, about 95% of the underground capital survived, including the subway system, underground parking, and underground storage facilities. Ernst Randzio calculated that in 1938 (and in terms of 1938 money), the value of the above-ground investment was 15.85 billion marks, the value of the underground investment 4.53 billion marks. (This ratio of about 3.5 to 1 was evidently similar to that in other cities.)

While about 70% of the above-ground investment survived the war, 95% of the underground investment remained intact.[11] Moreover, much of the damage to the pipelines and electrical lines could be repaired relatively quickly.

Restoring damaged utility plants to working order was sometimes more challenging. Münster's street lamps remained dark until 1948, and the city did not regain full electrical service until the beginning of 1950.[12] Stuttgart's electrical works were intact, but they lacked coal, and it was not until December 1945 that the city's steam power works were restarted. The city gas works began to function again the following month, although the lack of coal hampered both gas production and repairs to the damaged furnaces. Furthermore, Stuttgart observed that restoring utility service "was made difficult through the discharging of more than 500 workers, employees and officials due to their former affiliations with the Nazi party."[13] Nevertheless, the surviving investment in utilities, street surfaces, and urban transportation systems constituted enormous assets for the impoverished German cities, and the very existence of these assets exerted a great influence on the shape of reconstruction. Indeed, as surfaces were gradually cleared away, the layout of the street and utility systems often determined rebuilding sites.

For the German cities, rubble clearance posed a legal problem as well as a physical and economic one. If towns obviously assumed responsibility for removing rubble from the streets and the sites of public buildings, who should do so for private property? General legal practice required owners to maintain their property in accordance with local safety and health standards, but postwar conditions made this impossible in most cases. Efficient removal of the rubble required heavy machinery, a resource unavailable to most individual property owners. Besides, some owners were missing, and the ownership of some properties was unclear. The cities wanted to rebuild the ruined inner cities rather than concentrate all building activity in the undamaged suburbs, so clearance had to proceed, whatever the difficulties. On what grounds, then, could a community clear a property without the owner's consent, and what were the rights and obligations of the respective parties?

The initial basis for town action was the Reichsleistungsgesetz of 13 July 1938 in its revised version of 1 September 1939; this was a kind of enabling law that obliged and empowered the towns to enter a building to put out a fire, clear serious bomb damage, or make the site safe. For the public good the town could salvage what was possible from the rubble.[14] An alternative was the December 1940 Ordinance Concerning Measures for Clearance of War Damage (Verordnung über Neuordnungsmaßnahmen zur Beseitigung von Kriegsfolgen). Although these laws had been introduced and used by the Nazis, they were not abrogated by the allied occupying forces when the war ended, and local town authorities continued to invoke them as the legal basis for rubble clearance. Frankfurt, for example, passed a special rubble removal law in December 1945, based on the Reichsleistungsgesetz. The continued use of the provisions of the Reichsleistungsgesetz was challenged in court by owners who sought compensation for the value of the building material taken. They argued that as they had paid once for that material, they should not have to pay again—possibly even buying it back from the city—when they rebuilt. The towns, on the other hand, contended that the cost of clearance normally exceeded the value of the salvaged building materials, and the owner actually gained from the removal of the rubble since he now had a building site that did not require an outlay of additional personal funds for rubble removal.

Although the courts usually ruled in the towns' favor, they still pressed for new state rubble clearance laws to strengthen their position. Both towns and property owners found it troubling to have to rely upon laws promulgated by the authoritarian Nazi state instead of new, democratic legislation.[15] Hamburg, for example, passed a new law on 31 July 1948. Northrhine-Westphalia did so on 2 May 1949.[16] These laws clearly granted towns responsibility for rubble removal but typically allocated state funds to cover most of the costs.[17] One authority estimated that 2.5–4% of the total cost of reconstruction was for rubble clearance.[18] A property owner could apply for permission to clear his own property, in which case he retained title to material salvaged from the ruins, but generally the community did the work and claimed ownership of the rubble. Only when the value of the salvaged material exceeded the cost of clearance did the town pay the owner the difference. In applying these laws, a few unclear points had to be worked out in practice. When, for example, was a ruin so badly damaged that it presented a hazard, or, if there was no hazard, when did the public interest require demolition of a ruin anyway? Some owners felt that the cities should also remove debris from cellars. Cologne and Münster declined to do so, arguing that future building codes might not allow for the rebuilding of cellars, and in any case the owner could easily do that clearing by hand, in contrast to the removal of the above-ground mass of rubble, which required heavy machinery.[19]

The legal question was only one of the many issues facing the towns when they began clearance. Who would actually do the work, and how would it be organized? Some rubble clearance, of course, began as soon as the fighting stopped. Major streets were cleared with allied help, and property owners and tenants worked with their hands to make usable space in the ruins. The removal of the great masses of rubble, however, became a large-scale task for city-owned and private construction firms. As rubble clearance competed for labor and machinery with building projects already in progress, shortages of labor, fuel, and machinery were a constant problem for local authorities.

In the first year after the war, the shortage of labor, especially skilled labor, was quite serious. Many workers were still incarcerated in prisoner-of-war camps. The chairman of a large Frankfurt construction company reported that 10% of his firm's construction workers had died during the war. Many workers, moreover, lived outside the city and were reluctant to come into the center because of the cost and difficulty of travel and because wages and working conditions were often better in the suburbs or countryside.[20] The American military authorities in Bavaria determined that in June 1938, nearly 300,000 workers had been employed in construction or in the building materials industry. In February 1946, only 52% as many workers were employed in those sectors, and by the end of that year the figure rose only to 75%.[21]

   Demands of the Allies exacerbated the labor shortage throughout the early years. Munich's reconstruction office reported that up until the spring of 1946, the occupation authorities absorbed the largest block of construction workers. In December 1945, the military government employed 6,900 workers on its own building projects, while the railroad employed 1,800, the post office 350, other public agencies (including the city) 2,600, and the private sector 5,850.[22] These figures indicate more than the high priority enjoyed by military construction. The Allies supplemented their workers' wages with food and clothing, which was otherwise in short supply. In Berlin up to 30% of the construction workers on private and city projects claimed to be ill and failed to report to work, but few did so on military projects, which boasted high productivity rates.[23] Food shortages—the food ration in the American zone dropped to 1,180 calories per person daily in May 1946, a prime time of year for construction—meant ill-nourished private and city workers, who naturally achieved less.[24]

   The authorities tried a number of strategies to augment the supply of construction workers. Some help came from building workers who were refugees from the eastern lands. Prisoner-of-war camps provided another source of labor. Requests to the military government led to the release of skilled construction laborers for work on authorized projects.[25] In the fall of 1945, Berlin's Technical University stipulated that matriculated students devote hours to clearing rubble from the university grounds.[26] A law of the military government explicitly empowered German authorities to employ women "on building and reconstruction work, including rubble clearance," and photographs from the period frequently show women pulling down piles of rubble and passing debris along in buckets.[27] During the blockade of Berlin, when the cutoff of most shipments of building materials forced a much higher number of workers than normal to turn to rubble clearance, about 35% of the employees clearing rubble were women.[28] Engaged in hard, untraditional, but absolutely crucial work, these women—*die Trümmerfrauen*—labored heroically. Günter Grass immortalized Berlin's Trümmerfrauen in a wonderful poem, "Die große Trümmerfrau spricht," from which two stanzas read:

> Trümmerfrau Trümmerfrau
> singen die Kinder—
> will mit dem Ziegelbrenner Ziegelbrenner
> heut eine Wette machen Wette machen—
> es geht um viel Schutt.
> Amen Amen.
> Hingestreut liegt Berlin
> Staub fliegt auf,
> dann wieder Flaute.
> Die grosse Trümmerfrau wird heiliggesprochen.
>
> Rubble woman rubble woman
> sing the children—
> wants to make a wager make a wager

today with the brick burner brick burner—
it's a matter of much rubble.
Amen amen.
Berlin lies strewn about.
Dust blows up,
then a lull again.
The great rubble woman will be canonized.[29]

Many city authorities sought to force former Nazis to work for a specified number of hours clearing rubble. Stuttgart called on former Nazi party members to toil several unpaid weekends and four to five weeks of paid labor. Some 1,800 former Nazis cleared over 100,000 cubic meters of rubble in 1945.[30] In Cologne nearly 20,000 former Nazis worked six days each in 1946 and 1947, while 101,000 men and 72,000 women, none obligated to do so by their political past, volunteered for one day's labor.[31] In Münster, 500 former Nazis worked alongside some 4,000–6,000 citizens who volunteered their labor to clear rubble during an 11-week period beginning in July 1945.[32] Munich shipped in 500 former Nazis from an internment camp in Moosburg in a special train to work on rubble clearance.[33] When the Munich Social Democrats urged the city council to pass a resolution mandating further labor for "politically compromised persons," the Christian Democrats countered with a resolution promising special treatment in denazification trials for those who volunteered their labor.

Berlin, women clearing rubble on the Hagelberger Straße, Kreuzberg, 1949.
(Source: Landesbildstelle Berlin, 1 NK, 184 802.)

Berlin, clearing rubble using a temporary rail cart near the Reichstag building, 1946. (Source: Landesbildstelle Berlin, 4 RBau, 172 325.)

Neither resolution passed. By that time city officials recognized that the use of such labor was no longer very productive, since meaningful clearance was now done by heavy machinery rather than unskilled compulsory labor.[34]

The appeal for voluntary labor, termed "honorary service" (*Ehrendienst*), was widespread but often controversial. When Munich called on all adults and older schoolchildren to volunteer their labor, one senior Gymnasium student protested that this was no different from the labor service and Ehrendienst under the Nazis. (In fact such honorary service went back to World War I.)[35] Like the compulsory labor for former Nazis, appeals for voluntary labor ceased after 1947. They no longer succeeded in getting volunteers, and, as the Munich city council noted, the productivity of this type of labor had dwindled considerably.

In addition to obtaining sufficient labor, cities also struggled to find adequate machinery. In December 1945, the first head of Munich's reconstruction office listed the resources necessary to clear the rubble within three years. He needed 12,000 workers (including at least 4,000 regularly employed by firms contracted for rubble removal), 65 steam locomotives, 450 rail cars, and 155 other vehicles. Each month the machinery would consume 1,266 tons of coal, 37,275 liters of diesel fuel, and 60,375 liters of gasoline. He lacked not only the labor force, but also 40 locomotives, 150 cars, 120 of the other vehicles, and the fuel.[36]

Even if labor, machinery, and fuel were at hand, rubble clearance had to be organized and administered. Though some cities, like Hamburg, had estab-

Berlin, *Trümmerfrau* in Schöneberg, 1955. (Source: Landesbildstelle Berlin, 1 NK 40781.)

lished a rubble clearance office during the war, the months following the war found city administrations in a chaotic state. Cologne's land office (Liegenschaftsamt), for example, was responsible for acquiring and maintaining city land holdings as well as keeping track of land ownership and land transactions in the city. Before the war some 200 individuals had worked for that office. When the American troops arrived in Cologne, only 1 civil servant and 5 lower-level employees remained. By October 1945, the office had increased its staff to 18 civil servants, 35 lesser employees, and 3 manual laborers. About one-third of the city's employees had been Nazi party members, and they had to be screened. Only if no charges were filed against them could they return to work.[37] Most city offices were shorthanded and lacked adequate working space and facilities, although their tasks were greater than ever before.

The cities approached the task of organizing rubble clearance in different ways. Hamburg and Cologne created special rubble removal offices, which set priorities, acquired equipment, and designated dumping sites. Some of the work was done by city crews, but much was contracted out to local construction firms.[38] In Berlin during the last six months of 1945, a total of 254 different firms received 380 contracts for clearance of 549 sites designated by the city.[39] Both the city and the private firms tried to recover their costs by salvaging building materials from the rubble and selling them.[40] Frankfurt and Pforzheim established new corporations, in which private firms and the city were partners, to specialize in rubble clearance and salvage. The city of Frankfurt contributed RM 900,000 of the founding capital of a salvage firm, the Trümmer-Verwertungs-Gesellschaft m.b.H; the firms Philipp Holzmann A.G., Weyss & Freytag A.G., and Metallgesellschaft A.G. each contributed RM 200,000. The city thus retained a controlling interest while turning practical management over to the private sector.[41] In Stuttgart the city and the company that ran the local streetcar system each contributed RM 600,000 to found the Gemeinnützige Gesellschaft für die Trümmerverwertung und -beseitigung. This nonprofit company for the salvage and removal of rubble, legally independent of the city, was run by a board made up of four senior city officials, four members of the town council, and three members of the streetcar company.[42] In this way public control of the company was assured.

Removal or salvage—those were the two options for handling the rubble. Usually the two overlapped, but not always. Munich decided quickly that little economic gain would occur from attempting mass salvage of used building material because sand and gravel were abundant and cheap in the immediate vicinity. That city also found it too expensive to clean old bricks for reuse.[43] Frankfurt and Stuttgart, on the other hand, opted for salvaging as much as possible. Both cities lacked ready supplies of cheap sand and gravel, and neither had the space to dispose easily of unprocessed rubble.[44]

In either case, where could the rubble be put? Whether by truck or by special narrow-gauge trains, the rubble had to be hauled out of the inner cities. Hamburg was fortunate to have at hand unused canals that could be filled in, and it also used the rubble to strengthen the banks of the Elbe. Hamburg also used rubble to raise the level of one whole bombed-out area,

Nuremberg, park built upon rubble heap. (Source: Stadt Nürnberg Hochbauamt, Bildstelle und Denkmalsarchiv, L43 44/21a, photo Hochbauamt, 1985.)

Hammerbrook, which had been built originally on marshland and had perpetually suffered from bad drainage and defective sanitation.[45] Finally, special train lines carried excess rubble to low-lying dumping grounds to the east and west of the city.[46] Many cities, including Cologne, Berlin, and Munich, used the rubble to fill in, enlarge, or landscape city park lands, adding hills or contours to previously flat parks. Munich constructed the grounds for the 1972 Olympic games in a park formed partly by rubble deposits. Cologne hoped to use fully one-half of its 24,000,000 cubic meters of rubble to prepare the ground for a new main train station to replace the one near the cathedral, although ultimately that project remained unfulfilled.[47] Essen used rubble to fill in sinkholes and other depressions left from earlier mining, to strengthen dikes, build new road and rail beds, and to enlarge the airport.[48] During the blockade, Berlin trucked its rubble to the airports at Tegel, Tempelhof, and Gatow to build new runways.[49]

Varied and complicated programs emerged for salvaging building materials from the rubble. A national association of experts on rubble processing (Deutsche Studiengesellschaft für Trümmerverwertung) was founded to collect information and disseminate advice. Many cities had ambitious plans for rubble salvaging. Münster calculated that about 40% of the rubble could be salvaged: 10% in intact building stones, 2% in usable sandstone, and about 30% in whole bricks or pieces of brick that could be processed into wall blocks or roofing tiles.[50] Ministerialrat B. Wedler, the leading proponent of rubble processing in

Berlin, presented the following argument for a massive commitment to processing in that city. He estimated that it would take 25 years to clear Berlin's rubble using 42,000 workers continuously. This would cost RM 2.6 billion. Utilizing hand-sorting techniques, materials worth RM 450 million could be salvaged. However, if 35 efficient rubble processing plants with an hourly capacity of 25–30 cubic meters were built, then rubble clearance over the same 25 year period would require the labor of only 2,600 workers, half of whom would be women, and the total cost would be RM 650 million. Because the value of the salvaged and reprocessed building material would be RM 650 million, the rubble clearance would actually pay for itself.[51] (The complicated political situation in Berlin in fact prevented any such massive program from being implemented.)

The most important programs of rubble reprocessing were in Stuttgart, Frankfurt, Hamburg, Bremen, Braunschweig, Nuremberg, Kiel, Mannheim, and Düsseldorf, with the first three far out in front.[52] Stuttgart's efforts were probably the best known due to the proselytizing all over Germany by Lord Mayor Arnulf Klett on behalf of rubble processing. This city also made an effort to involve its citizens in rubble salvage by staging an exhibition in the middle of the town to demonstrate what kinds of building materials could be salvaged and how much could be saved.

H. G. Eberlein, the engineer who ran Stuttgart's rubble-processing firm, estimated that 67.8% of the rubble left from buildings destroyed by explosive bombs and 57.25% of that left by fire bombing could be salvaged. In the former case, 13.45% of the rubble consisted of whole bricks and 30.65% of broken bricks. The broken bricks were sorted by size and crushed if necessary, and the excess plaster content was separated out. Since coal was in very short supply, Eberlein also calculated that erecting walls made from concrete or building stones produced by using brick fragments required only 38–53% as much coal as putting up walls made with new bricks.[53] Klett reported in 1950 that the city's rubble-processing firm had met 30–50% of the demand for gravel, sand, wall bricks, chimney bricks, and roof plates, without which one-third less would have been built in the city. The use of processed rubble then reduced the cost of putting up walls by 30–40% and reduced by 6–8% the overall cost of building.[54]

Table 2.1 lists the accomplishments of Stuttgart's rubble-processing program up to the time that its processing firm closed its books on 31 October 1953. By that date the materials salvaged or processed from the rubble furnished enough to build the walls of 10,000 of the 42,593 dwelling units constructed since the war as well as 28,000 ceilings and 26,000 chimneys—a phenomenal achievement.[55] Such figures reflect the serious commitment made by Stuttgart to rubble processing, and cities similarly committed reported like figures. Hamburg's plants could process 600 cubic meters of broken brick every eight hours. By 1953, some 500 million building blocks and bricks had been salvaged or manufactured out of 20 million cubic meters of cleared rubble, along with 51,000 tons of salvaged iron and another 76,500 tons of scrap metal.[56] By the end of December 1945, Berlin had already salvaged 50 million bricks, enough to put up 2,500 dwellings.[57]

TABLE 2.1.   Rubble Processing and Salvage in Stuttgart: Output of
the Gemeinnützige Gesellschaft für die Trümmerverwertung und
-beseitigung in Stuttgart m.b.H. (TVB) 1946 through October 1953

Rubble removed	
By the TVB	3,370,000 cubic meters
By others	1,350,000 cubic meters
Total	4,720,000 cubic meters
Rubble processed	
By the TVB	660,500 cubic meters
By others	54,500 cubic meters
Total	715,000 cubic meters
Salvaged material	
Bricks	10,500,000 bricks
Stones	30,800 cubic meters
Scrap metal	20,700 tons
Usable iron	2,700 tons
Other metals	200 tons
Produced from split brick	
Building stones	27,000,000 pieces
Chimney stones	210,000 running meters
Roof tiles	1,143,000 pieces
Cast wall and sidewalk plates	68,500 square meters

Source: SAS/Trümmerverwertung und -beseitigung/Statistik/ "Leistungsangaben der
TVB für die Zeit von 1946–31. Okt. 1953."

The speed with which the cities cleared away the rubble depended upon
the amount of damage, the ease with which the rubble could be carted away,
and the commitment to salvage and processing. Frankfurt and Essen moved
rather slowly, clearing building sites individually rather than by blocks. Of the
large cities, Munich, Kiel, and Stuttgart cleared the quickest. By mid-1949,
Munich had cleared about 80% of the rubble, with one-quarter of that
amount being held on temporary dump sites.[58] By 1952, Stuttgart had cleared
over 88% of its rubble.[59] Cologne, in contrast, had cleared only 13% by the
fall of 1949 and 33% by 1953. By 1956, when the total had reached about
60%, the process slowed down as only individual lots, rather than entire
blocks, remained to be cleared.[60]

Obviously, by the mid-1950s people wandering through the cities had very
different perceptions of the progress achieved. Some back streets and low-
priority areas must have looked very much as they had in 1945. Other areas
were completely cleared and presented vast, open areas awaiting rebuilding.
Still others had already been redeveloped, erasing evidence of the war's damage. (Even today one can still stumble across bits of rubble, just as one can
still see the marks left by shells or bullets on facades that were never refin-
ished or on the sides of old buildings not concealed by other structures.) All in

all, about half of the rubble in the Federal Republic had been cleared away by 1951, and a lot of what remained was not immediately visible.[61] By the mid-1950s, the age of rubble was past.

Material for Rebuilding

Just as the Germans began at once to clear away the rubble from their homes and businesses, so they quickly began the long process of rebuilding—by hand, using whatever skills and material they could find. The desperate need for shelter and the disorderliness of local government meant that self-help—individual initiative—offered the only obvious and logical means of getting things going again.[62] And just as the reemerging local authorities sought to control rubble clearance, so they sought to control all parts of rebuilding. Skilled labor, fuel, and building material were in very short supply, whereas the demand for hospitals, schools, and other basic services, not to mention housing, reached crisis proportions. Only careful allocation of building material for approved building projects could ensure rational, efficient use of scarce resources. Inevitably, this situation spawned conflict between private initiative and public control, between what was practical and necessary and what was legal and in principle the "right" way to do things. Surveys found considerable discontent about the procedures for allocating building materials and approving building permits.[63] These conflicts found expression in the black market for building materials, "black" or unauthorized and unreported labor services, and "black" or "wild" construction projects, which lacked the necessary building permits. Both the military government and local German authorities lacked the power to prevent the development of an intricate and vast black market.

Instead, the growing black market threatened to overwhelm all possibility of rationally controlled reconstruction until the currency reform of mid-1948 finally defeated it. Unfortunately, its illegality means that it cannot be studied directly through public documents. It is the other side of the struggle, the measures to control building, that can be followed and from which much of the illegal activity can be inferred. The supply of building materials, the supply of labor, the granting of building permits, and the passage of building control laws were interrelated with each other, with forces outside the building industry, and, always, with the black market.

Prior to the currency reform the greatest problem plaguing the building industry was a shortage of materials. In November 1944, Germans working on reconstruction planning calculated that cement production must be increased by 40% over 1939 levels, building blocks by 50%, roof tiles by 100%, building lime by 150%, and building stones by 100%.[64] The situation of course deteriorated further with six more months of fighting. The shortages varied from region to region and zone to zone, depending upon what was produced where, but data from the American zone illustrates what was happening.

In 1949, upon preparing a major statistical analysis of the reconstruction

TABLE 2.2.   Building Materials in U.S. Zone

Item	Unit	Total Requirements for Munich	Estimated Requirement, U.S. Zone, 1946 1st Quarter	Total Production, U.S. Zone, Dec. 1945, Jan., Feb. 1946
Cement	Metric tons	333,400	412,570	163,667
Lumber	Cubic meters	447,600	632,800	472,630
Roofing tiles	Each	107,800,000	60,308,000	15,507,000
Roofing paper	Square meters	478,000	8,997,000	2,117,752
Glass	Square meters	710,000	3,441,000	1,661,230
Lime	Metric tons	190,400	62,020	61,736
Plaster	Metric tons	12,905	18,780	7,200

Source: SAM/Bauamt-Wiederaufbau/1095, "Statistik," II, Section X; OMGUS Monthly Report (February 1946): 18.

situation in Munich, officials estimated that the materials needed to rebuild Bavaria's capital would fill 162,000 railroad cars![65] Although the requirements for Munich were rough guesses, it is illuminating to compare them with U.S. government figures, as presented in Table 2.2, for materials production and needs in all of the U.S. zone for a three-month period in 1945–46. In most categories, zonal production lagged well behind zonal needs. And even if somehow all of the production for this three-month period could have been shipped to Munich, the city would still have needed more cement, roofing tiles, lime, and plaster.

However, this represents only a small part of the picture. In the first year of the occupation, a healthy proportion of all building materials was siphoned off by the military government for the construction of its own administrative buildings, housing for the occupation army, and facilities on the new military bases. In July 1945, the Americans appropriated virtually all of the lumber production.[66] In the first quarter of 1946, military procurements absorbed about 65% of glass production, 80% of plywood, 30% of wallboard, 14% of roofing tiles, 15% of bricks, and 32% of cement.[67] Most of the 50,000 tons of cement produced in August went to the American army.[68] Considerable quantities of lumber were exported to the British zone, where pit timbers were desperately needed to revive coal production in the Ruhr.[69]

Things were made worse by the fact that, quite apart from the huge demand, the total production of building materials lagged behind prewar figures. Statistics were compiled from reports of private firms, and these figures probably underreported actual production. In 1950, when the federal minister for the Marshall Plan asked the Association of Chambers of Industry and Commerce of Northrhine-Westphalia for production data, a Cologne chamber official noted that firms were afraid to give precise information "because they fear that these reports possibly might somehow be used against them politically."[70] During the occupation, private firms were undoubtedly even more reluctant to report all gains in production, not knowing whether such information might lead to an increase in taxes or a decrease in raw materials shipments. Production gains based on illegally acquired raw materials naturally failed to be reported as well.

That production levels were low, however, is not in question. In June 1946, production of cement in the U.S. zone was only 36%, lumber only 76%, and roofing tiles only 41% of the 1938 level, the last prewar year with more or less normal production.[71] Production in the spring and summer of that year had increased since the war's end, but it fell from one-third to one-half in the late fall and winter of 1946–47, due to harsh weather and shortages of coal and power.[72] Production rose again in the spring of 1947, and the requirements of the military began to decrease, but widespread shortages continued to prevail. In Bavaria in the first quarter of 1947, the U.S. army still requisitioned 83% of new brick production, nearly 90% of cement, and 54% of roofing paper.[73]

What lay behind the lagging production? It was not, as one might think, due to any massive destruction of production facilities. Building materials were usually produced in outlying areas which had escaped heavy bombing. The problem was that the plants could not produce to full capacity due to fuel (i.e., coal) shortages, skilled labor shortages, lower labor productivity resulting from inadequate food and clothing, and breakdowns in the transportation network (itself dependent on coal) which supplied raw materials and moved the finished goods to distribution points.[74] All agreed that coal production presented the greatest impediment, and hence German and allied authorities concentrated on getting the Ruhr minefield back to full capacity.[75] Table 2.3 gives production figures for Bavaria in 1946, while Table 2.4 shows the flagging production levels in the combined British and American zones. Although brown coal could be burned in power plants, it was unsuitable for many kinds of industrial production.

To the extent that they could, the occupation authorities and officials of the German state governments sought to allocate available building supplies to the various states according to the size of the state and the need for materials. Table 2.5 presents the distribution key as of mid-1947. Such figures, of course, pertain to those materials that were officially accounted for, and they do not, as far as I can tell, include materials gained from local salvage

TABLE 2.3. Production of Building Materials in Bavaria, 1946

Material	Unit	1938 Production	1946 Production	Production Capacity	Percentage of Capacity Used
Cement	Tons	949,000	365,000	634,000	57 %
Lime	Tons	504,000	192,000	360,000	53 %
Gypsum	Tons	36,000	14,900	36,000	41 %
Bricks	Piece	1,003,000,000	173,000,000	1,000,000,000	17.3%
Roofing tiles	Piece	223,000,000	73,000,000	252,000,000	29 %
Light fiber sheets	Square meters	14,000,000	1,540,000	10,000,000	15.4%

Source: NA/RG 260, OMG Bavaria/ Manpower, 105²/13: (Box 85) File 11: Paul S. Nevin, Chief, Trade and Commerce Branch, "Memorandum on Distribution of Building Materials," 28 November 1947, p. 2.

TABLE 2.4.   Industrial Production, Bizonia, 1949 (1936 = 100)

Commodity Group	1947 Actual	1948–49 Estimated
Hard coal	53	75
Brown coal	101	104
Electric power	118	136
Iron and steel	22	45
Sawmills and plywood	71	76
Stones and earths	35	82
Glass and ceramics	54	82

Source: OMGUS and Control Commission for Germany (British Element). Statistical Handbook of Bizonal Recovery Programs for Fiscal Years 1948/49—1949/50—1952/53 and Summary of Economic Progress, US/UK Occupied Areas of Germany (January 1949).

operations. Although pivotal representatives of the states developed it, some were quite unhappy with the distribution key. The organization representing Bavaria's cities complained that Bavaria in general and its cities in particular were not getting their share of material.[76] Moreover, the allocation and distribution system was often cumbersome and sometimes barely functioned at all. For example, the city of Regensburg had to get its cement from a plant 300 kilometers away, even though there was a cement plant only 24 kilometers from the city. Roofing paper came from a plant 250 kilometers away, though a factory only 10 kilometers away also produced roofing paper.[77]

The movement of some kinds of materials, such as new lumber, plywood, and massive construction steel, permitted close monitoring. Smaller items, and material from small plants, were harder to follow. How much building material eluded official accounting, and how much material that at one time

TABLE 2.5.   Apportionment of Building Materials in Bizonia, by State

State	Percentage
Bavaria	15%
Württemberg-Baden	10
Hesse	12
Northrhine-Westphalia	27.5
Bremen	2.5
Hamburg	6.5
Schleswig-Holstein	7
Berlin	6.5
Other (incl. export to other zones)	13
Total	100

Source: BHSA/ MWi (1952–53)/ 10166/ Report of Verwaltungsamt für Wirtschaft des amerikanischen und britischen Besatzungsgebiete, 8–9 May 1947.

was included in the official accounts never reached officially approved building sites? The Bavarian minister of labor, responsible for the distribution of building materials in his state, estimated that fully 40% of all material flowed into the black market.[78] One American official estimated that "approximately 60% of all construction was done with material secured through other than regular channels."[79] In cities, where controls were easier to enforce, perhaps a majority of construction was done with properly allocated materials, but in some rural areas all building material was obtained illegally. The effects of these irregular dealings were sometimes blatant. For example, a 9 January 1947 article in Munich's *Süddeutsche Zeitung* complained that 53 new buildings with 407 apartments had been structurally completed, but they remained empty because the material for finishing the interiors (heaters, ovens, flooring, staircases, bathroom fixtures, etc.) was lacking. Additionally, the windows were being stolen from the unfinished apartments, but meanwhile restaurants and retail establishments managed to find supplies of material to complete their interior construction.[80] City officials complained in turn about the plethora of building activity going on in rural areas, where the lack of stringent controls encouraged country residents to come to the city to pilfer materials from the rubble or acquire them on the black market.[81] Complaints such as these resounded throughout Germany. It seemed that there was always plenty of material to rebuild a bar, movie theater, restaurant, or shop, while the large, officially planned and sanctioned housing projects suffered defeating materials shortages.

When one thinks of the black market, one imagines people standing, somewhat furtively, on the edge of some square, exchanging cigarettes for a ham or a piece of family jewelry for some other object of immediate value. How this worked with building materials, especially in some quantity, is much harder to visualize. Surely no one stood on a street corner with a few tons of cement or coal to trade! A few cases, reported by U.S. occupation officials, will illustrate these kinds of transactions.

First, the case of a single individual. An artist in Regensburg wished to enlarge his studio by using attic space, but, although the plans were approved, he could not obtain permission to acquire the necessary building materials. Eventually he used seven cartons of cigarettes, obtained from American clients, plus RM 2,500, to acquire the materials.[82] Presumably the artist got the materials through a contractor, who had also come upon them illegally.

But how did a contractor get material? The example of the Kiefersfelden cement factory in southern Bavaria near the Austrian border illustrates this nicely. By 1947, this plant produced about 120 tons of cement daily, a quarter of its capacity. (Some 50% of the capacity was lost due to coal shortages, 25% to power shortages.) Twenty-five percent of the production went to the French zone in Austria. Sixty to sixty-five percent went into normal, approved distribution channels. The remaining 10–15% was exchanged for supplies, spare parts, and services needed to keep the plant going. This cement thus disappeared from official accounting, and no one could say how it was used. Moreover, since the official price of cement was only about 2% of the black market price, everyone at the plant assumed that some material was siphoned off for those prepared to pay.[83] Thus certainly more than 15% of the total production was diverted to the black market.

This kind of barter, or "compensation trading" as it was called, was initially legal, at least up to a level of 10% of production, since the authorities recognized that the practice did indeed supply factories with materials not otherwise available. Abuses, however, became so common by the fall of 1947 that state governments and the bizonal government tried to outlaw compensation trading, though to little effect, since all parties found such trading normal, fair, and necessary. Sometimes compensation trading reached enormous scales. An investigation of five Bavarian brick factories showed that during the first nine months of 1947, fully 59% of the production of the plants went for compensation trading. This excess trading primarily obtained illegal coal, which made possible an increase of brick production by 70%. Of the 12,228,000 bricks produced, 5,022,400 escaped the legally authorized channels of allocation and distribution. Of these only 43% could be directly accounted for, with 22% of that portion being exchanged for coal, 16% being used as compensation for the labor of rebuilding and repairs, 8% going to employees, and 54% being used to acquire other materials and machinery.[84]

Another example demonstrates how the building industry functioned in the early years after the war. From 1940 until the very end of the fighting, the construction firm Bährle AG, owned and directed by Dr. Albert Speck, had fulfilled a variety of large contracts in Germany, France, and the occupied territories in the East.[85] The latter contracts were for the Organisation Todt, the German government's agency in charge of large construction projects. In the spring of 1945, Speck withdrew his equipment and men to Bavaria, where he felt that he had the best chance of avoiding allied confiscation of his heavy equipment. In fact, in exchange for repairing some airfields for the Americans, he actually received additional equipment. By the summer of 1945, however, he decided to move to Cologne, in part because of the proximity of brown coal deposits, which were important for fuel, and in part because of the advice of an acquaintance in Bavaria who was a director of the Agrippina Insurance Company. He arrived in August with 14 large trucks, an entire freight train full of heavy equipment, including 3 large excavators, and some 70 men. Initially the equipment was housed in a part of the exhibition grounds in Deutz, but the city soon made available a parcel of land. He founded a new firm called Rhein-Beton.

Rhein-Beton's first major contract was with the city of Cologne and resulted from Speck's possession of the excavators. Over a year-and-a-half period, the firm cleared the suburb of Lindenthal of rubble, in the process laying down some 11 kilometers of temporary track for rubble cars. While erecting a small mountain of rubble near the university, the firm salvaged a wide variety of building materials. Other important contracts came from the Agrippina (via the earlier friendship in Bavaria) and other insurance firms. According to Speck, in those days no one bothered about obtaining permits for building or for building materials. One just built. The Agrippina had its own house architect who simply came to the building site and issued instructions rather than supplying blueprints. After the currency reform, Rhein-Beton started buying properties near the city center where the buildings were damaged but repairable, signaling a move into housing construction. In the early 1950s the firm pioneered the construction of housing with modern conveniences for widows and other single persons who only wanted or could only afford a single-room apartment.

The bottleneck for Speck's business was building material. Enough was salvaged from the rubble for the firm to trade building blocks for food. Cement was also obtained through illegal trading. Speck dispatched one excavator and two or three trucks to work for a coal producer. He was compensated with coal, which he then sent to a cement factory in exchange for cement. He found lime for mortar in the refuse heaps of a plant that produced carbide gas—lime was an unused and previously unwanted by-product of the gas—and traded surplus lime for other needed materials. This mode of operation involved some risk. At one point the local tax office came to investigate all this illegal activity, but the firm escaped penalty by quickly consigning its records about cement trading to an oven.[86] The firm also provided housing and food for its workers, in addition to their wages. Indeed, food remained such a problem in the Rhineland that Speck's wife, who still lived in Bavaria, sent food hidden in a truck disguised as a hearse, complete with casket. In short, barter, or "compensation trading," was essential to the success of Rhein-Beton and allowed Speck to function profitably even under the prohibitive conditions of a weak currency and scarce materials. When money was suddenly scarce after the currency reform, the Agrippina helped tide the firm over with a large payment in D-marks in compensation for current and anticipated projects.

Since most black market exchanges went unreported and unprosecuted— indeed, since many were viewed benignly by the German authorities, who recognized the benefits of allowing some shortcuts in the otherwise rigid and inflexible system—it is impossible to say whether the preceding examples are typical. They do show, however, that a vast amount of building material was available on the black market to small and large contractors who had something to exchange, whether it be other wanted commodities or some kind of useful labor.

Labor in the Construction Industry

Just as the shortage of building materials and fuel hampered reconstruction, so did serious shortages of skilled and unskilled labor. Some of the reasons for the labor shortages are obvious. Germany's heavy casualties in the war had reduced the number of available workers, and many more potential workers were incarcerated in POW camps. The general slowdown in construction during the war meant that building workers—if they were not in the army— had acquired other skills and found employment in other industries. The same was true for young men who in peacetime might have become apprentices in

TABLE 2.6. Construction Workers in Munich, December 1947

	Skilled	*Unskilled*	*Total*
Estimated demand	23,711	25,254	48,654
Currently employed	14,964	12,875	27,839
Labor shortage	8,747 (36.9%)	12,379 (49%)	21,126 (43.4%)

Source: SAM/Bauamt-Wiederaufbau/1095:III, Section XII.

the skilled building trades. During the war such a normal augmenting of the labor market did not take place.

The shortages, as noted, seriously undermined the industry. In 1947, Hamburg's building firms estimated that whereas 45,000 men should be employed in construction, only 11,000–12,000 were actually employed.[87] Table 2.6 shows the size of the labor shortage in Munich at the end of that year. The labor shortages were so severe that advertisements of openings simply had no audience; there were no available workers.

The situation worsened during the first years after the war due to the priorities set for the allocation of available workers. In Munich in December 1945, some 40% of all construction workers were assigned to projects of the occupation forces, which drew men away from construction of housing and public buildings. Construction of railroad facilities also enjoyed a higher priority than other kinds of civilian and private projects.[88]

Cities and private firms hoped to augment their labor forces by drawing upon the pool of rural construction workers, as had normally been the case before the war, but that proved very difficult. The grim condition of the bombed cities and particularly the lack of urban housing made rural workers unwilling to come to the cities. At best they might find themselves living in makeshift barracks, which were much less pleasant than quarters in undamaged rural towns. Hence a vicious circle developed: the lack of urban housing meant fewer construction workers and less production of building materials, which in turn made it all the harder to increase the amount of new urban housing. Moreover, in the countryside workers enjoyed fewer restrictions in their activities, better wages, and more foodstuffs available outside the rationing system.[89] Indeed, restricted diets and inadequate or unsuitable work clothing and shoes tended to make the workers who remained in the towns less productive than rural workers and of course less productive than workers had been before the war. (The same factors apparently also kept women—who had been very active during the initial phases of rubble clearance—from accepting various kinds of manual labor.)[90] As a result, urban authorities complained that more building occurred in the countryside than in the bombed towns, and that urban workers were leaving the towns for the countryside.

Finally, illegal building projects—projects lacking building permits—also acted as a drain on the labor supply. Even as the number of construction workers approached prewar levels, productivity remained low as workers commonly took sick leave from officially sanctioned projects in order to work

TABLE 2.7.   Size of Berlin Construction Firms

Number of workers	Employees				Firms			
	1939		1946		1939		1946	
	Number	%	Number	%	Number	%	Number	%
1–20	9,487	8.3%	12,757	11.2%	1,776	77.5%	1,662	64.5%
21–100	15,395	13.4%	32,804	28.7%	330	14.4%	649	25.8%
101–1,000	44,558	38.8%	60,962	53.4%	165	7.2%	238	9.5%
1,000+	45,413	39.5%	7,690	6.7%	20	0.9%	6	0.2%
Totals	114,853	100%	114,213	100%	2,291	100%	2,515	100%

Source: Harry Wild, "Struktur und Beschäftigung des Berliner Bauhauptgewerbes," Neue Bauwelt 2 (1947): 4.

on illegal projects which paid higher wages.[91] Moreover, after-hours work, whether on illegal jobs or just clearing and repairing one's own property, consumed the worker's energy and lowered regular productivity.

Widespread illegal building disrupted the construction industry in other ways too. Consider Table 2.7, which presents data on the size of construction firms in Berlin. By the end of 1946, the number of workers had risen to the prewar level. At the same time, however, the number of firms had grown, while the size of the average firm decreased significantly. Twenty large prewar firms employed more than 1,000 workers each, and together they had employed nearly 40% of the laborers. In 1946 only 6 firms employed more than 1,000 workers, and only 6.7% of the labor force worked for such firms. By the spring of 1948 there were 3,600 construction firms, but only 12 employed more than 500 workers each.[92] The small and often undercapitalized firms accepted illegal projects because property owners were willing to pay a premium to get something built at the same time that the firms had to pay premium wages to hold workers. Therefore, the big firms and the city government, which were the prime contractors for major projects, including rubble clearance and mass housing, found it hard to attract enough workers.

Legal and Illegal Building

How much illegal building was there? Some idea can be gained by examining figures on building permits. The issuing of building permits served, at least in principle, several functions. First, they provided authorities with a way to ensure that new and reconstructed buildings met current standards for health and safety. Second, they ensured that new buildings harmonized with the current town plan and current zoning provisions. Third, they enabled authorities to impose priorities on construction activity, so that projects deemed essential were put up before those considered less critical. Fourth, permits enabled the authorities to regulate the use of building material. Approved, essential projects merited material while projects lacking a permit did not. Finally, as part of denazification, persons considered undeserving because of their past political affiliations could be denied permits in favor, for example, of victims of the Nazi regime.

In practice, of course, circumstances undermined these ambitious principles. To rigorously control all construction activity through the issuing of permits, local government would have required a small and efficient army of trained evaluators and inspectors working in close contact with related agencies and supported by effective law enforcement. None of this was remotely possible during the chaotic postwar years, when local governments were regrouping and struggling to adapt to new conditions. Local governments barely managed the routine tasks faced in normal times, much less the crush of an extraordinary number of permit applications and large numbers of illegal projects. Moreover, the building bureaucracy itself was shorthanded because so many officials had been removed from office on account of their former membership in the Nazi party.[93]

The granting of permits occasioned frequent complaints. In Bavaria it was said in the early years that only "BMW"—*Bäcker, Metzger, Wirte* (bakers, butchers, restaurateurs)—obtained building permits because they could offer something in exchange for materials. And indeed in Würzburg in 1947, these groups accounted for 37.4% of the 1,800 projects under way, compared to only 13% for housing and public building projects.[94] Likewise, complaints surfaced about former Nazis, some of whom got permits without any subterfuge simply because they had access to materials. Often it seemed that the main criterion for getting a permit was the possession of the necessary material, whatever the source, even though theoretically material could be allocated only after the permit was granted.

The total number of permit applications varied from city to city, as did the number finally approved. From May 1946 to mid-March 1947, of 900 applications submitted in Münster only 20% were acted upon.[95] Stuttgart, a larger city, had some 7,300 submissions in 1949 and was able to approve 83%, processing the applications within three to five months. In the first five years after the war, Stuttgart granted permits for 17,353 projects with a value of DM 282 million.[96] In Cologne, a heavily damaged city, permit applications ran about 6,000 per year from the late 1940s into the early 1950s, with approval granted to one-half to two-thirds of those submitted.[97] Table 2.8 shows the type and value of approved and pending construction in Düsseldorf in early 1948.

Up until the currency reform, probably as much illegal building occurred as legal building. An official of the American military government wrote that the attitude of Munich's building office was "'if a man can build without disturbing the Munich contingent [i.e., the official allocation of materials to the city], bless him and let him go ahead.'"[98] In other words, if one could get materials to build, and as long as the building met the local codes, local authorities were usually loath to stop a construction project just because it lacked a permit. Any reconstruction seemed better than leaving the city in ruins while waiting for better times. When the Americans requested some spot inspections, the Munich building inspectors examined 1,963 building sites between January and April 1947. Fifty-six percent lacked permits![99]

TABLE 2.8.   Construction in Düsseldorf under Approved Permits, 1 March 1948

Project Type	In Progress	Value in RM	Pending	Value in RM
A. WITH BUILDING MATERIAL DISTRIBUTED THROUGH OFFICIAL CHANNELS				
Transportation	3	638,000	0	0
Public utilities	4	538,950	0	0
Commercial/industrial	122	3,451,977	23	360,592
Food industry, agriculture	117	1,946,790	3	212,650
Public buildings	90	5,714,006	4	88,700
Housing	816	11,032,862	62	281,333
Other	10	658,500	3	20,430
Totals	1,162	23,981,085	95	963,705
B. WITH BUILDING MATERIAL NOT DISTRIBUTED THROUGH OFFICIAL CHANNELS				
Transportation	1	58,950	0	0
Public utitilies	0	0	0	0
Commercial/industrial	80	856,747	12	139,985
Food industry, agriculture	11	154,064	1	12,000
Public buildings	8	230,100	0	0
Housing	256	2,519,699	19	240,473
Other	5	97,800	2	6,300
Totals	361	3,917,360	34	398,758
Totals, A and B	1,523	27,898,445	129	1,362,463

Source: HSANRW/ NW 73/Bd. 36, Baulenkungsamt Düsseldorf, Nachweisungen über die am 1.3.1948 laufenden Baumaßnahmen, report of 4 December 1948.

Under existing law, it was difficult to stop illegal building. In most places the fine for building without a permit was a mere RM 150, a pittance in the days of the black market. Those in a hurry to build simply accepted such fines as part of their costs. A city could order a halt to illegal construction, but an enormous commitment of time and energy was required to enforce these orders. Cologne reported stopping 1,134 projects through mid-1947 and imposing 600 fines. From mid-1948 to mid-1949, Cologne halted 3,092 projects and levied 718 fines, requiring 8,600 visits to building sites. During that same time permits were granted for construction of 4,762 dwellings and 1,236 commercial buildings, and offices mainly directed their energy to approved projects.[100] Moreover, in order to prevent illegal construction from being renewed, it was sometimes necessary to visit a site repeatedly or even station a policeman there. Over a two-year period ending in September 1947, Münster issued 880 injunctions to stop work on unapproved projects. In the end, however, only 20 cases were brought to court, resulting in 6 convictions and fines from RM 100 to RM 300.[101]

The situation cried out for change, but of what sort? Some city officials, planners, spokesmen for the building committees of the cities' associations, and even those officials of the military government who dealt directly with such matters argued for more thoroughgoing controls. A central agency should be created—whether at the state level or in each city—that would allocate all building material, assign all construction labor, allocate housing, set priorities for construction, plan overall rebuilding, license construction firms, issue building permits, and enforce all decisions.[102] This view also harmonized very well with the longstanding desire of the planners for a comprehensive building law.

On the other hand, a very strong argument could also be made for reducing rather than increasing controls. Many controls proved to be ineffective, and after the Nazi era neither the citizenry nor the military government really wanted a large, powerful German government. Moreover, it was expected that currency reform would remove most of the motivation behind the black market. A freer economy, not a more restricted one, would make it possible to rebuild Germany rapidly. Private initiative, innovation, and self-help should be encouraged. In short, much of the illegal activity should simply be made legal. This argument had the backing of architects' associations, the chambers of commerce and industry, and the building industry.[103] It was also an argument in tune with the thinking of the founders of the new Federal Republic, who were committed to a free market economy.

The path chosen lay between these two extremes. Generally, people felt that black-marketing in building materials and illegal building demanded more draconic punishment. Berlin's city planner Karl Bonatz called for a system that would guarantee rapid court decisions, because "otherwise people have simply no respect [for the law]."[104] In late 1948, a Munich official, complaining that illegal building had grown to such "frightening proportions" that it had become "a sanitary, social, and safety menace," wanted to raise the fine for illegal building to DM 20,000.[105] By the fall of 1947, bills were already under consideration in several states and by the Länderrat that would have sharpened the penalties for illegal building. The minister for reconstruction in Northrhine-Westphalia, when distributing copies of the draft bill for that state to the cities' associations and other interest groups, wrote that "over the long term one cannot do without a strong building control law based on a broad point of view."[106]

In fact conditions "in the short term" changed very rapidly once the currency reform had taken place. The black market disappeared altogether, and the amount of illegal building immediately decreased. The problem was no longer one of building material and labor shortages but of financing, and the cities' associations and the city governments now wanted to encourage building, not hinder it with bureaucratic obstacles. Northrhine-Westphalia passed a building control law on 9 February 1949 (Baulenkungsgesetz) that was a shorter and simpler version of the one proposed in 1947. It stated that "building projects may be prohibited if they are (a) not urgently required or not deserving promotion in the interest of the community or if they are (b) uneconomic either from the point of view of planning or because of their nature or mode of construction."[107] Violators faced fines of from DM 1,000 to DM 2,000 and in serious cases imprisonment of up to a year and a fine as great as DM 20,000.

By 1949, however, the cities no longer saw the law as terribly useful, and apparently it was seldom enforced.[108] In November 1951, the members of the building committee of the German cities' association, which included some of Germany's leading city planners, bemoaned the fact that illegal building continued to undermine their efforts at planned reconstruction, but they also recognized that there were "constitutional and political drawbacks to giving building administrations and police [sufficient] direct disciplinary authority" to deal effectively with illegal building. The best that one could hope for was that an occasional high fine or demolition of an illegal project might serve as a "frightening example" to those contemplating violation of the law.[109]

The regulatory efforts of the first postwar years were thus a failure in terms of lawmaking and enforcement. They failed to ration labor or materials; they failed to halt black market trade in building materials; they did not prevent illegal building. Moreover, this unsuccessful effort sapped the energies of understaffed local governments and created hostility between citizens on the one hand and local, regional, and occupation authorities on the other. It is also true that widespread illegal activities and the manifest weakness of the authorities helped undermine any commitment to a planned, organized reconstruction on a broader level. The failure of regulatory efforts probably reinforced skepticism in some circles about the desirability and need for a comprehensive town planning and building law.

Would Germany have been better off without having attempted to regulate building? In spite of the failure of these efforts, probably not. For one thing, regulation symbolized politically an attempt, however flawed, to make reconstruction fair and equitable. The reasons for the failure—the weakness of local government in relation to the economic and political strengths of certain groups in the population—were not sufficient to let reconstruction take its own course. Had that been the case, those who had suffered most in the war would have continued to bear the brunt of the recovery, a position no one could morally accept. Nor was there sufficient confidence right after the war that a free market economy—even if the Allies had allowed such a thing to appear— would of itself solve all allocation problems. Indeed, in the early postwar period a strong sentiment prevailed, especially among working-class Germans, that the time was ripe for some sort of regulated, if not socialized economy. It took a recovering economy, reinforced by the backlash against developments in Eastern Europe and in the Soviet zone, for confidence in the market mechanism to develop, and even then, as Ludwig Erhard formulated it, it was for the "social" market economy that the new Federal Republic opted.

Finally, there was a general acknowledgment that the city planners were quite right when they argued that unregulated building would lead to a replication of the defects of the prewar cities, blight the urban landscape with "temporary" buildings that would likely become permanent, and block needed comprehensive urban reforms. One could not hold these fears and at the same time openly abandon regulation. The only solution was really a compromise: accept illegal activities as largely unavoidable and wait for better conditions to materialize.

3

The Face of Reconstruction: Architectural Style

Relatively few Germans have offered praise for the shape which urban reconstruction took. They commonly have lamented that too few of the buildings were rebuilt in their prewar style, though sometimes they have complained that the modern buildings were poorly designed, plain and boring, or inappropriate for their setting. The objects of these criticisms are usually large commercial buildings, such as department stores, banks, and offices, along with public buildings, such as town halls. Poor quality is attributed to haste, as well as an inability to transcend Nazi aesthetic values, and a lack of talent and imagination on the part of architects.

In fact, it was by no means a simple, straightforward matter to design new buildings amidst the rubble left by the war. The architects who rebuilt Germany approached their task fully aware of the bitter controversies that swirled around the three stylistic traditions dominant in Germany during the previous decades. Usually grouped under the rubrics traditional, modern, and neoclassical, these styles coexisted in time and space. They were controversial because debates about architecture and debates about political behavior and values had been hopelessly tangled since the 1920s. Architects, planners, and politicians fundamentally agreed that the nature of the built environment largely shaped the behavior of the people living in that environment. "Democratic" architecture and urban design, in other words, would instill the Germans with democratic values; Nazi architecture and urban design would make the Germans strong of will, patriotic, and committed to the party and the Führer. During the 1920s, traditionalists and modernists vied for the right to represent the spirit of Germany, and, as Barbara Miller Lane has noted, "The Nazis inherited a political view of architecture from the Weimar Republic."[1] Certainly the debate over architectural style from 1919 to 1945 was heavily laden with political rhetoric. In fact, the rhetoric about the political content of architecture was more sharply defined than the architecture itself.

After 1945, most architects wanted to concentrate on actual building rather than discussions about style, and all circles, in any case, rejected the monumental neoclassicism favored by Hitler. The public rhetoric from architects about architecture, initially quite heated, soon cooled down, although architectural practice and scholarly discussion of German architectural history continued to be shaped by the political and aesthetic dichotomies of the Weimar and Nazi years. This debate rages even today. Indeed, since the 1970s the tone of this discussion has been quite sharp, though it is not always clear whether the scholars think that the built environment shapes behavior or reflects preexisting, basic social and political relations. A collection of essays published in 1979, for example, examines the arts, architecture, and media during the Third Reich. The editors' motivation in producing such a book was their fear that fascism and Hitler were becoming "fit for good company" (*salonfähig*) again because of a tendency to treat German fascism in abstract, aesthetic terms that failed to criticize its content politically or morally.[2] They titled the book *Die Dekoration der Gewalt*, which translates as the decoration of violence, force, or power. In an essay published in 1983, the architectural historian Joachim Petsch argued that merely "the use of the stylistic category of neoclassicism for the official architecture of the Third Reich is a monstrous neutralization [*eine ungeheure Verharmlosung*] and elevation of this architecture."[3]

The other side of the argument has been most provocatively advocated by the architect Leon Krier. Calling Hitler's architect Albert Speer "without a doubt the most famous architect of the 20th Century," Krier declares:

> Exorcism is not a form of judgement but of vengeance. Ignorant anti-Nazism (and anti-fascism) is just like the National Socialist anti-Semitism, a destructive form of self-affirmation. The traces of Nazism had, one thought, been successfully blurred by blowing up its arresting symbols, but the ghost still spreads fear and confusion. For two generations now, the German people have spared no sacrifice to prove to the free world that they had finally silenced the World [*sic*—Word] of Stone. . . . The destruction of German culture is no mere accident of warfare but, on the contrary, a super-human act of self-denial. In its industrial reconstruction, Germany has disavowed its individuality and its history. It is a truly heroic achievement, and the result of so much toil and sacrifice is futility and ugliness. . . . Germany may be the most advanced industrial nation in Europe, but it is also its ugliest country.[4]

Krier admires and applauds the architectural monuments of the Third Reich as powerful, seductively beautiful objects of art, categorically denounces the demolition of the undamaged remains of these monuments, and "dares" his readers to "find beauty in an architecture which has clearly and intentionally served to legitimize a political system we despise."[5] Krier aggressively sought to rehabilitate Albert Speer and reestablish monumental neoclassicism as a legitimate architectural style by viewing architecture primarily as art. "*Archi-*

tecture," he proclaims, "*is not political. It is an instrument of politics, for better or for worse.*"[6]

In order to understand both the actual developments in postwar architecture and the debates about architectural design, it is necessary to examine briefly the main currents that preoccupied the German architectural community. They all had their origins in a rejection of the architecture of the latter two-thirds of the nineteenth century. By the beginning of the twentieth century, the eclectic historicist monumentalism of official architecture had more or less exhausted itself. Whether neo-Romanesque, neo-Gothic, neo-Baroque, or neoclassical, the huge buildings of Imperial Germany had been darkened by industrial pollution, and their gloomy bulk seemed too "Prussian" for many Germans. The professors of architecture at the main academies, along with their students, sought to develop new ideas on design. This led some to modernism and some to a new kind of traditionalism, but both groups remained critical of nineteenth-century buildings.

The Bauhaus and Deutscher Werkbund

At the end of World War I, a group of young architects, reacting against the costly, chaotic consequences of that war and the dominant position in the architectural and artistic world still held by their teachers, recognized the potential for radical change inherent in the creation of the infant Weimar Republic and founded a new movement in architecture and modern design. This movement had rooted itself in the radical revolutionary turmoil of 1918. In late November of that year, Bruno Taut founded the Arbeitsrat für Kunst, a council for architects and artists dedicated to shaping a new, progressive Germany. Five months later Walter Gropius assumed leadership of the council, thereby gaining an organizational platform for his ideas.[7] Filled with the excitement and enthusiasm generated by the revolution and the expected transformation of German society, the modernists channeled this energy into the creation of new architecture.

The new movement had several sources. Most important was the Deutscher Werkbund, an organization of progressive craftsmen, artists, and architects founded before World War I, but the modernists also borrowed ideas from the Austrian Jugendstil movement, the Dutch De Stijl group, Russian Constructivism, traditional-minded teachers like Heinrich Tessenow and Paul Bonatz, and prewar German industrial architecture. However much they borrowed, the group of architects around Gropius nevertheless claimed to represent something distinctly new and uniquely modern.[8] In the public mind, the movement quickly became associated with the Bauhaus, a school of design in the town of Weimar and headed initially by Gropius. Bauhaus architects loudly denounced the architecture of the previous century and rejected historical styles as representative of undemocratic, authoritarian societies. The only appropriate architecture was one that fully sympathized with the industrial, urban, and now democratic society of the 1920s.[9] The Deutscher Werkbund declared in 1925 that it sought "to achieve a new aesthetic form [*Neugestaltung*] and a new order for economic, social, and spiritual life on the basis of new conditions."[10] The "new building," in other words, was more than just an exercise in design; it was invested with specific political and social meaning. The existence of the new German republic, however fragile, seemed to offer progressive planners and architects an opportunity to put their dreams into practice.

The modernists thus established positions for themselves not only through actual design projects but also through the use of polemics, and many of their supporters identified themselves with the left side of the Weimar political spectrum. Martin Wagner, a progressive planner, architect, and Social Democrat from Berlin, wrote in 1929: "Can any form of state sink deep historical roots without letting building stones speak for them? A state that does not build and build outstandingly simply does not live."[11] He believed that the new German democracy had to be represented in the form of important, modern, architectural endeavors, and indeed, clients for the progressive architecture often consisted of the democratic institutions of the republic—city and state governments and cooperative building societies.

Leaving aside the declared purpose of modernist architecture, how can the new modern style be characterized? Modern architecture first appeared around the turn of the century in Germany, but no single modern style emerged. Barbara Miller Lane lists the quite varied work of Paul Bonatz, Peter Behrens, Paul Schultze-Naumburg, Heinrich Tessenow, Bruno Taut, Hans Poelzig, and Walter Gropius as all contributing to the break from historical antecedents. By World War I, several trends were evident: the use of "simplified cubic masses, assembled asymmetrically and wholly unadorned"; decoration—when it existed—consisted of simple windows, balconies, and doors placed asymmetricallly, or bright panels of color.[12]

Some commentators reduced the new style to the advocacy of flat-roofed instead of pitched-roofed buildings, and, indeed, many of the arguments with the traditionalists were over roof lines.[13] The new building style went beyond flat roofs, however. Whereas the traditional architects promoted the use of traditional materials, which usually meant brick or brick covered with stucco, the Bauhaus and other innovative architects promoted the use of "modern" industrial materials: concrete, glass, and steel. Moreover, the use of these new materials broadened design possibilities. Buildings could be taller, with a much greater window surface to let in light, so they could appear weightless and partly transparent. Thus the use of glass addressed both aesthetic concerns and the hygienic concerns of the critics of the tenements of the nineteenth-century industrial city.

Although the new style emphasized clear, geometric shapes, the buildings were often sited to give a sense of movement and plasticity, in contrast to the heavy, solid masses of nineteenth-century buildings.[14] The emphasis on new materials was accompanied by a deemphasis on external, nonstructural decorative elements. Facades became clean, simple, and rational, reflecting the functions of architectural elements and the uses of the building. Because of this practical orientation, the new style was sometimes called "functionalism" (*Zweckmässigkeit*) or "the new objectivity" (*die neue Sachlichkeit*).[15] The new materials also lent themselves to new building techniques. In theory at least, major parts of the new buildings could be prefabricated. In 1922 and 1923, the Bauhaus exhibited designs for standardized housing, labeling them "dwelling-machines," itself a polemical term.[16] As Lane wrote, for the modernists "the minimal dwelling meant a rejection of *things*, a concentration on the simplest and most universal *forms*, and the erection into an aesthetic dogma of a way of life simple enough for the poor and therefore appropriate for all."[17]

From practically the moment of its founding, the Bauhaus and its programs suffered attacks by the political right as un-German, foreign, leftist, and decadent. The attacks were usually political in nature rather than substantive critiques of Bauhaus designs.[18] In spite of the controversy surrounding the new building style, and its lack of appeal to common citizens, the Bauhaus style spread rapidly through Germany after 1924. New housing, public administration buildings, schools, commercial and industrial buildings appeared in cities all over the country. Apart from the large housing projects of Frankfurt and Berlin, probably the best known examples of the new style were the Bauhaus building in Dessau and the 1927 building exhibition of the Deutscher Werkbund in Stuttgart known as the Weissenhof Siedlung. The latter was directed by Ludwig Mies van der Rohe, and individual houses and apartments were designed by the leading proponents of the new style, including Gropius, Bruno Taut, and the Swiss-born French architect Le Corbusier. The press gave marked attention to the exhibition, and thousands visited the white, geometric, flat-roofed complex on a hill.[19]

The Weissenhof exhibition enjoyed international acclaim. A group of the leading modern architects in Germany, including some who contributed to the Weissenhof complex, had organized themselves into what they called "the Ring," which participated in 1928 in the founding of the International Congresses for Modern Architecture (CIAM), dedicated to the promotion of the new style throughout the world.[20] On the eve of the Great Depression, architectural modernism seemed clearly ascendent.

At the same time, that very international success signaled the loss of modernism's earlier social and political content. It was beginning to become a "mere" style that might be incorporated in any kind of building.[21] In a letter written in 1934, Gropius wrote: "The layman really cannot know that it is all the same movement, whether it is called 'architectural Bolshevism' in Germany, 'Western bourgeois style' in Russia, or 'official fascist style' in Italy. . . . But precisely this madhouse of bewildering and contradictory conceptions is proof that the new architecture has absolutely nothing to do with this or that political structure."[22] Moreover, the success of the Weissenhof Siedlung also called forth a new organization of traditionally minded architects. Calling itself "the Block" as a counterpoint to the Ring, the group included some of the most prominent south German architects: Paul Bonatz, Paul Schultze-Naumburg, and Paul Schmitthenner. Traditionalism went on the offensive.[23]

Heimatschutz and Traditional Architecture

The modernists were not the only contenders for popular approval. Probably more people favored traditional over modern architectural designs. The traditionalist side of the spectrum derived in part from purely architectural concerns, in part from the growing strength of a historic preservation movement at the beginning of the twentieth century, and in part from the Heimatschutz movement. The latter was strongly shaped by the widespread hostility toward the spreading metropolises.[24]

In a general sense the traditionalists used architectural styles with historical antecedents in the buildings of a particular region, but without simply emulating the grandiose features of the Gothic or Romanesque.[25] Inspired primarily by regional domestic architecture, traditionalists stressed the use of native building materials and the quality of handicrafted (as opposed to prefabricated) construction.[26] In northern Germany, a traditional style usually meant the use of exposed brick with simple, baroque decoration. In other regions the style leaned toward simple cottages set in a garden, with steep, pitched roofs and plastered exterior walls.

Some architects, like Schultze-Naumburg and Tessenow, designed houses in traditional rural styles, while at the same time sharing some modernist elements, especially a functional simplicity of design. In Hamburg, Fritz Schumacher designed housing projects that combined modernist with traditionalist ideas. The placement of multistory apartment buildings reflected modern ideas about exposure to sunlight and air. Some of his buildings had flat roofs, others pitched roofs. The exterior walls were of exposed brick, with decoration in the detailing of doors, windows, and balconies to provide variation, but the decorations were not simply historicist replicas of local motifs.[27] When Schumacher worked in Cologne in the early 1920s, he proposed the construction of a neo-Romanesque cloister for the south side of the cathedral, and for the areas around the town hall and the Romanesque church of Groß St. Martin he suggested building new housing in the form of the single-family, two-story house traditional in Cologne. Although not dogmatic about architecture, and quick to acknowledge that his ideas countered the current purist trend in historic preservation, Schumacher felt that in this case preserving the artistic sense of the historic Rhine frontage demanded laying aside "theoretical scruples."[28]

The German historic preservation movement derived from the aftermath of the destruction of historic monuments during the French Revolutionary and Napoleonic periods. First Prussia (in 1815) and subsequently other German states promulgated laws that empowered government agencies to take measures to conserve designated historic monuments and to oversee any changes made in such monuments. In 1907 a Prussian law extended the concept of conservation to include ensembles and not just individual buildings.[29] Some cities created their own preservation offices. Cologne, for example, established an office in 1912.[30]

The effectiveness of these agencies, which at best had small staffs, often depended more on the abilities of individual officials and on public interest than on the force of law, but the spread of the historic preservation movement is evidence of a growing concern with the impact of urbanization and industrialization on the traditional urban and rural landscape to which many Germans were romantically attached. One of the key figures in the movement, Georg Dehio, stated: "We do not conserve a monument because we consider it to be beautiful but because it is a piece of our national existence."[31]

Preservationists generally favored protecting or restoring existing monuments, as opposed to recreating buildings that had disappeared, but the preservation movement could also accept something like the rebuilding of the late Baroque tower of the Michaelis Church in Hamburg, which had collapsed in 1906, because it was an intrinsic part of the history of that city. The conservation of a national heritage and a national tradition did not altogether preclude modern building, since modern buildings could be erected with minimal impact on the traditional urban silhouette and local landscape, but historic preservationism generally provided support for traditional rather than modern architecture.

A third and closely related source of traditionalism was the Heimatschutz movement. The Bund für Heimatschutz was formed in 1904, with the architect Paul Schultze-Naumburg as its head. Concerned with the relationship between the natural and built environments, the movement sought to demonstrate how bad planning and bad building ruined landscapes. Prior to World War I, there was considerable contact between the Heimatschützer and the Deutscher Werkbund as Schultze-Naumburg was a founding member of both. Like the modernists, the traditionalists shared a profound dislike of most of the architecture that appeared during industrialization. They considered it spiritually and physically unhealthy. One scholar recently noted that "Heimatschutz writers argued for a built environment that was modern, functional, and of high quality and aesthetic merit, but one in which the continuity of tradition remained sure and clear."[32] The architects associated with the Heimatschutz movement concentrated on domestic architecture and what was called *Wohnkultur*, which might be translated as the domestic environment. Tessenow designed small, simple, single-family homes, while Schultze-Naumburg built larger, more comfortable homes in the Biedermeier style for the middle class. In both cases, the houses were located not in the heart of big cities but in rural suburbs, where residents could enjoy fresh air and greenery.[33]

In a fascinating development, the traditionalists, the Heimatschützer, and the modernists in the Deutscher Werkbund collaborated during World War I in a first German exercise in reconstruction. Parts of East Prussia were twice occupied and damaged by the Russians in October 1914, and the Prussian government quickly decided to underwrite reconstruction. Participating architects ranged from modernists like Hans Scharoun to traditionalists like Schultze-Naumburg. All agreed that the small, backward East Prussian towns badly needed technical modernization, but they also agreed that the outward form of the new buildings should be traditionally East Prussian. In fact it proved difficult to identify such a style. Instead, the architects invented models for farm houses, workers' settlements, and other buildings that passed for authentic, regional buildings. Although these models were not in fact really East Prussian, they strongly influenced the image of what came to be considered regional architecture all over Germany throughout the 1920s.[34]

From the middle of the 1920s on, the traditionalists and supporters of the Heimatschutz movement leaned toward the right, becoming more and more vocal in their opposition to modernist rivals and adopting increasingly racist and nationalistic language. In addition to Schultze-Naumburg, leading opponents of the Bauhaus included Emil Högg, a professor at Dresden's Technische Hochschule, Konrad Nonn, editor of the *Zentralblatt der Bauverwaltung* and *Denkmalpflege und Heimatschutz*, and Paul Schmitthenner, a professor at the Technische Hochschule in Stuttgart. Indeed, Stuttgart, where Paul Bonatz and Heinz Wetzel also taught, became the best known center of traditionalism.[35] The traditionalists attacked the new architecture in terms of style and on its supposed lack of practicality. Flat roofs and glass walls were, they contended, impractical in a wet, cold, northern European country.[36] (The Stuttgart Weissenhof buildings were thus considered more appropriate for Arabs than for Germans.) They also attacked it on philosophical grounds; Högg argued in 1926 that prefabricated, standardized housing would lead to "uprootedness, spiritual impoverishment and proletarianization" of the Germans who lived in those buildings because they would lack any solid, historical tradition with which to identify.

In 1931 in *Heimatschutz und neue Baugesinnung*, Rudolf Esterer wrote: "It is not glass, steel, and concrete, not all the new materials and ugly forms of construction that is responsible for the destruction and devastation of our home town landscape against which the Heimatschutz movement has been vainly struggling . . . but men in a cultureless period, who have not technically mastered the new materials."[37] The Heimatschutz supporters could accept some modern elements in traditionally styled buildings, but they could not accept the modernists' principles or the claim that modernism embodied all that was valid in architecture. True German housing would root the Germans in the soil of their native land. German housing must not be designed according to universalist principles; it must be organically derived from the German landscape, climate, and historical traditions.[38] The advocacy of traditional styles thus took on a nationalistic tone.

Nazi Architecture and Neoclassicism

The political left was most closely associated with modernism in architecture while political conservatives most often advocated architectural traditionalism, but the Nazis were the only political party to take a strong position on architectural style. As is well known, Hitler presented himself as a frustrated architect, and he always professed an interest in monumental urban architecture. It was only in 1930, however, that the party joined the conservative side in specifically denouncing the Bauhaus, though even then the denunciations formed part of a general attack, in the name of German culture, on modernism in all of the arts.[39]

The Nazis' rejection of modern architecture at this juncture resulted from the growing influence of the antiurban ideas of Richard Walter Darré and the appointment by a Nazi minister in Thuringia of Paul Schultze-Naumburg as head of the architecture school in Weimar—the very place where the Bauhaus had been founded a decade earlier. Darré's doctrine of "blood and soil" endorsed traditional housing on individual land parcels and opposed industrialized, mechanized housing in the modern style.[40] Such ideas reinforced Schultze-Naumburg's own campaign against the Bauhaus and its supporters. Schultze-Naumburg became the most vocal spokesman for the Nazis in architectural matters. In 1932, he was joined by Konrad Nonn, Paul Schmitthenner, and others in founding the Kampfbund deutscher Architekten und Ingenieure to initiate propaganda against the modernists. This propaganda claimed to expose the close connections among architectural modernism, cultural Bolshevism, Judaism, and almost everything else the radical right detested in German society.

With the collapse of the German economy in the Great Depression, little money remained for new building construction. Prior to the Depression, one third of all buildings—especially large new housing projects—had been financed at least in part by the state; the Depression meant that this most important client stopped commissioning buildings. As most of the public housing had been designed by the modernists, these architects now found themselves with little work.[41] The propaganda campaign waged by the political right compounded their difficulties. In the fall of 1932, the Nazis on the Dessau city council managed to shut down the Bauhaus, forcing its relocation to Berlin, where it survived only until August 1933. After the Nazis seized power in January 1933, they forced a number of the leading modernist architects and planners out of their positions, and some left for the Soviet Union, Britain, Turkey, or the United States, while others spent the next decade building private houses.[42] No law was passed prohibiting modernist architects from designing buildings, but Nazi domination of the organizations of the building profession, combined with the selective purges, meant that few major commissions, if any, would be awarded to the modernists.

The cooperative building societies that had been responsible for most of the housing construction were consolidated into the Nazi German Labor Front. The German Architects Association (Bund Deutscher Architekten) and the Deutscher Werkbund were merged after 1933 into the Kampfbund deutscher Architekten und Ingenieure under the leadership of Gottfried Feder.[43] This organization, in turn, was absorbed in 1935 by the Reichskulturkammer in Goebbels's Propaganda Ministry. The new regime thus seized control of the architectural profession at the same time that it began to determine which large building projects could be constructed.

However virulent their incessant broadsides against the Bauhaus and the Ring architects, and however effective in depriving the modernists of jobs and commissions, the Nazis did not yet in fact offer an alternative set of architectural values beyond vaguely advocating "rooted" German traditions. Indeed, it was not clear in the first months after the Nazi seizure of power whether the Nazis really opposed all forms of architectural modernism, and some modernists still hoped to continue working in Germany.

In February 1933, modernists like Gropius, Wilhelm Riphahn, and Mies van der Rohe were among those invited to submit entries in a competition for a new Reichsbank building, and Peter Behrens, Fritz Schumacher, and Martin Wagner served on the prize jury. Mies van der Rohe's submission won one of the six prizes, even though it was a thoroughly modern design, and virtually all of the proposals included strongly modernist features, such as a lack of ornament, flat roofs, and functional, cubic masses. In January 1934 another competition was announced, this time for a "House of Labor" for the German Labor Front. Again leading modernists entered; their ranks included the Luckhardt brothers, Otto Bartning, Hans Schwippert, Martin Elsässer, Adolf Abel, and Gropius. Abel submitted a design for a building in the shape of a swastika, and Gropius's drawing included large Nazi flags and banners.[44] Today these designs, which suggest the willingness of the modernists to compromise with the National Socialists, are an embarrassment to the modernist camp, but they indicate that the relationship between architecture and politics was still not sharply defined.

In fact, the ambiguous attitude of the regime remained unresolved. The two agencies supposedly responsible for determining what architects should do and which architects would get commissions, the Kampfbund deutscher Architekten und Ingenieure and the Reichskulturkammer, proved unable to dictate the designs of all buildings, which were instead determined by whichever ministry or part of the government commissioned the building. A wide range of styles was used for different kinds of buildings. For example, a northern Romanesque style showed up in the Ordensburgen and Nazi party schools, and traditional, "völkish" domestic styles were used in some housing projects.[45] The Nazis willingly utilized the modernist architectural vocabulary in many industrial buildings. As late as September 1944 Herbert Rimpl, a leading designer of industrial architecture during the Nazi years, could declare that in industrial buildings "the standard is not the human being but the machine, and in fact the machine as means of production and as end product. The doors of an airplane factory are not determined by the height of humans and also not by ideas of either representative state buildings or of cults but simply by the size of the airplanes, which move into the hall." Such constructions had their own logic and thus demanded a different form of building than either religious or other secular buildings.[46] Clearly the Nazis were not about to endorse the historicism advocated by some of the traditionalists, and some traditional architects were critical of the regime's building programs.[47]

In spite of this plurality of styles, it is commonly asserted that a typical Nazi style of architecture existed because an official style did dictate the design of great representative buildings.[48] Hitler was attracted to the classical architecture of the ancient Roman empire because he believed the Romans served as models for the Germans and because he believed in a racial tie linking the ancient Greeks and Romans with the Nordic race of Germans. He greatly admired Paul Ludwig Troost's neoclassical design for the House of German Art in Munich, which corresponded to his own preconceived ideas about representative architecture. By the end of 1933, Hitler had endorsed Troost's neoclassicism as the appropriate style for the architecture expressly intended to represent the Nazi state.[49] Neoclassical buildings were to embody physically the great strength and will of the party, the state, the nation, the German people, and their Führer.

Hitler remained personally involved in the building program of his regime. He set forth programmatic outlines, contributed his own sketches, chose architects, and approved designs for some major projects—especially Speer's plans for the Party Congress grounds in Nuremberg and the plans of Speer and others for the huge architectural complex that would characterize the redesign of Berlin, Linz, Munich, Hamburg, and other cities. He viewed models of the projects and at times ordered modifications of the plans.[50] Furthermore, the Nazis launched a propaganda campaign asserting that their buildings, particularly the monumental, neoclassical buildings of the party and state, did indeed represent a unique style; they claimed that the "stones" of these buildings spoke the "word" of the movement.[51]

Actually neoclassicism was widespread at this time. In Germany there were examples from earlier regimes.[52] Albert Speer placed his own work in the tradition of late eighteenth- and early nineteenth-century Prussian neoclassicism, particularly the work of Karl Friedrich Schinkel and Friedrich Gilly.[53] Moreover, monumental neoclassicism was hardly unique to Germany. One could find neoclassical government buildings, exhibition halls, museums, schools, banks, and theaters all over Europe and in America as well. At the same time that Hitler planned to embellish the capital city of the Third Reich with neoclassical monuments, in Washington the Americans built the neoclassical National Gallery, Supreme Court, and Jefferson Memorial to enhance the neoclassicism of the Capitol Building and the White House.[54]

Be that as it may, monumental neoclassicism was trumpeted by Nazi propagandists as the great contribution of their movement to a revival of German culture. They successfully convinced both their supporters and their enemies that monumental neoclassicism embodied Nazism and that a distinctly National Socialist architecture broke from and rejected previous architectural traditions.[55] Furthermore, in the great Nazi architectural projects, architecture and urban design were expressly political and ideological. Buildings, however, were not to be simply symbols of Nazism. Individual buildings and complexes of buildings were to be functional, serving as administrative centers, locations for ceremonial display, meeting halls, parade grounds, train stations, and the like, while simultaneously impressing those who worked there and those who visited with the great power of the regime and with their own powerlessness as individual citizens.[56] Hitler equated functionality with beauty. Indeed, at one point he declared that "the final measure of beauty was a 'crystal-clear accomplished functionality.' "[57] He also equated power with size. In explaining why he was ordering the construction of such huge buildings, Hitler remarked that "only through such mighty works can one give a people the consciousness of being the equals of any other great country, even America."[58] In addition, the colossal scale also resulted from the desire to have huge masses of people experience a collective identification with the spirit of the buildings. Friedrich Tamms, professor of architecture in Berlin and a designer of Hitler's Autobahn network, stated that these buildings "must contain something unapproachable that would fill people with wonder, but also with awe."[59] Colossal architecture was to be public theater on a colossal scale. It was to be both representative and manipulative.[60]

It is in its intended function, then, that the unique character of National Socialist neoclassicism may be found, rather than in its formal architectural elements.[61] Certainly this was the opinion that Speer formed during his years in prison after 1945, and he became highly critical of his own work as Hitler's architect. On reflection, he found the scale of the Nazi buildings not simply gigantic but out of proportion even on their own terms. Even Hitler, had he ever been able to appear in the proposed great hall in Berlin, would have been reduced to insignificance. In addition, Speer feared that the buildings would have been so domineering as to preclude any real urban life. Worst of all, they might have been boring.[62]

Postwar Architecture

Although few of the neoclassical monuments planned by the regime were ever built, the impression made by the propagandistic claims about that architecture was so successful that the Allies refused to allow the "word in stone" to survive the demise of Hitler and his party. Consequently, the allied occupation forces continued to demolish Nazi buildings even after the war's end. Hitler's chancellery in Berlin, for example, could have been repaired, but instead the Allies razed it, salvaging the marble for the Russian war memorial in Treptow.

The powerful mythology surrounding Nazi architecture also meant that postwar German architects inherited a very murky legacy in the area of design. That which was overtly National Socialist—monumental neoclassicism—was condemned and ridiculed. For example, Rudolf Pfister, editor of the relatively conservative journal *Der Baumeister*, derided Troost's Haus der Deutschen Kunst and the Temples of Honor on the Königsplatz in Munich as little more than "carpentry in stone," and he castigated Hermann Giesler's party school buildings on the Chiemsee as a "gigantic act in tastelessness."[63] But what about all the other kinds of buildings to be found in the Third Reich, especially those in traditionalist or modernist styles? If undamaged, they escaped demolition. Moreover, except for Albert Speer, architects who had worked for the Nazis were not prohibited from practicing their profession under the allied occupation or in the new Federal Republic.

Questions about appropriate styles for rebuilding and the purpose and content of architecture in the new Germany abounded, surfacing regularly in heated debates. Klaus von Beyme recently suggested that postwar architecture can be grouped in three categories: reconstruction literally true to the damaged original, new building that attempted to emulate traditional styles through adaptation to local conditions, and completely new building in a modern style.[64] Wiltrud and Joachim Petsch suggest another category which they call "half-modern," a mixture of new forms and materials combined with traditional forms, such as traditional roof lines or an axial, symmetrical layout, but I think that contemporaries found such buildings to be modern.[65] The first two categories really belong together, since both attempted to recapture the historic atmosphere and spirit of individual cities, and they will discussed in a subsequent chapter.

Still another category, however, dominated much of the reconstruction in terms of sheer quantity, although it perhaps fails to merit the title architecture. Every West German city contains street after street lined with apartment buildings, three to five stories high, with plain, plastered facades painted in dull colors, often simply gray. If built on a main street, the ground floor usually contains shops. Except to the extent that they adhered to local codes about height and setback from the street, such buildings were neither modernist nor adapted to local architectural traditions. Rapid construction, rather than appearance, dictated style, and these apartments might fit into a category called "utilitarian building." In the intervening decades many of these structures have been "modernized" by adding another floor, new windows, or perhaps a new facade for the ground-floor business, but they are nonetheless recognizable as postwar housing. To the extent that they have been well-maintained, these apartment buildings have contributed positively to urban life, even if city residents no longer consciously "see" them and architectural critics dismiss them.

What about modernist architecture in the decade or so after the war? In a 1951 essay describing a Marshall Plan program in Germany, Bernard Wagner observed that the "Nazi regime systematically strangled any new ideas in architecture, thoroughly eradicated the earlier modern spirit and saw to it that German architectural schools produced nothing but obedient servants in the National Socialist conception of art and architecture."[66] Hence American sponsorship, he felt, was needed to revive modernism. In a book entitled *New German Architecture*, published in 1956, the authors bemoaned "the poor quality of the early post-war period" and complained that few buildings "reflect the true character of our age" or serve as hallmarks of outstanding architecture. Worse still, the large quantity of new housing seemed "almost untouched by any imaginative or artistic endeavours." "400,000 new dwellings a year need not necessarily add up to a cultural achievement!"[67] The passage of time has only cemented this view, and architectural historians agree that too little really good architecture was produced during the first decade of reconstruction. Wolfgang Pehnt spoke of "the wretchedness of postwar architecture."[68] Dieter Hoffmann-Axthelm denounced the postwar scene as "an architectonic no-man's land."[69] Christoph Hackelsberger liberally sprinkled his study of architecture in the 1950s with epithets: building was "sterile,"

"catastrophic," and "hideously plastered"; "a scandalous declaration of bank-
ruptcy," "belonging, with few exceptions, to the most miserable architectural
botches of all time."[70]

Is this devastating criticism fully justified? The hostility of these contemporary critics results from their high aesthetic, social, and political expectations
as well as their knowledge of modern architecture throughout the Western
world in the past four decades. Because they are all to the left of center
politically, they would normally identify "good" architecture with modern,
trend-setting architecture rather than with traditional architecture or with a
project in historic preservation. They share this position with modernist commentators after the war. Thus the editor of *Baukunst und Werkform* unequivocally asserted in early 1948: "A truly good architect will always at the same
time be a modern architect."[71]

All of the critics admit that there was some outstanding building during the
difficult, impoverished postwar years. A reading of the books by the critics
mentioned above or those by other architectural historians in fact reveals an
extensive list of praiseworthy modernist buildings.[72] These buildings earn their
accolades because they combine visible functionality with the use of modern
building materials: glass, steel, and concrete. Some emphasize the cubism of
the Bauhaus tradition; others feature playful, dynamic, curved lines and suggest lightness rather than the solidity of some starkly cubist designs. America
had supplanted Germany as the center of modern architecture, but surely the
production of important modern buildings in postwar Germany was no worse
than in other war-torn countries. Conceding that there was some good architecture, however, does not help explain why more was not produced.

The explanations for this failure all center on the difficulties experienced
by the modernists in postwar Germany. The generational split separating
older and younger architects, for example, resulted in a dearth of pertinent
experience. Older architects, such as Tessenow, who had trained and worked
before World War I, competed with a "younger" generation of men who had
trained in the 1920s and early 1930s. If the younger architects had worked at
all in Germany between 1933 and 1945, it was mostly on government projects,
though a few had built for industry or designed private houses. Their numbers
were augmented by thousands of contractors upon whom the Nazi Reichskammer der bildenen Künste had bestowed the title "Kammerarchitekt." By
the time the war ended, this younger generation was already 30 to 45 years old
and out of touch with the excitement generated by early modernism.[73] Prime
examples of modernist building had to be sought outside of Germany, in
Scandinavia or Britain, or in reports and exhibitions of American architecture. Friedrich Spengelin, for example, wrote that for his generation of younger architects, the high-rise housing projects of Fred Forbat in Stockholm
were "a Mecca."[74] Because of the enormity of the task at hand, both the older
and the younger generation of architects found ample opportunities to build,
but neither produced consistently innovative and exciting buildings.

Indeed, the magnitude of the task of reconstruction exceeded the capaci-
ties of both generations, no matter how qualified. Too many cities required

planning, too many buildings needed to be built. Younger architects who had received formal academic training but had been prevented by the war from gaining practical experience and young men whom the war had kept from academic study jumped at the chance to build, and the number of individuals designing buildings grew rapidly. Over 700 architects submitted entries for the competition for the 15 housing projects funded by the Marshall Plan.[75] Before the Nazi era, the Association of German Architects (Bund Deutscher Architekten, or BDA) of Munich/Upper Bavaria had had 80 to 100 members. In 1947, when there were only 3,500 qualified masons in the area, 1,000 individuals, most of whom called themselves architects, sought building permits in the region. This represented a wholesale appropriation of a formerly reserved professional title. In 1952, the head of Hannover's building department complained that 60% of the applications for building permits were inadequately prepared because the submitters lacked basic professional qualifications.[76] Such a situation hardly encourages innovation. Too few of the new architects possessed any real vision, and too much construction resulted from the rote application of formulas by architects and contractors. The results, en masse, could not help but be boring.

The situation, moreover, inevitably provoked a conflict between established architects, anxious to protect both the reputation of their profession and their incomes, and the younger generation, fighting for contracts that could make their reputations. The established architects demanded passage of a law protecting the use of the title "architect," setting a fee schedule, and ensuring that only registered architects (i.e., those listed as "Architect BDA") be allowed to present and approve building plans.[77] A similar demand had been published by the BDA in April 1933, when the architects' guild had tried to protect itself against the watering-down of the profession by the Nazis, but the moral ground of this association had been undermined by the fact that, upon being "coordinated" into the Nazi-organized Reichskammer der bildenden Künste, the conservative BDA leaders had excluded many modernists from the profession.[78] After the war, the BDA naturally avoided such ideological distinctions, but just as naturally nonmembers resented the influence of the architectural establishment. One engineer argued that "an architect cannot today 'demand' that he be protected from the difficulties and consequences of a lost war through professional privileges."[79] Nevertheless, in their occupation zones, the Americans and British approved laws that required the licensing of architects, while the French passed a law in the Saarland that restricted the use of the title "architect" to those clearly qualified and also created an "architects' chamber" to oversee and represent the profession. No national law defining the position of architects was passed in the Federal Republic, but the states eventually passed laws of their own.[80]

Another problem plaguing architectural innovation had to do with whether contracts should be awarded primarily to independent architects or to architects working within the building administrations of the cities, the cooperative housing corporations, or other institutions that commissioned buildings. Independent architects complained bitterly to the BDA that institutional insiders

monopolized all the major projects, and the BDA took up the cry. BDA
president Otto Bartning compared the impact of the "hydra of the building
bureaucracy" to a cancerous illness. By trying at the same time to commission,
plan, design, and construct, the building bureaucracy deliberately undercut
independent and creative architects.[81]

This was not just sour grapes: some places legally sanctioned this bureaucratic monopoly. In Bavaria, according to an ordinance of 30 June 1949, all
state buildings were to be built by architects directly employed by the appropriate agencies, which is to say "house" architects.[82] In Cologne, private
architects lodged complaints against "general planner" Rudolf Schwarz both
for showing favoritism to friends in the awarding of contracts and for intervening in competitions to his own advantage.[83] In Stuttgart, independent architects vehemently protested when Walter Hoss, the head of the building office,
presented his own design for the new town hall after all the other entries in an
open design competition had been submitted and judged by a jury on which
he sat.[84]

In general, the institutional architects, especially bank architects, were
highly conservative, and there may be some truth to the charge that these
architects disguised buildings infused with the spirit of Nazi heroic neoclassicism by clothing them in glass.[85] The massive bank buildings on Unter-
sachsenhausen and the Gerling company's headquarters in Cologne serve as
examples. Even when independent architects did win contracts for public
buildings, they often felt obliged to compromise their designs to satisfy local
building officials.[86]

Yet another problem affecting postwar architecture was that the ranks of
the modernists from the Weimar era had been thinned by emigration or death.

Stuttgart, the reconstruction of the town hall on the Marktplatz, 1931, 1946, and 1961. The original town hall building could have been restored, but the style of architecture was unpopular. The new town hall design, which was very controversial, called for a much larger and more dominant building. The flat roof lines and geometric shapes, however, harmonize with the rest of the new reconstructed buildings on the square. (Source: Landesbildstelle Württemberg, negative numbers 24643, 42406, F627139.)

Pioneers of the years 1910 to 1933, such as Gropius, Mies van der Rohe, Hilbersheimer, and Taut, had disappeared, while most Nazi-era architectural practitioners were still present and vigorous, if now less likely to trumpet their views. German modernists tried in vain to get Gropius and Mies to return to Germany, or, short of moving back, to contribute to German periodicals and participate in German architectural competitions. Mies, for example, turned down a professorship in architecture at the Kunstakademie in Düsseldorf.[87] The émigrés, however, were not willing to move back. They were fully engaged in major projects in their new countries and took time only for an occasional visit or entry in a competition.

In any event, the modernist complaints that their circle was too small to be heard was only partly true. Many modernists, such as Hans Scharoun, Adolf Abel, Otto Bartning, Richard Döcker, Hans Schwippert, Egon Eiermann, and Rudolf Schwarz, held influential positions in planning offices and academies in Germany after the war.[88] They won important commissions, sat on the juries in architectural competitions, and trained a new generation of students. This did not, however, keep some of the modernists from *feeling* beleaguered.[89] The most modern plans for new urban housing came from Hans Scharoun in Berlin and the French architects Marcel Lods in Mainz and Georges-Henri Pingusson in Saarbrücken. Scharoun planned a new Berlin in the form of an undulating ribbon or band with much high-rise housing. Lods and Pingusson, both followers of Le Corbusier, planned modern new cities with residential skyscrapers.[90] In all three cases, however, the plans and their planners were dismissed before the modernist buildings could be erected.

The fact that the defense of architectural modernism was generally more muted after 1945 than in the 1920s was not due to an absence of combatants in the modernist ranks. Energetic debates on architectural principles persisted, and the *Baukunst und Werkform*, for example, printed outspoken attacks on traditionalism. Hermann Mäckler asserted in its pages that virtually all of the entries in the competition for the rebuilding of the St. Paul's Church in Frankfurt offered little more than Nazi architecture in "miniature."[91] In 1949 *Neue Bauwelt* printed the Charter of Athens (the international manifesto of architectural modernism), with a critique of the manifesto and a rejoinder to the critique, although much of the debate focused on issues of functionalism in planning rather than on architectural style.[92] On the other side, *Der Baumeister* often published bitter attacks against the modernists.[93] These debates simply failed to command the attention of most architects. Rudolf Hartog, an architecture student in Darmstadt in the early 1950s, wrote that "the conflict between the Bauhaus style and traditional style affected us only marginally because we felt that both were part of the past and were no longer able to provide new guidelines." In fact, Hartog stated, "one tried to avoid any particular style altogether. . . . Consequently one can argue that no uniform style can be found in the architecture of the 1950s."[94] Rather than perpetuating the old struggle, proponents of the conflicting styles sometimes tried to resolve their differences. This was one of the purposes of a well-attended meeting in Darmstadt in 1951, for example, and when the few modernists in Munich formed a local chapter of

the Deutscher Werkbund, they staged discussion evenings with the traditionalists rather than confronting them.[95] Martin Elsässer urged his professional
colleagues to reject any "totalitarian" claims to correctness; conflicting opinions were useful in promoting fruitful discussions, but excessive dogma was
harmful.[96]

Many of the modernists who worked in Germany devoted their energy to
reconstruction planning as well as to the design of individual buildings. Working under extraordinarily difficult physical conditions, such architects as Rudolf Schwarz in Cologne, Hans Schwippert in Aachen and Düsseldorf, Richard
Döcker in Stuttgart, and Werner Hebebrand in Frankfurt were often overwhelmed by the magnitude of their many tasks. Standing amidst the ruins of
the bombed cities, Rudolf Schwarz wrote to Mies in 1947:

> We are standing on the Rhine, or more exactly in Cologne and Frankfurt, on
> the last line of defense of the West, beyond which there is no more retreat,
> and the West ends just a hundred kilometers from us. One feels like a soldier
> who has just been sent to the last barrier that can still be defended and who
> no longer asks if he can hold out. It sounds so artificial, but we believe that
> we must hold this position or fall doing so—since I feel my existence is
> identical with the West, however old-fashioned that may be. We must muster
> up whatever can still be gathered together, in order that once more a last
> glimmer of the old declining light shines over the world—our world, which
> has become so small—so that this ancient Volk once more sees the purpose of
> its existence and in thinking about this grasps what stands before it.[97]

These words exude melancholy and weariness, not eagerness to engage in
ideological battle over architectural styles.

Additionally, conflicts *within* the modernist movement rose more clearly
to the fore after the war and weakened its ability to provide leadership. As
noted earlier, architectural modernism had become, even prior to the war,
mere style. Dubbed the "international style" at the 1932 Museum of Modern
Art exhibition, it had increasingly lost its radical social purpose. In the 1920s
modernism had suffered from an unresolved tension between standardization
and functionalism on the one hand and the creation of new aesthetic forms
with new materials on the other. The largest client in that decade, municipal
governments and firms building subsidized housing, had stressed standardization and utility, and only later, beginning in the later 1920s and continuing in
the years of exile, had clients commissioned public buildings like theaters and
schools that presented modernist architects with the opportunity to pursue the
path of inventive forms. After the war, the huge demand for housing forced
building in standardized forms, while clients like the Catholic and Protestant
churches encouraged more imaginative designs and exerted less financial pressure on the architects.

Standardized housing, pioneered in the 1920s, was no longer a promising
innovation in the 1940s and 1950s; it was simply necessary, and few expected it
to result in exciting buildings. Consider the anecdote related by Ernst Neufert,
the wartime guru of standardization in Speer's ministry, in his contribution to

Berlin, cooperative social housing erected on Bayrischer Platz in Schöneberg. The photo is from 1955, and the style is typical of such apartment complexes throughout West Germany. (Source: Landesbildstelle Berlin, 43211.)

the catalog for the 1951 Constructa building exhibition in Hannover. He reported that an industrialist once stated: "'I plan my industrial buildings for their internal utility; outside the whole thing can look like a penitentiary.' " "Now," Neufert commented in all seriousness, "even penitentiaries can be beautiful, with large masses of walls and small, barred windows."[98] After the Third Reich, such statements did not augur well for outstanding architecture. In fact, the influence of Neufert's thinking and writing about the use of standard elements in building can be seen in thousands of nearly identical, unimaginative residential and commercial buildings.

The best modern architecture in the first decade or so of reconstruction found expression in schools, theaters, memorials, and museums, rather than housing. The 1957 International Building Exhibition in Berlin (the Interbau) finally initiated construction of modernist housing, but this too was more an exercise in form and urban planning than a housing program. It also brought to the surface another split within the ranks of the modernists. In 1951, Rudolf Schwarz declared that "the phrase 'modern architecture' is in itself nonsense" and that "nothing really right came from the [new] objectivity for the simple reason that things in themselves have no sufficient form whatsoever." Later he attacked the Bauhaus proponents for being too polemical and dogmatic, and Martin Wagner launched attacks on functionalism for having lost its original content.[99]

The deficiency of imaginative postwar architecture also resulted from the catastrophe of the Nazi experience, which ultimately and thoroughly discredited not only neoclassicism but also the ideas of monumental and representational building.[100] Writing about Cologne, for example, Hans Schmitt warned against all monumentality and grandeur in architecture, arguing that neither government nor industry had any intrinsic right to build on a massive, monumental scale. Such structures, both during the Nazi years and during the Bismarck years, had led to "an honoring of the banal" and a "thorough uglification of all cities."[101] The Nazi conception of monumentality had been based in part on sheer size and in part on imposing new perspectives through which people might view and experience the huge monuments. The bombing allowed some cities to create new perspectives on remaining historic monuments, but few Germans favored retaining large open vistas in the inner cities for future new monuments.

Entirely typical is a letter from Max Taut, a Berlin modernist of the older generation, to Mies van der Rohe. Taut wrote:

> Mostly I think about how one can best and most quickly get a roof over one's head. The smallest and most modest tasks seem to me to be the most important at this moment, especially since I do not believe that we will be in a position very soon to be able to build as we once could. We will have to limit ourselves to the most simple building, and even then, before we can properly begin [with large-scale reconstruction], which will occur perhaps decades from now, we will have to be satisfied with provisional buildings . . . . I am really not against fantasies and every now and then design "castles in the air," but one must not thereby forget and neglect the true realities. I think that it is a disease of us Germans, that especially when we are poor, we are most attracted to grandiose poses and thus kick over the traces.[102]

Otto Bartning, soon to be elected chairman of a reconstituted BDA, wrote in 1947 of infusing architecture with "modest respectability" and "calm mastery."[103] Such modesty was particularly characteristic of the bulk of the new construction, namely housing. One author declared that "housing should look like housing and not like the palace of a maharaja or a museum for local history. And a building for social housing should appear modest and not suggest that something special is hidden behind massive stone facades or powerful flowing lines."[104] Hanns Adrian, now Hannover's chief planner, has said that in the 15 years after the war the goal was not to decorate Hannover or to build an attractive city, but to solve efficiently the housing problem.[105]

Similarly great caution permeated discussions about "representative buildings." As Berlin was no longer a capital city and Prussia had been abolished along with the Third Reich, there was nothing to represent there, at least until the 1957 building exhibition sought to make modernism representative of democracy. Only in 1949 was the new democratic state established under the tutelage of the Allies, and prior to that date no real national client existed to commission and build representative buildings of any sort. After 1949 the

Federal Republic adopted a self-effacing stance, struggling to avoid calling attention to itself. Bonn was considered a provisional capital rather than the permanent seat of a democratic government. The federal states, the Länder, were mostly new creations as well.

And what sort of style might be considered appropriate to a new democratic society? In 1930, Hans Gerhard Evers wrote that "it is the mistake of liberalism to see the state embodied primarily in its citizens, so to speak in its soft parts. . . ."[106] The Federal Republic was a liberal state; what should the "hard parts" look like? Once Bonn was chosen as the capital, Hans Schwippert, a modernist architect, designed the new parliament building as a modern, open, light-filled structure, but it is hardly monumental or "representative" in the sense that pre-1945 architects like Evers understood that term. A member of the historic preservation branch of the state government of Hesse recently praised the office buildings of the Oberfinanzdirektion and Bundesrechnungshof in Frankfurt as good examples of representative, democratic architecture because they are clear, simple, and functional.[107] But do those who work there or those who visit these buildings really find them democratic?

In fact, designing representative democratic buildings was and is difficult for two reasons. First, representative architecture requires a spirit of confidence and enthusiasm. In the early 1920s, and in spite of the lost war, modernist architects believed that profound social change—perhaps resulting in socialism—was at hand, and their manifestos and buildings were infused with an optimistic, crusading, even utopian spirit. Certainly Hitler and Speer brought great confidence and enthusiasm to their building program after 1933. Post-1945 architects, however, lacked such vibrant optimism.[108] Very few of those who spoke of reconstruction as a unique opportunity to correct past wrongs embodied sufficient enthusiasm to overcome the trend toward modesty and mediocrity.

Second, the attempt to determine what kind of architecture was appropriate for a democracy proved troublesome. As stated earlier, neoclassical forms were immediately rejected because of their association with Nazism. One critic observed in 1979 that "the attempt to interpret in architecture a pluralistic, democratic republic is still a lasting historical and psychological complex, especially for the generation that [in 1979] is today over fifty years of age, as a result of the trauma of the Nazi period, which left the architectural scene with much anxiety and a feeling of being cramped."[109] Designing solemn, quiet churches for reflective believers or massive bank buildings to represent the power of the energetic capitalist economy proved much simpler than capturing in form and space so elusive a concept as democracy.

Johannes Cramer and Niels Gutschow noted that "emotions, feelings, and personal pronouncements, like those that had shaped the architectural discussions in the second half of the 1920s, were not there. In their place stood functional components, technical arguments, and the instrumentalization of architecture. . . . It almost seems as if the ability to understand form as an expression of a new social order had been lost."[110] It may be that innovative, lasting architecture derives from an ability to incorporate, transcend, and transform past social and political experience and past artistic vocabularies into a future-oriented expression. For some time after the war, Germany could neither transcend nor transform its past; it had to be satisfied with either suppressing memory or trying to reconcile the present with the past, thereby beginning the slow process of healing the wounds of the Nazi era.

A final explanation for the relative paucity of good modern architecture is simply that modern architecture was not very popular among the German people. To some Germans, especially those on the right, the reappearance of modernism in postwar Germany represented nothing more than the importation of what now seemed "American" noncontextual architectural forms.[111] For Germans in the middle of the political spectrum, modernism may have triggered disturbing memories of the unsettled radicalism of the early Weimar years and seemed entirely inappropriate for a people intent on achieving stability. It was legitimate to ask, in any case, whether a distinctively German form of modern architecture existed, and the desire to rebuild a devastated Germany in a modest German style is certainly understandable. Stuttgart's influential Lord Mayor Arnulf Klett, for example, in discussing the design of a new town hall, said: "We should examine whether the proposed building honestly and without false posturing expresses our preconception and our current image of the city hall of Stuttgart, the capital of the Swabian state."[112] Klett was not a reactionary, rigidly opposed to modernism; he wanted architecture appropriate to its setting, architecture that would have meaning for the citizens of his city. To the extent that they shared such sentiments, modernists were more likely to join forces with the traditionalist architects than to fight them.

The German scholar Gerhard Fehl recently argued that "seamless transitions" marked German architectural history: *Stunde Null*—zero hour—did not exist.[113] This is certainly true in the sense that basic programmatic positions and practices in architecture, formulated during the creative years between 1910 and 1933, had been submerged in the public consciousness by propaganda proclaiming a unique Nazi building style, but had reemerged after 1945. Christoph Hackelsberger incorrectly describes 1950s German architecture as a case of postponed modernism. Modernism never perished. It survived, although sometimes barely, always struggling with traditionalism, its old opponent. After 1945, a more moderate tone suffused the debate, while other obstacles hindered an immediate flowering of modernist architecture, primarily the intense need to clear away the rubble and build new housing. Still, modernist architects were there and at work, and modernism emerged as the dominant force in the late 1950s.

Ironically, the architecture that was built to last, to be eternal, proved remarkably short-lived. Hitler promised that his buildings were "intended for the millennia of the future," and both he and Speer fully expected those buildings to be impressive ruins upon the passing of millennia.[114] In fact the ruins that stand as monuments to the Third Reich were neither built by the Nazis nor do they celebrate Nazism. Instead they are the grim reminders of the bombing that gutted truly historic architecture. Nazi monumental neoclassicism, rather than modernism, amounted to a discontinuity in German architectural history.

Is architecture political, or is it the architects who are political? Do individual buildings have meaning beyond their formal elements? The German experience fails to provide clear answers. The political left and right both sought to build political architecture, and sometimes the designers, their clients, and the people who used the buildings shared common beliefs so strongly that they heard the stones speak. But "stones" may not in fact tell the truth after all.[115] Nazi buildings that survived both the war and the postwar demolition remain in use today. The House of German Art in Munich and the Berlin Olympic stadium, for example, do not impress a racist, volkish, aggressively nationalist ideology upon visitors, however the quality of their architecture is assessed. Nazi symbolic and decorative motifs had been simple in comparison to the architectural vocabulary of the pre-1918 monarchies and consequently could be removed rather easily.[116] Hartmut Frank recently observed that unless one knows what happened at Auschwitz, the remaining buildings of that terrible camp appear as nondescript factory buildings lacking any ideological content.[117] Building stones thus said less about political values than the proponents of the main architectural traditions in this century believed.[118] During the process of urban reconstruction, it proved much more important that architects design and build whatever was needed than that they build in one particular style.

4

The Face of Reconstruction:
The Role of Historic Preservation

The old inner cities, the *Altstädte*, where the bomb damage was often the most severe, represented far more than centers for housing, commerce, or government. They physically embodied Germany's urban history and culture. Hence debates about reconstructing the old inner cities were as much about historical symbols and values as about architectural elements or the technical dimensions of modern planning. The art historian Jürgen Paul recently noted that "the 'beautiful old city,' with its naturally and historically shaped individual physiognomy, occupied a central, identity-determining place in the national cultural consciousness of the conservative, idealistically-oriented, educated German middle class in the nineteenth century."[1] That remained true in the twentieth century as well. Much of the German population harbored a deep romantic attachment to the picturesque silhouettes and the urban landscapes of the old cities. Modern architecture and urban planning seemed to threaten the very core of urban residents' sense of being. They responded to this threat by generating massive popular support for the reconstruction of major monuments and for traditionalist, adaptive architecture. Some cities also revived the Heimatschutz movement.

Discussion about the restoration, preservation, or even complete reconstruction of old buildings in an inner city focused on the perceptions of both planners and the public about the city's essential, inherent character. Those who favored a maximum of rebuilding in the old form were also making an argument for reestablishing continuity with the past. Shortly before his death, Paul Clemen, one of the founders of the preservation movement in Germany, declared that such a reconstruction was "not only a precondition for rebuilding the nation . . . in the spirit of a historically-conscious, humanistic culture, but also an obligation [in order] to make it again possible for future generations to experience historical continuity."[2] In tune with most preservation officials and the public, however, Clemen did not seek to revive continuity or identification with some political form of German state as it had existed under the Hohenzollerns, in Weimar, or under the Nazis. Instead, the German nation needed to revitalize a cultural heritage grounded both in physical artifacts and in the realm of the spirit.

The kind of arguments made by Clemen and the Heimatschutz supporters underline once again continuities in ideas, organization, and personnel that predate the Nazi period. There were powerful representatives of traditionalism on the scene in 1945, including some of the same champions that had made it an important force early in the century. Tessenow and Fritz Schumacher, for example, were both still alive, although advanced age limited their activity. As planners, modernists claimed them, but as architects they had always stood closer to the traditionalists. Having maintained a low profile under the Nazis, their prestige could lend legitimacy to traditionalism and free it from association with Nazism.

Another important spokesman for traditionalism was Paul Schmitthenner, who enjoyed a new popularity in spite of a bitter controversy about his rehabilitation.[3] A vocal critic of the modernists in the late 1920s and early 1930s, and a committed Nazi, he had nevertheless published an article in 1943 in which he distanced himself from the monumentalism of Speer and his colleagues.[4] After the defeat of France in 1940, Schmitthenner managed rebuilding of the destroyed Alsatian town of Lauterburg, applying such traditionalist principles as the retention of the basic street layout and the use of local building materials and forms.[5] This approach made Schmitthenner a favored consultant after the war in Freudenstadt and Mainz, towns that chose a traditionalist form of reconstruction and enlisted his help in resisting modernist rebuilding programs coming from outside. Although Schmitthenner's influence in reconstruction incensed modernists, they attacked his style more than his Nazi associations. The modernist journal *Baukunst und Werkform*, for example, observed that Schmitthenner had not really been that important in the ranks of official Nazi architects and that it would be "at the least highly problematic" to contend that "Schmitthenner's architecture had anything to do with political doctrine."[6] The architectural historian Hartmut Frank argued persuasively that "Schmitthenner was not really attacked for his Nazi activities, but rather because of the extraordinary popularity of the traditional, locally-oriented architecture that he represented in an especially qualified form. This architecture could express itself very well in the context of the reserve and modesty necessary during reconstruction."[7]

Local Heimatschutz associations, revived and reinforced by citizens' groups that often referred to themselves as "friends of the rebuilding of the old city," once again advocated traditionalism. They preferred to be known by names other than Heimatschutz, because the Allies tended to ban organizations that had existed during the Third Reich. During those years, the Heimatschutzer had been busy "restoring" their towns to match idealized pictures of the towns' supposed appearance at some favored moment in the past. Houses from the Baroque era, for example, were given "medieval" facades, or original plastered facades were stripped of their plaster to reveal supposedly authentic brick construction—activity which discomforted local preservation officials.[8] On the other hand, in some places these same officials had participated in urban renewal projects during the mid-1930s in which many old buildings were demolished and replaced with new, though tradition- ally styled buildings.[9] After the war, these Heimatschutz groups advocated rebuilding in a form that would preserve the "historic character" of German cities, that is to say, to rebuild in a traditional rather than modern architec- tural style.

A few topics generated no argument. Traditionalist and modernist archi- tects, planners, and citizens agreed that a major historic monument—which usually meant a religious or government building predating 1830—should be preserved if undamaged and restored if only moderately damaged.[10] Co- logne's cathedral, for example, even though partly medieval and partly nine- teenth century, merited restoration. In Munich everybody simply understood that the Residenz, the huge royal palace near the center, would be rebuilt, and that new towers, faithful reproductions of the originals, would again top the Frauenkirche. Everywhere preservation offices urgently tried to prevent further deterioration of major bombed monuments and repaired or rebuilt them whenever possible. At the same time, very few found aesthetic or cul- tural value in preserving buildings erected after 1871, which were considered heavy and pompous.

There was also an unspoken consensus that the preservation, restoration, or reconstruction of historic buildings applied almost exclusively to the shell of the building. Modern architecture requires a clear relationship between form and function, and facades are supposed to reveal interiors, even if the walls are not made of glass. "Historic" buildings (again, those built before 1830), on the other hand, which usually featured inadequate lighting, ventila- tion, and plumbing, underwent significant interior modernization even though exterior facades were restored or reconstructed to be nearly identical to their prewar condition. Damaged or destroyed interior decoration of major monuments was seldom replaced, and ceilings, window frames, and other elements were commonly simplified. Historic buildings given new functions— as museums, as university buildings, as administrative offices—certainly mer- ited interior renovation, but those used as private houses and business were likewise modified and modernized. Historic replication of the facade, roof- line, and basic structure sufficed, since no one wanted to work or live in medieval conditions.[11]

The problem that confronted postwar German planners and builders, therefore, was how, and under what conditions, to rebuild the damaged shell. Should all major monuments that had been completely destroyed be recon- structed? What was to be done about lesser monuments that had been badly damaged? What about older private houses and businesses that had been bombed or those that survived the raids but now impeded other projects? And even if restoration was to take place, should the buildings be restored to their 1939 status, their 1933 status, the form in which they had originally been built in the distant past, or some intervening form? Should the remains of some historic building be preserved as ruins and thus as monuments to the war? These questions generated various and often contradictory responses, and preservationist officials, planners, architects, and citizens often found themselves bitterly at odds.

Principles of Historic Preservation

The war inflicted vast destruction on Germany's historic architecture. A report by the American military government in February 1947 concluded that 54% of the 1,616 important architectural monuments in its occupation zone had been damaged.[12] The bombing had been even heavier in the British zone. It is indicative of the Germans' will to rebuild those monuments that, as an extensive recent survey of war damage in the Federal Republic has concluded, "None of the architectural monuments which have a firm place in German architectural history were [permanently] lost, with the sad exception of the palace in Braunschweig."[13] What was lost, and not just in the bombing but also after the war in the demolition of repairable and even undamaged buildings, were thousands of lesser buildings, private houses and businesses that were not considered major monuments.[14]

Laws governing historic preservation had existed in some German states and cities since the early nineteenth century, but scholars agree that the power and influence of preservationist officials was based primarily on the personal prestige of the individual official and on public sentiment intent on preserving the remains of the past.[15] Consequently, in the immediate postwar years, most preservationist officials sought to stake out positions that would enjoy broad support yet not compromise their professional beliefs. Faced with enormous pressures, officials often looked for such positions in vain. The increased demand for rapid construction of commercial buildings, spurred by the reviving capitalist economy, heightened the already pressing need for new housing. Additionally, preservation officials competed for financing, skilled labor, and building materials, sometimes impossibly scarce resources.

In a statement of principles published in June 1947, the Preservation and Museum Council of Northwest Germany argued that the basic task of historic preservation was to save "the historic character of the old inner cities and the *Heimatgefühl* [feeling of being at home] of the inhabitants." In practice this meant not so much the preservation or reconstruction of individual buildings as the preservation of the traditional street layout and the exclusion of modern architecture (especially large-scale projects) and most automobile traffic from the old city center. Irregular, curved, or angled streets, varied building lines, and the dominance of pedestrians, it was argued, would provide the proper historic ambience, even if many of the buildings were in fact new.[16] In Munich in June 1948, when 47 senior preservation officials from all over Germany met for the first time, Hermann Deckert, the state conservator of

Lower Saxony, declared that the chief purpose of preservation was to conserve the "individuality" of each city against the pressures of modernization.[17]

At the same meeting, Georg Lill, the director of the Bavarian State Office for Historic Preservation, argued against rebuilding individual structures that had been leveled by the bombing. He also rejected moving historic remains elsewhere just to preserve them, derisively referring to such practices as "museum-like in the worst sense of the word." Furthermore, additions or even large-scale repairs to historic buildings should complement rather than imitate the old style, presumably by employing architectural elements characteristic of traditional, regional styles.

Postwar statements about historic preservation mirrored prewar thinking. Preservationists *and* modernist architects in both periods argued that historic buildings should not be reconstructed because original buildings were works of art. Just as a destroyed Rembrandt repainted by a contemporary and hung in a gallery would ring false, so a reconstructed building would necessarily fail to achieve the originality, beauty, and value of its prototype. Alfons Leitl pointed out that people had esteemed the famous copies of the Vermeer paintings as long as they believed the paintings to be genuine, but immediately devalued and disparaged them once they had been exposed as forgeries. He feared that while architectural copies would not fool those who watched them rise, future generations would not know that the buildings were mere reproductions.[18] In 1947, a group of 38 prominent architects and critics, including modernists like Leitl, Hans Schwippert, and Richard Döcker and traditionalists like Tessenow and Fritz Schumacher, signed a manifesto declaring that "the destroyed heritage must not be reconstructed in its historic form; it can only arise in new forms for new tasks."[19] Munich architect Robert Volhoelzer, also a signer of the manifesto, added: "To want to rebuild in the old form or perhaps to copy what had been destroyed is false. What is gone should remain gone. . . . We don't want to design [cities as] museums, but rather we want the courage to develop creatively something living, though, if possible, something of equal value" with what was destroyed.[20] An architect-planner from the Ruhr wrote that contemporary Germans no longer embodied the "mystical submersion" or "humble piety" charactistic of the middle ages that might justify rebuilding Gothic churches, nor did they boast the confident, "articulate, princely cheerfulness" that produced the buildings of the Baroque.[21] Indeed, concentrating on rebuilding old buildings might only inhibit the growth of new architectural ideas really in tune with the modern age.

Dissent, however, quickly appeared, especially in the debate about reconstructing the Frankfurt house in which Goethe had been born and spent part of his youth. A relatively undistinguished building, it had been modified already in the early nineteenth century and had contained period furniture, though not pieces owned by Goethe. Allied bombing had reduced the house to rubble, although the furnishings had been saved. The citizens of Frankfurt, the foundation that owned the house, and some preservationists favored erecting a copy of the structure as it had stood just prior to the air raids. They prized not simply the house but Goethe himself as a special symbol of what was good and valuable in German culture.[22] At the 1948 Munich meeting of preservation officials, Gerhard Strauss of Berlin defended the decision to reconstruct Goethe's house, even though it had been leveled, because it served an important public function, namely to remind Germans of the chief figure in German enlightenment and classical culture. Rebuilding the edifice would thus reestablish continuity with a treasured past.

Of those who opposed rebuilding the Goethe house, some cited the classic theory of historic preservation: preserve what exists, but do not recreate what has vanished. Otto Völckers wanted to know what would happen if the rebuilt house were destroyed again. Should one then make a copy of a copy?[23] But it was Walter Dirks who addressed the central issue of what it meant to attempt to revive a sense of continuity with the past. In an oft-cited article, he expressly argued against trying to reestablish a form of continuity that bypassed the Nazi era. "There are connections," he declared,

> between the spirit of the Goethe house and its fateful destruction. . . . That the Goethe house collapsed in rubble has its own bitter logic. It was not an oversight that one could have corrected, not some sort of mistake in the course of history; there is justness in its ruin. And therefore one should acknowledge it. The destruction of this house belongs just as much to German and European cultural history as does its construction. . . . We should not try to erase this last chapter—the destruction—of its long history.[24]

Germany's intellectuals, Dirks felt, had contributed to Hitler's rise and thus to the destruction of this building through their arrogant otherworldliness. The ruins of 1945 were a just and proper monument to the failings of German history. Franz Meunier observed that no mere coincidence accounted for the proximity of Buchenwald concentration camp and Goethe's real home, where he lived and worked, in Weimar.[25] In the minds of these critics, there *should* be a zero hour, a discontinuity, a break in German history. One must accept what happened, including the destruction of the old German culture, and summon the courage to begin again.

The Goethe house was in fact faithfully rebuilt, and the controversy about this single undistinguished structure eventually faded away. Leading preservationist officials, however, came to realize that the conservation or restoration of a few major monuments would not enable cities to retain their historic character in the face of modernization. In a 1948 pamphlet, one author argued that historic buildings could be viewed as symbols, as historical documents of a past age, as works of art, and as raw material for research in the technical practice of building. The latter two categories rendered meaningless a complete reconstruction or even major modification with modern means. On the other hand, if the building enjoyed symbolic importance or served as a historic document—and here the St. Paul's Church and the Goethe house in Frankfurt come to mind—then major restorations, reconstruction, or major modifications were entirely justified.[26]

Typical of this turnaround was the 1953 keynote speech given by Rudolf

Esterer, president of the Bavarian Office for the Administration of State Palaces, Gardens, and Lakes, to the annual meeting of the German Academy for City and Regional Planning, which convened in Munich. An outspoken critic of modern architecture and modernist architects in the early 1930s, Esterer now acknowledged that the decisive issue for *planners* was traffic management, which demanded a statistical, scientific approach.[27] Nevertheless, he insisted that planners conceptualize the preservation of the Altstadt in different terms. The Altstadt had always represented the true "soul" of the city, the feature that defined its unique character and personality. Admittedly, cities destroyed in the past had been rebuilt using new styles of architecture, even international styles like the Baroque, but still reconstruction had remained local in spirit and characterized by local artisans using local materials and fitting their work into the existing framework of street and property lines. Consequently buildings of different styles harmonized with one another and the personality of the city was saved. The present difficulty, Esterer argued, was that modern architecture, in addition to being international in style, had become purely mechanical and industrial in technique and impersonal in nature. Filling an old city with modern buildings would thus destroy its personality, its soul. In this sense the individual parts of the city mattered less than the whole, and in order to preserve what was most essential, the city's uniqueness, it might be better to build copies of destroyed historic buildings than to introduce new modern buildings that might stand just as comfortably in any city in the world.[28]

This change from a narrow view of preservation and restoration, in which only individual buildings largely undamaged should be saved or restored, to one which emphasized the character of an area or quarter as an ensemble, even if that meant complete reconstruction of a totally destroyed building, seems entirely reasonable from our perspective today, and even then it matched the sentiments of the citizenry better than the narrower, purist position. Implementing the change, however, proved extremely difficult due to the legacy of the debate on modern architecture that raged during the 1920s and 1930s. Preservation officials who advocated such policies feared sounding like the traditionalist and Heimatschutz architects who had gravitated toward Nazism before the war. In the first years after 1945, a supposedly pro-Nazi mentality was associated with the desire to "save the soul" of an old city by utilizing traditional styles and methods, reconstructing what had been lost, and banning modern architecture, just as the proponents of modern architecture neatly aligned themselves with supposedly progressive and democratic values. Such positioning was of course simplistic. One cannot equate Nazism and historicism any more than one can say that the modernizers were all democrats. Nevertheless, political recriminations unavoidably informed the discussions on postwar preservation and modernization in the old cities.

Preservationist officials never settled upon an entirely consistent theoretical platform for reconstruction, nor did they succeed in determining consistent priorities. Some historic monuments were rebuilt as close to the original as possible; others included major alterations or incorporated bits of architecture from different styles and periods.[29] Where the state governments owned important buildings, the state paid for much of the rebuilding and state officials made the decisions on reconstruction. The state of Bavaria, for example, spent more than DM 30 million on 18 major projects in Munich alone between 1945 and 1950.[30] The Protestant and Catholic churches, often with their own financial backing and architects, controlled the reconstruction of religious buildings, with or without the help and advice of town preservation officials. Sometimes the churches obtained assistance from other countries, an option seldom if ever available for rebuilding historic houses.[31] Individual owners of private, secular buildings were usually left to their own devices.

Cities tried to resolve the preservation issue in a variety of ways. Some opted strongly for modernization, preserving only isolated monuments or small ensembles. Others made a major effort to retain the historic character of their inner cities. Hamburg, Berlin, Frankfurt, Hannover, and Stuttgart are good examples of the former; Münster, Freiburg, and Nuremberg of the latter. Lübeck, Cologne, and Munich fall in between.

Modernizing Cities

West Berlin and Hamburg both chose modernization without devoting too much thought to issues of historic preservation. Hamburg already enjoyed a relatively modern street system and most buildings dated from after the great fire of 1842. Only a few medieval buildings had survived the fire, and they were clustered in the area of the Cremoninsel, an "island" formed by a ring canal on the edge of the harbor. There had been discussion before, during, and after the war about making the area a special historic zone. In 1937, Hans Bahn, the director of the Historic Preservation Office of Hamburg, had made such a proposal, calling for a radical renovation of everything in the area except the historic buildings. Though the chief local Nazi official approved the idea, no action was taken on it because that kind of project took a back seat to planning a completely new street system for the area along the Elbe as part of redesigning Hamburg as a representative Nazi city. Indeed, between 1939 and 1942, it was reported that 21 valuable buildings in the proposed preservation zone had been demolished because they failed to meet safety standards.[32]

In terms of total damage, Hamburg was one of the most badly hit of all German cities, although the inner city was less badly damaged than surrounding districts. Moreover, even though the famous firestorm that followed the devastating bombing raid of 1943 had caused extraordinary destruction and loss of life, the fact that most Hamburg buildings were of brick or stone meant that outside walls and foundations of ruined buildings could often still be used. As a consequence, many of the nineteenth- and early twentieth-century government, office, and commercial buildings could be restored, but with interior modernization. In the main, however, historic preservation efforts in Hamburg's inner city concentrated on restoring the few major monuments, such as the five main churches and the town hall (the primary piece of Wilhelmine architecture). In 1947, the preservation office had to function on a meager budget of RM 12,500, hardly enough to undertake a major program of reconstructing historic buildings.[33] Hamburg rebuilt, as it had in the past, with an eye to the future more than the past.

To save some sense of the old Hamburg, preservation officials revived the project of creating a historic zone on the Cremoninsel. Since many of the buildings listed for preservation in the proposals of the Nazi years had been destroyed in the war, Bernhard Hopp, the city's chief preservation official, advocated Fritz Schumacher's idea of moving the scattered remains of historic commercial buildings from other parts of the city to this small area. He also fought a rear-guard action against city planners, who suggested building a major thoroughfare across the Cremoninsel. The attitude of the planning office is well characterized in Oberbaudirektor Otto Meyer-Ottens's declaration that the Cremoninsel should not be allowed to become a "curio cabinet." In the end, the preservation office achieved some of its aims. A few buildings were restored on the island, and new buildings were erected that reflected in style and material the original scale and ambience of the area.[34]

In Berlin, the older sections that contained the most important monuments were located in the Russian sector, formerly East Berlin. Authorities in both halves of the city were committed to modernization, and in West Berlin very few historic buildings stood in the way of modern planning, since the existing street pattern was already generous in scope. Historic preservation, therefore, played a minimal role in West Berlin's reconstruction. In the 15 years after the war, countless ruins of public and private buildings from the Wilhelmine period were demolished to make way for new structures. Buildings from the latter part of the nineteenth century that had survived the war were preserved because of their immediate utility, not because they were deemed historically worthy of preservation, although there were a few exceptions to this rule. The tower of the Kaiser Wilhelm Memorial Church at the end of the Kurfürstendamm, saved in response to public pressure, is a well-known example of a ruin preserved as a monument to the war.[35] The remains of this rather ugly neo-Romanesque church, constructed in 1895, stand on an island in a sea of traffic, along with a new, modern church and campanile made of blue glass designed by Egon Eiermann and built between 1959 and 1963. This bizarre ensemble has become one of the symbols of West Berlin.

Rebuilding the badly damaged royal palace in Charlottenburg proved to be the largest and most important project of historic reconstruction and preservation in West Berlin. While city authorities contemplated tearing down these remains, East German authorities decided in 1950 to raze the ruins of the Hohenzollern palace built by Andreas Schlüter. West Berliners protested vehemently because the walls of the palace were still standing and reconstruction was entirely possible. Since West Berlin wanted to distinguish itself from the authoritarian regime in the East, the demolition in East Berlin provided the necessary impetus to preserve and restore the Charlottenburg palace in the West, now one of the city's major historic attractions.[36]

Some late nineteenth-century buildings with generous proportions and

Berlin, Unter den Linden, with the ruins of the Kaiser Wilhelm Memorial Church and the new church and tower by Egon Eiermann. The ruins of this rather ugly nineteenth-century edifice were kept as a memorial to the war. The ensemble has become the landmark of West Berlin. (Source: Landesbildstelle Berlin, 4 CHA-Ku-10-67, 75803.)

interesting facades have recently come under the care of the city conservator, but others from that period, especially in the Kreuzberg area, are slated for demolition in urban renewal programs. At the same time, in recognition of Berlin's leading role in the birth of modern architecture, interest has grown in preserving some of the better examples of early twentieth-century architecture. The most visible preservation activity in recent years, however, has taken place in East Berlin, where major efforts were at last under way to restore what remained of the old city center.

During the long period from the middle ages into the nineteenth century, Frankfurt am Main existed as an independent city-state and a major banking and commercial center. In spite of having served as the coronation city for the Holy Roman Emperors since 1562, Frankfurt's architectural character resembled that of a small bourgeois town. Some 2,000 private houses and few truly distinguished buildings graced the city. The seat of the weak Germanic Confederation from 1816 to 1866, in 1848 Frankfurt hosted the unsuccessful revolutionary German national assembly, which met to draw up a liberal constitution for a united national state. Since political power and patronage resided in Vienna and Berlin, however, none of this activity inspired important architecture in Frankfurt. When Prussia annexed the city in 1866, Berlin became the financial capital of Germany. No longer a state capital or an independent city, Frankfurt sought to assume a new modern identity.

An important step in that direction was taken in 1925, when the architect Ernst May was chosen to head the Frankfurt planning department. A member of the progressive Ring group and the Deutscher Werkbund, May designed and utilized standardized construction techniques to build new, very modern suburban housing projects that became models for other progressive architects.[37] First the Depression and then the victory of the Nazis put a stop to Frankfurt's building program, and May himself left in 1930 to accept a commission to build new cities in the Soviet Union. After the war, however, mayors Kurt Blaum and Walter Kolb and planning office leaders Eugen Blanck, Werner Hebebrand, and Herbert Boehm revitalized Frankfurt's commitment to modernism. Because the inner city lay in ruins, modern principles might easily be applied to the whole city and not just the suburbs, as had been the case under May. Moreover, modernization figured in the dream of Frankfurt's officials that their city might someday be celebrated as the capital of a new, modern German democracy. The Economic Council (Wirtschaftsrat) of the combined British and American zones met in Frankfurt, and with Berlin enmeshed in the struggles of the growing Cold War, several leading banks and corporations transferred their headquarters to Frankfurt. The city clearly called for investment in the future, not a return to the past. Echoing the urban renewal projects in the late 1930s in Frankfurt, planner Herbert Boehm viewed the Altstadt as a petit bourgeois slum badly in need of thorough urban renovation.[38] Land parcels in the old city were too small for modern construction, so the city rigorously consolidated and replotted property lines to make space for wide streets and large, economically viable buildings.[39] The 1948 town plan called for the demolition of 35% (51 of 145) of the still-standing remains of monuments that predated 1840.[40]

The minimal historic preservation efforts focused primarily on four reconstruction projects: the destroyed Goethe house discussed previously, the badly damaged St. Paul's Church, the cathedral, and the Römer complex of the town hall. The motive informing these projects was to provide the city with certain symbols; theories about proper historic preservation were of small importance.[41] The first priority was to restore by 1948 the St. Paul's Church, a building of little architectural distinction but historically important as the meeting place of the revolutionary national assembly of 1848. Its reconstruction would appropriately symbolize the creation of a new German democracy with Frankfurt as its capital, and hence the city felt justified in soliciting contributions from other, equally badly bombed cities. By November 1947, the contributions totaled RM 1.8 million, fully two-thirds of the cost of reconstruction. Not without dispute, Frankfurt selected a design by an architectural team headed by Rudolf Schwarz and Eugen Blanck, both modernists. The design called for only a partial restoration of the church as it had existed before the war.[42]

Frankfurt's lack of official support for a program of historic preservation generated its share of criticism. The chairman of a Hessian architects' association and the chairman of a society of Friends of the Old City went on Radio Frankfurt in the summer of 1948 to attack the modernizers, going all the way back to Ernst May. This attack was strong enough to call forth a rebuttal by Werner Hebebrand, head of the city's planning department until September 1948. (He subsequently served as Hamburg's planner during the 1950s.) Hebebrand declared that no one would want to live in the tiny old streets and houses that critics of modernization wanted to rebuild. Friedrich Lübbecke of the "Friends of the Old City" in turn responded with a nasty attack on both May and Hebebrand. He called May "a Mussolini of architecture" who would have forced all buildings to be built exactly alike.[43]

This bitter exchange did not, however, alter the city's stand on modernization. With the fate of Berlin in doubt, Frankfurt once again housed Germany's major banks, and its airport became the most important in the Federal Republic. Both of these developments merely corresponded to Frankfurt's new image as a progressive, forward-looking city. Following the example of the United States, the banks and other corporations erected modern skyscrapers to highlight their importance to Germans and to the world, and Frankfurt went on to become perhaps the most modern—its critics might say the most Americanized—of West Germany's cities, replete with traffic-clogged thoroughfares and smog-obscured views of the commercial downtown.[44] In recent years some citizens have yearned to salvage something of the past, whether by preserving some of the nineteenth-century buildings in the area around the train station, restoring the old opera house, or constructing brand new pseudo-medieval, half-timbered buildings on the square across from the Römer.[45] It is too late, however, to recapture any real sense of Frankfurt's historic character; most of the city's traditional architecture is gone.

Modern planning took clear precedence over historic preservation in Hannover as well. Of the 1,600 half-timbered buildings located in the oldest parts of the city, only 32 survived the war. Monumental buildings included the Gothic Marktkirche and Kreuzkirche, a number of Baroque buildings from Hannover's period of glory as seat of the Guelf dynasty, an enormous nineteenth-century opera house, and a massive early twentieth-century town hall. Although the street patterns and building lines in most of the inner city were medieval, the city expansions of the Baroque era and the nineteenth century and finally the construction of the train station and opera house gave part of the inner city and its surrounding area the more modern character typical of Germany's royal residence cities.

The primary goals of Hannover's postwar planning included building a modern street system that would route most traffic around the inner core rather than through it, reviving the inner city as a commercial, cultural, and residential focus, and thoroughly renewing the older parts of the city. Very large commercial buildings, such as the Continental Rubber skyscraper and the major buildings serving the Lower Saxon state government, were deliberately located outside the city center in an effort to preserve a sense of the former proportions of the old city and to prevent an excessive growth of traffic there, but with few exceptions even the buildings in the old inner city are modern.

As elsewhere, of course, major monuments such as the Marktkirche were restored. The royal palace, built in various styles from the late seventeenth through the early nineteenth century, was preserved only in part; major new additions enabled the building to function as the seat of the state parliament. The ruin of the gutted Aegidien Church was preserved as a memorial to the war. However, since it stands in isolation, surrounded by modern buildings and minimally traveled streets, very few people probably encounter this memorial. As far as private, secular buildings go, historic preservation was concentrated in an area of about five small blocks in which several half-timbered buildings still stood. Those on the Knochenhauerstraße were moved to the Kramer and Burgstraßen, thus forming a kind of preservation district like that proposed for the Cremoninsel in Hamburg.

Bordered by the Marktkirche to the east, the Leine Palace to the south, the Kreuzkirche to the north, and the Leine river to the west, this "historic" area has become a busy and popular island in a sea of modernity. Well-attended attractions include a regular flea market held along the river embankments, a museum of history, and the state theater of Lower Saxony. Additionally the Leine Palace serves as a meeting place for the state parliament. Because the area is small in relation to the rest of the inner city and few truly old buildings remain, the preservation island does not really convey the character of an old city. The modern courtyard and abstract fountain in front of the Ballhof theater, for example, lend a modern rather than traditional air to this partly mid-seventeenth-century building. Nevertheless, the "historic" area does function as a kind of counterweight to the city's modern architecture and the two-level pedestrian mall that leads from the train station to the Marktkirche.[46]

Like Hannover, Stuttgart had once been a royal residence city, with a large palace from the eighteenth and nineteenth centuries located in the city center and many small, late-medieval, half-timbered houses on narrow streets. A series of bombing raids reduced the central area almost totally to ruins. As early as 1941 Paul Bonatz prepared a memorandum containing plans to modernize the city and improve traffic flow.[47] After the war, both Stuttgart's town planners and preservation officials of the city and of the state of Württemberg agreed that the inner city should be modernized, though they hoped to retain at least some sense of the former street pattern and to avoid overbuilding with high-rise commercial buildings.

Given the degree of destruction and the inclination toward modernization, only major monuments would be scheduled for reconstruction in their prewar form. Thus the Old Palace across from the Stiftskirche on the Schillerplatz, the Königsbau, and the New Palace on the Schloßplatz merited restoration, while the formerly built-up area behind the New Palace was to be cleared for gardens. The most important church, the Stiftskirche, was restored, but several other damaged churches were demolished and replaced by new buildings. Likewise, the small private residences, almost totally destroyed, were not rebuilt.

The biggest controversy in terms of preserving the city's architectural heritage concerned demolishing the ruins of the palace of the crown prince

Hannover, Burgstraße, 1972. The old half-timbered buildings were brought to this site from other locations to form an ensemble in a "historic" quarter. To the left is the new historical museum of the city. (Source: Archiv-Bild des Presseamtes der Landeshauptstadt Hannover, photo by Hans Wagner.)

Former Russian Embassy, Stuttgart, 1941 and in ruins in 1952. This interesting building was obviously restorable, but it was demolished to widen a street. (Source: Landesbildstelle Württemberg, no negative number and 40902.)

Stuttgart. This sequence illustrates the kinds of sacrifices of historic architecture made in the name of traffic improvements. The first photo shows the ruins of the Kronprinzenpalais from the Königstraße in 1949. The building was burned out but restorable. It was demolished first to widen a road and make way for new, modern buildings. Then a new tram line was built (the photo is from 1974). The tracks were later moved to an underpass and replaced by a low-capacity road and the edge of a pedestrian mall. (Source: Landesbildstelle Württemberg, negative numbers F93123, K429125.)

(Kronprinzenpalais) in order to create an artery between the Schloßplatz and Schillerplatz. The debate failed to generate much heat, however, as even the preservationists valued modernization more than the palace.[48] Richard Döcker, one of the spokesmen for Stuttgart's prevailing modernists, argued that "we must use the opportunity and think ahead and plan for the next 50 to 100 years. Our descendents expect that of us. Should we take a crooked path and waste a clean, clear solution merely to save a few stones of the Kronprinzenpalais?"[49]

One of the most pleasant features of Stuttgart's inner city today is the extensive and beautifully landscaped public garden that begins on the northern edge of the restored new palace. However, the other sides of the palace are bordered by the open Schloßplatz and the Academy garden, and the palace appears to be an isolated historic building in the middle of a modern city. The restored state art gallery, dating from around 1840, is similarly isolated, in this case cut off from the city core by the wide thoroughfare now called the Konrad-Adenauer-Straße. Though Stuttgart boasts larger restored monuments than Hannover, they do not form a compact mass like Hannover's group of historic buildings.

Determined Preservationism

Cities particularly intent on preserving the historic character of their inner cores include Nuremberg, Münster, and Freiburg. All three had been proud of an important architectural heritage, and all had witnessed the virtual obliteration of that heritage by the war. They chose to reconstruct buildings of key importance while allowing or encouraging the construction of new buildings that would blend into the traditional image of the city, thereby giving the impression of a larger historic ensemble.

Reconstructing the old city of Nuremberg, in which more than 2,500 historic buildings had been devastated by the bombing, demanded considerable sensitivity. Hitler had admired Nuremberg as *the* German city, and the occupying American army authorities and probably also many Germans associated it with the huge Nazi party congresses, immortalized by Leni Riefenstahl in the film *Triumph of the Will*. Some allies wanted the old city to be razed completely or left standing as permanent ruins. Nuremberg's citizens naturally rejected both of these alternatives.[50]

By 1947, numerous proposals for reconstruction of the Altstadt had been submitted. These derived from the planning office as well as from competitions staged both for architects and for all citizens. From 1940 to 1945, Heinz Schmeissner had served in one position or another as the city's chief planner until the Allies arrested him for refusing to reveal the location of the Imperial regalia. From 1945 to 1949, Robert Erdmannsdorffer, whose ideas tended to correspond with those of Schmeissner, directed the planning process. In 1947, the year he was released from jail, Schmeissner entered a competition for Nuremberg's reconstruction as a private architect and won first prize. In 1949, he resumed his work as chief planner, a position he held until his retirement in 1970.

After September 1948, the planning office was advised on reconstruction by a private organization known as the Curatorium for the Rebuilding of the City of Nuremberg. This organization included local architects, engineers, representatives of economic institutions and the arts, and members of the city administration. Schmeissner himself served as the managing director until he took over the city planning office. Although the Curatorium lacked legislative and executive power, it enjoyed sufficient prestige to press advice on both government and private citizens. It established basic reconstruction principles to shape general policy and created an architectural quality subcommittee (Baukunstbeirat) to review individual projects (which by the end of 1954 numbered 793).

Schmeissner declared that "it was extraordinarily important psychologically that as early as 1947 an Altstadt competition had visually demonstrated what could be made of the city once again by restoring those architectural monuments that could still be restored."[51] Rebuilt or repaired historic buildings rather than modern buildings and traffic patterns, in other words, were to determine the visual quality of the inner city. A 1955 report summarizing the Curatorium's activities observed that Nuremberg's leaders had quickly recognized "that a reconstruction of the earlier city portrait [*Stadtbild*] in the sense of a formal copy was to be unconditionally rejected. With careful preservation of the few remaining old buildings and tactful attention to the greater conception of the historical city structure, there should instead be a synthesis of the old with the new, and the new should reflect the materials and forms of our times."[52] Variety was important. Those areas featuring still-standing old buildings, in which the traditional sense of the whole area was to be retained, required pitched, tiled roofs and customary building materials, but in totally destroyed areas flat roof lines and new materials were perfectly acceptable. The Curatorium made it clear, however, that the city's creative modern architecture must stand the test of time. Nuremburg was not a laboratory for experimental architecture, nor would it tolerate "brutal blunders"—massive projects out of proportion in the inner city.[53] Finally, in keeping with its preservationist bent, the Curatorium opted to retain the basic street pattern, except for some minor modifications to improve traffic flow. Most traffic, however, was to be routed around the inner city, rather than channeled through it.[54]

Adherence to these general principles resulted in the successful preservation of the architectural unity of the old city. Major monuments were rebuilt, and no new large buildings were constructed. In roof line, color, form, and often in materials, architects adapted their new buildings to mesh with the old styles.[55] The city lacked a formal policy advocating construction of copies of totally destroyed buildings, and it inconsistently determined the point at which damage precluded restoration. Therefore some copying of the old took place. Most public funds in the area of historic preservation financed the rebuilding of public monuments, while the owners of historic private residences struggled to rebuild on their own. Nor did the city take the lead in buying up old homes for restoration. On the contrary, many historic buildings were torn down when private owners lacked the funds or the desire to restore

Nuremberg, Albrecht-Dürer Platz, nos. 14–18. These pictures illustrate a good effort at adaptive architecture. The first photo, dated 1935, clearly suggests three attached buildings, with variety in facades and roof treatments. The second picture, from 1957, shows the rebuilt structure. The roof line is now continuous and the windows standardized. Only the gutter downspout suggests that this might not be seen as a single building. Nevertheless, the proportions and pitch of the roof suggest the old building. (Source: Stadt Nürnberg Hochbauamt, Bildstelle und Denkmalsarchiv, C6114/1, photo Staatliche Bildstelle; N89/X, photo Hochbauamt.)

Nuremberg, south–northwest corner of the main market square. These three pictures illustrate the difficulty faced by postwar architects and preservation officials. In this case, they wished to restore the historic character of the square, but which point in the past should be considered the norm? The first picture, from 1880, shows a market colonnade that was demolished in 1895. The second photo, from 1921, shows the colonnade gone, but also changes in the decoration on the facades fronting the square. The final picture, from 1968, shows the restored square, with drastically simplified, modernized, and standardized facades. (Source: Stadt Nürnberg Hochbauamt, Bildstelle und Denkmalsarchiv, photo 1, KS 65/IIIa, 1921, photo by Ferdinand Schmidt; photo 2, B 65/II, photo Hochbauamt; photo 3, FiH.2966, photo Hochbauamt.)

them. In 1942 Nuremberg listed 2,580 historic buildings; in 1970 only 400 remained, including 260 residences.[56] Though much was thus lost, the amount retained or rebuilt ensures that pedestrians have frequent visual contact with historic buildings. Moreover, Nuremberg's physical landscape complements its historic landscape. The restored castle on the hill, the buildings and bridges along or over the Pegnitz River, which flows through the city's center, and the medieval walls that enclose it all contribute to the historic sense of the center, in spite of the many vanished old buildings and the new modern architecture.

Smaller than Nuremberg, the town of Münster in Westphalia lacked encircling walls and a dramatic physical setting. Heavily damaged in the war, the city in November 1948 listed only 18 secular and 9 religious buildings marked for restoration or reconstruction.[57] Nonetheless, like Nuremberg, Münster succeeded in creating the air of a historic city in its center. It did so by reconstructing key monuments, retaining much of the old street and property layout, and requiring that new buildings in proximity to historic buildings utilize traditional proportions, colors, and materials.

Widespread agreement guaranteed the preservation of the layout of the Altstadt. Hans Ostermann, the town's leading architect, Heinrich Bartmann, the city's new building director, Edmund Scharf, the head of the local preservation office, and Wilhelm Rave, the Westphalian provincial conservator based in Münster, all spoke out in the first year after the war in favor of keeping the old streets, with only a few minor modifications to ease traffic flow. Bartmann declared that Münster's special character rested in its individual shops and houses, the predominance of pedestrians, and the "spatial relationship of the streets and squares." Any changes must not lead to a "dilution of [this] spatial configuration."[58] Rave, who played a more active role than conservationists in most other towns, stated that the layout of the historic city was "an obligatory legacy."[59]

At the same time, most favored the construction of new buildings rather than copies of destroyed ones, with the exceptions of the Gothic town hall and the adjacent Baroque Stadtweinhaus. Only when more than half of a building remained would restoration be attempted, and in those cases true artisanal materials and methods would be used.[60] New buildings would coordinate with the traditional styles and forms, "proportions and rhythm" of the remaining old buildings.[61] Bartmann rejected "stylistic masquerades and modish forms," and Rave argued that in the Altstadt "little room" existed for either "the so-called modern architecture" or for "new, large-scale urban planning."[62]

The most important project was the rebuilding of the Prinzipalmarkt. This broad street, on which the old town hall had been located, was lined with narrow, three-story houses, round-arched arcades, and shops faced with Renaissance or Baroque gabled facades at street level. During the nineteenth and early twentieth centuries a number of buildings on the street had been altered, some adding a full fourth floor and others neo-Renaissance facades. In an effort to control further changes, a 1904 building ordinance mandated continuities in parcel width, building height, and the shape of the arcades, while leaving the final character of individual facades to the discretion of the owner. This unusual ordinance sought to protect the basic structure of the area, not just its external face.[63] Only a couple of these buildings survived the war unharmed, and in 1945 a consensus determined that the old facades should not be copied. Instead, in keeping with the 1904 law, the facades should be left open to individual variation and change.

As early as August 1945, Hans Ostermann requested a permit to rebuild one of the buildings on Prinzipalmarkt, a move that triggered a dispute not over the shape of the building but over materials. Ostermann's decision to use exposed brick instead of either rough stone or plaster countered popular sentiment, even though the old city contained other brick buildings. Ostermann lost out, and the facades on the street were rebuilt, not as exact copies of the old, but nevertheless with considerable uniformity in style. More neo-Renaissance and fewer Baroque facades grace the postwar street, and more buildings have a full fourth floor, but the parcel size remained unchanged and almost all of the arcade arches are more or less the same as before the bombing.[64] This retention of the old land parcel boundaries was unusual in Germany at this time; most other cities, including Nuremberg, rationalized and enlarged building lots.

Münster's trend toward strong conformity with historic building traditions was embodied in a 1951 renewal and expansion of the pre–World War I ordinances. The new law prohibited any reconstruction or alteration that harmed or even significantly altered "the character or the impression which they made or had made" on 24 streets or squares, 14 religious buildings, 12 public buildings, and 34 private buildings. For the Prinzipalmarkt and three other streets the law stipulated the maximum facade height, prohibited changes in the size and number of arcade arches, and required that facades be of either yellow-gray rough stone or plaster.[65]

Private citizens and merchants supplied both the impetus and most of the funds for rebuilding the two best known buildings on the Prinzipalmarkt, the town hall and the Stadtweinhaus.[66] Although very controversial, the structures were rebuilt as copies. Both buildings had been extensively modified in the nineteenth century, so the debate centered on whether to reconstruct them as they had been just before the war or as they had been before the earlier modifications. Proposals for the town hall were solicited from Bartmann, Heinrich Benteler, the chief architect in charge of restoration of the cathedral, and Jobst-Hans Muths, who had won a competition on reconstruction of the inner city. Muths's ideas were quickly rejected as not fully thought out. Benteler proposed a supposedly purer Gothic facade, rejecting even the use of those original pieces and stones that had been salvaged from the ruins. He wanted, however, to retain the nineteenth-century alterations to the interior. Bartmann steadfastly opposed copying what had been destroyed. The city council decided to split the responsibility and charged Bartmann with the interior and Benteler with the exterior facade. Responsibility for the interior, however, was soon turned over to Conservator Scharf, when Bartmann withdrew to assume a professorship at the Technical University of Darmstadt. Scharf also opted for a modernized interior.[67]

The same arguments informed discussions about the Stadtweinhaus. Bartmann advocated a new approach; Benteler a copy of the old. In a March 1951 council subcommittee meeting, Benteler contended that "our age has, to be sure, good conductors, but composers are lacking. This is a sign of the times. Likewise in architecture we can copy better than we can create something genuinely new."[68] Because of the difficulty in financing reconstruction, the council delayed making a decision until 1954, when it opted for Conservator Scharf's plan of partially copying the old building.

Remarkably, although Münster possesses few historic buildings, some of its historic buildings are more or less copies, and most of the Prinzipalmarkt facades are adaptations rather than originals, still it impresses observers as a historic city with a clear identity. Indeed, in spite of the earnest commitment to preserve the fundamental structure of the inner city, major alterations have been made for schools, the university, museums, and city and state administrative buildings. Only a few streets in the very center have retained the old parcel size and historic building proportions. Clearly Münster's identity as a historic city is derived from that central area, where reconstruction was undertaken in such a way that, in the consciousness of both residents and visitors, it succeeded in symbolizing the entire city, including the modernized sections. Form, height, style, proportion, materials, and colors combine to create an effective ensemble.[69]

Just as Nuremberg's traditionalist-oriented reconstruction benefited from the continuous involvement of Heinz Schmeissner, Freiburg's benefited from the presence of Baurat Joseph Schlippe, who dominated reconstruction in that city. Even before the war, he had drawn up plans for a careful renewal of neglected areas of the old city while respecting the historic street structure and architecture. The city was destroyed in a raid in late November 1944, and the embers from the fires had barely cooled before Schlippe energetically set about salvaging anything that could be saved. By October 1945, he was ready with a reconstruction plan. Though subsequently modified in 1948 in order to widen some streets, this plan enjoyed the support of both the city government and the citizenry.

Freiburg's highest priority was the preservation of the cathedral, the centerpiece of the city and the dominant shape in its skyline. Here Freiburg benefited from Swiss donations of roofing tiles. Other churches, the old town hall, the old university building, the Basler Hof, and other major secular monuments were also shored up and rebuilt. Lowest priority went to private houses, many of which were lost. As important as the reconstruction of the major monuments was, the new buildings in the old city center were intended not so much to replicate the exact style of the old buildings as they were "to convey a genuine sense of preservation" through "a quiet, unobtrusive adaptation in proportions and materials" of the new to the old.[70] Like Münster, Freiburg refrained from radically redrawing property lines to produce larger building lots. Hence the use of common materials, colors, roof lines, and traditional house shapes and sizes all contributed to a continuity with the historical character of the city, even though the majority of the buildings were in fact new. Freiburg did not copy itself. Rather, in the words of Jürgen Paul, "It was more the revitalization of a trusted architectonic structure in which one saw not only artistic value but also the expression of a particular form of life, namely the historic city as a visible and vital form of unbroken national-historical continuity."[71] Reconstructed Freiburg succeeded in embodying once again the essence of the "German" city so dear to the hearts of the middle-class public.

Modernization and Preservation

Although all of the cities discussed thus far debated the relative merits of modernization and historic preservation, each clearly opted for one or the other. In Munich, Cologne, and Lübeck, this was not the case. Modernizing impulses in the planning offices were resisted by forces favoring reconstruction more or less true to the prewar shape of the cities.

Munich is probably the best liked city in West Germany, and much of its popularity must be attributed to the restoration and preservation of what was primarily an architectural legacy of the nineteenth century. The capital city of Bavaria since the thirteenth century, Munich had its share of major churches and palaces in all leading styles, but the city experienced its greatest transformation after the prince elector was granted the title of king in 1806. The following century saw the building of impressive, wide avenues and the construction of numerous large neoclassical buildings, including a significant enlargement of the royal residence. By the early twentieth century, little pre-1800 architecture other than the major monuments remained. After 1945, Munich, like Hamburg, faced the task of rebuilding an already fairly modern city, though Munich had suffered far more inner-city destruction in the war than had Hamburg. One early postwar inventory listed only 120 "older" buildings and monuments, of which about 30 dated from before 1800. The rest originated in the nineteenth century.[72]

Several parties participated in the discussions about rebuilding Munich's historic buildings, including citizens' groups, the city government, the Catholic church, and Bavarian state conservationists. Moreover, this was clearly a resumption of discussions about artistic and architectural values begun in the 1920s, in terms both of ideas and participants. Leading modernists included Robert Verhoelzer and Hermann Leitenstorfer, and Georg Lill and Rudolf Esterer enjoyed considerable influence in the traditionalist camp.[73] The state of Bavaria, which owned and administered many of the largest buildings in Munich, had enormous clout. Led by Lill, the director of the state office for historic preservation, and Esterer, head of the office for the administration of state palaces, it took responsibility for rebuilding the many state-owned buildings in the city. Both men also served on the planning and architecture commissions that advised the city. As one authority observed, the state acted quickly to preserve its "self-image and historic continuity as legal successor and heir to the monarchy."[74]

The huge royal palace topped the list of historic restoration projects undertaken by the Bavarian state. Lill and Esterer had already begun preparation for restoration in May 1944, and on 16 February 1945, before the war's end, a citizens' association called the Friends of the Residenz was formed to support the rebuilding effort.[75] Reconstruction work commenced in July 1945 without offering the public an opportunity to dissent, although clearly the project had broad support. The rebuilding of the Residenz constituted the largest single project of historic reconstruction and preservation undertaken in postwar Germany, with over DM 60 million spent by 1976. Ravaged and gutted by the war, the palace's still-standing walls permitted restoration of the external structure. Most of the movable furnishings and decorations, including some of the painted and gilded stucco, had been removed and protected, so some of the rooms could be recreated in their original form. Parts of the palace, where the loss in internal substance had been greater, were assigned new functions, such as housing the Academy of Sciences, the Max-Planck Society, and the new Herkulessaal concert hall.[76]

The city of Munich assumed primary responsibility for its own buildings, such as the old and new town halls, and for the overall layout of the city. In the very first reconstruction plan, submitted in 1946, Karl Meitinger stated that it was necessary "under all circumstances . . . to save the image of the Altstadt," but at the same time he rejected copying buildings that had been totally destroyed in favor of promoting new architecture. He went on to say that "even in the old city one must not hang absolutely and one-sidedly on the old and in particular one must pay proper attention to questions of traffic." Meitinger recognized that increased traffic might intrude upon the structure of the old city, which would be a "nightmare" for conservative proponents of urban planning, but he believed that historic preservation should not dominate reconstruction planning.[77] Though Meitinger no longer served as chief of the city building office after mid-1946 (hardly an important Nazi, he nevertheless "voluntarily" retired before a possible denazification procedure might mandate such a move), he continued to be a member of the advisory city planning commission and commission on architecture, and his views were consistent with the other main city spokesmen on reconstruction, Hermann Leitenstorfer and Helmut Fischer.[78]

Fischer strongly believed that the inner city had been changing long before the war, gradually losing its resident population and gaining more "city" functions in terms of commerce and administration. Blindly rebuilding the inner city to its historic specifications would ignore these changes, which were sure to continue once the city recovered from the war.[79] Fischer was willing to sacrifice "even perhaps buildings that in their form are good" to make way for "larger-scale solutions" to urban problems, and he noted that in the debates about whether to rebuild the inner city in a modern or traditional style, "no one can in fact specify just what this traditional style is. The old city evolved between 1156 and 1800 and since then the majority of profane buildings have been 'modernized.' "[80]

The conflict between the impulse to modernize and the desire to reconstruct the old city silhouette emerged most distinctly in the planning of the central square, the Marienplatz. The late nineteenth-century neo-Gothic town hall dominates the square, but on the eastern side of the square stood the ruins of the smaller, late Gothic old town hall. Nearby, though not actually on the Marienplatz, are the Frauenkirche and the Peterskirche, two important churches whose towers, once rebuilt, could be seen from the square. In September 1948, a competition solicited ideas on how to rebuild the square. The key issues were whether to reconstruct the old town hall, with its attached tower gate, and whether to demolish the buildings between the Peterskirche and the square, thereby opening up the square and providing a clear view of the church.

Discussion dragged on for over two years before a decision was reached. The reconstruction office, headed by Fischer, opposed creating new vistas that had not been there before, and Fischer himself favored demolishing the old town hall, which he considered an obstacle to the smooth flow of traffic through the square.[81] To the city council Fischer stated: "In the beginning was the street and everything else came afterward. Without streets there would be no Munich!" He warned that rebuilding the old town hall would be taking a step toward "making Munich's inner city into a museum," since it would block the traffic flow into the center.[82] Fischer also opposed a public referendum on the planning of the square, saying that "as desirable as it is under democratic principles to have as broad and active participation of the population as possible in questions of the reconstruction and redesign of Munich, a referendum on such questions poses the danger that the city administration might find itself bound by a result that lacks a [properly] expert foundation."[83] He feared—correctly—that popular opinion might force the reconstruction of the old town hall against the objections of the planning office.

City planner Leitenstorfer reluctantly admitted that it might be possible to reconstruct the main part of the old town hall, but he opposed rebuilding its destroyed tower, which he, like Fischer, thought would just be in the way, and he considered opening up a view of the Peterskirche a manifestation of "false romanticism."[84] Defending the old town hall because it embodied "so-called historic values" was "dangerous," and he further observed that "a value that is exclusively historic in our innermost of hearts is simply outmoded and no longer fully defensible against the just demands of life and the times. The question is more whether these old remains still mean something for us, the people of today and tomorrow—I would almost like to say—without considering their history."[85]

In the end, popular will prevailed over the expert opinions of the planning office, and Leitenstorfer had to concede that rebuilding the old town hall and its tower would be acceptable and that traffic patterns could be adjusted. Thus in 1951 Hans Högg, Leitenstorfer's successor as Stadtbaurat, stated that "the old gates are characteristic of the fact that Munich is not a colonial city of the American West but rather a city that has grown, has a particular heritage and urban structures of beauty, for which one must be ready to make sacrifices."[86] Fischer, it will be recalled, had wanted to sacrifice the old for the new, not the new for the old.

In fact, public support in Munich for the reconstruction or restoration of many well-known edifices was strong and organized. Citizens' groups raised funds for the rebuilding of such things as the towers on the Frauenkirche, the Peterskirche, and the Chinese pagoda in the English Garden.[87] The city government sometimes found these groups obstacles to implementing their plans, although Karl Sebastian Preis, the head of Munich's reconstruction office until his untimely death in 1946, had helped foster this public effort on behalf of historic monuments. On his initiative, and with the backing of the mayor and town council, the churches, the heads of the institutions of higher learning, the chamber of commerce, and even Bavarian Minister President Wilhelm Hoegner, a special fund (*Kulturbaufond*) was created to help pay for reconstruction. An appeal encouraged the public to donate to the fund, since the city's coffers lacked the sums necessary to underwrite restoration of all of the damaged historic buildings.[88]

By May 1946, in spite of 4,358 donations totaling over RM 375,000, the trustees realized that other means for raising funds had to be found. They decided to produce and sell special postcards and art prints, through which they hoped to raise another RM 800,000. In fact, by the time of the currency reform in June 1948, the fund had raised over RM 1,150,000 and spent some RM 750,000 on numerous projects. (The largest single gift of RM 130,000 came from a Munich harness-racing association.) The June 1948 balance of almost RM 400,000 was revalued to nearly DM 38,000. By July 1953, an additional DM 344,000 had been raised. As private gift-giving had virtually ceased by mid-1950, most of this sum had come from such things as the postcard sales or donations from the city or other government agencies.[89]

The state of Bavaria, the city government, the Catholic church, and private groups and individuals thus all joined forces in giving Munich its special blend of historic, nineteenth-century, and modern architecture. In many cases, Classical and Baroque facades were repaired, although interiors were modernized as buildings gained new functions. New buildings in the inner city tended to follow traditional building lines and adapt elements of local architectural styles, such as painted plastered facades. Arcades were introduced to provide extra space for widening streets without setting back the building lines. In contrast to Frankfurt, many of the banks in the inner city chose to forgo large, representative buildings.[90] It should also be recalled that the American military government played a role in shaping the face of Munich. Although it encouraged the rebuilding of major historic monuments, it mandated the demolition of several Nazi-era buildings, most notably the temples of honor on the Königsplatz. The Haus der Kunst on the Prinzregentenstraße was allowed to remain standing.

Reconstruction in Munich has its critics. The most famous is Erwin Schleich, who in 1978 launched a polemic against the city precisely in the area of historic preservation. In a book entitled *The Second Destruction of Munich*, Schleich documented many cases where buildings that had suffered only moderate damage were torn down and replaced with nondescript or ugly modern ones or where virtually undamaged buildings were demolished to create open spaces.[91] Schleich has gained some notoriety in Munich and elsewhere in Germany for his polemic, but the record of postwar destruction of buildings of some historic value cannot refute the basic success of Munich's reconstruction.

The cities of Cologne and Lübeck had both possessed a large number of extremely important historic buildings. Cologne had been noted for its many medieval churches; Lübeck for its medieval and Renaissance merchant houses. Both cities experienced uneven, controversial attempts to combine modernization with historic reconstruction and preservation.

Cologne, a city with a very rich architectural heritage, had had a preservation office since 1912. The conservator, who reported directly to the lord mayor, could designate a building, fountain, or the like, as worthy of preservation, but such a designation had only moral, not legal force. (A preservation law for Northrhine-Westphalia was not passed until 1980.) Nevertheless, the conservator enjoyed considerable prestige in a historic city like Cologne.

Hans Vogts, conservator from the 1920s through the early postwar years, had long felt that fully one-third of the Altstadt was badly in need of renewal, and he had played an active part in the 1930s renewal project in the area around Groß St. Martin's church.[92]

That project was mostly completed by 1942, when the air raids reached Cologne. As he watched his "charges" fall victim to the bombs, Vogts tried desperately to save what he could while developing his own conception of how reconstruction should proceed after the fighting ceased. For the salvaging tasks he needed labor and material to improvise temporary roofs, shore up walls that threatened to collapse, and rescue works of art from the ruins. From mid-1943 on, such resources were hard to come by, and he sought help from any source, including Albert Speer and the forced foreign laborers of the Organisation Todt, the heavy construction outfit that built military installations in the occupied territories. At one point Vogts even discussed a strategy for winning Himmler's backing. Looking ahead to the end of the war, Vogts naturally started with the preservation and restoration of as many of the major monuments as possible. Beyond that, he hoped that it would be possible to save the *character* of the *entire* old city, rather than just saving a few buildings as museum pieces. The city's character, he felt, derived from its small streets and single-family houses built on small land parcels. Hence he opposed the construction of large-scale rental housing units on rationalized parcels of land. Moreover, he felt that housing and shops should be built close to the large monuments, as they traditionally had been. For Vogts, this issue of proximity formed "the main problem in the entire reconstruction effort." He believed that it would be a mistake to retain open spaces around the medieval churches and create vistas and views that had never existed in the first place.[93]

Toward the end of the war, while Vogts prepared his office for the task of rebuilding Cologne's monuments, some prominent local architects and writers developed their own ideas about reconstruction of the historic city. Whether published or submitted as memoranda to the city's postwar mayor or building office, the proposals of Carl Oskar Jatho, Hans Schmitt, Karl Band, and Theo Merken all advocated the retention of all or most of the original street plan and rebuilding on a "human" scale to avoid the monumentalism of the nineteenth century as well as the large, characterless buildings of commercial capitalism. Jatho and Schmitt, however, wanted new, creative architecture to revitalize Cologne's urban landscape and life and suggested locating modern buildings on the old lots. The ruined churches, similarly, should be rebuilt by master architects in styles exuding a modern spirit. In contrast, Band and Merken, like Vogts, urged the restoration or reconstruction of the major religious and secular monuments, although they allowed that some might be rebuilt in a modern style.[94] Band even supported building copies of destroyed old buildings if it was necessary to reestablish the right style and character of a street or square.[95] Vogts too accepted such reconstructions and also additions and modifications to historic buildings—assuming they manifested the right spirit and were erected with appropriate materials—if old buildings thereby gained new functions.[96]

Thirty-three old churches had been located in Cologne's old city. Of these, four small ones had been totally destroyed in the war, but the rest, while badly damaged, could potentially be restored at least in part. In late 1946 and early 1947, the fate of these churches was the subject of public lectures staged in the great hall of the university. Most speakers agreed that the churches should not be preserved as ruins, and all agreed in rejecting the accretions of the nineteenth century. Probably the strongest sentiment to emerge from these forums was the encouragement for architects to build new churches in new styles on the old sites but to allow plenty of time—perhaps generations—for the completion of this process to ensure the construction of outstanding buildings truly in tune with the new age. (Interestingly, Lord High Mayor Pünder and former Mayor Konrad Adenauer, the grand old man of Cologne politics, both expressed impatience with the lengthy discussions. They wanted the city to get on with actual reconstruction rather than engage in lengthy, seemingly endless, debates!)[97]

Beginning in 1948, the plans of Rudolf Schwarz, the actual head of Cologne's reconstruction planning office, gradually became public. He advocated not only rebuilding the churches but making them the focal points of revived "quarters," or neighborhoods (ignoring the cautionary observations of both the Catholic church and Vogts's chief assistant, Hanna Adenauer, Konrad Adenauer's niece, that some of those inner-city parishes no longer contained enough parishioners to support them). The basic street structure ought to be retained, he thought, except for major new high-capacity traffic arteries that would cut through the city in both north–south and east–west directions. Schwarz argued that medieval Cologne had existed *only* in its churches, major secular monuments, and the street layout, since almost all of the buildings in the old city in fact dated from the nineteenth or early twentieth centuries.[98] Consequently, apart from the restoration of the major monuments, the buildings in the old city should be modern but at the same time embody the spirit of local architecture. Schwarz contended that Cologne's buildings should not imitate "Swabian" architecture, with little bay windows, gables, and other artificial "pleasantries." Instead, it should be "hard, objective, and imperial" without being Prussian. Inner-city housing should consist of small, single-family units with gardens.[99]

Although Schwarz's popularity waned and he left office before his plans were fully approved and implemented, for the most part his ideas carried the day—at least initially. The conservator's office identified some 230 religious and secular buildings and monuments that merited preservation or restoration, but the administrative reports show that the bulk of the restoration funds were spent on rebuilding the old churches. In 1950, of DM 284,000 spent on projects supervised by the conservator's office, 92% went for work on churches.[100] The Catholic church assumed chief responsibility for the repairs on the cathedral and the rebuilding of other churches, though church officials made rebuilding decisions in consultation with the conservator's office. In fact, almost all of the old churches were rebuilt more or less in their prewar form, though not as exact replicas of what had existed in 1939, and most

Cologne, the Romanesque church of St. Aposteln, built in 1021, was carefully restored, but it stands at the corner of a busy, auto-filled street, and when viewed from Neumarkt, it contrasts sharply and unharmoniously with a typically large, formulaic, uninteresting commercial building to the north. (Source: Verkehrsamt der Stadt Köln, photo by R. Barten.)

featured significant interior modifications. Only three modern churches were built in the area of the old city.[101] Today Cologne's many inner-city churches are underused, but they do constitute dominant features in the old heart of the city.

Eventually a few major secular monuments, like the town hall, were also restored, and a few old burgher houses were saved, but the so-called Altstadt, composed mostly of new buildings adapted to old styles or recreations of destroyed buildings, is confined to the tiny quarter around the church of Groß St. Martin, itself reconstructed to match its prewar appearance. Ironically, the urban renewal plans of the 1930s had called for eliminating almost all of the old building lines and buildings in precisely this area. Most of the large buildings dating from the nineteenth century were demolished. For example, the nineteenth-century opera house on the Ring, burned out but repairable, was disliked by Cologne's citizens because they identified the style of that period with Prussian domination. The city planning commission had briefly considered restoring the old opera house as a bank but eventually decided to demolish it.[102] Likewise, the owners of a number of intact houses in the Neustadt (the area just outside the Ring), built in the late nineteenth or early twentieth century, either demolished them to make room for more modern buildings or

modified them in ways that often clashed with their surroundings.[103] In this regard, Cologne's experience resembled that of Munich and many other cities.

As Schwarz had hoped, the street pattern of the old city was more or less retained, but a great many narrow streets were significantly enlarged. This, along with the major arteries cutting through the inner city, makes most of old Cologne a city more for automobiles than for pedestrians. Although the two most important shopping streets, both of which retained their original width, were reserved for pedestrians, the shops are so thoroughly modern that visitors would hardly know that the streets formed part of "historic" Cologne. Because large firms could buy land cheaply in the years after the war, they purchased adjacent parcels to accommodate sizable buildings that dwarfed the remaining historic buildings. The scale of the old architecture, one of Schwarz's key ideas, was thus abandoned.[104]

Today Rudolf Schwarz is remembered more as an important modern archi-

Cologne, Auf dem Wehrbrand Gasse, looking toward the church of Groß St. Martin, 1935 and 1980. This narrow street is part of the small area in Cologne where there was a serious attempt to recreate the historic city. (Source: Photo 1, Rheinisches Bildarchiv, 137264; photo 2, Verkehrsamt der Stadt Köln, no. 2565, photo by Christian Dalchow.)

tect than as the planner of postwar Cologne. His hand can be seen in one of the most successful attempts to blend historic remains with new interiors and functions. Schwarz and Karl Band collaborated on rebuilding the old Gürzenich meeting hall as a modern concert facility. They incorporated some of the original walls and also included windows that allowed visitors to look out into the ruins of the adjacent St. Alban's Church, preserved as a memorial to the war.[105] Schwarz's plan for a reconstructed Cologne, one that would artfully blend the old and new and thereby reestablish continuity with the past, was never fully implemented. In spite of its restored churches, the area inside the Ring—historic Cologne—was fundamentally rebuilt as a modern, busy city.

The issues of preservation in Lübeck differed somewhat from those in Cologne, partly because political overtones from the Nazi years spilled over into the postwar debate on reconstruction. Located on an island in the Trave, Lübeck had preserved its medieval architectural heritage to a much greater extent than Cologne. That was part of the problem. During the 1930s, city planner Hans Pieper recognized that much of Lübeck demanded thorough renovation. The traditional style of building, which combined a merchant's place of business and home, had become badly outdated. Too small and poorly arranged for modern needs, the housing in many parts of the old city tended to be damp, poorly ventilated, and dimly lit. Pieper wanted to open up some of the densely built blocks, but he also sought to preserve the city's silhouette and avoid what he called silolike skyscrapers.[106]

At the same time, the local Heimatschutz movement, with right-wing, antimodernist overtones, advanced its own program for change in Lübeck. Not only were some block interiors and courtyards cleared, but, more important, facades were altered to bring them into harmony with what was regarded as the city's "true" architectural style. That meant that some genuine Baroque, plastered facades were stripped of their plaster covering and redone in exposed brick in a supposedly Gothic style. Such projects made Lübeck more "medieval" than it ever had been![107] All of this activity of the 1930s played an important role in the postwar debates.

Lübeck was attacked by the British on 28–29 March 1942, in a raid that left one-fifth to one-sixth of the old city in ruins. Sixteen percent of the street fronts and somewhere between 1,750 and 2,000 buildings were completely destroyed.[108] The major monumental buildings and a section of old merchant houses near the city hall and Marienkirche incurred significant damage. Many walls in this area remained standing, but the Nazis, placing high priority on the quick clearing of streets, demolished a number of historic buildings to make the streets safe. They devoted no thought whatsoever to the question of historic preservation.[109]

The war obviously prohibited large-scale reconstruction, but preliminary planning on the rebuilding of Lübeck did begin. Shortly after the bombing, Pieper invited Konstanty Gutschow of Hamburg to visit the city and make suggestions on rebuilding. Gutschow rejected the recreation of the old buildings as "erroneous and unfeasible," and he also rejected "embarrassing historicist building." He argued instead for new architecture that respected Lübeck's building tradition. The normally small, elongated property parcels, he felt, provided the key to the city as a "total work of art." These should therefore be retained, though it would be necessary to clear out the inner courtyards of the blocks. Some streets should be widened to meet modern traffic needs, and on these land parcels should be consolidated to make possible larger buildings, appropriate to modern commercial needs. Done properly, the overall artistic quality of the city would be preserved, even with the structural modernization of the bombed area.[110]

Pieper, as well as city building director E. Weise, clearly agreed. In a February 1943 memo, Weise spoke of the city's desperate need for major traffic arteries. He wanted to preserve as much as possible but noted that in addition to the demolition of ruined buildings, some 600 meters of house fronts would have to be razed for street widening. He favored rebuilding the major churches, although perhaps with modern steeples, but he felt that the housing in the old city should be drastically reduced in favor of new government adminstration buildings and new commercial buildings.[111] Pieper also wrote of the need for modern, wide sidewalks, sufficient automobile parking, proper facilities for business and city government, and a general renovation of housing, which he considered seriously inadequate.[112] Preservation ideas clearly took a back seat to modernization hopes for the old city.

Pieper continued in office at war's end and readied his plans by the summer of 1945. He died in the spring of 1946, and his son, who also served in the building administration, published his father's plans later that year. That book constitutes one of the earliest fully developed reconstruction plans for postwar Germany.[113] Pieper argued forcefully for new streets, new property lines, and modern buildings in the destroyed areas. The desire to preserve the traditional street and property lines, he declared, must not be allowed to obstruct modernization of the old city, for only modern houses and businesses would prove economically viable. As Pieper's son at one point noted, both he and his father believed that "the city was first of all an economic organism, much like a large firm, that above all should be functional and find its organic beauty in its usefulness." For that reason, "the living tasks of the city appear to be more important than its art-historical values."[114]

To support his argument, Pieper marshaled statistics showing that even before the war, Lübeck was no longer really a medieval city. In 1939, some 39% of all buildings in the old city dated from after 1870, and the bombing leveled 11% more of the older, historic structures. Moreover, of the old city's 3,200 buildings, only 21.4% had possessed gables that predated the nineteenth century, and only 5.2% of the old buildings had featured exposed brick, compared to nearly 48% with plaster facades. It was patently wrong, therefore, to claim that gables and exposed brick characterized the "true" Lübeck style. In fact, architectural styles had constantly evolved over time, and modernization of the old city merely perpetuated that traditional process of change.[115] Pieper's arguments also implicitly attacked the right-wing, Heimatschutz restorations of the 1930s. As a compromise, he suggested the possibility of "rebuilding a quiet street around one of the churches as an [open-air] city museum by moving to that site buildings from other parts of the city that had to be sacrificed for street widening and remains of monuments destroyed during the war."[116] This would have created a preservation island like those in Hamburg and Hannover.

Pieper's plans unleashed a storm of criticism. Local architect Emil Steffann drew up a plan that called for preserving the original street and property lines, except for a relatively low-capacity traffic circle that would surround a pedestrian zone in the center of the island. Hans Ewers, a former

senator, prominent member of the preservation council, and local leader of
the conservative German Peoples Party (DVP) before the war, supported
Steffann, as did a local newspaper, the *Norddeutsche Echo*, which also denigrated Pieper's plan as a product of the Nazi era predicated on a military
victory that would finance a radical redesign of the town.[117] Ironically, in
Lübeck the modernist position was denigrated as being Nazi in spirit! The
Overbeckgesellschaft, a local civic society, engaged Heinrich Tessenow, who
had always favored modest, traditionalist architecture, to create a new plan.
Tessenow called for diverting traffic around the old city and cautioned that
new streets built for today's auto traffic could easily be outdated in 50 years.
Hence sacrificing historic buildings to accommodate present traffic volume
would be shortsighted and irresponsible.[118]

None of these plans struck city officials as the answer to Lübeck's reconstruction problems, and in mid-1947, the city engaged a new planner named
Georg Münter, who strongly supported the idea of constructing modern buildings and streets. Rebuilding in the old style would make Lübeck little more
than a "Häufung romantischer Winkel"—a "heaping of romantic nooks."[119]
Münter's vehement stance reflected his belief that the opponents of modernization were the historicists who had been close to the Nazis in the 1930s.

Others joined the fray. Spokesmen for the preservationist cause urged the
retention of original parcel size and the utilization of traditional architectural
motifs and materials.[120] The *Lübeckische Nachrichten* attacked the building
administration as authoritarian and expressed fear of an emerging "Müntero-
grad."[121] The local Bund Deutscher Architekten, the professional association
of architects, also split over the issue. The majority supported reconstructing
with traditional building styles on the original parcels, and the BDA chairman
complained that Münter and the building administration showed favoritism in
granting contracts to a smaller group of architects who advocated modern
construction with steel reinforced concrete and glass.[122]

The two sides locked horns in 1949 over the competition for the reconstruction of the historic main market square adjacent to the Gothic town hall. The
Overbeckgesellschaft and others complained that no members of the prize
jury represented preservation ideals. Hermann Deckert, the conservator of
Lower Saxony, was immediately added to the jury.[123] At the end of the competition, Deckert claimed that all prize winners were committed to preserving
the historic values embodied by the market and would neither add new monumental buildings nor copy the proportions or style of the town hall.[124]

Nevertheless, when the city building administration made public its plans
for the square, as the reconstruction law of Schleswig-Holstein required, critics quickly perceived that in fact some major changes were in the works. In
order to improve the traffic flow on the Kohlmarkt, the street on the south
side of the market square, Münter planned to have the new row of buildings
on that side moved a few meters to the north, thereby reducing the size of the
original square. In effect, this meant that property owners who sacrificed
some of their land for the wider street would be compensated by land lopped
off the square. Moreover, the south entrances to the square were to be relo-

Lübeck, view from the Petrikirche tower down onto a modern parking garage built right next to and overwhelming classic examples of the city's Renaissance and Baroque merchant houses. This garage has become one of the better known examples of ill-conceived reconstruction aimed at modernizing an old city. (Source: Michael Brix.)

cated in such a way that the first thing one saw upon entering would be neither the Marienkirche nor the town hall but the neo-Gothic post office, which had survived the war intact. This outraged the preservationists. A new organization devoted to preserving the city's character, the Vaterstädtische Vereinigung Lübeck, had been formed in 1949, and it published an "official" protest against the building administration's plans for the market in its journal.[125]

In the end, the building administration emerged victorious. The market square was indeed reduced in size. The low buildings which were put up on the south side and on the north side between the Marienkirche and the square itself featured exposed brick and a simple, unimaginative style that was supposed to complement the historic buildings on the square. Eventually cars were excluded, but for a number of years the square served as a parking lot. This central place in the city thus had the benefit of neither a harmonious

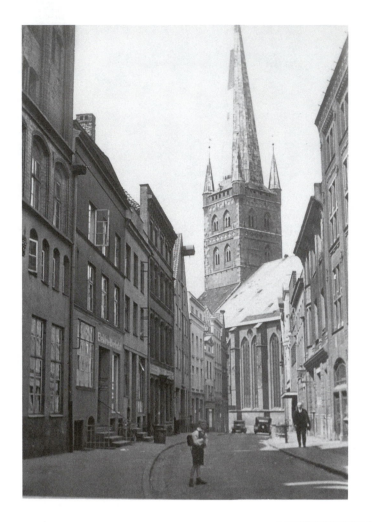

Lübeck, the Schmiedestraße, looking toward the Petrikirche. These all show the same view, about 1930, immediately following the bombing, and about 1975. The rounded shape of the parking garage is directly in front of the medieval church. Here the styles clash strongly. (Source: Museum für Kunst und Kulturgeschichte der Hansestadt Lübeck.)

recreation of the old nor creative modern architecture.[126] In spite of the excellent rebuilding of the major monuments such as the cathedral, the Marienkirche, and some individual historic houses, the main thrust of Lübeck's first decade of reconstruction was modernization, not preservation. Wider streets, improved traffic flow, some large apartment projects in the ruined area north of the Marienkirche, and large, glass storefronts were the not entirely happy result. In the bombed areas, the contrast between the old buildings that survived the war or those recently restored and the supposedly modern buildings is stark and often jarring.

Nevertheless, overall Lübeck gives the impression of a historic rather than modern city. Lübeck is fortunate that many historic buildings survived both the war and the process of reconstruction. Even though some of the new structures are disproportionately large, the island contains no skyscrapers, and the historic silhouette, when viewed from afar, remains unmarred. The island is small enough that the many historic houses, major monuments, remaining small streets and passageways, and overall silhouette suffice to give Lübeck its distinctive character.

Conclusion

The beginning of this chapter noted that inner-city reconstruction involved a debate over how to incorporate the legacy of an urban past into postwar planning. The experience of the cities described here demonstrates that planners usually sought to modernize the inner cities to accommodate new urban functions, while citizens' groups most often called for recreating the past and saving or reviving the unique historical character of each city, even if that meant copying destroyed buildings. The planners supported the preservation of the basic street layout, partly for economic reasons and partly to conserve a city's character, but that was easiest to manage in cities that already possessed a relatively modern street system. Where this was not the case, extensive changes often led to a considerable loss of historic substance. Planners sacrificed damaged but restorable buildings and also undamaged buildings to street widening and large commercial complexes. Many privately owned historic buildings, especially residences, were demolished.

Why were so many still-standing facades and buildings demolished when they could have been rebuilt? Some argue that the juggernaut of the Economic Miracle and the dictates of capitalism required building new, efficient structures at the expense of the old, traditional edifices. Others attribute the demolitions to the lack of building materials and skilled labor, a fear of collapse, or property owners' desires to use the land differently. In fact, planning departments, supported by the architectural profession, ordered the destruction. Architect Friedrich Spengelin observed that "for us, an acknowledgment of guilt blocked access to a compromised past and forbade the reconstruction of the bourgeois city."[127] Even before the economy began to recover, most cities opted for modern reconstruction plans. Planners focused less on individual objects and more on broad, functional questions such as public health, traffic flow, and safety.[128]

Preservationists struggled against this trend. Historic preservation lacked a strong legal foundation, but that deficiency only partly explains why it failed to exert much influence. After the war, professional preservationists entertained a very narrow conception of their task and were not at all eager to be closely associated with conservative citizen groups that might mire historic preservation in a controversy about Nazi architectural tastes. The general dislike of mid- and late-nineteenth-century architecture and of historicist architecture meant that little effort was exerted to save buildings that postdated the 1830s, and no one showed interest in preserving modern architectural monuments of the twentieth century. Such buildings had been roundly attacked by the Nazis, and modern architecture had not yet entered the historical consciousness of the urban population. Even in the case of many very old architectural monuments, the reaction against historicism created difficulties in determining just how to restore buildings worthy of being saved. The consequence of these considerations was that the desire to preserve or reconstruct the historic city— as opposed to individual monuments—usually gave way to modernization, and, as discussed earlier, the preservationists themselves often advocated modern cities and rejected attempts to transform an inner city into a museum of some past age.

Nevertheless, it is clear that the efforts of the preservation and Heimatschutz movements were not without some success. The inner cores of some major cities still convey a sense of the past, and residents and visitors are unquestionably attracted to these "historic" sections. As Jürgen Paul notes, the rebuilt cities are neither "entirely new cities nor entirely capitalist cities." Strong local cultural traditions forced the planning departments to save more of the old cities than they usually desired.[129] In Lübeck the number of undamaged or restored historic buildings was so large that the city retained its character in spite of plans for modernization. In Hamburg, the "historic" inner city was actually already relatively modern before the war and hence still viable. The most creative efforts to find a workable compromise between modernization and historic preservation occurred in Freiburg, Nuremberg, and Münster, where inner-city reconstruction featured traditional roof lines, building materials, colors, and proportions, so that new buildings harmonized with restored major monuments and formed large ensembles that manage to convey prewar impressions of the cities. This is true even though some historic buildings were demolished after the war and some buildings are merely copies of what had been destroyed. Historic recreations and adaptive architecture have contributed to the livability and urbanity of Germany's big cities. Modernist fears of a revival of nineteenth-century eclectic historicism proved to be unfounded, and over time the cities came to reflect a compromise between historic and modern forms and styles.

The place of historic preservation is much more established in West Germany today than it was in the decade after the war. In the 1960s and 1970s, critics of urban life argued that a strong policy of modernization without a significant commitment to historic restoration and preservation had been a mistake because residents no longer felt rooted in their cities. Since then Germans in large numbers, including planners, have begun to pay close attention to their disappearing urban heritage and to take firm action to preserve what has not been destroyed by decades of war and rebuilding. Moreover, they are able to profit from the lessons learned in those cities that succeeded in preserving their traditional character even while building anew.

5

The Housing Problem

Postwar Germany experienced a serious, immediate housing crisis. Fully 22% of the 1939 housing stock in the area that became the Federal Republic was totally destroyed or so badly damaged as to be unsalvageable; another 23% suffered some degree of damage. The number of homeless people was further swollen by the influx of refugees from the east. Between 1945 and 1950, some 600,000 refugees settled in Northrhine-Westphalia alone. Five years after the war, 11% of these still lived in camps or other emergency housing.[1] These disheartening figures quite naturally preoccupied planners and politicians. Nonetheless, at least among themselves, they also viewed the postwar housing crisis as part of a greater, long-term housing problem in urban Germany.

The impact of rapid industrialization and urbanization on housing conditions in Europe's cities is well known. Fed by a high birth rate and migration from rural areas during the latter two-thirds of the nineteenth century, the number of city-dwellers grew at a rate far exceeding the growth of the housing stock.[2] Inner-city housing became more and more crowded. Small buildings added upper floors; courtyards and open spaces, choked by new buildings, disappeared. Existing dwellings were subdivided, or tenants simply took on subtenants willing to pay for a bed. Police and fire regulations allowed authorities to limit the height of buildings and to insist on fire walls between buildings, but until the end of the nineteenth century much of the urban growth in Germany was unplanned and uncontrolled, and speculators feasted on the need for housing for the new urban masses. The results were catastrophic: German cities suffered from some of the highest population densities in Europe and subsequently endured appalling hygienic conditions. Berlin's infamous *Mietskasernen* was one of the worst examples. Enormous blocks of "rental barracks" that lined the wide, straight streets leading out of the center, the Mietskasernen featured stale air, little or no sunlight, serious overcrowding, and insufficient sanitary facilities, all of which dramatically increased

Berlin Kreuzberg, prewar housing around Chamissoplatz, 1978. Much of the lightly or moderately damaged housing stock was repaired and put back into service. The "rental barracks" form of the dense apartment blocks is clearly visible. (Source: Landesbildstelle Berlin, 4LuA Luftaufnahme, 208 979.)

disease rates. Criminality, immorality, and political radicalism within the working class and the destitute were also blamed on urban slums.[3]

For the well-to-do, the easiest solution to urban congestion was flight, and they often built single-family homes set in gardens in outlying districts. "Villa" architecture enriched the architectural heritage of Germany, but these suburbs failed to offer a solution to the housing problem of the cities, even though the image of the private villa became an ideal of elegant living. Although attractive, new suburbs on the model of the garden city, like the 1910–12 Hellerau project near Dresden, provided too little housing to reduce the density of the big cities.[4] City authorities weighed two options: they could either rehabilitate or redevelop slum areas or construct new, low-cost housing outside the central area. Both options were pursued during the first three decades of this century, although with varying intensity in different cities.

Slum clearance and redevelopment, even when it enjoyed political support, proved a difficult, time-consuming undertaking. In Hamburg, for example, the city government decided five years after the cholera epidemic of 1892 to embark on a massive program of urban renewal, including the construction of new housing for those displaced by the renewal program. This program continued, in fits and starts, until 1943, when the city was largely destroyed.

All cities which undertook urban renewal projects had to purchase prop-

erty or confiscate it by right of public domain. Because the law assured property owners fair compensation, redevelopment drained town resources. In
terms of housing, the purpose of redevelopment was to reduce population
densities and turn lower-class districts into proper middle-class residential
areas. That meant relocating current residents, some of whom refused to
move and yielded only to force.[5] Moreover, renewal projects reduced the
amount of available housing, at least until new housing built elsewhere could
absorb those evicted from the centers. Thus, while slum clearance remained a
firm goal of city authorities and a priority for parties across the political
spectrum, it never became a feasible way of alleviating Germany's housing
shortage. During the 1920s, when the German economy was disrupted by the
consequences of the lost war and the great inflation, city authorities were
unwilling to sacrifice even substandard housing, and urban renewal projects
were postponed.[6] Large-scale housing construction on newly improved land
was more promising, however, and provided valuable experience that could
be tapped after 1945.

Cooperative Housing

The construction of working-class housing dates at least back into the eighteenth century, when capitalist firms provided laborers with housing in the
hopes of maintaining a stable and dependent labor force.[7] The nineteenth
century saw the creation of corporations for *Gemeinnützige Wohnungsbau*, or
housing construction for the common good, which sought to provide workers
with inexpensive and healthy housing. Capitalist employers invested in these
corporations, from which they expected a fixed rate of return, partly out of a
sense of social responsibility and partly to assure their labor supply.[8] Though
worthwhile, these projects were not extensive enough to make a real dent in
the demand for housing.

The housing shortage grew worse after the turn of the century, leading the
Social Democratic party to call for reform legislation. During World War I,
the Prussian government began to fear that discontent over housing coupled
with tensions arising from the prolonged war might incite a social explosion.
Consequently, in March 1918, the conservative Prussian government passed a
law designed not only to stimulate new, modern housing construction but also
to facilitate the introduction of many innovations in urban structure, such as
parks and recreation areas. Adopted and adapted by the government of the
Weimar Republic and the parties of the Weimar Coalition, the law established
the legal framework for large-scale public subsidies for new housing.[9]

The beginning of the new republic, strongly backed by the Social Democratic party, raised great, often utopian hopes for urban reform, even though
the housing situation further deteriorated after the war because of the rising
number of new households (due to an increased marriage rate) and an influx
of refugees from territories occupied by the victorious Allies.[10] Reformers
hoped to build inexpensive, low-density housing set in greenery with ready

access to shops, public facilities, and the workplace. This goal reflected the enthusiasm of the reformers for the garden city movement as well as their hostility toward the industrial city.[11] The ideal was a one- or two-story cottage, but the enormous demand required that much of the housing take the form of multistory apartment complexes, including small apartments for single men and women. Situating and designing such buildings to provide a maximum of air and light were primary considerations. For models, housing reformers and town planners looked to the buildings constructed at architectural exhibitions, a tradition that began at the Darmstadt exhibition of 1901 and led to the 1927 Weissenhof exhibition in Stuttgart.[12]

The economic disruptions caused by the lost war, revolution, demobilization, and the great inflation meant that far more planning than actual construction occurred during the first years of the republic. Once the inflation ended in 1924, however, housing construction boomed until the onset of the depression. The majority of new housing was privately built, but between 40 and 50% consisted of cooperative housing financed by national, state, and local governments, as well as by private cooperatives or housing corporations formed by almost every kind of occupational group. Some cities founded their own public housing corporations. Seventy percent of all new housing built between 1924 and 1930 received some public funding, primarily from revenues generated by a special tax on properties that had gained in equity during the inflation, which had allowed mortgages to be paid off with devalued money. The proceeds of this *Hauszinssteuer*, first introduced in Berlin, were used to finance low-interest mortgages.[13]

Because large-scale housing projects necessarily involved town planning offices, cities exercised direct influence on the design of housing projects, even when the cooperatives chose the architects. Because the construction of detached single-family housing units, the ideal of most conservative German architects, failed to solve the housing crisis, city planning offices and cooperative housing corporations turned increasingly to modernist architects, who had been preaching the virtues of standardized housing construction. Walter Gropius, in his "Principles of Bauhaus Production," described the modernist approach to housing construction as "a resolute affirmation of the living environment of machines and vehicles; the organic design of things based on their own present-day laws, without romantic gloss and wasteful frivolity; the limitation to characteristic, primary forms and colours, readily accessible to everyone; simplicity in multiplicity, economical utilization of space, material, time and money. . . . The home and its furnishings are mass consumer goods."[14] Such statements appealed to left-center city governments, and modern housing projects went up all over Germany.

The three best known centers for progressive housing construction were Frankfurt, Berlin, and Hamburg. In Frankfurt, Ernst May, who headed the municipal building offices from 1924 to 1930, supervised the construction. A member of the Deutscher Werkbund and the Ring group of progressive architects, May had become a partisan of the English garden city movement while working under Raymond Unwin in England. His housing projects in suburban

Frankfurt—some 15,000 new dwellings—combined garden city ideas with the new style of architecture propounded by the Bauhaus and other radical architects.[15] Although the modern style of the buildings did not particularly appeal to the workers for whom the housing was intended, high demand ensured full tenancy.

In Berlin, thousands of new housing units were erected, mostly by cooperative housing corporations, the largest of which was the trade union Gemeinnützige Heimstätten-Aktiengesellschaft, or Gehag. Martin Wagner, a director of the Gehag, then planner in the Schöneberg section of Berlin, and finally chief planner of the whole city, and the architect Bruno Taut served as Berlin's guiding spirits.[16] Both applied the principles of the new architecture to mass housing construction, and both utilized prefabricated elements to try to lower costs through standardization. The flat-roofed Horse-Shoe Settlement in Britz was their most famous project. Another important project was the 1929 Siemensstadt development, housing put up by the Siemens electrical firm and designed by several modernist architects, including Gropius, Hugo Häring, Hans Scharoun, and Otto Bartning. In Hamburg, city planner Fritz Schumacher directed the construction of large housing projects in several parts of town. These too featured modern approaches to structure, layout, and site planning.

Although not identical, these new housing projects shared certain characteristics. Instead of closed apartment blocks surrounding interior courtyards, the modernists designed rows of buildings at different angles from the street or oriented by the compass in an effort to maximize the sunlight and air reaching each apartment and to provide green, open spaces. Some of the buildings were lower than traditional apartment blocks—two or three floors rather than five or six—which in turn lowered the density of the projects. Flat roofs predominated, and facades were usually either plain or minimally decorated with brightly colored paint or balconies. Inside, the designers provided central heating, modern plumbing, built-in kitchens, and a compact floor plan. Because the housing projects were built on the edges of the cities, the planners provided for such things as community buildings, schools, parks, and shops. Partly self-contained, the suburban housing settlements thus were virtual new towns. Unfortunately, rents still exceeded the resources of most working-class families, but the settlements nonetheless provided needed, valuable, and modern additions to the urban housing stock.[17]

Modernist architects were not the only ones flourishing under the housing boom. Conservative architects continued to build apartment buildings for private investors and for cooperative housing corporations formed by white-collar workers, professional groups, and government bureaucrats. They also built detached or semidetached houses in traditional styles, with pitched tile roofs and facades derived from local building customs. Traditionalist architects were also influenced by the garden city movement, however, and joined the modernists in situating new housing in greenery. They also tended to value simplicity in design and the inclusion of modern amenities.[18]

Housing Policy under the National Socialists

The housing policy of the Nazi regime can be divided into two phases. The first, which lasted until November 1940, was guided by the movement's antiurban ideology. The second, which lasted for the remainder of the war, reflected a shift toward accepting great cities and celebrating the triumph of technological and industrial rationalism. Elements of both phases would continue into the years of postwar reconstruction.

Early Nazi hostility toward large cities was based primarily upon criticism of slum housing for urban workers—a criticism shared by people across the political spectrum. Considered a product of unrestrained liberal capitalism, when speculators indulged in "orgies" in the land and housing markets, bad housing had created the "decadent big cities."[19] The ideology of *Blut und Boden* (Blood and Soil) called for housing produced with traditional arts and crafts techniques and situated in greenery, thereby enabling Germans to become "attached to the soil." Nazis viewed the large (and modern) cooperative housing projects characteristic of the late 1920s with disfavor. This ideological prejudice against massive, subsidized housing projects was reinforced by Nazi priorities: rearmament came before housing.

The preferred form of housing in the early Nazi years was the small *Siedlung,* or settlement, much like those built by Tessenow and other traditionalists before World War I. An example is the Mustersiedlung Ramersdorf in Munich, constructed in 1934 for unemployed and part-time workers. The Nazis promoted this project, along with others in Stuttgart, Düsseldorf, and Frankfurt, as a building exhibition of new housing forms.[20] Another example of this style is the Kameradschaftssiedlung begun in 1936 in the wooded Berlin suburb of Zehlendorf for members of the SS. This project eventually contained 606 rental units in small buildings and 305 single-family detached houses.[21] Even if constructed by housing cooperatives, however, these settlements were supposed to be financed privately. Government revenue raised by the Hauszinssteuer, used in the 1920s to subsidize cooperative housing projects, was diverted elsewhere, and by 1934 only 2.1% of the new housing received public financing, compared to almost 50% in 1928. With Germany still reeling from the effects of the Great Depression, the privatization of housing construction nearly brought new housing construction to a standstill. Instead, additional housing units were made available by refurbishing and dividing existing buildings.[22]

The early Nazi housing program also took aim at the hated Großstadt: inner-city slum clearance projects were carried out in Hamburg, Cologne, Frankfurt, Braunschweig, and other cities. There is no doubt that these slum areas were long in need of renovation, and the Nazis' reinvigorated renewal programs had begun or been planned before they came to power. Under the National Socialists, city authorities suddenly possessed the necessary power and financial and ideological backing to implement renewal plans that had been gathering dust. In 1933, when Konstanty Gutschow prepared a pro-

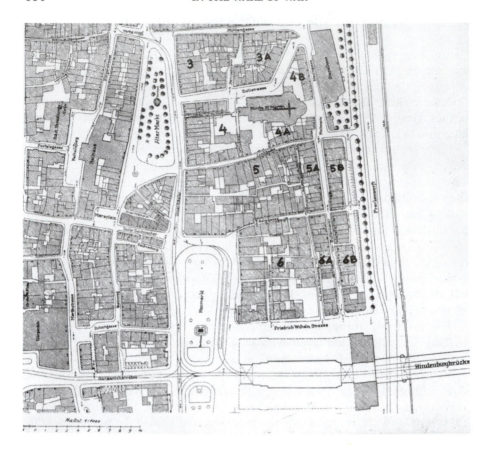

posal for renewal of one block in Hamburg, he justified the project by arguing:

> The home is the living space of the family, and the family is the [basic] cell of the state. Inadequate housing conditions necessarily create asocial elements and enemies of the state. A cartographic presentation of impoverished housing in a city corresponds almost down to each individual dwelling with the location of communist voters in earlier elections . . . . The elimination of such housing is a basic political task for the state, which can thereby get at the root of the evil.[23]

Stuttgart's Mayor Karl Strölin stated the ideological underpinnings of these projects even more baldly in 1935. Since the slums harbored "asocial elements of all kinds," who tended to foster Marxism, they should be razed and their residents relocated to new settlements. These new settlements, however,

> should fundamentally be reserved for the racially most valuable parts of our population. Thus it will in each case be necessary to examine carefully the inhabitants of these slums. The decidedly asocial elements should be harshly

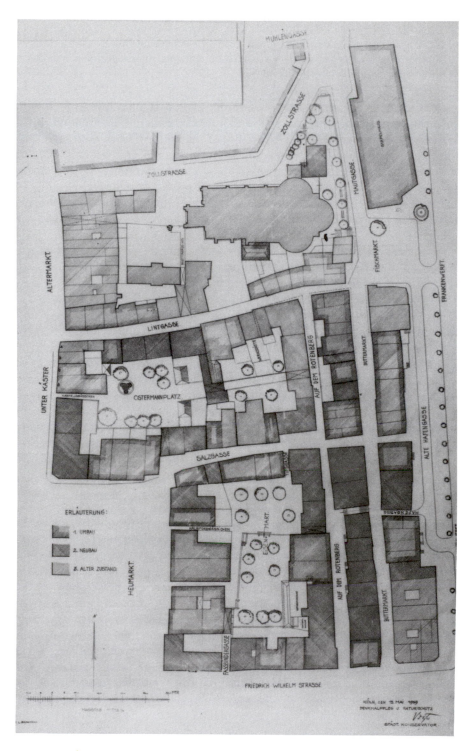

Cologne, quarter around the church of Groß St. Martin. The first photo shows the property lines in 1927. Blocks designated with numbers were considered in need of renewal. The second photo shows the 1939 plans for part of this area. Parcels of land were to be consolidated and the interiors of the blocks opened up for trees and air. (Source: Rheinisches Bildarchiv, nos. 76 989, 76 991.)

seized and brought where they can either be reeducated or, if that is no
longer possible, permanently guarded, for example in labor camps, work
houses, or similarly closed facilities.[24]

Such statements bear witness to the determination of city authorities to demolish substandard housing whatever the cost to the residents. The renewal projects brought improvements in the quality of the housing stock, although they
failed to increase the number of available housing units. In Braunschweig, for
example, the renewal area originally included 1,367 dwellings. Of these, 340
were demolished and 1,027 improved, while only 6 new units were built.[25] In
the projects carried out in Hamburg through 1937, two thousand new housing
units were constructed, 20% less than had previously existed in the renewed
areas.[26]

Beginning in 1936, several developments combined to change the nature
of Nazi housing policy. The first was the founding of two new cities. The Stadt
der Hermann-Göring-Werke (now Salzgitter) housed the workers of the new
steel works constructed under the Four-Year Plan, and the Stadt des KdF-
Wagens (now Wolfsburg) housed the workers of the new Volkswagen plant,
part of the "Strength Through Joy" (Kraft-durch-Freude) movement promoted by the German Labor Front (Deutsche Arbeitsfront, or DAF). The
second development was the program for the redesign (Neugestaltung) of
several German cities as representative Nazi cities. Third, the success of rearmament and industrial expansion convinced technocrats that they could
provide technical solutions to large problems. The Organisation Todt, for
example, formed to undertake huge military construction projects and headed
by the engineer Fritz Todt, was instrumental in pushing for greater rationalization and standardization in all areas of the economy. Finally, once the war
began, the initial victories promised not only expansion of the Reich but also
the colonization of conquered lands to the east and the possibility of massive
urban reform through population relocation.

The plan to create the two new industrial cities is extraordinary, given the
earlier antiurban and anti–industrial tone of Nazi ideology and propaganda.[27]
Built in the Braunschweig area, both new towns were to become large cities
with substantial working-class populations. Total populations would range
from 90,000 to 300,000. In scope, therefore, both cities went well beyond the
ideal new cities of 20,000 inhabitants advocated by Gottfried Feder, who, as
head of the Kampfbund deutscher Architekten und Ingenieure and then
Reichssiedlungskommissar from 1934 to 1935, had been the main Nazi spokesman on urban planning in the early years.[28] The layout of the housing blocks
was modern (row apartments positioned to get sunlight, etc.), although the
outward form of the buildings was traditional. Each city was to contain representative Nazi structures, such as a great square or stadium for mass assemblies, and factory buildings were to manifest a functional rather than modern
appearance. These two cities represented a massive state commitment to
housing construction, a complete reversal of the earlier privatization policy.
Moreover, by the end of the 1930s, more and more new housing was being

constructed in cities with over 100,000 inhabitants: 46% of the new housing built in 1939 was built in large cities, compared with a low of 39% in 1935 (and a high of 58% in 1928).[29] All told, during the Nazi years over 53,000 new housing units were built in Hamburg, a total not much different from that of the Weimar Republic.[30]

The Neugestaltung programs, especially those of Albert Speer for Berlin and Konstanty Gutschow for Hamburg, entailed massive redevelopment of densely built-up areas in Germany's two largest cities. The programs required demolition of large amounts of housing, which would have necessitated the building of considerable new housing in the suburbs. Thus in both cities the responsible architects' plans shifted from the design of individual monumental buildings to broader urban planning, including the planning of large housing projects. In Hamburg, for example, Gutschow calculated that there was already a housing shortage of 35,000 dwelling units: 30,000 additional units would be needed to replace housing demolished in the course of the Neugestaltung project, and 5,000 units were needed to replace cottages in other areas slated for development. He further projected a population increase of 800,000 (the result of the victorious war and consequent growth of Hamburg's world-dominating port), which would require another 200,000 units. Thus Hamburg alone needed to construct 270,000 new housing units. That figure virtually matched the total number of units constructed in the entire Reich in 1938.[31]

Since the total costs of the redesign programs were huge, planners began to think about cost-effective housing construction, which meant that by the beginning of the war in 1939, "modern" styles and materials increasingly gained adherents in Nazi circles. As was common in the Third Reich, different agencies became involved in planning housing construction. Initiatives came from the Reichsarbeitsministerium, which had been responsible for government housing policy since the Weimar era, the German Labor Front, the Plenipotentiary for the Regulation of the Building Industry (Generalbevollmächtigter für die Regelung der Bauwirtschaft: first Todt, then Albert Speer), the offices responsible for planning the Neugestaltung projects, and finally from a group in Albert Speer's ministry working on postwar reconstruction planning. The efforts of these agencies overlapped and sometimes conflicted.

The "Führer's Decree for the Preparation of German Housing Construction after the War," issued on 15 November 1940, signified the shift toward modernism.[32] This document marked what two scholars recently called "a turning point, which in its conceptual, technical, and organizational dimensions made possible a breakthrough in the progressive rationalization and modernization of housing policy and in the building industry and thereby helped create the first significant preconditions for the building boom in mass housing in the 1950s and 1960s."[33]

Hitler was himself involved in the discussions leading up to promulgation of the decree, which contained several important provisions. It created the position of Reichskommissar für den sozialen Wohnungsbau (Reich Commissioner for Social Housing), a position to which Robert Ley, head of the DAF, was appointed. The commissioner was to work with the Generalbevoll-mächtigter für die Regelung der Bauwirtschaft in fulfilling a government obligation to create a housing program that would meet the needs of an expanding population after the victorious conclusion of the war. The government was to supervise land acquisition and consolidation, approve architectural design, and promote economical production techniques that would guarantee excellent low-rent housing conditions. Wherever possible, "standardization and rationalization" would be the norm. The decree even specified that future housing units would range from 62 to 86 square meters in floor space, depending upon the size of the family, and that each would include a private bathroom with a shower.

The concept of "social housing" was new.[34] In part it was a variation on the earlier tradition of cooperative housing, and such cooperatives were to carry the burden of new housing construction. This represents an important ideological shift in its rejection of both completely private and exclusively government-financed construction. Initially massive subsidies were necessary, but the housing cooperatives were expected to become self-supporting. The concept addressed more, however, than simply the means of capitalization. Hans Wagner, a senior official under Ley, defined social housing as "that housing which can be mass produced to meet the average needs of the broad masses."[35] Another official referred to social housing units as *Volkswohnungen,* and Ley stated that he viewed housing construction in the same way as the building of the people's car, the Volkswagen.[36] In becoming advocates of industrialized housing production, the Nazis came very close to propounding the same theories advanced by the vilified Bauhaus.

Social housing thus implied not only a type of production but also the nature of the eventual consumer of the mass-produced good. After the war, the terms "social housing," "cooperative housing," and "subsidized housing" tended to be used interchangeably. But it should be emphasized that under the Nazis, the concept of social housing reflected a Nazi vision of totalitarian social engineering. New housing would combine with improved technology, social peace, population growth (encouraged by healthy housing), and colonization of the conquered lands to the east to raise the productivity of the new German society and breed a stronger German race. This authoritarian approach to housing dictated building standardized housing for people without asking them how they wished to live.[37]

In 1941 the Nazis called for the construction of 6 million new housing units in the 10 years following the (presumably victorious) war at a cost of RM 60–80 billion, a sum that approximately equaled the cost of armaments and the construction of fortifications in western Germany between 1934 and 1939. New housing demands grew, of course, with the bombing, and the scale of the housing plans expanded proportionately.[38] One of the ways in which the Nazis proposed to cut housing production costs was by exploiting the "human reservoir" of concentration camp inmates or the labor of the defeated Poles.[39]

Where exactly did this all lead? Eight competitions for the design of new housing forms were held between December 1940 and December 1942, and eight exhibitions of model houses were organized between March 1941 and August 1942.[40] Ley convened a meeting of leading planners in December 1941 to discuss housing questions, and these men then chaired subcommittees to examine specific issues, such as the relationship between housing and the work-place.[41] A new journal entitled *Der Soziale Wohnungsbau in Deutschland* (re-named in 1943 *Der Wohnungsbau in Deutschland*) was published to disseminate new ideas. For 1941 and 1942, the journal reported that work was planned, under way, or completed on 50,000 new housing units at 47 locations.[42]

Though the regime remained committed to the idea of detached single-family houses and small settlements, most of this new housing took the form of multistory row houses. Following modern ideas, closed blocks were gener-ally avoided. Curving streets and varied placement of the buildings in relation to the streets helped lessen monotony. In a concession to traditionalism, the exteriors were supposed to represent regional styles, but in fact they tended to be similar and resembled barracks.[43] Indeed, similarities exist between these buildings and the housing erected during the "first" reconstruction of East Prussia during World War I, when identifying suitable regional styles proved difficult.[44]

In 1943 and 1944, due to the turn in the war and the increasing monopoliza-tion of industry by Speer's Armaments Ministry, further production of large housing units ceased, and Ley and his group began designing temporary hous-ing for those whose homes had been destroyed by the war. They designed one- or two-room cottages or bungalows, composed of mass-produced basic elements, fabricated in some cases by concentration camp inmates. These *Behelfsheime* were to be constructed on small plots of land that could also contain vegetable gardens. After the war they would be converted into ga-rages or workshops.[45] By the end of the war, some 300,000 of these dwellings had been completed or were under construction.

As an integral part of these activities, officials in the housing program unequivocally demanded that fixed standards be set for building design and construction.[46] This was done with a full awareness of the examples of Ernst May and Fritz Schumacher during Weimar, and some of the men working on standardization during the war years had been members of the Weimar-era institute that did research on standardization, the Reichsforschungsgesell-schaft für Wirtschaftlichkeit im Bau und Wohnungswesen.[47] One of the most important products of the wartime standardization effort was the 1943 publica-tion of Ernst Neufert's massive *Bauordnungslehre*, which, along with his 1936 *Bauentwurfslehre*, became required reading for architects and construction engineers.[48] Neufert had worked for Walter Gropius before the latter left Germany and, beginning in 1938, he worked as a standardization specialist for Speer. Neufert's efforts formed a major contact point between Ley and his group and the architects and planners working for Speer and Konstanty Gutschow in Hamburg.

As suggested earlier, Ley's social housing organization was not the only agency working on housing. Significant activity in this area was generated by the Neugestaltung projects and Speer's ministry, and this too helped direct

National Socialist housing policy into channels that would lead into the post-war period. The most important figure here was Konstanty Gutschow, the architect responsible for the redesign of Hamburg. Gutschow had turned his office into a center for work on urban planning that rivaled Speer's as the most important in Germany. His approach to dealing with the housing crisis differed from that of Ley and, in the end, provided a needed counterweight to Ley's emphasis on constructing Behelfsheime.

An energetic and innovative planner, Gutschow had begun to develop his own ideas on housing by 1940.[49] As part of the preparation of a new general plan for Hamburg, he suggested that new housing be constructed in what he called the *Ortsgruppe als Siedlungszelle*, settlements of about 8,000 inhabitants, with mixed types of housing and appropriate social and cultural amenities.[50] These settlements were really garden suburbs for the large city, rather than the small new cities proposed by Feder. Gutschow's idea could also be applied to already built-up areas that might be redeveloped at a later date. To guarantee that Hamburg's cooperative housing corporations built new housing in keeping with his ideas, Gutschow appointed consulting architects to work with each housing corporation.[51] After the bombing raids began to inflict serious damage, Gutschow's office worked to coordinate the efforts of the housing corporations to repair damaged housing and construct new residential units.[52]

By 1941 Gutschow had come into conflict with the head of the DAF, Robert Ley, and with that agency's Hamburg director, Wilhelm Tegeler. The disagreements lasted until 1943 and culminated in Gutschow ceding many of his responsibilities in Hamburg. Tegeler's diversion of building materials to new housing construction incensed Gutschow, who felt that constructing air-raid shelters and reinforcing existing buildings to survive bombing demanded precedence. After Hamburg suffered the great air raids of July and August 1943, Gutschow became convinced repairing damaged buildings was the best solution to the emergency housing situation. Such work could be accomplished far more quickly and efficiently than constructing a comparable amount of housing through the Behelfsheim program of Social Housing Commissioner Ley, which Gutschow dismissed as "utopian." Gutschow eventually became a forceful critic of all proposals for temporary or emergency housing.[53]

Gutschow's conclusions about housing were the result of the continuous research efforts undertaken by his office on many aspects of urban planning and building. He gathered information from as many sources as possible and, always confident of his conclusions, sought to disseminate his findings widely. In June 1943, for example, he invited Neufert, Speer's adviser on standardization, to speak on that subject before an audience of 245 representatives of local government, the building industry, and finance.[54] When Gutschow resigned as Hamburg's planner (though not as Architekt für die Neugestaltung Hamburgs) in November 1943, the high quality of his work recommended him to Speer, who appointed Gutschow to a newly formed Arbeitsstab Wiederaufbauplanung bombenzerstörter Städte, or Working Staff for the Reconstruction Planning of Bombed Cities.[55]

Nominally the creation of this Working Staff entailed a division of labor between Ley and Speer. Speer's Working Staff was to work on general planning; Ley's office was responsible for housing. In practice their activities overlapped, and areas of disagreement immediately emerged between the two groups over the question of housing. As noted in early 1942 by Rudolf Wolters, Speer's chief assistant in the field of building, Speer and the Neugestaltung architects were designing cities "to mirror the mighty political will and military achievements" of an expanding Reich. The lines of National Socialist cities should be "clear, soldierly-strong." This vision did not jibe at all with the picturesque, semirural impression that Ley's group wanted to give their housing projects.[56]

Under Gutschow's leadership, the Arbeitsstab approached the housing question quite differently from Ley, even though both agreed on the necessity of rationalization and standardization. General guidelines for standardization of planning and construction were drawn up in the summer of 1944 and distributed in November to 69 individual planners and planning offices all over Germany.[57] Obviously this increased the influence of Ernst Neufert, the chief spokesman for standardization.

The Arbeitsstab went well beyond issuing guidelines, however. Gutschow undertook a study of rebuilding a bombed area of Hamburg and arrived at six different approaches featuring a variety of layouts and building types. In every case, housing blocks were to be opened up to light, air, and greenery. The density of the area would be reduced from the prewar figure of 60,494 to anywhere from 16,288 to 33,251 inhabitants.[58] Noting that "the English in their many publications on reconstruction planning always use the same three-fold programmatic division," Gutschow circulated a letter on 20 April 1944 to 18 planners and architects, indicating his views on housing priorities and soliciting their views on "(1) the repair of damaged housing; (2) the construction of temporary housing in different forms; and (3) the 'correct' form of constructing new housing."[59]

Most respondents agreed that the best housing form consisted of two-story, single-family row houses, even in inner-city areas, since the density of the old, closed housing blocks should be reduced in any case.[60] This model also conformed best with the guidelines in the 1940 housing decree, which were still in effect. Building detached single-family homes was impossible for large cities, however, because it required too much land and because demographic trends predicted growing urban populations rather than migration from the city. The key issue was to build healthy Großstädte, metropolises where good housing would help overcome the earlier class conflicts that had beset the cities and increased the communist electorate. Most respondents also agreed on standardization in construction, with appliances, steps, building blocks, fireproof concrete roof elements, and other elements being standardized and mass produced.[61] They considered the outward form of the new housing to be of lesser importance.

There was some dissent. Julius Schulte-Frohlinde, now a professor in Munich and an old Heimatschutz supporter, wanted to use local materials and forms and endorsed only moderate standardization, but he also noted that "reconstruction was a unique opportunity to eradicate [*ausmerzen*] everything bad in construction and building forms which had been piling up in the course of centuries."[62] Hans Stephan, on Speer's Berlin staff, observed that many mayors feared standardization and rapid reconstruction because they were "proud of their unique city silhouettes, rich in forms that had developed over centuries" and thought that standardization would bring a "desolate," "soulless schematization" to their rebuilt towns. And Rudolf Hillebrecht, Gutschow's chief aide in Hamburg, argued that housing should not be considered a mere consumer object, which the push for standardization threatened to make it. Such views, of course, echoed the debates between the modernists and the traditionalists and Heimatschutz movement in the 1920s.

Between July and November 1944, the Arbeitsstab hosted five conferences in Wriezen, a town outside Berlin, where a dozen or more planners and architects met to discuss various aspects of reconstruction, including housing. Gutschow introduced an idea here that he later developed in detail for Hamburg. He argued that each city should survey its bomb damage and then designate areas for high-priority, immediate reconstruction. These areas, or *Wiederherstellungsgebiete*, should be of relatively recent origin, modern in design, and in such a condition that invited quick and efficient repair or rebuilding. With proper planning, this approach could provide considerable housing in a short time and at reasonable cost.[63]

Though the participants at the Wriezen meetings still favored the model of two-story single-family row houses, Hans Stephan pointed out that the value of the investment in undamaged underground utilities would necessitate retaining at least the major streets in a city like Berlin, and it would probably also compel retention of large, closed housing blocks which were not damaged—however desirable it might be to redesign and renew these areas completely.[64] In reporting Speer's opinions on the subject, Rudolf Wolters noted that the minister had been circumspect and denied responsibility for the housing issue, "but that he would answer very precisely, if he were to have to decide on it." Speer was strongly inclined to endorse Neufert's standardization project, two-story, single-family row houses for small cities, but he felt multistory housing for large cities was acceptable and necessary. Wolters also noted that Speer liked the idea of competition between the Arbeitsstab in his ministry and the group working for Ley, since such a competition would show who could really develop the best proposals and instruments for housing construction.[65]

In fact, the recommendations of the group around Speer and the Arbeitsstab and the group around Ley in the end were not very far apart. They continued to disagree over the priority to be given the Behelfsheime, which Ley saw as a "weapon in the war against the housing blockade" imposed by the enemy bombers.[66] Ley, however, had finally also come to grips with large cities. In March 1944 he published a remarkable essay on housing and the city, which highlights the changed views of the Nazis on big cities. Therefore it is worth citing at length:

A massing of tens of thousands of settlements and single homes is hardly a city. Cities however are there and will always be there. Consequently we must of necessity also devote ourselves to multistory building. . . . We are used to seeing the city as dangerous for a people, as a kitchen for biological illnesses. The city tears individuals from the ties of a local community, which they still recognize in the village, and offers them the possibility of living a life of their own choosing, anonymously and uncontrolled by the community. This image derives mainly from the fact that our cities were built inorganically, that they have lost the communal context of the local central cell. But when we face the fact that we have cities and must build new cities, then we must also develop a new, positive orientation toward the city. I am convinced that a city, even a Großstadt, need not present a biological and political danger for our people if it is built correctly.[67]

Though Ley committed suicide in October 1945, and though some planners, like Gutschow, were removed from their posts by the denazification process, other former National Socialists with similar beliefs could—in terms of their planning philosophy—easily move on to join in postwar reconstruction.

Three men aptly illustrate this ability to move without prejudice into the postwar era. Johannes Göderitz, Hubert Hoffmann, and Roland Rainer, all of whom worked on housing theory within the German Academy for City, Reich, and Regional Planning, were ideologically more modernists than Nazis.[68] Göderitz had worked during the 1920s as a planner and architect in Magdeburg, but his association with the progressive town planning ideas of Ernst May forced him to retire in 1933. From 1936 to 1945, he found work in the German Academy, which was chaired by Reinhold Niemeyer, the head of Frankfurt's planning office during the 1930s and also a follower of May. Hoffmann, a student of the Bauhaus and member of CIAM, continued his close contacts with the modernists in and outside of Germany until the war started. Called to military service in 1940, he was released from duty two years later to work as a town planner and by early 1944 had joined forces with Göderitz. Rainer, who completed his studies in Vienna in 1935, had by 1938 begun research on housing for the Germany Academy for City, Reich and Regional Planning. Though he spent the war years as an infantryman, he nonetheless continued to work with Göderitz and Hoffmann in 1944–45 on housing and planning theory. In the last year of the war, these men drafted a book, *Die gegliederte und aufgelockerte Stadt*, which, though published only in 1957, most clearly formulated the fundamental planning ideals of the postwar years. At the heart of their planning model, about which more will be said in the next chapter, lay ideas on housing.

What was needed was to design cities following the logical progression from elementary, biological needs. One should start with families bearing and raising lots of children, which means starting with ideal housing forms and moving from there to other urban functions and structure. In Rainer's view, the healthy development of children was possible only if they grew up with a garden; thus "the question of housing is a question of town planning and biology."[69] Houses with gardens, in other words, constitute the foundation upon which town planning and reconstruction planning should be based.

But what kind of house with garden? The detached single-family house sited on its own plot was "biologically superior" for the family, but this was impractical.[70] To disperse the bulk of the population of the metropolis into detached single-family homes would require too much land and be too expensive, and the necessary scale would move too many families too far away from the central cultural facilities. However, it could be shown that two-story, single-family terraced row houses would provide almost as ideal conditions for garden settlements. In a settlement with 30 dwellings per hectare net building land, the gardens attached to or very near the homes would range from 218 to 275 square meters. If it proved financially necessary to increase the density of a settlement to 80 dwellings per hectare, one would have to build multifamily row houses up to five stories in height, and this would greatly reduce garden size. A development of this density would mean that, if it consisted of single-family terrace houses, the gardens would be only 5 square meters in size, but five-story multifamily buildings would still allow for acceptable gardens of up to 66 square meters per dwelling because less land would be covered by buildings.[71] Apartment buildings with more than five stories, however, would bring only diminished returns. There would be no gains in free land for gardens, and they would cost more to build. Still greater densities would of course also have equally negative consequences; they would begin to approximate the much-despised "sterile desert or steppe" of the metropolis of stone.[72]

Freestanding single-family houses could, of course, be sited virtually anywhere on the building plot, but this is not the case with attached row or terrace houses, especially when they rise above two stories. If living in nature meant living in gardens, it also meant living with maximum exposure to sunlight. It was necessary to pay close attention to the shadows cast by large buildings, since shadows would be harmful to garden areas. Site planning thus required careful calculation of the angles of sunlight at different times of year, and such calculations, particularly in the work of Rainer, led to the rather schematic, linear layout of proposed garden suburbs.[73] Göderitz, Rainer, and Hoffmann argued that garden city settlements in England, nevertheless, demonstrated that such residential areas need not be "monotonous," even when made up of "more or less identical, standardized small houses."[74]

The work of Göderitz, Rainer, and Hoffmann proved highly influential after the war, and all three enjoyed successful careers in spite of having worked for the Nazis. Göderitz returned to Braunschweig in 1945 as its chief planner, as a professor at the technical university, and as a leading authority on planning law and urban renewal. Rainer returned to Vienna, where he quickly published several essays on housing and planning, cleansed of Nazi-sounding phraseology, but consistent with ideas developed during the war.[75] He became an important modernist architect and teacher and for a brief time served as Vienna's planner. Hoffmann worked as a planner and independent (and modernist) architect, first in Dessau and then from 1948 to 1959 in West Berlin.

The legacy of National Socialist activity in the area of housing is thus complex and in some respects contradictory. Early policy and practice, along with the Führer decree of 1940, established the idea of small settlements or suburbs, with single-family detached houses or row houses set in greenery. This was an ideal in the sense of furthering physical health but also in the sense of furthering the sociopolitical struggle against class conflict and communism. The change toward social housing combined this ideal with the older organizational form of cooperative housing and committed the government to an extensive program of government subsidies and technocratic planning. During the war, there was new research and thinking about temporary housing, but large-scale housing projects, including multistory housing in inner cities, also gained currency. Planners recognized the need to accept the Großstädte as givens; the antiurban tenor of Nazi ideology played a steadily diminishing role. One had to rebuild the badly bombed cities, and one could not blithely proceed on the assumption of a victorious war.

In the plans themselves, outward architectural forms were deemphasized in favor of standardization of production. The initial impetus toward standardization came early in the war, when housing authorities vied with other agencies for resources. At the end of the war, the argument for standardization applied equally well to a shortage of resources caused by the bombing, the unsuccessful war, and general scarcities. The programs for prefabricated social housing construction, in particular, brought together under a Nazi roof modernist and conservative ideas on housing and architecture.

Altogether we find here a bundle of ideas, institutions, and practices that, once stripped of Nazi phraseology, could be applied to the task of postwar housing construction. The 12 years of Hitler's Reich thus produced a peculiar synthesis of certain aspects of modernism and traditionalism that coexisted with the official, monumental building program that Hitler loved. One scholar has described this synthesis as "reactionary modernism," another as "camouflaged modernism."[76] Whichever term one prefers, there was undoubtedly a strong modernist current present. One consequence of this strange alliance was that after the war, modernists, conservatives, and former Nazis found that they could work together in building housing for Germany's desperate population.

Postwar Housing

How bad was the housing shortage at the war's end? The available figures usually refer to dwelling units, not buildings or individual houses, since most urban buildings contained multiple housing units. Estimates vary, but within Germany's 1939 borders there were about 16 million housing units for a population of about 60 million inhabitants. By the war's end, around 2.5 million of these units had been totally destroyed and made uninhabitable. Another 1.6 million were classified as heavily damaged, meaning that 50 to 80% of each dwelling was in ruins, uninhabitable except for perhaps the cellar, and beyond any simple repair. In all, about 25% of the housing stock

TABLE 5.1.   Urban Housing Losses in Bavaria

	Number of Dwellings Lost	Percentage of Bavarian Losses	Percentage of City's Total Housing
Bavaria, excluding the 4 main cities	48,795	21.7%	
Munich	82,000	36.4%	33.2%
Nuremberg	61,319	27.3%	49.3%
Würzburg	20,453	9.1%	74.7%
Augsburg	12,423	5.5%	24.0%
Subtotal, 4 cities	176,195	78.3%	39.1%
Total, Bavaria	224,990	100%	

Source: SAM/ Bürgermeister und Rat/1976: Key for division of aid as of 3 May 1950.

was totally destroyed or heavily damaged, and in cities with prewar populations greater than 250,000 (excluding West Berlin), an average of 45% of the
housing stock was destroyed. The damage was worst in the inner cities, where
total destruction ranged from 50 to 90%. In Münster, for instance, only 3.1%
of the housing stock had escaped any damage, while 62.7% was uninhabitable. Only 6.4 million dwelling units nationwide—about 40% of Germany's
total stock—were undamaged, and many of these were in rural areas.[77]

Consider the damage in Bavaria, as represented in Table 5.1. Each of the
four largest cities suffered a greater housing loss than the average for Bavaria
excluding those cities, and more than three-quarters of Bavaria's housing
losses were concentrated in those four cities, which contained only 16% of
Bavaria's population in mid-1949. Würzburg suffered devastating losses indeed, losing 75% of its prewar housing stock. Munich's losses were more
moderate, but in the four central Altstadt districts, 64% of all buildings had
been totally destroyed.[78] On the whole, the housing stock in what became the
state of Northrhine-Westphalia—the most urban of the West German states—
suffered the most, with 30% destroyed or badly damaged, compared with
12.5% in Bavaria and only 4.1% in Baden. (In this context one should consider Bremen, with a 48.5% loss, and Hamburg, with a 53.5% loss, as cities
rather than as states.)[79]

Of the cities which had had more than 250,000 prewar inhabitants, 14 lost
more than 50% of their housing stock. Five experienced housing losses
of more than 100,000 units (Berlin, Hamburg, Cologne, Dortmund, and
Essen).[80] The three days of fire-bombing in Hamburg in July 1943 resulted in
263,000 dwelling units totally destroyed or very badly damaged. Most of the
destruction was of multiple-unit buildings—apartments—rather than single-
family houses. This meant that the poorer segments of the population suffered
much more than the wealthy, many of whom had homes in the outlying
suburbs.[81] Proportionally Cologne was worst hit among the big cities, losing
70% of its 250,000 prewar dwellings, but of cities with fewer than 250,000
prewar inhabitants, the housing loss ranged from Würzburg's 74% to 99% in
Düren![82] Nobel laureate Heinrich Böll found the claims of the various cities to

be the most badly destroyed "a most German and perverse form of one-upmanship," but the degree of damage was of more than anecdotal importance. It was used as a guide for the apportionment of state reconstruction funds.[83]

During the war, people had fled or been evacuated from the ruined cities. They sought shelter in the outer suburbs or the countryside with relatives, friends, or even strangers. For example, of the 132,800 people who lived in Münster in 1939, only 23,500 remained in May 1945. An American intelligence report of February 1945 noted that the destruction of housing, concentrated in the cities, had been offset by a combination of military and civilian deaths, a decline in the founding of new households, population migration, and programs of new construction and repairs of damaged buildings. The low urban populations at the war's end, in other words, could find shelter, but occupation authorities would have to prohibit people from returning to the cities in order to prevent a real crisis in the availability of housing.[84]

Although authorities urged the people not to return immediately to the bombed cities, once the fighting ended, the former inhabitants began to flood back to their former homes. Cologne's prewar population of more than 750,000 had shrunk to 40,000 by March 1945 but jumped to 450,000 by December of that year. Table 5.2 illustrates the repopulation of the bombed cities during the decade after the war.

The influx of former residents into the cities was augmented by large numbers of refugees from eastern parts of Germany that became parts of the Soviet Union and Poland and a bit later by people deserting the Soviet occupation zone for the Western zones. To take the case of Münster, 23% of the 1955 population, now 16% larger than in 1939, consisted of refugees from the eastern territories.[85] Although many of the refugees were settled in smaller

TABLE 5.2.   Urban Population Change

City	17 May 1939	29 October 1946	13 September 1950	1953	1954
NUMBER OF INHABITANTS					
Hamburg	1,698,400	1,406,200	1,605,600	1,722,800	1,752,000
Cologne	768,400	489,800	594,900	670,000	688,800
Essen	664,500	520,600	605,400	660,900	678,700
Dortmund	537,900	436,200	507,300	580,900	598,200
Bremen	557,900	488,400	588,600	607,900	623,000
NUMBER AS A PERCENTAGE OF 1939 POPULATION					
Hamburg	100	82.8	94.5	101.4	103.2
Cologne	100	63.7	77.4	87.2	89.6
Essen	100	78.3	91.4	99.5	102.1
Dortmund	100	81.1	94.3	108.0	111.2
Bremen	100	87.5	100.1	109.0	111.7

Source: HASK/5 (OSD)/ 38/ "Zahlen über Zerstörung und Wiedererstehen der Stadt Köln," p. 3.

towns, some also found their way to the big cities. By January 1950, over 1,930,000 refugees had settled in Bavaria. Of these, 69,000 took up residence in Munich and constituted 8.5% of the city's total population. Nuremberg's 21,600 refugees constituted 6.2% of its population, and Augsburg's 19,200 constituted 10.5%.[86]

The housing needs of the military and civilian personnel attached to the victorious and occupying allied armies further aggravated the housing situation right after the war. In 1939, according to an American intelligence report, 115,653 people had lived in Darmstadt in about 34,692 dwellings. In August 1945, some 65,644 Germans lived in the city in 15,184 dwellings. But in and around the city, 8,700 American troops resided in housing that could have sheltered 10,000 German civilians.[87] In Frankfurt, Germans inhabited 121,205 dwellings (half of which were in need of repair), and allied military forces occupied another 6,262 dwellings.[88] In Mannheim, the Americans appropriated some 4.5% of the available housing.[89] In Hamburg, British forces confiscated 1,361 single-family homes and 645 apartment houses in addition to assuming control of the undamaged big hotels.[90] Such confiscations occurred all over Germany.[91]

Eventually new quarters would be built for allied military personnel—a process that itself caused difficulties since it consumed large quantities of building materials and labor, a subject discussed in an earlier chapter—but immediately after the war, occupying military forces naturally commandeered the German housing in the best condition, often forcing the German inhabitants to vacate on very short notice, leaving their furnishings behind and taking only a few essentials with them.[92] In some cases Germans tried to resist eviction. In Regensburg, the Americans complained that the Thurn and Taxis palace was placed under the protection of the historic preservation office primarily to keep the Americans out of aristocratic housing. The Americans also accused the Germans of manipulating housing occupancy figures for their own purposes, reporting higher densities than actually existed in order to prevent the Allies from reallocating available housing. One officer observed that "it is evident that too often housing offices use density statistics as a drunkard uses a lamp post, for support and not for illumination. In Landshut one set of figures appeared when space was requested for additional refugees and another smaller figure when the city was bidding for the seat of the Regierung [district government] administration."[93]

In theory, Germans compromised by their participation in the Nazi regime were the first to lose their dwellings, which were allocated not only to the military but also to individuals designated as victims of the regime, such as former concentration camp inmates. Whether it worked that way or not, the confiscation of housing created much bitterness. As late as the fall of 1949, in the wealthy suburb of Marienburg on the southern edge of Cologne, 160 families had to vacate their homes to make temporary space for the British occupation staff—which itself had left quarters in Bonn now needed because that town was the new national capital. The evicted included the general directors of two very large insurance firms and Hans Gerling, the head of the important Gerling firm. The Germans protested that the dislocation of such men would harm the entire Cologne economy.[94]

Moreover, local officials assigned to the homeless housing that was empty for any reason. Under regulations established by the military government in Cologne, for example, housing would not be assigned to (1) anyone who had not had an official residence in the city prior to 1 January 1942; (2) members of the Nazi party prior to 1 March 1933; (3) Nazi party functionaries from the rank of block leader upwards; (4) members of the SA (Storm Troopers) with or above the rank of Scharführer; (5) members of the SS; (6) anyone not currently registered with the police as a Cologne resident; (7) those claiming a right to practice a business or trade but lacking a permit from the military government or the responsible licensing authority; and (8) anyone possessing another dwelling in Cologne or outside the city. The resulting turmoil, in which some had their housing confiscated, some were denied housing, and others were favored in obtaining housing, resulted in a situation rife with controversy and charges of unfair treatment.[95]

All of this meant that housing conditions were very bad in 1945, and they remained that way for quite some time. The German Cities Association called "the solving of the housing problem" "a question of the very existence of our people."[96] Families crowded into shared dwellings or sublet rooms, and people lived in cellars, makeshift huts, and the backrooms of shops. Those who found nothing else were herded into various kinds of emergency housing, such

Emergency housing becomes semipermanent. Quonset (or Nissen) huts in Berlin Amalienhof, 1956. (Source: Landesbildstelle Berlin, 1 NK, 49 334.)

as Quonset huts or abandoned German military barracks. Germans simply lived wherever they could. In 1947 authorities in the British occupation zone estimated that 9.1% of the population lived in refugee camps, some form of temporary housing, or in shelter improvised in the rubble.[97] This became a vivid setting for postwar novels, but before we romanticize life amidst the rubble, we should remember that the shelter found in the ruins was usually cold, damp, and often dangerous.[98] In every bombed city there were hundreds of buildings that the bombing had made structurally unsafe. People insisted upon setting up housekeeping anyway, and local authorities found themselves in the tense situation of having to evict people in order to demolish buildings in danger of collapsing. Cologne's 1951–52 administrative report noted that 11 persons had died and 32 had been injured when parts of damaged buildings had caved in. The following year the city administration reported that it had demolished 957 dangerous buildings, after evicting 1,863 persons. The next year saw 878 demolitions and 1,571 persons evacuated.[99]

Housing repairs and new construction could not keep up with repopulation and the other demands on the housing stock. For example, though by 1954 Cologne contained two and a half times as many dwelling units as it had in 1945, that number amounted to only 65% of the 1939 total, while the population had climbed to nearly 90% of the prewar figure. The housing density in 1939 had been 3.06 persons per dwelling and 0.79 person per room. Density figures for 1954 reported 4.23 persons per dwelling and 1.15 persons per room, an increase respectively of 38% and 46%.[100] In Stuttgart in March 1950, the mayor worried that 15,273 families totaling 43,794 persons sought housing, which required some 14,600 dwellings and 28,800 rooms. But in all of 1949, only 12,868 rooms had become available on the housing market.[101] One authority estimated a housing shortfall in Germany of 6.5 million dwellings in 1949. Even in the most productive prewar years, only 300,000 dwellings had been constructed annually. If Germany could construct 200,000 new dwelling units each year under existing conditions, it would take over three decades to make up the shortage, even assuming that none of the existing (and often damaged or substandard) housing stock was taken out of service.[102]

Before examining the efforts made to solve the housing problem, it should be emphasized that one of the greatest achievements of reconstruction was the massiveness and speed of housing construction. In the first months and years, people applied skills acquired during the war to repair whatever they could, create shelter in the rubble, and build temporary housing. Property owners slowly began to repair the damage to their buildings with the help of local authorities. Between the war's end and October 1945, Hamburg managed to repair 100,000 dwellings, create 10,000 new dwellings in cellars or buildings not previously used for housing, and construct 2,000 temporary units. Konstanty Gutschow had organized this program, and the British forces subsequently asked him to continue to head the planning and building office. Although they were aware of his background as Hitler's planner for Hamburg, the British respected his reputation for efficiency and competence.[103] Some military barracks, if not seized by the Allies, were converted to civilian housing. The Behelfsheim program begun by the Nazis now appeared in the form of Quonset huts (or Nissen huts) supplied by the Allies. In 1946–47 in Hamburg alone, 40,000–60,000 people were housed in such huts.[104]

Extensive new construction began only after the currency reform. Between 1949 and 1955, an average of about 450,000 dwelling units were completed yearly in the Federal Republic, compared to about 300,000 units yearly between 1927 and 1930, the prosperous years of Weimar. By the early 1960s, the housing crisis had been overcome.[105] This was an impressive accomplishment, even if, as noted in Chapter 2, the architectural quality of this housing left much to be desired in the eyes of critics. This accomplishment resulted in good part from the Germans drawing upon their complex heritage in housing policy, as discussed previously.[106]

Given the circumstances in which the Germans found themselves in 1945, it was natural to view the construction of massive amounts of housing primarily in technical terms: How could resources be used most efficiently to produce new housing? How could one most quickly put a roof over one's head? Some of the early postwar reconstruction plans reflected the same kind of reforming fervor that informed the housing planning in the 1920s and under the Nazis. Perhaps because the housing problem was so pressing, however, people began to view housing outside the context of general urban and reconstruction planning. Germans of all political persuasions, including former National Socialists, could speak quite safely about housing construction and help formulate housing policy precisely because the problem could be conceptualized in relatively value-neutral, quantitative terms. Indeed, concentration on technical questions may have helped shield former Nazis from legal, political, and ideological attacks.[107] Certainly the magnitude of the housing crisis enabled former political opponents to work together.

The cities and states (*Länder*) of the Western occupation zones and then later the Federal Republic shared a broad consensus on housing construction. Private individuals were encouraged to do as much as possible themselves—and without recourse to the black market—to repair their homes and make them habitable if at all possible. Beyond individual efforts, institutional help was needed. Local, state, and national government should provide financial assistance, and nonprofit cooperative or social housing corporations, whether privately or publicly owned, should assist in organizing and implementing construction projects. Because temporary housing in fact wasted resources, permanent, standardized housing should be built that maximized the sunlight and fresh air in each dwelling. In the inner cities, apartment blocks of three or four stories were appropriate; in suburbs, the model should be two-story row houses.[108]

This program shared characteristics with that promoted by the Nazis during the war, although stripped of Nazi racial-ideological content, and in many respects it resembled the program of leftist housing reformers during the Weimar Republic. Indeed, the parties of the 1920s which had supported housing reform—the Social Democrats, the People's party, and the Center—reemerged after 1949 as the SPD, Liberal, and Christian Democratic parties, and all three supported what was generally called social housing. In this sense, a significant part of the urban reconstruction program remained above partisan politics. While the Social Democrats viewed social housing as the long-term ideal, the conservative parties understood it as a transitional stage that would give way to individual, private home ownership, once the economy recovered.

No one doubted, however, that government would play a central role in the housing market. For example, in March 1947, seven leading Bavarian banks, in consultation with the Munich Chamber of Commerce, submitted to the Bavarian ministry of finances a proposal for a construction financing law. This proposal, submitted by a group of conservative institutions, contained the following observations:

> Whether, for example, one advocates a planned economy with enthusiasm or as a result of cool, perhaps even regret-filled considerations, makes no great difference in practical terms because of its necessity. . . . The proposal endorses the necessity of a planned economy in these areas, but it would like to see planning promoted "with a gentle hand" and, whenever possible within the realm of the planned economy, the proposal would attempt to encourage private initiative. . . . The period of housing construction by speculators belongs to the past. . . . The goal [is] a synthesis between a planned economy and private initiative.[109]

Two years later, Helmut Fischer, head of Munich's reconstruction office and manager of the Bavarian Reconstruction Council, argued that one of the central failures of the government between 1930 and 1933 was its inability to promote the building industry as a solution to the problem of mass unemployment. An "elastic housing construction program," he believed, would absorb the unemployed, stimulate the entire economy, and thereby "ban the threatening danger of a new radicalization."[110] The Social Democrats acknowledged conservative support for public intervention in the housing market in their 1949 proposal for a social housing bill—a bill which was to become the basis of the first federal housing law—and agreed with Federal Housing Minister Eberhard Wildermuth that "the number of communist voters in European countries stands in inverse proportion to the number of housing units per thousand inhabitants."[111] Social and political stability demanded rapid housing construction, whether it be social housing or private housing. Significantly, no stigma was attached to living in subsidized social housing. In postwar Germany, virtually everyone needed assistance, and the overwhelming need for social housing probably increased the measure of social integration in the rebuilt cities.

Because social housing had been concentrated in the larger cities, the damage to this sort of housing had been particularly great. Even before the creation of the Federal Republic and the passage of the first Federal Housing Law on 24 April 1950, social housing corporations had initiated repairs. In the state of Northrhine-Westphalia, 65,000 of the 85,000 uninhabitable apartment buildings at the war's end had been social housing. By 1950, fully 90% of the

Hamburg-Eilbeck. The first photo shows temporary housing in Quonset huts in an area largely leveled in the bombing. The large structure standing in the middle is an above-ground, reinforced concrete air-raid shelter. Such shelters were built in many German cities, and they proved far too costly to demolish. Consequently, they were left standing, surrounded by rebuilt structures. The Eilbeck shelter, painted a bright color, is visible above the new social housing constructed in this area. (Source: Staatliche Landesbildstelle Hamburg, nos. 7681, C5303.)

lightly or moderately damaged units and 50% of the totally destroyed or badly damaged units had been repaired or rebuilt. Most of this work was completed by the social housing corporations before the currency reform and without outside help. Interestingly enough, 41.5% of this social housing had consisted of small settlements and single or two-family houses rather than large apartment blocks.[112] Employers, especially in large industries, also invested in social housing independently from state-sponsored programs. This phenomenon reflected the longstanding tradition of paternalism in German industry and the hope that such efforts would tie workers to their companies.[113]

Economic stability came to the Western occupation zones with the currency reform of June 1948, and the establishment of the Federal Republic in May 1949 brought political stability as well as a new source of funding for housing. For the first time in Germany, a federal housing ministry was created. Although many cities had enacted their own social housing programs since the 1920s and were thus already involved in housing construction, the 1950 Federal Housing Law encouraged a flow of new financial resources into the housing market. The law was designed to stimulate housing construction by making available funds for loans and subsidies for social housing and by granting property-tax relief for new private housing and repaired or rebuilt dwellings. Rents were controlled for publicly funded housing in order to guarantee the availability of housing to people with low incomes.[114]

The principle for dispensing federal funds to the states was worked out in complicated negotiations.[115] A distribution formula was weighted so that 50% of the apportioned amount was based on population size, 25% on the degree of destruction, and 25% on the level of industrialization. The high percentage for population was a response to the enormous influx of refugees. Efforts to settle them in relatively undamaged areas created a demand for housing that went well beyond needs resulting from war damage. The financial apportionment can be illustrated by examining the federal housing ministry's plans to distribute funds in 1953. Of the DM 400 million budgeted, DM 75 million would be used by the federal government for resettlement projects, DM 5 million was to be put in a special fund, and DM 20 million was to be set aside as a reserve, perhaps for use in reconstructing city centers. The remaining DM 300 million was allotted to the states according to the distribution formula in Table 5.3.

Each state worked out similar distribution formulas to divide funds among cities, where the money would often be commingled with local resources.[116] Figures 5.1 and 5.2 graphically represent what happened in the housing market in the large city of Munich. Figure 5.1 shows that public subsidies for housing construction grew rapidly at first and stabilized after 1950, although the percentage of the city budget devoted to housing dropped after 1952. Figure 5.2 shows that privately financed housing grew faster than both social housing and subsidized housing as the German economy recovered during the mid-1950s and as some of the prewar and wartime controls on rents and property values—which had dampened private investment in housing—were gradually relaxed.[117] The relationship between private and publicly financed housing varies from city to city, however, with northern cities emphasizing

TABLE 5.3.   Distribution Key for Federal Funds, 1953

Schleswig-Holstein	6.48%
Hamburg	4.27%
Lower Saxony	14.85%
Northrhine-Westphalia	28.20%
Bremen	1.34%
Hesse	7.99%
Rhineland-Pfalz	4.55%
Bavaria	16.17%
Baden-Württemberg	10.15%
West Berlin	6.00%
Total	100.00%

Source: HSANRW/ NW 305/333/ Bundesministerium für Wohnungsbau,
Ministerkonferenz, 28 November 1952.

public subsidies and social housing more than southern cities. Of the 106,214
dwellings built in Hamburg between 1946 and 1952, some 53% were publicly
subsidized. Forty-two percent of the 89,000 units built between 1949 and 1952
were in social housing projects.[118] The social housing emphasis in the north
probably resulted from the greater concentration of wartime urban and housing planning there.

Of what did the subsidies consist, and where did the money come from?

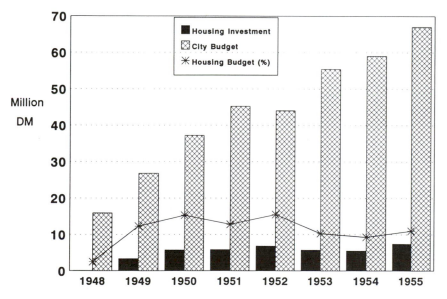

FIGURE 5.1. Munich city housing investment.
Source: Helmut König, *München setzt Stein auf Stein* (Munich, 1958), p. 120.

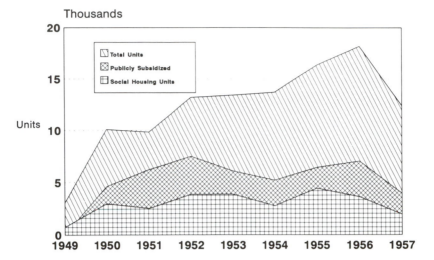

FIGURE 5.2. Munich: housing by type.
Source: Helmut König, *München setzt Stein auf Stein* (Munich, 1958), p. 120.

Everyone agreed in 1945 on the need for government aid, particularly in housing construction, and the archives and professional journals contain numerous proposals for implementing this.[119] Several kinds of public subsidies for housing were adopted, including low-interest or interest-free loans, waivers on normal property taxes and fees, and reduced fees for land improvements such as street and sewer construction. Such exemptions considerably reduced normal city revenues, which might otherwise have been used in rebuilding city-owned properties, but governments also raised money from regular taxation and from special taxation, such as taxes levied on property undamaged during the war.[120] Those whose property escaped the war unscathed thus shared the burden of reconstruction. The Nazis had passed such an "equalization of burdens" act during the war, and the Hauszinssteuer of Weimar had anticipated the principle by taxing property that had appreciated in real value during the inflation in the 1920s.

After the war, the state of Bavaria passed a special emergency levy for housing construction. Owners of undamaged buildings were to pay from 0.3% to 0.5% of the value of the building as determined either by calculating the 1914 cost of the building or by consulting fire insurance valuation estimates.[121] Although owners of the property often opposed such measures, most agreed that everyone had to shoulder some of the burden of reconstruction.[122] Other funding devices included tax-advantaged savings plans to encourage individuals to put money aside for future mortgages and contracts between tenants and property owners whereby tenants loaned funds to the owners to repair, enlarge, or construct apartment buildings in return for long-term leases and fixed low rents.[123]

As noted previously, the special attention to social housing did not mean that all housing was publicly subsidized, nor did it mean that all subsidized

FIGURE 5.3. Financing of housing, 1950–54.
Source: As in Table 2.

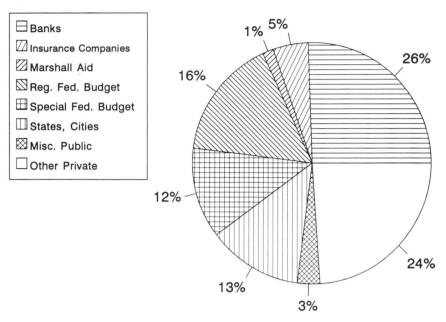

housing was publicly owned. British authorities reported that private owners constructed 72% of all residential buildings completed in 1950, public corporations 6%, and non-profit enterprises 22%.[124] Table 5.4 and Figures 5.3 and 5.4 indicate the sources of financing for the period from 1950 through 1954 for the entire Federal Republic. In 1950, the investment of DM 3.8 billion in housing

FIGURE 5.4. Financing of housing, 1950–54.
Source: As in Table 2.

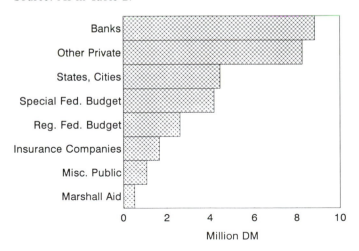

TABLE 5.4. Financing of Housing (DM in millions)

Source	1950		1951		1952		1953		1954		Total	
	DM	%	DM	%	DM	%	DM	%	DM	%	DM	%
Financial institution												
Banks	1,154	30%	950	20%	1,212	19%	2,108	27%	3,421	38%	8,845	28%
Insurance companies	257	7%	259	6%	313	5%	390	5%	444	5%	1,663	5%
ERP (Marshall aid)	181	5%	192	4%	89	1%	37	0%	15	0%	514	2%
Subtotal	1,592	42%	1,401	30%	1,614	26%	2,535	32%	3,880	43%	11,022	35%
Public funds												
Regular federal budget	308	8%	346	7%	571	9%	664	9%	722	8%	2,611	8%
Special federal appropriations	670	18%	1,015	22%	651	10%	809	10%	1,038	12%	4,183	13%
State and city budgets	600	16%	700	15%	1,100	17%	1,050	13%	1,000	11%	4,450	14%
Miscellaneous	90	2%	155	3%	391	6%	224	3%	215	2%	1,075	3%
Subtotal	1,668	44%	2,216	47%	2,713	43%	2,747	35%	2,975	33%	12,319	39%
Other (private capital, loans from renters, etc.)	540	14%	1,083	23%	1,973	31%	2,521	32%	2,145	24%	8,262	26%
Total	3,800		4,700		6,300		7,803		9,000		31,603	

Source: Arthur Brunisch, "Der Wohnungsbau in der Bundesrepublik Deutschland 1945–1955," Der Architekt 4 (1955): 255.

amounted to more than a quarter of the total capital investment in that year in all sectors of the economy combined.[125] Public financing reached a high in 1951 of 47% and then fell steadily, with the financial markets and private capital sources consistently providing the largest share of housing funds. Figures for Hamburg for the years 1949 through 1952 (Table 5.5) indicate that private housing construction accounted for more than half of the new housing, in spite of a relative decline as increased public funding helped spur social housing. Furthermore, building authorities in many cities argued that rent levels needed to be raised from about one-sixth to one-fifth of gross income (i.e., to prewar, peacetime levels) as a means of stimulating further private construction of rental housing.[126]

Part of the public funding for housing came from the Marshall Plan. Even as they confiscated dwellings for their own use, the Americans encouraged new housing construction. They were encouraged in this both by their own wartime experience in planning and by German-born architects who had fled Hitler's regime in the 1930s. The debate over the usefulness of prefabrication, for example, was one common to both countries. Walter Gropius, at Harvard University since 1937, had participated in a group set up by Martin Wagner in Berlin in 1931 to develop designs for prefabricated, modular housing. Wagner was then Berlin's chief planner, and, like Gropius, had firmly believed that a democratic society required modern (and by definition democratic) housing and planning.[127] Their interest in this subject continued after the two men migrated to America. In 1941, Wagner and Gropius presented a joint paper advocating industrialized housing construction to a U.S. House Select Committee investigating war-related population migrations in the United States.[128] If prefabricated housing was touted as a solution to America's housing problem, surely it would work equally well for Germany. Members of the American military government also thought that Germany might be able to export simple prefabricated housing to other devastated countries and thereby im-

TABLE 5.5. Housing Construction in Hamburg (in dwelling units)

Housing Form	1949 Number	%	1950 Number	%	1951 Number	%	1952 Number	%	Totals Number	%
Private	9,950	70%	15,294	59%	13,747	53%	11,844	51%	50,835	57%
City social housing	1,971	14%	2,906	11%	2,597	10%	2,305	10%	9,779	11%
Other social housing	2,153	15%	7,522	29%	9,148	35%	8,706	37%	27,529	31%
Government employee housing	86	01%	174	01%	327	01%	380	02%	967	01%
Total dwelling units	14,160		25,896		25,819		23,235		89,110	

Source: Karl Sommer, "Der Wohnungsbau nach dem Kriege," in *Wohnungsbau in Hamburg* (Hamburg, 1953).

prove its foreign trade balance. With American encouragement, some effort was made in this direction.[129]

In 1949 the American military government invited two planners from Philadelphia, Samuel Zisman and Hans Blumenfeld, to visit Germany and advise both the Germans and Americans on the status of planning. They devoted two months to talking with German planners, architects, town officials, and students in planning and architecture.[130] As a result of their travels, Zisman and Blumenfeld reached the conclusion that the solution to the German housing crisis required American financial support. They found that the war damage, the lack of an extensive housing construction program under the Nazis, and the influx of people expelled from the former German lands to the east had created "intolerable overcrowding and unsanitary conditions" that posed "serious moral, social, and political dangers." "The seriousness of the situation," they argued, "makes it impossible to treat this problem as a matter of no concern to the [American] High Commission."[131]

The suggestions made by Blumenfeld and Zisman were similar to programs initiated by German housing reformers since the 1920s. The solution to the housing shortage included long-term planning of new housing projects, the creation of new legal and fiscal tools to enable impoverished property owners to rebuild damaged buildings, and basic changes in the design of housing units and construction techniques. Outmoded conservative German construction methods, for example, which sought to build houses that would last indefinitely, had to be replaced by modern forms, particularly prefabrication. The Germans needed to understand the concept of "functional obsolescence" and accept the idea of regularly replacing housing.[132] The financing of a massive program of housing construction could be accomplished either through deficit financing (prohibited by the Allies) or through foreign assistance. The latter would of course include Marshall Plan counterpart funds, which Blumenfeld and Zisman felt would be "one of the most productive uses to which these funds could be put."[133]

With the advent of the Marshall Plan, the Americans did in fact exert considerable influence on housing construction. They feared that the lack of good housing for lower income groups—workers and refugees—might undermine their policy of democratization, and one official observed that "the potential danger of several million people housed under deplorable conditions is difficult to exaggerate."[134] The Americans felt that current rents for existing housing were too low, and taxes, interest rates, and building costs for new housing were excessively high. They acknowledged that new sources of funding for housing were desperately needed in the new West German state. As noted earlier, the Federal Housing Law of 24 April 1950, which made available a variety of governmental subsidies and tax credits, provided the framework for funding most of the new construction, but counterpart funds under the Marshall Plan also made an important contribution and enabled the Americans to influence the shape of reconstruction. In addition, under an agreement with the Federal Housing Ministry, European Recovery Program (ERP) funds were to be allocated in accordance with the provisions of the

Federal Housing Law. That meant that ERP-financed housing had to be social housing consisting of dwellings built "at the lowest possible costs at such places where the demands . . . is [*sic*] considered most urgent." Rents were to be kept low, and persons assigned to the housing should be working in areas essential to economic recovery (such as mining, industry, or export trades) or else belong to categories of especially needy persons, such as refugees from the east or those disabled by the war.[135] At the same time, the allocation of funds and the assignment of completed housing units should reflect some measure of social equity.

The Americans pursued several goals simultaneously. In keeping with the overall aim of the Marshall Plan and as suggested by the agreement with the federal housing minister, they wanted most of all to help stimulate the German economy. Upon seeking the American High Commission's assistance in obtaining financial aid for housing, individual Germans were told that "housing is allocated with the view to increasing the general productivity of the German economy by bringing workers closer to their work, and by relieving labor shortages and inefficiencies. This policy does not permit us to direct our aid to those persons who perhaps have a greater claim to our friendship, appreciation and generosity."[136] In other words, economic growth rather than rewarding political loyalty guided American policy.[137]

Within the housing industry itself, Americans attempted to improve productivity by introducing greater efficiency. They were extremely frustrated by German unwillingness to build or live in temporary housing structures made of wood. German authorities always insisted on solid masonry construction that would last decades and repeatedly obstructed the building of prefabricated dwellings.[138] Even when architects favored new construction methods and designs, local bureaucrats stifled innovation by insisting that builders conform to any number of petty regulations or that the design of individual buildings harmonize with traditional local styles. The Americans hoped ERP funds would pressure the German bureaucrats to give up their traditional thinking and accept efficient, innovative construction processes.[139]

The first extensive American-sponsored housing construction program was the building of small residential settlements in 15 German cities.[140] The Americans hoped "to break traditional building methods" by releasing Economic Cooperation Administration (ECA) funds only if construction costs were held down through the use of standardized building techniques.[141] Cities wishing to participate had to provide suitable land near important industries and assume the costs of improving the land. To obtain widespread German participation in developing progressive designs and construction methods, a nationwide competition was announced in the summer of 1951. Some 3,300 dwellings were to be built in developments of from 200 to 300 units with DM 37.5 million in ERP funds. All were to be social housing projects in keeping with the provisions of the Federal Housing Act, but the Americans also wanted most of the housing units to become the private property of the residents.

The competition clearly fulfilled the goal of stimulating interest in the program. Individual architects or architectural teams submitted an extraordinary 725 entries, which an international committee then judged. Entries were evaluated on the basis of the quality of planning, arrangement of the housing units, building cost and efficiency, construction techniques, and appearance. The State Department asked Gropius to serve as the American co-chairman. He declined but sent in his stead Walter Bogner, a Harvard colleague who concurred with Gropius's ideas about town planning, modern design, and standardized construction techniques. The German co-chairman was Otto Bartning, president of the Association of German Architects (the BDA) and, like Gropius and Martin Wagner, a member of the 1931 Berlin group that had worked on prefabricated housing. Moreover, Bernard Wagner, the son of Martin Wagner and also an architect, served on the committee as an ECA housing consultant.[142] In an essay describing the ECA program, Bernard Wagner stated that it was intended to help German architects "pick up where Poelzig, [Mies] van der Rohe, Gropius and Martin Wagner left off" because the "Nazi regime systematically strangled any new ideas in architecture, thoroughly eradicated the earlier modern spirit and saw to it that German architectural schools produced nothing but obedient servants in the National Socialist conception of art and architecture."[143] This illustrates again that the ideology of modernism moved from Germany in the 1920s to America in the late 1930s and, sponsored by the United States, returned to Germany after the war in the ECA competition.

The prize committee spent 40 days traveling around Germany analyzing entries and examining prospective building sites. Many of Germany's best known architects had entered the competition, and the wartime activities or ideology of the participating architects obviously played no role at all in the decisions of the prize committee. The winners included architects who had prospered during the Nazi regime, such as Konstanty Gutschow and Hans Bernhard Reichow, and architects who had suffered, such as Werner Hebebrand. Losers included famous modernists like Hans Scharoun and conservatives like Hermann Rimpl.[144] Almost all of the 725 entries featured small row or terrace houses with small gardens according to the prevailing theory of ideal residential planning and house design.[145] As it turned out, only one of the 13 winning entries—in Bremen—was located in an urban area destroyed by bombing; the others were on the outskirts of towns, for which the prize committee incurred some sharp criticism. Costs were indeed kept down, but many bemoaned the small size of the dwellings, the paucity of imagination in site planning, and the poor quality of construction.[146]

In spite of these criticisms, or perhaps through them, this ECA-funded competition was clearly important. Another ECA-sponsored program, this time to provide housing for miners, was organized by James Butler, head of the housing division of the ECA mission to Germany. Everyone knew that the low level of coal production hurt all areas of the German economy and prevented a rapid rise in productivity. The lack of suitable housing for miners in the Ruhr coal fields contributed to this problem, and Butler suggested using ERP funds both to support "standardized and efficient construction" in terms of the external shell and the interior amenities and fixtures, and to establish "an incentive plan to distribute a greater share of the housing built to mines showing highest relative increase in coal production."

> We suggest building distinctive ECA housing projects, clearly identifiable as such and properly publicized at the outset, so that we can move immediately towards our prime objective, namely increased production through improved morale. We can do this by impressing the miners with the fact that they can expect to get good, inexpensive housing soon, housing which will be built within properly planned communities, not under the control of individual mines, but under their own control as members of a community and as private owners of individual houses contained therein.[147]

To guarantee that the design quality would be progressive (and not left in the hands of local officials), an international committee was again appointed to approve the designs for the miners' housing projects. The United States was represented by Mack Arnold, who had served on the earlier ECA prize committee, and Martin Wagner, now retired from Harvard and making his first trip back to Germany since fleeing in the 1930s.[148]

The nine miners' housing settlements, which were to contain some 5,000 dwellings, were supported with an infusion of DM 100 million in counterpart funds. In contrast to the earlier ECA competition, this one devoted more time to planning, and entries were solicited from the prize winners in the first ECA program to ensure that mistakes made in 1951 were not repeated. Planners also surveyed residents in the ECA projects and prospective residents in the miners' housing. Surveys taken a few years after completion indicated that the miners' projects were largely successful.[149]

The impact of the American-sponsored housing programs far exceeded its construction of 8,000 new dwellings. In 1958, Hermann Wandersleb of the Federal Housing Ministry claimed that housing construction and town planning had received "strong stimulation and experienced further development through the ECA competition. Repeatedly winners of large planning competitions have stated that the prize-winning entries were based on the ECA planning."[150] Freed of American control, German planners and architects designed larger, more substantial housing units than the Americans had thought necessary, but the ECA settlements, now viewed as model projects and objects of research, stimulated new thinking among Germans in the field. The American insistence on standardization, moreover, reinforced German efforts in this direction. Standardization helped cut and control costs and also provided authorities with an instrument for guiding reconstruction.[151]

How important, however, was the overall financial contribution of the Marshall Plan to housing construction in Germany's bombed cities? Of the DM 1.187 billion in counterpart funds available during the first year of the Marshall Plan, DM 81.5 million was committed to housing construction.[152] Among other projects, this money financed 779 units in Bavaria, 280 of which were in severely bombed Munich, and 3,155 units in Baden-Württemberg, including 741 in Stuttgart. In a September 1951 report, James Butler noted that nearly DM 450 million in ECA counterpart funds had gone into housing and that the 100,000 housing units which the ECA had helped finance amounted to about "one out of every five constructed since the initiation of ECA aid to housing." Nevertheless, he estimated that West Germany needed at least DM 40 billion more to reach prewar levels of housing.[153] In fact, the Marshall Plan provided only 5% of the total financing for housing in 1950 and by 1952 contributed almost nothing. Only 1.63% of the total of DM 31.6 billion invested in housing between 1950 and 1954 came from Marshall Plan aid.[154] That sum is not insignificant, but it fell far short of German expectations that American aid would rebuild the bombed cities. The availability of Marshall funds in other areas of the economy, however, undoubtedly freed up monies in the financial markets for housing, so the effect of Marshall aid should not be dismissed lightly, even if its direct impact was negligible.[155] Charles Maier has asserted that Marshall aid to West Germany functioned "as . . . the lubricant in an engine—not the fuel—allowing a machine to run that would otherwise buckle and bind."[156] Throughout West Germany in the 1950s, the financial machinery of public agencies and private institutions made ample credit available for the subsidy of housing construction.

If massive state involvement in housing construction signified a continuation of policies initiated during the Weimar years and resurrected by the Nazis during the war, continuities are equally strong in questions of design for housing projects. Leaving aside the issue of architectural style, the main—and related—issues were the location of housing, the general form of a project, and the type of construction.

In determining the location of new housing, planners and developers faced the choice of building on new, sometimes unimproved land on the edges of the cities or on the sites of demolished buildings within the cities. There were compelling arguments for each option. The former could draw on the experiences of the progressive housing projects of the 1920s, which consisted of row houses built with optimum site planning. Free of rubble, and usually boasting simpler patterns of land ownership than in the inner cities, this land easily accommodated the planning and construction of large-scale projects. Indeed, the very absence of war wreckage made the locations more aesthetically attractive than the rubble-filled cities. Building on new land was also initially cheaper by some DM 4 per square meter of living space, at least if hidden costs such as commuting into a city to work were overlooked.[157] Additionally, property owners in the inner cities, often impoverished by the destruction and the costs of rubble clearance, found it impossible to start any new construction.[158] Moreover, some inner-city areas were placed under a construction ban until new plans were developed. Advocates of suburban housing could also draw upon the strong antiurban sentiments nurtured by Germans on both the left and the right for over a century.

This antiurbanism can be seen clearly in the statements of many postwar planners and in the essays written by private citizens. When Munich's planner Helmut Fischer asked, "Do we want to rebuild progressively dying inner-city housing?" he was simply restating the widely shared opinion that inner cities had become unhealthy and unpleasant places to live and that, as a result, the population had been abandoning them in favor of better housing in the suburbs.[159] Those who advocated building on undeveloped land thought reconstruction should accelerate this trend by encouraging "a thorough depopulation of the inner city."[160] These planners also wanted to avoid future concentrations of population in inner cities because they felt high population density had increased the casualties during the bombing raids. Good site planning for new housing, with buildings surrounded by greenery, would lessen the likelihood of a bomb-induced firestorm and would also make rapid evacuation or flight from a city possible. Planning housing with an eye to a future war, however, was not a topic openly discussed with the public.[161]

Finally, the idea of decentralizing the population was in perfect harmony with the planning ideal advocated by the modernists in the Charter of Athens, namely, that urban areas should be separated "according to their functions [as places of] work, housing, transportation, recreation, culture, and administration. . . . The old inner city can no longer come in question as a place to live. Its main meaning will be derived from being a focal point for administration, culture, and business."[162] Based on these arguments, new residential suburbs were erected all over Germany.

On the other hand, persuasive arguments supported rebuilding housing in the inner cities. In spite of the destruction, such building was practical since some of the damaged inner-city housing was in fact relatively modern in terms of siting and basic structure. Where the walls and foundations were usable, rebuilding rather quickly could produce a large number of housing units at relatively modest expense. Konstanty Gutschow regularly invoked this argument in making the case for Hamburg's reconstruction. Toward the end of the war, he had drawn up plans for declaring certain sections of the bombed cities targets for immediate reconstruction, and he began implementing these plans when the war ended. Major construction firms were invited to study the designated areas and submit proposals for efficient reconstruction using industrial techniques, and architects were invited to submit ideas on how buildings could be better located within blocks to provide light and air.[163]

Rebuilding inner-city housing blocks along the lines suggested by Gutschow would have continued the urban renewal projects of the Weimar and Nazi eras. In a tortuous statement indicating his attempts to disassociate himself from the Nazi regime, Gutschow argued that it was necessary to "bind Germans with the German soil. However, we want to be careful that this slogan, which appeared in 1918 out of the experience of the First World War, which quickly bogged down in further production of Mietskasernen, which was then utilized by Nazi propaganda, and which was unable to resist the psychosis and vanities of the Großstadt, this slogan must now be clearly chosen with full awareness of the direction to take to [authentic] settlements."[164] When Gutschow was relieved of his position in the fall of 1945, a former employee in his wartime office, Arthur Dähn, took over the city housing office and implemented Gutschow's plans, and Hamburg served as a model for other cities on how to rebuild quickly.[165]

Hamburg-Dulsberg, residential street with social housing. The bombing burned out the brick buildings, but they could be repaired quickly. The photos show the ruins and the finished apartment blocks. (Source: Staatliche Landesbildstelle Hamburg, nos. 7982, 19878.)

It was also argued that it was both costly and harmful to the cities to begin with housing construction in the suburbs. Paying for roads and other improvements for properties that would be tax-exempt if new social housing were erected strained city coffers. Diverting resources away from inner-city reconstruction would result in abandoned damaged buildings or ugly open spaces where the rubble had been cleared but upon which no one could afford to build.[166] Furthermore, a study of population trends indicated a growing demand for small housing units for single persons, and such housing suited cities better than suburbs.[167] Social housing firms, which had long invested in inner-city housing, also argued that the inner cities could be made livable. They observed that even under ideal conditions most of the population would still live in the inner city or close to the inner city, rather than in distant suburbs.[168] Finally, some argued that only inner-city housing could restore a city's historic vitality. Middle-class town houses, presumably with middle-class residents, would rejuvenate civic spirit and energy.[169]

Over the long term, of course, it was possible to build housing in suburban settlements and in the inner cities. Single-family, two-story row houses were built on newly improved land, while multistory apartment blocks were erected in the cities proper. Apartment towers typically consisted of 3- to 6-story buildings, although Hamburg's Grindelhochhäuser provided a notable exception. The British initiated construction of this 15-story complex for their own occupation administration personnel in 1946 but turned it over to the Germans for completion when it became clear that Hamburg was not going to become a major political and administrative center for Germany.[170] The Grindelhochhäuser proved to be one of the largest inner-city housing projects put up in the early 1950s.

Of the residential buildings constructed in 1950, some 40% were single-family houses, 33% duplexes, and only 27% contained three or more dwellings. In general the dwellings were small; those built in 1950 averaged 3.25 rooms per dwelling.[171] Until 1954, three-room apartments comprised the bulk of West Germany's new housing units, reflecting a strong demand from single persons and particularly single women.[172] Even the 15 settlements sponsored by the Marshall Plan, which, with the exception of a project in Bremen, consisted of row houses on the edges of cities, were generally small dwellings, with 40 to 50 square meters of total floor space.[173]

The questions of the location of housing, ideal form, and means of construction all converged at the Constructa Building Exhibition in Hannover in 1951, which, like its predecessors in Weimar and under the Nazis, revolved around the central theme of planning and constructing housing. This was actually not the first postwar building exhibition. In 1946, Hans Scharoun, Berlin's first postwar planner, staged an exhibition of plans for the rebuilding of the capital and exhibited five models of prefabricated, standardized, single-family homes.[174] Because of the relative isolation of Berlin, however, the models received scant attention, and skepticism remained about the value of prefabricated housing.[175] Another building exhibition was staged in Darmstadt in 1951 in the hope of establishing continuity with the pioneering

Darmstadt exhibition of 1901, but none of the 11 solicited proposals, all for public buildings like schools, clinics, and theaters, were in fact built at the time.[176] As a result of the paucity of such exhibitions, Constructa drew the attention of planners, housing officials, architects, and construction firms from all over the Federal Republic.

Hannover's new city planner, Rudolf Hillebrecht, originally proposed the Constructa in 1949, after visiting impressive housing projects in Britain.[177] Based on standardized housing models and boasting a high level of built-in equipment, these homes were occupied by very contented residents.[178] Hillebrecht thought the Constructa exhibition could provide other German architects and planners with comparable insights about housing. Formerly Konstanty Gutschow's chief assistant in Hamburg, Hillebrecht employed his former boss to help develop a reconstruction plan for Hannover and to serve as an expert adviser for the building exhibition. As a result, Constructa bears the imprint of the group of men involved in wartime reconstruction planning.

Constructa was divided into numerous sections on the exhibition grounds and also featured demonstration building projects in Hannover proper. Visitors could study displays on regional and town planning, construction techniques and materials, and especially housing, the exhibition's primary focus. Planning exhibits examined the location of housing; technical exhibits presented means of furthering industrialized, standardized construction of housing; and model houses and the demonstration projects showed what could be done.

In his introductory statement for the catalog, Federal President Theodor Heuss—a former member of the Deutscher Werkbund—said that although he hoped standardization would lower housing costs, another goal of the exhibition was to help overcome "the gulf between the 'technical' [*Ingenieurhaften*] and the 'artistic' [*Künstlerischen*]"—the gulf between modernism and traditionalism—that had caused so much controversy throughout the century.[179] In his statement of the goals of the exhibition, Fritz Suppert similarly assured participants that "Constructa does not want to look back into the past any more than necessary"—an indication that the organizers saw it as a vehicle of reconciliation.[180] The roster of participants in itself suggests an attempt to heal past conflicts. There were model homes by modernists like the Luckhardt brothers and Werner Hebebrand and exhibition pavilions by Gutschow and Ernst Neufert, the former spokesman for standardization in Speer's ministry. A special pavilion honored three masters, Peter Behrens, Hans Poelzig, and Heinrich Tessenow, all of whom had combined certain aspects of modernism with certain aspects of traditionalism. The catalog includes essays by Federal Housing Minister Wildermuth as well as articles by planners like Gutschow and Wilhelm Wortmann, who had held important positions during the war. In an attempt to clear the air, Hillebrecht arranged a private meeting during the exhibition for a number of architectural opponents.[181]

Johannes Göderitz and Roland Rainer, basing their approach on wartime work on housing, prepared the section of the exhibition on forms and building techniques. They examined several housing forms but recommended row houses with gardens as most appropriate for "urban conditions." Though clearly all kinds of housing would be found in urban areas, Göderitz and Rainer stressed, as they had in 1944, "the racial/biological [*volksbiologisch*], ethical, and health advantages of the single-family house with a garden."[182]

Designed by Gutschow, the demonstration housing projects manifested in their variety an openness to different approaches.[183] In the inner city, an area around the Kreuzkirche was redesigned with three- to five-story apartment blocks surrounding a group of two-story row houses, with the reconstructed church as the dominant feature. A model of low-density, inner-city housing with good light, air, and landscaping, it remains much admired today. On the Hildesheimer Straße, just outside the center, Gutschow and Friedrich Wilhelm Kraemer designed a large apartment block, though difficulties in arranging the land transfers delayed the completion of construction until 1952, preventing visitors from viewing this project in its final form. Seven kilometers out, at Am Mittelfelde, a small new settlement of two- and three-story row houses was built. Hillebrecht described the settlement's architectural form in terms of its "harmlessness" and maintained that the designers sought a "clean and simple building and had no ambitions for extravagance."[184]

Hillebrecht's choice of words is revealing, because they suggest both the modesty and the conciliatory nature of this most important exhibition since the end of the war. Modernists and traditionalists alike joined to produce useful, pleasant, modest housing. In spite of the appeals for great accomplishments in reconstruction, Constructa did not exactly fulfill the goals originally expressed by Heuss. Large quantities of housing were indeed built in the 1950s, and though much of it resembled the Constructa models, it was not the industrialized, standardized housing advocated by the reformers of the 1920s, the housing specialists in the Third Reich, or the reformers of the early postwar era, even if individual elements became more or less standard. Nor did Constructa produce great architecture. Important architecture, as opposed to functional housing projects, begins to appear only in the second half of the 1950s, and this was best seen at a second great building exhibition, the Internationale Bauausstellung Wiederaufbau Hansaviertel in Berlin—the Interbau of 1957.

First proposed in 1951, the Interbau came to fruition after several years of site planning and organization.[185] In 1953, Berlin Bausenator Karl Mahler declared that the exhibition "should not be a building fair [presumably like Constructa] but rather a clear endorsement of the architecture of the Western world. It should demonstrate what we consider to be modern city planning and proper housing, in contrast to the false ostentation of the Stalinallee [in East Berlin]."[186] Significantly, the publication of Göderitz, Rainer, and Hoffmann's 1944 manuscript, *Die gegliederte und aufgelockerte Stadt*, coincided with the opening of the Interbau, in which all three men participated.[187] Their book was the clearest presentation of housing ideals that had been developed since the 1920s.

The Interbau, however, did not in fact embody the kind of housing settlements proposed by Göderitz and his colleagues. Instead, nearly 50 buildings were erected by some of the most important modernist architects from the Western countries. Primarily social housing, the buildings ranged from 7 to 18 stories. The housing ministry was critical of the large size of the buildings, and Theodor Heuss felt there was too much devotion to pure form and the technical mastery of modern materials. The problem was that the Interbau had become a showcase for architecture, not housing, no matter how many dwelling units the Hansaviertel might contain. The era of modesty—the term Hillebrecht used to describe the housing projects of Constructa—was clearly past. A few more years were needed for West Germany to overcome the housing shortage, but it did so on the basis of programs already in place. The towers of the Interbau indicated that conceptually and intellectually the period of reconstruction from the war was over.

6

Town Planning
to 1945

While all Germans struggled with the postwar housing crisis, town planners urgently sought to control and direct reconstruction, including the building of new housing, through meticulous, systematic planning. Planners all over the Federal Republic believed they had an obligation to lay the groundwork for cities of the future, not simply to rebuild the cities of the past. Many of the central issues addressed by the planners have already been touched on, including the best location for housing construction, the retention or modification of the historic street pattern, the renewal of slum areas, and the desire to reduce population densities in the inner cities. Earlier chapters considered these issues in the context of the construction of individual buildings or smaller ensembles. This chapter examines the broader framework within which reconstruction planners conceived their task.

It is important to reemphasize that town planners, at least in terms of ideas and practices, did not start with a tabula rasa in 1945. No zero hour separated postwar planning from previous planning theory and practice. Prewar planning models, including detailed proposals for urban reconstruction, helped shape later propositions, even if they had to be modified or rewritten to suit postwar conditions.[1] During the war, reconstruction plans were based on planning experiences earlier in the Nazi period as well as on Weimar initiatives. An analysis of planning, therefore, must begin not with 1945, but with planning traditions from before 1933 and throughout the Nazi era. Indeed, because so much important reconstruction planning occurred during the Third Reich, this chapter is devoted to the period up to 1945. The following chapter addresses postwar planning.

Planning Traditions before 1933

Town planning as a distinct discipline in Germany developed at the beginning
of the twentieth century, although planning had taken place sporadically before then. For example, in the Baroque era, in Germany as elsewhere in
Europe, new streets, gardens, and governmental buildings had been carefully
laid out to represent the power and prestige of aristocratic rulers. Karlsruhe is
a good case in point. Such planning enterprises, however, were exceptional.
Until the nineteenth century, when steady population growth and migration in
the context of industrialization brought rapid change, virtually all of Germany's cities retained the basic structure that had characterized them for
centuries.

Controlling dynamic urban change, particularly its dangerous, unhealthy
manifestations, led to initial planning efforts in the second half of the nineteenth century. Several developments eventually merged to form the basis of
German urban planning, including town extension plans, the garden city
movement, regional planning, and programs for urban renewal.[2]

At first, most city governments attempted to control and shape urban
expansion or extension (*Stadterweiterung*) in areas beyond the confines of the
historic cores.[3] This proved difficult. Civil law codes protected private property from arbitrary seizure by the state, and property owners were free to
develop their land as they saw fit. Moreover, initial planning efforts were
usually schematic and almost always inadequate. For example, under the
Prussian *Fluchtliniengesetz* of 1875, the police could determine the location of
roads (which usually followed existing rural roads), improve the land through
the construction of utilities (while passing on the costs to property owners),
and set minimum building standards for hygiene, fire prevention, and safety.
In practice this usually meant that they could determine the setback of buildings from the street and regulate building height. To reduce land-improvement
costs in new areas in Berlin, blocks were sometimes 300 to 400 meters in
length, which in turn resulted in the construction of the infamous rental barracks, the Mietskasernen of closed blocks of buildings of uniform height,
discussed in Chapter 5. City authorities, consequently, wanted to initiate more
positive planning. Vienna in 1858, Cologne in 1880, and Munich and Vienna in
1893 staged important competitions for the design of ring roads and new outer
districts. Juries included architects and engineers as well as political figures,
and these competitions entailed systematic consideration of such matters as
population densities, land use, and urban transportation. These events indicated that city planners were moving toward a synthesis of aesthetic and
structural design.[4]

In Cologne, for example, Joseph Stübben won the competition for the
design of the large area acquired by the city after the city walls were demolished. Part of his plan was purely extension planning—the creation of the
Ring, a magisterial boulevard inspired by the Paris of Haussmann, and the
layout of new residential streets—but Stübben's plan also involved parts of the
existing old city. Streets in the old city were lengthened to reach and cross the

Ring. Stübben also proposed moving the main train station from its place near the cathedral to a new location outside the Ring.[5] Stübben was later involved in extension planning in many European cities, and his 1880 book, *Der Städtebau*, became one of the early standard texts for German town planners.[6]

Whereas German ideas on town extension planning and zoning developed primarily as a response to the problems accompanying rapid change in their own cities, the model of the garden city or garden suburb was largely imported from Great Britain at the beginning of the twentieth century, although contemporary anti-urban German writers aired some similar ideas.[7] As conceived by Ebenezer Howard, garden cities were to be new, largely self-sufficient cities, complete with industry, commerce, cultural facilities, and housing, at some distance from, though in contact with an established urban center.[8] They were to embody at once social reform, land reform, and environmental reform. Cooperative land ownership would preclude speculation in housing construction and prevent the worst manifestations of industrial capitalism. A stable, healthy community would be formed, with the working and middle classes living together in modest housing of varied types surrounded by gardens and common green areas. Howard and almost all subsequent town planners simply assumed that living amidst greenery had a salutary effect on all people and would produce positive ethical values and behavior. Indeed, the working class would adopt the values of the middle class, generating a hitherto unimaginable measure of social harmony. A network of such communities would in time allow for the dissolution of the chaotic, unhealthy metropolises. On a limited scale, Howard and his followers succeeded in putting their ideal into practice, and the first garden cities of Letchworth and Welwyn became meccas for planners all over the world.

The transfer of the English model to the Continent necessitated fundamental changes in Howard's ideal. Building entire new cities, for example, proved impossible for most garden city enthusiasts. Instead, planners usually settled for the creation of garden suburbs (purely residential areas set in greenery, but without industry and the full range of cultural facilities envisaged by Howard), or for green satellite cities (partly self-contained settlements, but dependent on a metropolis that still exercised most central functions), or for the introduction of significant new green areas into existing cities (urban parks and green belts).[9]

The Germans did not, therefore, slavishly copy the English model.[10] After having served in the German embassy in London, the architect Hermann Muthesius wrote a three-volume study of English housing which presented the ideas of the British garden city movement to German architects and planners. The prevalent antiurban, anti–industrial sentiment in Germany accepted and encouraged the idea of new towns consisting of houses in greenery, built by skilled, traditional craftsmen rather than by industrial technology. Indeed, from the beginning the German garden city movement contained elements of social darwinistic, *völkisch*, and racial thinking, and these elements continued to play a role in planning theory at least through the 1950s.[11] The first German garden settlement, although more a garden suburb than a true garden city, was Hellerau, outside of Dresden, designed in 1908 for the Deutscher Werkbund by Richard Riemerschmidt, Muthesius, and Heinrich Tessenow. The influence of the garden city model could also be seen in the 1910 Berlin Town Planning Exhibition and in the garden city of Staaken designed by Paul Schmitthenner.

Throughout the 1920s, Germany's most important town planners made significant attempts to implement garden city ideals. Fritz Schumacher, Hamburg's planner from 1909 to 1933, spent the years 1920–23 in Cologne, where he planned that city's noted green belts with the support of Lord Mayor Konrad Adenauer. In Frankfurt in the latter half of the decade, Ernst May designed his much-admired new residential suburbs, which followed the contours of the landscape and thereby harmonized with nature.[12] May had in fact worked with Raymond Unwin in Britain before World War I and was thoroughly familiar with the English garden cities. Planners Martin Wagner and Bruno Taut likewise set new housing developments in Berlin in greenery. Though all of these planners were considered progressive, with membership in the Deutscher Werkbund or in modernist architectural circles, conservatives also endorsed the ideal of living in greenery, close to nature.

Another important new trend in German planning—planning on a regional scale—was reflected in the Greater Berlin competition of 1910. Extension planning had been limited to the specific new area to be built up, and the garden city movement had directed its attention to the creation of what were really garden suburbs. Regional planning, in contrast, sought to calculate the impact of the urban dynamic on small towns and villages outside the original boundaries of the large city, and, in fact, often served as preparation for incorporation of these towns and villages.

In general, however, the legal basis for regional planning was too weak to be effective. Imperial Germany was a federation, and the boundaries between states made regional planning difficult if not impossible. Even within Prussia, the largest state, strong traditions of local self-government obstructed effective regional planning. In 1920 the Prussian government created a regional planning association, the Siedlungsverband Ruhrkohlenbezirk, to resolve conflicts between the economic and administrative divisions in the densely populated Ruhr industrial region, but the association lacked any legal prerogatives and instead had to rely upon the persuasiveness of its members to exercise any authority.[13] In Hamburg, Fritz Schumacher strongly advocated regional planning, which he believed was essential to solving Hamburg's planning problems, but he never succeeded in overcoming the resistance of surrounding towns and districts to full-scale regional planning for a greater Hamburg.[14]

Almost by definition, regional planning, the garden city movement, and town extension planning had relatively little impact on the existing inner cities because everyone assumed that replanning the central areas of old cities was highly unlikely. Only a catastrophe, such as the great fire in Hamburg in 1842, would make replanning of streets and building lines and the introduction of fire-safety standards possible, but until World War II, no one imagined that such catastrophes would become the common experience of Germany's cities.[15] At best, planners could hope to implement modest programs of urban renewal in inner-city areas beset with especially deplorable working-class housing. The previous chapter examined some of these programs for urban renewal, such as Hamburg's response to the cholera epidemic of 1892. These programs sought primarily to improve the housing stock, but whether urban renewal consisted of clearing away large areas of old buildings or of clearing away buildings in the centers of blocks, the possibility of laying out new streets existed. The creation of the Mönckebergstraße in Hamburg is a case in point.[16] Thus renewal of inner-city housing could lead to broader planning for the city centers.

Schumacher's work in Cologne merits closer examination for two reasons. First, it reveals most clearly the way in which extension planning, garden cities planning, regional planning, and urban renewal combined to produce comprehensive town planning. Second, Schumacher has been consistently and widely admired as a model of the modern planner, one who gave the thorough study of topography, demographic and social trends, transportation needs, industry, and trade higher priority than aesthetic considerations in preparing new plans.[17] In his 1923 book on Cologne, Schumacher suggested that his planning there be seen as a paradigm of "general problems in town planning" and not merely as an isolated treatment of a single city.[18] Schumacher felt that all planners could learn from the attempts to solve typical urban problems, particularly in housing and transportation. Consequently he deliberately "omitted from consideration political conditions of the present and the future"— even though writing during the debilitating political and economic upheavals of the French occupation of the Ruhr and the great inflation.

Schumacher was no hater of great cities, and his remarks on urban conditions should not be understood as a part of the antiurban tradition in Germany. Even so, he worried that explosive, unplanned urban growth since the onset of industrialization had created "a city without a soul, since the soul of an organic work of art is nothing more than the expression of its intrinsic harmony." The greatest problem was housing, as unrestrained private entrepreneurs forced 85% of the population to live in unsuitable conditions.[19] A solution to this problem rested not in the aesthetics of architectural form—be they modern or traditionalist—but rather in social and technical questions. The conflict of interests resonating in modern society makes this a challenging approach. "In times past," Schumacher noted, "when a single, overriding will, whether it be embodied in the church or in an absolute ruler, determined the form of the community, it was not necessary to worry about this difficult task." In contrast, planners now shouldered the onerous responsibility of finding "the correct balance between compulsion and freedom in shaping the existence of a metropolis."[20]

For Schumacher, solving the problems of a great metropolis demanded looking at the relationship between open spaces and complexes of buildings, not merely single buildings. This approach determined his design for the extension of the city into the area beyond the Neustadt planned by Stübben in the 1880s. This new area, once an outer ring of defensive fortifications, would contain housing, cultural, and community facilities for 80,000 to 90,000 inhabitants. Most important, the area would be characterized by extensive green areas—parks, meadows, paths, and gardens. Schumacher did not plan a new garden city but rather made nature and greenery part of an organically growing urban structure. The green belt that resulted from Schumacher's plans remains a monument to his work in Cologne.

Schumacher did not, however, limit his thinking to town extension in this one area. On the contrary, he anticipated continued population growth. Whereas 535,000 people currently lived on the Left Bank of the city and 164,000 on the Right Bank, he estimated that the future would find 1,260,000 residents on the Left Bank and 900,000 on the Right. Such growth would necessitate the building of huge amounts of housing, schools, churches, hospitals, government buildings, community cultural centers, and of course new industrial and commercial centers. This growth, Schumacher argued, should not follow the traditional form of urban expansion in concentric rings. Instead the new metropolis should be a radial city, with planned growth along the radial arms of the transportation network and with clear separation of urban functions. The radial arms would organically link Cologne to outlying towns and villages. When fully implemented, the structure of the new city would be quite different from the old. In terms of land use, purely commercial areas would increase from 15.2% to 21.8%, purely residential areas would increase from 29.7% to 50%, and areas of mixed use would decline from 55.1% to 28.2%. The percentage of small, two-story houses would grow from 8.8% to 54.2%, which of course promised the end of the Mietskasernen as the dominant form of housing. People would instead live in small "colonies" of 5,000 to 10,000 with convenient transportation links to shopping and work.[21]

The Altstadt, the historic city center inside the Ring, would continue to exist as a mixed area of housing, commerce, government, and culture and serve as the spiritual focus for the metropolis. Schumacher did not, in other words, contemplate dismembering the city into smaller entities. Nevertheless, some major changes were needed in the inner city. Areas of outdated, inadequate, excessively dense housing had to be renewed, and new transportation needs had to be addressed. Schumacher called for renewing the area south of the town hall, improving transportation flow through the old city along east–west and north–south axes by widening existing streets and cutting new streets through existing blocks. Such fundamental changes had been postponed for far too long, he observed, which "hasn't made it easy for us. The role of the destroyer of the old is not entirely our fault."[22]

To balance the architectural dominance of the cathedral, Schumacher proposed constructing a new monumental building at the western end of the suspension bridge between Cologne and Deutz. With two towers 49 meters high, the building would be massive enough to provide a strong presence on the river but not so large as to compete with the towers of the church of Groß St. Martin or the cathedral.[23] He would have preferred to move the main train station, a disruptive feature in the inner city, to a location outside the Ring, but he recognized that the same economic reasons that prevented such a move under Stübben still persisted and called instead for building a new passenger station that would at least relieve the burden on the central station.

Schumacher's greatest achievement in Cologne was the creation of the green belt. New housing settlements did not follow his designs, and his plans for the inner city were not realized, though some features, such as the new arteries through the inner city, would reappear in planning under the Nazis and again after World War II.[24] In any event, as a planner (though not as an architect), Schumacher anticipated many of the ideas expressed in the 1932 Charter of Athens, which constituted an international manifesto of Europe's (and Germany's) modernist architects. Thesis 77 of the charter declared that planning must focus on a city's four essential functions: housing, work, recreation, and traffic—the system uniting the first three. The modernist, functionalist approach to urban planning was largely technical in nature, as rational, mechanical calculations about the functional needs of cities and their inhabitants lay at its center, and plans that included green belts or skyscrapers resulted from these calculations. More architectonic, the traditional, conservative approach on the other hand addressed the aesthetic design of structures (height, volume, surface materials, proximity to other buildings or spaces) and their relation to surroundings.[25]

The onset of the Great Depression proved frustrating to Germany's town planners. As a discipline, planning had made great strides as a variety of regional and town planning concepts had been developed and subjected to a lively public discussion. Although the planning process had become increasingly sophisticated, the economic crisis, combined with existing legal restraints and growing political instability at the end of the 1920s, considerably diminished the prospects for urban planning. Some planners opted to leave. Ernst May, who had hoped to impose his ideas on all of Frankfurt and not just on new suburbs (Frankfurt was to be "The New City" of the future), migrated to the Soviet Union, where he found the tantalizing prospect of building a new model industrial city in Magnetogorsk.[26] Although others were less attracted by the dictatorship of workers in the east, they shared May's frustration with conditions in Germany. Rudolf Schwarz, then in Aachen, wrote in 1932:

> The Reich is like a construction site, where all the preparations have been made for beginning the foundations for a new architecture. The pile of building materials, which awaits a new direction, grows ever larger, as does the number of men, who wait for plans and projects, now that the old ones can no longer be realized. . . . But time is wasted, material squandered. A clear conception of what to do is lacking. No one risks anything, no one seizes the initiative, and those who have the power do not see that a [new] design must be created.[27]

The frustrations of many planners and architects soon ended, at least if they were willing to work for and with the new Nazi regime, which, unlike its predecessors, was willing to implement the necessary legal and financial conditions to put new designs into practice.

Urban Planning during the Third Reich

Urban planners were extraordinarily busy under the Nazis. Beginning with the implementation of the urban renewal programs proposed prior to 1933 and suspended because of the economic and political crises that afflicted the Weimar Republic, planners moved on to creating new residential suburbs and new industrial cities, implementing regional planning, redesigning 23 large cities according to guidelines determined by Hitler, and, finally, planning for reconstruction of the cities bombed in the war. Because much of this planning activity carried over into reconstruction planning after 1945, it is essential to determine the extent to which this activity evolved out of planning efforts begun before 1933. Planning during the Third Reich was more than just Nazi planning, though National Socialist ideas were naturally very influential. Nazi ideas and vocabulary on race and *Blut und Boden* constantly recur, for example, and the political organization of the community formed the core of most planning during this period.

Moreover, for planners, perhaps the most attractive feature of the Nazi regime was that it fostered unbounded confidence in the possibility of total planning with the firm backing of the state. For the first time, German planners could truly think about planning the entire urban environment; the National Socialists would provide both the financial resources and the legal framework to make such work possible. What Baron Haussmann did for Paris under Napoleon III now seemed possible in Germany. A strong authoritarian element informs all town planning activity, especially when planners look at entire cities. Their task is to provide rational, professional, imaginative solutions on a scale that far surpasses the competence of individual residents. They are tempted, therefore, to impose these solutions upon a city as if by decree and dismiss the objections of residents and property owners as narrow and self-centered. To planners, democratic planning—planning with the participation and consent of the citizenry—seems counterproductive. Even noted planners on the political left like Ernst May and Martin Wagner, both of whom went into exile, temperamentally shared this authoritarian streak, and it is hardly surprising that most planners could reconcile themselves to working under the Nazis, even when the worst features of that regime had become apparent.[28]

Some town planning activities between 1933 and 1945 were discussed earlier: the urban renewal programs in such cities as Hamburg, Cologne, Braunschweig, Frankfurt, and Kassel; the building of new residential suburbs in such cities as Berlin and Munich. The renewal programs, it will be recalled, demolished substandard housing, reduced population densities, opened up the interiors of blocks, and in some cases introduced new streets through the block centers. On the Marktgasse, Kassel even introduced what may have been the first inner-city pedestrian street.[29] The housing programs of the early Nazi years erected small, traditionally styled cottages in green settings, intended primarily for the party faithful. Whether in redeveloped inner cities or in new suburbs, healthy housing was supposed to strengthen political support for the regime.

Regional planning also gained the support of the new government. In Berlin, Gottfried Feder, a leading figure in the early "coordination" of the architectural profession, taught regional planning at the Technical University from 1933 to 1941. December 1935 saw the creation of a Reich Office for Regional Planning, the dissolution of all regional planning associations, and the formation of 23 new associations. Expansion of major cities through incorporations followed. In 1932, a regional plan had been developed in Stuttgart which went into effect in 1936 and included the incorporation of several suburbs.[30] Under city planner Hans Bernhard Reichow, Stettin grew from 82.17 square kilometers in 1937 to 458.84 in the fall of 1939. Reichow planned to expand the city to the north along the Oder in a ribbonlike pattern that followed the contours of the landscape rather than taking a more traditional, circular form.[31] In January 1937, regional planning led to the formation of Greater Hamburg—long a goal of Fritz Schumacher, who had been forced to retire in 1933—and opened the way for comprehensive planning for the Hamburg region. Here the desire for rational planning intermixed with Nazi political aims. Hamburg Reichsstatthalter Karl Kaufmann justified the city's expansion by assuring that providing new space for housing would undercut Marxism and Bolshevism. In addition, it seems likely that the regime also viewed regional planning for Hamburg in terms of industrial expansion and rearmament.[32] Mainz likewise had incorporated a number of neighboring villages in 1930, and it added more in 1938. In 1940 its planners developed a regional plan from which they believed future town planning must derive. A future Mainz, they thought, would be part of a regional "ribbon city" organized around its transportation network.[33]

The planning of new cities was both theoretical and practical. On the one hand, Feder sought to develop a new theory of organic town planning in his influential book *Die neue Stadt*, published in 1939 and widely read into the 1950s.[34] A product of the antiurbanist current long present in Germany, Feder called for decentralizing the population into smaller garden cities of 20,000 inhabitants. Existing large cities should be broken up into smaller "cells," in which all features of urban life could be rationally planned: the exact number of schools, utilities, cultural facilities, government and party offices, and so forth. As had followers of the garden city movement, Feder calculated the ideal size of a city partly on the basis of optimal movement by foot or bicycle between home, workplace, and schools, and he believed that a city of 20,000 encouraged residents to maintain the ties to the land and nature that characterized healthy villages.

On the other hand, two significant new cities were actually built: the Stadt des KdF-Wagens (City of the Strength-Through-Joy Auto of the German Labor Front, now Wolfsburg), planned by Peter Koller, and the Stadt der Hermann-Göring Werke (City of the Hermann Göring Works, now Salzgitter), planned by Herbert Rimpl.[35] The former was the site of the Volkswagen plants, the latter the site of new steelworks for armaments production. The layout of these new towns accorded with modern planning concepts. Industry was located downwind of the rest of the city, housing was set in greenery, a rational street grid facilitated transportation flow, and so forth.

The Representative Cities Program

These varied planning activities paled in comparison to the nationwide program for the redesign (Neugestaltung) of a large number of existing cities either as representative Nazi cities or as urban centers which manifested Nazi power and ideals. Planners worked on projects that, if realized, would have altered the historic urban structure significantly more than the measures outlined in previous urban renewal plans. These new projects thus set a precedent for comprehensive planning that planners looked to when facing the task of reconstructing the bombed cities—even though the bombastic monumentalism of the Neugestaltung plans had necessarily receded in importance.

The program for redesigning the cities began in Berlin. Hitler made Speer general building inspector for the capital in January 1937 and promulgated a law empowering the state to redesign designated cities nine months later. The highest priority was assigned to Berlin as the national capital, Nuremberg as the site of the party congresses, Hamburg as Germany's greatest port, Munich as capital of the Nazi movement, and Linz as a center for art and culture. Speer was the key figure for Nuremberg, having already designed the congress grounds; Konstanty Gutschow emerged in 1939 as the planner for Hamburg; and Hermann Giesler, the brother of Munich's Gauleiter (the chief regional party leader), was appointed general building director for Munich in 1938. (He was also given responsibility for Linz and Weimar.) In most of the other cities, local planning offices assumed the task of replanning.[36]

Hitler's program dictated that all cities feature certain traits: a very broad, long avenue (suitable for mass parades) that culminated in a forum or large square, a huge hall to accommodate assemblies of 50,000–100,000 people, and massive party buildings. Other huge buildings—hotels, recreation facilities, offices, transportation facilities—were to line or cap the new boulevard or to be sited near the central buildings. Everything was designed on a monumental scale to intimidate and manipulate residents and visitors and to convince them of the overwhelming power of the Third Reich. Architecture and planning joined to produce settings for mass political theater.[37] Berlin's domed assembly hall was to dwarf St. Peter's, Munich's new train station was to be the largest in the world, Hamburg was to have a party skyscraper and suspension bridge to match if not exceed even the biggest in America. Hitler's and Speer's interests in urban planning were architectonic: both started with a concept of architecture and imposed it on the map of Berlin.

Some plans called for retaining the existing historic core of the redesigned city and others called for fundamental transformations. The new plans for Hamburg and Stettin left the old city centers intact. In Cologne, on the other hand, major changes were in the offing even before the Neugestaltung program began. New forum and party buildings were to be built across the Rhine from the old city center, but improving the transportation system required that a wide east–west thoroughfare be cut through the old city on its way across the river, and a new north–south axis was also planned. Two new train

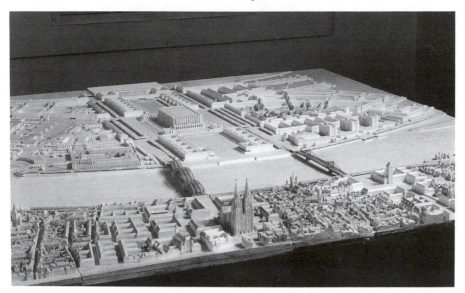

Cologne, model of the Nazi plans for the redesign of the city. On the east side of the Rhine one can see the huge forum. Massive new blocks were also planned for the area north of the cathedral and on the southern edge of the old city. (Source: Rheinisches Bildarchiv, no. 137 355.)

stations would replace the old one near the cathedral, and the site of the old station would then be redeveloped. Everywhere massive new buildings would replace the smaller traditional homes and businesses. During the war, this kind of thinking fed on itself until the entire old city was replanned. Almost all of the old street patterns and virtually all of the older buildings, except for the major monuments, would have disappeared.[38]

Similarly, proposals for Stuttgart, submitted by Konstanty Gutschow, by Paul Bonatz, and by the city planning office, all entailed major changes in the old city, with the construction of new axes and the demolition of many old buildings.[39] The same was true for Hannover, as evidenced in Karl Elkart's proposals.[40] New monumental buildings typically graced the edges of the old centers, although not on heretofore open, unbuilt land. Areas developed in the nineteenth century were to be unhesitatingly sacrificed for the new plans. The traditional buildings defining the historic silhouette, such as churches and town halls, would remain but would be challenged by the second concentration of huge buildings. Appropriate new traffic arteries would connect the old and new centers with each other as well as with the new Autobahn network.

The implementation of such sweeping plans demanded the purchase or confiscation by city land offices of acres of valuable land, the demolition of vast numbers of existing buildings, and the relocation of tens of thousands of businesses and residents into substitute buildings to be erected elsewhere in the city or in the outskirts. Thus plans for the central avenue and mandatory monumental buildings necessarily spilled over into broader urban planning for new residential suburbs and altered transportation networks, which in turn raised possible jurisdictional conflicts between the traditional city building offices and the extraordinary offices for Neugestaltung. This planning activity was thoroughly authoritarian, as citizens very rarely had access to the plans. Planners drew up their designs as if the city were a blank tablet upon which they could impose their ideas at will—and with the powerful backing of the regime. At the same time, moving into broader urban planning areas required planners to consider the functional needs of modern cities as well as the political and aesthetic dimensions of monumental planning.

Of Speer, Giesler, and Gutschow, the three main Neugestaltung architects, Gutschow enjoyed the greatest long-term impact on German town planning. Giesler worked in relative isolation in the south, where his work influenced only his own narrow circle. Speer became armaments minister in February 1942, which effectively diverted his attention and energy away from town planning. Gutschow, in contrast, established a broad network of collaborators and coworkers who shaped thinking on planning in much of northern Germany during the war and continued to be highly influential after 1945. Although the preceding chapter examined some of his activities, the unusual importance of this Hamburg planner merits further attention.

A native of Hamburg, Gutschow studied in Danzig and Stuttgart (where Heinz Wetzel and Paul Schmitthenner were his most important teachers) and then began his professional career in 1926, working two years in the Hamburg city building office and one year as city planner in Wandsbek, a Prussian town bordering Hamburg.[41] Fritz Schumacher served as chief city planner of Hamburg during these years and was engaged in a protracted struggle to acquire neighboring Altona, Wandsbek, and other Prussian towns on Hamburg's borders. Gutschow had a good opportunity to observe and appreciate Schumacher's methodical approach to planning, and Schumacher's relationship with Gutschow became that of master–pupil.[42] After 1930 Gutschow practiced as an independent architect, winning a number of competitions and establishing his reputation as a city planner, although little was actually built in those years because of the Depression. He then vaulted into prominence when Hitler selected him to redesign the Elbe shoreline in Hamburg.[43]

Hitler wanted the focal point of Hamburg—its main commercial, governmental, and political functions—moved away from the Alster and relocated on the Elbe between the St. Pauli Landungsbrücken and the western suburb of Altona. He envisioned a skyscraper housing the regional (*Gau*) party offices and an enormous suspension bridge over the Elbe that would welcome (and impress) incoming vessels, and he viewed the proposals for the city building office in 1936 as inadequate. Additionally, Altona had to be incorporated into Hamburg, something achieved by the creation of Greater Hamburg in January 1937. In August a limited competition for a new design for the Elbe shore was announced. Only Paul Bonatz of Stuttgart, Werner March of Berlin, Erich zu Putlizt of Hamburg, and Gutschow were invited to submit entries.[44]

Required, like his competitors, to work within Hitler's stipulations, Gutschow used the same architectural vocabulary as the architects planning other representative Nazi cities. His most original contribution was a new major traffic artery along the Elbe, lined with commercial office buildings. Closely tied to both the harbor and the old city, this commercial avenue was to relieve the congestion of the old center but not to replace it. Altona was to receive a new flow-through train station, and a huge parade ground was to be built between the station and the skyscraper on the river, with neoclassical buildings, some for the party, on both sides. Of the competitors for the Hamburg award, Gutschow alone traveled to the United States to study existing skyscrapers, determine methods of their construction, and familiarize himself with the logistics of such a structure. He never particularly liked the idea of the massive bridge, however, and his proposals for it fell well short of the Führer's grandiose vision. Indeed, Hitler never approved Gutschow's designs for either the suspension bridge or the skyscraper.[45] In fact, Hitler once referred to Gutschow as "that Hamburg dwarf."[46] Nevertheless, in January 1939, after viewing the proposals in the Chancellery in Berlin, Hitler declared Gutschow the winner of the competition.

First as Architekt des Elbufers and after 1941 as Architekt für die Neugestaltung der Hansestadt Hamburg, Gutschow had an unusual position. According to the decree of 26 April 1939, he remained a free and independent architect, contracted to work under the supervision of Karl Kaufmann, the Reichsstatthalter of Hamburg.[47] He was not, in other words, part of the city administration and did not hold a bureaucratic office. In this private capacity he eventually gathered together an office of some 250 employees, with his closest assistant, the young architect Rudolf Hillebrecht, supervising the most important sections of the firm.[48]

It became immediately apparent that the 1939 Neugestaltung project would spill over into other areas of city planning. Large tracts of land had to be purchased and the occupants relocated. Since a major housing shortage already afflicted Hamburg, this meant constructing housing for hundreds of thousands of persons over the course of the 25 years it would take to complete the project. The Elbe project also required redesigning the rail and highway arteries of the city. By inclination more a city planner than architect, Gutschow naturally saw the need to prepare a general building plan (*Generalbebauungsplan*) that incorporated his Elbe project into an overall city plan.[49] Normally such a task was the province of the city building office, but Gutschow received a contract to draw up a general plan by January 1941 from the Reichsstatthalter.

Gutschow here drew upon his knowledge of earlier planning undertaken by Schumacher. Gutschow was never inclined simply to impose his ideas on the city, even though he undoubtedly had the authority to do so. He felt that effective implementation of any set of plans required the full cooperation and support of all major groups in the city, and consequently he printed and distributed over 300 copies of the general plan to various government offices, private architects, and interest groups for comment and criticism.[50] This was not democratic planning—the general public was not consulted—but it contrasted remarkably with the secretive planning going on in other cities.

Gutschow also moved quickly to involve other planners, architects, and agencies actively in his projects. He asked prominent local architects to evaluate components of his Hamburg planning ventures and subcontracted parts of them to some 150 independent architects in and around Hamburg. Such assignments were valued sources of work and income, and Gutschow's largesse greatly enhanced his reputation and influence. He insisted that all employees in his office participate in a continuing education program that he organized at the Hansische Hochschule für bildende Künste. Over four semesters between 1940 and 1942, between 50 and 160 architects attended lectures and seminars on the plans for Hamburg and on redesign projects in other cities, as well as on the planning of new cities like Wolfsburg. Lecturers included Schumacher and Gutschow's teacher Wetzel. When war conditions made it impossible to continue this program at the school's buildings, Gutschow staged seminars, lectures, and special excursions out of his office in Altona, and he mimeographed some of the material for distribution to employees seeing active military service.[51]

The plans of 1940, like planning elsewhere at this time, were based on the false premise that the war would be brief, victorious, and not inflict much damage on Germany.[52] The Generalbebauungsplan was in many respects a general economic plan for the city. Gutschow anticipated that Hamburg's population would grow by at least 500,000 and that the turnover in the harbor would double. Consequently he slated the harbor for major expansion and planned the construction of new residential suburbs, which would be connected to the city center by rail lines and the new Autobahn network. An estimate of projected costs, prepared in September 1940, totaled RM 3 billion, *not* including 1.5 billion for the bridge, 193 million for the Autobahn ring, 120 million for the Gau skyscraper, 594 million for railroad construction and the airport, and 125 million for other city-owned projects.[53]

One of Hamburg's most pressing traffic problems was the lack of a major street to carry east–west traffic along the southern edge of the old city close to the Elbe and the harbor. The Neugestaltung project's proposal to create a major axis along the river just to the west of the old city, however, would only increase the traffic flow into that area. The difficulty for planners was that any new artery would necessarily cut through one of the few areas of truly old buildings that had survived the great fire that destroyed much of the city in 1842. In mid-1940, Gutschow's office organized a competition for the design of an east–west traffic artery. The 126 entries were judged in January 1941, but the project was not carried out because of the war.[54] In 1948, when Gutschow no longer held his position, a similar competition was announced, and many of the same architects submitted proposals. Since a number of these men either had been employed by Gutschow or had worked with Gutschow's office, and since Gutschow himself published the most thorough analysis of the competition, prewar and wartime ideas continued to resonate in postwar planning.[55]

A second major problem facing Gutschow's office was housing. Planning many new suburbs with low-density housing close to the workplace and with plenty of access to sun and greenery did not sufficiently address this issue, as many of the problems concerned existing housing. In the area of the Elbe project, Gutschow organized an enormous sociological and economic study of the 224 blocks that would be affected in order to determine the full impact of his plans. He also commissioned a study of the relationship between housing, workplace, and commuting in Hamburg. The study revealed that only 300,000 of Hamburg's 800,000 employed residents lived close to their places of work, and 54% commuted farther than 3 kilometers. Moreover, under normal conditions, nearly one-third of the population apparently changed residences each year. The study concluded that a massive exchange of residences to move people closer to their jobs was not unreasonable. This proposal was strongly criticized, however, and Gutschow decided instead to construct new social housing (subsidized or constructed by the city) wherever possible.[56] He arranged for 10 approved architects to advise the 10 social housing construction firms operating in the city to ensure that their plans harmonized with his overall plans for the city. Once again, however, the war brought a halt to almost all new construction.[57]

Finally, and also important for postwar housing construction, the city began systematically to acquire the property called for by the Neugestaltung project. In February 1939, a freeze on construction was announced for the whole area included in the project. Beginning in March 1939, and continuing through April 1943, the city land office (not Gutschow's office) began to procure property through either purchase or trade, eventually acquiring some 700 parcels.[58] This land proved immensely valuable to the city after the war. Some parcels were used for social housing construction, while others were traded for land desired by the city for other purposes. Most of the funds for the land purchases had come from the Reich in the form of tax rebates, not from the city treasury.

In the process of developing general building plans, Gutschow and his colleagues in Hamburg and friends and colleagues in neighboring cities invoked a set of concepts that evolved out of the planning movement prior to 1933. The models of the *Stadtlandschaft* (the city in a natural landscape) and the Ortsgruppe als Siedlungszelle (local chapter of the Nazi party as basic residential cell) were developed and expanded to address the ramifications of urban growth and expansion. Although these models appear in Gutschow's 1940–41 Generalbebauungsplan, after 1943 they became central to considerations about rebuilding the war-damaged cities.

Drawing on both the garden city movement and the planning models in Gottfried Feder's book *Die neue Stadt*, Gutschow conceived the Ortsgruppe als Siedlungszelle as a system of organizing new residential settlements.[59] Five thousand to eight thousand residents would live in settlement "cells" (*Zellen*) consisting of mixed types of housing located in greenery, which would encourage the mingling of social classes and avoid the development of a suburb of villas. (Here Gutschow shared the reformist ideal of Ebenezer Howard's garden city model.) Four such cells (which would approximate Feder's ideal size for new towns) would be grouped around central community buildings, with housing units oriented to maximize exposure to sunlight. Gutschow's innovations included dispersing the cells to help shield them from the consequences of air raids (and this in 1940) and grouping the cells along the organizational lines of the local party chapter (*Ortsgruppe*), which was also divided into cells. A socially and biologically healthy population would thus be closely integrated with the new political order. Gutschow circulated his proposal widely, to general praise, including the strong endorsement of Fritz Schumacher.

The second planning model used by Gutschow, that of the Stadtlandschaft, is best understood as a city embedded in the natural landscape, rather than as an urban landscape or cityscape. Based also on the garden city movement as well as on Ernst May's planning models, the Stadtlandschaft was clearly expressed by Hans Bernhard Reichow in his extension planning for Stettin and later in essays by Wilhelm Wortmann, the regional planner for Bremen.[60] Reichow and Gutschow knew each other from student days in Danzig, and Wortmann and Gutschow had collaborated on planning competitions in the late 1920s as employees in Fritz Schumacher's planning office. Both Reichow and Wortmann actively participated in the seminar-lecture series on planning that Gutschow organized in Hamburg.

Reichow conceived of an expanded Stettin as part of a Stadtlandschaft. Outside the historic core, the city would take the form of ribbons or bands of housing, industry, roads and rail lines, and green areas along the Oder. Cells of residences would be no more than 30 minutes walking distance from work and community and party buildings. Modernist planners of the 1920s had also proposed linear cities, but in contrast to their rigid grid layout, Reichow designed his bands to follow the existing landscape, thus bending and flowing naturally like the river. The green areas would serve as truck gardens, not merely sterile parks, and feature undulating footpaths for strolling pedestrians. Urban growth would therefore be based on organic rather than abstract and schematic planning.

Gutschow, Reichow, and Wortmann became the spokesmen for the concepts of Ortsgruppe als Siedlungszelle and Stadtlandschaft in northern Germany during the war. As the latter concept was not particularly political, it could be easily adapted to postwar conditions, in contrast to the former, which could not be called upon without being stripped of its political connotations and reformulated to express the concept of neighborhood. Both approaches then comprised part of the standard vocabulary of postwar planners.

From Representative Cities to Reconstruction

The war, however, moved both the planning for monumental, representative cities and general town planning to the back burner. The victory over France had been a brief stimulant; Hitler quickly visited Paris, and his favorable impressions of the grand boulevards and great monuments were conveyed to

German planners. Britain's effective resistance, on the other hand, in combination with the onset of the bombing of Germany and the prolonged war with the Soviet Union, relegated planning for new monumental buildings and broad avenues in Germany's cities to a far less urgent position than prosecuting the war.

Although instructed in 1942 to cease work on anything not related to the war effort, planners in fact did not stop drafting Neugestaltung plans. Speer's office in Berlin, Gutschow's in Hamburg, Giesler's in Munich, and planning offices in other cities sporadically produced drawings and models in which the Führer retained an interest, even as the war turned against Germany. Furthermore, the eastward expansion of the Reich in the early war years gave German planners the opportunity to apply their ideas to rebuilding towns in the occupied territories.

Wilhelm Wortmann's work in Bremen is a good example of the attempts to continue with comprehensive regional planning during the years before the air war forced German planners onto the path of reconstruction planning. In November and December 1943 Wortmann circulated memoranda on new planning for the city (which had not yet been extensively destroyed) and surrounding region.[61] The November essay began with a long citation from Alfred Rosenberg's 1930 book, *Myth of the Twentieth Century,* in which Rosenberg called for the relocation of the population of Germany's metropolises into smaller cities, urban centers with populations of no more than 50,000–100,000. This decentralization of the population he considered cultural and "spiritual necessities." In addition to alleviating the racial and demographic unhealthiness of huge cities, decentralization would provide the best protection in "possible wars" against air raids with high explosives and poison gas bombs.

Wortmann "fully endorsed" Rosenberg's propositions. He argued that Bremen's three-decade-long falling birth rate had produced an overaged population that boded ill for the future and mortally endangered the city. The combination of disastrous demographic trends and danger from the air required a thorough dispersal (*Auflockerung*) of housing, industry, and commerce, and a restructuring (*Gliederung*) of the existing city including extending the city into new industrial and residential areas to the north and south. One fourth of the population of the whole city and 100,000 of the 180,000 currently living in the old city and in the newer area across the Weser, he concluded, should be relocated into new Siedlungszellen.

In the December essay, Wortmann advocated building new residential cells amidst "permanent greenery" in harmony with the natural landscape of the Weser Basin. Green areas would support agriculture and small truck gardens, and residents would have quick and easy access to their workplaces, which would be built nearby. He urged, however, that the resultant Stadtlandschaft, not be considered a mere mechanical equivalent of "zoning for lower buildings, reduction of population density, general dispersal, and ample introduction of greenery into built up areas." Instead each cell would form a true community, with no "crass differences between 'villa suburbs' and 'working-class suburbs.' " Each cell would derive its unique character from local conditions, but, as part of the larger national community, each would "consciously" be organized along the same lines as the political organization of the *Volk*.

Planning for towns and cities in the conquered territories in France and in the east was based on similar concepts. In 1941, a reconstruction office was created for rebuilding damaged towns and redesigning existing towns in occupied Lorraine.[62] Headed by Clemens Weber, the town planner of Saarbrücken, the office employed a number of men associated with architectural modernism, including Rudolf Schwarz, Emil Steffann, Walter Hoss, and Richard Döcker. This wartime work in the *Westmark* allowed these men to practice their profession and be excused from military service. Viewing their jobs as a kind of "inner emigration," they ignored the fact that their activity was premised on the expulsion of large numbers of French citizens to make room for future German settlers. The Hermann-Göring Works planned new industrial facilities in the region, and Herbert Rimpl, chief architect for the Göring Works nationwide, opened a branch office and also employed modernists, including Alfons Leitl, to design factory buildings. After the war Schwarz planned in Cologne, Steffann in Lübeck and Cologne, and Döcker and Hoss in Stuttgart. Leitl became editor of the influential journal *Baukunst und Werkform*. These architects formed a close group and frequently contacted each other to share and exchange ideas.

The work of Rudolf Schwarz is especially interesting. Prior to 1941 he had worked only as an architect and not as a planner. For Diedenhofen in Lorraine, he developed ideas about integrating modern housing settlements, consisting mostly of single-family houses with gardens grouped around a primary school, into an existing urban and natural landscape. The urban structure, he thought, should take the form of a flowing ribbon city, with bands of industry, greenery, and housing that followed natural topographical contours. The "crown" of the new city should be what Schwarz called a *Hochstadt,* a central place in which structures supporting the ennobling functions of worship, culture and education, administration, and economic leadership would be located. There was insufficient time to put these ideas, which had no specific Nazi content, into practice, but Schwarz later tried to apply his wartime model to the reconstruction planning of postwar Cologne.

Planning activity also progressed in the eastern occupied lands, as evidenced by a planning ordinance issued on 30 January 1942 by Heinrich Himmler in his capacity as Reichskommissar für die Festigung deutschen Volkstums. Entitled "Guidelines for the Planning and Design of Cities in the Annexed German Territories in the East," it was distributed by Reichskommissar für den sozialen Wohnungsbau Robert Ley to party leaders and housing commissioners and offices throughout the Reich.[63] Konstanty Gutschow circulated his copy of the guidelines among his colleagues with the notation that they constituted "an excellent formulation of urban planning which has general importance beyond the application to the work in the East."[64]

The guidelines called for "an organic connection between town and countryside," a network of small cities of 15,000 to 20,000 inhabitants, and a few cities of medium and large size, though large cities generally should be discouraged, since they were an "economic and above all a biological burden on the Volk." Urban planning should be integrated within the framework of regional planning, guided by the Reich. Since the Germans considered existing cities on what had been Polish territory to be culturally German, they sought to preserve the outward forms of historic centers, but at the same time it was essential that the cities serve modern purposes. Only on what had been Russian territory would existing cities be completely razed and new towns founded. Moreover, the guidelines stressed that "the primacy of common use before private use must also be expressed in urban design." The plans for newly founded cities and newly built areas in old cities must be derived "from the spirit and needs of the present time." Urban design should acknowledge and respect the different uses of land and buildings and should strive to create an organic whole that had inner coherence and harmonized "with the natural forms of the landscape." Residential districts should be organized into "cells" of up to 5,000 inhabitants, corresponding to the equivalent political organization of the party. Single-family homes and row houses were the best residential form, and footpaths and bicycle paths would link housing to work areas and to inner and peripheral green areas. The location of industry should minimize negative environmental consequences, and industry, housing, and public services should be carefully dispersed to lessen the impact of possible air raids. The transportation and road network should be laid out according to future needs: through traffic should be routed around the city center, not through it, and sufficient parking space should be allotted for the growing number of motor vehicles.

This ordinance summarizes many of the planning concepts then circulating in Germany, concepts being discussed and developed by Gutschow, Reichow, Wortmann, and others. The guidelines make no mention of monumental buildings or streets, nor do they address the particular form of community buildings, although actual construction is assigned to the party. Hence urban planning figured far more than architecture in conceptualizing these new communities. Seen from the perspective of those in the east who would be displaced or massacred to make room for new and redesigned "German" cities, the guidelines assumed the possibility of total planning on a horrible, inhuman scale. From the perspective of the German planning profession, the guidelines formed a useful synopsis of what they considered the technical, apolitical foundation of good urban design.

Reconstruction Planning

Once the air war had begun to reduce German cities to rubble, planners refined the concepts and models developed originally for town extensions and for new cities and applied them to plans for *reconstruction* (*Wiederaufbau*) of the bombed cities. However shocked they may have been at the degree of destruction wrought by the bombers, planners recognized an opportunity to introduce even greater changes in the old inner cities than had been envisaged in the Neugestaltung programs. They all agreed that the cities should not be rebuilt as they had been; the flaws of the past should not be reproduced. By definition, reconstruction planning, with few exceptions, meant planning largely new inner cities.

A great many reconstruction plans were drawn up between the spring of 1942 and the end of the war, although none reached the public eye. The most important area of planning activity was the Arbeitsstab Wiederaufbauplanung zerstörter Städte (Working Staff for Reconstruction Planning of Destroyed Cities) in Speer's ministry. The preceding chapter discussed its contribution to the question of housing policy. In some cities the regular town planning or historic preservation offices assumed the task of reconstruction planning, whether or not the Arbeitsstab was also working on planning for that city. Private citizens also advanced plans and suggestions, acting either on their own out of affection for their native cities or perhaps with the hope of gaining some future employment. Though most of this activity had no impact on postwar rebuilding, it merits brief examination because it reveals the wide range of reconstruction thinking during the final years of the war.

The first instance of comprehensive reconstruction planning is to be found, appropriately enough, in Lübeck, the first city to suffer extensive damage from area bombing. As seen in Chapter 4, on historic preservation, the city commissioned Hans Pieper to prepare reconstruction plans shortly after the bombing. Working practically alone out of his home, Pieper drafted an argument for modernizing not only the destroyed areas but also the overall street network of the old city. Like most people, he recognized that the traditional Lübeck gabled buildings were simply inadequate for modern housing and business purposes. They permitted too little light and air and contained very small rooms. Many merchants had already moved to more spacious housing in the suburbs and turned their former homes in the old city into warehouses—badly suited ones at that. Immediate needs required consolidating the small, elongated building lots and creating ample open space in the interiors of blocks. This would entail relocating some of the population into satellite suburbs of 5,000 inhabitants. Streets had to be widened, and "parking places in the old city must be created under all circumstances."[65] As is clear from the 1946 published version of Pieper's work, he did not settle upon a single reconstruction plan but rather offered a number of suggestions for changing the street pattern and rebuilding whole blocks.

Two other architects began to work on reconstruction plans for Lübeck at the same time as Pieper. Carl Mühlenpfordt was hired by the Lübeck merchants' association (Kaufmannschaft), whereas it appears that Darmstadt professor Karl Gruber simply worked on his own, although he had previously been employed by Lübeck in 1938–39 for modifications of the historic city hall.[66] Both advocated a very conservative approach to reconstruction, arguing for retention of the basic street layout and the construction of new buildings in keeping with the style of the traditional Lübeck burgher house. Although Gruber did not demand a literal copying of the old and recognized the necessity of consolidating building lots, he believed that the proportions and "rhythm" of the old city should guide new construction.[67] The conservative approach of Mühlenpfordt and Gruber appealed to the citizenry of Lübeck, but it ran counter to the prevailing planning climate, which had little sympathy with recreating the past.

Behind the scenes and beyond the planning offices and the offices for Neugestaltung, speculation about the shape of reconstruction took place all over Germany. Some suggested radical innovations, as evidenced by the following examples from Hannover, Hamburg, and Cologne.

In the fall of 1943, Gerhard Graubner, a professor at the Technical University of Hannover, proposed rebuilding the bombed cities primarily in view of the likelihood of future wars.[68] Called *Wehrstädte*, these new fortress cities would, like their medieval predecessors, protect and guarantee the safety of their citizens in the event of war. Graubner advocated placing all major transportation lines (train tracks and trunk roads), important utilities, and war-related industry underground in bombproof caverns. This would be easiest if cities were erected in naturally hilly landscapes, which would require the abandonment of many existing cities. In central areas above ground, bomb-proof high-rise bunkers would house businesses, administrative and cultural facilities, and some residences. These bunkers would have direct access by elevator to the underground transportation network. Most housing would be dispersed into suburbs, and buildings in all sections of the new city would be separated by large green areas. Surface traffic would be limited to pedestrians, bicycles, local trams, and automobiles. Graubner proposed testing his ideas on Stuttgart, which lay within a ring of hills, and Hannover, which had already endured damaging air raids. He suggested turning Hannover's catastrophe into a virtue by abandoning much of the former city for a new fortress city.

An alternative to abandoning bombed cities permanently was temporarily to return bombed areas to nature. A month after Hamburg was devastated by bombing in late July 1943, the landscape architect Max Schwarz submitted to the Neugestaltung office a proposal calling for the afforestation of the destroyed areas. He thought the ruins should be completely leveled, graded, covered with mud, and then planted. Eventually a new urban landscape—a Stadtlandschaft—would grow, and when, after a generation or so, the area was rebuilt, this new landscape would provide the natural contours for healthy reconstruction. Another idea for abandoning the bombed sections of Hamburg came from the regional planning office, which suggested relocating at least one-third of the city's population into the countryside. A future Hamburg would then be a dispersed city, not the densely built-up city of the past.[69]

In an essay about Cologne's rebuilding, written in 1944 but not published until 1946, Hans Schmitt called for the retention of the city's traditional small building lots and the historic street pattern, but otherwise he argued for a completely new city.[70] Declaring that "old Cologne is as dead as a masterpiece that has been destroyed by time or fire," Schmitt believed that the city should reject any attempt to copy the old, whether with decorative facades or with historicist imitations of buildings from earlier periods. He warned against the type of urban renewal of the 1930s, the romanticism of the nineteenth century, and the construction of new axes, whether in the style of Haussmann or the Nazis. In his opinion, an axis through Colgone would be "brutal and stupid," "a monstrosity." He considered it a "cardinal error" to locate the train station next to the cathedral and then build the railroad bridge as an axis lined up with the cathedral. All monumentality was little more than "honoring the banal," and it would be a gross mistake to destroy a rebuilt city with roads and parking places for automobiles—products of an amoral technology.

Schmitt envisioned a rebuilt Cologne as consisting of new terraced houses with gardens on flat roofs constructed on the old building lots. He wanted to retain the narrow streets, not out of romanticism but because they brought intimacy, and augment them with new arcades and interesting passages. He wanted to move the train station outside the Ring and run tram and bus lines tangentially to the inner city. Reconstruction, he warned, must be kept out of the hands of housing speculators if population density was to be reduced. The whole inner city—with housing, commerce, and "city" functions—should be made into a huge pedestrian zone, and he insisted on "a *radical ban on autos in the inner city*."

Too radical for publication under the Nazis, this program, like the proposals of Graubner and Max Schwarz, proved far too radical for postwar reconstruction as well. The efforts of the Arbeitsstab Wiederaufbauplanung proved much more important for eventual reconstruction than the kind of radical suggestions for Hannover, Hamburg, and Cologne.

The Arbeitsstab was organized out of Speer's ministry between December 1943 and July 1944, with Rudolf Wolters as its head.[71] Its legal basis was an edict issued by Hitler (through Speer) on 11 October 1943, ordering Speer to begin preparations for planning the reconstruction of the destroyed cities. Speer announced the edict in a speech of 30 November and then in a long letter (based on the speech) sent to the various Gauleiters. The new planning activity clearly marked a break with the monumental, architectonic thrust of much of the Neugestaltung effort. Postwar reconstruction was to be practical, quick, and efficient. Speer noted:

> For the time being, a reconstruction plan will not consist of planning individual administrative buildings, businesses, and so forth in their artistic details, but rather it will have as its sole task to determine the shape of the larger street systems and reconstruction areas and thereby develop a system for reconstruction in the destroyed cities and on their peripheries. . . .

> In planning particular attention must be given to the fact that here is a unique opportunity to make the cities again livable in terms of traffic, since there can be no doubt that, with further development of traffic, our cities, like London and New York, will be ruined economically by the urban contradiction between the growth in traffic on the one hand and, on the other, the unfavorable width of the streets and the relationships between streets. . . .

> It is not necessary here to determine architectonic details. This can be the subject of a second phase of reconstruction planning.[72]

Planners were thus to devote their main attention to the functional requisites of urban life, especially traffic. The emphasis on traffic planning was perhaps encouraged by the experience of the Autobahn builders, some of whom now served on Speer's staff. In any event, the need for efficiency and economy required utilizing the existing street system rather than building grand axes as had been advocated in earlier Nazi planning. To encourage lower population densities, reconstruction planning would include opening up the interiors of blocks of housing and not rebuilding badly destroyed central cities in their prewar form.[73]

The core of the Arbeitsstab consisted of about 20 architects and planners, mostly from northern Germany. This may have reflected the transportation difficulties of 1944, but it is also clear that Munich, for example, did not take the Arbeitsstab very seriously. Speer's rival in Munich, Hermann Giesler, delegated Hans von Hanffstengel to attend meetings of the group because von Hanffstengel had previously worked in Gutschow's office in Hamburg, but planning in Munich continued to focus on Neugestaltung, not reconstruction.[74] Though the nominal director of the Arbeitsstab was Rudolf Wolters, Konstanty Gutschow acted as Wolters's representative and established himself as the real leader of the group. He used the Arbeitsstab to create an extensive network of correspondents throughout the Reich. Other key members of the staff included Hanns Dustmann, Ernst Neufert, Herbert Rimpl, Friedrich Hetzelt, Friedrich Tamms, Reinhold Niemeyer, Willi Schelkes, Julius Schulte-Frohlinde, and Hans Stephan.

The work of the Arbeitsstab Wiederaufbauplanung was divided into several areas: developing a uniform system to evaluate bomb damage, preparing a set of generally applicable standards and guidelines for future planning, developing housing prototypes, landscape planning for green areas, regional planning, and the drawing up of actual plans for the 42 cities designated for initial reconstruction. In all cases the thrust was technical, not architectonic. The appearance of rebuilt cities mattered less than how they met basic urban needs.

Appropriately, the first set of instructions—prepared by Gutschow—to be distributed to city planning and building offices nationwide showed how to draw up maps and gather statistics that depicted accurately the range and type of damage sustained in the bombing. It was important to know exactly which buildings were damaged, the extent of the damage (light, heavy, etc.), and whether the damage affected roofs, walls, floors, cellars, foundations, or other structural elements. Such information, presented both cartographically and statistically, would provide the basis for developing an effective reconstruction strategy. Planners could designate which areas merited repair or reconstruction and which should be razed for new development, and an accurate knowledge of the degree and type of damage would help in estimating labor and material requirements. The instructions were printed and distributed in July 1944, and many cities did in fact set about surveying the damage and preparing appropriate maps and statistics. By the time the war finally ended, of course, further bombing had rendered most of the maps and data obsolete, but the process did establish the method for the first postwar surveys.[75]

At the same time, the Arbeitsstab produced what were called "provisional city planning guidelines" (*Vorläufige städtebauliche Richtwerte*) that addressed a number of key topics: planning techniques; the relationships between land, water, and population; open areas, including parklands, recreational areas, cemeteries, and unbuilt military lands; buildings of all sorts; and all means of transportation. The guidelines suggested, for example, that cities have one theater seat for every 40 to 80 inhabitants, and, following a decree Hitler made in 1940, that in the future at least 80% of the housing consist of four-room dwellings of at least 74 square meters (almost 800 square feet) of floor space, in order to provide ideal conditions for the large families that would be needed to make up wartime population losses. Main streets with streetcar lines on their own rail island should be at least 50 meters wide. As examples of successful high-capacity thoroughfares, the guidelines mentioned Berlin's east–west axis and Unter den Linden, Vienna's Kärntner Straße, Paris's Champs Élysées, Hamburg's Jungfernstieg, and Düsseldorf's Königsallee.[76]

This was an ambitious handbook, and Gutschow recognized that, unlike the guidelines for damage reports, planning guidelines and norms would have to remain flexible enough to be useful under widely varying conditions. Initially Gutschow hoped for widespread voluntary cooperation and compliance from Germany's city planners, but in fact it was primarily Gutschow's own employees, colleagues, and friends from northern Germany who worked hardest on the guidelines and supported them. In August 1944, Gutschow wrote to his friend Wortmann that he was thinking about trying to get Reichsführer Himmler to "commit himself" to the work of the Arbeitsstab. He believed that Himmler's support would put pressure on uncooperative planners, but nothing ever came of this suggestion to coopt the head of the SS.[77] The Arbeitsstab nevertheless persevered and distributed the guidelines on 11 November 1944 to 69 leading city planners and city officials throughout Germany. On 17 January 1945, Gutschow complained to Wolters, his superior in Berlin, that things were not progressing as hoped. He felt that some sort of pressure must be applied to force city planners to meet deadlines and comply with the Arbeitsstab guidelines.[78] The unrelenting war, however, and the pessimism it engendered combined to frustrate Gutschow's efforts. Like the damage surveys, the guidelines nevertheless helped postwar officials and planners organize the process of reconstruction.

In addition to preparing and distributing guidelines, the Arbeitsstab held several meetings outside of Berlin in Wriezen during the summer and fall of 1944, in which different planners gave reports on various aspects of city planning or on reconstruction plans for individual cities.[79] Chapter 5 described the extensive discussions devoted to postwar housing at the second meeting in August and the fourth in October. Also at the second meeting, Willi Schelkes reported on the planning of urban green areas to provide recreation and relaxation facilities for residents and thereby promote their good health. He asserted that "it is better to construct and maintain green spaces than to build hospitals." In addition to serving as an "ordering element in urban space," separating residential areas from other areas and providing visual and aural relief from traffic, green areas were vital to the defenses against air raids, since only there did flak batteries have enough space to operate. He considered planning of green spaces, therefore, too important to leave to landscape architects; it belonged to the province of the general planner.[80] Reinhold Niemeyer spoke on developments in regional planning and lamented that after 1933 the Reichsstelle für Raumordnung—the agency in Berlin responsible for overseeing regional planning—had been a "complete failure."[81] Other topics at the Wriezen meetings included planning for industry (its location by type, proximity to transportation and labor, environmental impact, and protection from air raids), the capacity of the building industry to cope with the needs of rebuilding, and how best to organize reconstruction.

In spite of Speer's call for practical, limited, economical reconstruction planning in his programmatic letter of December 1943, the members of the Arbeitsstab clearly placed their work in the context of broad, general urban planning.[82] They sought to set the agenda not only for immediate reconstruction but for long-term planning. Thus they spoke of seeking "optimal solutions," formulating "ideal plans," and proceeding with "large-scale planning."[83]

Finally, the Arbeitsstab also began the formulation of concrete reconstruction plans for individual cities. Although Speer had promised that Arbeitsstab members would serve as advisers to planners already employed by the cities, in some cases the Arbeitsstab advisers took over for local building officials. Friedrich Tamms, for instance, began work on a reconstruction plan for Lübeck, forcing Hans Pieper and local private initiatives into the background. Gutschow himself worked on plans for Kassel and Wilhelmshaven in addition to Hamburg. It took some time for the Arbeitsstab and the Gauleiters to settle on which planner was to work where, and the resultant delays meant that in some cases reconstruction planning either never really got started or remained very sketchy, as was the case in Düsseldorf and Stuttgart.[84]

It is difficult to assess the *direct* influence of the planning activities of the Arbeitsstab on postwar reconstruction. None of the wartime reconstruction plans were implemented unchanged after 1945. At a minimum, Nazi axes and monumental buildings had to be deleted from the plans, as did planning language that smacked of Nazism. Pieces of the wartime reconstruction plans, however, do reappear after 1945, which makes examining a couple of these plans in detail worthwhile. Because of his preeminence during the war, Konstanty Gutschow's reconstruction planning for Hamburg is especially noteworthy.

By 1944, Hamburg differed strikingly from the city of 1940 for which Gutschow had prepared his earlier general building plan. In spite of the best efforts of the Amt für kriegswichtigen Einsatz to prepare for bombing raids, Hamburg suffered some of the worst destruction of all German cities. Gutschow approached reconstruction planning for Hamburg by building upon his 1940 plan and methods, but with new considerations. An updated plan needed to respond to the destruction, anticipate immediate postwar needs, such as finding jobs in the building industry for large numbers of demobilized soldiers, and identify the tasks meriting highest priority, such as rapid housing

construction. Furthermore, the short-term, high-priority items had to be properly integrated into long-term plans.[85] Gutschow felt that the events of the war
had validated the direction taken in his earlier plan: "A general opening-up of
the body of the city; the building of settlement 'cells' surrounded by greenery;
the locating of new settlements in a ribbon-like east–west direction; stronger
development of Harburg and other areas on the southern bank of the Elbe;
and the relieving of the central 'City' through the creation of a second 'City.' "
Only in totally devastated areas did he favor a complete redrawing of property
and street lines, truly redesigning Hamburg.[86] Such areas provided planners
with a tabula rasa upon which they might implement proposals for solving the
problems that had resulted from the unplanned urbanization accompanying
industrialization.

Reconstruction planning for Hamburg was to be the work not only of
Gutschow's office but of his whole circle of friends and colleagues. He drew
up a list of 73 projects, such as the laying out of certain new streets and the
planning of various small sections of the city. Though a few of these projects
were assigned to his office colleagues, most were parceled out to 39 architects
and planners who either lived in Hamburg or were otherwise in close contact
with Gutschow through his earlier planning for the redesign of Hamburg as a
representative Nazi city. He also organized a series of evening seminars,
where members of his circle presented their ideas for criticism.[87]

Gutschow meticulously examined the contributions of his coworkers, and
he was open to—although he did not always accept—their criticism of his
ideas. Both Gustav Schleicher and Ernst Zinsser questioned the monumental
scale of some of the buildings planned for the Elbe Neugestaltung project,
arguing that they were out of proportion to the buildings of the old city.
Although the reconstruction plans were not supposed to emphasize monumental building projects, Gutschow reacted strongly: "'Man as the measure of all
things'—easily said! . . . And yet how different the proportions of temples
and cathedrals. A proportion is nothing absolute, but rather an expression of
race, man, and time. . . . The Elbe forum of the new Hamburg is to be the
midpoint of the Reich in the north and also the world harbor for the
Reich. . . . Beauty of the truly grand, 'the monumental.' Experience Paris-
Versailles." At the same time, Gutschow rejected suggestions that seemed to
overemphasize the new "City" at the expense of the old. The main train
station, for example, would remain where it was because the old center would
still retain its "City" functions.[88]

By mid-July 1944, Gutschow was ready to present a version of his reconstruction plans in the form of a new general plan to a scheduled meeting of city
planners, mayors, and Gauleiters who would be involved in reconstruction of
their own cities. The meeting was canceled due to the worsening military
situation and increasingly difficult travel conditions, and instead Gutschow
presented the plan to the members of the Arbeitsstab for reconstruction planning on September 17.[89]

The 1944 plan contained many of the ingredients of the earlier plan: the
new "City" along the Elbe, the opening up of the old "City," new housing

settlements on both sides of the Elbe, the Autobahn ring, the doubling of the harbor, and the introduction of major new "green" areas. The layout of the rebuilt city would also conform to the topography of the Alster and Elbe. The emphasis on neighborhoods (*Nachbarschaften*) as the guiding concept for new settlements and for the reconstruction or redesign of old residential areas is somewhat stronger than in the 1940 plan, probably because the possibility of creating neighborhoods throughout the entire city had not existed in 1940.

Gutschow also tried to plan housing in a way that would eliminate the class divisions that so characterized prewar cities. New housing, whether in older areas or new settlements, should be varied in size, layout, and design, so that people of different backgrounds, ages, and occupations would live together in a common neighborhood. Finally, the plan called for the designation of so-called reconstruction areas (*Wiederherstellungsgebiete*) of relatively recent origin, modern in design and low in density, that could be repaired or reconstructed very quickly and thus immediately provide large amounts of housing to replace that which had been destroyed. Gutschow suggested that the areas of Barmbeck-Nord, Dulsberg, and Jarrestadt would be appropriate for such designation. These three areas, plus Hamm and Horn, were the primary focus of Gutschow's attention during 1945. He also worked on or solicited memoranda on such topics as methods of salvaging building material from rubble, improving traffic flow around the main train station, and partially redesigning the old inner city. (The central problem here was still where and how to build a functional east–west traffic artery through the old city near the Elbe.)[90]

The actual plans and supporting documents for the five high-priority reconstruction areas were not completed until September 1945, well after Germany's defeat. Although the collapse of the Reich and the arrest or flight of key Nazi officials undermined the political basis for Gutschow's position in Hamburg as Architekt für die Neugestaltung, his original contract was not supposed to end until 1959. Consequently, in spite of the turmoil, he continued to work on his reconstruction planning. In August 1945, for example, he prepared a memorandum designating 18 places where streets should be widened or straightened to improve the flow of traffic.[91] Recognizing the importance of his work and not yet involved in an intensive "denazification" effort, the English, who occupied Hamburg, instructed the new lord mayor to have Gutschow continue to work on reconstruction planning. Oblivious to or unconcerned with the profoundly altered political circumstances, he did just that.

The plan for these five high-priority reconstruction areas consisted of seven parts: an explanation of the overall strategy; a detailed analysis of the damage following the guidelines of 1944; building plans for the five areas; memoranda from five large construction firms (one for each designated area) delineating a construction schedule and construction techniques and estimating labor and material needs; an analysis of financing possibilities; a discussion of basic requirements for practical implementation of the plans; and a conclusion.[92] In 1939, the five areas together had contained 33,646 dwellings. Of these, 25,913 had sustained at least 30% damage by 1945. Gutschow proposed reconstructing 22,951 dwellings, gaining 3,924 dwellings by dividing some very large units, and constructing 7,122 new units. Including the 7,719 units that survived the war, the five areas would then have a total of 41,716 housing units, a gain of 8,870, or 19.3%. He estimated the cost at RM 200,846,000, or RM 5,806 per unit. These figures included the expense, as estimated by the construction firms, of removing the rubble or reprocessing it to salvage building stones and gravel. Several sources would finance the project, including a tax amounting to 50% of the profits earned by the owners of the buildings and a tax on renters (that would effectively raise rents). Much of the capital, however, would have to come from public funds. Finally, to implement the plans, Gutschow called for a strong new building law that would grant the authorities the power to impose building freezes, redraw property lines, and guide reconstruction by carefully controlling building permits and the allocation of materials.[93]

Gutschow did not stop with the preparation of these plans. Just as he had done with his earlier plans, he distributed copies to dozens of officials and architects soliciting comments "so that many forces will feel themselves also responsible for a creative general city plan."[94] Finally, in his concluding report to the city government of 2 October, he suggested a number of ways to streamline the bureaucracy in the building administration in order to manage more effectively the process of reconstruction.[95]

By now Gutschow's career as a city planner for Hamburg had ended. He had been too prominent, too close to the seat of power to escape the reaction against the Nazi regime. Although paid through December 1945, his contract was officially terminated in October.[96] (Since he had never been a member of the official bureaucracy, he could not be removed from office, as was the normal procedure under denazification.) He never again worked as a planner in Hamburg, but undoubtedly because he had involved so many other architects in his six years of planning for Hamburg, a great many of his ideas were in fact eventually implemented, some by former employees who went to work for the city building office.

A second interesting, although ultimately less influential example of reconstruction planning was that of Karl Elkart in Hannover. Elkart's earlier plans for the Neugestaltung of Hannover had called for major new arteries to be cut through the heart of the old city and new monumental buildings to dominate the city's architecture. Backing away from this earlier model, Elkart's reconstruction plans stressed the importance of forming a Stadtlandschaft like Reichow and Wortmann had advocated. The city's structure should be organically related to the local topography, especially the Leine River, and major green areas should intrude into the city center. Traffic arteries were still needed, but widening existing streets and redesigning key squares and intersections should make cutting broad new paths unnecessary. A new east–west axis would curve around the Marktkirche and Leine Palace so that these two major buildings remained the dominant features of the city. Likewise no structural changes in the location of the train station and rail lines were needed. "The reconstruction of Hannover can fundamentally occur on the same location and using the existing important installations."[97]

Like all planners, Elkart proposed reducing the population density in the city center to only 60–80 dwellings per hectare instead of the current 140–200. (Of course most of this housing no longer really existed after the bombing of the city.) Much of the population would live in new suburban "cells," Ortsgruppen along the lines proposed by Gutschow. The important monuments in the city center would be rebuilt or repaired and provide a focus for the city, while new cultural and administrative buildings would be built along a zone about one kilometer from the railroad station. The forum and Nazi party buildings would be built in the southwest near the Maschsee. Though Elkart did not say so, these monumental buildings would in fact not dominate the city as had been proposed before the war. Indeed, the main feature of reconstruction would be the retention of Hannover's unique nature as expressed in its characteristic buildings.

When the war ended Elkart turned reconstruction planning over to Otto Meffert, the director of the city's town extension office. Elkart turned 65, the mandatory retirement age, in 1945, although his retirement became official only the following year. He did not, therefore, attempt to force his ideas on the city, and in 1948 reconstruction planning took a new direction under Rudolf Hillebrecht. Nevertheless, Elkart's reconstruction plans in the last year of the war demonstrate an interesting attempt to combine features of all phases of Nazi-era planning with the realities and consequences of the war damage.

The members of the Arbeitsstab went about their work amidst constant destruction with surprising energy and commitment. Konstanty Gutschow in particular was indefatigable. In addition to planning for Hamburg, Kassel, and Wilhelmshaven and practically running the Arbeitsstab, Gutschow maintained an extensive correspondence with his colleagues and friends in other cities. Between the beginning of January 1944 and March 1945, for example, he exchanged 11 letters with Gerhard Graubner in Hannover and 25 with Wilhelm Wortmann in Bremen.[98]

Wortmann, at least, had the sense to question what they were doing. In August 1944 he wrote to Gutschow: "As before I have strong doubts, whether it is at all right to be continuing these planning activities right now." Gutschow promptly wrote back:

I too have been afflicted more than once by doubts, whether one can really answer for . . . the use of our last resources on reconstruction planning in the middle of this war. I have to tell myself all kinds of rational reasons in order to convince myself and then to be able to concentrate again on my work. Only one thing is certain: when we finally come to reconstruction in practice, it will have been useful that a small circle of men will not have begun at that moment to think but rather have been racking their brains over it for some time and at least will be far enough along to know where the problems are.

In September Wortmann responded:

The enemy stands on our borders and the war is driving irresistably towards its resolution. At this moment a few dozen planners are supposed to occupy themselves not only with the basic questions of reconstruction but beyond that to prepare partial plans for a selected section of a city and indeed a detailed example on a scale of 1:500. I cannot reconcile these things.[99]

Perhaps both men were right. Time, energy, and resources were wasted on plans that were never implemented. At the same time, Gutschow correctly anticipated that those engaged in wartime reconstruction planning would be prepared to lead the reconstruction effort after the war.

7

Planning and Planners
after 1945

The end of the war only momentarily halted the feverish reconstruction planning that had been going on since late 1943, as the occupying armies temporarily assumed the responsibilities of local government and purged government offices of leading Nazi enthusiasts. Only in a few cities could the chief wartime planners–Kiel's Herbert Jensen, Freiburg's Joseph Schlippe, and Lübeck's Hans Pieper, for example–continue working. Most senior planners were removed from office or allowed to resign. Sometimes the purge affected lesser officials as well, although this varied widely from place to place. Naturally the central agencies in Berlin that had sponsored urban planning were abolished along with the Reich government. The members of the Arbeitsstab Wiederaufbauplanung, planners in Speer's ministry and in the German Labor Front, scattered across Germany, seeking refuge in cities where they hoped to be able to work, either as private architect/planners or as employees of new city governments or even as employees of the occupying powers.

Despite the inauspicious conditions, most of the wartime planners did in fact find new jobs, which enabled them to bring into the postwar period the models, concepts, and practices developed before 1933 and during the Nazi era. Although it became clear very quickly that the Allies wished to revive local (and democratic) government and let planning remain a German responsibility, it took a few months for the dust to settle. Planners had to find working space, collect statistics and other data, and begin the time-consuming process of drafting plans. While they tried to concentrate on the forward-looking activity of planning, they often had to direct attention to the immediate tasks of clearing rubble and supervising temporary construction. In any case, they were able to put their professional training and experience to use.

The Postwar Planners

There is no question that reconstruction planning after 1945 remained in the hands of the generation of planners who had gained definitive experience between 1933 and 1945.[1] That is only to be expected. Reconstructing a badly bombed city was an enormously complex task, and city administrations and town councils naturally sought qualified, experienced planners to organize and direct all aspects of rebuilding.

Of the few representatives of the Weimar generation of planners still around in 1945, most hoped that Fritz Schumacher and Heinrich Tessenow would link postwar work to the pre-Nazi era. Schumacher had been forced to retire at age 63 in 1933, and though he had maintained fairly close contacts with Gutschow's group in Hamburg and Wortmann's in Bremen, his postwar image remained that of an untainted, saintly figure.[2] Too ill to do more than write, Schumacher nevertheless prepared a hefty reader on planning that included contributions ranging from the ultramodernist (Le Corbusier) to the conservative (Paul Bonatz).[3] He wrote commentaries on planning in Bremen and Hamburg, as well as general essays in which he called for practical planning to include artistic, technical, social, and economic perspectives.[4] Tessenow consulted on the rebuilding of Rostock and on planning in Lübeck but, like Schumacher, was too old to provide real leadership. Schumacher died in 1947; Tessenow in 1950.

The men who had made the Technical University in Stuttgart a leading planning center were also no longer available.[5] Paul Bonatz had emigrated during the Nazi years to Turkey, though he had not been pressured to do so. (He had designed Autobahn bridges and had returned during the war to consult on new plans for Stuttgart.) He chose to remain in Ankara and returned to Germany only for occasional consulting jobs. Heinz Wetzel died in 1945. Paul Schmitthenner expected to play a role in reconstruction planning, and he was invited to submit proposals for Freudenstadt, a small town in the Schwarzwald, and for Mainz. In both cases he was caught between rival factions with strongly conflicting views on planning, and his ideas did not enjoy the success he hoped for. As noted earlier, he was denied his professorial position in Stuttgart due to his prominence under the Nazis, in spite of being cleared in a denazification hearing.

Ernst May, whose pioneering work in Frankfurt in the 1920s had been one of the most frequently cited examples of modern planning, had left Germany in 1930 with many of his Frankfurt coworkers to plan new industrial cities in the Soviet Union. When his work there was frustrated, he emigrated to Africa and worked as a planner and architect in Kenya and Uganda. He returned to Germany in the early 1950s, but not as a town planner. In 1954 he became head of the planning section of the trade unions' huge social housing firm, Neue Heimat.[6]

German planners in the modernist camp entertained high but ultimately unfounded hopes that Walter Gropius and Martin Wagner, two of the most influential figures from Berlin in the 1920s and both in exile in America, would migrate back to Germany and assume leadership of postwar planning. In the late 1920s, while Wagner served as chief planner (*Stadtbaurat*) of Greater Berlin and after Gropius had left the Bauhaus in 1928, the two had collaborated on housing projects in that city. Since neither could expect to keep working under the Nazis, who considered them subversive examples of cultural bolshevism, both went into exile. Dismissed from his post in 1933, Wagner took a job in Turkey, while Gropius moved first to England and then to the United States. The two men came together again in 1938. Soon after Gropius became head of the department of architecture at Harvard University, he arranged for Wagner to join the department as assistant professor of housing and regional planning.[7]

During the war both wrote essays on planning which made no distinction between the problems of decayed American cities like Boston and the bombed-out cities in Europe. The problem, they believed, was essentially the same: the industrial metropolis of modern capitalism required radical reform. They further argued that democratic assemblies should assign the task of comprehensive planning to a "great artist planner and builder" or, better yet, to a select team of such individuals. These artist-planners alone could anticipate and incorporate future needs into their plans.[8] After 1945, old German friends expected Wagner and Gropius to return to Germany and assume the role of artist-planners.

Prewar German colleagues inundated Gropius with letters beseeching him to throw his weight and prestige behind progressive planners and architects in their feuds with conservatives and holdovers from the Nazi regime. Hans Scharoun, Berlin's first postwar planner and an architect who had worked with Gropius and Wagner on the Siemensstadt housing project in 1929, asked Gropius to join other progressive Berlin architects in protesting the rehabilitation in Baden-Württemberg of Paul Schmitthenner.[9] Likewise, Gropius's old friend Richard Döcker hoped Gropius would help squelch the resurgence of conservatives in Stuttgart.[10] Otto Meyer-Ottens, Hamburg's city planner, also sought Gropius's help, not so much against former Nazis as against planners and architects "whose way of thinking was now more than outdated."[11] A group of architects in Düsseldorf urged Gropius to oppose the appointment of Julius Schulte-Frohlinde as a planner in that city.[12] When Erich Kühn, himself a planner and official of the reconstruction ministry of Northrhine-Westphalia, created a new academy for research and teaching in the area of planning, he asked Gropius to join the faculty, and, if that were not possible, at least to lend his name as a sponsor.[13] In the fall of 1951, Chancellor Konrad Adenauer invited Gropius to lead a special "commission on new settlements" that would study German housing conditions and work with the housing ministry.[14]

To such requests Gropius always responded that he considered himself an American and that he was deeply committed both to his duties at Harvard and to his own architectural team in Cambridge. Although willing and happy to make gestures that cost little, such as writing a letter or an article, he would not focus his attention on Germany and entertained no thoughts of moving back.

Gropius did, however, make one journey to Germany expressly to advise Americans and Germans on urban reconstruction. Asked to provide General Lucius Clay, the head of the military government in the American zone, with a report, Gropius traveled to Berlin in August 1947, where he observed the condition of the city, spoke with officials, old friends, and colleagues, and made public speeches. From Berlin he went to Hannover, Frankfurt, Stuttgart, and Munich, again giving public lectures and conducting informal talks with smaller groups. Gropius was openly astonished and appalled at the extent of the destruction of the German cities. The ruins and devastation far exceeded his expectations and seemed to leave him even more depressed about the prospects for reconstruction than were the German planners responsible for the job. In response he called for a psychological reconstruction of the spirit to precede actual planning and rebuilding.[15]

To his distress, Gropius's trip stirred up quite a bit of controversy, and it is clear that his observations provided little of value to anyone. Apart from propounding his well-known ideas on urban planning, and perhaps providing some measure of inspiration for his German friends, he implicitly criticized Karl Bonatz, the newly appointed planner of Berlin, when he heaped praise upon Bonatz's predecessor Scharoun and joined Scharoun in calling for bold, new, visionary planning for the bombed city. Bonatz angrily replied that Gropius knew too little about conditions in Berlin to make informed and meaningful criticisms of the efforts of the hard-pressed planning office and that his ideas were too vague to be instructive.[16] Gropius's published report to Clay also included a somewhat muddy attack on the attempts to standardize construction through the establishment of set norms for the whole country.[17]

Finally, while in Frankfurt, Gropius hinted that he and his Harvard students would work to prepare a proposal for a master plan for the rebuilding of Frankfurt. This idea was enthusiastically received, but when city planner Werner Hebebrand wrote Gropius wondering about the status of the project, Gropius replied that he had given up on it. Reconstruction planning, he said, should be done by the Germans themselves. Gropius's refusal to pursue this project further underscores his American orientation and his perception that he no longer shared the interests and concerns of the Germans.[18] Comfortable in his role as a teacher at Harvard and as a vocal proponent of the "new building," his publications on planning and architecture tended to be general statements directed to a universal audience concerned with universal problems, rather than to a German audience concerned specifically with the bombed German cities. In spite of his correspondence with former colleagues, Gropius had clearly distanced himself from his German past.

Whereas Gropius shied away from extensive involvement in German postwar affairs, Wagner welcomed it. In contrast to Gropius's emphasis on teamwork, joint effort, and compromise, Wagner's assumption of the role of dogmatic idealist, the fighter willing to take up arms for his vision of new cities, alienated Germans and denied him the opportunity to work again in Germany. Indeed, although there was some talk of making him Scharoun's successor in Berlin or Meyer-Ottens's successor in Hamburg, Wagner traveled briefly to his homeland only once, in 1953, to serve as a consultant on American-sponsored housing projects.[19] His standing fell precipitously when he began publishing polemics on German reconstruction without basing them on any firsthand observations. He lambasted German planners and architects for a singular lack of vision, arguing that the "spiritual rubble" left over from the Nazi era needed to be cleared away well before the physical rubble left from the bombing.[20] Wagner felt that the terrible conditions in Germany's cities made a radical, even revolutionary approach to reconstruction necessary and practical, rather than utopian. Only sufficient courage and vision would rebuild the cities in a worthwhile way, and he made it clear that, in his opinion, the current generation of German planners sorely lacked such qualities.

As one might expect, rebuilding in Berlin drew Wagner's particular attention. When Karl Bonatz presented the framework of the new town plan in the fall of 1947, he rejected Wagner's ideas as utopian. Too many of the old structures still stood, too much of the underground infrastructure of the city was undamaged, and too many people needed immediate shelter in the old city for anyone to seriously contemplate pulling up stakes and constructing a new Berlin on virgin land—one of Wagner's central proposals.[21] Wagner replied with a sarcastic, biting "open letter" in which he argued that his ideas were more practical and economical than those of Bonatz and that Bonatz was merely a naive architect of the old school, without real training and experience as a city planner. The insulting character of Wagner's letter offended Bonatz and other Berlin builders; indeed, Wagner's colleague Gropius also found his tone offensive.[22]

Unfortunately, the tone of this letter typified Wagner's polemics. Earlier he had condemned those who were critical of his ideas as "architectural illiterates."[23] The polemics were, at least in part, an attempt to confront the legacy of Nazism. In 1948, Franz Rosenberg, then a member of the planning office of Braunschweig, asked Wagner to come to Germany instead of sending critical articles from America. "If you do this," Rosenberg wrote, "you will be doing something better than if you spend your time educating a generation of American students."[24] Wagner replied:

> Your invitation to come to Germany is truly tempting, and I would have long ago put this idea into action, had I truly believed that my time had come. It *has not*! Why? Because my chance, that is, *your* chance and the chance of the younger generation has not yet come. First the political twilight, by which Hitler seized the rudder, has to be cleared away. First the ministerial chairs and the chairs of the privy counsellors have to be shaken before it can be worth my while to invest the rest of my life in an action which is worth little more than starving. When my time calls me, then I will come, you can be sure of that.

The conditions for which Wagner hoped, of course, did not exist.

To be sure, the provocative tone of Wagner's writing attracted attention to his conceptualization of modern city planning. When Wilhelm Seidensticker published a brief survey of new planning concepts, for example, he included Wagner's ideas for a radical, sweeping redesign of Boston as one of nine theoretical models. The Boston plan was also displayed as part of an exhibit on town planning at the Constructa building exhibition in Hannover in 1951.[25] Rudolf Hillebrecht sounded out Gropius about Wagner's suitability for taking over reconstruction planning for Hamburg.[26] Gropius discouraged Hillebrecht from putting forward Wagner's name. In strongly Germanic English (and it is revealing that he chose to write in English), he wrote: "[Wagner] is always a violent fellow, knowing front attacks only, without any subtle quality of tackling difficult problems with others. Wherever he has worked he had violent clashes in practice. He is a research man and does very good work there but as soon as he steps into polemics he hits people right in their center and that is what he does also in his articles written for Germany. His attack of Bonatz is, I think, of doubtful value and has an offending effect."[27]

Gropius's harsh judgment of his long-time colleague certainly hurt Wagner's chances of returning to Germany as a city planner. The relationship between the two men had begun to deteriorate as early as 1940, when Wagner criticized Gropius for abandoning the progressive positions of the 1920s in favor of more fashionable, comfortable projects. He feared that Gropius was more interested in building theaters and grand public buildings than prefabricated housing for the masses, more interested in architecture than in facing "the most urgent social, economical and artistical problems of our time."[28] Although they collaborated on a number of essays and public appearances during the war, a steely bitterness characterized their disagreements by the fall of 1948. Gropius finally severed any further collaboration, concluding his last letter to Wagner: "the rest is silence!"[29] Wagner denounced Gropius as a compromiser; Gropius despaired of Wagner's pigheadedness. The result of all this was that, to the dismay of their old German friends, neither played a significant role in reconstruction planning for Germany. Wagner's polemical diatribes undermined his chances of returning to work in Germany. Gropius later designed a building for the Interbau building exhibition in Berlin and helped inspire the huge Berlin residential suburb that bears his name (Gropiusstadt), but he did not contribute to reconstruction planning.

As the older generation of planners failed to assume the lead in reconstruction planning, that responsibility fell on the shoulders of those who had worked as planners under the Nazis. This is not to say that no one suffered for his Nazi connections. Albert Speer was sentenced to 20 years imprisonment as a war criminal. Though not officially prohibited from doing so, Konstanty Gutschow and Hermann Giesler never again headed planning offices. Wilhelm Wortmann left his position as Bremen's town and regional planner in 1945. Heinrich Knipping had to resign his office in Mainz. Herbert Rimpl departed Salzgitter for Wiesbaden. Although reappointed in 1949, Heinz Schmeissner was initially dismissed in Nuremberg for having helped hide the imperial regalia of the old Holy Roman Empire from the Americans. Michael Fleischer, who had planned in Cologne during the 1930s before going to

Danzig, returned briefly to Cologne in 1945 only to be dismissed because of his Nazi background. Paul Schmitthenner in Stuttgart and the landscape architect Alwin Seifert in Munich lost their academic chairs. Munich's Karl Meitinger avoided a denazification hearing by taking early retirement in 1946.

Many of these men, however, continued to influence reconstruction planning in one way or another. Gutschow and Wortmann, for example, worked extensively as consultants in Hannover and Bremen. Hans Bernhard Reichow, who fled his position as Stettin's planner at the war's end, helped plan housing settlements in Hamburg as a private architect. Schmeissner was reappointed in Nuremberg in 1949, the same year in which Knipping became Hagen's planner. And while the planning offices in most of the cities changed their top personnel after the war, the new officeholders could hardly claim spotless records. Indeed, it is remarkable that so many individuals who had been associated with wartime reconstruction planning found new positions as postwar planners. The most prominent included Rudolf Hillebrecht in Hannover, Heinrich Bartmann in Münster, Johannes Göderitz in Braunschweig, Helmut Hentrich and Hans Heuser in Krefeld, Friedrich Hetzelt in Oberhausen and Wuppertal, Hans Stephan and Walter Moest in Berlin, Rudolf Wolters in Coelsfeld, Werner Hebebrand in Frankfurt and Hamburg, Herbert Boehm in Frankfurt, Franz Rosenberg in Bremen, Friedrich Tamms and Julius Schulte-Frohlinde in Düsseldorf, Walter Hoss in Stuttgart, and Rudolf Schwarz in Cologne.

The data available on these planners affords a sketch of a typical career. Born about 1900, members of this group characteristically studied in Berlin, Munich, Stuttgart, or Darmstadt immediately after World War I.[30] During the 1920s and early 1930s they tended to work as fledgling independent architects or in lower positions in town planning offices and in the meantime entered planning and architectural competitions and built networks of professional contacts and friendships. After 1933 they were employed in one way or another by the Nazi regime, although this did not necessarily require party membership or ideological conviction. In their late twenties to early forties, they found the prospect of finally putting into practice ideals that planners had developed in the previous decade exciting and became deeply attached to those ideals. Since rebuilding bombed cities comprised the major planning problem during the war, they worked on reconstruction planning under the auspices of one Nazi agency or another, most likely the Arbeitsstab Wiederaufbauplanung. Rightly or wrongly, they viewed their work as largely apolitical and technical and considered themselves members of an international movement that sought to cure the ills of urban life through planning. Strong critics of the unplanned metropolis, they nevertheless viewed great cities as the raw material for the exercise of their trade.

They considered the Nazi defeat and its replacement by a democratic form of government no obstacle whatsoever to continuing these planning activities. As apolitical technocrats, they considered their central planning concepts and models applicable anywhere—and everywhere.[31] Consequently they went to work in a new location, either as an official planner or as an independent architect/planner, entering planning competitions or serving on competition juries. They maintained their wartime professional friendships but did not hesitate to cooperate with those who opposed Nazism ideologically.[32] National professional associations provided them with forums for the exchange of ideas.[33]

Viewing this generation of town planners as carriers of a set of ideas shaped by more or less common experiences underscores the extraordinarily pervasive continuities in planning. It bears repeating, however, that most of the planning concepts themselves predated the Nazi regime, and it would be a distortion to label postwar reconstruction planning a mere continuation of Nazi planning just because the planners had worked under the Nazis.[34]

Planning Models

The first 15 years after the war witnessed a very broad consensus on the fundamental goals of urban planning. Planners of all generations and all political backgrounds invoked the same concepts and vocabulary.[35] The components of this consensus are familiar.[36] Housing must have adequate sunlight, fresh air, and proximity to greenery. The population density of old, inner-city residential areas must be reduced. The relocated population should live in new, carefully planned suburbs or residential "cells" or settlements (Siedlungen). Both the suburbs and the inner-city residential areas should function as neighborhoods, each with its own cultural activities. The whole population required green spaces for recreation, and these areas should integrate built-up areas and the natural topography of the site into an urban landscape, an organic Stadtlandschaft. A meandering, flowing city, in which perspectives changed as one moved through the urban landscape, was immensely preferable to a mechanical, schematic grid.[37]

Rebuilt cities demanded proper zoning that separated industry from residential areas but kept the populace in close proximity to worksites. Zoning should clearly articulate all essential urban functions, and areas in which industry, housing, and commerce had been mixed together should be zoned for a single activity. Though the inner city should shape the identity of the citizens by serving central cultural, governmental, and economic functions, this central place, or "city crown," should not be completely filled with buildings. Here too open space was needed. Throughout the city buildings should be loosely rather than tightly grouped. The street and transportation network should be modernized and the central area freed of through traffic. Within the center citizens should be able to conduct their shopping and business excursions by foot, and workers should be able to reach their places of work either by foot or on bicycle. The form of the new city—and they were to be new rather than old cities—should be derived from human needs, not from aesthetic premises that might satisfy a photographer's eye but fail to serve inhabitants.[38]

As one planner put it, "It is self-evident that we in Germany will generally use the extensive destruction of our cities to change the entire urban structure."[39] In most cities the bombing had already wiped out the worst of the prewar slums; slum clearance now meant rubble removal, and urban renewal was part of the general renewal of the inner city. As Göderitz, Rainer, and Hoffmann put it, the new city was to be an "organically articulated and dispersed city." The city of stone must be transformed into a living organism, with its parts defined by logical, natural spatial relationships. This organic city should consist of cell-like units that developed in a healthy, natural fashion. (Contemporaneous sketches of such cities rather resemble dividing amoebas.)[40] Urban functions were compared to bodily functions; the transportation system, for example, was considered analogous to the circulation of the blood. Beyond this, the organic city was intrinsically linked to nature and inherently able to "fulfill the biological needs of men."[41] In Rainer's words, "Greenery would flow into the city, rather than be closed off in individual courtyards or limited to public parks." It would constitute "a coherent, borderless spatial landscape" that would give residents "an entirely new spatial feeling."[42] Flowing greenery and landscape, and not just transportation arteries, would articulate and tie together the neighborhoods, urban cells, and districts into a larger city, a biologically healthy entity free of the evils of the metropolis of stone. If possible, regional planning—made most difficult by the immediate postwar political conditions in Germany—should organically link larger urban units together.[43]

The American theorist Kevin Lynch has argued that there are three primary, normative models for urban planning.[44] Cosmic planning derives the form of the city from the means of exercising political or religious power. Such a model would apply to town planning in the Baroque era, to towns dominated by the church, and to Nazi planning. Mechanical planning, according to Lynch, conceives of the city as a regular machine, laid out in a fixed, mechanical fashion to expedite the function of its essential parts, such as industrial production, commerce, and housing. Such a city might be designed as a grid, like some American cities, or as a linear band, as in the designs of Le Corbusier. Organic planning sees the city as an organism whose parts have functions—industry, housing, and so forth—but which also experiences a kind of life-cycle of health and sickness, growth and contraction. Here the planner approaches the city as a physician or naturalist rather than a mechanic. Such thinking was typical of much of the late nineteenth-century antiurban planning but also reverberated in the models of planners like Reichow.

The guiding concepts of postwar German planning clearly combined the second and third of Lynch's normative models: the mechanical and the organic. Only a few postwar planners were guided by a sense of the cosmic function of a reconstructed city. Moreover, the concerns of the German planners were overwhelmingly structural, not aesthetic. Far less concerned with how the city looked than with its ability to function in a rational, healthy fashion, they felt that the aesthetic impact of the city would derive from the restoration and preservation of major monuments and new or adaptive archi-

tecture. As seen earlier, planners generally opposed the sentimental reconstruction of an entire bombed city in its prewar form.

When discussing the state of German architecture in the years after the war,
Alfons Leitl observed that even though Germans had been cut off from international developments during the war, "there is evidently a secret co-ordination
of artistic impulses that extends beyond frontiers."[45] The same held true for
planning. The German planning models developed in earlier decades to solve
the problems of the industrial city in Germany had enjoyed international currency.[46] And, after all, modern town planning everywhere derived from the
same urban problems. Extensive prewar international contacts within the garden city movement and within CIAM (International Congresses for Modern
Architecture) were revived after the war, and versions of the Charter of Athens, the document which best embodied the ideals of functional, organic urban
planning based on considerations of housing, the workplace, recreation, and
traffic, appeared in German beginning in 1947.[47] British planners lectured in
Germany in the early postwar years, and some German planners participated
in study tours of Britain. Göderitz, Rainer, and Hoffmann illustrated their
planning theory with examples of English and Scandinavian garden cities, as
did two of Cologne's postwar planners, Rudolf Schwarz and Eugen Blanck.[48]
That German planners saw their own basic concepts in terms of an international movement made it all the easier for them to view themselves as apolitical
experts seeking to solve technically complex problems.

The planners worked under considerable pressure. How were planners to
design economically healthy and functional cities when it was unclear whether
the Allies would insist on the complete deindustrialization of Germany? How
could regional planning be undertaken with Germany divided into occupation
zones? How were planners to realize their ideas amidst the chaos of the
collapse and abolition of the previous central government, the contradictory
expectations of the occupying powers, and differences between the states and
cities which had thrown the legal powers of planning authorities into total
uncertainty? (The legal problems are the subject of Chapter 8.) The planners
wanted to do a thorough, careful job and resist the pressures of "capitalistic
speculation" and "land speculators," which had undermined initial planning
efforts in the nineteenth century.[49] Philipp Rappaport noted the importance of
avoiding hasty, provisional building because "Germany is much too poor to
have to rebuild twice."[50] On the other hand, while property owners and
business executives accepted the need for urban planning, they also argued
that "we cannot wait decades, until all of the highly desirable demands of the
urban planners have been fulfilled."[51] The public supported planning in the
first years after the war, but it also demanded concrete results from town plans
that best facilitated rapid reconstruction.

The Extremes

Just as the Arbeitsstab Wiederaufbauplanung had begun to develop standardized planning models and procedures that could be used by bombed cities all

over Germany, so there was some effort to develop standardized planning techniques after the war. Erich Kühn, head of the planning group in the reconstruction ministry of Northrhine-Westphalia, and Hans Schwippert, an architect and professor at the Technical University in Aachen, produced several such drafts of planning guidelines, but they found little resonance in the profession. Philipp Rappaport, director of the Ruhr regional planning association, observed that "a truly experienced urban planner does not need [such guidelines], and for the inexperienced planner they are insufficient" to replace years of training and practice.[52] Instead of governing by specific prescriptions, postwar planning was therefore shaped by general concepts in which nearly all believed and which left ample room for widely divergent approaches.

The most radical reconstruction plans were drawn up for Berlin, Mainz, and Saarbrücken, though in all three cases radical planning eventually succumbed to more pragmatic proposals. Whereas local architects drew up the radical plans for Berlin, in the western cities such plans came from the pens of French architects imposed upon local governments by French military authorities. Since the Saar remained under French control for the first decade after the war, its planning activity was relatively unknown in the rest of Germany, and it has only very recently received scholarly attention.[53] The cases of Berlin and Mainz, therefore, are used to illustrate radical reconstruction planning.

Planners in Berlin were more concerned with building a modern metropolis than with rebuilding a historic capital.[54] Beginning in the early eighteenth century, central Berlin was consciously built up to represent the growing power and prestige of the Prussian state. Hence, the idea of representative architecture informed most planning for the city. In the early 1920s, Bruno Taut spoke of the *Stadtkrone*, or city crown, in describing a central urban core that contained symbolically representative important buildings.[55]

Obvious difficulties beset this kind of thinking after World War II, however. Instead of becoming the dominant city on the European continent as Hitler had envisioned, Berlin lost its governmental functions altogether, was occupied by the four victorious Allies, and had a very uncertain political future. The historic state of Prussia had been abolished, and at least for the time being, no new German state emerged to replace the Third Reich. In the western occupation zones, representative architecture was severely discredited, as was the idea that a city's design should reflect the power of the state.

Reconstruction planning got under way quickly in Berlin.[56] Almost as soon as the city was conquered, the city government appointed Hans Scharoun to head the building office and assume the responsibility for planning reconstruction. A leading modernist architect in the 1920s who had participated in the design of the Siemensstadt housing project, Scharoun had received no public commissions during the Nazi years, although he had remained in Berlin and designed a few private residences. During the war, Scharoun and several like-minded colleagues organized an informal "collective" to discuss their ideas for a new postwar and post-Hitler Berlin. Given the chance to design a rebuilt Berlin, he struck out on a radical path. Fully aware of the obstacles presented by the division of Berlin into four sectors occupied by Allies with varying approaches to urban problems, Scharoun nonetheless sought to plan for Berlin as a unified city. He hoped to interest the Allies by presenting plans for Berlin as "an example" of designing a new metropolis.[57]

The *Kollektivplan,* the joint proposal of Scharoun and his team (though usually associated primarily with Scharoun), was revealed to the public in an exhibition mounted in the Hohenzollern Palace in August 1946. It called for a radical reorganization of the city based upon a transformation and redistribution of property ownership. Instead of a city that expanded in concentric rings, which had been the historic pattern and still formed the basis of Albert Speer's plans for a Nazi Berlin, Scharoun wanted to spread the city out in a "ribbon" system following the course of the Spree River. In this way Scharoun hoped to create a true Stadtlandschaft, an "urban landscape" harmonizing topography and buildings.[58] Inhabitants would reside in distinct neighborhoods dispersed throughout this landscape, and a grid of high-capacity motorways would accommodate most traffic. He took it for granted that Berlin would remain Germany's capital and proposed that a "City" core, containing the state administrative buildings and major cultural buildings, would remain where it had been before the war. A pure landscape, the park of the Tiergarten, would form the center of this core.[59] Although this City was to "reflect the unity of Germany," the true focus of the plan concerned the relocation of industry and housing.[60] Scharoun and his colleagues proposed moving industry to an area near the Havel and dispersing housing to several areas well away from the City. Following accepted modernist planning principles, he supported strictly separating urban functions and preventing the intermingling of housing, industry, shopping, culture, and government.

The same exhibition also featured a different, more cautious plan. The "Zehlendorf plan," prepared by a team headed by Walter Moest in the building office of the district of Zehlendorf, was primarily a traffic plan for a great metropolis. It called for a series of concentric ring roads that in many respects resembled Speer's earlier plan, even though Moest expressly refused to speak of axes and "representative" roads and buildings and rejected Speer's plans as too schematic.[61] Moest insisted on staying within the "realm of the possible" and avoiding "the false expansiveness" typical of the Nazi years. One of the tasks of reconstruction was to demonstrate to the world that "the German spirit did not live solely in utopias."[62] Moest reasoned that too many buildings, streets, and utilities had survived the war to permit serious contemplation of any radical restructuring of the city.

Scharoun's plans and the Zehlendorf plan were based on the functionality of large cities rather than on judgments about how a capital city should look. Given the magnitude of Germany's recent defeat and destruction, neither devoted much attention to the idea of Berlin as a capital city. Some architects found this disturbing. Hans Josef Zechlin urged his colleagues to think not just of rebuilding but also of building "a more beautiful Berlin," one where the historic buildings on traditional squares would gracefully harmonize with their surroundings.[63] Max Taut, a 1920s modernist and now head of the architecture department at the Academy of Fine Arts, sought to combine functional planning with modern architectural form. He called for creating a number of new "urban cores" with commercial and administrative buildings of steel and glass rising over subway lines and lining broad avenues.[64] In one of the other few essays that addressed the form of the new core area, Paul Mast called for constructing a new national house of representatives (on the American model) to serve as the "structural and architectonic heart of the city." He imagined accompanying this building with a new "temple of justice" and a house for a national president. A major capital needs "imposing beauty," Mast argued, but "the City must represent an economically, socially, and politically transformed Germany, although not become a skyscraper city with unsolvable traffic problems."[65]

These many proposals failed to produce any dramatic results. On the contrary, the all-Berlin legislature ousted Scharoun as chief planner in October 1946, and his radical proposal for a totally new city, which had never enjoyed broad public support, became little more than a point of discussion for a future generation of planners.[66] On questions of practicality the Kollektivplan incurred harsh criticism. A leading Social Democrat, for example, argued that imposing an entirely new street system on the city would waste the billions of marks invested in underground utilities. Furthermore, the "chessboard system of roads" was "nothing other than a ten-fold magnification of the crossed axes of the National Socialists," who "were never as radical in the destruction of existing investment." The creation of new residential settlements solely for workers was also rejected. "This authoritarian allocation of housing is a mockery of every democracy; socialism wants freedom of movement and a healthy social mixture of the population, not pure workers' quarters."[67]

Karl Bonatz (brother of the conservative architect Paul Bonatz) replaced Scharoun and directed his own planning efforts along the lines of the Zehlendorf plan, basing future planning upon the layout of the existing historic city and putting traffic planning "in the foreground." Warning against "chasing after utopias," Bonatz insisted instead on pursuing practical goals.[68] He rejected the "revolutionary" plans of the Scharoun collective, especially its grid system of roads, and argued that in fact Berlin really did function as a radial city.[69]

The city parliament endorsed Bonatz's practical approach, believing that the task of city planners was to solve the problems of an existing city, not fantasize about an ideal city.[70] The Berlin blockade, the split in the city government (and in the building department), and the creation of the two new German states naturally forced planners in West and East to reformulate their thinking. They found themselves trying simultaneously to address the needs of the whole city and to plan for a divided city. In West Berlin, Walter Moest and Richard Ermisch proposed redesigning much of the old City so that one could "experience a modern world city even in the historic streets." In part this transformation was to come through the construction of a skyscraper "in the sense of Le Corbusier" at the corner of the Leipziger and Friedrichstraßen.[71] The proposal emphasized a world city, however, more than a capital city for a new Germany.

Bonatz's planning office, on the other hand, concentrated on traffic planning and designing small areas, such as the space surrounding the Bahnhof
Zoo and the Kurfürstendamm. In spite of his criticisms of Scharoun, Bonatz
gave the construction of high-capacity roads a high priority. Hence, a competition was organized in 1948 by the West Berlin building administration for a
design for the area around the Gedächtniskirche, and in the following year the
building administration presented its own plans for this area.[72] There was
heated disagreement in the press about the predominance of traffic considerations in the official plan and whether this area was in fact intended to become
a new City center to rival the historic City in East Berlin. Bonatz denied this
allegation, although in fact it was true. Approved in 1954, the final plans
advocated reconstructing the area with buildings in a modern style.[73] Eventually two dominant structures emerged: the modern Europa Center and the
Memorial Church complex, which included the ruins of the old Gedächtnis-
kirche and the new, modern church by Egon Eiermann.

In 1949, East Berlin became the capital of the new German Democratic
Republic, but the division of the city and the poverty and insecurity of the
East German regime had a lasting impact on its reconstruction. East Berlin's
planners talked about rebuilding their part of Berlin as a representative socialist capital, but their efforts were characterized by debilitating indecisiveness
about appropriate goals. The Soviet sector between the Brandenburg Gate
and Alexanderplatz contained Berlin's most important architectural monuments and buildings that symbolized the historic Prussian and German capital. The East German regime failed to implement a coherent policy with
regard to these buildings during the first postwar decade. The East German
government did repair the main damage to the buildings on the museum
island and the Brandenburg Gate, and it also announced its intention of
restoring the Frederickan Forum and the Gendarmenmarkt buildings, a project which took decades to complete.

The primary focus in East Berlin was on the design of a new street that
would represent the ideals of a socialist Germany.[74] The Frankfurter Allee,
the main artery in a badly bombed area, was renamed the Stalinallee and was
to be lined with a solid front of five- to nine-story apartment houses. Pronouncements by Lothar Bolz, minister for construction, and by the regime's
head, Walter Ulbricht, determined that the architectural style was to be "national" rather than modernist and was to draw on the classicism of historic
Berlin.[75] They envisioned a new national capital of a democratic, socialist
Germany growing out of reconstruction. An important section of the general
town planning principles officially decreed in 1950 was the mixing of urban
functions. In contrast to West Berlin, housing, the workplace, shops, cultural
buildings, and so forth, were not to be relocated into separate areas but were
to coexist as they traditionally had in European cities. East German building
law facilitated planning by lowering compensation levels and thereby making
the confiscation of private property easy and inexpensive. Theoretically, at
least, East German planners encountered far fewer obstacles in their efforts
to introduce major innovations than did their West German counterparts.

East Berlin's planning principles called for a central core with monumental buildings to serve political, administrative, and cultural functions, along with huge squares and streets for political demonstrations. A central axis would run from the Brandenburg Gate down Unter den Linden to Alexanderplatz and then down the Stalinallee. The dominant building was to be a government tower 200 meters tall. Under the leadership of Richard Paulick and Edmund Collein, and with the collaboration of several architects, including Hermann Henselmann, who emerged as the chief architect of East Berlin, these plans went through several metamorphoses but culminated in very few actual results other than demolition of some and restoration work on other buildings on Unter den Linden (like the opera). To the outrage of West Berliners, the Hohenzollern Palace on the Spree was torn down to make way for the huge assembly square called for in the design for a socialist capital city. Although the Palace interior had been gutted by the bombing, the walls remained standing, and the building could have been restored.[76]

Thus, during the first 15 years after the war, and despite a professed interest in representative architecture, the historic center of Berlin was not revived as the core of a socialist capital for the German Democratic Republic. Not until the early 1960s, when the political climate and official taste in East Germany had changed from "national" to modern and progressive, did new construction finally get under way. The result was a television tower instead of a government skyscraper on Alexanderplatz, and a low, glass-covered Palace of the Republic on Marx-Engels Platz, the huge, deserted demonstration square.

West Berlin's planners responded in several ways to these activities in the East. They adamantly denied that East Berlin alone could be a capital city and sharply criticized the work of their former colleagues in East Berlin.[77] In 1950, planners under Bonatz developed a general land use plan for Berlin—though in reality now for West Berlin.[78] East Berlin's claims to represent the whole city were challenged again by a 1957 design competition in the West for "Hauptstadt Berlin," Berlin as a capital city. Because the 151 submissions simply ignored the division of the city, they were of no practical import.[79] West Berlin responded to the demolition of the Hohenzollern Palace by resolving to restore Schloß Charlottenburg, the main Baroque palace in the western part of the city. Although the extent of its damage had engendered discussions about tearing it down, the action in East Berlin made its restoration a patriotic and symbolic act. In reaction to the opening of the first buildings on the Stalinallee, West Berlin announced an international competition for a new housing development in the Hansaviertel that would represent the progressive democracy of the Federal Republic. A competition was staged for the design of the completely cleared area in 1953, and the first residential towers of the Hansaviertel opened as part of the 1957 International Building Exhibition.[80]

A second city in which the planning debate was initiated by the presentation of a radical new design was Mainz. The French military government asked Marcel Lods, a French modernist architect, follower of Le Corbusier, and proponent of the planning principles in the Charter of Athens, to prepare a reconstruction plan for Mainz, which in mid-1946 became the capital of the French occupation zone.[81] Lods set up an independent planning office, where he was joined by Adolf Bayer, who had worked on reconstruction planning for Mainz during the war. A student of Otto Ernst Schweizer of Karlsruhe, Bayer was one of the main German advocates for the concept of the ribbon city.

The first draft of Lods's plan was ready in May 1946. Though subsequently refined, it remained essentially unchanged until Lods left Mainz in April 1948. The street pattern of the old historic core around the cathedral would remain basically the same, although some streets would be widened and only the major monuments restored. The old core clearly figured only minimally in Lods's thinking. He concentrated instead on the entire area to the north and west of the old center, which he wished to redesign completely. Here the bulk of the population was to live in high-rise, slablike apartment buildings sited in greenery. The road system was laid out as a rectangular grid. The civic center of the new city—the governmental and commercial center—would lie in a redesigned area between the old center and the new residential district. Lods advocated relocating industry, a new airport, and the major rail and Autobahn lines across the Rhine, and he pictured Mainz as part of a new ribbon city that would stretch through Wiesbaden to Frankfurt.

The Lods plan quickly generated opposition, first within the city administration and then, after it was publicly presented in January 1948, within the general public. The reasons are obvious. In addition to altering the entire character of the city, huge property transactions, the relocation of commerce and industry, and the resettlement of the population would have required much more extensive resources and would have taken a much longer time than the citizens would tolerate. Furthermore, the Lods plan ignored the fact that the area north of the Rhine lay within the American occupation zone and was therefore beyond the jurisdiction of Mainz's planners. The citizens of Mainz simply wanted to return to the city they knew and to some sense of normalcy. They did not want to wait or make sacrifices for the realization of this utopian scheme.

Mayor Emil Kraus and official town planner Erich Petzold sought to undermine Lods by calling in Paul Schmitthenner, Petzold's teacher, to draft an alternative plan. Schmitthenner was pleased to do so, but no sooner had he begun working than Adolf Bayer persuaded the French to demand Petzold's dismissal in November 1946 and to install Richard Jörg as his replacement. Jörg was not enthusiastic about the Lods plan, but he also apparently feared Schmitthenner and prevented him from presenting to the public his ideas for the reconstruction of Mainz, which were in any event limited to the old center. Schmitthenner repeatedly criticized the Lods proposal as utopian and unrealizable, although he agreed with some of Lods's traffic planning schemes and would have permitted the building of skyscrapers on the outskirts of the city.

Petzold castigated Lods in criticisms published in March 1948, arguing that the French design would lead to "the unrestrained organization, mechanization, depersonalization, and collectivization of our lives." Shortly thereafter, the city council soundly rejected the Lods plan.[82] Aware of the impending cessation of the military occupation, the French authorities made no attempt to force the city to accept the Lods plan, and Marcel Lods left Mainz in April. Bayer went to work for the city planning office in May, and he collaborated for two years with Jörg on plans for parts of the city. In 1950 Bayer left to become the planner in Offenbach, and in 1952 Jörg moved to Mannheim. Years elapsed before their successors introduced a new set of general plans for Mainz.

Neither the Scharoun/Kollektiv plans for Berlin nor Lods's plans for Mainz—both calling for radically modern ribbon cities—were implemented. Instead, both cities turned to more conservative, more practical approaches that were also far less comprehensive. The resulting partial planning of Mainz and Berlin thus resembled that of most other West German cities.

Reconstruction plans at the other end of the spectrum sought to conserve as much as possible of the prewar city center. The first maxim of the conservative approach dictated retaining the historic street pattern, the *Grundriß*. Another tenet advocated retaining the traditional size of building lots, particularly respecting the width of the lot on the street. Adhering to this concept would guarantee the reappearance of the traditional proportions of the damaged city, whether the new buildings were adaptive or new architecture. Conservative planners had no intention, of course, of recreating the overcrowded, unhealthy slums destroyed in the war. They therefore advocated opening up overbuilt blocks on the inside and called for some street widening. To preserve the cities' historic proportions, they sometimes introduced arcades to make space for pedestrians on widened streets.

A good example of such conservative planning is Freiburg.[83] Freiburg was bombed relatively late in the war, in a single raid on 27 November 1944. The attack destroyed one-fifth of the housing stock and many important historic monuments, mainly in the northern half of the city. The reconstruction planning of Joseph Schlippe sought to retain the romantic and charming character of the historic town. This required rebuilding major monuments in the old center and excluding large new buildings that supported "City" functions. Such government and commercial buildings might displace housing and smother the intimate life of the center. Most traffic was routed around the compact core along a new ring road fed by widened north–south streets. New hotels, banks, and office buildings would be built on the outside of the ring. Areas totally destroyed by the bombing would feature new building blocks with small gardens and open spaces in interior courtyards, which would also reduce the density of the central area. Although some streets had to be widened, the center's historic street pattern remained unchanged. Fourteen percent of the built-up area of the Altstadt was lost to streets during rebuilding. The planning office appointed architects to consult on the rebuilding of each block, and once construction was finished, most property owners could return to their previous locations.

If Freiburg typified conservative planning for a relatively small city—as did Nuremberg and Münster—Cologne provides an interesting example of conservative planning for a major city with a very large historic Altstadt. From early 1946 until 1952, reconstruction planning in Cologne was directed by Rudolf Schwarz. Among postwar planners, Schwarz was unusual in two ways. First, he continued an active architectural practice in and outside of Cologne. Second, while most planners saw their task in urgent, practical terms, Schwarz tended to philosophize about urban life and the modern world, and his thinking was always shaped by his strong Catholicism.

Though as an architect and church builder he was always considered more of a modernist than a traditionalist, he had begun to question modernist principles already by 1932, when he wrote:

> In the nineteenth century one built bourgeois cities, from which evolved the sinister economic cities with their laughable skyscrapers, administrative palaces, and comical traffic problems, cities as cults of salesmanship, built for men for whom everything was venal, everything saleable . . . . But that is already now past. At this moment, when the East has announced the dictatorship of labor and introduced the cult of the machine, that seems to us as the introduction of our own outdated proposals.[84]

After the war, Schwarz hoped to build cities in a new society, a socialist society dedicated to doing God's will and righting injustice.[85]

Town planning, he believed, was "not a matter of science but of history, an act done in a historical moment and in a given historical situation."[86] "Therefore every work should foresee its own reversability. *A good plan must build in the dynamic of history which will someday overcome it* . . . . To know that is good, because it means that there is no objectivity. . . . Pure objectivity would be the death of a historical movement."[87] Moreover, the town planner knows "that in order to remain fruitful, history needs an unused stock of chaos, and he incorporates this chaos in his own planning . . . . He gives this chaos space, enormous free space, and he also allows space for contradictions in his plans and in his own soul, and he concludes his proposal in an act of audaciously humble trust in the eternally unplannable."[88]

This perspective and language made Schwarz a sought-after speaker and essayist, but turning his ideas into concrete planning for Cologne sometimes proved more difficult. His plans for Cologne derived from his wartime work in Lorraine. Schwarz argued that previous planners had been blind to the fact that there were now two standards for planning. The first was the human body itself; the second, technology, emanated from the human mind. With machines humanity had succeeded in doubling itself, and the living environment now must accommodate not simply humanity but humanity and their machines. Cities must therefore be double cities.[89] Hence the new Cologne should not be a radial or circular city with a single core but rather a curved ribbon city, shaped by the natural landscape of the Rhine basin and developed around two poles. The historic Altstadt would dominate the south, and a new garden city housing some 300,000 people who worked in nearby industrial plants would characterize the north. The new pole in the north, Schwarz

argued, should become a true, independent urban center, but it would be false
to expect older suburbs, like Marienburg to the south, whose inhabitants had
always commuted into the Altstadt to work or to use cultural facilities, to
function independently of the historic center.[90]

The plan for a new city center to the north shares many of the features of
the radical plans of Scharoun and Lods, though in marked contrast to Lods,
Schwarz strongly preferred single-family row houses to apartment towers.
Schwarz was deeply committed to living in greenery. He wrote that as a
prisoner of war he discovered the desire for a house with its own garden was
the "only" thing that alleviated the "suffering and deprivations" of his fellow
prisoners and penetrated "the inner hearts of these disillusioned men."
Schwarz also noted the extraordinary number of truck gardens maintained by
Cologne residents. Even during times of economic prosperity, perhaps one-
fourth of the city's families nurtured such gardens, though they often had to
go a long distance to work in them.[91] In April 1947, in preparation for the visit
of the Lord Mayor of Birmingham, Schwarz indicated his intention to build
many new small suburbs consisting of single-family homes or duplexes with
gardens, all the while admitting that this might seem utopian when only 40
new buildings were in fact planned for the city for all of 1947. Nevertheless,
Schwarz believed that such garden settlements were essential for the working
class. In addition to enabling the workers to "plant for themselves necessary
vegetables, fruit, and flowers," "this beautiful, meaningful activity" would
encourage their children to "learn and prepare themselves for a life that
would have a more valuable content than that of the life of a worker currently
living in a great city." Schwarz expected "eventually to transplant the greater
part of the working population into such new settlements."[92] His sketch of the
new city closely resembles the proposals for "organic" cities produced by
Hans Bernhard Reichow.

In contrast to his garden settlement plans, Schwarz's ideas for the old city
center were markedly conservative. He felt that the old city should support
both residential and cultural functions. People should reside in single-family
homes, not in rental barracks or "termite piles."[93] Homes should be small, not
"freestanding villas in large parks, but rather like our parents' homes: three-
story row houses with terraces looking toward the small gardens in the rear."[94]
The houses themselves need not adhere to any traditional architectural style,
but the proportions must remain traditional.[95] The old city quarters, which
Schwarz imagined as peaceful parishes, would comprise the fundamental units
of the reconstructed Altstadt. A rebuilt church would be the dominant architectural feature as well as the moral heart of each quarter. And "we want to keep
the comfortable smallness of the traditional old streets. Otherwise they will no
longer be what they were but instead traffic will rush through them."[96] Additionally, the Griechenmarkt quarter should be rebuilt as a model of inner-city
housing.

To fulfill its status as a *Hochstadt,* a central place for worship, culture,
administration, and commerce, the old city should be divided into different
quarters in which these functions should be concentrated.[97] Like the curving

ribbon city, this idea of the Hochstadt carried over from Schwarz's wartime planning. He categorically refused to consider reconstructing the large buildings of Stübben's age, arguing instead that the architecture of the late nineteenth century should disappear.

Only by retaining the historic street pattern and the small size of traditional building lots could this rebuilt Altstadt serve as a Hochstadt and as a residential area.[98] Although this would effectively shield the quarters from excess traffic, something still had to be done about traffic through the center. Schwarz dismissed the two 72-meter-wide axes planned by the Nazis as the result of "an embarrassing predilection for the schematic and an equally fatal aversion to reality." Such axes would grossly undermine the proportions of the small streets and homes. He had to admit, however, that 72 meters was not too wide if one wanted to accommodate streetcars, autos, parking spaces, and bicyclists.[99] Cologne needed traffic arteries, but Schwarz felt that roads only 18 meters wide would suffice. The streets carrying most of the traffic should clearly separate individual city quarters from each other but not destroy them. Inside each quarter one should be able to get everywhere by foot. Schwarz also wanted to remove the other main disruptive transportation medium—the railroad—from the inner city. Like all planners before him, he wanted to move the main train station away from the cathedral to a location outside the Ring.

In spite of conceding that some wider streets were needed to serve as north–south and east–west traffic arteries, Schwarz's plans for the old city in many respects embodied a wish to return Cologne to a quieter, preindustrial city. The new Cologne should arise out of the city's earlier history.[100] When the first version of the reconstruction plan was finished, Schwarz wrote to Mies van der Rohe:

> We have finished the general planning for Cologne, but it is something which the representatives of determined modernism will presumably abhor. As I see again and again, I am basically a very conservative man for whom it is ever more difficult to believe in the visions of some of our modern friends. . . . In Cologne one cannot, like some of the idealists of modern building believe, toss everything together and rebuild according to some abstract new plan. Thus in essence my planning has become ultraconservative, which also draws the stormy approval of our population.[101]

Though his ideas enjoyed broad popular approval, they were only partly realized. Schwarz was bitterly disappointed. Upon leaving office in 1952, he wrote to the mayor: "Our planning in my eyes has remained at least a 50% failure, since I began it in the high hope of a new social order, one which would give also the little man, deprived of his rights, a place in the sun. Nothing has come of this, and what remains is that later automobiles will be able to drive better through our city."[102] Schwarz blamed the failure to fully implement his plans on uncooperative officials in other agencies, inadequate planning and building laws, and the financial problems of the city caused by the currency reform of 1948. This view was shared by his successor, Eduard Pecks, though it was Schwarz's abrasive personality as much as anything which undermined his position as Cologne's planner and thereby prevented fuller realization of his ideas for the reconstruction of the city.[103]

Although the old street pattern was essentially preserved, the north–south and east–west arteries were built significantly wider than Schwarz had wanted. They became, in fact, jarring discontinuities in the city fabric which current planners are now struggling to eradicate. In spite of years of negotiations, the train station remained by the cathedral.[104] The old city is hardly a haven of single-family homes, but reconstruction did rid the city of the nineteenth-century style of rental barracks. There are far too few parishioners to invest the rebuilt churches with enough energy to become viable foci for the inner-city districts. Needless to say, the dream of a socialist society carrying out God's will remains unfulfilled. The Altstadt does serve as a Hochstadt, with the cathedral, a new opera house, museums, the town hall, the buildings of the West German radio and television network, and numerous buildings housing major banks and insurance companies. The Griechenmarkt-Viertel was not completed until the second half of the 1950s, too late to serve as the model intended by Schwarz.[105] The new residential settlements were built to the north, but more as suburbs rather than as an autonomous urban center, and this area utterly fails to function as a second pole in a double-centered ribbon city.

Despite Schwarz's partial success in Cologne, conservative planners enjoyed far more success than radical planners in implementing their ideas because the conservative approach generated considerable popular support. The conservative plans did not threaten to overturn all property relations and promised to preserve the traditional image of the city—so fundamental to the personal identities of the inhabitants. Conservative planning was particularly successful in smaller cities, and, as seen, less so in larger, more dynamic cities like Cologne.

Pragmatic Planning

Only a small number of cities contemplated clearly radical or conservative approaches to reconstruction planning. Most favored pragmatic approaches that tended to advocate modernizing cities rather than recreating them in their prewar forms.[106] Planners compromised and struggled to accommodate both the wishes of the citizenry for rapid rebuilding of the city in its historic form and the planners' dreams of structurally modernizing the city according to the models endorsed by the profession. As Rudolf Hillebrecht once commented, town planning was the "art of the possible."[107]

What was possible for the city centers was pursuing the policy of decongestion on the one hand and developing a street system better able to handle the demands of motorized traffic on the other.[108] Massive destruction and the subsequent depopulation of the central areas had already initiated the process of reducing densities; planners sought to make that change permanent. They attempted to control new housing construction in outlying areas, promote residential garden settlements and healthy new neighborhoods, and guard against new slums built by speculators. At the same time, they designed new blocks of buildings for the inner cities with fewer residences and more open space in the interiors. As seen in an earlier chapter, they often encouraged social housing as a means of achieving these aims. They also initiated policies of voluntary or mandated consolidation of property parcels, which will be considered in subsequent chapters.

The policy of decongestion, at least in the first 15 years, was carried through with considerable success. In 1885, for example, 57,588 persons lived inside the walls in Nuremberg's Altstadt. Thereafter the Altstadt's population declined to some 45,000 people. With reconstruction, the population of the Altstadt dropped still further to only about 20,000. The number of workers in the central area had decreased significantly, presumably in response to a decline in the number of employers. Of the Altstadt's 3,807 buildings in 1939, some 69% belonged to private individuals and 43% were occupied by owners. In 1969, there were only 1,694 buildings in the Altstadt; 72% of them were owned by private individuals but only half as many were occupied by owners. There were fewer but now much larger building lots, making it possible for social housing corporations but also for enterprises like department store chains to build large buildings.[109] The trends for Munich are similar. In 1871, some 50,000 people, or 30% of the population, lived in the center. In 1933, about 33,000, or 4%, remained. In 1956, only 16,000 people, 1.7% of the population, lived in the center, a figure unchanged since 1945.[110] Reconstruction, therefore, reinforced a process that had begun before the war and was greatly accelerated by the bombing.

The cities of Kiel and Aachen aptly demonstrate the process and implementation of pragmatic planning by German cities. In Kiel, pragmatic, progressive reconstruction planning went relatively smoothly and quickly. Herbert Jensen, head of Kiel's building and planning office since 1935, had worked on reconstruction planning for the city during the war, and he saw his work as a continuation of the planning of the 1920s and early 1930s. This earlier planning emphasized decongestion of the central area, better functional zoning, and the construction of new residential garden suburbs.[111] The site of important war industries, particularly shipbuilding, Kiel had rapidly expanded prior to 1939. After the war, the Allies dismantled or demolished virtually all of the war-related industrial plants that had survived the bombing, in effect cutting off the city's major source of economic well-being. However, because large numbers of refugees settled in Schleswig-Holstein, the city's population quickly reached prewar levels.

Jensen realized that Kiel's viability required a reorientation of the city toward other purposes. Small and medium nonmilitary industry had to be encouraged to provide employment. The central area needed to be rebuilt as an attractive site for the new state government, the university, and commerce. The first general plan was ready in May 1946. While the plans were being drawn up, rubble was being cleared and used as fill to widen the shore along the harbor, and land parcels which had been more or less cleared were planted with grass and shrubbery. In 1948, a design competition was staged to solicit ideas for a new street layout.[112] Konstanty Gutschow and Hans Bernhard Reichow were among those submitting entries. As always, Reichow called for organic planning, meaning the utilization of the natural topography, the creation of a green area in the center and parks along the shore, "cell-like neighborhoods" of new housing sited in greenery, and the opening up of densely built inner-city blocks.[113]

By 1949, Jensen had completed a reconstruction plan for the bombed area. It called for major street changes, including creating a new artery that would run from the north side of the train station to a widened Holstenbrücke Straße (from 16 to 40 meters) and then north over the widened Bergstraße and Holtenauer Straße. This artery would carry much traffic through the city, with bypass roads on the outskirts for vehicles that wanted to avoid the center. A row of single-story shops was built along the Holtenauer Straße, with multistory apartment buildings erected at right angles to the street, a design that was intended both to reduce street noise in the apartments and to provide space between the apartments for greenery. Space was also left in the central area for parks. Building lots were to be consolidated to allow more rationalized construction and open up the interiors of blocks. The key to realization of the Kiel plan was the largely voluntary cooperation of property owners in redrawing the land parcels.[114]

In all, Jensen saw the plan as an attempt to create a Stadtlandschaft, an urban landscape.[115] It is not surprising that Jensen's reconstruction plan, which was steadily implemented, enjoyed wide praise from other planners. Roland Rainer, for example, saw Kiel's reconstruction as an example of "progressive urban planning, based on the findings of modern planning theory, which does not disappoint but rather fulfills or perhaps even exceeds the great expectations of 1945."[116]

Aachen's pragmatic reconstruction planning was the work of Wilhelm Fischer, the third person to assume responsibility for planning after the fighting ended. The first was the architect Hans Schwippert, whom the Americans appointed after they seized the city in the fall of 1944. Though primarily concerned with the urgent need to repair housing and revive services in the badly damaged city, Schwippert also drafted a preliminary outline of ideas for rebuilding.[117] He called for reducing the density of the central city, introducing greenery, and improving traffic conditions by widening the existing three concentric rings around the center. Schwippert placed great importance on restoring the thermal baths as the city's economic focus, and he also argued that, in contrast to prevailing planning theory, it was not necessary to relocate all of the city's textile industry to areas zoned purely for industry because this industry did not produce a lot of dirt and noise.

In 1945, Karl van der Leyden was made head of the city building office, and he turned planning over to Professor R. von Schöfer of the Technical University, who apparently did very little. Hence, in February 1948, a new planning office was created, and Wilhelm Fischer, an assistant to von Schöfer at the university, was given a contract to direct reconstruction planning. Fischer remained an independent architect outside the city government, however, until van der Leyden's retirement at the end of 1956, at which point Fischer finally became a city official.[118]

Fischer clearly saw his job in practical terms. In 1953, he argued that "it would be absurd in Aachen's planning to want to corset the city's body in purely theoretical ideas. All of these ideas—satellite cities, the city of quarters, the ribbon city—are purely theories for theory's sake and are dangerous."[119] "Uninfluenced and undiverted by the arguments of the many theoreticians of urban planning," Fischer instead sought to produce plans that could be implemented, although, like planners elsewhere, he saw the destruction as an opportunity to cure the ills of a city that had grown too rapidly at the turn of the century.[120]

The medieval city of Aachen had grown around the ancient cathedral. As it grew, three rings of defensive walls had been built and then torn down and turned into streets—the last in the nineteenth century. Located in a natural basin only five kilometers from the border with Holland and Belgium, Aachen had expanded primarily toward the east in the nineteenth and twentieth centuries, in the direction of Germany and the Rhine, and the thermal baths and textile and metal finishing industries had formed the basis of the economy. By 1939, the population had expanded to 162,000. In September 1944, forced evacuation to the east had reduced the population to a mere 3,000, but by the fall of 1946 it had rebounded to 110,000 and by the fall of 1952 had reached 140,000.

Population density had always been highest in the central core. Whereas the prewar average for the whole city had been 387 persons per hectare, the most crowded areas housed over 700 persons per hectare. Fischer sought to reduce the average density to 335 and the maximum in the center to 500, with densities of only 200 per hectare in the suburbs. This required the relocation of some 15,000 persons—over 10% of the population—to new residential settlements, of which Fischer planned 16.[121] He also planned to improve living conditions by relocating most industry to areas zoned for that purpose and creating new green areas. For 2 such green areas, 18 parcels of land in the hands of 9 different owners were scheduled for expropriation by the city.[122]

Improvements in the street network were also needed. In 1939, there had been one motor vehicle for every 19.1 persons in the city. In 1952, there were 18.6 persons per vehicle, but Fischer predicted that the future would see 8 to 10 persons per vehicle, a level that would choke the old streets.[123] On the one hand, Fischer favored preserving the historic Grundriß, the layout of the streets. Except for the most important monuments, the war had destroyed virtually all of the important domestic and secular architecture, and he encouraged architecture that emulated traditional proportions, colors, forms, and materials, while maintaining that the "face" of the city existed primarily in the Grundriß.[124] On the other hand, he also had to acknowledge a "certain primacy" of traffic planning. "Only where the structure of a city is perceivable from the clear order [of the street network] is orientation possible and the growth of identification [Heimatgefühl] with one's town guaranteed. Only through the separation of superior and subordinate traffic arteries is it possible to create this order."[125]

Fischer argued against approaching traffic planning as an end in itself. A functional street system should make the city more livable for people, not machines. It better suited human character that streets, even major arteries, bend and curve rather than follow a perfectly linear path. Bends in a street, squares, and intersections of differing sizes created new visual perspectives. To implement the desired improvements in the street system, Fischer planned 78 projects, most of which involved widening old streets from 2 to 30 meters.[126] He also planned north–south and east–west arteries through the city, though these were to be tangent to the ring roads and not run through the center.

All in all, this reconstruction plan avoided radical changes in the structure of the city while seeking to "heal" the ills of earlier decades through the application of the basic principles to which all contemporary planners subscribed. Fischer's reconstruction planning for Aachen was unsentimental and straightforward, and it won both official and public approval.

Traffic Planning

Traffic planning was central to the radical plans for Mainz and Berlin, the conservative plans for Freiburg and Cologne, and the pragmatic plans of cities like Aachen and Kiel. Often traffic planning took precedence over other planning goals. It would be possible to present an almost unending list of citations in which major planners proclaimed that traffic planning formed the heart, the *Kernstück*, of their efforts.[127] The following two examples demonstrate the preoccupation with traffic. Karl Josef Erbs published a book on planning principles in 1948, in which he cited a statement—highly critical of the prevalent attitude toward traffic, but accurate—by the pioneer planner Karl Henrici: "The Lord Traffic, a twin of capitalism and main representative of materialism, has soared to a world-ruling position, has seized for itself science and technology, has changed from servant to master. Its name need only be pronounced and the whole world swoons in devotion and makes way, so that it can set forth unhindered on its favorite chosen path."[128] Similarly, Herbert Jensen, the planner of Kiel, declared that "if the old cities are or should be part of a modern city, then they have to be appropriately opened up in terms of traffic or they will remain or become limited in their economic value. There are always enough closed off 'islands' of sufficient size for historic reminiscences and historic preservation."[129] In a 1953 address to the German Academy for Town and Regional Planning entitled "The Competition between Traffic and City Planning," Jensen stated: "To be a junction and assembly point of traffic, that is, to serve the exchange of goods, money, labor, ideas, and culture—that was the original and is today still the task of cities. . . . Traffic is for the city's body the life-giving flow of blood, the streets are the arteries. . . . We live in an age of traffic. Traffic is trump; we live in fact in an intoxication, an ecstasy of traffic, and of motorized traffic at that."[130]

The tone of these statements resonates throughout postwar planning dialogues. Planners saw traffic as absolutely essential to urban viability. Appropriate traffic patterns not only brought life to cities; they sustained that life by functioning as clear, pulsating arteries in which the energizing force of metropolitan areas circulated. The dominance of traffic over other aspects of city life was incontestable, and planners necessarily accorded traffic considerations the highest priority.

The term artery had long been used in describing traffic flow. It derives from the depiction of the growth of cities in organic terms and fit perfectly with the model of the natural, living city, featuring abundant greenery and residential "cells." As the planners clearly realized, major motorways were destined to form an essential part of the urban landscape in the machine age.[131] As noted previously, thesis 77 of the Charter of Athens declared that planning must focus on a city's four essential functions: housing, work, recreation, and finally traffic—the system that linked the other three functions together.

In confronting the key issue of traffic, planners in several cities, such as Munich, Stuttgart, Cologne, and Hamburg, hoped to relocate main railroad stations in order to increase their capacity and ease surrounding motor traffic. Some suggested excavating bombed-out areas to bury the tracks, but none of these ideas was ever acted upon because the state railroad was autonomous and therefore impervious to local town planning. Rail authorities entertained their own ideas and priorities and saw no compelling need to move rail lines, although they welcomed improvements to access roads and the area in front of a train station.

For city planners, then, traffic planning meant street planning, and they hoped to create what Hans Bernard Reichow later called "die autogerechte Stadt," the automobile-ready city.[132] After the war planners and citizens welcomed the growth of automobile traffic as a sign of vitality, recovery, and normalcy. The old, inner cities required changes to accommodate this new energy, and streets were often widened even though such work frequently entailed removing historic facades, demolishing potentially restorable damaged buildings, undercutting facades to create arcades for pedestrians, and appropriating former sidewalk space for roads or parking. In addition to street widening, the city centers usually needed new streets cut through formerly built-up areas. New traffic arteries formed from these *Durchbrüche* can be found in Düsseldorf (Berliner Allee), Cologne (Nord–Süd-Fahrt), and Hamburg (Ost–West-Straße), to name but three well-known examples. Since these new arteries sounded all too much like the great ceremonial streets planned by the Nazis, planners often went to great lengths to assure that these new roads were built to efficiently move *traffic* not marching hoards, and that they were absolutely not intended to serve as "representative" streets. Unlike the Nazi *Prachtstraßen*, which were to be lined with massive neoclassical buildings, the architecture on these postwar arteries was not considered important.

Finally, the inner cities would be surrounded by high-capacity ring roads. Feeder streets might come in from the suburbs like spokes of a wheel, or they might join the rings on tangents, reducing the number of crossings. Vehicles crossing the city to connect with points outside the city would normally be kept out of the inner city, confined to the Autobahns or ring systems. Some through traffic would, however, still cross the inner city on the new *Durchbruchstraßen*, because the economic health of the Altstadt required that it not be an isolated island. Planners expected that this redirection and channeling of traffic would relieve congestion in the inner cities and make life easier for pedestrians. Improved traffic conditions, along with a more functional layout of the city (i.e., relocation of industry) and better housing, would revitalize inner cities.

Hannover, Hamburg, Lübeck, Düsseldorf, Stuttgart, and Munich illustrate the main thrust of postwar traffic planning. In all of these cities, planners chiefly used a technical rather than architectonic approach in their work, though the ease in implementing their ideas varied somewhat from city to city. Munich, for example, did not always grant technical traffic planning top priority, although it did consider street construction vital.

Of all of Germany's bombed cities, postwar Hannover long enjoyed the reputation of being a model of progressive reconstruction planning. The high reputation of both the city and its planner Rudolf Hillebrecht rested on the remarkable cooperation between citizens and the planning department, a model inner-city housing project, but chiefly on Hannover's traffic planning. In early 1948, the first postwar planner, Otto Meffert, submitted a plan that called for relieving through traffic by creating a double ring road, with part of the inner ring running along the west side of the Leine River. Several plans drawn up by a team led by Hans Högg at the Technical University kept variations of Meffert's rings but also advocated redesigning the Steintorplatz and widening the Georgstraße to facilitate traffic flow through the city. Shortly after Hillebrecht's appointment to succeed Meffert in mid-1948, still another team of independent architects and officials set to work on a plan, one which retained some of the features of the earlier plans but called for enlarging the outer ring and having tangents rather than radial streets serve as feeders. (This feature resembled Karl Elkart's 1944 proposal.)[133]

Another source of planning ideas was the Aufbaugemeinschaft Hannover, a private organization formed by owners of inner-city property. For this organization Konstanty Gutschow prepared a lengthy technical analysis of the history of the inner city, of its likely future development, and of the various traffic plans prepared to date. Finally, Hillebrecht organized a public competition to solicit ideas for the redesign of the inner city. The competition addressed a number of issues, including land use and questions of form (*städtebauliche Gestaltung*), but traffic considerations weighed most heavily.[134] After analyzing and reviewing all of these sources, the planning office drew up final street plans in collaboration with the Tiefbauamt (in charge of actual street construction) and a representative of the Technical University's planning department. Hillebrecht mediated the proceedings.

The result was a concept of Hannover, now the capital of the Land of Lower Saxony, as the hub of a large region. Traffic would flow easily to and from the city, but not through the inner city. Instead it would use the new system of rings and tangents. The tangent and radial streets, like the Lavesallee, would curve, in contrast to the linear axes planned by the Nazis. To further divert high levels of traffic from the inner city, skyscrapers could be built only outside the inner ring, and buildings inside the ring could not exceed the proportions typical of the historic core, a decision based partly on technical and partly on aesthetic grounds. Streets in the Altstadt were widened enough to facilitate the traffic that did flow through the inner city and leave open the possibility of a subway system. Planners provided for a pedestrian shopping street (not a pedestrian zone, a concept of the 1960s) and for some mingling of functions to ensure that the inner city did not become a purely administrative, cultural, or shopping center. It was quite important that people still live in the Altstadt, although under modern conditions.[135] Hillebrecht not only won approval for his ideas from the city government, but he also successfully sold his ideas to the citizenry. Consequently, planning and actual construction moved at a pace that earned the envy and admiration of planners from other cities.[136]

In many ways Hamburg's new traffic planning followed the wartime planning for the city's redesign as Hitler's representative port. A 1940 competition for the design of an east–west axis on the southern edge of the inner city along the Elbe was repeated in 1948, with some of the same architects submitting proposals. Building director Otto Meyer-Ottens argued insistently that this artery would serve traffic and not parades of "brown battalions or victorious armies," like the Nazi axes. He added, "We also do not want people to have to live on these traffic arteries as we are planning them. It is systematic murder for the individual resident every day to have to experience and put up with the smell, noise, and dirt of a major artery."[137] In fact the function of the new street, carrying a high volume of traffic, varied very little from that of the wartime plans.

Other key features included a new bridge alongside the old Lombardsbrücke over the Alster, a new tunnel under the Elbe in about the same place that Hitler had wanted to build a great bridge (postwar Hamburg rejected a bridge as too expensive), and improvements to the road along the old city wall. Altona's old train station was to remain, but the planners recommended that the land that would have been used in the Nazi-era plans to build a new flow-through train station be left as an open green area in the event that future needs warranted a new station.[138] The purpose of all this, as Otto Sill, the later director of the Tiefbauamt put it, was "high-capacity roadways and generously and lucidly designed squares for traffic."[139]

In Lübeck, a number of experts presented their ideas for the reconstruction of the inner city and particularly for traffic planning.[140] Almost all of the suggestions for Lübeck's reconstruction began with the premise that the bombing provided a unique opportunity to widen streets, improve traffic flow, and generally open up the city. Lübeck was one of the few old Hansa cities in which both the old street pattern and a large number of very old merchant houses had survived into the twentieth century. Moreover, the old city was built on an island in the Trave River, and that island had best suited long-distance traffic crossing the river, which resulted in severe congestion. Stadt-baudirektor E. Weise noted in February 1943 that the city would expand upon plans under way since 1940 that called for widening certain streets (Breite-straße, Mühlenstraße, Beckergrube, Kanalstraße, Holstenstraße, Wahm-straße, Krähenstraße) to 20–25 meters. These widened streets would form arteries capable of carrying a substantial volume of north–south and east–west traffic. The project would require the demolition of from 480 to 700 linear meters of housefronts *in addition* to what had already been destroyed in the bombing. The resulting streets, however, would not be straight axes. Indeed, planners were advised to avoid "rigid linearity in street lines" in favor of curves and changing perspectives.[141]

In a preliminary essay in 1943, Hans Pieper spoke out even more strongly for change. He observed that Altstadt streets were too narrow; some side-walks were only 0.7 meter wide. "Today's traffic," he asserted, "demands exactly the opposite: evenness, breadth, and clarity in the traffic system. This must be said once and for all." Moreover, *"under all circumstances parking places must be created in the Altstadt."*[142] Pieper saw reconstruction of the bombed old city as an opportunity for introducing desperately needed modern improvements to the street system, and this perspective informed his full-scale reconstruction study published posthumously in 1946.[143] Hans Pieper's work was systematic and highly technical, and it accorded traffic planning, rather than the reconstruction of historic Lübeck, the top priority.

The priority of function over form is also clearly present in the reconstruc-tion proposal begun in 1944 and finally submitted by Friedrich Tamms to the city in 1947. Arguing for a "regeneration" of the old city, Tamms asserted that reconstruction had to be premised on a clear sense of Lübeck's economic and sociological nature and a realization that traffic was the "vita activa" of the city.[144] To be sure, an ideal solution to Lübeck's traffic problems was probably beyond reach, since it would require several new and prohibitively expensive high bridges to route most through traffic around the Altstadt. Moreover, such bridges would not necessarily be a good idea for Lübeck, since the economic health of the city depended partly on the handling of freight going through it. Finally, Lübeck's proximity to the border of the Soviet zone raised uncertainties about what would happen to the city's former eastern hinter-land. Hence widening streets and improving traffic flow in the Altstadt seemed preferable to and far more practical than erecting bridges. Planners observed that wider, newer streets have a natural advantage over old, narrow ones because they greatly ease traffic flow and increase parking space. "That is a fact, which in the future cannot be estimated too highly."[145] The indepen-dent architect Emil Steffann considered historic preservation the top priority and called for creating a traffic-free historic zone around the Marienkirche and the town hall. In criticizing this proposal, Tamms denigrated Steffann's plan as "a graphic plan; that is, he starts with an image, with a firm opinion, instead of with a study of the real forces in urban life, from which alone the true form can be developed. . . . Everything else is just decorative planning, graphics; that is, they ignore what is actually alive."[146]

For some time after Hans Pieper's death, Lübeck's planning decisions were in a kind of limbo. Pieper's successor, Georg Münter from Wismar, was not hired until September 1947, and it took some time for him to establish himself in office. The building administration continued to work on the technical aspects of planning, while public debate focused on the Steffann plan, which enjoyed the support of conservative citizens, who generally opposed any major alterations in the Altstadt. This conservative position got a major boost in November 1947, when Heinrich Tessenow submitted his reflections on Lübeck's reconstruction.[147] Tessenow was very pessimistic about *any* real solution to the traffic problems of major cities, including Lübeck. Widening old streets or cutting through new ones, all at great expense and entailing the loss of much historic substance, could only make traffic flow "at best no better than *approximately* good, *approximately* fluid." Old buildings were unquestionably of value, he admitted, but one nonetheless had to admit their inadequacy in fulfilling modern functions. Traffic conditions had to be improved, but it was likely that in 50 years the magnitude of traffic would exceed all expectations and render current solutions obsolete. Consequently, Tessenow recommended that bombed areas be kept open and unbuilt as much as possible, so that they could be used at some future date when needs could be more realistically assessed. Meanwhile, the city should make do with a system of one-way streets that would bring some improvement at little cost.

Once Münter had taken charge, it became clear that he thought along the same lines as Pieper and Tamms. The city should be viewed as an economic organism, whose life-giving fluid was the traffic that flowed in the streets. Lübeck was not defined simply by its historic buildings, although these should not be gratuitously destroyed either. He declared:

> The spirit with which the building administration prepares a plan should be that of life itself. Economic and traffic considerations should be considered first and their requirements given form from an artistic point of view. The spirit of clarity should inform the whole, just as it informed the *ancient* city plan. The building administration has rejected the idea of designing the inner city according to "views." That would produce a false romanticism, the atmosphere of a bratwurst stand.[148]

In concrete terms, this meant that the building administration ruled out the idea of a traffic-free zone in the inner city. "Simply strangle the traffic? It is the most important function of the economy. A ban on motor vehicles in the inner city would mean the economic ruin of the inner city. The city would become a museum. That must not happen."[149] Moreover, unless most traffic used the crossing of the Breitestraße and the Wahmstraße, several other streets would have to be widened, which meant moving or demolishing several remaining old houses and housefronts. Hence it was essential that this intersection, where the Kohlmarkt bordered on the south side of the historic Marktplatz, be redesigned to increase traffic capacity. The war had destroyed the buildings along the south side of the square, and the city staged a competition to solicit suggestions for the redesign of that area. The competition pitted traffic needs against historic preservation, a contest in which traffic was bound to prevail.[150] Technically based planning, focused on traffic issues, had constituted the main thrust of reconstruction planning in Lübeck ever since the bombing and naturally continued to dominate it.

Having completed his proposal for Lübeck, Friedrich Tamms moved in 1948 to assume the position of chief city planner in Düsseldorf.[151] An expert road and bridge builder—his specialty in the 1930s—Tamms immediately broadened an existing 1947 proposal by the building office by suggesting extensive changes in the street layout, including major *Durchbrüche*. Without hesitation, he called on his former colleagues in Speer's Working Staff, Hans Dustmann and Konstanty Gutschow, for advice. Tamms wanted to make Düsseldorf a modern economic and administrative center, which required "certain corrections in the city's structure. . . . The healthy functioning of the urban economic organism will depend on it in the future. One can compare the urban organism of a city with the biological organism of a human body. . . . It would be unforgivable, especially in consideration of coming generations, if one did not use the few advantages, which the destruction offers the cities, for a general healing."[152] In contrast to Schwarz's plans for Cologne, which featured neighborhoods built around dominant church buildings, Tamms envisioned Düsseldorf as an open city in which traffic arteries, the Rhine bridges, and modern commercial towers formed the dominant architectural features.

In Düsseldorf, as in other cities, some streets were to be widened, and a ring road would handle long-distance vehicles. New bridges over the Rhine were needed to funnel traffic onto tangents along the inner city. The most controversial part of Tamms's plan called for a major new artery, 45 meters wide, just east of and parallel to the Königsallee. This street, today the Berliner Allee, would route a considerable volume of traffic through the heart of the inner city. Tamms encountered opposition both from local property owners and from a vocal group of local architects, the Architektenring Düsseldorf. This latter group drew up its own plan and issued appeals for support to modernist architects in other cities and to Walter Gropius and Martin Wagner in America. The Architektenring's members opposed any increase of traffic through the city center and instead proposed a double ring system. They believed that Tamms's new "parallel street," as it was then called, would become a grand boulevard (Prachtstraße) and devalue the Königsallee. Moreover, upon considering the wartime positions of Tamms and his friends, they suspected that Tamms planned a grand axis in the Nazi style.[153]

Tamms knew, however, how to win his case. Like Hillebrecht, he had undoubtedly learned from his experiences with members of the Working Staff for Reconstruction Planning how to persuade and manipulate the public. He mounted a highly convincing exhibition of his proposals and delivered carefully prepared speeches. Road building was his specialty, and he triumphantly carried the day, brushing aside critical comments and alternative proposals submitted by concerned citizens.[154] By 1955 he could be satisfied that Düsseldorf had three main north–south and three main east–west arteries as well as broad avenues in the central business district.[155]

In Stuttgart, where traffic considerations again lay at the heart of reconstruction planning, the building office had a very difficult time selling its ideas to the public. For a time Paul Bonatz had led the planning for that city as one of Hitler's representative Nazi cities. In 1941, he prepared a major memo entitled "Stuttgart, Städtebau und Verkehrsfragen," in which he called for a new, flow-through train station closer to Bad-Cannstatt, a grand boulevard connecting the station with the old city, and a new "city" with administrative and economic functions situated between the new station and the old center, which would remain the cultural center.[156]

Some of these ideas persisted in the planning goals of postwar Stuttgart. In April 1947, a group from the Technical University under Carl Pirath prepared a general traffic plan that was largely adopted by the reconstruction office headed by Walter Hoss and submitted to the city council for approval that summer.[157] This *Verkehrsgerippeplan* called for moving the train station, but not until some future date when more resources would be available. Otherwise, the most important features of the plan advocated creating a new, high-capacity artery to the northwest of the existing train station (today the Theodor-Heuss-Straße, Friedrichstraße, Heilbronner Straße) to relieve traffic on the Königstraße and improve traffic flow in front of the train station. (This would relieve the existing bottleneck on the relatively narrow Rote Straße.) In addition, the Neckarstraße, on the southeast side of the train station and the Schloßgarten, was to be improved (part of this is called the Konrad-Adenauer-Straße today). Finally, the plan called for building an artery to connect these two streets by widening the Planie, which ran between the Neues Schloß and Altes Schloß. This required demolition of the Kronprinzenpalais, a bombed building whose facade still stood and which could have been restored. This traffic plan, it should be noted, was approved long before any general town plan was ready for discussion.

There was dissatisfaction with the *Verkehrsgerippeplan* in several quarters. The city had imposed a ban on new inner-city construction while planning was under way, and property owners, eager to start building, became increasingly angry as the planning process dragged on. Property owners were also unhappy about the amount of land that might be expropriated for street construction. Many citizens protested what they considered an excessive modernization of their city and decried the building administration's tendency toward arrogance and secrecy.[158] Conservationists naturally objected to the demolition of the Kronprinzenpalais. In support of the conservative view, art historian Hans Fegers, a member of the reconstruction advisory council, warned that although it would be "irresponsible to neglect today's tasks out of historical considerations and interests," it would be equally disturbing if "in many places pure traffic questions are obviously accorded a superior place to archi-

tectonic form. I want to state very strongly," he continued, "that the architectonic form of our cities should not only, and not even in the first instance be
made dependent on considerations of traffic needs."[159] Even Bonatz, when
asked for his opinion, eventually abandoned some of his earlier views and
favored rebuilding the Kronprinzenpalais and using one-way streets to solve
the traffic problem.[160]

Hoss's position was that Stuttgart had to rebuild as a modern city, not one
tied to a romanticized past. "We must think like modern men and seek a vital
connection between content and form. . . . I do not believe that we need
musty and narrow passages like closed-in Italian cities. We do not want to
look into a fairyland around every corner. Our sense of life demands free and
open spaces, filled with air and light—which are in any case self-evident
demands of modern city planning."[161] Hoss and his supporters eventually
prevailed, and the new traffic network was constructed, but the debate left a
residue of bitter feelings about reconstruction planning in Stuttgart.

The clearest statement of Munich's planning priorities was published by
Karl Meitinger. Meitinger had been the city's regular planner throughout the
Nazi period. During those years, however, the planning process had been
dominated by the special office of Hermann Giesler, who had been charged
by Hitler with the redesign of Munich as the capital city of the Nazi movement. Though in effect shunted aside, Meitinger worked on reconstruction
planning on his own, and he was able to produce a polished proposal shortly
after Munich's city government began to function again after the war's end.

Believing that architecture was more important than purely technical considerations of traffic flow, Meitinger declined to make traffic planning the top
priority for the historic city core. In his quest to reestablish Munich's status as
a center for arts and tourism, he argued that the central area must not be
overrun by automobiles.[162] He limited traffic improvements to the ring streets
around the inner core and the radial streets leading into the city. Grand axes
were to be avoided: "One thing must be said; problems about huge Durchbrüche and the creation of monumental axes in Munich did not exist before
and are not evident today."[163] Meitinger listed 16 projects for improving the
city ring, 12 for improving east–west traffic flow, 14 for north–south traffic
flow, and 20 for other improvements.[164] He advocated widening several
streets in the inner city, usually by creating arcades for pedestrians, which
freed sidewalks for streets. The most significant changes were to be in the
Angerviertel, although the central Marienplatz was also slated for widening.
Meitinger also called for moving the main train station farther away from the
central city.

Concern for pedestrians also was at the heart of proposals made by Adolf
Abel of Munich's Technical University. In 1947 he suggested the creation of a
large pedestrian zone extending north from the Marienplatz. He wanted pedestrians, not motor vehicles, to dominate the old city center; hence a pedestrian
plan must accompany any plans for motorized traffic. Indeed, Abel advocated
hollowing out many of the old building blocks and transforming them into
pedestrian shopping areas which were totally isolated from traffic.[165]

After Meitinger retired, responsibility for reconstruction was divided between the planning office under Hermann Leitenstorfer and a new office for reconstruction, headed first by Karl Sebastian Preis and then by Helmut Fischer. Leitenstorfer was more architect than planner; Preis and Fischer were by nature technicians. As a result of the friction between these men and the conflicting jurisdictions, Meitinger's plan surfaced as the unofficial guideline for reconstruction. An architectonic rather than technical approach thus remained the norm for inner-city traffic planning, as can be seen in the 1949–50 debate about redesigning the Marienplatz.

Both Leitenstorfer and Fischer wanted to aid traffic flow by widening the square with arcades and tearing down the ruins of the medieval town hall, which blocked the eastern end of the square. In this case both cited technical rather than architectonic arguments in support of this plan. In a statement to the city council, Leitenstorfer asserted that "above all the necessity of designing the square in view of modern traffic conditions means that it can no longer be viewed as a medieval square."[166] In a rather bizarre exaggeration, Fischer commented: "In the beginning was the street, and everything else came later. Without the street there would be no Munich."[167] Because the overall sense of inner-city planning endorsed the preservation of the historic Gestalt, however, the majority of the entries in the competition for the redesign of the square called for the reconstruction of the old town hall. The public and the city council agreed, and the two planners were forced to abandon their technically conceived solution to traffic flow through the Marienplatz, although many of the other suggestions for improving the street patterns made by Meitinger, Fischer, and other planners, were ultimately implemented, including the ring road around the inner city.

Among the consequences of traffic planning, there is no doubt that widening streets and creating new arteries resulted in a considerable loss of historical substance: damaged buildings that could have been restored were torn down, and the character of others was radically changed by the opening up of space around them. In retrospect, since many of these street alterations proved inadequate and were subsequently abandoned in favor of pedestrian zones, that loss seems shortsighted and costly. The debates about new traffic arteries always included discussions about retaining the historic street plan, the *Stadtgrundriß*, which, along with existing historic buildings and the historic Gestalt (height, roof line, building materials), constituted the essence of the Altstadt. As it happens, the small, twisted streets of the historic street plan proved far more amenable to conversion into pedestrian zones than did the

Hamburg, the area around the Michaeliskirche. The first photograph shows the vacant areas where bombed buildings had been cleared away and the lines drawn by the planners for an east–west artery. The second picture shows the completed artery in the 1960s. The new road clearly constituted a brutal separation of parts of the historic city core. (Source: Photo 1, Freie und Hansestadt Hamburg, Baubehörde-Lichtbildnerei, no. 6368; photo 2, Hamburg, Landesbildstelle/ SAH Plankammer 131-4/Ost53.)

broad traffic arteries that had to be abandoned when they proved incapable of
handling increasing volumes of traffic. Third, even where the Durchbrüche
still function as main traffic arteries, they have sometimes undermined the
fundamental character of the inner city. Thus, for example, Cologne's Nord–
Süd-Fahrt, Hamburg's Ost–West-Straße, and Stuttgart's Konrad-Adenauer-
Straße–Neckarstraße all constitute unpleasant breaks in the continuity of the
urban landscape. Finally, the early concentration on technical traffic planning
sometimes meant that architectural form was neglected. Hannover, for instance, has often been criticized for its undistinguished buildings, however
progressive the layout of the streets.[168]

In explaining why postwar planning activity resulted in these miscalcula-
tions, some have argued that although the concept of modern traffic planning
was basically sound, the extensive underground capital investment in sewers
and in water, power, and gas lines which survived the war relatively undamaged left responsible planners in Germany's impoverished cities no choice but
to retain most of the old street structure, even though they realized that those
streets would be inadequate to cope with future automobile traffic.[169] On the
other hand, those cities that did widen streets and create new traffic arteries
were unable to accomplish even greater modernization because state and
national legislators refused to define property rights in a way that permitted
extensive expropriations of private property.

This was a favorite complaint of the planners, and Chapter 8 addresses the
subject of new planning law. Generally, however, this complaint is not very
convincing. In fact, city planners usually succeeded in implementing new
plans that they thought would work for the postwar period and well into the
future. The difficulties of expropriation and the necessity of using existing
utilities were usually not decisive, although in some cases they may have
prevented planners from fully realizing their plans.

More important, those who oversaw reconstruction grossly underestimated both the speed of German recovery and the phenomenal growth in the
use of motor vehicles. It was common right after the war to talk about reconstruction in terms of a lengthy process spread out over two or three generations, and planners thus thought they had years and years to plan and build.
The sudden prevalance of private motor vehicles surprised almost everyone.
Hillebrecht, for example, said that he believed the poverty of the German
cities and the German people would mean that decades would elapse before
most Germans could afford their own cars. Only at some distant date would
Germany perhaps achieve American proportions of 1 auto for every 10 inhabitants.[170] When Friedrich Tamms completed Düsseldorf's reconstruction plans
in 1949, he noted that in 1939 there had been 1 motor vehicle for every 28
residents. He expected that "in the future," Germany could expect to reach at
most an approximate mean between America's current satiation and Europe's
prewar condition.[171]

The "future" arrived quickly. In 1937, Stuttgart boasted 1 motor vehicle
for every 16.2 residents. In 1949, the year in which the city council debated
cutting a major artery through the inner city, motor vehicle registration in-

FIGURE 7.1. Registered motor vehicles in Cologne.
Source: HASK/ Köln, Generalverkehrsplan (Cologne, 1956), p. 108.

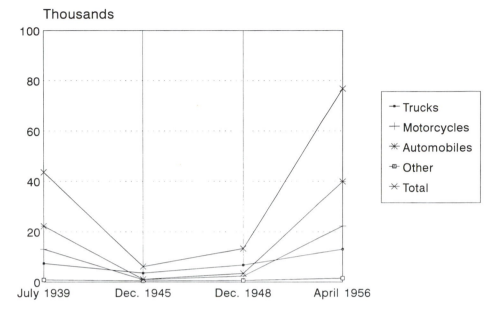

Thousands

creased 46% over the previous year, and the city had 1 vehicle for every 20.7 residents. The following year saw 15.6 residents per vehicle, 1951 saw 13 per vehicle, and in 1952 there were 11.3 residents per vehicle. By 1960, the ratio had diminished to 1 vehicle per 10.8 inhabitants. By 1970, the ratio had been slashed to 1 per 4.08 inhabitants.[172] Figure 7.1 and Table 7.1 show the rapid growth in total motor vehicles and in personal automobiles in Cologne. Obviously these increases far outstripped the expectations of the planners. Before the war, Munich had regulated traffic with a mere 12 traffic signals, and only 4 more were added by 1950. In 1955 Cologne had only 72 traffic signals.[173] It is no wonder that within a decade after their construction, new arteries were hopelessly overwhelmed.

Finally, it is possible that postwar traffic planning *overvalued* the role to be

TABLE 7.1.   Registered Motor Vehicles in Cologne

	July 1939	*End 1945*	*End 1948*	*April 1956*
Total	43,618	6,194	13,335	76,751
Automobiles	51%	18%	26%	52%
Trucks	17%	58%	51%	17%
Motorcycles	30%	16%	18%	29%
Other	2%	8%	5%	2%

Source: HASK/ Stadt Köln, *Köln. General Verkehrsplan,* mimeo (Cologne, 1956), p. 108.

played by automobiles in the inner cities.[174] As traffic exceeded the capacity of the new arteries, old narrow streets, the cores of building blocks, even some of the larger avenues were converted into pedestrian zones which prohibit all vehicular traffic except that essential for relevant deliveries. The pedestrian zones now are found everywhere in Germany.[175] Access is by foot or public transportation, and often these zones are connected to major train stations with active passenger service. The pedestrian zones are usually open, though sometimes they connect with glassed-over galleries between buildings or in the cores of building blocks. Natives and visitors tend to regard these vital pedestrian zones as affirmations of the success of German urban planning, although in fact the flourishing pedestrian zones bear witness to the failure of most postwar inner-city traffic planning. Most of the pedestrian zones, after all, used to be streets that carried cars, buses, and streetcars, often in great volume.

Conclusion

Postwar planning has been criticized as sharply as postwar architecture and housing. Vittorio Lampugnani, for example, has argued that because postwar planners pursued predetermined goals and failed to respond to actual conditions, reconstruction was "preprogrammed for basic failure." Town planning, Lampugnani feels, "was almost without exception a sad chapter in the history of building."[176] In fact, however, postwar planning was always molded by a dialectical struggle between abstract models and realities of which the planners were quite aware. None of the numerous utopian reconstruction plans drawn up at the end of the war was implemented.

The planners themselves thought that the deficiencies in reconstruction came not from pursuing planning ideals but from being forced to abandon those ideals due to economic conditions. In addition, after only five years of reconstruction, when many of the new town plans were reaching final form or final approval, Germany's planners began to fear that they were losing control of the reconstruction process. Herbert Jensen spoke of a "crisis of planned building."[177] Although he welcomed the unexpected high volume of new building, Rudolf Hillebrecht noted that, in spite of planners' efforts to the contrary, there was too much unplanned construction activity that contradicted the basic principles of good urban design. Much of the new housing in outer areas was erected in planned suburbs, but this "legitimate" activity was accompanied by a lot of "wild," uncontrolled housing construction. In some inner-city areas builders once again filled in block interiors with housing, which threatened to return population densities to unhealthy prewar levels. Attempts to relocate industry away from housing and implement functional zoning were resisted by some businessmen, and areas designated for commerce and industry tended to be overbuilt.[178] In addition, the public, or that part of the public in a position to build, had its own ideas about what it wanted. Planners soon sensed that the great opportunity of 1945 had faded away.

A large group of planners had come to the task of reconstruction well prepared. They shared common experiences and common ideas, and they saw themselves as technocrats, problem solvers, and decision makers. They wanted effective laws and administrations that had the authority to put their ideas into practice, efficient mechanisms that could turn lines drawn on paper into brick, concrete, and asphalt. But democracy often is an inefficient political process in that it encourages public participation and involvement in policy decisions.

The planning profession was deeply ambivalent about public input. Herbert Jensen asked: "Is democracy in a position to combine the achievements of many individuals into an achievement of the whole? . . . Is democracy capable of a systematic, creative cultural achievement?" He understood the public's fear of strong government after 12 years of the Third Reich, but he felt that the public needed to go beyond seeing freedom as freedom merely from some form of oppression to seeing freedom as the "freedom to" do things.[179] Alfons Leitl wondered: "Can anyone be surprised that democracy in this country often was misundertood to mean freedom from any control, and that the obligation to practice self-discipline in public matters was forgotten?"[180] The authoritarian tendency in the profession, a tendency which had helped make it possible for so many planners to work comfortably during the Third Reich, was still very strong.

There were many complaints about excessive secrecy in the planning department and about planners treating citizens as mere objects.[181] In a democracy like the Federal Republic, authoritarian planning was really not possible, and the profession groped toward a new, more political role. As Otto Meyer-Ottens of Hamburg admitted, "We [the planners] have still not learned how to act and think democratically."[182] Fritz Schumacher wrote that "we artists have become politicians of building," but by that he meant only that the planner had to join forces with and guide other specialists—engineers, sociologists, and economists. To the very end he believed that "urban planning is *nothing* political but instead something social-cultural (and moreover something artistic) ."[183] Politics was not artistic.

The technical nature of planning made involving the public difficult, if not impossible. Sometimes competitions were as useful for opening up the planning process to the public and removing the veil of secrecy as for soliciting valuable new ideas.[184] Exhibitions of plans and speeches by planners were intended primarily to persuade the public that the planner possessed good judgment, not to make planning an open and democratic process. The activities of reconstruction associations in Bremen and Hannover were praised for including those affected by planning in the process, although this applied mainly to property owners rather than the general public.[185] Moreover, the reconstruction associations in Hannover and Bremen were more the exception than the rule. Not until the latter half of the 1960s did it become common practice to systematically involve the public in urban planning, in spite of Rudolf Hillebrecht's 1957 conclusion that a healthy, organic, urban society was also a political society: "Urban planning was therefore not aesthetic or aestheticizing but rather political planning." Its goal was, or at least should be, the city as polis.[186]

The city as polis, as a city of citizens actively participating in formulating public policy, also implies a different kind of city from that implied by the prevailing planning model of the reconstruction years. Indeed, the image of the polis anticipates the different planning model of the mid-1960s and 1970s. Only then did planners begin to favor density over decongestion and dynamic urbanity over the distinct separation of urban functions. Planners then had to find ways of accomplishing these goals without further overburdening a street system already gridlocked by the growing mass of private autos. This problem remains today.

8

Reconstruction and Building Law

"Town planning is town-planning law turned into stone," or so believed Germany's postwar planners.[1] Convinced that only strong planning and building laws could turn their plans into reality, all wanted to see the jumble of inherited state and local ordinances transformed into a new, coherent body of law. They feared that without new laws, the rebuilt cities would reproduce the flaws that afflicted the unplanned cities of the previous century.

Not surprisingly, urban planners were well-prepared to address the legal issues raised by reconstruction. The realm of building and planning law manifested extraordinary continuity from the end of World War I into the post–World War II era. In the 1920s, a group of planners had begun work on a comprehensive building and planning law that sought to structure the planning process, define public and private rights and obligations, and delineate the limits that could be placed on private ownership of land. The destruction during the war raised new issues, such as whether to distinguish between previously undeveloped land and land the bombing had leveled. Basically, however, the planners who had long worked on planning law sought to adapt their programs and ideas to the new situation and arrive at a modern, comprehensive law that would guide immediate reconstruction as well as all future building.

During the first five years after the war, building law was the basis of a broader nationwide discussion than virtually all other aspects of reconstruction, including the question of rebuilding historic monuments. Most decisions on urban reconstruction were made locally, and local self-government was universally accepted as a foundation for revived political life. The strong desire for a national planning law thus conflicted with equally strong efforts to retain local autonomy; advocates of legal uniformity and clarity found them-

221

selves sometimes in bitter opposition to advocates of reconstruction planning tailored to local needs. The legalists were enormously influential during the five years after the war. By the end of 1950, all West German states, with the exception of Bavaria, had passed reconstruction laws. No comprehensive national planning law, however, was passed. The complex, overlapping, subtly intricate maneuvers involved in lawmaking reveal the development of many of the basic concepts of urban planning and fundamental conceptualizations regarding property rights and politics in postwar Germany.

The Framework: Building Law and Proposals for Reform to 1945

The growth of a body of planning law paralleled the growth of town planning in Germany in the late nineteenth century. Several states had enacted laws regulating zoning, building height and setback from the street, and expropriation of private property for such public uses as new roads (*Staffelbauordnungen* and *Fluchtliniengesetze*). Toward the end of the century some passed laws enabling towns to redraw property lines (*Umlegungsgesetze*) so that the size and orientation of land parcels would conform to zoning standards.[2] In 1892, Franz Adickes, the reforming mayor of Frankfurt, introduced a bill in the Prussian Diet that would have permitted *Umlegungen* in Prussian towns of over 10,000 inhabitants. The bill would also have enabled towns to confiscate property for widening streets, redeveloping slums, and for building new housing on vacant land. Opposed on the one hand by property owners and on the other by many town representatives who feared losing local powers of self-administration, the bill was repeatedly defeated. It finally passed in 1902, but in a form that applied only to Frankfurt. An important provision in the law dictated that when property lines were redrawn for previously undeveloped land, up to 35% of the property could be expropriated for streets and public squares without compensation to the owners. The assumption was that the owner's loss would be made up by gains that would accrue from the improvements built by the town. This law, usually referred to as the *lex Adickes*, was subsequently adopted by several states.[3]

These laws, however, usually sufficed for laying out streets but typically failed to address the issue of what was erected behind the street facades. None of the existing planning laws could prevent the construction of the terrible urban slums that blighted the landscape of Berlin and other industrial cities. Only the extraordinary conditions that prevailed at the end of World War I allowed the passage of housing legislation that contained provisions increasing town planners' prerogatives.[4]

The Prussian Housing Law of 1918 provided a legal framework within which Prussian planners, such as Martin Wagner in Berlin, could begin new, modern housing projects. The states of Saxony, Hamburg, and Thuringia also passed new planning legislation between 1919 and 1932. Nevertheless, much remained to be done. In the first place, existing town planning laws were still designed primarily or exclusively to deal with the expansion (or extension) of towns or with the creation of new towns, not with renewal or redevelopment of the old cities. Second, the laws failed to clearly define the planning process. How should a proper city plan evolve, and what safeguards should the public be able to call upon during the planning process? The discipline of city planning was not yet widespread enough to provide a common approach to these issues. Finally, much greater clarification was needed on the most politically sensitive of questions, the expropriation of private property for public uses.

The Weimar constitution of August 1919 was ambivalent on private property rights. On the one hand, articles 153 and 155 stated that the possession of private property brought with it obligations, such as sacrificing personal interests for the public good. On the other hand, these articles also stated that private property could be expropriated only with "appropriate compensation," an ambivalent phrase left to the courts to define. If, for example, a new city plan caused property values to escalate suddenly, did the city have to pay owners the full, newly inflated value or could it merely pay the prespeculation price for the parcels of land that were to be made into a public street or garden? Payment of full market value usually meant that cities could ill afford to implement renewal or development programs. Finally, planners wished for greater uniformity in law and practice. The great variety of city, state, and national laws resulted in wildly inconsistent planning and building policies, which naturally confused builders and authorities alike. In 1923, Fritz Schumacher declared that "only when we have laws . . . that simplify and generalize property expropriation and consolidation by public authorities and make building permits not just dependent on street construction but on general economic principles can we to some extent bring together contemporary ideas about urban planning and realize those ideas."[5]

An attempt to address these deficiencies in the building laws was made shortly before Hitler's rise to power. A group of men in the Reich Labor Ministry, led by Wilhelm Dittus, prepared a comprehensive national building and planning law.[6] The draft of the law was submitted in 1931 and was being debated by the Reichstag in 1932, when the final collapse of the parliamentary process precluded any further legislative action. The draft did not, however, disappear completely. A few provisions found their way into the more limited Suburban Housing Law (Wohnsiedlungsgesetz) promulgated in September 1933, such as those granting towns the right to designate an area for housing development and impose a general prohibition on all building in that area while plans for its development were being completed. In addition, Dittus, Ludwig Wambsganz, and others, continued to work on a comprehensive law within the Labor Ministry throughout the Nazi period, and they prepared a new draft as late as March 1942. At the same time, work was under way on laws addressing what could be considered sections of a comprehensive law. The Deutsche Akademie für Städtebau, Reichs-und Landesplanung prepared drafts for a new land law and a law on urban renewal.[7]

These drafts dealt explicitly with some of the deficiencies in the prewar planning laws. For instance, in order to strengthen the rights of the community in relation to the rights of private property owners, it was proposed that all land be placed under the sovereignty of the Reich. Although the concept of private property would remain, owners would in fact hold title in trust for the community and would therefore find their options of using the land severely restricted.[8] The planning process itself was to be broken up into several clearly specified mandatory and legally binding stages. The drafts also granted towns extensive powers to expropriate private property and provided means for thwarting land speculation during the planning process.[9] Herbert Boehm, a Frankfurt planner, observed that the proposed laws included risks, since planners received the "total right to shape" (*totale Gestaltungsanspruch*) cities, but that overcoming the "unlimited individualism" that had hitherto wreaked so much havoc more than justified such provisions. "There is thus nothing else we can do," Boehm claimed, "than to accept discipline, give the Führer principle [*Führerprinzip*] its due in the area of urban planning, put the right man in the right place, and put at his side advisors and, if needed, a controlling organ composed of the truly best architects and economists and thereby attempt to reduce if not completely eliminate" this danger.[10]

At the same time, the Nazis promulgated a number of pieces of planning legislation, including the Suburban Housing Law discussed in Chapter 5. Most important was the Law for the Redesign (Neugestaltung) of the German Cities, decreed on 4 October 1937. This law granted a specially appointed building commissar wide-ranging, almost unlimited power to plan and execute plans. The commissar's authority was based not on the town government but on the authority of the Gauleiter or, as with Speer in Berlin, on the backing of Hitler himself. This law directly applied the Führer principle to town planning. Owners of private property were now powerless to prevent the forced sale or outright expropriation of large tracts of inner-city land, and in several designated cities, acquisitions of property for planned areas continued into the early years of the war. Under the terms of the law, owners were entitled to "appropriate compensation" for property expropriated, which led to extensive discussions among legal experts about what was appropriate. Was the state obliged to compensate owners for the book value of the land and buildings, or did it also have to reimburse such things as the cost of relocating a business, setup costs in the new location, special wages to employees to keep them from changing jobs during the transitional period, and profits lost through the loss of clients that might result from the relocation?[11] Since the Neugestaltung of Germany's cities seldom got beyond the planning stage, however, the 1937 law was not as extensively applied as it might have been had the war not intervened.

The laws promulgated by the Nazis were based on an arbitrary and authoritarian regime and were hence declared void by the military government in 1945. Opponents of comprehensive city planning sought to discredit postwar efforts to pass a comprehensive building and planning law by arguing that such a law was no less than an attempt to continue or revive Nazi legislation, a charge that weakened but did not stop the campaign for new laws on which to base reconstruction.

The Postwar Debate: Defining the Scope of a New Building Law

Most postwar planners desired a comprehensive reconstruction law, but they recognized that the passage of such a law might be difficult and time-consuming. Local authorities, however, needed an immediate legal basis for their actions. Local and state laws regulating rubble clearance and the allocation of building supplies and labor (discussed in Chapter 2) often were based on ordinances from the Nazi era and dealt only with the emergency situation existing at the war's end, not reconstruction planning.

The director of Cologne's land office argued that cities should simply continue invoking the 1937 law for Neugestaltung but replace references to Gauleiters and other Nazi officials with current governmental labels.[12] Although the 1937 law was too closely tied to Hitler's megalomaniac urban visions for this suggestion to be accepted, other planning laws promulgated during the Third Reich were utilized. Aachen, for example, applied a 1937 property consolidation ordinance and a 1940 ordinance for planning in response to war damage in preparing the city's first reconstruction plans.[13]

In Hamburg in September 1945, Wilhelm Bahnson, a senior official in the building law office, argued that rebuilding could be guided sufficiently by merely reinterpreting existing "building police" regulations. Since the building police were already legally empowered to restrict private property rights in the interest of public health, one only needed to see that the bombing had created an urban housing situation that threatened public health and welfare. Consequently, Bahnson felt that the city government could simply decide how to rebuild housing and then use the existing police regulations to implement that decision.[14] Although ineffective and ill-suited to postwar conditions, this approach informed activity in Hamburg until the city passed a building law in 1949.

Echoing his assertions of the 1920s, the aged Fritz Schumacher in 1945 called for granting city planners extensive powers to set and enforce reconstruction priorities and to control the land market.[15] Concrete proposals for investing planners with such authority came from several cities. An official in Munich's building office drafted a strong reconstruction law in early 1945. In 1946, the town of Pforzheim drew up both a reconstruction plan and a proposed reconstruction law which, it was argued, would promote "reconstruction from the city center outward" and would create "an organically growing townscape," the healthiest path for urban rebuilding. The key provision of this law facilitated the voluntary formation of nonprofit cooperatives (*gemeinnützige Genossenschaften*) that would arrange for the redrawing of property lines according to modern guidelines, arrange financing, and then start actual construction.[16] Another important early proposal came from Frankfurt. Led by its first postwar mayor, Kurt Blaum, the city sought to steer a course between "unhealthy egotism," by which he meant uncontrolled private rebuilding, and "unhealthy socialism," a situation in which rebuilding was completely in the hands of the public authorities.[17] The latter, in Blaum's opinion, had led to "fantastic" and simply impractical plans, but the former would fail to clear out the overcrowded old city and consolidate tiny land parcels to make way for modern buildings. Frankfurt proposed to extend the powers of earlier laws on redrawing property lines (the *lex Adickes*) in order to make it easier to force both consolidation of parcels and actual rebuilding according to new zoning regulations. Owners of expropriated land were to be compensated at the current assessed value. In the case of damaged buildings for which it was difficult to decide on a fair "current value," the value as of October 1936, when prices had been frozen, was to be the standard for compensation.[18]

By this time, Wilhelm Dittus and Ludwig Wambsganz were spearheading the campaign for passage of a national comprehensive building and reconstruction law. As already noted, both had worked on the 1942 draft law in the Labor Ministry and as legal authorities for the building and housing section of Berlin's city government after the war. Wambsganz called for *"creation of a balanced, systematic, organic, unified, and conclusive legal instrument—a new planning, building, and land law*, that would replace the existing, mosaic-like hodge-podge [*Mischmasch*]."[19] He and Dittus rejected proposals for special laws that treated reconstruction as an isolated process. In most cases, they argued, it would be impossible to clearly distinguish between reconstruction and normal building activity. How, for example, would such laws categorize a building erected to replace a destroyed building but in a different form or on a different site? And what about areas containing undamaged buildings, partly damaged and restored buildings, and brand new buildings put up on previously open land? Or "what if, while rebuilding a given area, it was decided to demolish an old, undamaged building in order to improve traffic conditions? Could that be called reconstruction?"[20]

Support for a national building law was widespread. *Der Bauhelfer*, *Neue Bauwelt*, *Die neue Stadt*, and other leading journals for architects and planners carried numerous articles calling for new reconstruction laws. Between 1946 and 1954, the German Academy for Town and Regional Planning (Deutsche Akademie für Städtebau und Landesplanung) and its state branches entertained some 25 lecturers who discussed and hotly debated proposed innovations in planning law.[21] The German Association for Housing, Town and Regional Planning (Deutscher Verband für Wohnungswesen, Städtebau und Landesplanung), which also had sponsored work on building law during the war, called for close cooperation between all federal states in all four occupation zones in drawing up a simplified, unified building law. Like Dittus and Wambsganz, the association argued that no distinction should be made between reconstruction of war-damaged cities and extension of cities in peacetime, since the basic issues were the same. The most important point was that the public interest outweigh purely private interests. A new law must offer simple, effective solutions to the issues of property consolidation, expropriation, and compensation. It must also control land speculation and tax away unearned profits.[22] With the decline of public interest in socialization in the western zones, it was necessary to find a way to distinguish between specific expropriations for the purposes of city planning and more general expropriations for the purpose of some sort of socialization. Some people cited the

English city planning legislation of 1947–48 as a model for progressive planning and property law.[23] In any event, all agreed on the urgency of enacting a building law.

At this point those concerned with reconstruction law in the Soviet occupation zone were still participating in the general discussion in Germany, if somewhat marginally. Soviet land reform measures, whereby large landholdings were confiscated without compensation, applied to the countryside, not the towns. Therefore, between October 1945 and March 1947, the five states in the Soviet zone passed urban reconstruction laws. Surprisingly, only the Saxon-Anhalt law provided for regular expropriation of land without suitable compensation. Elsewhere the laws followed the practice of the Weimar constitution or other early planning laws.[24]

Basing his ideas on the 1947 Saxon law, Professor A. Heilmann of Halle in the Soviet zone published a proposal for a building and land law that he felt could be generally applied. Like his Western colleagues, Heilmann wanted a general planning and building law, not one limited to either reconstruction or expansion of cities. If existing political circumstances precluded a unified and comprehensive law, a series of laws dealing with rubble clearance, land reform, and the financing of construction must be enacted. In any event, he insisted that the law specify that the rebuilding of the cities was "solely and genuinely a task for the self-administration" of the towns, and that state supervision accord with "democratic administrative practice."[25]

Heilmann's draft law contained a number of interesting clauses. The sale or transfer of building land would require official permission, which could be denied in the event of price discrepancies or questions of public interest. In addition, the town would always have a first option to purchase any property offered for sale. If the overall reconstruction plan determined that it was in the public interest, a town could consolidate or expropriate land parcels or place them in trust. Indeed, with "appropriate compensation," whole areas could be expropriated. Heilmann's law called for dividing planning into two stages, a preliminary plan that would indicate streets and building lines (*Teilbebauungsplan*) and a final plan (*Durchführungsplan*) that would include stipulations about building materials and labor. During the planning and building process, a ban on unapproved construction would be imposed for the whole area slated for rebuilding. Finally, property owners in an area planned for reconstruction would be given a time frame within which they had to rebuild according to the plan. If they failed to meet this requirement, either because they were unable to or because they "maliciously" (*böswillig*) chose not to, the town could confiscate their property or place it in the hands of a cooperative that would undertake the desired building. Though not part of his draft per se, Heilmann noted that in the Soviet zone, a "forced mortgage" (*Zwangshypothek*) had been imposed on all undamaged and partly damaged property to raise funds for financing reconstruction. He considered this an equitable adjustment of burdens, since otherwise those who by chance had lost everything in the war would also have had to shoulder alone the cost of rebuilding.

Dittus responded to Heilmann's proposed law at some length. He acknowledged that Heilmann's carefully thought out draft addressed many central problems, but he contended that it did not go far enough. Too much remained unspecified. His 18-point commentary asked, for example, how building cooperatives would be established and how they would function. How would a legal obligation to rebuild be applied in cases in which single-story buildings stood among four-story buildings? Would owners be forced to add three more floors? Dittus found the provisions on expropriation sorely inadequate because they failed to detail procedures and seemed too limited to the task of immediate reconstruction. Furthermore, the first-purchase option was not broad enough to guarantee towns the necessary building land. In short, Germany still needed a thorough, comprehensive law that covered all eventualities.[26]

In articles published in 1948, Dittus and Wambsganz spelled out what they believed should be covered by a new building law. The fundamental premise was that henceforth all building had to be carefully planned, and planning had to be anchored in law. "Even the all-powerful Speer," they observed, "had found it useful to underpin his unchecked building aspirations with wide-ranging legislation."[27] A new law would "clear the way for city planning to fulfill its key task, [namely] to give the planner the necessary freedom to plan and implement his plans."[28] The law must cover all above- and below-ground building, deal with all aspects of land ownership and use, and clarify the relationship between private ownership of land and buildings and the rights and obligations vested in public authorities. It should also prescribe in detail the planning process itself and indicate the respective functions of planners and the *Baupolizei*, the building police or inspectors who would enforce building regulations. Finally, the law must harmonize and unify building practices for all of Germany. This required modifying or replacing older laws and reconciling variations in the laws of different states. Otherwise, planners, property owners, architects and contractors, politicians, and the public would misunderstand each other, and fruitful planning would be impossible.

The extent of private property rights proved the most controversial and difficult issue. As Dittus pointed out, in the course of the nineteenth century the rights associated with land ownership had become more and more absolute, and land owners could successfully block virtually any kind of urban plan that was not perceived to be in their own interest. During the Weimar Republic and also under the Nazis, however, the trend had been reversed, and land owners confronted an increasing number of restrictions and the growing power of the state to expropriate private property. Naturally the planned reconstruction of Germany's bombed cities necessitated serious limitations on the right of private ownership of land, but, as Dittus admitted, the majority of the population still preferred a system of private property over any other. For this reason, any new building law would have to be designed and phrased very carefully to account for both the needs of the planners and the desires of the citizenry. Indeed, it would be preferable to avoid the word "expropriation" (*Enteignung*) altogether because of its many negative connotations.[29]

Dittus listed 16 aspects of the private property question:

1. The law must recognize planning as more important than any unlimited right of private owners to build as they saw fit.

2. It must provide for the possibility of redrawing property lines.

3. Towns had to be able to rid themselves of minuscule land parcels.

4. Where there was to be no compensation, a justly proportional distribution of burdens would be imposed on owners.

5. The law must provide for consolidating parcels to form large building lots.

6. Towns had to be able to acquire building land, especially on sites where the overall plan called for special construction.

7. Towns had to be able to acquire other land to compensate owners of expropriated land.

8. The law must define ways of turning over building land to those willing and able to build.

9. All construction must be consistent with the plan. If some property owners were unwilling or unable, or were perhaps missing, the law must grant towns the means to realize the construction plans.

10. Towns must have the ability to require owners to undertake new construction, repairs, or alterations when the plan called for such activity.

11. The law must provide for exchanges of property within different parts of a town or at even greater distances.

12. Up to a specified percentage, towns needed the authority to force owners to foresake part of their land without compensation when the land was desired for public purposes.

13. Formulas for compensation had to exclude changes in property values that resulted from new planning.

14. Building permits could be awarded only to projects consistent with the town plan.

15. Land could be subdivided only with official permission.

16. To rationalize the building process, it had to be possible for towns to assume management of actual construction.

Dittus rejected as unessential (1) the power to place property in the town's hands as trustee, since there were other ways of arranging private trusteeship; (2) the option of first purchase, since that would involve too much administrative work; (3) the need of owners to obtain official permission for merely selling land; and (4) the power to require firms or trades to relocate because their location was unsuitable.

If a comprehensive national building law, as proposed by Dittus and Wambsganz, had incorporated these limitations on private property, city planners might indeed have prevailed over any objections of private land owners. Such a law eluded postwar Germany, however.

Dittus and Wambsganz were upstaged by Johannes Göderitz. Göderitz, it may be recalled, had worked as a planner in Magdeburg until the Nazis arrested him because of his membership in the Social Democratic party. Once released, he went to Berlin, where he served as executive director of the German Academy of Town and Regional Planning for the rest of the war. In that capacity he worked with Dittus on the 1942 draft law in the Reich Labor Ministry. The summer of 1945 found him planning reconstruction for the town of Braunschweig. Drawing on his work on the earlier draft, he immediately proposed his own broadly worded reconstruction law. This proposal was forwarded to the Zonenbeirat, the British zone's governing council in Hamburg, which accepted it as a possible basis for a national building law.[30]

Göderitz's draft was subsequently reworked by a special committee of the revived national German Cities Association (Deutscher Städtetag); by representatives of the Ruhr regional planning authority (Siedlungsverband Ruhrkohlenbezirk), including its director Philipp Rappaport; by a specially appointed commission that included Andrew Grapengeter, who drew up a building law for Hamburg in 1949; by Erich Kühn, who later became a key official in the reconstruction ministry of Northrhine-Westphalia; and by representatives of the housing section of the Central Labor Office (Zentralamt für Arbeit) of the British zone, where Göderitz also worked and which was dominated by Social Democrats, who shared that party's traditionally strong interest in centralized town planning.[31] The result was a draft of an *Aufbaugesetz* that was published in August 1947 and given very wide circulation in all parts of Germany. Because it was published by the Zentralamt für Arbeit in the town of Lemgo, it was normally referred to as the Lemgo draft.

Although analogous in many respects to the positions expressed by Dittus and Wambsganz, the Lemgo draft also incorporated some fundamental differences. Dittus and Wambsganz emphasized planning, suggesting a four-stage planning process, beginning with overall regional planning and moving to detailed, binding plans for specific parts of the community. The Lemgo draft provided for only two stages. It called for a broad town plan (on a scale of 1:2,000 to 1:10,000) showing overall land use, and an implementation plan (Durchführungsplan) for the specific area.[32] Recognizing the necessity of imposing limitations on private property, the Lemgo draft stated that "it is self-evident that the rebuilding of the cities and villages is unthinkable without encroachments on private property." As a first step, the draft granted towns the option to purchase any property offered for sale in an area designated for rebuilding, a measure Dittus thought unnecessary.[33]

The clauses in the Lemgo draft intended to dampen land speculation were milder than Dittus would have wanted, but otherwise Göderitz's proposal dealt with the basic property issues in much the same manner as Dittus. The draft authorized towns to impose a five-year ban on building in a designated area and let them expropriate without compensation up to 10% of built-upon and 35% of unbuilt areas for community roads or recreation areas. Land could also be expropriated for housing or commercial development, with appropriate compensation normally taking the form of a parcel of land elsewhere in the town. The towns could expropriate land just to gain parcels to compensate the owners of other expropriated land. The draft included provisions for the voluntary or mandatory redrawing of property lines and the consolidation of small building lots. Owners could be issued a deadline for building, rebuilding, or repairing a building, after which the property could be assigned—once the original owner was compensated—to someone willing to build.

The Lemgo draft proved very influential. The states of Schleswig-Holstein, Hamburg, Lower Saxony, and Northrhine-Westphalia all passed reconstruction laws that closely followed the Lemgo draft, and it strongly shaped the reconstruction laws of Baden-Württemberg, Hesse, and Rhineland-Pfalz.[34] Nevertheless, the Lemgo draft did not, as its sponsors had hoped, become the basis of a national law. Powerful opposition to a national law came from Bavaria, which alone of the states did not pass a new reconstruction law, and, until mid-1949, Germany lacked a national legislature that could pass such a law.[35]

Moreover, important differences distinguished the laws of the states and made agreement on a uniform law unlikely. Variations generally concerned (1) the percentage of an owner's property that could be expropriated without compensation (anywhere from 10 to 35%); (2) the length of time that a general ban on building could be imposed (usually three to five years, sometimes with an extension allowed); (3) the exact process through which land parcels could be consolidated; (4) the terminology used for planning stages and for intermediary bodies created for supervising changes in landholdings; and (5) the structure of the planning process. Berlin, for example, adopted a building law written by Dittus himself. This law spelled out the planning process, which entailed four stages, in far more detail than the Lemgo draft. The Berlin law also contained a stronger provision for dealing with increases in property values due to new planning, calling for negating those increases by taxes which would underwrite public expenditures for streets, utilities, and the acquisition of land slated for compensation in expropriation cases.[36] The Baden-Württemberg law of 18 August 1948, to cite another example, left it to implementation ordinances to determine just how a number of key provisions—a town's first option to purchase a property, the process of parcel consolidation, and the ability to force an owner to build—would work. To the despair of planners, the implementation ordinances were not promptly enacted. Professor Hugo Keuerleber of the Technical University of Stuttgart and a member of the city planning commission raged: "it is a catastrophe that the building law has been passed by the legislature in its current form. A wide-ranging reconstruction is impossible with this building law."[37]

Opposition to the New Laws: Property Rights and Politics

The states' reconstruction laws were not passed without opposition. Hamburg's law, for example, was passed only after it was debated in 17 long meetings held by the relevant parliamentary subcommittees in which representatives of various economic interests participated. Objections were typically raised over the encroachments on private property or the scope of the planning process. Representatives of private property, such as the chambers of commerce, mortgage banks, and land and home owners' associations, argued that the reconstruction laws simply gave the towns too much arbitrary power over private property. Others felt that the possibility of expropriating up to

35% of a property without compensation smacked of "socialist tendencies."[38] In addition, the prolonged ban on construction in an area being planned would hinder the overall rebuilding effort and impose an unfair burden on affected property owners.[39] If, for example, a property owner was unable to rebuild within the specified time period, the planner could simply transfer the right to build to the owner's chief competitor. Finally, applying to undamaged areas measures designed to modernize destroyed areas was grossly unfair. Opponents of the new reconstruction laws wanted to restrict them to the emergency at hand, rather than broaden them into general planning and building laws.[40]

The second kind of opposition rejected the perceived tendency to give a government agency—in this case town planners—too much leeway to function in the kind of arbitrary, undemocratic fashion to which they had become accustomed. In Düsseldorf, the Association of House and Property Owners complained in November 1949 that planners continued to invoke—with the sanction of the state reconstruction minister—Nazi emergency laws promulgated to deal with clearing away bomb damage.[41] The Lemgo draft called for sending the initial plan to state authorities for approval, without permitting public review. Implementation plans were to be made available to the public only one month before final action, and any objections had to be referred to higher administrative authorities, with no possible appeal to the regular courts. In contrast, private property owners demanded codetermination rights (*Mitbestimmungsrechte*) during planning and legal safeguards against bureaucratic action that threatened their interests.[42]

Only in Bavaria, however, did the opposition prove strong enough to prevent passage of a comprehensive building law. Here, bureaucratic infighting dissipated the early momentum for passage of such a law. In fact, three different reconstruction laws were proposed and rejected during the first six years after the war. Because the Bavarian case demonstrates just how powerful the opposition to new planning legislation could be, it merits a closer look.

The first proposal, dated 1 December 1945, came from the Munich city government and was drafted by Karl Sebastian Preis, the chief official in the housing office.[43] Called an Emergency Construction Law (*Aufbaunotgesetz*), it would have created a special new state agency or ministry to organize the reconstruction effort, with a reconstruction commissioner or commissar in each city to supervise the work on the local level. The law contained many of the provisions common to most of the reconstruction laws. First, the town had to prepare an overall land use plan for the area in question, after which a construction ban could be imposed during the planning and rebuilding process. The law obligated and authorized towns to clear rubble from private property and granted to them ownership of the rubble for the purpose of salvaging usable building materials. Once plans for the area were complete, the town could expropriate land for building housing and roads as well as for public open spaces. Owners were entitled to appropriate compensation, unless the expropriated property was less than 10% of the whole piece and the remainder was sufficiently large for building. In cases of redrawing property lines, up to 20% of built-upon and 35% of unbuilt-upon property could be expropriated without compensation. Permits would be issued only to buildings that conformed to current regulations, harmonized with the general planning scheme, and demonstrably filled a recognized need. The state would assume responsibility for allocating building material and could also assign certain building firms to certain projects, in order to maintain a high level of efficiency. Finally, the law provided for severe penalties to discourage or punish those who violated the new provisions.

Preis presented his proposal to a gathering of Bavarian city mayors in mid-December. His ideas appealed to city officials, since he suggested creating a state ministry that would allocate funds and resources but would leave control and direction of reconstruction in local hands. The mayors endorsed the proposal, as did the members of the Bavarian Cities Association (Bayerischer Städteverband).[44] Upon being forwarded by the city government to the Bavarian state government, however, Preis's draft met immediate opposition. On 19 December 1945, a representative of the Bavarian Labor Ministry declared that the military government had charged the ministry with overseeing all activities concerning housing, the production and allocation of building materials, construction financing, building law, and planning. The ministry intended to work through regional and local Siedlungsämter, housing offices primarily responsible for new residential settlements. This would result in some administrative decentralization without giving too much autonomy to the cities. The labor minister saw no need for a new reconstruction ministry, special reconstruction commissars, or any sort of special reconstruction offices on the local level.[45] The ministry praised the Preis law as an interesting contribution toward eventual passage of a housing bill, but in essence it dismissed Preis's proposal for strong, centralized management of reconstruction.

At issue, of course, was who was to assume control of the rebuilding effort—the towns, a special ministry, or one of the regular ministries. The appointment of an engineer to deal with rubble removal in Munich by the Labor Ministry incensed city officials. Notwithstanding the fact that Munich served as the state capital, they adamantly denied that the Bavarian government might initiate and implement reconstruction programs there. Preis denounced what he regarded as the violation of the city's traditional legal right of self-administration. He believed that, if left on its own (though with a financial subsidy from the state), Munich could clear away the rubble in three years. Moreover, Preis declared that he had now read through the military government's laws, and the Labor Ministry's claim of complete jurisdiction over reconstruction clearly usurped authority.[46]

In a letter to the mayor, Preis argued that the administrative structure advocated by the Labor Ministry would result in the same kind of overlapping competencies, bureaucratization, and inefficiency that had characterized the Nazi period. His own proposal, in contrast, would simply and efficiently augment the existing administration without violating the principles of urban self-administration and responsibility.[47] Mayor Scharnagl, in turn, wrote to Minister Seifried that the actions of the Labor Ministry amounted to a "sharp encroachment on the self-administration rights of the towns" that was "entirely dictatorial" in nature.[48] In March, Bavarian big city mayors "strongly applauded" the mayor of Augsburg's attack on the Labor Ministry and his endorsement of Preis's draft for an emergency reconstruction law.[49]

The Labor Ministry remained steadfast. Indeed, it found support in the Munich Chamber of Commerce, in which a subcommittee headed by officials of the Bavarian Mortgage and Exchange Bank (Bayerische Hypotheken- und Wechselbank) evaluated Preis's draft. The Chamber of Commerce rejected Preis's idea of special commissioners, which it felt came too close to the kind of "commissioners" (*Sonderbeauftragter*) often used by the Nazis. The chamber also objected to many specific provisions in Preis's draft, especially those that gave towns wide powers to expropriate private property without fully compensating owners.[50] In the final draft of his proposed law, dated 11 April 1946, Preis deleted the suggestion for reconstruction commissioners and acknowledged the authority of the Labor Ministry, although a parenthetical comment expressed his continuing disagreement on this issue. On 8 August 1946, a formal ordinance distributed throughout Bavaria set forth the broad responsibility of the Labor Ministry (as opposed to the cities) in matters of housing and construction.[51]

Preis's proposal was dead, although it continued to circulate in official circles for some time.[52] Other proposals for new building laws soon joined Preis's suggestions as the basis of discussions, but they did not fare any better. In April 1948, the power to supervise housing and reconstruction was taken away from the Labor Ministry and turned over to the state Building Authority (Oberste Baubehörde) in the Interior Ministry, which had traditionally been in charge of construction projects by the state of Bavaria.[53] Shortly thereafter, two senior councilors in that agency began work on a comprehensive building law for Bavaria. A Dr. Vierling and Ludwig Wambsganz, who had worked with Dittus in Berlin on the original proposal for a national building law, took as their starting points the draft for a Hessian law and the Lemgo draft, both prepared by Göderitz.[54] They realized, however, that their prospects were dismal. In a meeting with Munich officials, Vierling admitted that "internal discussions were proceeding extraordinarily slowly" and that the likelihood of either the ministers or the state parliament approving any kind of measure that included expropriation without full compensation was minimal.[55]

The strength of the opposition more than justified their pessimism. As early as August 1947, Wilhelm Hoegner, then deputy minister president and minister of justice, had written to Munich's mayor arguing that the expropriation clauses in Preis's draft violated Bavaria's new constitution and hence were unacceptable.[56] The same objection would presumably apply to the draft of Vierling and Wambsganz. A member of Bavaria's agricultural office complained that the State Building Authority was seeking comprehensive powers that would allow it to regulate the production of building materials through the allocation of coal and iron. Under current conditions, such authority would in effect allow building officials to control the whole economy, not just construction.[57] The Munich Chamber of Commerce passed a resolution complaining that the new draft failed to consider all relevant economic factors and urged that the authors consult with the chamber.[58] Even Helmut Fischer, who had succeeded Preis as head of Munich's reconstruction office after the latter's death in May 1946, and who also served as managing secretary of the Bavarian Reconstruction Council (Bayerischer Aufbaurat), objected to the new draft. Though convinced that the lack of a good building law seriously impeded reconstruction planning, he nevertheless found the law proposed by the Oberste Baubehörde too protracted and complex. Such a draft would take far too long to enact into law.[59] In fact, though the draft was published in March 1950, its proponents never succeeded in getting it through the conservative Bavarian legislature.

Almost in despair, in the fall of 1949 Bavaria's four largest and most badly damaged cities—Munich, Augsburg, Würzburg, and Nuremberg—proposed an emergency reconstruction law that would apply only to those cities. In his cover letter to the state government, Munich's Mayor Wimmer stated: "It may be that in early 1946 the time was not yet ripe for a reconstruction law. Today, however, it is overripe."[60] But again a strong opposition surfaced. First, the Bavarian Administrative Court ruled that the provisions of a 1923 law, whereby a town could expropriate without compensation up to 35% of virgin land during the process of introducing improvements (streets, sewers, etc.), could not be applied to built-upon land that had been damaged in the war, since property owners had already paid for the original improvements. Moreover, as the Bavarian constitution required compensation for any expropriation, a major constitutional revision would have to precede passage of any such emergency reconstruction law.[61] In a report to the main committee of the Bavarian Cities Association, Helmut Fischer acknowledged that the draft submitted by the four cities had no chance of passing. It faced opposition from the ministries, the trade unions, the financial institutions, the property owners' organizations, and the architects' groups.[62] The Chambers of Commerce of Würzburg and Nuremberg urged approval of the law, mainly because they recognized the urgent need for *some* law, but, along with the Chambers of Commerce of Augsburg and Munich, they too objected to the possibility of expropriation without compensation and to the wide-ranging and possibly undemocratic powers given to the building administration.[63] Fischer was right. The cause was hopeless, and Bavaria never passed a comprehensive building law.

The Struggle for a National Building Law

Other states did, however, pass laws which, on the surface at least, had much in common and seemed to indicate that West Germany might well pass a national building law after all. Indeed, the enactment of so many similar state laws marked a considerable achievement in light of the political fragmentation that existed prior to the creation of the Federal Republic. Buoyed by the success on the state level, the building committee of the German Cities Association

(Deutscher Städtetag), which included most of West Germany's leading town planners, convinced the association to continue lobbying energetically for a national building law. The German Association for Housing, Town and Regional Planning also lobbied for a new law.[64] French planning authorities in their occupation zone and visiting American planning experts all pressed for national planning and building legislation.[65] While a constitution for the new republic was being drawn up there was a call for both a federal building law and a federal reconstruction ministry to cope with the complex and overlapping issues of planning, financing, building, and compensation for war and reconstruction losses.[66] The Basic Law (the new constitution) was approved in May 1949, and the first cabinet included a Ministry for Housing, which assumed responsibility for matters in the area of building. Dittus moved from Berlin to fill a new position in the housing ministry in Bonn, where he set to work on his proposed law.

Obstacles quickly appeared. Since the national ministry was for housing rather than for general reconstruction, officials were uncertain about whether to initially introduce a law limited to housing or whether a general building law should be proposed first. A housing law draft garnered immediate opposition due to its expropriation provisions, which would have granted the federal government considerable direct influence over local expropriation proceedings. In Northrhine-Westphalia, for example, the state's reconstruction minister and representatives of industry condemned these provisions. Responding to a request from the Städtetag that he evaluate an early proposal for a federal housing law, Philipp Rappaport, director of the Siedlungsverband Ruhrkohlenbezirk, recommended to Reconstruction Minister Steinhoff that the whole question of expropriation be avoided for the time being, since no agreement in the Bundestag was likely. He also harbored apprehensions that the federal government might deprive towns of some of their revenues and use them for housing, undermining civic independence.[67] Steinhoff, in turn, strongly protested to Bonn. He viewed the centralization of housing construction at the federal level as "providing an authoritarian position of power which is not consistent with the federative character of the Basic Law." Indeed, he argued, "this practice of 'governing through decrees' should, in the context of a democratization of public life, be decisively opposed," and he castigated the current draft of the housing ministry as mirroring "an enabling law of the national socialist Reich."[68] The union of employers' associations of Northrhine-Westphalia (Vereinigung Nordrhein-Westfälischer Arbeitgeberverbände) also wrote to Federal Housing Minister Eberhard Wildermuth to express their fear of placing too much power in the hands of the federal government, which they thought might well disrupt the process of rebuilding.[69]

When the federal government's First Housing Law (Erstes Wohnungsbaugesetz) finally passed and became effective 4 April 1950, it contained no provisions for expropriation. The law specified that towns, states, the federal government, and other bodies all had an obligation to acquire and make available land for housing construction, but it said nothing about how this should be done. In accordance with the wishes of most of the states, all of the provisions for expropriation had been removed.[70] The bill sought to stimulate housing construction by providing funds for loans and subsidies for social housing and by granting property tax relief for new private housing and housing being repaired or rebuilt.[71]

This was obviously not a comprehensive building law. Even so, Helmut Fischer of Munich complained that the new law seriously infringed upon the self-administration rights of the towns. It required them to subsidize certain kinds of housing and make available building land at the same time that it reduced one of their primary sources of income, local property taxes. These provisions, he said, made an adequate legal basis for planning and land reform all the more necessary.[72] As it stood, the federal housing law addressed only a small part of the reconstruction problem.

In early June, Dittus presented his latest draft of a comprehensive law to the housing minister. He tried to defuse the controversial issue of land expropriation, which he felt was now stigmatized by the "odium" of mass expropriations in the Soviet zone. He talked instead of the procurement of inexpensive building land for housing.[73] In general, however, the draft followed his Berlin building law.[74] Published in the fall, some 2,300 copies were distributed to interested organizations, individuals, and government agencies.[75] While Dittus's law was circulating, the housing ministry prepared a more limited law, which dealt expressly with expropriation of land for housing construction, to supplement the federal housing law. A draft of this Land Procurement Law (Baulandbeschaffungsgesetz) was presented to the cabinet in December 1950.[76]

Support for legislative action was widespread. At a conference of organizations designed to encourage and sponsor reconstruction, Dittus's draft was acclaimed by Herbert Boehm of Frankfurt—a planner who in 1935 had called for the application of the Führer principle to town planning—as "the Magna Charta of German city planning," and the conference called for the Bundestag to pass a comprehensive law immediately.[77] When the Bundestag passed the First Housing Law on 28 March 1950, it also passed a resolution calling for prompt submission of a law that would resolve the questions of expropriation of land for building.[78] In addition, associations lobbying for city interests continued to call for a comprehensive law.[79] At the big Constructa building exhibition in Hannover in July 1951, Wambsganz, Dittus, and Göderitz combined to prepare an exhibit on building law and repeat their call for a federal law.[80]

Nevertheless, some remained firmly opposed to such a law. One Cologne official observed that the draft seemed to be going counter to current legal opinions on the issue of obligatory compensation.[81] In an evaluation of Dittus's draft submitted to and widely circulated by the Munich Chamber of Commerce, F. W. Kärcher of the Bayerische Hypotheken- und Wechselbank denounced the law as a "true bureaucratic concoction" that "turned city planning into something absolute and forced the individual into a particularly scanty role." Dittus's attempt to substitute the word procurement (*Beschaffung*) for expropriation (*Enteignung*) reminded Kärcher of the "euphemisms of totalitarian states, which included terms like liquidate, organize, and the like." Clearly

Dittus had "a complete misunderstanding of the ideas of a democratic state," and instead he "sought to create a pure tyranny of planners."[82]

The law's sponsors persevered. A May 1951 meeting of state and federal officials led to the creation of a special committee headed by Andrew Grapengeter, president of the Landesverwaltungsgericht of Hamburg and an expert on building law. This committee studied the expropriation issue in detail and submitted to the housing ministry an extensive survey of various existing building laws.[83] Hoping both to produce a better draft law and to gain broader support, in the fall of 1951 Wildermuth appointed a new commission consisting of representatives of the states, academic specialists, and planners, to examine once again all aspects of a building law.[84] On 13 September 1951, when the Bundestag debated a resolution, sponsored by all the major parties, demanding that a draft of a comprehensive, unified building law be presented to the legislature by the end of the year, Minister Wildermuth declared that the new building law would be "comparable perhaps to the Civil Code [*Bürgerliches Gesetzbuch*] in importance" and even more difficult to draw up.[85]

Hoping to clarify the constitutional question, the cabinet, the Bundestag, and the Bundesrat in October 1952 jointly petitioned the Supreme Constitutional Court to rule on several important questions: whether building and planning law in fact fell within the jurisdiction of the federal government, to what extent such a law might allow planning authorities to impose their will on property owners in such matters as the consolidation of parcels of land, and whether the expropriation provisions of the state reconstruction laws and the draft law of the housing ministry were in conflict with Article 14 of the Basic Law.[86] That article states: "Property carries obligations. Its private use should also serve the well-being of the public." (Eigentum verpflichtet. Sein Gebrauch soll zugleich dem Wohle der Allgemeinheit dienen.) The article allowed expropriation in the public interest, but only as spelled out by legislation which also determined the nature and extent of compensation. Legal redress was possible by appeal before the regular (as opposed to administrative) courts. The planners believed that the article's reference to obligations and the well-being of the public took precedence over compensation when, because of the poverty of the towns, compensation itself was detrimental to the public welfare. They argued that the Basic Law's fundamental premise that the state had public, social obligations should be "more than a formula."[87]

While the court considered the question, the state of Hamburg drew up an initiative for altering the Basic Law in order to clarify the public responsibilities of property owners, enable easier expropriation of land for public use, and route legal appeals to the administrative courts, rather than the regular courts, which were considered much slower.[88] Both the special commission in the housing ministry and the committee headed by Grapengeter agreed with the terms of the initiative and supported calls for amending the constitution.[89]

Even before the high court reached a decision, however, the majority of the cabinet and the Bundesrat made it clear that they opposed revising the Basic Law. In the end, the housing ministry failed to overcome the resistance of the cabinet and the states and secure the necessary backing to push the comprehensive building law through the Bundestag. Wildermuth died in March 1952, and the best that his successor, Fritz Neumayer, could obtain was passage of the Land Procurement Law in the summer of 1953. It was a compromise bill that conformed to the constitution. The wording of the compromise was initially hammered out in several conferences between the cabinet and the Bundesrat and then in more than 40 sessions of the Bundestag committees on law, housing, and reconstruction.

The most important of the Land Procurement Law's several objectives concerned encouraging housing construction.[90] The law also sought to develop "the ties of the broad masses of the people to the land," which in fact meant giving the flood of refugees from the east firm ties to their new homeland. It sought to promote the construction of housing on already improved property (i.e., on land where former buildings had been destroyed), rather than on unimproved land in the outer suburbs. At the same time, the law permitted the procurement of land for green and open areas deemed necessary for a suitable housing project, such as a planned suburb. This, it was felt, would help keep overall reconstruction within the framework of organic town planning. Finally, the law allowed communities to expropriate land to use as compensation for land expropriated elsewhere in the community.

Under this law, three kinds of land could be expropriated, as long as the proposed project fitted in with approved city planning: vacant land, land where earlier buildings had been either destroyed or badly damaged, and land that was minimally and insignificantly used. The latter included property on which there was only a temporary building or a small, single-story shop surrounded by large, multistory commercial buildings. Perhaps the most important provision was that *anyone*—individuals, private organizations or corporations, or public agencies—could initiate expropriation proceedings. The law assumed that private land owners lacked the ability to carry out such projects. To start expropriation proceedings, for example, it was necessary to have made a good-faith attempt to purchase the property at a fair price, and to demonstrate an ability to begin actual construction within one year after the expropriation had taken place (two years in the case of a town). Property owners could defend themselves against expropriation by proving an ability and desire to build and then actually starting construction. If either the old or new owner failed to start construction within the specified time or if construction was suspended, new expropriation proceedings could begin.

Expropriation had to be accompanied by just compensation, and towns were required to establish special offices to oversee the process. Although based on the 17 October 1936 value (when the price freeze went into effect), compensation figures recognized real improvements, assessed at a fair current value, as well as any legal encumbrances on the property. Excluded from compensation were any increases in value that had resulted from the mere existence of new town planning or from the initiation of the expropriation process. Original owners could claim compensation in various forms, including a substitute piece of property, money, or an alternative dwelling. Legal redress was to be to a newly created chamber of the regular state court system.

It was just as well that the Land Procurement Law omitted the strong expropriation clauses originally proposed by Dittus. In June 1954, after reviewing the Dittus draft of a comprehensive building law, the Supreme Constitutional Court ruled that the federal government did not have primary jurisdiction over all aspects of building. It rejected Dittus's broad conception of land law and ruled that the states had jurisdiction over building regulations and taxation of land that had increased in value. On 26 November 1954, the regular Supreme Court, after examining a case from Stuttgart, ruled that a prolonged and general ban on building amounted to a type of expropriation which required compensation. Then on 21 July 1955, the Supreme Constitutional Court ruled that any expropriation that did not allow for "sufficient" compensation was unconstitutional and hence void.[91] These court decisions not only appeared to prohibit a strong, comprehensive national building law, but they also undercut the existing state reconstruction laws. Now every planning enterprise threatened to be delayed indefinitely by unhappy property owners who sought legal redress.[92]

Politics, Democracy, and the Law

City planners despaired at these devastating blows against the heart of their comprehensive building laws. They criticized the new Germany for being unable to place public interests above private interests. At the annual congress of the German Academy for City and Regional Planning in 1955, Wilhelm Blunck, assistant director of the Siedlungsverband Ruhrkohlenbezirk in Essen and an early collaborator of Göderitz's, declared:

> City planning in a democracy requires finally that the makers of the Basic Law indicate the contents and limits of property, whose ownership supposedly carries obligations and whose use supposedly serves the welfare of the public, and second that they specify in appropriate legal clauses the type and extent of the compensation due in cases of expropriation—the taking-away of or limitation of property. Democratic city planning further requires that this compensation, as stated in the Basic Law, must be in terms of a just balance between the interests of the public and the parties concerned.[93]

At the same 1955 congress, Herbert Jensen, Kiel's city planner, asserted: "It is not city planning that has lost an opportunity; no, the problem is much more serious and much deeper. *Democracy has lost an opportunity*, or better, *it is in danger of losing a unique opportunity*."[94]

What was the opportunity being lost? The planners were disillusioned by more than the court decisions on expropriation. In a 1949 pamphlet describing an exhibit in Hannover on building law, Guido Görres expressed some of the deepest convictions of planners. "Planning must necessarily come before all creating and designing," he wrote. "Everything that is unplanned is ugly. It cannot be anything other than repellent, since it lacks spirit. . . . The purpose of the building law is to stimulate, indeed to force communities to be more active than before in the area of building. The law will first of all call forth strong planning activity, which, however, must everywhere lead to a complete fiasco unless one makes sure that truly able and experienced men are drawn into the planning process from the beginning."[95] Consequently, when the voters, politicians, and courts failed to give the planners the legal framework they desired, they perceived a real threat both to their profession and to the very process of planning. Without strong planning laws, the most qualified individuals would not become planners, reconstruction would be unsystematic and haphazard, and Germany would be blighted by the reappearance of ugly cities.

In fact, by 1955 the basic course of reconstruction was fairly well set, and any major changes would have been arduous and costly. Even the Land Procurement Law had been enacted so late that it failed to help much in rebuilding the old inner cities. Ultimately, planners had to rely on persuasion rather than the coercive power of the law. A federal building law was not enacted until June 1960, about 30 years after the first draft had been submitted to the old Reichstag.[96] It was not, however, the strong law that Dittus and his colleagues had worked for, and, in any case, it was passed too late to be of use in rebuilding the bombed cities.

Critics of reconstruction, like Alexander Mitscherlich, have blamed the predominance of private property rights in the West German legal system for the failings of contemporary German cities.[97] The issues of expropriation and compensation were central to the debate over all building laws after the war, and private property owners were among the most vocal in their opposition to the proposed laws. There were, however, other compelling reasons that help explain why no comprehensive building law was passed during reconstruction. No agreement could be reached, for example, on who had jurisdiction over the rebuilding process—the towns, the states, or the federal government. Each wished to exert control, and though most states and some cities did pass reconstruction laws, significant differences between these laws remained that could not be easily glossed over. Finally, strong objections greeted the procedures contained in the draft laws. For many people sensitive to the excesses of the Nazi era, it was simply unacceptable to give city planners the power to make arbitrary decisions. However admirable the goals of the planners, such concerns were surely legitimate. It was not merely the revival of capitalism and private property in the Federal Republic, therefore, that precluded the passage of a comprehensive building law.

How important was the failure to pass a comprehensive national building law? Some cities achieved much even without a comprehensive federal law. Bavaria's bombed cities were reconstructed without a federal or a state reconstruction law and in spite of the complaints of Bavarian city authorities that reconstruction was impossible without such a law. Elsewhere, state reconstruction laws, even though legally challenged, gave city planners considerable leverage. Up until the 1954 and 1955 Supreme Court decisions, merely the threat of applying the expropriation clauses of the state laws spurred recalcitrant property owners to cooperate with city authorities. In both Hannover and Hamburg, planners sometimes told property owners that if they did not cooperate voluntarily, the city would confiscate 35% of the property under the local reconstruction law and also refuse the owner a building permit. Because going to court would hold everything up for years, it was in the owner's interest to settle things amicably. But most of the time threats were not necessary to gain cooperation. In both cities, the use of expropriation via the law courts was negligible.[98]

Finally, the preoccupations of postwar planners—in particular their fixation on traffic planning—was such that even the benefits of a comprehensive building law might not have made much difference for the quality of the cities. Certainly, laws facilitating the expropriation of property would have given planners more freedom to implement their plans. How they would have taken advantage of this freedom is another question. In any event, it remains to be seen just how town planners went about putting their ideas into practice without the laws of which they dreamed but finally despaired.

9

Organizing Reconstruction

No one believed that isolated individuals could rebuild Germany's cities. For decades Germans had thoroughly organized political, economic, social, and intellectual life. Individuals had articulated and sought to realize their goals through a wide variety of associations, some voluntary and private, some mandated and led by government agencies. The Nazis in particular, with their corporatist philosophy, had attempted to regiment every aspect of German life, including the profession of architects and planners. Late in the war, as noted previously, they began organizing urban reconstruction as well. Although the excesses of that regime were universally recognized and condemned after 1945, most still expected the Germans to organize the postwar reconstruction effort fully and carefully. As Alfons Leitl put it in *Baukunst und Werkform* in 1948, "Planning is organizing, and our town planning is organized town planning."[1]

The organization of reconstruction meant several things. It referred to the overarching technical legal structure of reconstruction as well as to individual agencies responsible for realizing reconstruction goals. Tasks tended to be categorized by their urgency or scope. Emergency or immediate tasks included repairing utilities, streets, and hospitals and other buildings that provided essential services and erecting emergency housing for the homeless. Slightly longer term tasks included clearing rubble, salvaging building materials, demolishing dangerous ruins, issuing building permits, and allocating building materials. Long-term tasks included overall planning of inner-city reconstruction and constructing new suburbs (a process itself broken down into several carefully defined stages), making necessary alterations in property lines and ownership, obtaining financing, and supervising actual construction. Each of these tasks conceivably merited the creation of a new institution. Although cities assumed the primary responsibility, reconstruction agencies could also exist on the regional and national level. Moreover, to avoid competition, the relationships between different organizations had to be carefully defined.

In principle at least, it was entirely possible to turn urban reconstruction over to existing ministries and town building administrations, once they had been denazified and augmented with branches to deal with new phenomena such as rubble clearance. Some places did utilize existing structures and hence enjoyed a good measure of institutional continuity. But often key aspects of reconstruction were turned over to new, extraordinary organizations that functioned alongside traditional agencies. The new organizations were either special government departments or private commissions or corporations. Here too there were pre-1945 precedents that could be followed. This chapter examines some of the more important of these new organizations in terms of the circumstances that led to their birth and their subsequent relationships with other reconstruction-oriented organizations.

Generally these organizations were supposed to make the process of reconstruction—from decisions about individual buildings to the implementation of new town plans—effective and efficient in spite of the extraordinarily difficult situation. Everyone wanted government reconstruction agencies to function more smoothly, quickly, and imaginatively than in the past, and to forsake some of the authoritarian activity that typically defined German bureaucracies. At the same time, however, greater efficiency could not be allowed to become a rationale for the type of coercive behavior manifested by agencies of the Third Reich. Consequently, most encouraged the efficient but voluntary cooperation of private citizens in the rebuilding effort. The most interesting organizational forms produced an effective working relationship between government and the public. In other cities, conflicts within or between agencies led to a hostile relationship between local government and the public, which, in turn, hindered the rebuilding process. In these cases, where Germany's much-vaunted organizational talents failed, the cities might have made better progress if they had simply turned to the traditional building administration.

The Role of the Allied Occupation Governments

Up until the creation of the Federal Republic, the occupation authorities had the power, if they chose to exercise it, to determine the course of reconstruction. The Allies could not, however, agree on a common reconstruction policy—the infamous Morgenthau Plan to return Germany to a rural state being a prime example. They did attempt to control the issuing of building permits and the allocation of labor, building material, and energy supplies within their respective zones, although they acted not so much out of concern for reconstruction of the towns as for management of the whole economy. Allied policies calling for deindustrialization and then reindustrialization of Germany helped determine which industrial plants could produce building materials and in which quantities and which construction firms would be allowed to function. Since the Allies needed and mandated the construction of housing and other facilities for their own troops, they thereby helped determine initial reconstruction priorities. In general, however, this type of activity did not have a major long-term impact on the nature of rebuilding.

Almost as soon as the war ended, the occupying forces set about reestablishing viable municipal governments, to which the Allies assigned responsibility for most decisions on the local level. As part of the process of reestablishing a national polity, the Allies also allowed the state governments to create joint committees to advise on economic measures to aid reconstruction, especially of housing.[2] At the same time, the Allies behaved quite differently from each other when it came to the affairs of cities in their zones. The philosophies of the Allies toward planning helped determine the extent of their intervention in urban reconstruction. The British and French supported planning, the Americans did not, and the differences are worth examining briefly.

The British, in their occupation zone, encouraged the formation of strong, often centralized organizations for business, labor, and the professions, and in turn these organizations often became the basis for nationwide organizations after 1949. The British themselves had a well-established tradition of town planning and had passed comprehensive planning legislation for the rebuilding of their own bombed cities during the war. From the beginning, they required that all building permits in their zone receive final approval from British officers, although in cities like Hannover, which had effective planners, the English would defer to the town building offices, which were thus able to control building activities.[3] Rudolf Hillebrecht reported that he and his fellow planners in the northern cities were relieved that the British did not adopt the American policy of laissez faire. British support for thorough urban planning made it much easier for German planners to shape and pursue reconstruction plans, although the British did not dictate either the nature of those plans or the organizational structures through which they were realized.[4]

Of the Western Allies, the French had the most powerful tradition of centralized government, and they too clearly supported urban planning. During the war the Vichy regime had developed a strong central reconstruction ministry and enacted strong planning legislation, which the postwar French government subsequently adopted.[5] The French were prepared, therefore, to intervene dramatically in reconstruction planning in their occupation zone. As noted, they imposed the French architect Marcel Lods, a disciple of Le Corbusier, on Mainz, where they envisaged a highly modernist urban reconstruction along the lines of the Charter of Athens, and they forced the dismissal of the conservative planner Erich Petzold, even though the population clearly preferred a conservative approach to reconstruction planning.[6] In Saarbrücken the French military governor appointed a French team to prepare plans for a modernist reconstruction.[7] By the spring of 1946, they considered creating a commission to supervise urban and regional planning, zoning, architectural design, and actual construction, with the expectation that they could develop a model for organized reconstruction that could be applied beyond their zone, perhaps even in France. Such a commission would, in effect, introduce modern, French-inspired reforms.[8]

In response to sharp conflicts in Mainz and Trier over reconstruction planning, such a commission was finally created in July 1948 under the direction of Albert de Jaeger. In selecting the German members of the Conseil supérieur d'architecture et d'urbanisme, Jaeger did not limit himself to architects and planners in the French zone, nor did he follow any strict ideological line. The nine Germans appointed included conservatives Paul Bonatz (then living in Turkey) and Paul Schmitthenner and modernists Richard Döcker and Otto Ernst Schweizer, although the conservatives did outnumber the modernists. De Jaeger chose as his assistant Ernst Hamm, a member of the Reich office for regional planning in Berlin during the war and author of a number of articles about the Germanization of the conquered territories in the east.[9] The council also had seven French members. Its mission was to examine and advise on plans for the rebuilding of Trier, Mainz, Freiburg, and other cities in the French zone.[10]

In Trier, a conflict had developed between Fritz Thoma, a private architect engaged by the mayor to prepare a reconstruction plan for the inner city, and Alfons Kraft, the head of the city building administration. The ensuing deadlock impeded construction and generated considerable impatience and resentment among citizens. Although the Conseil supérieur decided in favor of Kraft, final planning in Trier continued to be delayed, and the dispute between the citizens and city government lasted several years.[11]

The Conseil supérieur generally worked very slowly. The first of only two plenary sessions was in August 1948. It opened in Coblenz and then moved to Mainz, Freiburg, and Baden-Baden. The second, in Baden-Baden with excursions to Mainz and Freiburg, occurred in February 1949. Because the council members advocated divergent concepts about urban planning, Hamm was assigned the task of developing a standardized planning methodology.[12] The council also collected material for reports on reconstruction efforts in several cities. In a fashion reminiscent of the Arbeitsstab Wiederaufbauplanung during the war, the council, at its last meeting, divided up into teams to examine and then advise on planning in eight cities within the French zone.[13] General Koenig, the French zonal commander who attended that meeting, urged council members to be thorough and responsible in their planning, even if that took considerable time. In fact, the council moved so slowly that its impact was negligible, and it was subsequently dissolved after the creation of the Federal Republic. Nevertheless, it did serve as a short-lived international forum for discussion about urban planning.

The Americans exhibited much less interest in town planning or planning of any sort than the French or British. They gradually recognized the pressing need for massive housing construction, both to replace the housing damaged in the war and to provide new housing for refugees and displaced persons, and they urged the Germans to build modern, mass-produced, inexpensive housing units. Generally, however, the Americans failed to generate a consistent, high-level American policy on what, if anything, to do about helping the Germans repair their war-torn communities.

In a June 1944 letter to Secretary of State Cordell Hull to inquire about plans for occupied or liberated parts of Europe, Secretary of War Henry Stimson noted that "our military civil affairs agencies have confined themselves to the relatively restricted field of relief and rehabilitation and, in the absence of any definition of national policy of economic reconstruction, have obviously been unable to point their activities toward any such program." In his reply, Hull indicated that a "policy pertaining to rehabilitation and reconstruction" was being considered, but in the meantime any relief effort would be limited to that "which perhaps would prevent suffering and unrest among the civilian population."[14]

Whatever policy the Americans were contemplating, it had little to do with physical reconstruction. A policy planning committee for Germany had already recommended that there be "minimal interference with established administrative mechanisms and procedures" and that "municipal services [and] municipal enterprises" should remain under local German control.[15] In July 1944, it was proposed that the Organisation Todt, the Nazi heavy construction program that operated mostly in the territories occupied by the German armies, be continued after the war, but with new supervision and with forced foreign labor replaced by voluntary or "semivoluntary" German labor. Although nothing ever came of this plan, it was thought that this organization, highly experienced in large-scale engineering and construction, might assist major reconstruction projects in Germany as well as in areas that had been occupied by Germany.[16]

The American military government worked without the benefit of a clear-cut policy that might have resulted in organized aid for physical reconstruction. Instead they reinstituted German municipal administrations and viewed rebuilding as the province of municipal housing and construction offices. Moreover, by the fall of 1945, cost-cutting had forced the reduction of military government staffs, and physical reconstruction was an area that could easily be turned over to the Germans. Although military government officers did not always like the way city officials pursued reconstruction, the Americans seldom intervened in local decisions on rebuilding priorities, town planning, or architecture.[17]

General Lucius Clay certainly wanted to help alleviate the housing crisis, but he felt duty bound by the Joint Chiefs of Staff Directive JCS 1067 not to take any steps to improve the German standard of living. (JCS 1067 envisaged a harsh, punitive occupation, including the deindustrialization of the German economy.) In time he became comfortable invoking the escape clause that allowed measures to prevent "disease and unrest" in order to take steps to get crucial segments of the economy functioning again, but he always considered housing construction a task for the Germans. Nevertheless, in February 1947 his staff assisted Herbert Hoover, who had been asked by President Truman to study conditions in Germany, in preparing a report on the deplorable housing situation, and Clay himself recognized that housing comprised a major, long-term capital problem. Still, in his opinion "it was an entirely German problem."[18]

As escalating tensions between the United States and the Soviet Union led policymakers in Washington to adopt an increasingly cold-war mentality, General Clay realized that he could not expect to proceed indefinitely in the American zone on the basis of JCS 1067, even loosely interpreted, nor could he realistically expect to be able to coordinate American policy in Germany with Soviet policy. One result of this shifting political landscape was Clay's invitation to Walter Gropius to come to Germany as a visiting consultant on housing and city planning.

During his 1947 visit (discussed in Chapter 7), Gropius called for strong new planning and building laws that would facilitate massive realignment of property lines, the creation of a new research institution to investigate all aspects of urban life, and a strong central ministry to organize the process of reconstruction. Personnel should be drawn from the ranks of "the best technical experts . . . chosen for their ability rather than for party membership."[19] In the same way that Clay had persisted in working for U.S.–U.S.S.R. cooperation on Germany, Gropius suggested creating a national Institute for Planning and Building Integration under the auspices of the Institut für Bauwesen in the German Academy of Sciences, if the military governments could support such an organization. Although the academy was located in the Soviet sector of Berlin, it was headed by Gropius's friend Hans Scharoun, who lived in the Western part of the city. Gropius suggested that further gains in specialized knowledge could be obtained from more visits to Germany by appropriate foreign experts as well as from visits by "well-chosen Germans" to America. He also observed that the existing "shortage of manpower and materials" mandated "a rationalization of building methods."[20]

Gropius's recommendations for centralized organization of reconstruction went unheeded. When a German planner later wrote to Gropius asking for a copy of his recommendations to Clay, Gropius replied that "it was mouldering, like so much else, in the archives of the occupation army."[21] The same was true of similar recommendations made by Hans Blumenfeld and Samuel Zisman after their visit to Germany in 1949. They criticized the progress of reconstruction and American policy and felt that German reconstruction suffered from a debilitating lack of coherent, centrally directed, long-range planning. Obviously central planning could not occur until the formation of a central government, but Blumenfeld also noted that "the emphasis on the rights of the individual versus the state, healthy and natural as a reaction against the totalitarian tyranny of the Nazi Regime, has been frequently turned, in the dogmatic way characteristic of much German thinking, into opposition to any restriction of private activities, even where such restrictions are clearly in the interest of the great majority of the people."[22] In fact, "with the current aversion of German public opinion against officialdom, there is a tendency to consider *any* kind of private agency . . . as more democratic than any public agency."[23]

This tendency was potentially dangerous. German government agencies had been denazified, but some towns seemed to turn to private, voluntary planning organizations "as vehicles to bring back into positions of power persons who are ineligible for public office because of their political pasts."[24]

Moreover, "the carrying out of the currency reform without a simultaneous 'Lastenausgleich' [equalization of burdens] shifted economic power from the states, municipalities, cooperatives, and building societies to the owners of real estate and commodities. This has made condemnation for public purposes extremely difficult. In addition it has led to a misdirection of resources into non-essential building ."[25] Even the requirement that all levels of government operate on balanced budgets acted to undermine long-range planning because it restricted the judicious use of credit.

Blumenfeld and Zisman urged American High Commissioner John McCloy "to encourage the establishment and continued effective activity" of a strong, federal planning agency along the lines of state planning agencies in North-rhine-Westphalia and Lower Saxony, and they felt that the High Commission itself should maintain a high-level planning committee to help coordinate regional and town planning activities. They pointed approvingly to the Franco-German council on planning in the French zone. They argued that such central planning offices should address broad problems, while actual construction should remain in the hands of local city planners. They also recognized that some German cities, such as Hamburg and Frankfurt, had historically had strong local planning offices, and they recommended against transplanting American urban planning practices, which they considered comparatively weak, into postwar Germany.

To shape public opinion in favor of stronger urban planning and changes in the methods of housing construction, Zisman and Blumenfeld suggested that the High Commission support and help rehabilitate the German Association for Housing, Town and Regional Planning as a full-fledged member of the International Federation for Housing and Town Planning. They also strongly encouraged American support for cultural exchanges, preferably run by private rather than public organizations and specifically by German agencies rather than the American government.[26]

In the end, however, the Americans failed to endorse a highly organized and centralized urban reconstruction program for Germany, and the American contribution to rebuilding consisted of encouraging rationalized housing construction under the ECA program. The American government preferred to let local authorities or, even better, individual property owners handle rebuilding. Indeed, the absence of a strong official American policy spurred at least one attempt in the United States to galvanize private support for German reconstruction, but it had no success whatsoever.[27]

The Allies, who approached reconstruction in varied ways in their respective zones, also failed to coordinate or reconcile their efforts in the jointly occupied city of Berlin. The Soviets, who initially occupied the city, appointed Hans Scharoun as chief planner, and he quickly organized a team to prepare plans for a radically new layout of the city. Fully aware of the obstacles presented by the division of Berlin into four sectors occupied by Allies with distinct approaches to urban problems, Scharoun nonetheless sought to plan for Berlin as a unified city. He hoped to tempt the Allies with his plan by presenting it as "an example" of plans for a new metropolis.[28] Simultaneously, planners in the American sector worked on their own plans, which based reconstruction on the city's traditional form. Both sets of plans were put on public display in an exhibition mounted in a usable area of the old Hohenzollern Palace in August 1946. Upon the Russians' insistence that Scharoun be dismissed because he was too apolitical for their tastes, the all-Berlin legislature ousted him as chief planner in October 1946. The new city government chose Karl Bonatz as his successor. Bonatz rejected Scharoun's approach as too impractical and opted instead for the plans developed in the American sector.

The Berlin blockade, the split in the city government (and in the building department), and the formation of the two new German states further impeded effective reconstruction planning and naturally forced city planners to reorient their thinking. Because the basic documents, maps, and materials rested in the Soviet sector, planning was seriously disrupted by the division of the city in 1948. In response, the West Berlin planning office under Bonatz tried to plan simultaneously for the whole city and for a divided city. This was difficult. For example, when the West Berlin building administration organized a competition in 1948 for designs for the area around the Gedächtnis-kirche and in the following year presented its own plans for this area, there was a heated debate in the press about whether the official plan devoted too much attention to general traffic considerations and whether this area was in fact intended to become a new "City" center to rival the historic "City" in East Berlin, which in fact it was.[29]

The split between East and West was not the only allied contribution to the chaos of reconstruction in Berlin. Each allied force had different policies on materials allocations, building permits, and the like. The Soviet Union, for example, confiscated plants that produced building materials, although in at least one instance, two formerly private cement and lime–plaster plants which they had confiscated were "given back" to Karl Böttcher (the head of the Hauptamt für Aufbau/Durchführung in the city building office under Scha-roun) as if the plants had been Böttcher's own property.[30] Black market trading between sectors undermined any rational organization of the building industry. Hence, not only did final reconstruction planning for Berlin lag behind that of other cities but purely private, self-help rebuilding efforts also failed to produce as much building as in the West.

Berlin did, however, subsequently become the focus of the largest single American program to aid rebuilding of a German city. Once isolated from West Germany, the city became a unique political symbol and thus acquired a special claim to assistance. Not only was it necessary to stimulate the city's economy to ensure that pressures placed on it by the Soviet Union could be resisted, but it was also vital that the city *appear* healthy. A democratic Berlin must look functional and vibrant. By 1958, the total value of counterpart funds in Germany, when converted into credit in a revolving fund, equaled some DM 13 billion. About one-third of this, DM 4.5 billion, went to Berlin alone.[31]

Most of the Marshall Plan aid to Berlin during this period targeted four areas: an investment program which channeled funds into the rebuilding of factories, office buildings, retail stores, and hotels; a program to help underwrite orders for goods produced in the city; support for the city's operating budget; and a reconstruction program that by 1960 had spent DM 208 million on such things as clearing rubble, 233 million on housing, 43 million on schools and other buildings for social services, 466 million on new utilities, subways, streets, and bridges, and 120 million on the repair of green areas like the Tiergarten.[32] In addition to this infusion of Marshall aid, the Americans also contributed to specific building projects, such as the Kongreßhalle.[33] The American effort in this one city easily dwarfed the aid offered to any other West German city. This massive American support for Berlin was not, however, the result of a policy to aid urban recovery. On the contrary, it resulted from political sympathy for this particularly beleaguered city.

State and National Reconstruction Agencies

Many German planners favored some kind of relatively strong centralized organization of reconstruction. Hillebrecht and Arthur Dähn, a wartime colleague in Hamburg and later head of Hamburg's housing office, published a book in 1948 calling for thorough state planning of the economy generally and city reconstruction in particular.[34] Philipp Rappaport, director of the Ruhr housing association and also director of the German side of the Central Labor Office (Zentralamt für Arbeit) in the British zone, tried to get the German Cities Association (Deutscher Städtetag) to endorse the creation of a German Central Office for Reconstruction in the British Zone, which he hoped would evolve into a national ministry.[35] Rappaport continued to lobby for such a ministry when the Federal Republic was established.[36] In Munich in 1945, Karl Sebastian Preis urged creation of a Bavarian reconstruction ministry and the appointment of reconstruction commissars in all bombed cities.[37]

Not surprisingly, city planners sought a central organization that empowered city planners and not one that imposed constricting rules and procedural dictates upon them. They envisaged state or federal ministries that would exercise firm control over the economy while granting planners all the building material, labor, and financial support they requested. They also sought full legal powers to make sweeping changes in the layout of the old cities. In essence, they felt that the cities should be self-governing, but because reconstruction was too large a task to be completely self-financed, they also sought limited state involvement. Either the planners failed to conceive of a better way of asserting their hegemony over reconstruction or they suffered from great naiveté in propounding this scheme, for surely state and federal reconstruction ministers managing the economy and distributing funds would insist on exerting considerable influence over decisions about the utilization of these resources.

The new federal government created in 1949 contained a housing ministry but not a reconstruction or building ministry. Even though it allocated substantial funds, the housing ministry was relatively weak because of its nontraditional status and its concentration on one specific issue.[38] Indeed, once the housing crisis was solved, the ministry would undoubtedly be dissolved. The existence of a federal ministry also implied not only the possibility of central direction but also the potential for conflicts between the ministries and the cities and between the states and the federal government. In an attempt to reduce the differences between state building and housing agencies, the federal government established a coordinating committee that functioned much like the coordinating committee under the Allies.[39]

Unlike the federal government, most of the states did establish reconstruction ministries. In Northrhine-Westphalia, for example, the ministry for reconstruction was organized like a city building administration. It included nine departments: general matters; housing policy, statistics, small settlements; city planning and rubble removal; building standards and permits; building and housing law; financing of housing construction; allocation of housing; building inspections and the production and allocation of building materials; and buildings and other surface construction owned by the state.[40] In any of these areas the ministry might issue regulations and require consultation with city officials, in addition to actually controlling the flow of funds and materials. In some cases, the ministry enjoyed remarkably broad reach. A memo issued in April 1947 detailing procedures for cracking down on black market activity, for example, was sent to 145 persons and organizations, including 57 officials on different levels, 4 church organizations, 10 interest group organizations like the Cities Association, 7 trade unions, and 67 chambers of commerce and umbrella associations for one or another industry related to building.[41] Finally, the ministry included a city planning committee, headed by Erich Kühn, which included participants such as Rappaport and Münster's planner, Heinrich Bartmann. This committee examined and commented on plans prepared by the cities in the state.[42]

The state of Bavaria, typically something of a maverick among German states, created an interesting special commission instead of a reconstruction ministry to consider questions of statewide importance that dealt with reconstruction. The creation of this Bayerischer Aufbaurat was announced in July 1948. Its purpose was to provide a forum in which experts could criticize proposals submitted by the state government and at the same time present its own ideas. This format, it was hoped, would mobilize broad forces in support of rebuilding.[43] The work of the Aufbaurat was to take place in four committees: overall planning, technical questions, financial questions, and legal or administrative questions. The business manager of the new organization, and chairman of all four committees, was Helmut Fischer, the head of Munich's reconstruction office.

From the beginning, it was clear that financial and legal issues rather than city planning itself would monopolize committee discussions. Certainly questions of architectural form would hardly ever be broached. The composition of the membership at the time of the first meeting, broken down by affiliation in Table 9.1, dictated this ordering of priorities. Although the membership list changed for later meetings, it was always heavily weighted against town plan-

TABLE 9.1.   Membership in the Bayerischer Aufbaurat

State and county government officials	16
City officials	5
Banking and insurance	4
Associations of renters, property owners, home builders	4
Building industry, engineers	6
Chambers of commerce, industry, crafts	2
Postal service, railroads	2
Refugee association	1
Farmers association	1
Associations of cities, villages	2
Affiliation not given	5
Total	48

Source: BHSA/Bayer. Staatskanzlei, 19 July 1976/ 75 (2653)/ Bayer. Aufbaurat: Organization, 22625, Verzeichnis der Mitglieder, 11 October 1948, with the business manager Fischer included.

ners and architects, a circumstance that manifested itself in the actual work of the commission. When Fischer reported on the activities of the Aufbaurat for the period from July 1949 to August 1950, for example, he stated that there had been 32 committee meetings. However, the general planning committee had met but once, and the technical committee, which might have considered specific architectural issues, not at all. The most productive work had gone into proposals for financing construction, while the committee on law had discussed and decided to oppose passage of the new comprehensive building law requested by the cities.[44] Clearly this Bavarian Aufbaurat served more as a forum for conservative property interests than as a representative of comprehensive planning. This focus accorded beautifully with the consistently conservative tenor of the state, as well as with the orientation of Helmut Fischer, its manager and the individual who not coincidentally spoke most often in the meetings. To the extent that this organization affected the passage of legislation, especially on financing, it was doubtless influential, but except for Fischer, Bavaria's city planners could not have been very satisfied with it.

The National Associations and Their Affiliates

Although Germany lacked a national reconstruction ministry, the process of urban reconstruction was at least in part organized nationally through a few influential private associations. In fact, at a meeting of the Arbeitsstab Wiederaufbauplanung in 1944, Karl Maria Hettlage had urged that centralized coordination and leadership of reconstruction be placed in the hands of the major private associations rather than in the hands of a government agency.[45] Throughout the period of military occupation following the war, such associations helped compensate for the lack of a national government by providing a forum for the exchange of knowledge and experience. This exchange in turn helps account for some of the similarities in reconstruction that transcended local and state boundaries.

The natural home for these organizations would have been Berlin, the former capital. An Institute for Building was established by the German Academy of Sciences in the Soviet sector of Berlin (Institut für Bauwesen an der Deutschen Akademie der Wissenschaften) in October 1947, with the architect Hans Scharoun as its head. With its 11 sections addressing such issues as housing, standardization, transportation, and historic preservation, the Institute for Building was conceived as a national institution, but the political situation in Berlin limited its activities primarily to that city. In 1950 it was transformed into the German Academy of Building (Deutsche Bauakademie) and put under a new director, Kurt Liebknecht, who ensured that the academy endorsed the Soviet approach to city planning and architecture. This alienated the western members, who subsequently abandoned the institute, leaving it without any influence in the West.[46]

With the Academy of Sciences out of the picture, the most prestigious and influential organizations included the German Cities Association (Deutscher Städtetag) and particularly its building committee, the German Federation for Housing, Town and Regional Planning (Deutscher Verband für Wohnungswesen, Städtebau und Raumplanung), and the German Academy for Town and Regional Planning (Deutscher Akademie für Städtebau und Landesplanung). All represented revivals of organizations that had existed before 1933, when they experienced Nazi "coordination" and succumbed to Nazi control. To some extent their membership overlapped, since all of the most important city planners, mayors, and city managers as well as many important architects subscribed to one or more of these organizations. Many of the leading figures have been previously discussed. They included Rudolf Hillebrecht of Hannover, Philipp Rappaport of Essen, Arnulf Klett of Stuttgart, Helmut Fischer of Munich, Herbert Boehm of Frankfurt, Herbert Jensen of Kiel, Heinz Schmeissner of Nuremberg, Johannes Göderitz of Braunschweig, and Wilhelm Dittus of Berlin. Often the most valuable discussions took place in committee meetings and small "working" sessions attended by the most important and prestigious planners, but large, plenary meetings also gave planners and officials from small towns an opportunity to exchange views. Some 700 persons, for example, attended the June 1948 meeting of the German Federation for Housing, City, and Regional Planning. They heard Sir George Lionel Pepler, president of the International Association for Housing and City Planning, Jacqueline Tyrwhitt, head of the London School for Planning Research for Regional Development, and Max Lock, head of the planning department of the city of Portsmouth, report on developments in English town and regional planning. These keynote addresses were followed by a presentation of various aspects of the planning for the rebuilding of Frankfurt, the meeting's host city.[47]

At one time or another, all of these national organizations discussed and passed resolutions on the major issues: building law, traffic planning, housing construction, historic preservation, rubble clearance and salvage, financing, and so on. The meetings of the German Academy for City and Regional Planning and its provincial affiliates concentrated particularly on regional planning, planning law, traffic planning, and planning abroad. Through their meetings, correspondence, and publications, members added to the information imparted by professional journals and kept abreast of activity occurring elsewhere. The associations lobbied state and national government officials and invited them to meetings. Indeed, these organizations provided the state and national governments with a clearly defined sense of what the city governments collectively wanted and needed.[48]

Lastly, established architects sought to influence reconstruction through their own professional association—the Association of German Architects (Bund Deutscher Architekten, or BDA). The relationship between the BDA and city building offices and other organizations could be rather tricky and tempestuous. Indeed, a major point of contention concerned the fundamental question of whether private architects even had a role in the planning and decision-making process. City officials felt that architects should be content with serving on advisory commissions and participating in planning competitions. The architects criticized the commissions for being too narrow and condemned the competitions for often being rigged against them. They demanded a formal, organized structure for participation in reconstruction planning.[49]

This conflict was particularly pronounced in Bavaria. Munich's BDA was founded anew in June 1945. Two years later, its president was urging the city to use independent architects in an organized, systematic fashion to advise on general planning and to act as expert referees in planning and rebuilding blocks and neighborhoods.[50] With the jurist-bureaucrat Helmut Fischer dominating the city's reconstruction apparatus, however, this plea went unheeded. Upon becoming business manager and effective head of the Bavarian Aufbaurat, Fischer's differences with the independent architects were magnified. The architects complained that the Aufbaurat ignored them since it considered only legal and financial questions and totally avoided issues of architectural form.[51] They also contended that Fischer shunted aside "cultural matters" and what he considered "peripheral issues, [such as] questions of architectural form."[52] Never one to avoid a fight, Fischer bluntly informed the architects that new planning, "if it is to be more than just a pipe dream," is possible only after such problems as land use, financing, and settlement of refugees have been resolved.[53] This heated argument continued into mid-1950, but Fischer's infighting skills proved successful in deflecting all attacks from the organized architects.

Organization at the Town Level

Traditional Practice

German cities had enjoyed a long tradition of self-administration and had always struggled to resist state and national interference in local affairs. Reconstruction was assumed to be a local matter, although that assumption was undermined somewhat in the cases of cities that also served as state capitals, and city officials felt free to organize the local reconstruction effort as they saw fit. The Allies, as noted previously, were not heavily involved in these matters, and no national reconstruction ministry existed. The state reconstruction ministries, under the state reconstruction laws, left primary responsibility for rebuilding in the hands of town governments. As described earlier, some towns assigned reconstruction to the traditional building administration, while others established new organizations to deal with what was recognized as an extraordinary situation.

Every German city had maintained some sort of building office before the war, and these offices naturally constituted a strong basis of institutional and practical continuity in urban planning and building after the war, in spite of sometimes significant personnel changes. Because Germany had not had a uniform system of local government, building administrations differed from city to city. Nevertheless, Lübeck's building office offers a general idea of the typical structure of such offices. In December 1945, a director responsible to the city council and mayor headed Lübeck's building administration. The office was divided into 13 subsections, which assumed responsibility for general administrative matters, parks and cemeteries, building inspections, army buildings, air force installations, city heating plants and machine shops, and city building activities at nearby Travemünde. Two sections (*Hochbauamt*) handled above-ground building activity, which included such things as planning and constructing new administrative buildings and housing, the evaluation and repair of bomb damage, and the rationing of building materials. Three sections dealt with surface and below-ground construction (*Tiefbauamt*), such as roads, bridges, and planning for a new subway. The Tiefbauamt also gathered statistical data. Finally, a section devoted to city planning and reconstruction included urban renewal projects, planning of new suburbs and other extensions of the city, and rebuilding of the historic old city.[54]

Most cities had a building office organized with subsections similar to those of Lübeck. Some cities added new sections to deal with rubble clearance, the rationing of building materials, and other matters somewhat beyond the traditional scope of the office and related to reconstruction, a process which would eventually be completed and give way to normal routines. In addition, all city governments maintained other departments or committees whose functions were closely related to reconstruction, such as land offices, which managed city properties and registered all property transactions, and housing offices, which ran city-owned housing projects. In Cologne, this committee (the *Städtebaukonferenz*) met almost weekly to evaluate requests for building permits. Cologne's committee typically included representatives of the major departments of city government, as well as the city conservator and a member of the local architects' association. From 1945 to 1948, the committee met 141 times and considered 2,995 requests for permits, an average of 21 per meeting.[55] Cities normally tapped local chambers of industry and commerce to assist in mediating between conflicting interests of the city and the private economy. Such compromises might include setting priorities for allocating building materials or granting of business licenses to construction firms.[56]

In addition, the city parliaments or councils had committees that analyzed and made recommendations on building or planning proposals that required legislative action and supervised the activities of the building administration. Cologne's city planning committee (*Stadtplanungsausschuss*) consisted of representatives of the various political parties and the city administration. It met every two weeks and considered from 6 to 20 issues each session. These ranged from minor alterations of building lines to the layout of a major artery and the purchase of land required for such a massive project.[57]

Finally, virtually every city featured organizations of citizens devoted to the reconstruction, restoration, and/or preservation of beloved historic monuments. These organizations raised funds for specific projects, sometimes helped the city choose an architect or builder, and regularly lobbied in the press and in city council meetings on behalf of their goals. In Munich, to cite but one example, a society called the Friends of the Residence raised funds for rebuilding the huge royal palace, while another society helped push through the reconstruction of the Peterskirche, and a special foundation raised money for the restoration of a number of other historic buildings and monuments, including such things as fountains.[58]

Most aspects of urban reconstruction, therefore, were highly organized, either by official building administrations or by private associations. A longstanding tradition even dictated the process of gaining advice from independent architects not employed by the city. Often before making final decisions on specific building projects or on broad planning, cities used a publicly announced competition as a mechanism for soliciting ideas other than those put forward by their in-house city architects. Almost all of the major cities staged competitions in the early postwar years—some as early as 1945.[59]

These architectural and planning competitions had existed and followed a set procedure in Germany since the late nineteenth century.[60] Cities initiated this process, endorsed by the German Association of Architects, by announcing the framework of the competition, in which the priorities of the city were specified as precisely as possible and competitors were provided with the necessary technical information.[61] The competitions might be limited to a single city or to a region, or they might encourage any qualified individual to submit an entry. Members of the building administration, representatives of the city council, a few independent experts (usually planners, architects, or professors of architecture or planning from other cities), and perhaps a leading local citizen or two, typically comprised prize juries. First prizes were not always awarded, and cities were not committed to use any of the submissions. City building administrations often adapted and combined the best ideas from prize-winning entries, although occasionally a prize winner's submission merited a contract based on its own specifications and vision.

Some criticized planning competitions as a waste of time and energy. Alfons Leitl and Philipp Rappaport, for example, argued that the complexity of the issues required a thorough mastery of large amounts of specialized data. The majority of competition entries, they felt, revealed that few of the participating architects had the time or competence to prepare useful designs. They concluded that in most cases town planning should be undertaken by the appropriate planning office, which could consult private architects should the need arise.[62]

A capable building administration director—one who was both an imaginative and thorough planner and a vigorous administrator and who had reasonably efficient and adequate personnel backed by a tradition of achievement—usually rendered other, outside efforts to administer and guide reconstruction superfluous. In some cities, key personnel and much of the organizational structure of the building offices carried over from the war years into peacetime. For example, Kiel's building director, Herbert Jensen, could move immediately to the task of reconstruction planning because he had no need to reconstitute the city's building offices. The same was true of Joseph Schlippe in Freiburg. Rudolf Hillebrecht, appointed head of the building administration of Hannover in mid-1948, quickly reorganized and consolidated some of the traditional sections to better suit them to current needs. Max Guther, appointed director in Ulm in 1947, headed the planning office, the land office, and the city's economic affairs office simultaneously and hence effectively controlled reconstruction in that city.[63]

Extraordinary Agencies

Although the city building offices normally directed planning and construction activities, important precedents set both before 1933 and under the Nazis placed authority in the hands of individuals who stood outside the city governments. Freed from the pressures of party politics and from the stultifying effects of bureaucracy, the independent architect was supposedly capable of approaching his task in a far more creative fashion than could be expected of a civil servant. Thus Fritz Schumacher had been invited as an outsider to plan for Cologne in the 1920s. Similarly, Konstanty Gutschow had worked independently for Hamburg under the Nazis and had headed a hardworking, efficient team of architects and planners. In 1944, as noted earlier, the Arbeitsstab Wiederaufbauplanung assigned and directed private architects to supervise reconstruction planning in bombed cities all over the Reich. Some cities, therefore, naturally thought that independent planners and organizations would also facilitate postwar reconstruction. They tried several different organizational forms with varying degrees of success. In northern Germany, where wartime reconstruction planning had been most advanced, this approach worked particularly well.

Postwar reconstruction in Hamburg proved complicated precisely because of the success of Konstanty Gutschow's wartime organization. During the war two organizations dealt with planning and building in Hamburg. Gutschow led a private but very large office that planned the redesign of Hamburg as a representative Nazi city, while the regular city building offices retained responsibility for existing streets, buildings, and so forth. Upon suspension of planning for a new Hamburg early in the war, Gutschow's office had assumed responsibility for emergency construction projects, such as air raid shelters, rubble clearance, and repairs of housing and other buildings. His office accomplished this work so adeptly that, for a time, the city offices had been merged with Gutschow's and placed under his control. Though he continued as the architect responsible for the redesign of the city, Gutschow resigned his city offices in late 1943, an act that upset and blurred lines of responsibility and accountability in the city building office, a situation which lasted until the end of the war.

In 1945, the newly arrived British occupation forces found the regular building offices functioning fairly well, undoubtedly because key officials like Hans Berlage of the planning department had served continuously through the war and into the postwar era. Nevertheless, the British apparently wanted a more efficient and active reconstruction office, and they asked Gutschow, not the regular building administration, to organize the reconstruction effort. One of Gutschow's reconstruction proposals, displayed in Figure 9.1, was based on his wartime thinking, which envisaged concentrating on five designated reconstruction areas. As he had done with his earlier 1940 plans, he distributed copies of his proposals to dozens of officials and architects "so that many forces will feel themselves also responsible for creating the general city plan." He also proposed methods for streamlining the bureaucracy of the building administration.[64] Gutschow, however, had been too prominent, too close to the Nazis to be able to continue to plan in Hamburg. His contract was terminated in December 1945.

Although war losses and denazification had considerably reduced the personnel levels of most city governments, Hamburg's building office had held up rather well. Table 9.2 indicates the condition of the staff of the Hamburg building offices before and after the war. The number of personnel was actually greater in 1949 than before the war, partly because the building administration had absorbed most of the staff of Gutschow's private office.

In spite of the strength of the building administration and its continuity in personnel, Hamburg's city government still began the postwar period by creating an extraordinary committee (a Stadtplanungsausschuss) to initiate new city planning. During its first five months, from September 1945 to February 1946,

TABLE 9.2. Hamburg Building Administration Personnel

	1939	1949	Positions unfilled	POWs	Total positions
Civil servants	755	395	203	68	666
Salaried employees	1,043	1,457	255	95	1,807
Wage-earning workers	3,663	3,096	741	214	4,051
Total	5,491	4,948	1,199	377	6,524

Source: BSH/ Baudeputation Protocols, vol. 1, session 19, 31 January 1949, pp. 6–7.

Contents in Catchwords:	Appropriate Drawings and Illustrations

1. The emergency plan as a result of the general plan. Methodology for chronological rebuilding. 5 reconstruction areas: Jarrestraßenviertel, Barmbeck-Nord, Barmbeck-Dulsberg, Hamm, Horn. Areas where building prohibited.

Emergency plan with illustrations

2. Conditions. Damage to buildings. Type and size of damaged housing. Inhabited housing. Housing in cellars.

For each of the 5 reconstruction areas:
a) Damage map, 1:10,000
b) Reconstruction plan, 1:10,000

3. Proposal. Necessity of partial but insignificant alterations. Rational for demolitions. Design of roof lines. New building. Number of dwellings. Division of dwellings.

c) Example of blocks to be opened up.
d) Model for changing common green areas inside the residential blocks into truck gardens.

4. Urban planning structure. Building density. Housing density. Comparisons with areas of older buildings and planning goals. Commercial needs: arrangement of commercial courtyards, a shopping district. Public needs: schools, post offices, etc.

As examples from different areas:
a) Plan of a commercial courtyard
b) Administrative buildings and their impact
c) Schools and school districts. Housing density as example, before the destruction, today, and after rebuilding

5. Economic questions in construction Organization of large building sites. Production of prefabricated building elements. Consumption of building materials. Transportation. Economic plan for building industry. Organization.

Workshops for prefabrication of building elements
Plan for organizing a large building site
Transportation plan

6. Financial questions. Earlier conditions. Depreciation of mortgages. New financing. Rents.

7. Economic consequences for city utilities, facilities. Traffic. Supplies. Upkeep of streets. Waste. Schools, post offices, etc.

8. Practical implementation. Fundamental suggestions. Burdens on property owners. Time tables for beginning construction. Unrestricted and forced building.

Source: SAH, Baubehörde I/B2 Wiederaufbauleitung, E9.

FIGURE 9.1. Organization plan for the "reconstruction areas," Hamburg, 8 August 1945.

this six-member committee was comprised of three city officials, including Berlage, and three private architects with experience in planning. Architect Gerhard Langmaack chaired the committee until March, when his departure resulted in a period of restructuring. In September Otto Meyer-Ottens, the new chief of the building administration, assumed leadership of the committee, while the private architect Friedrich Ostermeyer accepted responsibility for preparing the detailed plans.[65] In mid-1947, upon completion of the preliminary general plan, the planning committee was dissolved, and the building administration took charge of all aspects of reconstruction.

In creating a special committee composed of both officials and private architects, Hamburg clearly reacted to the uncertain political reputation of planning in the city during the war. Gutschow and his team had been very effective, perhaps more effective than any other planning group in Germany, but Gutschow's Nazi affiliation left him politically tainted, and suspicion likewise fell on senior members of the building administration. The advantage of creating a special planning committee was that it could function outside the regular bureaucratic machinery and therefore avoid too much political scrutiny. At the same time, such a committee could tap valuable experience accumulated during the war years. As the political climate stabilized and the building administration resumed its normal functions and routines with Meyer-Ottens as its head, such a committee was no longer needed, and it was dissolved.

The northern cities proved particularly adept at devising strategies and creating special committees to gain general public support for their projects and voluntary cooperation from property owners in the areas designated for reconstruction.[66] In Kiel, Jensen's building office, for example, had completed a new general town plan by May 1946. In 1948, Jensen organized a competition to solicit designs for rebuilding the inner city, and in April 1949, he proposed a major redrawing of property and street lines in that area, especially along the Holtenauer Straße, the major thoroughfare in the inner city. A leading town banker helped Jensen work out details which affected property owners, and completed plans were approved within a year. At this point new organizations were created under the reconstruction law of Schleswig-Holstein to implement the necessary property consolidations, trades, or sales. Next, a building corporation, the Aufbaugenossenschaft Kiel Holtenauer Straße, was established to finance and supervise actual construction.[67] By the end of 1952, the initial construction phase of this key project was completed—testimony to the effectiveness of Jensen and the city building office.

Hamburg likewise created a special organization to mediate between city planners and private property owners over questions of redrawing property lines. The Gesellschaft zur Förderung des Wiederaufbaus m.b.H. was founded jointly by an umbrella association of property owners' organizations, an association of housing corporations, and an organization that represented tenants. It enjoyed particular success in winning the voluntary cooperation of property owners in reconstructing the Hammerbrook area, a section of the city totally devastated by the bombing.[68]

The best known and most widely praised of the private associations established to further reconstruction were in Bremen and Hannover. The first postwar years in Bremen saw a flurry of organizational activity. The occupation forces demanded the resignation of Wilhelm Wortmann, the chief wartime city and regional planner, and replaced him with Klaus Tippel, an able man who had little experience in urban planning.[69] In January 1946, property owners on the Sögestraße, an important street in the inner city, founded a Reconstruction Association Sögestraße and engaged a private architect, Kurt Haering, to develop a reconstruction plan. Seven or eight similar associations were formed soon thereafter by property owners on other streets. Haering's proposals were presented to city authorities in October of that year, but differences with Tippel and uncertainty about the city's legal power to make planning decisions combined to prevent approval. In July 1947 these small associations combined to form an umbrella association (Verein "Wiederaufbaugemeinschaften Stadtmitte Bremen") to plan the rebuilding of the central city. Within a year, the new umbrella association had expanded its activities to include planning for the whole city, and the association was renamed the Aufbaugemeinschaft Bremen. This new name indicated that the organization's purpose had expanded from *reconstruction* planning to general planning. The association engaged nine private architects to develop plans and invited former city planner Wortmann to serve as technical adviser.

Another private organization, the Working Association for City Planning (Arbeitsgemeinschaft für Stadtplanung), simultaneously pursued planning activity in Bremen. Founded in 1947 at the urging of the local architects' association and a group styling itself a "union for urban planning," this association included nine private architects and four members of the city planning department who struggled to rejuvenate planning begun in Bremen in 1926 but abruptly halted with the onset of the depression of 1930. Four of the architects working for the Aufbaugemeinschaft Bremen also worked for the Arbeitsgemeinschaft.

Reconstruction planning for Bremen was thus clearly shared by the city administration and private planning organizations in a complicated arrangement which boasted several advantages. It involved prominent property owners and private architects in the planning process from the beginning, a situation which eased the process of actually implementing the plans and anticipated and hushed subsequent architectural condemnation of the chosen course of reconstruction. Additionally, the overlapping membership facilitated coordination with the city government and hence promoted a consensus about the actions to be taken. This arrangement also permitted the continuing influence of Wilhelm Wortmann, who enjoyed the confidence of the merchant community and often mediated between the city administration and property owners.[70]

In practice, this arrangement produced uneven results. On the one hand, the private reconstruction associations aptly managed the redrawing of property lines to consolidate small building lots. On the other hand, disagreements about planning, especially the location of new traffic arteries and the width of streets in the city center, were vociferous enough to warrant outside evaluations on several occasions. In 1948, for example, a committee of the German Academy of Town and Regional Planning was called in to reconcile conflicting plans, and eventually, on Wortmann's recommendation, Franz Rosenberg arrived from Braunschweig in early 1949 to provide new leadership in the city administration. Only under Rosenberg's direction was the city finally able to move ahead with reconstruction.

Other cities imitated the Bremen model of an Aufbaugemeinschaft includ-ing property owners, private architects, and city building officials, in spite of its difficulties. Hannover founded an Aufbaugemeinschaft in 1949 based on Bremen's model. The key figures in the Hannover reconstruction association were Rudolf Hillebrecht, who became director of the city building administra-tion in 1948, and Konstanty Gutschow, who served as technical adviser for the association.[71] Both had long been friends of Wortmann. Hillebrecht came to Hannover after having worked for three years in the building branch of the economic division of the British occupation government in Minden. Hille-brecht had not been a member of the Nazi party and suffered no negative consequences for his wartime work in Hamburg. In bringing Gutschow to Hannover, Hillebrecht displayed personal and professional loyalty by offering his friend and former mentor an opportunity to work again as a planner. The Aufbaugemeinschaft Hannover contained representatives of the city govern-ment, the Hannover Trade Fair, the local property owners' associations, credit associations, the chamber of commerce, labor unions, and leading con-struction firms.

The Aufbaugemeinschaft's several functions included serving as a forum for discussion of overall planning goals and specifically the 1949 competition for the redesign and reconstruction of the inner city. Along with the building office, it delegated "block architects" to work with property owners on the redesign of whole blocks and to facilitate voluntary property exchanges and consolidation. It also organized a clearing house for property transactions in the reconstruc-tion area. (Of the 1,000 affected land parcels, 20% were offered for sale, 11% exchanged for other parcels, 64% were to be built upon unchanged, and 5% still awaited a decision at the end of 1949.) The Aufbaugemeinschaft selected the area around one of the old inner city churches, the Kreuzkirche, as a model project for the building of new inner-city housing. This project became a center-piece for the Constructa building exhibition of 1951. Finally, under the auspices of the Aufbaugemeinschaft, Hillebrecht, Gutschow, and other members of the building administration participated in literally hundreds of meetings with vari-ous groups to discuss reconstruction plans.

The efforts of the building office under Hillebrecht and Hannover's Aufbaugemeinschaft were so successful that the city soon acquired a reputa-tion as the model for urban reconstruction in Germany. The combination of the building administration's vigorous leadership, the reconstruction associa-tion's impressive technical competence, and the willingness of both the city government and private citizens and organizations to work together proved ideal. Hannover's reconstruction experienced virtually no acrimony, and plan-ning and actual construction proceeded smoothly and fairly quickly. This was quite remarkable, given that theoretically up to 65 different steps were neces-sary merely to clarify property questions.[72] As one historian later put it, "Because nearly all problems were worked out in informal negotiations, . . . the decision-making process seems deceptively simple."[73]

In the south, Nuremberg organized its reconstruction effort in a rather simple and effective form as well. On the initiative of Mayor Otto Ziebill and with the unanimous support of the city council, a special committee known as the Curatorium for the Rebuilding of the City of Nuremberg was established in September 1948 as an independent forum for the discussion of reconstruction issues. Its members included architects, engineers, economists, representatives of different segments of the town's economy, educators, and other specialists. The Curatorium used its independence to help free the course of reconstruction from "bureaucratic restraints."[74] The considerable experience and impressive reputations of the committee's members infused the Curatorium's recommendations with enviable influence. Moreover, it was felt that the Curatorium's independence and prestige could particularly help this city—home of the spectacular Nazi party congresses—rebuild positively and rehabilitate "the name of the city of Nuremberg, which had suffered considerably from the political events of the past years."[75]

The Curatorium functioned until December 1954, when it was dissolved in accordance with its bylaws. Throughout its eight-year existence, it had 67 members, including 14 architects or builders, 11 members of the city council, and 9 members of the city administration. Seventeen persons served for virtually the entire period of the Curatorium's existence. Its work was performed in 26 committees that considered matters ranging from planning to social housing and building law to special exhibitions. Of particular importance were those committees that worked with the city's building officials on planning and the architectural committee. The latter reviewed plans for individual building projects and made recommendations for or against approval, thereby lending some stylistic coherence to reconstruction. In Nuremburg too, then, the key organization existed outside the city government, although members of the building administration also served on the Curatorium. Important reconstruction decisions, therefore, were always backed by the combined weight of the government and the Curatorium's experts and notables.

Like the mayor of Nuremberg, Munich's Lord Mayor Scharnagl also aspired to create a large, independent committee of leading citizens to provide advice and guidance on reconstruction. In the fall of 1945, he began to assemble such a committee, only to encounter immediate obstacles. First, he had problems getting the right membership. Fritz Schumacher, for example, declined to be a member, insisting that his 76 years, ill health, and residency in Lüneburg in the far north of Germany prohibited travel. At best, he could review written material.[76] Other early candidates for membership turned out to be tainted politically. One of the other Munich mayors suggested inviting the landscape architect Alwin Seifert, who had been responsible for landscaping the new Autobahn system during the Nazi era. When first approached about joining the reconstruction committee, Seifert declared that, although he had served as chief landscape architect for highways (Reichslandschaftsanwalt des Generalinspektors für das deutsche Strassenwesen) under the direction of the Organisation Todt, in fact "with his labor he served neither the Party, nor Dr. Todt, nor highway construction, but rather the beauty and health of our landscape, the eternal home of the Germans," and he then went on to detail his conflicts with various high-ranking Nazi officials.[77] Because of his party affiliations, however,

Seifert's Munich house had been confiscated and turned over to a former concentration camp inmate. When Seifert informed the occupant of his house that the forthcoming appointment to the reconstruction committee was the first step toward full rehabilitation and the regaining of his house, the former camp inmate reacted by sending the mayor some incriminating documents he had found in the house. In addition to enjoying the confidence of Hess, Himmler, Bormann, and Ley, Seifert had also been the landscape architect for the Nazi complex at the Obersalzburg. The personnel director of the city government subsequently remarked that, "given this political and military incrimination of Seifert, it is not advisable that he be involved in any sort of task connected with the reconstruction of the city of Munich."[78]

After overcoming these sorts of impediments, Scharnagl's reconstruction committee finally met in March 1946, having invited 90 notable town citizens to become members. The committee never really amounted to much, however, and certainly never achieved the prominent role enjoyed by Nuremberg's Curatorium. Its most important accomplishment was probably a reconstruction plan proposed by Karl Meitinger, but even this was laden with controversy and complications. During the war, a special office under Hermann Giesler had overseen Munich's redesign as "the capital of the movement." Meitinger, although not directly involved in that project, served as the city building director and found himself politically tainted. In the spring of 1946 he was granted early "retirement," which allowed him to keep his pension, a benefit forfeited by those abruptly removed from their positions by the denazification process.[79] His reconstruction proposal was indeed one of the first general reconstruction plans completed after the war. Although he wrote it while serving on Scharnagl's reconstruction committee, it was published in the name of the city building office, with a foreword by the lord mayor.[80] Publishing the first postwar plan under Meitinger's name would have meant ignoring or flouting political realities to an embarrassing extent by the reconstruction committee and the city government.

Countering the mayor's efforts to guide the reconstruction process through this large committee of notables, another proposal called for radically decentralizing reconstruction. In 1946, Otto Völkers, a leading member of the Munich architects' association, argued that property owners acting through specially organized block corporations rebuild the city block by block. In this case, initiative would come from the private sector, not government.[81] In certain respects, this proposal resembled the block associations in Kiel and Hannover.

Völkers's idea was not adopted, however, and probably for the same reason that Mayor Scharnagl's reconstruction committee was deprived of much influence, namely, the persistence of the directors of the city building administration in retaining control of reconstruction. Traditionally the city building administration had functioned as a cohesive unit, but in December 1945, a new department for reconstruction was established under Karl Sebastian Preis. Trained in finance and economics, Preis had headed the city utilities and housing offices prior to his dismissal by the Nazis in March 1933—the same time that Scharnagl had been ousted as mayor. When the American occupation forces reinstated Scharnagl in May 1945, he promptly recalled Preis to head first the housing office and then the new reconstruction office.[82]

Designated Section (*Referat*) 12, the reconstruction office's most important initial tasks included clearing rubble and salvaging building materials; repairing damaged buildings; planning and constructing new housing projects; organizing the construction industry, including allocation of labor and building materials; financing rebuilding; and general cartography. The organizational chart depicted in Figure 9.2, however, indicates that Preis entertained much greater ambitions for his office. Prepared by Preis in January 1946, the heavy lettering in this organizational plan equates the hierarchical level of the head of Section 12 (Preis) with the lord mayor. The mayor's advisory committee stands between the mayor and Preis, but it could advise only Preis, not other departments that dealt with reconstruction. The head of Section 12 is clearly responsible for directing the whole show. Preis's chart places Section 13, the traditional city building office, in a subordinate position, as well as six other sections of the city government that in fact enjoyed the same legal status as Section 12. He even subordinated the building section of the Bavarian Ministry of the Interior to Section 12. In spite of its seemingly arrogant assumptions, this chart did not reflect a passing fantasy. In December 1945, Preis had submitted a draft of a reconstruction law for Bavaria that called for installing a reconstruction commissar with wide-ranging powers in each city. Although supported by Munich and other large Bavarian cities, Preis's draft was opposed by the Bavarian state government and never became law. Moreover, Preis soon found himself feuding with the state over control of rubble clearance and building priorities in Munich.[83]

Nevertheless, Preis's ideas had a significant impact on the course of Munich's reconstruction. In a June 1946 letter to Schumacher, Mayor Scharnagl reported that his grand reconstruction committee was not functioning as he had hoped because "Stadtrat Preis . . . has mainly followed his own train of thought and has turned for help to those individuals whom he himself picked." Scharnagl complained that Preis had worked less on "large scale planning" than on "the more immediate tasks of the moment, especially rubble clearance." He added, "With the many demands on my own time, I have been unable to pursue my own ideas and goals of laying the basis for wide-ranging planning."[84] Scharnagl's analysis of the situation was accurate. As the organizational plan in Figure 9.2 shows, Preis viewed city planning as a small part of the picture—perhaps because it was subsumed under Section 13, the traditional building office.

Preis died in May 1946, and Helmut Fischer, another strong personality, replaced him. Like Preis, Fischer was an administrator by training and experience, not an architect or city planner. He too sought to control the whole reconstruction process, but it took him some time to consolidate his position. The leadership vacuum that had existed in Section 13 since the awkward retirement of Meitinger had finally been filled by the appointment of Hermann Leitenstorfer in August 1947. (Meitinger's effective date of retirement

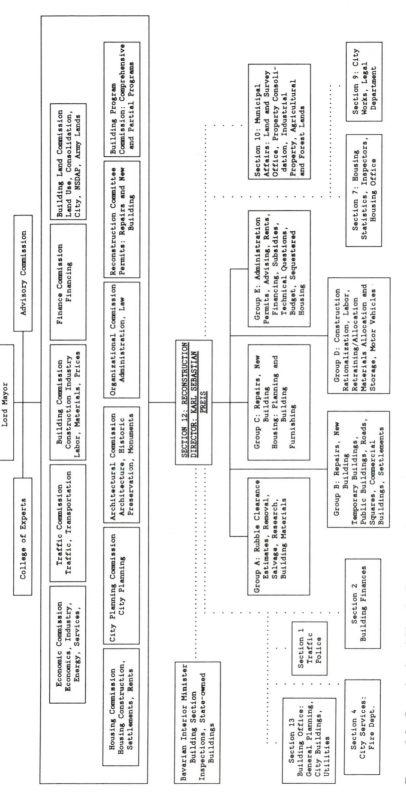

FIGURE 9.2. Organizational Plan for Reconstruction, Munich, January 1946.

Source: SAM/Bürgermeister und Rat 1204.

was 1 June 1946.) For the next three years, Fischer and Leitenstorfer competed for preeminence in leading Munich's reconstruction.

Tension between the two departments and their heads was evident by the
beginning of 1948. The city's personnel director urged the mayor to transfer
some of the building and repair projects on city-owned buildings that were
currently in Leitenstorfer's section to Fischer's section because the Stadt-
bauamt was supposedly "hopelessly overburdened."[85] Fischer could then assign these tasks to the Münchner Aufbau G.m.b.H. (or MAG). This private
building corporation was founded in January 1947 but not licensed by the
military government until March 1948. The city owned 60% of the capital,
and three associations of firms in the construction industry owned the remainder. In a closed session of the city council on February 24, Scharnagl argued in
favor of the transfer. Not only would it help relieve Leitenstorfer's department, but the MAG could function more efficiently than city departments
because, as a private corporation, it enjoyed greater "freedom of movement,"
especially in personnel matters. That is, it could simply hire workers as
needed, and was not burdened by bureaucratic or political restrictions.[86]

The Münchner Aufbau G.m.b.H., whose activities were directed by
Fischer, assumed responsibility for an ever-growing number of projects. The
resulting rivalry between Fischer and Leitenstorfer intensified to the point that
by August 1948, the mayor's office, the personnel office, and the executive
committee of the city council were all contemplating the consolidation of the
two departments under Fischer, especially since Leitenstorfer had been offered
a chair at the Technical University and might rather gracefully leave the city
government.[87] Fischer's department was evidently far more efficient than
Leitenstorfer's, which led some to argue that all of reconstruction should be
directed by an administrator trained in law (like Fischer). Others argued, however, that reconstruction demanded a leader with technical training in architecture or building (like Leitenstorfer). At best, the two rivals felt that some
clarification of responsibilities was in order. Fischer, moreover, observed that
reconstruction involved economics, land management, fiscal arrangements,
and law, not just planning, and that technically minded individuals simply could
not approach reconstruction from this broad perspective. He added: "The
reliance alone on new laws, laws for which many city planners yearn, appears to
be false; one must instead first try to make full use of the legal and economic
possibilities in existing laws."[88] This was an opportune observation, since it was
becoming increasingly clear that no general reconstruction law was going to
make it through the Bavarian legislature.

Although proposals for consolidation circulated into 1951, the two departments remained separate. Leitenstorfer held on until November 1950, when he
left for his university chair. His hand-picked replacement was Hans Högg, a
former city planner who had lost out to Rudolf Hillebrecht for the chief position
in Hannover. Högg was narrowly elected over two of Leitenstorfer's subordinates in the building office.[89] Högg succeeded in defending his department
against Fischer, whose attention was somewhat diverted as he had become a
leading figure in a new Bavarian reconstruction commission. Still Fischer maintained a commanding position in Munich, as is evident in Figure 9.3, which

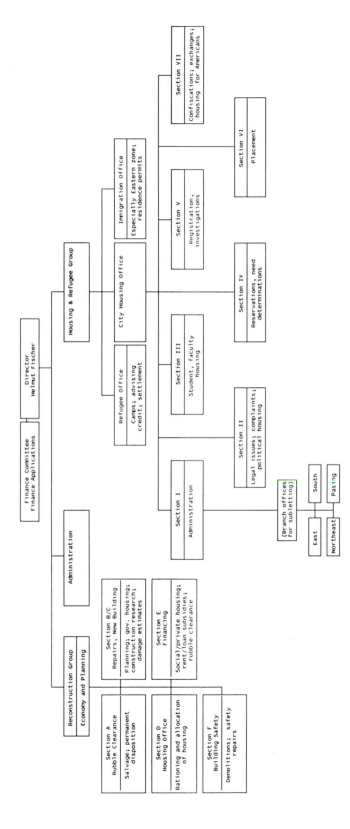

FIGURE 9.3. Organization plan, Munich Reconstruction Department, February 1951.
Source: SAM/Bürgermeister und Rat/1965.

shows the areas of competence in his department as of February 1951. More-over, Fischer was not just an administrator. He proved to be a masterful propa-gandist who effectively shaped reconstruction in Munich while buttressing his own position.

Some of the same kinds of personnel conflicts that beset Munich also existed in Stuttgart and Cologne. But where Helmut Fischer succeeded in prevailing both administratively and with the public, the key reconstruction officials in Stuttgart and Cologne fared less well, and the reconstruction effort suffered accordingly. These cities lacked the kinds of organizations that had helped make rebuilding a relatively smooth process in cities like Hannover.

Immediately after the war, architect Eugen Mertz was put in charge of Stuttgart's departments for planning and construction, and he quickly pro-duced a plan for rebulding the city.[90] This rather peculiar plan, which called for transforming Stuttgart into a spa resort, generated no support. The Allies dismissed Mertz, and in May 1946, the city established a special reconstruction office, the Central Office for the Rebuilding of the City of Stuttgart (Zentrale für den Aufbau der Stadt Stuttgart, or the ZAS). The ZAS had primary respon-sibility for repairs and reconstruction, labor and materials allocation, building permits decisions, planning and legal questions, the construction of city build-ings, and housing construction. Advised by a special committee made up of professors from the technical university, independent architects, preservation-ists, art historians, and representatives of labor and the building industry, the ZAS was initially headed by Richard Döcker and his assistant Walter Hoss, both of whom were trained architects who had worked as planners in the "Westmark" (in Alsace-Lorraine) during the war.[91]

Personnel and personality conflicts soon undermined this structure and rendered it much less efficient than its founders had hoped. Quarrels between Hoss and Döcker resulted in the latter's departure to the university and Hoss assuming control of the ZAS. (Döcker complained to Hans Scharoun that Hoss was an "opportunist," a man of "pretty words" who "won't lift a finger."[92]) Hoss sympathized politically with the left, and he supported passage of a strong comprehensive building law that would enable him to make sweeping changes in property holdings and redesign much of the basic street pattern. This natu-rally alienated the conservatives in the city council and raised cries of alarm and fear among the town's property owners, especially in the inner city. In the fall of 1948, the head of the town planning office, which continued to exist alongside the ZAS, began to feud with Hoss and leaked exaggerated and hence damaging rumors to the press and representatives of the property owners about Hoss's grand designs. Hoss denounced the planning official's manipulation of the public as "evil" and "a cardinal error."[93] The dispute spilled over into the city council, which reproached Hoss's opponent for not adhering to regular bureau-cratic procedures.[94]

Following this bureaucratic conflict, the property owners formed organiza-tions to confront and bitterly attack Hoss in a series of public meetings begin-ning in 1949.[95] To loud applause, Hoss was referred to as "'dictator' Hoss" and accused of refusing to listen to the "little man," the individual property owner.

Denouncing his plans as inappropriately grandiose for Stuttgart and the times, the owners saw Hoss as authorizing "a monstrous squandering of land and property."[96] Hoss, in turn, defended his plans and actions by observing that they had the almost unanimous support of the city council and its committees, and he accused his critics on those committees of being too cowardly to speak their minds at the appropriate time, and doing so only with the backing of a mob of irate and ill-informed citizens.[97] Lord Mayor Klett urged the warring members of the city administration and town council to be more temperate in their language and encouraged them to resolve their differences quickly and efficiently so that Stuttgart's reconstruction planning could proceed.[98]

The damage, however, had been done. Every important part of the rebuilding process was fought out in the city council, public meetings, the press, and sometimes in the courts. Indeed, it was a supreme court decision involving Stuttgart that finally dealt a fatal blow to all German planners who had hoped for a strong building law that would grant them the power to force major property realignments.[99] Stuttgart's rebuilding—especially the inner city—was slow and costly.

Unlike Stuttgart, which created a new governmental department (the ZAS) after the war to plan the rebuilding of the city, Cologne adapted an existing organization to oversee reconstruction. In February 1941, a so-called Planning Corporation (Planungsgesellschaft G.m.b.H.) to work on redesigning the city had been established by the Ernst-Cassel Foundation (which helped poor families pay their rent) and the Grund-und-Boden Gesellschaft (a building corporation), both of which had evolved out of the Gemeinnützige Aktiengesellschaft für Wohnungsbau, a social housing corporation created in 1927 and half-owned by the city. Thus, although the Planungsgesellschaft was a private company, the city had a financial interest in it and, under a contract with the local Gauleiter, Cologne paid the firm's expenses. When reconstruction planning began in 1944 under the auspices of the Arbeitsstab in Speer's ministry, the Planungsgesellschaft, rather than the regular city planning department, performed the work in Cologne.[100] After the war, rather than tapping its regular building administration offices to plan reconstruction, Cologne's leaders decided to utilize the Planungsgesellschaft, which they reorganized as the Reconstruction Corporation (Wiederaufbau G.m.b.H.) in December 1945.[101]

The city chose to work through this "new" corporation because it offered the advantages of city control without debilitating bureaucratic restraints. Moreover, such an arrangement protected sensitive personnel matters from the scrutiny of the public and allied occupation forces. The administrative board consisted of the lord mayor, the city manager and his two assistants, one of whom served as business manager, and former Lord Mayor Konrad Adenauer, who served as honorary chairman. Because Adenauer had communicated his desire to participate in reconstruction and wished to use his former home as his Cologne base, Lord Mayor Pünder instructed his subordinates to rush repairs on Adenauer's house. This was a bit tricky, since the city had bought Adenauer's house in 1937 and now appeared to be returning it to him as a gift, at a time when others struggled vainly to get building permits.[102]

Business manager Carl Schweyer divided the Reconstruction Corporation into two sections, one dedicated to planning and the other to "scientific" studies. Headed by the elderly economic historian Bruno Kuske, the latter featured an advisory committee of 14 members, including city conservator Vogts, writer (and friend of Adenauer) Carl Oscar Jatho, and the business manager of the chamber of commerce. Schweyer asked Michael Fleischer, who had worked for the Planungsgesellschaft early in the war and later gone to Danzig, to assume leadership of the planning section. Schweyer also established a separate planning commission, which included architects Eugen Blanck, Karl Band, and Wilhelm Riphahn. (In the fall of 1945, Adenauer had asked Riphahn to draw up a plan for rebuilding Cologne.)[103]

None of this proved satisfactory. Fleischer had trouble working with the planning commission, and, as a former Nazi party official, was soon dismissed by the Allies anyway. His replacement, architect Rudolf Schwarz, immediately asserted himself as the central figure in Cologne city planning and was named "general planner" in November 1946. He remained, however, outside the building administration, since he found "the world of the bureaucrat to be alien." He preferred working in an independent entity, which, as a senior city official put it, was "more mobile and less bureaucratic than a government agency."[104] Still, difficulties persisted. Schwarz had disagreements with Blanck, who left in 1946 for Frankfurt, and with Kuske.

Kuske's attentions were divided between preparing reports on the economic basis for reconstruction in Cologne and leading the economic division of the government of Northrhine-Westphalia. The reports for Cologne tended to be either theoretical statements or detailed summaries of old economic histories of the city, and Schweyer complained that "the long essays contain little that is of immediate use in practice."[105] Moreover, Kuske insisted that the corporation include former university librarian Hermann Corsten and former city archivist Erich Kuphal, both of whom had been party members. In a letter to Kuske, Lord Mayor Pünder advised exercising "restraint in employing former party members within the framework of the Reconstruction Corporation."[106] Kuske complained about Schwarz's sociological jargon, and Schwarz mocked Kuske's persistent, meaningless references to old books.[107] Finally, in August 1948, Schweyer informed Kuske that the currency reform demanded some retrenchment, which included abolishing the scientific division of the Reconstruction Corporation. He offered Kuske an unpaid directorship, which Kuske declined.[108] Kuske's actual contribution had been minimal. Perhaps his most interesting suggestion was a proposal to create a permanent, scientific advisory committee that would include "available, more active historians."[109]

Meanwhile, Schwarz, who now had full responsibility for the corporation, found himself increasingly disillusioned. He had expected the organization to promote rebuilding "not so much through bureaucratic measures as through independent decisions and actions," and he had assumed that the corporation would function as a "central office for reconstruction."[110] In fact, he complained, he spent much of his time soliciting cooperation from other city departments, with varying degrees of success.

If the individuals working for the Reconstruction Corporation were discontented, those outside expressed displeasure as well. In 1949, formal complaints denounced Schwarz's attempts to keep his plans secret, his continued activity as an architect apart from his work for the city, his arrogant personality, and his favoritism in awarding contracts to friends.[111] The city government became so concerned that it confidentially cautioned the "general planner" to restrain the "corrosive sarcasm" that was making enemies for him and the city.[112]

In June 1947, the Social Democrats and Communists in the city council urged that the Reconstruction Corporation be abolished in favor of the normal city offices, and the spokesman of the Social Democrats angrily complained about the Nazi-era origins of the corporation.[113] In the fall of 1949, the functions and remaining personnel of the Reconstruction Corporation were finally transferred to the planning section of the city building offices. Schwarz's contract, which expired at the beginning of 1952, was not renewed, and the Reconstruction Corporation withered away without being formally dissolved. The last document in the archives bearing the name of the corporation is dated 29 October 1953, and a note at the bottom, dated 24 July 1954, simply observes that the corporation was no longer active.[114]

Various associations of private citizens and property owners interested in Cologne's rebuilding complained—though never in the angry, bitter tone that characterized the disputes in Stuttgart—that the process was moving far too slowly.[115] Prior to 1951, however, Cologne lacked organizations that brought property owners and city officials together like the Aufbauförderungsgemeinschaften that served that purpose in Hannover and other cities. One city administrator attributed this partly to Rhenish individualism and partly to the absence of a suitably competent and strong personality.[116]

Finally, in 1951, four large building firms formed an association for the reconstruction of the old city (Altstadt-Wiederaufbaugesellschaft). This new company sought to turn the rebuilding of the Griechenmarkt quarter of the inner city into a model rebuilding project, but here, too, many years passed before planning was completed, the necessary property transactions had transpired, and actual construction was begun.[117] In short, in spite of its early start, Cologne never succeeded in organizing the reconstruction effort independently of the city's building offices.

Conclusion

The organizational forms chosen for urban reconstruction were intended to make the process more efficient without being too authoritarian or bureaucratic. Though they differed in detail, the extraordinary organizational structures created alongside the normal building administrations were generally similar throughout Germany. The national, regional, and professional organizations kept planners, city officials, and architects aware of developments elsewhere. Experiences were shared through meetings and publications, and the successes of cities like Hannover were well known.

Given this shared experience, it is noteworthy that reconstruction was organized more successfully in northern Germany than in southern Germany. The north enjoyed greater continuity in personnel from the war years into the postwar period, which enabled those cities to begin functioning effectively almost as soon as the war ended. In addition, the British and the French encouraged thorough city planning in their occupation zones. The north's crucial advantage, however, was manifested in the temperament and background of the leading northern planners, such as Hillebrecht, Jensen, and Wortmann, who were better suited to the job than southern planners like Hoss, Schwarz, and Fischer. The northern planners combined technical training in planning and architecture, practical experience, and a keen awareness of the necessity of involving the community in the planning process. The latter insight was something they had learned during the war, perhaps in part from observing the difference between Konstanty Gutschow's approach in Hamburg and Speer's in Berlin. Although planners ultimately made the key decisions, rebuilding was organized in ways that encouraged property owners and interest groups to participate early and often in shaping those decisions. The personal qualities of a few individuals, then, defined the organizations and lent them authority, respect, prestige, and the ability to accomplish difficult tasks. Structural consistency by itself was not enough to ensure organizational efficiency and productivity.

10

Conclusion

In 1945, German planners and architects agreed that the war's devastation offered Germany a unique opportunity to correct the failings of the urban blight produced by the industrial and population expansion of the second half of the nineteenth century. For them, this was the bright side of the catastrophe of World War II, and they envisioned a thorough modernization of the urban fabric. Consequently planners disliked the term *Wiederaufbau*—reconstruction—because it suggested a return to prewar conditions rather than a future orientation. As Darmstadt's chief planner Peter Grund asked in 1952, "Can we and do we want to be satisfied with restoring what has been destroyed? Haven't the spiritual and material bases of our lives to a great extent been transformed?" It was not the recreation of old cities that was needed but rather the building of new cities for modern conditions.[1]

The persistently high and naive hopes of postwar planners were constantly disappointed. In 1949, Hugo Keuerleber of Stuttgart feared that because the rebuilding process failed to produce truly new cities, "future generations will accuse us of having lost both the war and the peace."[2] In 1951, Rudolf Hillebrecht complained that illegal, unplanned construction endangered an orderly, organic reshaping of the cities, and in 1957 he admitted that "the phrase 'missed opportunities' hangs over the rebuilding of our cities like a dark cloud."[3] Though Hillebrecht acknowledged some planning errors, he consistently attributed the failings of reconstruction to a debilitating "lack of political insight" that might have coordinated and harmonized the legal, planning, and financial policies of local, regional, and federal authorities.[4] With more cooperation and better laws, planners could have done a better job. Similarly, Ernst May argued that German urban planners had missed a unique chance to design new cities because the new democracy hindered effective planning and encouraged private speculators to build in ways contrary to modern planning precepts.[5] In 1961, Herbert Jensen commented that the "obvious disorder dominating our immediate surroundings is extraordinarily embarrassing," particularly within the context of an epoch characterized by the scientific discovery of fundamental order in the natural world.[6]

Does this disappointment in having missed a great chance, this shame at inadvertently perpetuating disorderly cities, mean that postwar reconstruction was a failure? Those who condemn reconstruction as a failure and sharply criticize architects and planners may have forgotten that in 1945 Germans faced the enormous challenge of housing millions of people, rebuilding businesses, schools, hospitals, and government buildings, repairing streets and utilities, and restoring or reconstructing the major monuments that characterized each city. Not only was all this work accomplished, but it was completed much faster than anyone at the time thought possible. Within a decade or so after the war, cities that had been reduced to rubble and ashes were again livable and lived in. At least in a quantitative sense, and in terms of speed, reconstruction was a great success. Moreover, there can be no doubt that postwar housing marked a great improvement over the hated Mietskasernen, or that the streets of the rebuilt cities accommodated the demands of modern motorized traffic far better than the narrow streets typifying prewar Germany. Even if the cities failed to fulfill the expectations of the planners, reconstruction can hardly be flatly dismissed as a failure.

It is more difficult to judge the quality of reconstruction, although judgments about one aspect or another have been made throughout this study. There is no easy way of deciding, for example, whether function or aesthetics should inform such evaluations, or whether they should be limited to individual buildings and ensembles or broadened to encompass entire cities. In a 1948 essay expressing concern about the course of reconstruction, Franz Meunier cited Goethe's warning about the magical permanence acquired by stupid mistakes given physical form because the imagination was dominated by visual perceptions.[7] In fact, urban structures, whether buildings or streets or combinations of enclosed spaces and open spaces, constantly change and evolve, as do the values, perceived needs, and aesthetic standards of planners, architects, politicians, and the public. Neither the structures nor the qualities attributed to them are frozen in time. As buildings gradually decay, the foliage planted around them proliferates to conceal that decay. At any given time, some ugly, badly designed buildings and beautiful, well-designed buildings remain standing when others have long since been demolished. Except for selected monuments, it is normal for urban buildings to be replaced as they become run down or obsolete or as tastes change. Streets widened after the war to facilitate auto traffic are now being narrowed to discourage the use of private autos. Not only is nineteenth-century architecture, commonly despised by the postwar planners, now deemed worthy of preservation, but buildings from the era of reconstruction itself are being preserved as "documents" of that period. On the other hand, some of the "adaptive" architecture of reconstruction now seems sorely out of place because its intended environment has changed completely.[8]

Similarly, standards and expectations change too. While we might condemn a building or thoroughfare as ugly, inhuman, and disruptive of the surrounding environment, people in 1950 or 1955 might have considered it functional and harmonious. Small apartments designed for single persons may have seemed a very sound idea in the first decade after the war, inadequate in the decades thereafter, but perhaps desirable again today. Likewise, had the planners received the strong laws they demanded in order to rebuild on a grander and more modern scale, they would have built even more expansive traffic arteries that would be inadequate by now and that would have destroyed the unity and harmony of urban space.

The architects who design buildings and the planners who design public spaces necessarily start from some ideal conception that may or may not match the conceptions of subsequent users of the buildings and spaces. The users judge their environment according to their needs and values. And, to the chronic irritation of architects, users tend to modify and personalize their environment even when the changes violate the clarity of the original design and undermine the "art" of the architect or planner.[9]

Judgments also vary according to the context in which the urban landscape is experienced.[10] If one is driving rapidly through a city, for example, one is struck by events and objects at street level rather than by architectural details higher up on the facades of the buildings. Pedestrians are more likely to make aesthetic judgments about the facades of individual buildings or ensembles than to think about what lies behind the facades. And house guests tend to evaluate layout, size, quality of construction, comfort, and so forth, rather than worry about whether the exterior harmonizes with exteriors of neighboring buildings.

Tourists, who approach cities from still another vantage point, naturally arrive at different judgments about the quality of cities than do permanent residents. The English historian Peter Laslett once complained about the inability of tourists to understand their surroundings. Tourists, he says,

> seem to perceive [their surroundings] only as a sharper version of the technicolor poster displayed back home in the tourist agent's window . . . these are humans without personalities as far as you are concerned; you wish to know nothing further of them, they are physical objects only and have no moral import. . . . To have to recognize that you [too] have no personality when you are in the tourist situation . . . makes a moral weed of you. . . . For me anyway this is the strangest and the saddest element in the quality of life in the contemporary European city.[11]

I think Laslett is wrong. First, the perceptions of tourists are often sharp indeed, sometimes sharper than those of the permanent residents of a town, because the tourists are quickly struck by incongruities, unsuccessful buildings, or bad planning decisions that the residents have long since become accustomed to and no longer see at all. Indeed, tourists' questions and observations inspired this study. Moreover, even the permanent residents of large cities are frequently tourists in their own city. That is, they normally live within rather closely defined parameters—work, shopping, church, recreation, whatever—and never see much of the city. And when they do see it, they see it very much as tourists see it. Those who live on the outskirts are likely to come into the historic center as tourists, to visit the theater, to eat and drink, or just to walk around and breath an atmosphere different from that of the suburbs.

Whether people in cities possess or lack moral significance for each other is not so much a consequence of tourism as a reflection of urban life generally. Of concern here is how the normal mixture of residents and visitors experience a city. Because the rebuilt German cities include both modern and (rebuilt) old designs, they are anything but quaint, lifeless museum pieces. On the contrary, they have an undeniable vitality for all, and Germans freely criticize their cities. Düsseldorf residents, for example, complain that their preserved Altstadt is much too tourist-oriented, with its plethora of restaurants, and Hannover's citizens frequently bemoan their dull architecture. Inhabitants of Hamburg and Stuttgart complain about the traffic arteries, while citizens in Cologne simultaneously denounce postwar buildings as ugly and argue that too many chic modern buildings have been built, which has somehow rendered the old shabbiness rather comfortable and nice.

No one would claim that the postwar period marked a golden age of German architecture. Societies that energetically produced creative, imaginative architecture—such as Renaissance Florence, Amsterdam in Holland's Golden Age, or New York and Chicago in the early twentieth century—were relatively wealthy and dynamic, and both individuals and the society as a whole exuded self-confidence and achievement. Certainly postwar Germany lacked such wealth and confidence. A beaten nation, in which recalling past cultural glories could be considered suspect, Germany was in no position to look ahead with great confidence. The circumstances demanded humility and modesty.

Errors were undoubtedly made in that first decade. Planners badly underestimated the growth of motorized traffic and were too impressed by the poverty of the postwar years to be able to imagine the fabulous prosperity that was soon to follow. Even had they correctly anticipated the number of autos that would fill the streets, the planning concepts of the time could not have provided adequate guidance. No one anticipated that one day soon planners would need to discourage the use of private autos.

Aesthetic errors were also made. Everyone failed to appreciate the positive contributions of nineteenth-century architecture to urban life. The variety of facades and the sheer eclecticism of that period added a great deal of visual richness to city streets. Instead of demolishing most of the still-standing facades of burned-out buildings and clearing large areas for new buildings, city authorities could have saved more of the facades and attempted a slower, more careful kind of urban renewal, one that might have preserved more of the character of the prewar cities. Although some urged the cities to proceed cautiously and thoughtfully and avoid mistakes, the public generally demanded a massive, rapid construction effort. They had no patience at all for painstaking deliberations about the quality of urban life and consequently were willing to sacrifice remnants of the past at the altar of modernization.

The goals of functional separation and the reduction of population densities in the inner cities, central tenets of the postwar planners, resulted in city centers that were relatively lifeless in the evenings and on weekends because too few people lived there. At the same time, ultramodern apartment towers standing on the edges of cities, surrounded by lush green lawns but isolated from urban culture and daily commerce, turned out to be sterile and alienating. Only at the end of the reconstruction era did critics start arguing for a return to "urbanity," the sort of intense urban experience typical of the crowded urban quarters at the turn of the century.[12] In other words, planners belatedly recognized the virtue of some of the old dense residential districts, in which a very intense sense of neighborhood prevailed. The planners also erred in thinking that they could completely control urban development and steer it along a path of "organic" evolution. Some things could be planned, but others emerged from the dynamic of conflicting social forces and values. Rudolf Schwarz was right when he said that planners needed to accept the fact that some things simply resisted planning.[13]

In addition to quantitative and qualitative evaluations, German reconstruction begs a moral judgment as well. Though most of the ideas and concepts that shaped reconstruction predated the Nazis, it is nevertheless true that the planners and architects who rebuilt Germany belonged primarily to the generation that had worked more or less enthusiastically on the urban programs of the Third Reich. They had been attracted to and inspired by the possibility of planning and building on an unimagined scale under the Nazis, and they naturally considered themselves prepared for the great challenge of postwar reconstruction. Most planners and architects, whatever their wartime activities or positions, insisted on seeing themselves as apolitical. In an exchange of letters with Alfons Leitl in 1947, Gerhard Graubner stated: "An artist must remain true to his profession under all circumstances and not allow himself to be guided by the political or economic conditions of a changing time." In contrast, Leitl argued that the architect was necessarily political in the sense of being "engaged in public affairs," and he found it "terrible" that everyone, "the great and the small," claimed "to have been specialists and always absolutely unpolitical." When architects could not accept a regime, they should withdraw, as Tessenow had.[14] In fact rather few had withdrawn, and these same specialists rebuilt Germany after 1945.

German reconstruction was not, however, Nazi urban planning in disguise. The most distinctly Nazi ideas—the politicization of urban life, the monumental streets and buildings of representative cities, the neoclassical architectural forms—were absent after 1945. Does it matter then that so many of the leading planners and architects had worked for the Nazis? Is the comparative success of reconstruction tainted by the background of those responsible for it? This dilemma extended to all areas of German life. What Alfons Leitl said about architects—that "almost everyone . . . raised his hand high" in the Nazi salute—was true for most people who had held their jobs and prospered to any extent during the Third Reich.[15]

There is no simple answer here. It is perhaps easier to hold an individual responsible for the morality of his or her actions than to judge the moral content of a street or building. Thus condemning the use of slave or concentration camp labor in wartime building projects and holding those who conceived and implemented such actions responsible need not necessarily lead to condemnation of every social housing plan drawn up during that time. On the other hand, distinguishing between planners and architects and their products, whether buildings, neighborhoods, city centers, or traffic arteries, tends to isolate those projects in a nebulous ahistorical timelessness. German reconstruction occurred in a specific historic and social context and must be evaluated within that context. The architects and planners who practiced their trade in the Third Reich shed the vocabulary tainted by Nazism as easily as other Germans shed their uniforms, but this was a superficial change. Neither 1933 nor 1945 marked a fundamental break in the history of German architecture and town planning.

A combination of factors resulted in huge numbers of buildings being reconstructed surprisingly quickly. Necessity mandated a fruitful mixture of public planning and private initiative, public and private financing, and public and private construction. A highly advanced country in spite of the war damage, Germany possessed the technology, the labor skills, the management skills, and the incentive to rebuild energetically. Leadership came from a group of experienced planners and architects who had long been pondering how best to solve Germany's urban problems, including the question of rebuilding war-damaged cities. Although it took a while for sufficient financing and building materials to be collected, it should really come as no surprise that the Germans rebuilt as fast as they did, given the readily available stock of ideas and human capital.

The shape of reconstruction—decisions about restoring historic buildings, retaining historic street patterns, laying out new arteries, decongesting inner-city housing, and choosing architectural styles—was affected by long-term continuities in architectural, planning, and preservationist practice that dated to the early part of the century. The dominant trend had been toward modernization, an inclination that continued after the war. In Germany's rebuilding, therefore, continuity meant change, although German reconstruction rarely resulted in radically innovative architecture or new town plans. Instead, modernization manifested itself in incremental stages.

Although these continuities were essential for the course of urban reconstruction in Germany, the bombing campaigns and Germany's defeat in the war created a number of new conditions that transcended politics. Germans responded by collectively and individually searching for identity. The war had turned cities into mountains of rubble. While those who had remained in their homes grimly dug their way out of the ruins, unprecedented masses of people roamed about Germany as refugees, soldiers, or prisoners. They sought to return home or find new homes, to reestablish roots or sink new roots. Rebuilding a home or a business thus meant more than just acquiring a roof over one's head or making a living. The rapid return of former inhabitants to the bombed-out cities surprised nearly everyone, but people were simply trying to return to a world they had known before the war. By 1954, the population of most West German cities exceeded that of 1939. Many former residents had died in the bombing or during combat on the front, and a significant segment of the new population consisted of refugees from formerly German-held parts of Poland and Czechoslovakia and from Russian-occupied East Germany. These people struggled to establish new identities in a new Heimat, a new urban home. Novelist Heinrich Böll assessed this migration by observing that the search for one's old Heimat was tinged with melancholy, while searchers of a new one radiated optimism.[16]

To enable the citizens to identify with their home towns, it was vital that the cities be rebuilt on their old locations and that major architectural monuments be rebuilt. Thus churches, for example, were often reconstructed in neighborhoods with inadequate numbers of supporting parishioners. The quest for identity also tended to mandate that reconstructed homes and businesses resemble their prewar appearance. For this reason, roof lines and shapes, building heights, materials and colors often followed local tradition. Such German towns as Nuremberg, Freudenstadt, and Freiburg restored their identities through adaptive architecture. Germans returned to bombed cities and rebuilt them into *their* cities again. Most Germans (and most outsiders) agree that each city embodies unique characteristics, in spite of similarities in the style of social housing, department stores, and office buildings.[17]

The outward shape of reconstruction—that which formed the identity of the rebuilt cities—resulted from a dynamic interaction between local conditions and general trends. Thus, while historical preservationists tended to steadfastly oppose erecting copies of demolished buildings, powerful public sentiment demanded such copies for their symbolic and cultural value. Furthermore, the Protestant and Catholic churches generally rebuilt bombed places of worship with or without the agreement of preservationists. At the same time, even those who advocated replicating such structures as destroyed palaces supported the introduction of modern plumbing and lighting. In many such cases, preserved historic facades conceal very modern interiors.

Efforts to rebuild bombed quarters of cities in their historic form undercut the modernist goals of planners. Still-standing facades of bombed buildings had to be cleared away if streets were to be widened, if new modern housing was to be built, and if land was to be used more rationally. Planners, architects, and citizens often disagreed on whether appearance or functionality should guide reconstruction, and those disputes were worked out either within private organizations or in the public arena. Hence reconstruction varied widely, depending upon the degree of destruction and the particular constellation of forces defining reconstruction.

Moreover, most agreed that government, whether central, provincial, or local, had to assume a major role in rebuilding. Especially important was public financing of reconstruction, particularly with regard to social housing.

The citizenry shared a common belief that reconstruction should be planned rather than haphazard and that governmental organization and participation would ensure financing for housing as well as efficient management of such things as rubble clearance, fair allocation of building materials, allocation of public housing, and supervision of rent levels. Governmental action was also needed to restore and improve utilities, public buildings, and services and to rejuvenate public transportation systems. Germans believed that reconstruction should be guided by objective goals and technical necessities rather than politics or ideology, a view that of course greatly appealed to the generation of planners who had been active during the war. As demand for their skills rose, attention to their wartime activities diminished, rendering their recent pasts increasingly irrelevant.

Still, the public resisted giving government a completely free hand. Germans naturally rebelled against the excessive power exercised by the government and the Nazi party during the war and were wary of granting planners the kind of power they had enjoyed under the Nazis. On the other hand, the public also recognized the potential of strong government to accomplish efficiently and quickly large, complex projects. Hence German archives abound with petitions requesting government leadership and intervention as well as complaints about officials with dictatorial tendencies. Much reconstruction was planned, and done so in a more authoritarian than democratic fashion. Certainly, reconstruction was not left to the vicissitudes of free market forces.

Another common feature of rebuilding concerns financing. Funds raised by regular and special taxation, such as taxes levied on undamaged property, contributed most significantly to reconstruction. All Germans, even those whose property escaped the war intact, shared the financial burden of reconstruction. As noted, the Nazis had passed such an "equalization of burdens" act during the war, evoking a principle already present in a Weimar-era tax on property that had appreciated in real value during the inflation in the 1920s. Likewise, after World War II, new federal and regional equalization of burdens taxes were instituted. Hence, the consensus that everyone had to shoulder some of the cost of reconstruction resulted in adapting past financing procedures, which in turn exemplified the willingness of relatively wealthier segments of the population to help the less advantaged. In fact, it was during this period of general need that the willingness to share and sacrifice was greatest, not during the subsequent period of prosperity.

Another feature of rebuilding also concerns the prevailing sense of an interdependent community. Because the war left so many in dire straits and so many in need of housing subsidies, there was no social stigma attached to living in subsidized housing units. Hence, the experiences of the war dissolved some of the traditional social barriers separating the urban middle classes and the working classes. Workers and middle-class burghers, widows, and the elderly all needed assistance, and they all shared the desire to reestablish their identities within the context of the identities of their rebuilt cities. This is not to say that the rebuilt cities manifested perfect social integration. The wealthy suburbs emerged from the war with less damage than the centers, and many who could afford to do so abandoned the rubble-filled inner cities for comfortable single-family houses in nice suburbs. Nevertheless, urban poverty was not, as it were, simply set in stone and abandoned, and the influx of refugees surely changed the social mixture of the cities and helped make them less narrowmindedly provincial.

Finally, a spirit of cooperation generally prevailed in the bombed cities. Postwar Germany witnessed an efflorescence of citizens' groups dedicated to helping rebuild individual monuments or whole streets or quarters, such as associations that facilitated the redrawing of property lines. Although reconstruction laws enabled authorities to mandate such property adjustments, that involved the time and expense of pursuing complicated administrative and legal procedures. In many places, voluntary associations of property owners, acting upon the advice of local planners, went ahead and made the adjustments on their own, trading lots or buying out individuals who were unwilling or unable to rebuild. As long as they seemed reasonable, property owners usually accepted the proposals of planning authorities, even when those proposals entailed some personal sacrifice.

The rebuilding of Germany's bombed cities can be understood only in terms of the interaction between deeply embedded continuities dating from the turn of the century and Germany's unique postwar circumstances. The long process of urban modernization was suddenly accelerated by the opportunities created by the bombing. Hence the period of reconstruction—the decade after the war—rather quickly merged into the normal process and rhythms of urban change.

Visual reminders of the period of reconstruction, however, continue to mark German cities. Every city contains what Germans call *Baulücken*, gaps in streetfronts, where single-story shops, rebuilt hastily after the war, stand between multistory buildings. The city council of Cologne recently debated a proposed allocation of DM 5 million to reconstruct the Bayenturm, a destroyed medieval fortified tower that used to stand at the southern end of the city wall. Forty-five years later, proponents argue that rebuilding the tower would restore the silhouette of the southern part of city with a dominant feature, implying that the skyscrapers a bit farther to the south fail to do so. Such debates, as well as recurring suggestions about how to fill the *Baulücken*, however, are generally little more than footnotes to a remarkable process of urban recovery.

Still, there are compelling reasons for contemporary urban policymakers to reflect upon the lessons of postwar reconstruction. In the 1960s and again in the 1980s, Germans let the free market shape housing construction. As a result, Germany suffers from an acute shortage of inexpensive housing, a crisis exacerbated by the recent influx of refugees from East Germany, Poland, and other countries. Policymakers, in response, are invoking postwar models and creating new subsidies to encourage social housing construction. Speculators who keep building lots empty with the idea of earning future profit can now be forced, as they were after the war, to build or to yield their property to those who are prepared to build. Additionally, the press featured discussions about applying postwar reconstruction models to the urban renewal so urgently needed in what used to be East Germany, where large urban areas are in terrible condition because of decades of neglect, bad planning, and shoddy construction. Some suggested using the funds that still exist in the accounts of the Bank for Reconstruction in Frankfurt; others talked of instituting a new equalization of burdens tax to finance new housing and public buildings or to renovate old and dilapidated structures. The flood of West German architects, planners, and builders into East Germany suggests that they view the present as a new opportunity, comparable to the supposedly missed opportunity after the war, to solve the problems of urban life. The outcome of all this activity remains to be seen, but in contemporary Germany, postwar reconstruction—both its successes and failures—continues to be of great interest.

Sadly, cities continue to be destroyed in wars or by natural catastrophes, and as Martin Wagner and Walter Gropius argued in the 1940s, the consequences of urban blight can closely resemble the consequences of a bombing raid.[18] It has often been said that New York's South Bronx looks like a war-ravaged city. In the first couple of years after the war, Germans lived in cellars and makeshift shelters. Today Americans sleep in doorways and over subway vents in big American cities—some 80,000 in New York alone. If the Germans could successfully rebuild under the most disadvantageous conditions, what prevents prosperous America from doing the same? The tourists I accompanied to Munich many years ago wondered about this disparity between West German successes and current American failures. Could Americans perhaps appropriate some of the lessons of German urban reconstruction?

An essay written in 1954 by an important German architectural critic, Alfons Leitl, entitled "What's Wrong with German City Planning? The Lessons of Reconstruction," argued that German reconstruction planning, while perhaps successful in terms of speed and quantity, had failed to generate any really new styles of urban life. The reason, he felt, was that only citizens of an old democracy, not those of a new one like Germany, were likely to "recognize the superior needs of the group and the necessity for compromise on the part of the individual landowner." "Can anyone be surprised," he asked, "that democracy in this country was often misinterpreted to mean freedom from any control, and that the obligation to practice self-discipline in public matters was forgotten?"[19]

Although the United States is, by comparison, a very old democracy, when it comes to rejuvenating cities, too seldom do its citizens acknowledge the needs of others, appear willing to make even modest sacrifices, or possess self-discipline in public affairs. If learning from one's own history is difficult, learning from the history of other societies is even more challenging. Nevertheless, if the European model of urban recovery after World War II is indeed in some ways applicable to the revival of America's blighted cities, then Americans need to foster new attitudes about their cities, about the role of planning and of government, and above all about sacrifice and cooperation. For the rebuilding of Germany's bombed cities, such attitudes were just as important as any ideas about architecture or planning.

Notes

Archives and Archival Abbreviations

When citing sources from archival collections, I use the following procedure. The abbreviation of the archive is followed by the designation of the general series or collection and then by the designation of each subsequent subdivision, ending either with a page number or with the names and dates identifying the document. In order to make the notes more compact, where possible I have used the appropriate numbers rather than give the names of document series in full.

AdKB	Akademie der Künste, Berlin
ADST	Archiv des Deutschen Städtetags, Cologne
AHSL	Archiv der Hansestadt Lübeck
AIHKM	Archiv der Industrie- und Handelskammer Munich
AKB	Archiv Karl Böttcher, Berlin
ASKG	Archiv für Städtebau Konstanty Gutschow (Hamburg, Absteinach)
BDST	Bibliothek des Deutschen Städtetags, Cologne
BHSA	Bayerisches Hauptstaatsarchiv, Munich
BSA	Bauverwaltung der Stadt Aachen
BSBWB	Bibliothek des Senators für Bau- und Wohnungswesen, Berlin
BSH	Baubehörde der Stadt Hamburg
BSL	Bauverwaltung der Stadt Lübeck
HAA	Hamburg Architektur Archiv
HASK	Historisches Archiv der Stadt Köln, Cologne
HLH	Houghton Library, Harvard University, Cambridge, Mass.
HLL	Harvard University, Loeb Library, Cambridge, Mass.
HSANRW	Hauptstaatsarchiv Nordrhein-Westfalen, Düsseldorf

LAB   Landesarchiv, Berlin
LC   Library of Congress, Washington, D.C.
NA   National Archives, Washington, D.C.
RWWA   Rheinisch-Westfälisches Wirtschaftsarchiv, Cologne
SAA   Stadtarchiv Aachen
SAH   Stadtarchiv Hannover
SAM   Stadtarchiv Munich
SAS   Stadtarchiv Stuttgart
SB   Staatsarchiv Bremen
SH   Staatsarchiv Hamburg

As the reader will see, the papers of Konstanty Gutschow form one of the most important archival collections used in this book. I first studied this enormous collection in the Gutschow home, where Mrs. Konstanty Gutschow and Niels Gutschow gave me access to the material. After the death of Mrs. Gutschow and the sale of the family home, the collection was dispersed. The largest part, currently in the Hamburg Architektur Archiv, eventually will be turned over to the Staatsarchiv Hamburg. There is already a collection in the Staatsarchiv of papers generated in the course of Gutschow's work for the city between 1939 and 1945, and there is some duplication of material in the Hamburg Architektur Archiv. To a considerable extent, both of these archives use Konstanty Gutschow's own classification scheme in organizing the material. Other parts of the private Gutschow collection are currently in the hands of Niels Gutschow, in Absteinach, and Werner Durth, in Mainz. It has been impossible for me to determine if each of my original citations from the private Gutschow papers still bears the same classification signature, but I have checked enough to be confident that future scholars will be able to find anything I have cited without difficulty, although they may have to inquire in more than one place.

Introduction

1. The most important of these are Werner Durth, *Deutsche Architekten. Biographische Verflechtungen 1900–1970* (Braunschweig and Wiesbaden, 1986) and Durth and Niels Gutschow, *Träume in Trümmern. Planungen zum Wiederaufbau zerstörter Städte im Westen Deutschlands 1940–1950*, 2 vols. (Braunschweig and Wiesbaden, 1988). The latter is a treasure-trove of primary documents, which make up half of its more than 1,000 pages, a great many of which derive from the Gutschow papers. For a brief discussion of the problem of confronting an earlier generation, see Niels Gutschow, "Väter und Söhne," *Bauwelt* 75 (20 April 1980). The other major work on urban reconstruction to date, *Der Wiederaufbau. Architektur und Städtebaupolitik in beiden deutschen Staaten* (Munich, 1987) by Klaus von Beyme, examines reconstruc-

tion as a process lasting into the 1970s and also compares rebuilding in the Federal Republic with that in the German Democratic Republic. Based entirely on published material, this is an interesting and useful synthesis. The most recent survey is Gerhard Rabeler, *Wiederaufbau und Expansion westdeutscher Städte 1945–1960 im Spannungs- feld von Reformideen und Wirklichkeit*, Schriftenreihe des Deutschen Nationalkomi- tees für Denkmalschutz, vol. 39 (Bonn, 1990), a brief, rather schematic, but very nicely illustrated book. One should also consult the case studies in Klaus von Beyme, Werner Durth, Niels Gutschow, Winfried Nerdinger, and Thomas Topfstedt, eds., *Neue Städte aus Ruinen. Deutscher Städtebau der Nachkriegszeit* (Munich, 1992), a volume which discusses 12 West German and 6 East German cities. For an earlier attempt to define objectives for research on cities in the postwar era, and one which also raises the issue of continuities, see Lutz Niethammer, "Die deutsche Stadt im Umbruch: 1945 als Forschungsproblem," *Die alte Stadt* 5 (1978).

2. LC, MS Division, Spaatz Papers, Container 203, "Jeeping the Targets in the Country That Was." The group included Major General Anderson and Colonel Lowell Weicker of the bomber command. Weicker was a leading proponent of area bombing of cities.

3. The Germans expected that it would take decades, if not a half-century, to rebuild. See Anna J. Merritt and Richard L. Merritt, *Public Opinion in Occupied Germany: The OMGUS Surveys, 1945–1949* (Urbana and Chicago, 1970), pp. 103–4. A rare exception was the Cologne architect Karl Band. Based on his experience in an urban renewal project in the late 1930s, he thought that reconstruction would be possible in a mere 10 years. HASK/2/1313/ Band, "Gedanken zum Wiederaufbau unserer Stadt," 29 June 1945.

4. Hans Pieper, *Lübeck. Städtebauliche Studien zum Wiederaufbau einer histor- ischen deutschen Stadt* (Hamburg, 1946), p. 155.

5. As will be evident in the notes, there is already an extensive scholarly litera- ture in several of these areas, especially German architecture in the 1920s and 1930s. I rely heavily on these studies, though my purpose is different, since I am most inter- ested here in influences on postwar urban history.

6. Ludwig Neundörfer, "Inventar des Zusammenbruchs," *Baukunst und Werk- form* 1 (1947): 21.

7. Hans Scharoun, "Berlin," *Baukunst und Werkform* 1 (1947): 26.

8. Alfons Leitl, "Anmerkungen zur Zeit," *Baukunst und Werkform* 1 (1947): 13.

9. This was the specific purpose of a 1985 colloquium at the Technical University of Berlin. Karolus Heil, "Einige Anmerkungen zur Veranstaltung," *Wendezeiten in Architektur und Stadtplanung. Kontinuität in der Entwicklung nach 1945*, in Erich Konter, ed., Arbeitshefte des Instituts für Stadt- und Regionalplanung der Tech- nischen Universität Berlin, 36 (Berlin, 1986), p. 15. Heil called for an analysis of the "dialectic between continuity and discontinuity" in planning history and in the recent history of Berlin (p. 16). The confrontation with the Nazi past can, however, lead to intellectual difficulties. Thus in his contribution to the colloquium, Wolfgang Schäche argues that one can find the roots of Berlin's postwar developments in the urban planning of the early twentieth century at the same time that he insists that postwar reconstruction was determined and shaped by individuals, ideas, architectural styles, and planning practices from the Nazi years. See his "Von der Stunde Null und der Legende des Wiederaufbaues," idem, pp. 79 and 86.

10. See the essays in Jeffry M. Diefendorf, ed., *Rebuilding Europe's Bombed Cities*, (London and New York, 1990).

11. See Durth and Gutschow, *Träume in Trümmern*, pp. 278–79. This point was also made by Günther Kühne, longtime essayist on architecture and planning for *Bauwelt*, the leading German periodical in the field, in an interview with the author in Berlin, 9 November 1981. The content of the professional journals also changed in the mid-1950s. For example, the progressive journal *Baukunst und Werkform* absorbed another progressive journal, *Die Neue Stadt*, in 1954, but the pages of the new publication lacked almost entirely the passionate, crusading tone of the early postwar years.

12. A speech by Edgar Salin to the Deutscher Städtetag (German Cities Association) in June 1960 helped start the German debate over the validity of current planning concepts. That speech was published as "Urbanität," in *Erneurung unserer Städte*, Neue Schriften des deutschen Städtetages, no. 6 (Stuttgart and Cologne, 1960). See also Jane Jacobs, *The Death and Life of Great American Cities* (New York, 1961). An example of the German response to Jacob's book is Rudolf Hillebrecht, "Von Ebenezer Howard zu Jane Jacobs—oder: War alles falsch?" *Stadtbauwelt* 8 (1965).

13. Von Beyme, *Der Wiederaufbau*, pp. 91, 340. The same conclusion is reached by Axel Schildt and Arnold Sywottek, "'Wiederaufbau' und 'Modernisierung': Zur westdeutschen Gesellschaftsgeschichte in den fünfziger Jahren," *Aus Politik und Zeitgeschichte* B 6–7 (3 February 1989): 20. Erich Konter argues that "technocratic, formal functionalism" became dominant "toward the end of the 1950s." "Deutsche Planer und Architekten: Selbstverständnis und 'Standes'-Politik—Neubeginn oder Kontinuität?" in *Wendezeiten in Architektur und Stadtplanung—Kontinuität oder Bruch in der Entwicklung nach 1945*, Erich Konter, ed., Arbeitshefte des Instituts für Stadt- und Regionalplanung der Technischen Universität Berlin, no. 36 (Berlin, 1986), p. 58.

14. Joseph Schlippe, "Wie Freiburg wiedererstehen soll?" in *Freiburg in Trümmern 1944–1952*, Walter Vetter, ed. (Freiburg, 1982), p. 148.

15. For example, see Werner Durth, "Vom Sieg der Zahlen über die Bilder: Anmerkungen zum Bedeutungswandel der Städte im Denken der Planer," *Stadtbauwelt* 88 (1985): 364, and "Utopia im Niemands-Land," in *So viel Anfang war nie: Deutsche Städte 1945–1949*, Hermann Glaser, Lutz von Pufendorf, and Michael Schöneich, eds. (Berlin, 1989), p. 223. The reconstruction plans discussed by Durth and Gutschow in *Träume in Trümmern* were very often grandiose and utopian rather than humble, but for that reason they were seldom taken seriously, in contrast to the modest, pragmatic reconstruction plans that were put into effect in the first decade after the war.

16. Schildt and Sywottek, "'Wiederaufbau' und 'Modernisierung,' " p. 28.

17. At the beginning of this introduction I mentioned that much research remains to be done. In addition to the study of reconstruction in as-yet unexamined cities, there are other interesting problems to be studied. For example, church organizations, and in particular the Catholic church, assumed chief responsibility for the rebuilding of their respective churches all over Germany. Where there was a historic preservation law on the books and where the church in question was on the list of protected buildings, church officials consulted with preservation officials in making decisions on exactly how to rebuild. Towns and states often helped underwrite expensive restorations, but the churches shared the financial burden. To understand how this worked in detail requires examination of the appropriate church archives. Or, to take another example, little work has as yet been done on the fate of properties which had been owned by Jews before the war. Many were either confiscated by the Nazis or sold under pressure at below-market values. After the war, many such properties were then caught up in the so-called *Wiedergutmachungs* process of compensation for victims of the Nazis.

Chapter 1

1. Goethe, for example, built "ruins" in his park in Weimar.

2. John Brinckerhoff Jackson, "The Necessity for Ruins," in Jackson, *The Necessity for Ruins and Other Topics* (Amherst, Mass., 1980).

3. Albert Speer, *Inside the Third Reich: Memoirs*, Richard and Clara Winston, trans. (New York, 1970), p. 56. During the spring of 1945 Speer was ordered to contribute more directly to the creation of ruins when Hitler decided on his "scorched earth" policy for the collapsing Third Reich. To his credit, Speer worked to undermine this order. His motives were mixed. He did not want to destroy what was left of Germany's industrial capacity and transportation network partly because that would make it all the harder on the population but partly also because industry would be needed if the German armies should manage to fight on. He did not, however, worry about preserving buildings for their own sakes. On this see the last part of his memoirs and Gregor Janssen, *Das Ministerium Speer. Deutschlands Rüstung im Krieg* (Berlin, 1968), pp. 295ff, 310ff.

4. George F. Kennan, *Sketches from a Life* (New York, 1989), p. 194.

5. The British analysis of the air war contains an "Extract from the Report by the Police President of Hamburg on the raids on Hamburg in July and August 1943, dated 1st December 1943," which begins: "This short account of the course of the raids cannot, even though illustrated by figures, maps and photographs, give any idea of the destruction and terror. . . . The impression made by a gutted area is colourless compared with the actual fire, the howling of the firestorm, the cries and groans of the dying and the constant crash of bombs. It seems important to record this. Because the calamity is as much perceived in the process of destruction as in the accomplished fact." Charles Webster and Noble Frankland, eds., *The Strategic Air Offensive against Germany, 1939–1945*, vol. 4, *Annexes and Appendices* (London, 1961), p. 310.

6. The best recent summaries of the strategies behind aerial warfare are Michael S. Sherry, *The Rise of American Air Power. The Creation of Armageddon* (New Haven, Conn., and London, 1987), and Ronald Schaffer, *Wings of Judgment. American Bombing in World War II* (New York, 1985). See also Max Hastings, *Bomber Command: The Myths and Reality of the Strategic Bombing Offensive 1939–1945* (New York, 1979).

7. Sherry, *The Rise of American Air Power*, p. 26.

8. Haywood S. Hansell, Jr., one of America's senior air force commanders in World War II, recently summed up the strategy developed in the late 1920s and 1930s. That strategy concluded, according to Hansell, with the idea that "if enemy resistance still persists after successful paralysis of selected target systems, it may be necessary as a last resort to apply direct force upon the sources of enemy national will by attacking cities. In this event, it is preferable to render the cities untenable rather than indiscriminately to destroy structures and people." "The idea of killing thousands of men, women, and children was basically repugnant to American mores. And from a more pragmatic point of view, people did not make good targets for the high-explosive bomb, the principal weapon of the air offensive." *The Strategic Air War against Germany and Japan: A Memoir* (Washington, D.C., 1986), pp. 10, 13.

9. Sherry, *The Rise of American Air Power*, pp. 49ff, 70.

10. The moral issues have been explored by Sherry and Schaffer and by Earl R. Beck, "The Allied Bombing of Germany, 1942–1945, and the German Response: Dilemmas of Judgment," *German Studies Review* 5 (1982), as well as many others. All studies dealing with the dropping of the atomic bomb, the final act in the bombing campaign against enemy cities, address the moral issues.

11. See Hans Rumpf, *The Bombing of Germany*, E. Holt Fitzgerald, trans. (New York, 1962), pp. 24–27; Kenneth Hewitt, "Place Annihilation: Area Bombing and the Fate of Urban Places," *Annals of the Association of American Geographers* 73, no. 2 (1983): 262; and Webster and Frankland, *The Strategic Air Offensive*, p. 129. Another brief German account of the air war against Germany is to be found in Bundesministerium für Vertriebene, Flüchtlinge und Kriegsgeschädigte. *Dokumente deutscher Kriegsschäden*. 10 vols. in 7 (Bonn, 1958–1971), 1: 1–68. (Henceforth this will be cited as *Dokumente deutscher Kriegsschäden.*)

12. Webster and Frankland, *The Strategic Air Offensive*, p. 190. One should not minimize the German contribution to the air war. The RAF commented that the German raids on England during 1940 and 1941 had been severe, with 41,000 deaths, 350,000 houses destroyed, and 1 million people forced from their homes. Nevertheless, these attacks "produced no major interruption of the British war effort. . . . The British industries and British people possessed a degree of resilience and recuperative power adequate to sustain a greater shock than was in fact inflicted." Idem, p. 259.

13. Ibid., pp. 140, 195.

14. Robert Ley, quoted by Gerhard Fehl and Tilman Harlander, "Hitlers Sozialer Wohnungsbau 1940 bis 1945—Bindeglied der Baupolitik und Baugestaltung zwischen Weimarer Zeit und Nachkriegszeit," *Stadtbauwelt* 84 (1984): 395. For an example of guidelines for construction that would minimize possible bomb damage, see Tilman Harlander and Gerhard Fehl, eds. *Hitlers Sozialer Wohnungsbau 1940–1945. Wohnungspolitik, Baugestaltung und Siedlungsplanung*, vol. 6 of Stadt, Planung, Geschichte (Hamburg, 1986), pp. 397–401. As will be seen, it is surprising partly because of its scope, but I would note that when I first began talking to Germans about wartime rebuilding, there was unanimous agreement that nothing was done about reconstruction during the war itself. Most Germans seemed to have forgotten about wartime repairs.

15. LC, MS Division, Spaatz Papers, Container 203, Special Studies of Bombing Results no. 2, 19 October 1942. See Charles Messenger, *"Bomber" Harris and the Strategic Bombing Offensive, 1939–1945* (New York, 1984), pp. 207–9. Arthur Harris headed the British Bomber Command.

16. Webster and Frankland, *The Strategic Air Offensive*, p. 260.

17. Ibid., p. 289.

18. "Report by Air Ministry Intelligence in Consultation with Political Warfare Executive: Allied Air Attacks and German Morale—IV" in "Combined Bomber Offensive Progress Report: Feb. 4, 1943—Nov. 1, 1943, Section R," LC, MS Division, Spaatz Papers, Container 67. The comments about the "rumours" of "living torches" are remarkable, since the Hamburg raid used mostly incendiary bombs and produced a great firestorm, as the British had hoped.

19. It was the only raid that historic Lübeck suffered during the war. The first German city to suffer massive area bombing retains enough of its historic substance still to be, along with Bamberg and Regensberg, one of the most important examples of medieval architecture. That Lübeck was spared further damage appears to be due partly to the intervention of the banker Eric Warburg, a refugee from Hamburg, who persuaded the president of the International Red Cross to make Lübeck an exchange center for the correspondence of prisoners of war. Hartwig Beseler, Niels Gutschow, and Frauke Kretschmer, eds., *Kriegsschicksale deutscher Architektur. Verluste, Schäden, Wiederaufbau. Eine Dokumentation für das Gebiet der Bundesrepublik Deutschland*, 2 vols. (Neumünster, 1987, 1988), 1: x.

20. The best account is Hans Brunswig, *Feuersturm über Hamburg. Die Luftangriffe auf Hamburg im Zweiten Weltkrieg und ihre Folgen* (Stuttgart, 1978). See also the

report cited in note 2 above, and Martin Middlebrook, *The Battle of Hamburg: Allied Bomber Forces against a German City in 1943* (London, 1980). Also spectacular were the famous "1,000 bomber" raids against Cologne and other cities.

21. "The Combined Bomber Offensive Progress Report" for 4 February through 1 November 1943 states: "Damage to housing, combined with evacuation, has resulted in the final saturation of all suitable accommodation in Germany. . . . The housing situation and the general morale are both so bad that either might cause a collapse before industry became unable to sustain the war effort." LC, MS Division, Spaatz Papers, Container 67, p. 6.

22. Schaffer, *Wings of Judgment*, pp. 66–67, and also Schaffer, "American Military Ethics in World War II: The Bombing of German Civilians," *Journal of American History* 67 (1980); Sherry, *The Rise of American Air Power*, p. 162.

23. On this see the memoir of W. W. Rostow, *Pre-Invasion Bombing Strategy: General Eisenhower's Decision of March 25, 1944* (Austin, Tex., 1981). Also *Dokumente deutscher Kriegsschäden*, 1: 38.

24. *Dokumente deutscher Kriegsschäden*, 1: 45–46. For a table showing the dates of the most devastating raids, see Beseler, Gutschow, and Kretschmer, *Kriegsschicksale deutscher Architektur*, 1: xi.

25. See American Commission for the Protection and Salvage of Artistic and Historic Monuments in War Areas, *Report of the American Commission for the Protection and Salvage of Artistic and Historic Monuments in War Areas* (Washington, D.C., 1946). The materials of the commission are found in the National Archives, Record Group 239. For a discussion of the efforts of the commission, see also Gerald K. Haines, "Who Gives a Damn about Medieval Walls?" *Prologue* 8 (1976).

26. This is not to say that nothing was achieved by the Roberts Commission. It did, for example, succeed in finding, identifying, and returning a great many works of art that had been stolen by the Nazis.

27. Haines, "Who Gives a Damn about Medieval Walls?" p. 100.

28. Messenger, *"Bomber" Harris*, p. 191.

29. Sherry, *The Rise of American Air Power*, p. 205.

30. United States Strategic Bombing Survey, *The Effects of Strategic Bombing on the German War Economy* (n.p., October 1945), pp. 7–11.

31. Interrogation report in Webster and Frankland, *The Strategic Air Offensive*, pp. 382, 385, emphasis in printed version. The raids on the crucial ball-bearing factories at Schweinfurt, though relatively successful, produced damage that was repaired within two months. Hansell, *The Strategic Air War*, p. 86. See also David MacIsaac, ed., *The United States Strategic Bombing Survey*, 10 vols. (New York and London, 1976), and John Kenneth Galbraith, *A Life in Our Times* (Boston, 1981). A member of the survey team, Galbraith has remained highly critical of the bombing campaign.

32. See Fred Charles Iklé, *The Social Impact of Bomb Destruction* (Norman, Okla., 1958). Iklé calculated that at least 25% of the housing stock had to be destroyed before depopulation really began to occur (p. 52). Generally bad wartime conditions, plus bad news from the front, meant that perceptions of "relative deprivation" were lowered, which in turn slowed the collapse of morale. Because the housing supply was elastic, bombing "could not become decisive until technical developments made it possible to hit less elastic resources, such as transportation facilities and factories" (p. 75).

33. *Strategic Bombing Survey*, p. 13. This is the conclusion reached in an excellent new study by Alfred C. Mierzejewski, *The Collapse of the German War Economy, 1944–1945: Allied Air Power and the German National Railway* (Chapel Hill, N.C., and London, 1988). He also notes that the Soviet conquest of Upper Silesia, a major

industrial and coal center, was also of great importance in the collapse of the German economy.

34. In a "Preliminary Appraisal of Achievements of Strategic Bombing of Germany," Report by the director of the Overall Effects Division, Galbraith observed: "Germany's secret weapon it would appear was the energy and ingenuity with which she repaired and restored production plants that had been badly damaged." LC, MS Division, Spaatz Papers, Container 203. On the other hand, Sherry is certainly right in arguing that one should not therefore simply dismiss the strategic bombing campaign as unimportant. It tied up a large German air defense system, and vast resources did go into the repair of industry and housing. In short, the bombing campaign made up one part of the war of attrition. Sherry, *The Rise of American Air Power*, p. 158.

35. An interesting impressionistic account of the experience of city dwellers is by Earl R. Beck, *Under the Bombs: The German Home Front, 1942–1945* (Lexington, Ky., 1986). Beck discusses the many ways people coped with material shortages and spiritual turmoil caused by the bombing. For the experience of a single city, see Thomas Grabe, Reimar Hollmann, Klaus Mlynek, and Michael Radtke, *Unter der Wolke des Todesleben. . . . Hannover im Zweiten Weltkrieg*, 2 vols. (Hamburg, 1983).

36. Note for the archives by Rudolf Hillebrecht, SH/ Architekt Gutschow/ B23/ 12 May 1943, for comments on the difference between Hamburg and Berlin. "Gerade die verantwortlichen Leute in Berlin führen Abend für Abend weit außerhalb der Stadt, um bloß keinen Luftangriff zu erleben. In Hamburg träfen sich dagegen die verantwortlichen Leute nachts 1 Stunde nach Alarm, und das sei eben Front."

37. See my "Konstanty Gutschow and the Reconstruction of Hamburg," *Central European History* 18 (1985): 151–53; and Iklé, *The Social Impact*, p. 136. Eyewitness accounts of the bombing in several cities are to be found in *Dokumente deutscher Kriegsschäden*, Beiheft 1, *Aus den Tagen des Luftkrieges und des Wiederaufbaues. Erlebnis- und Erfahrungsberichte*.

38. Brunswig, *Feuersturm über Hamburg*, pp. 166, 188. As president of the Hamburg fire department, it was Brunswig's responsibility to face the attacks. His book is a sober, carefully reasoned account of Hamburg's experience.

39. *Dokumente deutscher Kriegsschäden*, Beiheft 1: 74.

40. Webster and Frankland, *The Strategic Air Offensive*, p. 315. See also Beck, *Under the Bombs*, pp. 60–71, for the experience of the raids in Cologne and Hamburg.

41. Brunswig, *Feuersturm über Hamburg*, pp. 401–9.

42. *Dokumente deutscher Kriegsschäden*, 1: 54, 57; Rumpf, *The Bombing of Germany*, p. 164; and Hewitt, "Place Annihilation," p. 266.

43. Such measures included shutting off gas lines, putting aside quantities of sand and water to combat fire bombs before the blazes got out of hand, and opening up tunnels and connecting doors between cellars, so that individuals would not be trapped and suffocate. For examples, see *Dokumente deutscher Kriegsschäden*, 2, part 2: 294–301. In 53 raids on Stuttgart, only 4,017 died because of such measures. Karl Strölin, *Stuttgart im Endstadium des Krieges* (Stuttgart, 1950), pp. 22–23.

44. Kurt Preis, *München unterm Hakenkreuz: Die Hauptstadt der Bewegung: Zwischen Pracht und Trümmern* (Munich, 1980), p. 251. Illustrations of evacuation plans are in *Dokumente deutscher Kriegsschäden*, 2, part 2: 302–39.

45. In Hannover, for example, local leaders discussed building a new city where all roads and train tracks would be underground, while all housing would be above ground, in the form of heavy bunkers. See Grabe et al., *Unter der Wolke des Todesleben*, p. 91. For landscaping proposals see Niels Gutschow, "Hamburg—the

'Catastrophe' of July 1943," in *Rebuilding Europe's Bombed Cities*, Jeffry Diefendorf, ed., (London and New York, 1989), pp. 118–20.

46. Hans Werner Richter, "Literatur im Interregnum," *Der Ruf*, no. 15 (1947), reprinted in *So viel Anfang war nie*, Hermann Glaser, Lutz von Pufendorf, and Michael Schöneich, eds., (Berlin, 1989), p. 9.

47. SAM/Bauamt-Wiederaufbau/1118/ K. S. Preis, "Der erste Schritt zum Wiederaufbau unserer Stadt. Eine amtliche Denkschrift des Referenten für den Wiederaufbau über die Beseitigung der Ruinen, der Trümmer und des Schuttes in München," n.d., but early December 1945.

48. *Dokumente deutscher Kriegsschäden*, 1: 55.

49. Hans Speier, *From the Ashes of Disgrace. A Journal from Germany 1945–1955* (Amherst, Mass., 1981), p. 11.

50. SAM/Bauamt-Wiederaufbau/1095, II, Section IX, no. 1.

51. Hans Ramm, "Aufräumung," in *Hamburg und seine Bauten 1929–1953*, Architekten- und Ingenieur-Verein Hamburg, ed. (Hamburg, 1953), p. 321.

52. Otto Dann, ed., *Köln nach dem Nationalsozialismus* (Wuppertal, 1981), p. 195.

53. SAM/Bauamt-Wiederaufbau/1106/ Speech by Fischer, Fall 1946.

54. NA/Dept. of State Interim Research and Intelligence Service, Research and Analysis Branch, R & A 3298, 29 December 1945, "Darmstadt: A Survey of Political, Economic and Social Conditions in a Medium-Sized German City," Field Memorandum no. 1010.

55. F. Jürgens, "Der Neubau des Hamburger Schulwesens," in *Neues Hamburg. Zeugnisse von Wiederaufbau der Hansestadt*, vol. 1, Erich Lüth, ed. (Hamburg, 1947), pp. 42–43.

56. Ernst Randzio, *Unterirdischer Städtebau: besonders mit Beispielen am Groß Berlin* (Bremen, 1951), p. 79.

57. NA/RG 260, Box 481, File 5, "History of Construction of Technische Werke," 3 November 1948.

58. Niels Gutschow and Renate Stiemer, *Dokumentation Wiederaufbau der Stadt Münster* (Münster, 1982), p. 25.

59. Erhard Mäding, *Beitrag der Städte zum Wiederaufbau der deutschen Wirtschaft. Bericht über deutsche Selbstleistungen im Sinne des Marshallplans*, typescript submitted to Bundesminister für den Marshallplan, April 1951, pp. 21–22. Copy in BDST.

60. Arthur Dähn, "Die Zerstörung Hamburgs im Kriege 1939–1945," in *Hamburg und seine Bauten 1929–1953*, Architekten- und Ingenieur-Verein Hamburg, ed. (Hamburg, 1953), p. 37.

Chapter 2

1. Some of the best evidence of this is to be found in photographs. Since inmates in their camp clothing were working on main streets in major cities, obviously a high proportion of the population must have witnessed their efforts and their condition. For the use of prisoners from Dachau in Munich, see Preis, *München unterm Hakenkreuz*, p. 225. Also SH/Architekt Gutschow/ B23/ report of Baupolizeiamt, 31 July 1942, and B7/ Advisory session of town councillors of 18 September 1942, on the use of foreign workers and POWs in clearing streets and in constructing temporary housing in Hamburg under the auspices of the AKE. At one point, Konstanty Gutschow, whose office ran the AKE and also was responsible for long-term planning in Hamburg, complained

to the Reichsstatthalter for the city that street clearance should be planned more carefully to avoid wasting fuel and salvagable building material. The Reichsstatthalter rejected the complaint out of hand, saying that "Die sofortige Beseitigung der Trümmer nach Fliegerschäden stehe an wichtigster Stelle." He didn't care how the rubble was cleared, only that the job be done quickly. SH/Architekt Gutschow/ B23/ protocol, 14 January 1942.

2. Beck, *Under the Bombs*, p. 87, quotes a Berliner who wrote: "We repair because we must repair. Because we couldn't live another day longer if one forbade us the repairing."

3. Order nine of the Generalbevollmächtigter für die Regelung der Bauwirtschaft, in BHSA/ II/ Geheimes Staatsarchiv/ Reichsstatthalter von Epp/ vol. 541/1.

4. Janssen, *Das Ministerium Speer*, p. 227.

5. Fehl and Harlander, "Hitlers Sozialer Wohnungsbau," p. 392.

6. SH/Architekt Gutschow/B7/Speech by Konstanty Gutschow to Ratsherrn, 26 January 1943.

7. SH/Architekt Gutschow/ B23/ Note for the archives, 7 March 1943, reporting on a trip to several Rhenish cities.

8. Rumpf, *The Bombing of Germany*, pp. 85, 91.

9. "Wiederaufbau Mitteilung des Bauausschusses," *Deutscher Städtetag,* no. 4 (1 December 1946): 9.

10. SAM/Bauamt-Wiederaufbau/1118/ Wiederaufbaureferant, Proclamation of the full assembly of the city council, 28 January 1947.

11. Randzio, *Unterirdischer Städtebau*, p. 61; BDST/Erhard Mäding, *Beitrag der Städte zum Wiederaufbau*, pp. 59–60.

12. Gutschow and Stiemer, *Dokumentation Wiederaufbau der Stadt Münster*, p. 27.

13. NA/RG 260, Box 481, File 5, "History of Construction of Technische Werke," 3 November 1948.

14. This discussion is based on Günter Ede and Emil Möller, *Trümmerrecht unter Berücksichtigung der Ruienhypotheken* (Cologne, 1949).

15. See RWWA/1/237/1, Bauwesen, Allgemeines, vol. 1 (1945–49), 4th meeting of the Bau- und Wohnungswirtschaftliches Ausschusses, Industrie- und Handelskammern of Northrhine-Westphalia, 18 March 1947, p. 86.

16. The Hamburg law is reprinted in Ede and Möller, *Trümmerrecht*; for the law in Northrhine-Westphalia, see the *Gesetz- und Verordnungsblatt für das Land Nordrhein-Westfalen* 3 (1949): 109–12.

17. The state of Bavaria attempted to use financial assistance to force Munich into accepting the state's priorities on rubble clearance. See Chapter 8 for a detailed discussion of developments in Bavaria.

18. BDST/Erhard Mäding, *Beitrag der Städte zum Wiederaufbau,* pp. 59–60.

19. See HSANRW/NW73–166–167, for correspondence on such matters.

20. Martin Arndt, "Wiederaufbau und Bauwirtschaft," *Wiederaufbau zerstörter Städte*, no. 5 (1947), pp. 19–20. What was meant, of course, was that 10% of the prewar construction labor force had died. During the war forced laborers had been extensively used in construction; they were no longer available to German contractors.

21. NA/RG 260/OMG Bavaria, Manpower Division, Box 7, Folder 6, "Statistical and Analytical Report Covering Period 1 May to 31 May 1947."

22. SAM/Bauamt Wiederaufbau/1112/ Report by Preis, 5 February 1946; and 1095/"Statistik," III, Section XII, no. 3.

23. Stadtverordnetenversammlung of Greater Berlin, I. Wahlperiode, *Stenographischer Bericht,* 31st Session (29 May 1947), report by Stadtrat Karl Bonatz, p. 25.

24. *Dokumente deutscher Kriegsschäden*, 3: 49–57.

25. For examples, see NA/RG 43/Allied Control Council-Germany, Documents 1945–48, Box 30, File DMAN/P (46) 177, "Communication from the Allied Secretariat Relative to 'Release of Prisoners of War Formerly Employed in the Building Industry,' " 3 December 1946; and NA/RG 260/OMG Hesse, Manpower Branch, Economics Division (orig. box 89–3), Folder 7: German Waterway Administration, Wiesbaden, to Capt. Jack H. Post, US Group CC, Transport Division.

26. Peter Brandt, "Wiederaufbau und Reform. Die Technische Universität Berlin 1945–1950," in *Wissenschaft und Gesellschaft. Beiträge zur Geschichte der Technischen Universität Berlin 1879–1979*, 2 vols., Reinhard Rürup, ed. (Berlin, Heidelberg, and New York, 1979), 1: 503.

27. Office of Military Government for Germany, United States (henceforth OMGUS) Monthly Report No. 13 (July 1946), on Law No. 32.

28. Josef Beule, "Der Stand der Enttrümmerung in den Westsektoren Berlins," *Neue Bauwelt* 4 (1949).

29. Günter Grass, "Die große Trümmerfrau spricht," in *Gesammelte Gedichte* (Neuwied and Berlin, 1971), p. 156.

30. Hermann Vietzen, *Chronik der Stadt Stuttgart, 1945–1948* (Stuttgart, 1972), pp. 362, 364.

31. Verwaltungsberichte der Stadt Köln, 1945–47, p. 86.

32. Gutschow and Stiemer, *Dokumentation Wiederaufbau der Stadt Münster*, p. 29.

33. SAM/Ratsitzungsprotokolle/719/2: Public session of 22 October 1946, pp. 1251–53.

34. SAM/ Ratsitzungsprotokolle/720/2: Session of 11 November 1947, pp. 2377–2400.

35. SAM/Bürgermeister und Rat/1966/ G. Baumrucker to Fischer, 5 March 1947, and reply of 24 March 1947.

36. SAM/Bauamt-Wiederaufbau/1112/K. S. Preis, "Der erste Schritt zum Wiederaufbau unserer Stadt. Eine amtliche Denkschrift des Referenten für den Wiederaufbau über die Beseitigung der Ruinen, der Trümmer und des Schuttes in München," 8 December 1945, p. 14.

37. *Verhandlungen der Stadtverordnetenversammlung, Köln* (1945): 38.

38. See HASK/ 171, no. 13: 3–4, contract between the city and an "Arbeitsgemeinschaft Trümmereisenaufbereitung."

39. Privatarchiv Karl Böttcher, Berlin, report to Magistrat, 29 December 1945.

40. See Ramm, "Aufräumung," p. 323.

41. *Dokumente deutscher Kriegsschäden*, 2, part 2: 133–35; and Arndt, "Wiederaufbau und Bauwirtschaft," p. 36.

42. Vietzen, *Chronik der Stadt Stuttgart*, p. 364.

43. SAM/Bauamt-Wiederaufbau/1118/Speech by Fischer, 28 January 1947, pp. 13–14.

44. A useful source for the varied approaches to this problem is the *Wiederaufbau-Mitteilungen*, published by the building committee of the Deutscher Städtetag and edited by Philipp Rappaport. Eleven numbers appeared as sections of *Der Städtetag*, with the last in February 1949. The bulletins included technical information on how to process rubble and a current list of relevant literature.

45. See [Oberbaurat a. D.] Glootz, "Wie kann der Hammerbrookplan durchgeführt werden?" and Otto Sill, "Der Durchführungsplan Hammerbrook," both in *Nordwestdeutsche Bauzeitung* 3 (1951).

46. Ramm, "Aufräumung," p. 321.

47. HASK/5/195, "Trümmerräumung und Trümmerverwertung. Halbjahresbericht vom 1.4. bis 30.9.49," p. 3.

48. Erich Heyn, *Zerstörung und Aufbau der Großstadt Essen* (Bonn, 1955), pp. 31–35.

49. Walter Nicklitz, "Die soziale Lage der Bauarbeiter," in *Berlin. Planung und Aufbau der Stadt* (Berlin, 1948), p. 108.

50. Niels Gutschow and Renate Stiemer, *Dokumentation Wiederaufbau Münster: Materialsammlung*, Beiträge zur Stadtforschung, Stadtentwicklung, Stadtplanung, vol. 6 (Münster, 1980), p. 53.

51. *Wiederaufbau-Mitteilungen,* no. 4 (December 1946): 8. The use of female labor was stressed probably because women would be paid less than men.

52. SAS/Trümmerverwertung und -beseitigung/Chronik, essay by Dr. Winternitz, "Stand der Trümmerräumung und -verwertung in der Bundesrepublik" from "Mitteilungen der Deutschen Studiengesellschaft f. Trümmerverwertung," no. 37 (October 1950): 285.

53. NA/RG 260, Box 481, File 5: Eberlein, "History of the Rebuilding of the City of Stuttgart, 5 November 1948."

54. HASK/2/1320/Klett, "5 Jahre Aufbau in Stuttgart," speech to Stuttgart Gemeinderat, 23 April 1950, pp. 11–12; see also Arnulf Klett, "Die Bedeutung der Trümmerverwertung für die kommunale Wirtschaft," *Der Städtetag*, new series, 4 (1951).

55. Kurt Leipner, *Chronik der Stadt Stuttgart 1949–1953* (Stuttgart, 1977), p. 109.

56. Ramm, "Aufräumung," pp. 323–24.

57. Privatarchiv Karl Böttcher, Berlin, report to Magistrat, 29 December 1945.

58. SAM/Bauamt-Wiederaufbau/1095/ II, Section IX, no. 19.

59. Leipner, *Chronik der Stadt Stuttgart*, pp. 108–9.

60. HASK/5/195/"Trümmerräumung und Trümmerverwertung. Halbjahresbericht von 1.4. bis 30.9.49," pp. 10–11; *Verwaltungsberichte der Stadt Köln* (1952–53): 116 and (1955–56): 167; and Ernest Thomas Greene, *Politics and Geography in Postwar German City Planning*, diss. (Princeton, 1958), pp. 111–12.

61. BDST/Erhard Mäding, *Beitrag der Städte zum Wiederaufbau,* pp. 120.

62. While doing research for this book, I lived in houses in Munich and Cologne which had suffered serious bomb damage and which had been largely rebuilt by the owners. Relatives brought wood and other material from the countryside and also contributed their skills and labor.

63. See Merritt and Merritt, *Public Opinion in Occupied Germany*, p. 151.

64. Joachim Steffens, "Bauvolumen und Baukapazität," p. 27, in Niederschrift, meeting of Arbeitsstab Wiederaufbauplanung in Wriezen, 11–12 November 1944, ASKG/Arbeitsstab Wiederaufbauplanung.

65. SAM/Bauamt-Wiederaufbau/1095/ "Statistik," II, Section X.

66. OMGUS, Monthly Report (June 1946): 20.

67. BHSA/MWi (1952–53)/10166.

68. OMGUS, Monthly Report (June 1946): 21.

69. OMGUS, Monthly Report (March 1946): 7.

70. RWWA/1/237/2/148, "Notiz für Herrn Dr. Schäfer," 4 April 1950.

71. OMGUS, Monthly Report (June 1946): 51.

72. OMGUS, Monthly Report (February 1946): 7, 9.

73. "Survey of Allotment of Building Material," prepared by the Bayerisches Staatsministerium für Arbeit und soziale Fürsorge, 9 May 1947, in NA/RG 260/ OMG Bavaria, Manpower Division, Labor Relations and Standards B1/ Statistical Reports 30 3/13 31 1/13 (Box 52).

74. See, for example, Verband industrieller Bauunternehmungen Groß-Hamburgs, "Bedeutung und Leistungsvermögen der hamburgischen Bauindustrie," *Baurundschau* 37 (1947): 506–8. Special issue, "Hamburg im Wandel."

75. OMGUS, Monthly Report (July 1945): 7, states, and this is typical, that "basic materials for the production of building materials exist in fairly adequate quantities in the U.S. Zone. The coal shortage is the principal limiting factor in the production of building materials, especially cement, glass, and roofing paper."

76. NA/RG 260/ OMG Bavaria/ Manpower 105¹/13 (Box 85) File 11: Resolution of the Bavarian Cities Organization on Questions of Reconstruction, 23 October 1947.

77. NA/RG 260/ OMG Bavaria/ Manpower 105¹/13 (Box 85) File 11: Samuel R. Rosenbaum, Field Operations Supervisor for Southern Bavaria, Memorandum for Chief, Executive and Field Operations Branch, "Target Project on Construction in Southern Bavaria," 14 October 1947, p. 4.

78. NA/RG 260/ OMG Bavaria Manpower Division, Box 52, Folder 9: "Building Program 1948," 22 October 1947.

79. NA/RG 260/ OMG Bavaria/ Manpower 105¹/13 (Box 85) File 11: Herman Stern, Field Operations Supervisor for Franken, Memorandum for Chief, Executive and Field Operations Branch, "The Use and Misuse of Building Materials," 14 October 1947, p. 5.

80. Clipping in SAM/ Bürgermeister und Rat/ 1971.

81. SAM/ Bürgermeister und Rat/1967/Protokoll über die Sitzung des Baustoff-beirats, 1 August 1947: 4–5.

82. NA/RG 260/ OMG Bavaria/ Manpower 105¹/13 (Box 85) File 11: Samuel R. Rosenbaum, Field Operations Supervisor for Southern Bavaria, Memorandum for Chief, Executive and Field Operations Branch, "Target Project on Construction in Southern Bavaria," 14 October 1947, p. 4.

83. Ibid., p. 8.

84. NA/RG 260/OMG Bavaria/ Manpower 105¹/13 (Box 85) File 11: Paul S. Nevin, Chief, Trade and Commerce Branch, "Memorandum on Distribution of Building Materials," 28 November 1947.

85. The following is based on a long interview with Albert and his son Jürgen Speck in Cologne, 19 March 1990, and on an essay by Albert Speck, "Das Dritte Reich, Krieg, Inflation, Währungsreform, Wirtschaftsbau: Wege, Um- und Schleich-wege, Pannen von 1934–1948 und danach," privately printed in Cologne, 1988. Trained as a corporate economist, Albert Speck served as business manager for the Wirtschaftsgruppe Bauindustrie in Berlin from 1934 to 1939, and he wrote several successful texts on accounting and bookkeeping in the building industry. As a contrac-tor for projects deemed important for the war effort, he was exempt from military service.

86. A legal complaint against Speck was filed by the building union on behalf of a former employee, who accused Speck of large-scale black market profiteering. The accusations were serious enough to warrant a quiet investigation by the city, quiet because they also feared a countersuit against the city by Speck. HASK/2/ 1329/ 11: P. J. Wingen to Staatsanwaltschaft Köln, Strafanzeige gegen Dr. Albert Speck, 29 Octo-ber 1947.

87. See Verband industrieller Bauunternehmungen Groß-Hamburgs, "Bedeutung und Leistungsvermögen der hamburgischen Bauindustrie."

88. SAM/Bauamt-Wiederaufbau/1112/ Report by Preis, 2 February 1946; and also *Verhandlungen der Stadtverordnetenversammlung,* Köln, Session 7 (23 June 1947): 200.

89. For example, NA/RG 260/ OMG Bavaria/ Manpower 105¹/13 (Box 85) File 11: Memo by Herman Stern, Field Operations Supervisor for Northern Bavaria, "Labor Shortages in Critical Labor Area Nürnberg in Relation to Housing Shortages" (3 December 1947): 3.

90. Ibid., p. 4.

91. For example, SAM/Bauamt-Wiederaufbau/1118/ Report by Fischer, 28 January 1947, p. 26.

92. Josef Beule, "Die Vereinigung Berliner Baubetriebe," *Neue Bauwelt* 1 (1946) and "Viel zu viele—und ohne Halt," *Neue Bauwelt* 3 (1948): 250–51. Berlin had tried to control this development through the creation in July 1945 of an association of building firms (Die Vereinigung Berliner Baubetriebe, or VBB), which sought, among other things, to coordinate the allocation of construction labor, the training of apprentices, and the reeducation of workers from other industries to give them construction skills. Complaints from the left that the VBB was merely a traditional capitalist entrepreneurial association led the Komanditura to abolish it in early 1947.

93. Konrad Peter, "Wir Architekten fordern . . . : Der Beamtete Architekt," *Der Bauhelfer* 2, no. 16 (1947): 22.

94. NA/RG 260/ OMG Bavaria/ Manpower 105¹/13 (Box 85) File 11: Herman Stern, Field Operations Supervisor for Franken, Memorandum for Chief, Executive and Field Operations Branch, "The Use and Misuse of Building Materials" (14 October 1947): 7.

95. Gutschow and Stiemer, *Dokumentation Wiederaufbau Münster: Materialsammlung*, p. 75.

96. HASK/2/1320/Oberbürgermeister Klett, "5 Jahre Aufbau in Stuttgart," speech delivered 24 April 1950, p. 9.

97. *Verwaltungsberichte der Stadt Köln,* (1953–54): 126; (1954–55): 136.

98. NA/RG 260/ OMG Bavaria/ Manpower 105¹/13 (Box 85) File 11: Samuel Rosenbaum, Field Operations Supervisor for Southern Bavaria, Memorandum for the Chief, Executive and Field Operations Branch, Manpower Division, "Target project on construction in Southern Bavaria" (14 October 1947): 6.

99. Ibid.

100. *Verwaltungsberichte der Stadt Köln* (1947): 84; (1948–49): 87.

101. Gutschow and Stiemer, *Dokumentation Wiederaufbau: Materialsammlung*, p. 77.

102. For example, BHSA/MWi (1952–53)/10153/ Hillebrecht for Ausschuss für Bau- und Wohnungswesen des Zonenbeirat to Bayer. Innenmin., 18 November 1947; and NA/RG 260/ OMG Bavaria/ Manpower 105¹/13 (Box 85) File 11: Memorandum to the Director, Manpower Division, "Survey of Relationship of Labor Shortages with Shortages of Housing and Reconstruction in Bavaria" (25 June 1948, summary of conclusions reached after study conducted in the fall of 1947).

103. For example, RWWA/1/237/4, Wiederaufbauausschuss, IHK Essen to IHK Cologne, 29 September 1948, with enclosed letters from several organizations.

104. Stadtverordnetenversammlung of Greater Berlin, I. Wahlperiode, *Stenographischer Bericht,* 31st session (29 May 1947): 25.

105. SAM/ Ratsitzungsprotokolle/ 721/3/ Closed session (14 December 1948): 3487.

106. ADST/6/22–05, Baulenkungsgesetz, letter of 8 March 1948; see also his letter to the Städtetag of 10 November 1947.

107. *Gesetz- und Verordnungsblatt für das Land Nordrhein-Westfalen* 3 (14 May 1949): 69.

108. ADST/6/22–05, Baulenkungsgesetz, correspondence between Deutscher Städtetag and member cities, November 1949ff.

109. ADST/ 6/00–00–10: 10th meeting of Bauausschuss (21 October 1951, Niederschift dated 26 November 1951): B1493, p. 4.

Chapter 3

1. Barbara Miller Lane, *Architecture and Politics in Germany, 1918–1945* (Cambridge, Mass., 1985), p. 3. For a brief introduction to the question of the influence of architecture, see Jon Lang, "The Built Environment and Social Behavior: Architectural Determinism Reexamined," in *VIA: Culture and the Social Vision*, vol. 4, Mark A. Hewitt, Benjamin Kracauer, John Massengale, and Michael McDonough, eds., (Philadelphia and Cambridge, Mass., 1980). The modernists and traditionalists both overestimated the ability of buildings to bring about long-lasting changes in deeply held cultural values.

2. Berthold Hinz, Hans-Ernst Mittig, Wolfgang Schäche, and Angela Schönberger, "Vorwort," in *Die Dekoration der Gewalt: Kunst und Medien im Faschismus*, Hinz et al., eds. (Gießen, 1979), p. 5.

3. Joachim Petsch, " 'Neues Bauen' und konservative Architektur der 20er und 30er Jahre," *Der Architekt* 4 (1983): 191.

4. Leon Krier, "An Architecture of Desire," in *Albert Speer, Architecture 1932–42*, Krier, ed. (Brussels, 1985), p. 218. Whatever one thinks of Speer's work, the language of Krier's essay, meant to be provocative, is offensive. Such statements (p. 227) as: "Auschwitz-Birkenau and Los Angeles are children of the same parents [industrial civilization]" and "There can no more be authoritarian or democratic architecture than there can be authoritarian or democratic Wiener Schnitzels" amount to a casual dismissal of what the Nazis did.

5. Ibid., p. 219. Krier also states: "Reading Heinrich Himmler's edicts concerning the future colonization of the Baltic countries, at no point does one have the slightest impression of studying the lucubrations of one of the most zealous murderers of history, but rather an elegant synthesis of all the best urban theories from Aristotle to Tessenow" (p. 221). One must not dismiss the author of this backhanded praise of Himmler as some odd fanatic: in 1986 Krier was named the first director of the new Institute of Architecture and Urbanism established in Chicago by the Skidmore, Owings, and Merrill Foundation (though he resigned the directorship in short order because of a disagreement on the terms of his appointment), and in the fall of 1987 his drawings of a future Washington were exhibited in the Octagon in that city.

6. Ibid., p. 227. Emphasis in original.

7. Iain Boyd Whyte, *Bruno Taut and the Architecture of Activism* (Cambridge, 1982) is the best source for this. The authorized biography of Gropius is Reginald Isaacs, *Walter Gropius*, 2 vols. (Berlin, 1983–84), but an excellent analysis of the development of Gropius's ideas is to be found in Winfried Nerdinger, "Walter Gropius—totale Architektur für eine demokratische Gesellschaft," *Jahrbuch des Zentralinstituts für Kunstgeschichte* 1 (1985).

8. The Werkbund was founded in 1907 to try to harmonize German artisanal traditions with the desire for modern design in many areas. See Joan Campbell, *The German Werkbund: The Politics of Reform in the Applied Arts* (Princeton, N.J., 1978). Lane, *Architecture and Politics*, p. 21, describes it as "an organization of architects, craftsmen, and businessmen formed to improve industrial design." The Germans were

of course not creating a new movement in isolation. The Werkbund was not unlike the Arts and Crafts movement of William Morris in Britain. The leading French modernist, Le Corbusier, had worked with Mies van der Rohe and Gropius in Peter Behren's Berlin AEG office before the war. German modernists were also aware of the modern designs of Frank Lloyd Wright.

9. See Joachim Petsch, "'Neues Bauen,' " p. 188; and Lane, *Architecture and Politics*, pp. 45–50. Architectural modernism has at times been labeled the "international" style. This is not inappropriate, since the modernists were rejecting "national"— which is to say historical—architectural styles. While the Bauhaus included crafts in its curriculum and sought to include finely designed utilitarian objects in architecture, it stressed industrial construction techniques, whereas conservatives in the Werkbund stressed individual, artisanal construction.

10. Quoted from W. C. Behrendt, "Geleitwort," *Die Form* 1 (1925): 1, quoted by Lane, *Architecture and Politics*, p. 130. "Neugestaltung" is the same term later used by the Nazis to describe what they sought to do in redesigning several cities as representative Nazi cities.

11. Martin Wagner, "Das neue Berlin" (typescript, Berlin, 1932), p. 230, as cited by Lars Olof Larsson, *Die Neugestaltung der Reichshauptstadt: Albert Speers Generalbebauungsplan für Berlin*, Stockholm Studies in the History of Art, vol. 29 (Uppsala, 1978), p. 121, n. 22. Copies of the Wagner manuscript are to be found in the Akademie der Künste and the Bibliothek des Senators für Bau- und Wohnungswesen, Berlin.

12. Lane, *Architecture and Politics*, p. 27 and generally Chapter 1.

13. See Richard Pommer, "The Flat Roof: A Modernist Controversy in Germany," *Art Journal* 43, no. 2 (1983). In his sharp attack on the architecture and planning in Berlin in the nineteenth century, Werner Hegemann noted that Schinkel, much admired by opponents of modernism for his classicism, had designed a building that was a cubic mass with a flat roof. Schinkel's Kavalierhaus in the Charlottenburger Schloßpark was thus a building, "die mancher deutsche Bürgermeister oder Rassentheoretiker als semitische oder marokkanische Baukunst mit blindem Eifer befehdet." Hegemann, *Das steinerne Berlin. Geschichte der größten Mietskasernenstadt der Welt* (Berlin, 1930), p. 179.

14. An interesting discussion of these contrasts is in Joachim Petsch, *Architektur und Gesellschaft. Zur Geschichte der deutschen Architektur im 19. und 20. Jahrhundert* (Cologne and Vienna, 1973).

15. *Sachlichkeit* does not translate very well. Lane, *Architecture and Politics*, p. 130, uses "practicality." She notes that the term was used in different ways. Gropius and Taut stressed architecture "as abstract form and only secondarily as a matter of functional planning and machine technology" (p. 132).

16. Ibid., pp. 58–59.

17. Barbara Miller Lane, "Architects in Power: Politics and Ideology in the Work of Ernst May and Albert Speer," in *Art and History: Images and Their Meaning*, Robert I. Rotberg and Theodore K. Rabb, eds. (Cambridge and New York, 1988), p. 293. One should note, however, that not all of the modernists were alike. Architects like Rudolf Schwarz and Hans Schwippert, both working in the Rhineland, were more modern than traditional, but they did not follow the purist line of the Bauhaus or the "new objectivity," instead continuing to use some traditional forms and materials.

18. Lane, *Architecture and Politics*, Chapter 3.

19. A recent study is Richard Pommer and Christian F. Otto, *Weissenhof 1927 and the Modern Movement in Architecture* (Chicago, 1990).

20. Lane, *Architecture and Politics*, 127.

21. As Gerhard Fehl observes, stripped of its social democratic content, there was then no reason why modernist style could not be used by the eclectic Nazis. "Die Moderne unterm Hakenkreuz. Ein Versuch, die Rolle funktionalistischer Architektur im Dritten Reich zu klären," in *Faschistische Architekturen. Planen und Bauen in Europa 1930 bis 1945*, Hartmut Frank, ed., Stadt, Planung, Geschichte, vol. 3 (Hamburg, 1985), p. 102. The term "international style" for modernist architecture was used as the title of a 1932 exhibition at the Museum of Modern Art in New York.

22. Quoted in Nerdinger, "Walter Gropius," p. 347. The letter was written to Friedrich Lörcher.

23. The manifesto of the Block is reprinted in Anna Teut, *Architektur im Dritten Reich, 1933–1945* (Berlin, Frankfurt, and Vienna, 1967), p. 29.

24. For the ideological bases of the Heimatschutz movement, see Klaus Bergmann, *Agrarromantik und Großstadtfeindschaft*, Marburger Abhandlungen zur Politischen Wissenschaft, vol. 20 (Meisenheim am Glan, 1970), pp. 121ff.

25. Petsch makes a distinction between conservatives and traditionalists. The former use historical forms, but they also resist social change, instead holding on to preindustrial, antiurban values. The traditionalist, according to Petsch, seeks peaceful social change and tries to combine modern values with historical forms. Petsch, "'Neues Bauen,' " p. 188. I am not sure this distinction is all that clear and useful.

26. See also Gerd Kähler, "Regionalismus ist kein Stil," *Bauwelt* 76 (1986), for a recent polemic against considering regionalism as a particular architectural style, as opposed to a list of formalistic elements.

27. Manfred Fischer, *Fritz Schumacher, das Hamburger Stadtbild und die Denkmalpflege*, Arbeitsheft zur Denkmalpflege in Hamburg, vol. 4 (Hamburg, 1977), pp. 59–62.

28. Fritz Schumacher, *Köln. Entwicklungsfragen einer Großstadt* (Munich, 1923), p. 273. None of the proposed buildings were built.

29. Regine Dölling, "Protection and Conservation of Historical Monuments in the Federal Republic of Germany," in *The Conservation of Historical Monuments in the Federal Republic of Germany*, Dölling, ed., Timothy Nevill, trans. (Munich, 1974), p. 10. See also Friedrich Mielke, *Die Zukunft der Vergangenheit. Grundsätze, Probleme und Möglichkeiten der Denkmalpflege* (Stuttgart, 1975).

30. See Hiltrud Kier, "Denkmalpflege in Köln," in *Glanz und Elend der Denkmalpflege und Stadtplanung Cöln 1906–2006 Köln*, Rheinischer Verein für Denkmalpflege und Landschaftsschutz (Cologne, 1981).

31. Quoted by Hans Gerhard Evers, *Tod, Macht und Raum als Bereiche der Architektur* (1939, rpt. Munich, 1970), p. 285.

32. Christian F. Otto, "Modern Environment and Historical Continuity: The Heimatschutz Discourse in Germany," *Art Journal* 43, no. 2 (1983): 150. This discussion is based on Otto's article.

33. See K. Michael Hays, "Tessenow's Architecture as National Allegory: Critique of Capitalism or Protofascism," *Assemblage* 8 (February 1989): 113. According to Hays, Tessenow sought a middle ground between capitalism and communism and became thereby petit bourgeois.

34. I owe this insight to Hartmut Frank, who shared with me his unpublished manuscript "3mal Wiederaufbau" and discussed his research on German architectural history at a conference on European reconstruction held 1–5 June 1987, at Bellagio, Italy. On rebuilding in East Prussia during and after World War I see Hartmut Frank, "Auf der Suche nach der alten Stadt. Zur Diskussion um Heimatschutz und Stadtbau-

kunst beim Wiederaufbau von Freudenstadt," in *Stadtgestalt und Heimatgefühl. Der Wiederaufbau von Freudenstadt 1945–1954. Analysen, Vergleiche und Dokumente*, H.-G. Burkhardt, H. Frank, U. Höhns, and K. Stieghorst, eds. (Hamburg, 1988), pp. 5–6.

35. See Max Guther, "Zur Geschichte der Städtebaulehre an deutschen Hochschulen," in *Heinz Wetzel und die Geschichte der Städtebaulehre an deutschen Hochschulen*, Ulrike Pampe, ed. (Stuttgart, 1982).

36. Lane, *Architecture and Politics*, pp. 81n, 128, 134.

37. Quoted in Otto, "Modern Environment and Historical Continuity," p. 155.

38. Lane, *Architecture and Politics*, p. 136.

39. Ibid., p. 148. Lane also discusses the broader antimodernism of the Kampfbund für deutsche Kultur.

40. Andrew Lees, *Cities Perceived. Urban Society in European and American Thought, 1820–1940* (New York, 1985), p. 283, and Lane, *Architecture and Politics*, pp. 153ff.

41. Joachim Petsch, *Baukunst und Stadtplanung im Dritten Reich* (Munich, 1976), p. 54. Teut, *Architektur im Dritten Reich*, p. 17, notes that a construction freeze was imposed on public buildings in Prussia, by far the largest of the German states. Her important book reprints many important documents from this period.

42. Lane, *Architecture and Politics*, pp. 171–84. Those losing their jobs and/or emigrating included Hans Scharoun, Hans Poelzig, Robert Vorhoelzer, Martin Elsässer, Johannes Göderitz, and Martin Wagner. Ernst May and Bruno Taut had already departed for Russia in 1930. Gropius left Germany first for Britain and then, in 1938, for the United States, taking Wagner with him. Gropius made at least one attempt to gain a commission from the Nazis, and Elsässer, in exile in Italy, expected the Nazis to get over their hostility to modernism. See Hartmut Frank, "Welche Sprache sprechen Steine? Zur Einführung in den Sammelband 'Faschistische Architekturen,' " in *Faschistische Architekturen. Planen und Bauen in Europa 1930 bis 1945*, Hartmut Frank, ed., Stadt, Planung, Geschichte, vol. 3 (Hamburg, 1985), pp. 15–17. Gerhard Fehl is surely correct that the purge of modernist architects was a product not just of ideology but also of the opportunity to take revenge on competitors. See his "Die Moderne unterm Hakenkreuz," p. 100.

43. Petsch, *Baukunst und Stadtplanung*, pp. 71–75, and Teut, *Architektur im Dritten Reich*, pp. 66ff, on the process of Gleichschaltung for architects.

44. Winfried Nerdinger, "Versuchung und Dilemma der Avantgarde im Spiegel der Architekturwettbewerbe 1933–35," in *Faschistische Architekturen: Planen und Bauen in Europa 1930 bis 1945*, Hartmut Frank, ed. Stadt, Planung, Geschichte, vol. 3 (Hamburg, 1985). This important essay reproduces some of the proposals.

45. Robert R. Taylor. *The Word in Stone. The Role of Architecture in the National Socialist Ideology* (Berkeley, Calif., 1974), pp. 92–93, 232.

46. Niederschriften, Tagung in Wriezen, Arbeitsstab Wiederaufbauplanung zerstörter Städte, 16–17 September 1944, p. 41, in ASKG/Arbeitsstab Wiederaufbauplanung.

47. Petsch, *Baukunst und Stadtplanung*, p. 182.

48. The debate about the the existence of such a style is often couched in terms of existence of "fascist," as opposed to Nazi, architecture. The former would also include the architecture of Italy, Spain, Vichy France, and other right-wing regimes. See, for example, Frank, *Faschistische Architekturen*. I think there are probably as many differences between the right-wing European regimes of this period as there are similarities, which is to say that I am uncomfortable about simply seeing Nazism as a variant of fascism. In any event, since the focus here is Germany, this question, though an important one, must be passed over.

49. For Troost's work in Munich, see Hans-Peter Rasp, *Eine Stadt für tausend Jahre. München—Bauten und Projekte für die Hauptstadt der Bewegung* (Munich, 1981), pp. 22ff.

50. See Jochen Thies, *Architekt der Weltherrschaft: Die "Endziele" Hitlers* (Düsseldorf, 1976), pp. 72–80, and the documents in Jost Dülffer, Jochen Thies, and Josef Henke, *Hitlers Städte. Baupolitik im Dritten Reich: Eine Dokumentation* (Cologne and Vienna, 1978).

51. Hitler used the phrase "the Word in Stone" in a speech at the German Architecture and Crafts Exhibition in Munich on 22 January 1938. In September 1934, Otto Klöppel urged architects to take up the challenge of renewing Germany through Nazism, declaring that "Steine lügen nie." Klöppel, "Der Baukünstler, ein Träger nationalsozialistischer Weltanschauung," reprinted in Teut, *Architektur im Dritten Reich*, p. 135. See Frank, "Welche Sprache sprechen Steine?" The point is also made by Lars Olof Larsson, though he is much less critical of Speer's work than is Frank. See Larsson, "Klassizismus in der Architektur des 20. Jahrhunderts," in *Albert Speer, Architektur. Arbeiten 1933–1942*, Karl Arndt, Georg Friedrich Koch, and Lars Olof Larsson, eds. (Frankfurt, 1978).

52. See Wolfgang Schäche, "Platz für die staatliche Macht," in *Die Metropole. Industriekultur in Berlin im 20. Jahrhundert*, Jochen Boberg, Tilman Fichter, and Eckhart Gillen, eds. (Munich, 1986).

53. Albert Speer and Wolfgang Pehnt, "Die Manipulation des Menschen," *Der Architekt* 4 (1983): 186. See also Georg Friedrich Koch, "Speer, Schinkel und der preussische Stil," in *Albert Speer, Architektur. Arbeiten 1933–1942*, Karl Arndt, Georg Friedrich Koch, and Lars Olof Larsson, eds. (Frankfurt, 1978). Speer was a student of Heinrich Tessenow in Berlin. Tessenow was himself a traditionalist, but one who mixed certain historical elements with modern elements. He built primarily houses, and he never supported the Nazis.

54. In an interesting study, Diane Y. Ghirardo indicates that in the 1930s fascist Italy more often chose modernist designs for public buildings than did the United States, but in both states architects sought to use architectural elements that convey political messages to the viewer. *Building New Communities: New Deal America and Fascist Italy* (Princeton, N.J., 1989).

55. See Hartmut Frank, "Monumentalität und Stadtlandschaft. Anmerkungen zu einer bösen Architektur mit einem Abstand von 45 Jahre," in *"Die Axt hat geblüht . . ." Europäische Konflikte der 30er Jahre in Erinnerung an die frühe Avantgarde*, Jürgen Harten, Hans-Werner Schmidt, and Marie Louise Syring, eds. (Düsseldorf, 1987), pp. 345–46.

56. Functionality also influenced the style of nonrepresentational Nazi buildings. Industrial buildings tended to be relatively modern in style. Hermann Göring's buildings for the Air Ministry were also relatively modern, including many with flat roofs and extensive use of glass. Lane, *Architecture and Politics*, pp. 200–204. See also Hans-Jochen Kunst, "Architektur und Macht. Überlegungen zur NS-Architektur," *Arch +* 71 (1983): 64.

57. Quoted in Nerdinger, "Versuchung und Dilemma der Avantgarde," p. 65.

58. Dülffer, Thies, and Henke, *Hitlers Städte*, p. 297.

59. Friedrich Tamms, "Das Große in der Baukunst," reprinted in Tamms, *Von Menschen, Städten und Brücken* (Düsseldorf, 1974), and in *Stadtbauwelt* 84 (1984): 425.

60. Speer and Pehnt, "Die Manipulation des Menschen," pp. 184–85. Speer says that "the only new thing" in his architecture was that it was "einen Rahmen für eine Kundgebung von mehreren hunderttausend Menschen." Stephen D. Helmer, *Hitler's*

Berlin: The Speer Plans for Reshaping the City (Ann Arbor, Mich., 1985), uses the term "manipulative aesthetics" (pp. 38–40), while Dieter Bartetzko, in "Versteinerte Gefühle—NS-Architektur als Wunscherfüllung," in *Stadtbauwelt* 92 (1986), points out the resemblance between Nazi architectural visions and the cinematic visions of Fritz Lang, in terms of both mythic heroic forms and the portrayal of the decadent metropolis. Photographs of the buildings planned for Berlin have been published in many places, including Helmer, *Hitler's Berlin*, and Larsson, *Die Neugestaltung der Reichshauptstadt*. For the buildings designed for Munich, see Rasp, *Eine Stadt für tausend Jahre*. For Cologne, Wolfram Hagspiel, "Die Nationalsozialistische Stadtplanung in und für Köln," *Geschichte in Köln* 9 (1981). There is a chilling and prophetic ring to the title of a book written in 1930 but published in 1939 by Hans Gerhard Evers: *Tod, Macht und Raum als Bereiche der Architektur*, which can be translated as *Death, Power, and Space as the Realm of Architecture*. Evers saw architecture as thoroughly political, historical, and national, though not necessarily racial, and the book is not explicitly Nazi in content or language.

61. It is also here that contemporary commentators disagree most sharply. Petsch argues that one must not separate pure form from intended function, while Larsson and Krier argue that neoclassicism must not be judged as evil just because its uses by the Nazis were evil.

62. Speer, *Inside the Third Reich*, p. 134, and Speer, "Vorwort," in Speer, *Architektur*, p. 8. Leon Krier, in his praise of Speer's projects, neglects Speer's own criticisms.

63. Pfister argues that there in fact was no "Nazi period style." The party buildings were huge but eclectic, while lesser buildings were simply mediocre. Rudolf Pfister, "Hitlers 'Baukunst,' " *Baumeister* 43, no. 2 (July/August 1946): 27, 31.

64. Von Beyme, *Der Wiederaufbau*, pp. 176ff.

65. Wiltrud Petsch and Joachim Petsch, "Neuaufbau statt Wiederaufbau: Architektur und Städtebau in Nordrhein-Westfalen 1945–1952," in *Aus den Trümmern. Kunst und Kultur im Rheinland und Westfalen 1945–1952, Neubeginn und Kontinuität*, Klaus Honnef and Hans M. Schmidt, eds. (Cologne and Bonn, 1985), pp. 76–77.

66. Bernard Wagner, "More Homes for Germans," *Information Bulletin of the Office of the US High Commissioner for Germany* (December, 1951). Wagner was the son of Martin Wagner, the former progressive city planner of Berlin who had moved to Harvard University with Walter Gropius in the 1930s .

67. Gerd Hatje, Hubert Hoffmann, and Karl Kaspar, *New German Architecture*, H. J. Montague, trans. (Stuttgart, London, and New York, 1956), p. vii. Though not a well written or persuasive book, the title and content of Martin Pawley's *Architecture versus Housing* (New York and Washington, D.C., 1971) suggests that during much of this century the two have not been particularly compatible.

68. Wolfgang Pehnt, *German Architecture, 1960–1970* (New York, 1970). The comment is about the first decade.

69. Dieter Hoffman-Axthelm, "Deutschland 1945–80—Der Architekt ohne Architektur," *Arch+* 59 (1981): 16.

70. Christoph Hackelsberger, *Die aufgeschobene Moderne. Ein Versuch zur Einordnung der Architektur der Fünfziger Jahre* (Berlin, 1985), pp. 33, 48, 54–55, 64. Hackelsberger does, however, admit that good housing projects were built in the Neue Wahr in Bremen and in Hamburg-Altona.

71. "Anmerkungen zur Zeit," no name, but normally by Alfons Leitl when not otherwise specified, no. 2 (1948): 5.

72. The following is a sample from Werner Durth and Niels Gutschow, eds. *Archi-*

tektur und Städtebau der Fünfziger Jahre, Schriftenreihe des Deutschen National-komitees für Denkmalschutz, vol. 33 (Bonn, 1987); most are to be found in one or another of the other architectural histories. Grindelhochhäuser, Hamburg (Bernhard Hermkes et al., 1946–56); Landesversorgungsanstalt, Munich (Wassili Luckhardt, 1955–57); Berlin Philharmonic (Hans Scharoun, 1956–63); Berlin Hansaviertel (Many architects, including Walter Gropius, 1957); Frankfurt Kaufhof (Peter Grund, 1950); Siemenssiedlung in Obersending, Munich (Emil Freymuth, 1954); Thyssen skyscraper, Düsseldorf (Helmut Hentrich, 1955–60); Konzerthaus/Liederhalle, Stuttgart (Adolf Abel et al., 1955–56); Gürzenich Concert Hall, Cologne (Rudolf Schwarz and Karl Band, 1949–55); Westfalenhalle, Dortmund (Walter Hoeltje and Horst Retzki, 1949–52); Schwarzwaldhalle, Karlsruhe (Erich Schelling, 1953); Fernsehnturm, Stuttgart (Fritz Leonhardt, 1953–55); churches in the Rhineland by Dominikus Böhm and Rudolf Schwarz. For other examples, see Christoph Mohr, "Überlegungen zum Denkmal-begriff der Nachkriegsarchitektur," and Michael Neumann, "Ängstliche Gedanken über den Kirchenbau der 50er Jahre," both in *Architektur und Städtebau der Fünfziger Jahre*, Schriftenreihe des Deutschen Nationalkomitees für Denkmalschutz, vol. 36 (Bonn, 1988). Petsch and Petsch, "Neuaufbau statt Wiederaufbau," p. 81, praise the architecture of the years 1948 to 1952 but find that of 1953 to 1957 generally deficient.

73. Hans K. F. Mayer, "Strömungen in der heutigen deutschen Architektur," *Der Aufbau* 8 (1953): 354.

74. Hans Martin Kampffmeyer, Friedrich Spengelin, and Wolf Jobst Siedler, "Zu Beginn der 60er Jahre hatten wir das Gefühl: Jetzt müssen wir von Grund auf neu anfangen," *Stadtbauwelt* 88 (1985): 332. See also Rudolf Hartog, "Architektur der 50er Jahre—Erlebnisse und Erfahrungen," in *Architektur und Städtebau der Fünfziger Jahre*, Schriftenreihe des Deutschen Nationalkomitees für Denkmalschutz, vol. 36 (Bonn, 1988). During the discussion at a conference in Hannover on 2 February 1990 on "Schutz und Erhaltung von Bauten der Fünfziger Jahre," Carl Bauer, an architect who had been at the Bauhaus in 1933 and who worked in Hannover in the early 1950s, reported that he and Rudolf Hillebrecht, the chief planner, went to Sweden in 1950 and returned with some 600 slides of the best in Swedish architecture. They used these slides repeatedly in meetings with property owners and architects in Hannover to influence the form of reconstruction in that city. The influence of Scandinavian and Swiss models was stressed by Winfried Nerdinger in his conference paper: "Materialästhetik und Rasterbauweise—Zum Charakter der Architektur der 50er Jahre," in *Architektur und Städtebau der Fünfziger Jahre: Ergebnisse der Fachtagung in Hannover, 2.–4. Februar 1990. Schutz und Erhaltung von Bauten der Fünfziger Jahre*, Werner Durth and Niels Gutschow, eds., Schriftenreihe des Deutschen Nationalkomitees für Denkmalschutz, vol. 41 (Bonn, 1990). Bauer's remarks are summarized on pp. 103–4.

75. Ulrich Höhns, "Neuaufbau als Hoffnung—Wiederaufbau als Festschreibung der Misere. Marshallplan und Wohnungsbau in der Bundesrepublik nach dem Kriege," in *Grauzonen. Kunst und Zeitbilder. Farbwelten 1945–1955*, Bernhard Schulz, ed. (Berlin, 1983), pp. 88–92.

76. BDST/6/00–00–11/ C 712, 11 Sitzung des Bauausschußes des Deutschen Städtetags, 21 and 22 April 1952, pp. 2–3 of a 37-page report by Weinbrenner to the committee.

77. Eugen Fabricius, "Architekt BDA," Otto Gühlk, "Einheitlicher Berufsver-band der Architekten," Günther Kühne, "Wer kann 'Architekt BDA' werden?" and Max Unglehrt, "'BDA' oder 'bda' oder Großberufsverband?" all in *Neue Bauwelt* 2 (1947), and Hans Matthus, "Wir Architekten fordern . . . ," *Der Bauhelfer* 2 (1947): 25–27, give the flavor of this conflict.

78. Teut, *Architektur im Dritten Reich*, p. 82.

79. Paul Mast, "Wir Architekten fordern . . . : Der Ingenieur," *Der Bauhelfer* 2 (1947): 27.

80. Konter, "Deutsche Planer und Architekten," pp. 59–62. Rhineland-Pfalz passed such a law in 1950, Bavaria in 1954, Baden-Württemberg in 1955, Schleswig-Holstein in 1964, Hamburg in 1965, Hesse in 1968, Northrhine-Westphalia in 1969, Lower Saxony in 1970, Bremen in 1971, and West Berlin in 1973.

81. AIHKM-München, XXII-157r/ Speech by Otto Bartning, president of the national BDA, to the annual meeting of the association, 12 July 1951. Bartning's complaint was discussed by Gustav Lampmann, "Architekt und Baubehörde," *Der Städtetag*, new series 4 (1951): 393–94.

82. Michaela Stauch, "Die Freunde des Neuen Bauens," in *Aufbauzeit: Planen und Bauen München 1945–1950*, Winfried Nerdinger, ed. (Munich, 1984), pp. 78–79.

83. HASK/2/ 1321/ Niederschriften über die Sitzung des Verwaltungsrats der Wiederaufbau-Gesellschaft, 31 May and 11 July 1949.

84. SAS/ZAS 78/Gutachten zum Entwurf Hoss, 1 August 1950. A special committee was set up to evaluate Hoss's design. Made up of mostly modernists, the committee condemned the design as "pseudomodern" and lacking a proper understanding of the relationship among materials, function, and site. The committee included Richard Döcker and Martin Elsässer and was chaired by Paul Bonatz. The committee concluded that had Hoss's entry appeared in the competition, it would not have ranked within the first 20. Hoss had to accept the jury's decision.

85. Hoffmann-Axthelm, "Deutschland 1945–80," p. 17.

86. AIHKM/XXII-157r/Speech by Otto Bartning, president of the national BDA, to the annual meeting of the association, 12 July 1951.

87. See Jeffry M. Diefendorf, "Berlin on the Charles, Cambridge on the Spree: Walter Gropius, Martin Wagner and the Rebuilding of Germany," in *Cross-Cultural Influences in Exile*, Helmut Pfanner, ed. (Bonn, 1986) for attempts to get Gropius and Wagner to return. The Mies van der Rohe papers in the Library of Congress contain letters from Hans Schwippert, Otto Bartning, and others, asking in vain for Mies to return, for example, Hans Schwippert to Mies, 17 January 1947 (General Office Files, Container 53); Otto Bartning to Mies, 30 March and 22 June 1955 and reply from Mies (General Office Files, Container 19); Hermann Blomeier, editor of *Bauen und Wohnen*, and Alfons Leitl, editor of *Baukunst und Werkform*, to Mies in 1947 (General Office Files, Container 18). See also Jürgen Paul, "Kulturgeschichtliche Betrachtungen zur deutschen Nachkriegsarchitektur," in *Architektur in Deutschland: Bundesrepublik und Westberlin,* Helge Bofinger, Margret Bofinger, Jürgen Paul, and Heinrich Klotz, eds. (Stuttgart, 1979), p. 14.

88. See the roster of participants in the Darmstadt exhibition and discussion there in 1951, in Otto Bartning, ed., *Mensch und Raum*, Darmstädter Gespräch, no. 2 (Darmstadt, 1952).

89. See, for example, the letters written during 1947 and 1948 to Hans Scharoun by Richard Döcker and Hugo Häring in AdKB/ Nachlaß Scharoun/Versch. 5.

90. Hartmut Frank, "Trümmer: Traditionelle und moderne Architekturen im Nachkriegsdeutschland," in *Grauzonen. Kunst und Zeitbilder. Farbwelten 1945–1955*, Bernhard Schultz, ed. (Berlin, 1983), p. 50; Werner Durth, "Mainz: Blockierte Moderne," *Arch+* 67 (1982); and Rémi Baudoui, "L'équipe degli urbanisti della Sarre," *Casabella* 567 (April 1990): 57–58.

91. Hermann Mäckler, "Anmerkungen zur Zeit," *Baukunst und Werkform* 1 (1947): 12.

92. *Neue Bauwelt* 4, nos. 37 and 43 (1949).

93. See Joachim Petsch, "Zum Problem der Kontinuität nationalsozialistischer Architektur in den Fünfziger Jahren am Beispiel der Zeitschrift *Baumeister,*" in *Die Dekoration der Gewalt. Kunst und Medien im Faschismus*, Berthold Hinz, Hans-Ernst Mittig, Wolfgang Schäche, and Angela Schönberger, eds. (Gießen, 1979).

94. Hartog, "Architektur der 50er Jahre," pp. 13, 15.

95. See the comments by Paul Bonatz and Alfred Weber in *Mensch und Raum*, Bartning, ed., pp. 91, 96. For Munich, see Stauch, "Die Freunde des Neuen Bauens," pp. 77ff.

96. Martin Elsässer, "Fruchtbare Polarität," *Der Bauhelfer* 3 (1948): 115.

97. LC, Mies van der Rohe Papers, Late Correspondence, Container 53, Schwarz to Mies, 21 May 1947.

98. Ernst Neufert, "Müssen Industriebauten häßlich sein?" in *Amtlicher Katalog der Constructa Bauausstellung 1951* (Hannover, 1951), p. 264.

99. Schwarz's statements are from Bartning, ed., *Mensch und Raum*, pp. 66 and 69. See also Schwarz's comments in his articles, with rebuttals, in *Baukunst und Werkform* 7 (1953) and 10 (1956). Excerpts can be found in Christian Borngräber, *Stil Novo. Design in den 50er Jahren: Phantasie und Phantastik* (Frankfurt, 1979). For Wagner, see my "Berlin on the Charles," note 32.

100. Kenneth Frampton, *Modern Architecture: A Critical History*, rev. ed. (London, 1985), notes that Sigfried Giedion, Fernand Léger, and José Luis Sert had argued in 1943 that "neither the monumentality of the New Tradition nor the functionalism of the Modern Movement was capable of representing the collective aspirations of the people." This was meant for democratic and fascist states.

101. Hans Schmitt, *Der Neuaufbau der Stadt Köln* (Cologne, 1946), pp. 24, 28. See also HASK/2 (OBM)/1322/ Speech by Prof. Reidemeister at 4th meeting of "Der offenen Kreis" of the Wiederaufbaugesellschaft, 12 March 1947.

102. LC, Mies van der Rohe Papers, Late Correspondence, Container 7, letter of 30 June 1948. The edge of the paper with the year has crumbled away, but the text reveals that it was written during the Berlin Blockade.

103. Otto Bartning, "Mensch ohne Raum," *Baukunst und Werkform* 1 (1947): 20.

104. Hans Schoszberger, "Gestaltung," quoted by Höhns, " 'Neuaufbau' als Hoffnung," p. 92.

105. Hanns Adrian, "Ideen, die überlebten," in *Architektur und Städtebau der Fünfziger Jahre: Ergebnisse der Fachtagung in Hannover, 2.–4. Februar 1990. Schutz und Erhaltung von Bauten der Fünfziger Jahre*, Werner Durth and Niels Gutschow, eds., Schriftenreihe des Deutschen Nationalkomitees für Denkmalschutz, vol. 41 (Bonn, 1990).

106. Evers, *Tod, Macht und Raum*, pp. 288–89.

107. Christoph Mohr, from the transcript of a radio discussion aired by the Süddeutscher Rundfunk, 1 September 1988, printed in *Architektur und Städtebau der Fünfziger Jahre*, p. 113.

108. Jürgen Paul, "Kulturgeschichtliche Betrachtungen," p. 13.

109. Helge Bofinger, "Architektur in Deutschland," in *Architektur in Deutschland: Bundesrepublik und Westberlin*, Helge Bofinger, Margret Bofinger, Jürgen Paul, and Heinrich Klotz, eds. (Stuttgart, 1979), p. 8.

110. Johannes Cramer and Niels Gutschow, *Bauausstellungen. Eine Architekturgeschichte des 20. Jahrhunderts* (Stuttgart, 1984), p. 83.

111. Joachim Petsch, "Architektur und Städtebau in den 50er Jahren," in *Bikini. Die fünfziger Jahre: Kalter Krieg und Capri-Sonne*, Eckhard Siepmann, ed. (Berlin,

1981), p. 230, makes this point, but he attributes it to the adaptation of the style by the unreconstructed right after the war, whereas I think one can see it clearly in prewar projects. Mies van der Rohe, for example, moved back and forth between expensive pavilion architecture (the German pavilion in Barcelona in 1929) and luxurious single-family detached houses. An example of the attack on modernism can be taken from Lübeck, where former town senator Ewers complained about "silo-like buildings, . . . uniform houses in a European-American-Asiatic style." AHSL/Hauptamt 15u/2–64–0-I/report in *Lübeckische Freie Presse* on Bürgerschaft meeting of 30 October 1950.

112. SAS/ *Amtsblatt*, no. 47, 22 November 1951.

113. Fehl, "Die Moderne unterm Hakenkreuz," p. 89.

114. Teut, *Architektur im Dritten Reich*, p. 189.

115. This point is argued by Hartmut Frank, "Welche Sprache sprechen Steine?" Hermann Hipp, "Der gewöhnliche Traditionalismus: Heimat im Dritten Reich," *Der Architekt* 4 (1983).

116. My thanks to James Shedel for this observation.

117. Frank, "Monumentalität und Stadtlandschaft," p. 344.

118. Lane, "Architects in Power," p. 308, offers a similar opinion, whereas her book *Architecture and Politics in Germany* tends to stress the political content of architecture.

Chapter 4

1. Jürgen Paul, "Der Wiederaufbau der historischen Städte in Deutschland nach dem zweiten Weltkrieg," in *Die alte Stadt: Denkmal oder Lebensraum?*, Cord Meckseper and Harald Siebenmorgen, eds. (Göttingen, 1985), p. 119. The role of the urban landscape in forming personal identity was a point made by Kevin Lynch in his classic *The Image of the City* (Cambridge, Mass., 1960). Lynch, *What Time Is This Place?* (Cambridge, Mass., and London, 1972) and David Lowenthal, *The Past Is a Foreign Country* (Cambridge, 1985), both offer stimulating discussions of the problems presented by the preservation of historic buildings. Celia Applegate, *A Nation of Provincials. The German Idea of Heimat* (Berkeley, Los Angeles, Oxford, 1990), argues that local Heimat, or hometown associations, helped Germans form a national identity out of local identity in the late nineteenth century and again after 1945. Rudy J. Koshar, "Altar, Stage and City: Historic Preservation and Urban Meaning in Nazi Germany," *History and Memory* 3 (1991), discusses the manipulation of preservationist ideas by the Nazis. Ursula von Petz, *Stadtsanierung im Dritten Reich*, Dortmunder Beiträge zur Raumplanung, vol. 45 (Dortmund, 1987), p. 9, notes that the middle classes idealized the individuality not just of architecture but also of the furnishing of the interior.

2. Paul Clemen, "Aufgabe der Denkmalpflege von heute und morgen," *Zeitschrift für Kunst* 1 (1947), quoted by Jürgen Paul, "Die kulturelle Grundssatzdebatte über den Wiederaufbau der historischen Städte nach dem Zweiten Weltkrieg in Deutschland," *Politische Studien* 2 (1988): 42, special issue, "Denkmalpflege: Andenken und Auftrag." See also Stefan Muthesius, "The Origins of the German Conservation Movement," in *Planning for Conservation*, Roger Kain, ed. (New York, 1981).

3. Only at certain moments did emotions deriving from past conflicts boil to the surface. At the war's end, Schmitthenner had been removed from his professorial chair in Stuttgart. Though he was then living in Tübingen in the French zone, he voluntarily underwent a denazification hearing in Stuttgart in the American zone. He was judged

"untainted" by Nazism, and he wanted his chair back. His cause was supported by traditionalists, the students, and also by the liberal Theodor Heuss, who remembered Schmitthenner as a cofounder of the Werkbund by later awarding him a medal. His rehabilitation was opposed by modernists, led by Richard Döcker and Hans Scharoun. He did not get back his university chair, and except for reconstruction proposals for Freudenstadt and Mainz, he had no other opportunities to participate in reconstruction planning. On Freudenstadt, see Niels Gutschow, "Freudenstadt: Ein Versuch über den Freiraum von Städtebau 1945 bis 1949—fern jeder Realisierungschance," *Stadtbauwelt* 84 (1984), and Frank, "Auf der Suche nach der alten Stadt."

4. Paul Schmitthenner, "Das sanfte Gesetz in der Kunst, in Sonderheit in der Baukunst," reprinted in part in *Stadtbauwelt* 84 (1984): 424.

5. Niels Gutschow, "Stadträume des Wiederaufbaus—Objekte der Denkmalpflege?" *Deutsche Kunst und Denkmalpflege* 43 (1985): 9.

6. "Anmerkungen zur Zeit," *Baukunst und Werkform* 2 (1948): 13. The comment is presumably by the editor, Alfons Leitl.

7. Frank, "Trümmer," p. 61. For the Schmitthenner affair, see pp. 56–64.

8. Niels Gutschow, "Die historische Stadt im Städtebau der vierziger Jahre: Leitbilder der Wiederaufbauplanung und des Aufbaus 1942–1952," in *Kriegsschicksale deutscher Architektur. Verluste, Schäden, Wiederaufbau*, Hartwig Beseler, Niels Gutschow, and Frauke Kretschmer, eds. (Neumünster, 1987), 1: xli.

9. For example, see Petz, *Stadtsanierung im Dritten Reich*, p. 151.

10. The meaning of the term monument in this context can be illustrated by the 1974 Hessian state law on historic preservation: "Cultural monuments worthy of protection within this law include objects, complexes of objects, or parts of objects whereby there exists public interest in their preservation for artistic, scholarly, technical, historical, or architectural reasons." Dölling, "Protection and Conservation," p. 12. The American army during the war cataloged historic monuments and works of art, mostly for the purpose of restoring art works to their rightful owners. See *Report of the American Commission for the Protection and Salvage of Artistic and Historic Monuments in War Areas*, and NA/RG 239, Box 73.

11. The proposals and projects of the 1920s and 1930s for urban renewal of what were considered slums in the old city centers usually called for the retention of interesting facades but for interior modernization. Petz, *Stadtsanierung im Dritten Reich*, discusses such projects in Berlin, Cologne, Braunschweig, Breslau, Frankfurt, and Kassel. More will be said about these projects in later chapters.

12. OMGUS Monthly Report No. 20 (February 1947): 11.

13. Hartwig Beseler, "Baudenkmale—Zeugnisse architektonischer überlieferung im Umbruch," in *Kriegsschicksale deutscher Architektur. Verluste, Schäden, Wiederaufbau*, Hartwig Beseler, Niels Gutschow, and Frauke Kretschmer, eds. (Neumünster, 1987), 1: xxxvii. The two volumes of this massive publication comprise a catalog of damaged buildings, organized by state and city, and indicating whether or not some sort of reconstruction took place. The most extensive of its kind on the Federal Republic, it still could not include every private "historic" home that was destroyed.

14. Petz, *Stadtsanierung im Dritten Reich*, pp. 97, 123. It is worth noting that large numbers of pre-1900 buildings had already been demolished in various prewar urban modernization projects. Thus in Frankfurt, a survey in the 1930s showed that 400 of the 2,500 buildings in the Altstadt had been torn down between 1872 and 1906, mostly during construction of the new train station and to widen streets. In Kassel, one-fifth of the 7,500 buildings in the Altstadt were scheduled for demolition in a Nazi-era renewal project.

15. Friedrich Mielke and Klaus Brügelmann, "Denkmalpflege," in *Die Stadt in der Bundesrepublik Deutschland*, Wolfgang Pehnt, ed. (Stuttgart, 1974). See also Gerd Albers, "Über den Rang des Historischen im Städtebau," *Die alte Stadt* 11 (1984).

16. HASK/171/426.

17. SH/Denkmalschutzamt 49/Auszug aus dem Protokoll der Tagung der deutschen Denkmalpfleger.

18. Alfons Leitl, "Die städtebauliche Seite," *Baukunst und Werkform* 5 (1951): 10. He was probably right in this. Several Germans of my acquaintance, all in their forties or younger, insist that Rothenburg ob der Tauber was not bombed. In fact, a raid on 31 March 1945 destroyed or damaged 28% of the historic city. Because it depended on tourism, the decision to rebuild in the old form as much as possible was virtually unopposed. The Bavarian Office for Historic Preservation oversaw the work. Major monuments were faithfully restored, but new buildings were required to fit in with their historic surroundings. This has proved to be a highly successful example of reconstruction of a small town.

19. "Ein Aufruf: Grundsätzliche Forderungen," *Baukunst und Werkform* 1 (1947): 29.

20. Robert Vorhoelzer, "Stimmen zum Neuaufbau deutscher Städte," *Baukunst und Werkform* 1 (1947): 28.

21. Philipp Rappaport, *Wünsche und Wirklichkeit des deutschen Wiederaufbaus*, Schriften des Deutschen Verbandes für Wohnungswesen, Städtebau und Raumplanung, no. 4 (Frankfurt, 1949), p. 13. For a similar statement regarding the rebuilding of Bremen, see Wolfgang Dronke, "Der Wiederaufbau historischer Altstadtkerne— dargelegt am Beispiel Bremens," in *Städtebauliche Aufgaben der Gegenwart mit besonderer Berücksichtigung Bremens. Der Wiederaufbau der freien Hansestadt Bremen*, Schriftenreihe der Bauverwaltung, no. 1 (Bremen, 1946), p. 62.

22. See, for example, Kurt Blaum, "Nochmals: Das Goethehaus," *Die Neue Stadt* 2 (1948): 74–75. The rebuilding of the Goethe house became a symbol of the conflict between preservationists and modernizing planners. For example, see "Planer, werdet hart," *Der Spiegel* 6, no. 1 (2 January 1952): 20–21. A discussion of the controversy in Frankfurt can be found in Bettina Meier, "Goethe in Trümmern—Vor vierzig Jahren: der Streit um den Wiederaufbau des Goethehauses in Frankfurt," *Germanic Review* 63 (1988).

23. Otto Völckers, "Der Streit um das Goethehaus," *Die Neue Stadt* 1 (1947): 75– 76. There is a brief survey of the controversy about the Goethe house in Hermann Glaser, *The Rubble Years. The Cultural Roots of Postwar Germany, 1945–1948*, Franz Feige and Patricia Gleason, trans. (New York, 1986), pp. 65–68.

24. Walter Dirks, "Mut zum Abschied. Zur Wiederherstellung des Frankfurter Goethehauses," *Frankfurter Hefte*, no. 8 (August 1947); reprinted in *Baukunst und Werkform* 2 (1948), along with a number of essays by other critics attacking the rebuilding of the Goethe house. The citation is from the latter journal, p. 27.

25. Franz Meunier, "Illusion als Schicksal? Die deutschen gebildeten Stände und der Wiederaufbau. Ein notwendiger Nachtrag zur Goethe-Haus," *Baukunst und Werkform* 2 (1948): 21.

26. Adolf Bernt, "Baudenkmale und Wiederaufbau. Versuch einer Ordnung," *Ausbausonderhefte*, no. 5 (Stuttgart, 1948).

27. See Chapter 3.

28. SAM/Bauamt-Hochbau/1068.

29. Beseler, "Baudenkmale," 1: xxv–xxxii, xxxvii.

30. BHSA/ Bayer. Staatskanzlei 75 (2653), Oberste Baubehörde (Fischer) to Bayer. Staatsmin. d. Innern, 19 April 1950, "Aufbauleistungen des Landes Bayern seit 1945," supplement 1: den staatlichen Hochbau.

31. Freiburg, for example, received roofing tiles from the Swiss for the damaged cathedral. For the attempts of Cologne to solicit money for church reconstruction from John McCloy, the American high commissioner, see correspondence, July–December 1950, HASK/2/198.

32. SH/Denkmalschutzamt 32/Bahn to Witt, President of Kultur- und Schulbehörde, 10 November 1937, and 38/5 January 1938; H. Becker (Verwaltung für Künst- und Kulturangelegenheiten), "Denkschrift zur denkmalpflegerischen Planung und Gestaltung der Cremoninsel," Hamburg, 1942, in SH/Wohnwirtschafts u. Siedlungsamt/29.

33. SH/ Denkmalschutzamt 32/ Berichte über denkmalpflegerische Probleme/ Memorandum by Bernhard Hopp, 15 December 1947. For a survey of preservationist activities in the city, in addition to Beseler, Gutschow, and Kretschmer, *Kriegsschicksale deutscher Architektur*, see Günther Grundmann, *Großstadt und Denkmalpflege. Hamburg 1945 bis 1959* (Hamburg, 1960). Hopp headed the office from 1945 to 1950, when he was succeeded by Grundmann.

34. SH/ Denkmalschutzamt 38/Cremon Insel/ Note for the archives by Hopp re talk with Oberbaudirektor Meyer-Ottens, 19 March 1947, and notes of meetings with property owners, 15 September 1949 and 16 February 1950; 32/Berichte über denkmalpflegerische Probleme/ typescript of discussion in Senate on 29 April 1948; Hopp, "Über denkmalspflegerische Probleme beim Wiederaufbau Hamburgs," *Baurundschau* 37 (1947), special insert on Hamburg: 125–26; and Konstanty Gutschow, "Zum Wettbewerb um die Hamburger Innenstadt," *Baurundschau* 39 (1949).

35. Günther Kühne, "Berlin," in *Kriegsschicksale deutscher Architektur. Verluste, Schäden, Wiederaufbau*, Hartwig Beseler, Niels Gutschow, and Frauke Kretschmer, eds. (Neumünster, 1987), 1: 140.

36. *Neue Bauwelt* 5 (1950), contains numerous articles and letters on this subject. Günther Kühne, a leading commentator on Berlin architecture since the war and for many years an editor of *Bauwelt* stated in an interview with the author on 9 November 1981 that the demolition of the Schloß in East Berlin virtually saved Charlottenburg. Now that the division of the city has ended, it is possible that the Schloß will be reconstructed from original plans and photographs.

37. See John Robert Mullin, "City Planning in Frankfurt, Germany, 1925–1932. A Study in Practical Utopianism," *Journal of Urban History* 4 (1977).

38. See Petz, *Stadtsanierung im Dritten Reich*, pp. 95–115.

39. See Herbert Boehm, "Städtebauliche Grundlegung für ein neues Frankfurt," and Heinrich Schütz, "Die Frankfurter Aufbau-AG im Wiederaufbau unserer Stadt," both in *Frankfurt baut auf*, Max Kurz, ed. (Stuttgart, 1954).

40. H. K. Zimmermann, "Der Wiederaufbau der Altstadt in Frankfurt am Main," *Deutscher Kunst- und Denkmalpflege* 11 (1953): 20, and Zimmermann, "Zerstörung oder Erhaltung," reprinted in Durth and Gutschow, *Träume in Trümmern*, 2:539. Zimmermann was the director of the city branch of the Hessian State Conservator's Office.

41. Zimmerman, "Der Wiederaufbau der Altstadt," pp. 19–27.

42. Durth and Gutschow, *Träume in Trümmern*, 2:479–85; Alfons Leitl, "Der Wiederaufbau der Paulskirche," *Baukunst und Werkform* 1 (1947): 99–103. For the solicitation of funds, see "Aufruf der Stadt Frankfurt am Main zum Wiederaufbau der Paulskirche," 20 January 1947 (partly reprinted in Durth and Gutschow), and the subsequent direct appeal for money, for example in HASK/2/1340. Cologne eventually

committed DM 1,657.31 for a window. Cities in the Soviet zone were generous in their contributions.

43. HSANRW/NW177/205/128 and 129.

44. Germany, however, has lacked a critic with the prestige of Great Britain's Prince Charles, who complains that modern architecture has made London "a stunted version of Manhattan" (ABC Evening News, 2 December 1988). The evils-of-modernism refrain is one that has been heard since the end of the war.

45. See Manfred Sack, "It's Real Counterfeit Architecture," *The German Tribune*, 25 December 1983; Hanns Adrian, in "Stadtplanung und Stadterhaltung in Frankfurt," in *Die Kunst unsere Städte zu erhalten*, Hiltrud Kier, ed. (Stuttgart, 1976), p. 178, declared this project to be a mixture of "Jahrmarktsarchitektur, Disneyland und Brauereinostalgie." See also Heinrich Klotz, Roland Günter, and Gottfried Kiesow, *Keine Zukunft für unsere Vergangenheit: Denkmalschutz und Stadtzerstörung* (Gießen, 1975).

46. See Dieter Lange, "Bemerkungen zu Denkmalpflege und Stadtentwicklung in Hannover," in *Die Kunst unsere Städte zu erhalten*, Hiltrud Kier, ed. (Stuttgart, 1976), pp. 215–17.

47. SAS/Hauptaktei, Gruppe 6: 6ll0–19: Bonatz, "Stuttgart, Städtebau- und Verkehrsfragen 1941."

48. SAS/ZAS 24, Beirat session of 6 September 1949 and ZAS 25, letter of Dr. Hans Fegers, an art historian on the advisory planning committee, to chief planner Hoss, 16 August 1951. This controversy attracted national attention. See "Planer, werdet hart," in *Der Spiegel* 6, no. 1 (2 January 1952): 21–22.

49. SAS/ZAS 25/ Beirat session of 10 August 1951.

50. Max Guther, Rudolf Hillebrecht, Heinz Schmeissner, and Walther Schmidt, "'Ich kann mich nicht herausdenken aus dem Vorgang der Geschichte, in den ich eingebunden bin'—Erinnerungen an den Wiederaufbau der Bundesrepublik: Hintergründe, Leitbilde, Planungen," *Stadtbauwelt* 72 (1981): 350.

51. Ibid., p. 362. See also Durth and Gutschow, *Träume in Trümmern*, 2:981ff for planning in Nuremberg.

52. Das Kuratorium für den Aufbau der Stadt Nürnberg, "Bericht über die Tätigkeit von 1948–1955," pp. 2–3. I used a copy of this mimeographed report in the library of the Deutscher Städtetag in Cologne.

53. Ibid., pp. 42–44.

54. Guther et al., "'Ich kann mich nicht herausdenken aus dem Vorgang der Geschichte,' " p. 372.

55. Erich Mulzer, *Der Wiederaufbau der Altstadt von Nürnberg 1945 bis 1970* (Erlangen, 1972).

56. Ibid., pp. 73–74, 81–85, 98–111.

57. Gutschow and Stiemer, *Dokumentation Wiederaufbau der Stadt Münster: Materialsammlung*, pp. 85–90. The text accompanying the document collection was published with the same title in 1982. What follows is derived from this excellent study.

58. Gutschow and Stiemer, *Dokumentation Wiederaufbau der Stadt Münster*, p. 66.

59. Gutschow and Stiemer, *Dokumentation Wiederaufbau der Stadt Münster: Materialsammlung*, p. 255.

60. Ibid., p. 71; and Gutschow and Stiemer, *Dokumentation Wiederaufbau der Stadt Münster*, pp. 17–19.

61. Gutschow and Stiemer, *Dokumentation Wiederaufbau der Stadt Münster: Materialsammlung*, pp. 28–30, 71.

62. Ibid., pp. 71, 256.

63. Gutschow and Stiemer, *Dokumentation Wiederaufbau der Stadt Münster*, pp. 122–27.

64. Ibid., pp. 131–33, 182–83.

65. Gutschow and Stiemer, *Dokumentation Wiederaufbau der Stadt Münster: Materialsammlung*, pp. 141–44.

66. This was typical of a number of cities, including Munich, where citizen groups spearheaded the effort to reconstruct the old town hall; see also the prolonged and bitter controversy in Hildesheim over the competition to redesign the ruined main square, a controversy in which the modernizers eventually triumphed. Stadtbaurat Haagen, "Die Gestaltung des Marktplatzes der Hildesheimer Altstadt," *Neue Bauwelt* 6 (1951).

67. Gutschow and Stiemer, *Dokumentation Wiederaufbau der Stadt Münster*, pp. 81–90.

68. Ibid., p. 95.

69. Ibid., pp. 67–72.

70. Joseph Schlippe, "Freiburgs Baudenkmäler und ihre Wiederherstellung," in *Freiburg in Trümmern 1944–1952*, Walter Vetter, ed. (Freiburg, 1982), pp. 161 and 184.

71. Jürgen Paul, "Der Wiederaufbau des Kornhauses in Freiburg i.B. und einige Betrachtungen über Architektur und Geschichtsverständnis," *Archithese* 11 (1974): 13.

72. SAM/Bauamt-Wiederaufbau/1119.

73. For a good treatment of the role of historic preservation in Munich during reconstruction, see Nina A. Krieg, "München, leuchtend und ausgebrannt . . . Denkmalpflege und Wiederaufbau in den Nachkriegsjahren," in *Trümmerzeit in München. Kultur und Gesellschaft einer deutschen Großstadt im Aufbruch 1945–1949* (Munich, 1984). In slightly altered form this also appears as "Denkmalpflege und Wiederaufbau," in *Aufbauzeit: Planen und Bauen, München 1945–1950*, Winfried Nerdinger, ed. (Munich, 1984). In the latter volume see also Michael Brix, " 'Möge München dereinst als Kronjuwel einer friedlichen Welt erstrahlen'—Formale Leitlinien des Wiederaufbaus Innere Stadt."

74. Heinrich Habel, "Denkmalpflege in München seit 1945," in *Die Kunst unsere Städte zu erhalten*, Hiltrud Kier, ed. (Stuttgart, 1976), p. 184. (The monarchy, it might be noted, had been abolished at the end of World War I!)

75. Krieg, "München, leuchtend und ausgebrannt," pp. 75, 83, 86.

76. Michael Brix, "Munich: Residenz and Nationaltheater," in *The Conservation of Historical Monuments in the Federal Republic of Germany*, Regine Dölling, ed., Timothy Nevill, trans. (Munich, 1974), pp. 40–44, and Habel, "Denkmalpflege in München," p. 184.

77. Karl Meitinger, *Das neue München* (Munich, 1946), p. 10.

78. SAM/Bürgermeister und Rat/ 1969: Stadtplanungskommission and Baukunstkommission, 15 March 1948.

79. SAM/ Bauamt-Wiederaufbau/1106/ Speech by Fischer, Fall, 1946.

80. SAM/ Bauamt-Wiederaufbau/ 1097/1/ Speech by Fischer, 1950, "Erhaltung oder Neugestaltung," p. 12.

81. SAM/Bürgermeister und Rat/1987/Bericht über die Vorprüfung, 7 January 1948; brochure, "Ideenwettbewerb Marienplatz," September 1948; and report by Fischer to the Stadtrat, 9 May 1949.

82. SAM/Ratsitzungsprotokolle/723/1: 57, 62.

83. SAM/Bürgermeister und Rat/1987/statement dated 18 April 1949.

84. SAM/Ratsitzungsprotokolle/722/16/Besprechung, "Wettbewerb Marienplatz," 25 April 1949.

85. SAM/Ratsitzungsprotokolle/723/1: 17–18.

86. SAM/Ratsitzungsprotokolle/724/22/ Bauausschuß session, 16 May 1951, p. 56.

87. See, for example, SAM/Bürgermeister und Rat/1988, 2056, 2057, for the activities of these associations. Holes had already been bored in the Alter Peter to demolish the still-standing walls when public pressure forced the city to accept reconstruction. See also Beseler, Gutschow, and Kretschmer, *Kriegsschicksale deutscher Architektur*, 2: 1386.

88. SAM/Bauamt-Wiederaufbau/1086a, "Aufruf an die Münchner Bevölkerung zur Beteiligung an der Schaffung eines Kulturbaufonds für den Wiederaufbau der Stadt Münchens," 19 February 1946.

89. SAM/Bürgermeister und Rat/1982/Kulturbaufond: minutes of trustees' meetings and annual reports.

90. See Brix, " 'Möge München dereinst als Kronjuwel einer friedlichen Welt erstrahlen,' " p. 32.

91. Erwin Schleich, *Die zweite Zerstörung Münchens*, Neue Schriftenreihe des Stadtarchivs München, vol. 100 (Stuttgart, 1978, rprt. 1981).

92. Kier, "Denkmalpflege in Köln," and von Petz, *Stadtsanierung im Dritten Reich*, pp. 135–56. For a discussion of preservationist ideas in planning in Cologne, see my "Städtebauliche Traditionen und der Wiederaufbau von Köln vornehmlich nach 1945," *Rheinische Vierteljahrsblätter* 55 (1991).

93. HASK/171/429. This volume contains several memoranda by Vogts making the same arguments.

94. Carl Oskar Jatho, *Urbanität. Über die Wiederkehr einer Stadt* (Düsseldorf, 1946); Schmitt, *Der Neuaufbau der Stadt Köln*; Band, HASK/2/1313/ 29 June 1945; Merken, HASK/30/58/ 31 December 1945.

95. Band, HASK/2/138/ 1 August 1946.

96. HASK/171/426/4 and 7 January 1946.

97. *Kirchen in Trümmern* (Cologne, 1948).

98. Speech to Stadtversammlung, Verhandlungen 1946; Rudolf Schwarz, *Das neue Köln—Ein Vorentwurf* (Cologne, 1950).

99. Rudolf Schwarz, "Gedanken zum Wiederaufbau von Köln," *Aufbau* 2 (Stuttgart, 1947), p. 23, special issue, *Grundfragen des Aufbaus in Stadt und Land*.

100. See the *Verwaltungsberichte der Stadt Köln* for 1950 for the statistics.

101. Hiltrud Kier, "Die Wiederherstellung der Kölner Altstadt-Kirchen," in Rheinischer Verein für Denkmalpflege und Landschaftsschutz, *Glanz und Elend der Denkmalpflege und Stadtplanung Cöln 1906–2006 Köln* (Cologne, 1981), p. 30. The city celebrated the completion of the task of rebuilding the city's Romanesque churches in 1985. See Hiltrud Kier, "Das Jahr der Romanischen Kirchen in Köln— wozu eigentlich?" and Christoph Machat, "Der Wiederaufbau der Kölner Kirchen," both in *Deutscher Kunst und Denkmalpflege* 43 (1985), and Machat, *Der Wiederaufbau der Kölner Kirchen*, Landschaftsverband Rheinland, Working Paper 40 (Pulheim, 1987).

102. HASK/2/ 136/ Stadtplanungsausschusses, Meeting of 20 March 1948.

103. Hiltrud Kier, *Die Kölner Neustadt. Planung, Entstehung, Nutzung*, Beiträge zu den Bau- und Kunstdenkmaleren im Rheinland, vol. 23 (Düsseldorf, 1978), pp. 210–12.

104. Hiltrud Kier, "Der Wiederaufbau von Köln, 1945–1975. Eine Bilanz aus kunsthistorischer Sicht," in *Die Kunst unsere Städte zu erhalten*, Hiltrud Kier, ed. (Stuttgart, 1976), pp. 232–34.

105. See John Burchard, *The Voice of the Phoenix. Postwar Architecture in Germany* (Cambridge, Mass., 1966), pp. 48–51.

106. AHSL/Bauverwaltung/ 39²/Akten des Bauverwaltungsamtes 20/ Pieper, "Lübeck als Gegenstand der Denkmalpflege," in *Lübeckische Angelegenheiten*, supplement to *Lübecker General-Anzeiger* no. 14 (17 January 1936).

107. Ibid.

108. Pieper, *Lübeck*, p. 22, and Durth and Gutschow, *Träume in Trümmern*, p. 814. Estimates vary considerably, partly because some surviving facades of damaged buildings that possibly could have been restored were subsequently demolished.

109. Otto Hespeler, "Der Umbau der Lübecker Altstadt," *Zeitschrift des Deutschen Akademie für Städtebau, Reichs- und Landesplanung* 33 (1938).

110. Gutschow's memo on Lübeck is reproduced in Durth and Gutschow, *Träume in Trümmern*, pp. 850–51. See also Michael Brix, *Lübeck. Die Altstadt als Denkmal* (Munich, 1975), p. 36.

111. ASKG/17–12–54.

112. AHSL/Hauptamt 15u/1/W7 Wiederaufbau/ 2 February 1943.

113. Pieper, *Lübeck*.

114. ASKG/17–12–55.

115. AHSL/Hauptamt 15u/2–64–9-I/Klaus Pieper, "Auseinandersetzung mit den Wiederaufbau-Ideen des Architekten Steffann," 21 February 1947.

116. Pieper, *Lübeck*, p. 88.

117. AHSL/Hauptamt 15u/2–64–0-I, for: Emil Steffann, "Ein Plan zum Wiederaufbau Lübecks," from *Lübeckische Nachrichten*, 31 December 1946; letter from Hans Ewers to Steffann, 30 December 1946; "Um den Aufbau Lübecks," from *Norddeutsches Echo*, 15 February 1947. The aged Fritz Schumacher criticized Steffann's suggestions because he felt they in fact worsened rather than solved the traffic problem. When his criticism was not published in the press, the architect Otto Siebert sent copies to Lübeck's city manager Helms. The Schumacher letter is dated 11 January 1947; the cover letter from Siebert, 27 January 1947. The Steffann plan is also discussed in Durth and Gutschow, *Träume in Trümmern*, p. 836.

118. AHSL/Hauptamt 15u/2–6/ "Wiederaufbau der Altstadt Lübeck." The report is reproduced, from a copy in Bremen, in Durth and Gutschow, *Träume in Trümmern*, pp. 860–63.

119. AHSL/Hauptamt 15u/2–64–6. In 1952 Münter left Lübeck for a position at the Technical University in Dresden.

120. Most clearly expressed in AHSL/Hauptamt 15u/2–64–5-16, 29 September 1949; *Lübeckische Blätter* 85 (1949).

121. Otto Willrich, "Ein Beitrag zum Wiederaufbau alter Städte: an dem Beispiel der Stadt Lübeck," *Die Kunstpflege* 2 (1948); Johannes Klöcking, "Denkmalschutz und Aufbauplan," *Lübeckische Blätter* 85 (1949).

122. AHSL/Hauptamt 15u/2–64–10/ 17 February and 21 July 1949.

123. Helmuth Ehrich, "—und von der Pflicht gegenüber unserer Stadt," *Lübeckische Blätter* 85 (1949).

124. See AHSL/Hauptamt 15u/2–64–7-I, II, III, and 8.

125. Hermann Deckert, "Wettbewerb um die Neugestaltung des Lübecker Marktes," *Der Bauhelfer* 5 (1950).

126. *Vaterstädtische Blätter* 2 (1951).

127. Kampffmeyer, Spengelin, and Siedler, "Zu Beginn der 60er Jahre," p. 330. Of course many technocratically oriented planners and architects felt no guilt at all; they simply wanted to move ahead with urban modernization.

128. Petsch and Petsch, "Neuaufbau statt Wiederaufbau," p. 74; Albers, "Über den Rang des Historischen im Städtebau," p. 220. The same point is made for Kassel,

where planners sacrificed restorable buildings "coolly and without any sentimentality." Volker Helas, "Die Architektur der Fünfziger Jahre in Kassel," in *Architektur und Städtebau der Fünfziger Jahre*, Schriftenreihe des Deutschen Nationalkomitees für Denkmalschutz, vol. 36 (Bonn, 1988), p. 62. Here too planners opted for radical modernization—in terms of planning, not architectural style—of the old central area.
129. Paul, "Der Wiederaufbau der historischen Städte," p. 118.

Chapter 5

1. Walter Frey, "Kriegsschäden und Wiederaufbau," *Der Aufbau* 8 (1953): 345; Petsch and Petsch, "Neuaufbau statt Wiederaufbau," p. 72.

2. For a brief introduction to this subject, see Wolfgang Köllmann, "The Process of Urbanization in Germany at the Height of the Industrialization Period," *Journal of Contemporary History* 4 (1969). More extensive analysis can be found in Jürgen Reulecke, *Die deutsche Stadt im Industriezeitalter* (Wuppertal, 1978) and Reulecke, *Geschichte der Urbanisierung in Deutschland* (Frankfurt, 1985). For a study of the consequences of bad housing on health, see Reinhard Spree, *Soziale Ungleichheit vor Krankheit und Tod. Zur Sozialgeschichte des Gesundheitsbereichs im Deutschen Kaiserreich* (Göttingen, 1981).

3. The classic indictment of the Mietskasernen in Berlin is Hegemann, *Das steinerne Berlin*. For material on the question of housing reform as a broader exercise in social control, see Lutz Niethammer, "Some Elements of the Housing Reform Debate in Nineteenth-Century Europe; Or, On the Making of a New Paradigm of Social Control," in *Modern Industrial Cities. History, Policy, and Survival*, Bruce M. Stave, ed. (Beverly Hills, Calif., and London, 1981). On housing reform prior to 1914, Nicholas Bullock and John Read, *The Movement for Housing Reform in Germany and France, 1840–1914* (Cambridge, 1985), and Brian Kenneth Ladd, *Urban Planning and Civic Order in Germany, 1860–1914* (Cambridge, Mass., and London, 1990).

4. The Gartenstadt Hellerau is discussed in Gerda Wangerin and Gerhard Weiss, *Heinrich Tessenow. Ein Baumeister 1876–1950* (Essen, 1976).

5. See Petz, *Stadtsanierung im Dritten Reich*, for a survey of renewal projects under the Nazis. A good discussion of this process in Hamburg is Michael Grüttner, "Soziale Hygiene und Soziale Kontrolle: Die Sanierung der Hamburger Gängeviertel 1892–1936," in *Arbeiter in Hamburg. Unterschichten, Arbeiter und Arbeiterbewegung seit dem ausgehenden 18. Jahrhundert*, Arno Herzig, Dieter Langewiesche, and Arnold Sywottek, eds. (Hamburg, 1983). For a long-term survey of urban renewal in Berlin, see Harald Bodenschatz, *Platz frei für das neue Berlin! Geschichte der Stadterneurung in der "größten Mietskasernenstadt der Welt" seit 1871*, Institut für Stadt- und Regionalplanung der TU Berlin. Studien zur Neueren Planungsgeschichte, vol. 1 (Berlin, 1987).

6. Petz, *Stadtsanierung im Dritten Reich*, p. 28.

7. For housing in Krefeld, see Wilhelm Kurschat, *Das Haus Friedrich und Heinrich von der Leyen in Krefeld* (Frankfurt a.M., 1933). The construction of housing for company workers by the Krupp works in the nineteenth and early twentieth centuries is the best known example of such paternalistic housing policy. Joachim Schlandt, "Die Kruppsiedlungen—Wohnungsbau im Interesse eines Industriekonzerns," in *Kapitalistischer Städtebau*, Hans B. Helms and Jörg Janssen, eds. (Neuwied and Berlin, 1970). See also Michael Honhart, "Company Housing as Urban Planning in Germany, 1870–1940," *Central European History* 23 (1990).

8. F. Allmers, *Die Wohnungsbaupolitik der Gemeinnützigen Bauvereine im Rhein-land von 1815–1914* (Cologne, 1925); Reinhard Dauber, "Die Anfänge der Wohnungs-politik und Bautätigkeit des Gemeinnützigen Wohnungsbaus im Rheinland," *Die alte Stadt* 7 (1980); and Dorothea Berger-Thimme, *Wohnungsfrage und Sozialstaat. Unter-suchungen zu den Anfängen staatlicher Wohnungspolitik in Deutschland (1873–1918)* (Frankfurt, 1976), pp. 55–70.

9. See Berger-Thimme, *Wohnungsfrage und Sozialstaat*, Part 2; and Lane, *Archi-tecture and Politics*, pp. 87–89.

10. Nicholas Bullock, "Housing in Frankfurt, 1925–1931—And the New Wohn-kultur," *Architectural Review* 163, no. 976 (1978): 335.

11. See Kristiana Hartmann, *Deutsche Gartenstadtbewegung: Kulturpolitik und Gesellschaftsreform* (Munich, 1976), and Andrew Lees, "Critics of Urban Society in Germany, 1854–1914," *Journal of the History of Ideas* 40 (1979). See Chapters 6 and 7 below for a more extensive treatment of planning concepts.

12. Cramer and Gutschow, *Bauausstellungen*.

13. A useful survey is Ronald Wiedenhoeft, "Workers' Housing as Social Politics," in *VIA: Culture and the Social Vision*, vol. 4, Mark A. Hewitt, Benjamin Kracauer, John Massengale, and Michael McDonough, eds. (Philadelphia, Pa., and Cambridge, Mass., 1980), and at greater length, Wiedenhoeft's revised dissertation, *Berlin's Hous-ing Revolution. German Reform in the 1920s* (Ann Arbor, Mich., 1985).

14. Reproduced in Ulrich Conrads, ed., *Programs and Manifestoes on 20th-Century Architecture*, Michael Bullock, trans. (Cambridge, Mass., 1970), pp. 95–96.

15. Mullin, "City Planning in Frankfurt," Bullock, "Housing in Frankfurt," and Lane, *Architecture and Politics*, pp. 90ff. Bullock examines efforts at standardization by May. The new housing projects in Berlin and Frankfurt are also discussed by David C. Anderson, *Architecture as a Means for Social Change in Germany, 1918–1933* (Diss., University of Minnesota, 1972).

16. See Wiedenhoeft, "Workers' Housing," pp. 114ff. On Taut: Whyte, *Bruno Taut and the Architecture of Activism*. On Wagner: Joachim Kempmann, *Das Ideengut Martin Wagners* (Diss., Technische Universität, Berlin, 1968), and Klaus Homann, Martin Kieren, and Ludovica Scarpa, eds., *Martin Wagner 1885–1957: Wohnungsbau und Weltstadtplanung: Die Rationalisierung des Glücks* (Berlin, 1985).

17. See Wiedenhoeft, "Workers' Housing," p. 115, and Hermann Hipp, "Wohn-ungen für Arbeiter? Zum Wohnungsbau und zur Wohnungsbaupolitik in Hamburg in den 1920er Jahren," in *Arbeiter in Hamburg: Unterschichten, Arbieter und Arbeiter-bewegung seit dem ausgehenden 18. Jahrhundert*, Arno Herzig, Dieter Langewiesche, and Arnold Sywottek, eds. (Hamburg, 1983), pp. 474–75.

18. Lane, *Architecture and Politics*, pp. 114–16.

19. Gottfried Feder, *Die Neue Stadt. Versuch der Begründung einer neuen Stadt-planungskunst aus der sozialen Struktur der Bevölkerung* (Berlin, 1939), pp. 13–14. See Hegemann, *Das steinerne Berlin*, for such criticisms coming from a supporter of modernist reformers.

20. Rasp, *Eine Stadt für tausend Jahre*, pp. 31–33. See also Johannes Cramer, "Wie wohnen? Neuer Anfang mit alten Konzepten," *Stadtbauwelt* 84 (1984), and Cramer and Gutschow, *Bauausstellungen*.

21. Dittmar Machule, "Die Kameradschaftssiedlung der SS in Berlin-Zehlendorf—eine idyllische Waldsiedlung," in *Faschistische Architekturen. Planen und Bauen in Europa 1930 bis 1945*, Hartmut Frank, ed., Stadt, Planung, Geschichte, vol. 3 (Ham-burg, 1985).

22. Manfred Walz, *Wohnungsbau- und Industrieansiedlungspolitik in Deutschland*

1933–1939 (Frankfurt and New York, 1979), pp. 39–40. Information on housing conditions in Hamburg is found in Susanne Back, Elke Pahl, and Anne Rabenschlag, *Wohnungsbau, Wohnungsversorgung und Wohnungspolitik im 3. Reich in Hamburg* (Diplomarbeit, Hochschule für bildende Künste, Hamburg, 1977, copy in Staatsarchiv Hamburg).

23. Quoted by Dirk Schubert, "Gesundung der Städte—Stadtsanierung in Hamburg 1933–45," in Michael Bose, Michael Holtmann, Dittmar Machule, Elke Pahl-Weber, and Dirk Schubert, ". . . *ein neues Hamburg entsteht* . . ." *Planen und Bauen von 1933–1945*, Beiträge zur städtebaulichen Forschung, vol. 2 (Hamburg, 1986), p. 65. As late as 19 January 1942, Gutschow continued to describe renewal measures in similar terms; urban renewal would be guided not by aesthetic or technical considerations but rather by "sociological considerations, in which the political position of the residents can be seen." Gutschow to Wilhelm Wortmann, SH/ Architekt Gutschow/ B136/ letter of 19 January 1942.

24. Karl Strölin, "Die Durchführung von Altstadtsanierungen," *Deutsche Kunst- und Denkmalspflege* 8 (1935): 145, quoted by Walz, *Wohnungsbau- und Industriean-siedlungspolitik*, p. 246.

25. Walz, *Wohnungsbau- und Industrieansiedlungspolitik*, pp. 242ff; Grüttner, "Soziale Hygiene und soziale Kontrolle," pp. 368–69; Hagspiel, "Die Nationalsozialistische Stadtplanung in und für Köln," pp. 97–98.

26. Schubert, "Gesundung der Städte," pp. 68–69.

27. The main studies of these cities are Walz, *Wohnungsbau-und Industrieansied-lungspolitik*, Christian Schneider, *Stadtgründung im Dritten Reich. Wolfsburg und Salzgitter* (Munich, 1978), and Roswitha Mattausch, *Siedlungsbau und Stadtneu-gründungen im deutschen Faschismus* (Frankfurt, 1981).

28. Feder, *Die neue Stadt*.

29. Walz, *Wohnungsbau- und Industrieansiedlungspolitik*, pp. 79–80.

30. See Elke Pahl-Weber, Michael Holtmann, and Michael Bose, "Der Wohnungs- und Siedlungsbau in Hamburg," in Bose et. al., ". . . *ein neues Hamburg entsteht* . . . ."

31. See Konstanty Gutschow, "Generalbebauungsplan 1940," p. 19 (copy in possession of author); also to be found in HAA/ Best. Gutschow; Walz, *Wohnungsbau-und Industrieansiedlungspolitik*, p. 75.

32. Reprinted in Harlander and Fehl, *Hitlers Sozialer Wohnungsbau*, pp. 131–32. This book contains both an excellent analysis of the housing question and an invaluable collection of documents, which makes up about three-fourths of the book.

33. Ibid., p. 11. On Hitler's role, p. 150.

34. Ibid., p. 107.

35. "Die Neuordnung des Deutschen Wohnungsbaues," reproduced in ibid., p. 183.

36. Jürgen Fischer-Dieskau, "Die Übergangsregelung für die Förderung des Wohnungsbaues im Kriege," and Robert Ley, "Grundsätzliches zum künftigen Wohnungsbau," both reproduced in ibid., pp. 194, 335.

37. For a fascinating argument about such ideological combinations, see Jeffrey Herf, *Reactionary Modernism: Technology, Culture, and Politics in Weimar and the Third Reich* (Cambridge, 1984). Modernist planners also tended to impose their ideas upon the consumers of their products.

38. Harlander and Fehl, *Hitlers Sozialer Wohnungsbau*, p. 19.

39. Ley's housing deputy Heinrich Simon observed that "in order to combat the danger that non-German rural laborers might become attached to their homes and thereby initiate an increase of their race and a 'völkisch' infiltration, their housing had

to be in the form of camps, so that one had them under supervision and control." "Die Deutsche Wohnungsbau nach dem Kriege," reproduced in ibid., pp. 17ff, 153.

40. Ibid., p. 433.

41. SH/Architekt Gutschow/B136/Grundsätze für die planmässige Vorbereitung der Wohnungsbauvorhaben nach dem Kriege, prepared by Hans Wagner, Geschäftsführer beim Reichskommissar für den sozialen Wohnungsbau, 3 December 1941. The group included Wilhelm Wortmann of Bremen, Hans Bernhard Reichow of Stettin, Konstanty Gutschow of Hamburg, Hermann Rimpl of the Stadt der Hermann-Göring-Werke, and Elkart of Hannover.

42. Harlander and Fehl, *Hitlers Sozialer Wohnungsbau*, pp. 434–36.

43. Ibid., pp. 42, 50–57.

44. See Niels Gutschow, "Hamburg—The "Catastrophe" of July 1943."

45. Harlander and Fehl, *Hitlers Sozialer Wohnungsbau*, pp. 71–83; 323–34, 361.

46. Thus in March 1941 Hans Wagner declared: "In die Sprache des Technikers übersetzt heißt das, wir müssen rationalisieren, wir müssen normen, wir müssen typisieren, wir müssen mechanisieren, wir müssen dazu übergehen, am laufenden Bank zu produzieren, wir müssen zur Serienherstellung kommen." "Die Neuordnung des Deutschen Wohnungsbaues," reproduced in ibid., p. 182.

47. Ibid., pp. 31, 106–7.

48. Leon Krier has recently stated that "Neufert's influence on contemporary building is in fact far greater than that of any master of modernist architecture." See Krier, "An Architecture of Desire," p. 230, n. 34.

49. On Gutschow, see my "Konstanty Gutschow and the Reconstruction of Hamburg."

50. See Elke Pahl-Weber, "Die Ortsgruppe als Siedlungszelle: Ein Vorschlag zur Methodik der großstädtischen Stadterweiterung von 1940," in *Faschistische Architekturen: Planen und Bauen in Europa 1930 bis 1945*, Hartmut Frank, ed., Stadt, Planung, Geschichte, vol. 3 (Hamburg, 1985).

51. SH/Architekt Gutschow/A337/Letter from Gutschow to Reichsstatthalter, 27 September 1940.

52. SH/Architekt Gutschow/A339–41.

53. Letter to Wilhelm Wortmann, 25 November 1943, in ASKG, folder labeled AFN 6, Verschiedenes 4, Briefwechsel. I examined this while it was still in the possession of Niels Gutschow. Other material on the dispute with the DAF can be found in SH/Architekt Gutschow/B23/ reports from the Amt für kriegswichtigen Einsatz of 19 June 1941, 12 May and 1 June 1943.

54. SH/Architekt Gutschow/B16.

55. The most complete study of the activities of this group to date is Durth, *Deutsche Architekten*. For discussions within the Arbeitsstab on housing, see pp. 222–28.

56. Harlander and Fehl, *Hitlers Sozialer Wohnungsbau*, pp. 235, 50–57.

57. SH/Architekt Gutschow/A44: Schriftenreihe D; ASKG/Wiederaufbauplanung zerstörter Städte/1. Allgemeines/8. Blaue Durchschläge: Verteiler list of 25 November 1944.

58. SH/Architekt Gutschow/A44/D4.

59. This and the replies are in SH/Architekt Gutschow/A44/D22/Wohnungsbau nach dem Kriege. The survey is also discussed briefly in Cramer, "Wie wohnen?"

60. This was the conclusion also reached by Roland Rainer, *Die zweckmässigste Hausform für Erweiterung, Neugründung und Wiederaufbau von Städten*, Denkschrift der Akademie für Städtebau (Breslau, 1944). This was a research project sponsored by the Deutsche Akademie für Städtebau, Reichs- und Landesplanung. Like many oth-

ers, Rainer viewed the destruction caused by the bombing as a wonderful opportunity to undertake proper inner-city renewal: "Dazu bietet der Wiederaufbau zerstörter Stadtteile bisher ungeahnte Möglichkeiten, neben denen alle bisherigen Versuche der Altstadtgesundung und degl. in jeder Beziehung bedeutungslos werden" (p. 23).

61. Durth argues, incorrectly I think, that Gutschow and his colleagues opposed Neufert's standardization efforts. It is true that Neufert was much more willing than they to build multistory apartment buildings, but even the two-story row house could be subject to standardized production techniques.

62. It is remarkable how often the architects and planners employ the language— whether racist, militaristic, or simply brutal—used by the Nazis in their war against the Jews. To cite another example, Hans Simon, noting in 1941 the need to consolidate some of the nearly 3,500 cooperative housing firms into more efficient units, stated: "Es ist nicht damit getan, daß 100, 200 oder auch 500 Wohnungsunternehmen liqui-diert oder fusioniert werden, die Lösung muß, wie immer im Dritten Reich, total sein." "Der Deutsche Wohnungsbau nach dem Kriege," reproduced in Harlander and Fehl, *Hitlers Sozialer Wohnungsbau*, p. 154.

63. "Hamburger Generalplanung," 16–17 September 1944 conference, Wriezen Protocols. The most complete set of the protocols of these meetings, assembled from the Gutschow papers and from the files of Hans von Hanffstengel, are in the hands of Werner Durth.

64. "Wohnungsbau, insbes. Wiederherstellung," at the 19–21 August Wriezen meeting, pp. 40–42. Stephan reported that he had assigned 11 architects to study possible ways of rebuilding a single, typical housing block. He found it very difficult to get these men to limit themselves to this task; instead they wanted to develop their ideas "at least in outline form about new planning for Charlottenburg or Wilmersdorf or metropolitan Berlin or metropolitan Germany or the necessary spatial planning required for all of Europe."

65. Wolters, "Ergebnis der Ministerrücksprache," Wriezen protocols for meeting of 11–12 November 1944, pp. 3, 5, 6, in ASKG/Arbeitsstab Wiederaufbauplanung.

66. Ley, "Grundsätzliches zum künftigen Wohnungsbau," reproduced in Har-lander and Fehl, *Hitlers Sozialer Wohnungsbau*, p. 339.

67. Ibid., p. 336.

68. For the following biographical sketches, see Durth and Gutschow, *Träume in Trümmern*, pp. 220–22.

69. Rainer, *Die zweckmässigste Hausform*. Rainer comes close to the racial Blut und Boden ideology of the Nazis in this work when he uses such phrases as "die volksbiologische Bedeutung der Wohnung" and writes about "bevölkerungspolitische Auswirkungen" of different types of cities and housing (pp. 7, 9). Proper housing will lead to greater numbers of healthy children, but Rainer does not suggest that any specific housing system is "Aryan." Göderitz, Rainer, and Hoffmann cite Bavarian statistics of 1939 to argue that families owning land had more children than those not owning land (p. 33).

70. Ibid., p. 15.

71. Johannes Göderitz, Roland Rainer, and Hubert Hoffmann, *Die gegliederte und aufgelockerte Stadt* (Tübingen, 1957), p. 56. I have also discussed this work at some length in "Cities of Rubble to Cities in Greenery: Postwar Reconstruction Plan-ning in Germany," *Planning History* 12 (1990).

72. Göderitz, Rainer, and Hoffmann, *Die gegliederte und aufgelockerte Stadt*, p. 25.

73. For example, Rainer's proposal for a Vienna suburb of 10,000 inhabitants in two- and three-story, single-family homes. Ibid., pp. 80–81. This model was prepared

for the 1957 International Building Exhibition in Berlin. Rainer's drawings of model housing in his *Die zweckmässigste Hausform* show remarkably uninspired, barracks-like buildings.

74. Ibid., p. 86.

75. Roland Rainer, *Die Bahausungsfrage* (Vienna and Zurich, 1947), and Rainer, *Städtebauliche Prosa: Praktische Grundlagen für den Aufbau der Städte* (Innsbruck, 1948).

76. Herf, *Reactionary Modernism*, and Werner Durth, "Getarnte Moderne. Planung und Technik im Dritten Reich," in *"Die Axt hat geblüht . . ." Europäische Konflikte der 30er Jahre in Erinnerung an die frühe Avantgarde*, Jürgen Harten, Hans-Werner Schmidt, and Marie Luise Syring, eds., and as reported in the *Frankfurter Allgemeine Zeitung*, 7 November 1987, p. 27.

77. *Dokumente deutscher Kriegsschäden*, 1:54, 57, and 2, part 2: 13; E. Wagenmann, "Grundlagen zum Deutschen Wohnungsbauprogramm 1945–1980," *Neue Bauwelt* 4 (1949); HSANRW/NW 177/109/51–65.

78. SAM/Bürgermeister und Rat/ 1969: Stat. Amt, "Der Bestand am Gebäuden und Wohnungen in der Münchner Altstadt," 15 February 1946.

79. *Dokumente deutscher Kriegsschäden*, 1:51–52.

80. Ibid., 1:52.

81. Dähn, "Die Zerstörung Hamburgs im Kriege 1939–1945," pp. 28, 30.

82. *Dokumente deutscher Kriegsschäden*, 1:53.

83. Quoted in Gerhard Brunn, "Köln in den Jahren 1945 und 1946. Die Rahmenbedingungen des gesellschaftlichen Lebens," in *Köln nach dem Nationalsozialismus*, Otto Dann, ed. (Wuppertal, 1981), p. 40.

84. NA/RG 43/European Advisory Commission/ Box 47, "A Preliminary View of the German Housing Position: The Altreich and the American Zone, as of January 1945," February 1945.

85. HSANRW/NW 177/109/51–65.

86. SAM/Bürgermeister und Rat/1976: Key for division of aid as of 3 May 1950.

87. NA/Dept. of State Interim Research and Intelligence Service, Research and Analysis Branch, R & A 3298, 29 December 1945, "Darmstadt: A Survey of Political, Economic and Social Conditions in a Medium-Sized German City," Field Memorandum No. 1010.

88. NA/OMG Hesse/ Manpower Branch, Economics Division, Box 8/118-1, Folder 1, Monthly Housing Reports, here the report for April 1947, prepared by the city's Obermagistratsrat.

89. Joachim Irek, *Mannheim in den Jahren 1945 bis 1949. Geschichte einer Stadt zwischen Diktatur und Republik*, vol. 1, *Darstellung*, Veröffentlichungen des Stadtarchivs Mannheim, vol. 9 (Stuttgart, 1983), p. 202.

90. SAM/Bürgermeister und Rat/ 1967: Report of the Wiederaufbaureferat to the Stadtrat, 17 December l946, on a trip to Hamburg.

91. See Irek, *Mannheim*, 1: 202.

92. For example, see John Gimbel, *A German Community under American Occupation. Marburg, 1945–1952* (Stanford, Calif., 1961), pp. 55–56.

93. NA/RG 260/ OMG Bavaria/ I. Manpower Division, Box 85, Folder 9: Samuel R. Rosenbaum, Field Operations Supervisor for Niederbayern-Oberpfalz to OMGB Regensburg, 8 August 1947, p. 3.

94. See RWWA/1/239/1/6:297.

95. *Verhandlungen der Stadtverordnetenversammlung, Köln* (1945): 43, 112–19.

96. Deutscher Städtetag, *Forderungen zum Wohnungsbau* (Cologne, 1949), p. 2.

97. *Monthly Statistical Bulletin of the Control Commission for Germany (British Element)* 2, no. 11 (November 1947), Table 18, p. 30.

98. Böll, for example, uses rubble as settings for *Und sagte kein einziges Wort* (Frankfurt, 1966) and *Gruppenbild mit Dame* (Cologne, 1971).

99. Verwaltungsberichte d. Stadt Köln (1951–52): 102, (1952–53): 112, (1953–54): 127; for Munich see SAM/Bauamt-Wiederaufbau/ 1047/1: H. Fischer, "Bekanntgabe in der Vollversammlung des Stadtrates, 12 December 1950."

100. HASK/5 (OSD)/ 38, "Zahlen über Zerstörung und Wiedererstehen der Stadt Köln," p. 11, Tables 9 and 10; a United States survey of 13 April 1946 indicates that in Berlin at that time there were 1.25 persons per room and about 12 square meters per person. NA/RG 43: Allied Control Council Germany, Documents 1945–48. File DMAN/SEC(47) 1, Manpower Directorate, 2 January 1947.

101. HASK/2/1320/ Oberbürgermeister Klett in speech to Gemeinderat, "5 Jahre Aufbau in Stuttgart," 23 April 1950.

102. Wagenmann, "Grundlagen zum Deutschen Wohnungsbauprogramm," p. 735.

103. See my "Konstanty Gutschow and the Reconstruction of Hamburg," and SH/ Baubehörde I B1/Abschlußbericht der Sonderabteilung "Wiederaufbauleitung," Anlage 11: Instandsetzungsaktion im Wohnungbau; Bauprogramm und Baubedarf. Gutschow was dismissed for political reasons at the end of September 1945.

104. Höhns, "'Neuaufbau' als Hoffnung," pp. 97–98.

105. Ulrich Blumenroth, *Deutsche Wohnungspolitik seit der Reichsgründung: Darstellung und kritische Würdigung*, Beiträge zum Siedlungs- und Wohnungswesen und zur Raumplanung, vol. 25 (Münster, 1975), pp. 313, 329, 399.

106. Some aspects of the housing campaign were discussed in Chapter 2, such as the rationing and/or regulation by various authorities of building materials and building labor.

107. Harlander and Fehl, *Hitlers Sozialer Wohnungsbau*, p. 138.

108. One can find this set of guidelines in many places. For example, BHSA/ Bayer. St. Min. d. Finanzen, 27.3.79/ 249–252 II-IX/ 248/ doc. 10828/ Min. Dir. Wolf, Bayerisches Arbeitsministerium, "Richtlinien für den Wohnungsbau in Bayern 1946," Munich, 21 March 1946. See also Deutscher Städtetag, *Forderungen zum Wohnungsbau*, for the housing program of the German Cities Association.

109. SAM/Bürgermeister und Rat/1969/Entwurf eines Aufbaufinanzierungsgesetzes sent by Wilhelm Biber, Bankdirektor of Bayerische Vereinsbank to Lord Mayor Scharnagl, 6 March 1947; BHSA/ Bayer. St. Min. d. Finanzen, 27.3.79/ 250 II-IX 249/ 8080/ copy of the proposal sent by the banks to the Finance Minister, 5 March 1947.

110. SAM/Bürgermeister und Rat/1972/ Bayerischer Aufbaurat, "Erfordernisse des Aufbaues in Bayern," p. 5.

111. SAM/Bürgermeister und Rat/1972, "Sozialer Wohnungsbau," SPD Bundestag—Fraktions Entwurf, December 1949. The proposal was originally made by the Gesamtverband gemeinnütziger Wohnungsunternehmen. Eberhard Wildermuth, "Begrüßungsansprachen," in *Um die Grundlagen des sozialen Wohnungsbaues: Kundgebung der Gemeinnützigen Wohnungswirtschaft des Landes Nordrhein-Westfalen* (Essen, 1950), p. 8. The 1,000 participants at this meeting represented banks, government agencies, and numerous social housing corporations. Wildemuth's statement, of course, echoed similar statements made by conservative, and Nazi, supporters of urban renewal projects in the 1930s.

112. A. Flender, "Die gemeinnützige Wohnungswirtschaft in Nordrhein-Westfalen," in *Um die Grundlagen des sozialen Wohnungsbaues: Kundgebung der Ge-*

meinnützigen Wohnungswirtschaft des Landes Nordrhein-Westfalen (Essen, 1950), pp. 22–26.

113. For example, see BHSA/MWi 11650/Report of 26 September 1950, from Vereinigung der Arbeitsgeberverbände in Bavaria to Staatsmin. Hans Seidel.

114. Social housing sponsored by this law was to be modest in size—32 to 65 square meters—with a rent of DM 1 to DM 1.10 per square meter, and with tenants assigned by the local housing authority. This rent was under the market level for uncontrolled rents. See my "Reconstruction Law and Building Law in Post-war Germany," *Planning Perspectives* 1 (1986).

115. For a report on these negotiations, BHSA/ MWi 11652/ Dr. Ringelmann of Bayer. Staatsmin. der Finanzen to Oberste Baubehörde in Staatsmin. d. Innern, 16 May 1949.

116. As would be expected, there were disagreements about the fairness of the distribution keys, and small cities complained that big cities enjoyed an unfair advantage. For example, ADST/ 6/22–15/ vol. 1/ Roser, Bürgermeisteramt Stadt Esslingen am Neckar to Städtetag, 7 January 1952.

117. The problem was that rents were frozen on older buildings and not on new, unsubsidized buildings, so that tenants in rent-controlled housing were paying only 10–15% of their income in rent. Spokesmen for the government and the housing industry felt rents should be allowed to rise to 20% of income, which would create new capital for housing investment. For discussion of this issue: BHSA/MWi 11652/ Arbeitsstab des Länderrats des Vereinigten Wirtschaftsgebiets für Wohnungsbau, to Länderrat, 15 May 1949; Fritz Kleffner, "Wohnungsmietstop und Wohnungsbau," and Paul Edelmann, "Mietpreisstop und Wohnungsbau," *Der Städtetag*, new series 2 (1949): 52–55 and 139–40; HASK/ Best. 2 (OBM)/2291/ Deutscher Städtetag, Bauausschuß, material distributed on 24 August 1949 for 4th meeting of committee; Gerhard Weisser, *Wünsche und Wirklichkeit des sozialen Wohnungsbaues in Westdeutschland*, Schriften des Deutschen Verbandes für Wohnungswesen, Städtebau und Raumplanung, no. 3 (1949): 9–15; and BHSA/MWi 11650/Dr. Jaschinski, "Memorandum zu Grundsatzfragen der Wohnungsbauförderung," 3 October 1951.

118. Karl Sommer, "Der Wohnungsbau nach dem Kriege," in *Wohnungsbau in Hamburg* (Hamburg, 1953), pp. 15–16.

119. For example, Ernst Runge, "Vorschläge zur Finanzierung des Wohnungsbaues," *Der Bauhelfer* 1, no. 3 and 4 (1946); the various proposals submitted in 1945 and 1946 by housing firms and financial institutions in BHSA/ MWi 11646.

120. Karl Horn, "Steur- und Abgabevergünstigungen im Wohnungsbau," *Der Städtetag*, new series 4 (1951): 299–300, estimated a loss of land tax revenues over 10 years at DM 700 million.

121. *Bayerisches Gesetz- und Verordnungsblatt*, no. 14 (1949): 135.

122. For an example of such opposition, BHSA/MWi 11653/Dr. Bessler, Syndikus, and Ludwig Beegen, Chairman of Haus- und Grundbesitzerverein Regensburg und Umgebung, to Wirtschaftsminister Dr. Seidel.

123. Edgar Siemens, "Die Wohnungsbaufinanzierung im Spiegel der Währungsreform," and Robert Deumer, "Pfandbriefaufwertung und Zwecksparen als Instrument des Investitionskredits," both in *Neue Wege zur Finanzierung des sozialen Wohnungsbaues* (Memmingen, 1948).

124. HLL/ Vertical Files, Central Statistical Office, British Element, Allied General Secretariat, "Housing in the Federal Republic of Germany," memorandum of August 1951, p. 6.

125. Jürgen Fischer-Dieskau (of the Federal Housing Ministry), "Wo kommt das

Geld für den Wohnungsbau her?" in *Amtlicher Katalog der Constructa Bauausstellung 1951* (Hannover, 1951), p. 119. Presumably this is the same Jürgen Fischer-Dieskau who worked for Ley in the Nazi years.

126. For example, SAM/Bürgermeister und Rat/1972/report by Stadtrat Fischer to Bayerischer Aufbaurat, 10 November 1948, p. 3.

127. See Martin Wagner, *Das neue Berlin* (1932), unpublished book manuscript in BSBWB. When Wagner visited the United States in 1929, he was critical of the American approach to housing. He concluded that the highly mobile Americans had no interest in building long-lasting, attractive houses. Rather they wanted to make money, and they did so by keeping construction costs low and the price of finished houses low, creating a mass market. Wagner also noted that whenever Negroes moved into an area, white people began to move out, with a corresponding rapid drop in property values. "Städtebauliche Probleme in amerikanischen Städten und ihre Rückwirkung auf den deutschen Städtebau," originally published in a special issue of *Der Deutsche Bauzeitung* in 1929, reprinted in part in *Stadtbauwelt* 96 (1987): 1802–3.

128. The paper was entitled "How to Bring Forth an Ideal Solution of the Defense Housing Problem?" See Gilbert Herbert, *The Dream of the Factory-Made House: Walter Gropius and Konrad Wachsmann* (Cambridge, Mass., 1984), pp. 138ff, 234ff.

129. NA/RG 59, Department of State Decimal File 1945–49/ Box 6778/862.502/4–2246: Robert Murphy, US Political Advisor for Germany to the Secretary of State, 22 April 1946, with OMGUS press release of 18 April 1946; RG 466 US High Commissioner for Germany (HICOG)/ Box 69/ File 504.21/ report on housing signed by Luther H. Hodges, chief, Industry Division, Office of Economic Affairs, but in fact written by James W. Butler, head of the housing division, ECA mission to Germany, p. 7. A commendation Butler received for the report, dated 5 April 1951, stated: "This is the first comprehensive, intelligent and constructive report on the German housing situation that has reached the Department [of German economic affairs] in the course of five years."

130. Born in Hamburg, Blumenfeld had studied in Germany and then worked there as an architect during the 1920s. He was a member of the German Communist party, and from 1930 to 1937 he worked in the Soviet Union, after which he emigrated to the United States. He resigned his job in Philadelphia in 1951 to protest the need to take a loyalty oath, though he did take the oath. In 1955 he went to Canada, where he spent most of the rest of his life. He died in 1988, having just published a new volume of memoirs, *Life Begins at 65: The Not Entirely Candid Autobiography of a Drifter* (Montreal, 1987). I have been unable to find further information about Zisman. It is likely that this visit was part of the OMGUS exchange program, which was taken over by the High Commissioner for Germany after mid-1949. Considerable hunting in the State Department, OMGUS, and HICOG records revealed little about the origins of this trip or the fate of its recommendations. Archivists at the National Archives report that many records from the transition period from OMGUS to HICOG were misplaced or are virtually impossible to track down. The following discussion is based upon a report submitted by Blumenfeld on 8 December 1949 to Fernando Eugen Ropshaw, who had been an OMGUS officer up to 1949 and who then moved to the State Department. "City Planning in Germany," NA/RG 59/ State Department Central Decimal Files/ Box 6778/ no. 862.502/12–849, and henceforth cited as "Blumenfeld report." A copy of the report, under Zisman's signature, was sent by Clarence Perry Oaks, chief, Political Affairs Division of the Office of the US High Commissioner in Bremen, to Bremen's Baudirektor Tippel, 8 December 1949. SB/4,29/1–981. A brief German version was published in 1950. S. B. Zisman and Hans Blumenfeld, "Allgemeines über Städteplanung in Deutschland," *Neue Bauwelt* 5 (1950).

131. Blumenfeld report, p. 12.

132. Ibid., p. 14.

133. Ibid.

134. US Political Advisor for Germany, "The Problem of Housing in the Bizonal Area," memo, 6 May 1949, HLL/ Vertical Files. It is interesting that during the Nazi years, German authorities pursued programs of slum clearance in part because they felt that bad, unhygienic housing conditions bred communism. See von Petz, *Stadtsanierung im Dritten Reich*.

135. NA/RG 466 (HICOG)/Box 69/ 504.21/ Official translation of letter from Federal Minister for Housing Wildermuth to the ministers (senators) of the Länder in charge of housing, 19 June 1950: Directives concerning the utilization of the ERP funds for the 1950 social housing construction scheme.

136. NA/RG 466 (HICOG)/ Box 69/ 504.21/ Sam Gillstrap to Erich Groeppler, 28 December 1950. This was a standard reply.

137. This is typical of the American retreat from earlier denazification and democratization policies. To take another example, the High Commission was asked in 1950 by several citizens to intervene when a group of houses in Zuffenhausen, near Stuttgart, were to be turned over to their former owners, who had been SS and Nazi party members. The housing settlement had been built in 1939 for politically reliable persons, taken over by the United Nations Relief and Rehabilitation Administration (UNRRA) for displaced persons in 1945, then turned over to the military government in 1947 but immediately seized by the city and given to victims of Nazism. The original owners sued to regain their homes and the German courts ruled in their favor. The High Commission felt this was unjust, and there was concern about having a settlement with a high concentration of former Nazis, but the Americans felt it was too late to do anything without causing other problems. NA/RG 466 (HICOG)/ Box 69/ report on Rotweg Housing Settlement by H. W. Weigert, 14 March 1950.

138. NA/RG 466 (HICOG)/Box 69/ 504.21/ office memo from James W. Butler to F. L. Mayer, 27 September 1951. In July 1949, at the moment of transition from OMGUS to the High Commission, the Americans considered making a documentary film that would encourage prefabricated housing construction by making "the 'reactionary builder type' the butt of comic ridicule in the film." NA/RG 260 (OMGUS)/ Shiplist 13 1/10, Container 5911/ Box 264/ Harold J. Hurwitz, OMGUS Information Services Division, to Mr. Stuart Schulberg, 6 July 1949.

139. NA/RG 466 (HICOG)/Box 69/504.21/report on housing signed by Luther H. Hodges, chief, Industry Division, Office of Economic Affairs, written by James W. Butler, p. 5.

140. For this program see Höhns, "'Neuaufbau' als Hoffnung."

141. NA/RG 466 (HICOG)/ Box 69/504.21/ memo from Luther H. Hodges, chief, Industry Division, Office of Economic Affairs, "Housing and City, Town, and Country Planning. Cost," 1 March 1951.

142. HLH, Gropius Papers, no. 416: Gropius to Otto Bartning, the president of the Bund Deutscher Architekten and the German cochairman of the committee, 6 October 1951. Other American members of the committee were Mack Arnold, a manufacturer of building materials from Greensboro, North Carolina, Charles M. La Folette (former director of the military government in Baden-Württemberg), Donald Monson (a former Detroit planner), William Wittausch (an official in the Washington housing administration), and James W. Butler, the author of the program and head of the housing division of the ECA mission to Germany. Bernard Wagner emigrated to

the United States in 1938, finished his studies in architecture at Harvard, served in the American army, and after the war worked for the National Housing Agency.

143. Bernard Wagner, "More Homes for Germans."

144. The full list of entries, along with 22 essays on the competition, is to be found in Hermann Wandersleb and Hans Schoszberger, eds., *Neue Wohnbau*, vol. 1, *Bauplanung* (Ravensburg, 1952). Gutschow's winning entry was in Hannover, Reichow's in Lübeck, and Hebebrand's in Bremen.

145. See Göderitz, Rainer, and Hoffmann, *Die gegliederte und aufgelockerte Stadt*.

146. See "Kritik aus USA" by the American members of the prize committee, in Wandersleb and Schoszberger, *Neue Wohnbau*, pp. 127ff. In noting that construction costs for the winning projects were 20% less than comparable German housing projects, Walter Bogner claimed that "a reduction of this magnitude, if applied to the 40 billion Deutsche Marks that will have to be spent for housing by the West Germans during the next 15 years, would result in vast savings. However, of greater significance at this time of world tension is the fact that methods seem to have been found whereby more housing can be built in a country where it is so desperately needed to keep workers contented and productive." "A Housing Development Program for Western Germany," Department of State, *The Record* 8, no. 2 (March–April 1952): 10.

147. NA/RG 466 (HICOG)/Box 69/504.21/ Special Miners' Housing Program from 1950/51 Reserve, 30 October 1951.

148. NA/RG 466 (HICOG)/ Box 68/ 504.21/ report of 13 December 1952. This was a truly international committee, with representatives from six countries in addition to those from West Germany and the United States.

149. Lotte Tiedemann and Emmy Bonhöffer, "ECA-Entwicklungsbauten—von ihren Bewohnern und von Frauen gesehen," in *Neue Wohnbau*, vol. 2, *Durchführung von Versuchssiedlungen. Ergebnisse und Erkentnisse für heute und morgen. Von ECA bis Interbau,* Hermann Wandersleb and Georg Günthert, eds. (Ravensburg, 1958), pp. 18ff.

150. Wandersleb and Günthert, *Neue Wohnbau,* p. 9.

151. For example, HSANRW/ NW 73: 239/ Prof. Dr. Ing. Hans Spiegel, Düsseldorf, "Forschungsaufgabe: Verbilligung des Wohnungsbaues durch die Einführung genormter Fertigbauteile und darauf aufgebauter Fertigungsmethoden für Werkstatt und Bauteile." During the war, Spiegel had worked on standardized temporary housing in the office of the Reichswohnungskommissar, along with Ernst Neufert.

152. Höhns, "'Neuaufbau' als Hoffnung," p. 102, n. 2.

153. NA/ RG 466 (HICOG)/ Box 26/ 504.21 (Bavarian Land Commissioner)/ K. Fredericks to George Godfrey, 4 December 1950, "Master List of ECA Financed Housing Projects in Bavaria," 3 November 1950; and Box 69, 504.21/ Simonson to Garrett, "List of Württemberg-Baden ECA Financed Housing (Revised)," 30 November 1950; Box 69/ 504.21/ Butler to Frank Miller, "Facts about German Housing," 8 September 1951. Butler broke down the ECA allocations to date (in millions of DM) as:

At-once aid program	81.3
Special refugee program	105.3
General housing program	108.0
1950 Ruhr miners housing (through mine companies)	23.3
1951 Ruhr miners housing	45.0
Berlin housing	50.0
Development projects housing	37.0
Total	449.9

154. Arthur Brunisch, "Der Wohnungsbau in der Bundesrepublik Deutschland 1945–1955," *Der Architekt* 4 (1955): 255. The bulk of the money came from private individuals, private lenders, cooperative housing associations, and local and federal government agencies.

155. On the subject of Marshall aid to Germany, see Manfred Pohl, *Wiederaufbau. Kunst und Technik der Finanzierung 1947–1953. Die ersten Jahre der Kreditanstalt für Wiederaufbau* (Frankfurt, 1973), and Manfred Knapp, "Reconstruction and West-Integration: The Impact of the Marshall Plan on Germany," *Zeitschrift für die gesamte Staatswissenschaft* 137 (1981): 424–25. A recent study of the impact of Marshall aid in Berlin is Wolfgang Bohleber, *Mit Marshallplan und Bundeshilfe. Wohnungsbaupolitik in Berlin 1945–1968* (Berlin, 1990).

156. Charles S. Maier, "The Two Postwar Eras and the Conditions for Stability in Twentieth-Century Western Europe," *American Historical Review* 86 (1981): 342–43.

157. For the Constructa building exhibition of 1951, a study was done of housing construction on new land and on land covered with the rubble of destroyed buildings. The results are described by Rudolf Hillebrecht, *Neubeubauung zerstörter Wohnflächen*, Schriftenreihe des Deutscher Verbandes für Wohnungswesen, Städtebau und Raumplanung, no. 7 (Frankfurt, 1952).

158. See, for example, an essay by Hochbauamt Direktor Tralau, 23 January 1951, in HASK/171/426/ pp. 2–3.

159. SAM/Bauamt-Wiederaufbau/1106/copy of speech delivered in the fall of 1946.

160. HASK/2/1312/Theo Nussbaum, "Die Neugestaltung Kölns," 1 April 1946.

161. See Rudolf Hillebrecht's statement in Guther, Hillebrecht, Schmeissner, and Schmidt, " 'Ich kann mich nicht herausdenken aus dem Vorgang der Geschichte,' " p. 371.

162. This is by Baudirektor Dr. Dronke, "Städtebauliche Aufgaben der Gegenwart mit besondere Berucksichtigung Bremens," speech to Senate, SB/ 4, 29/1–487 (14 December 1945): 10–11, but such statements were typical of postwar planners.

163. SH/Architekt Gutschow/A45/E9/Wiederherstellungsgebiete/September 1945/ VII/ Zusammenfassung; and A45/E2/ Beschaffung von Wohnraum, 1 June 1945.

164. SH/Architekt Gutschow/A45/E9/ Wiederherstellungsgebiete/September 1945/ VII/ Zusammenfassung.

165. Arthur Dähn, "Hamburg, dicht am Ozean: Eine Gesamtschau der Aufgaben, Problem und Leistungen," *Neue Bauwelt* 5 (1950), and Dähn, "Die Entwicklung des Wohnungsbaus," in *Hamburg und seine Bauten 1929–1953*, Architekten- und Ingenieur Verein Hamburg, ed. (Hamburg, 1953).

166. ADST/ 6/22–15, vol. 1, doc. A1012/minutes of DST committee with Baudirektor Dr. Döscher in Bundesministerium für Wohnungsbau, 8 July 1950; and A2080, summary of meeting of 19 January 1951, where the representatives of the cities urged the ministry to help concentrate reconstruction on inner-city housing, not new suburbs.

167. Hochbauamt Direktor Tralau, 23 January 1951, in HASK/ 171/426/ Section 2.

168. For example, Gemeinnützige Aktiengesellschaft für Wohnungsbau Köln, "Grundsätzliche Erwägungen zur Neubau-Planning," sent to Cologne's planner Rudolf Schwarz, 8 March 1947, in HASK/ 30/66.

169. Jatho, *Urbanität*; Schmitt, *Der Neuaufbau der Stadt Köln*. Jatho's argument, which is directed at the rebuilding of Cologne, presages the arguments of Hans Paul Bahrdt, "Nachbarschaft oder Urbanität," *Bauwelt* 51–52 (1960), and Jane Jacobs, *The Death and Life of Great American Cities*, which helped launch a movement against functional zoning in America and Europe. Schmitt's essay was actually written in 1944.

170. The British withdrew from the project in April 1948 because the administration of the combined Western zones was to be in Frankfurt. The project was turned over to the city, and construction continued until 1956 under a team of Hamburg architects for the city. The project was successful in the end, but the housing was too expensive for workers, and most tenants were white-collar employees and bureaucrats. See Sylvaine Hänsel, Michael Scholz, and Christoph Bürkle, "Die Grindelhochhäuser als erste Wohnhochhäuser in Deutschland," *Zeitschrift des Vereins für Hamburgische Geschichte* 66 (1980), and Axel Schildt, *Die Grindelhochhäuser. Eine Sozialgeschichte der ersten deutschen Wohnhochhausanlage* (Hamburg, 1988).

171. HLL/Vertical Files, Central Statistical Office, British Element, Allied General Secretariat, "Housing in the Federal Republic of Germany," memorandum of August 1951, p. 5.

172. Elke Pahl-Weber, "Im fließenden Raum. Wohnungsgrundrisse nach 1945," in *Grauzonen. Kunst und Zeitbilder, Farbwelten 1945–1955*, Bernhard Schulz, ed. (Berlin, 1983).

173. Höhns, " 'Neuaufbau' als Hoffnung," pp. 88–92.

174. Hans Scharoun, "Zur Ausstellung 'Berlin Plant,' " and Karl Böttcher, "Von der Retorte zum Kunststoff-Montagehaus," both in *Neue Bauwelt* 1 (1946); Scharoun, *Hans Scharoun. Bauten, Entwürfe, Texte*, Peter Pfankuch, ed. Schriftenreihe der Akademie der Künste, vol. 10 (Berlin, 1974). The *Neue Berliner Illustrierte*, no. 2 (Sept. 1946), carried pictures of the five model houses—an American, Russian, English, French, and German type—named for each of the occupation powers. Böttcher, who directed the program, designed the houses and continued to advocate rationalized housing construction after he left the Berlin city government. See Karl Böttcher, *Bericht über meine Arbeit* (Berlin, 1989), pp. 46ff, 60ff.

175. Karl Böttcher, who developed one of the models, told the author in an interview on 28 October 1981 that even at the time he felt a skilled mason could raise a wall as fast and as economically as it could be done with prefabrication. In Hamburg, one of the firms (Philipp Holzmann AG) asked by Gutschow to study a housing block for immediate reconstruction also questioned prefabrication. See ASKG/A45/E9/Wiederherstellungsgebiete/30 January 1946/Beurteilung der bauwirtschaftlichen Durchführung nach den Vorschlägen der Firmen. Some armaments firms, including Messerschmidt and MAN, sought to produce standardized housing units. MAN built a few homes with walls made of metal plates. The public much preferred homes made of traditional materials such as brick. Christoph Mohr discussed this housing in "Architektur der 50er Jahre ohne Namen—Erfahrungen aus der Provinz: Ein Bericht über Erfassung, Bewertung und Auswahl in Hessen," in *Architektur und Städtebau der Fünfziger Jahre: Ergebnisse der Fachtagung in Hannover, 2.–4. Februar 1990. Schutz und Erhaltung von Bauten der Fünfziger Jahre*, Werner Durth and Niels Gutschow, eds., Schriftenreihe des Deutschen Nationalkomitees für Denkmalschutz, vol. 41 (Bonn, 1990).

176. Cramer and Gutschow, *Bauausstellungen*, pp. 208–12.

177. Ibid., pp. 213–22; *Amtlicher Katalog der Constructa Bauausstellung 1951* (Hannover, 1951); and "Aus dem Bericht des Preisgerichts über den Constructa-Wettbewerb nr. 1," *Baurundschau* (1950): 357–70.

178. Rudolf Hillebrecht, "Neuer Wohnungsbau in England," originally printed in *Gemeinnützige Wohnungswirtschaft*, no. 6 and 8 (1949), reprinted in part in *Stadtbauwelt* 96 (1987): 1804–5.

179. Heuss, *Amtlicher Katalog der Constructa Bauausstellung 1951*, p. 2. In 1948 Gropius made a trip to Germany. He came away with doubts about the value of

prefabrication. In particular, he was put off by the fact that Ernst Neufert, his former office employee before leaving for America, continued to be the spokesman for standardization, even after his years of working for Speer. Gropius, "Reconstruction: Germany," *Task*, no. 7–8 (1948).

180. *Amtlicher Katalog der Constructa Bauausstellung 1951*, p. 40.

181. See my "Berlin on the Charles, Cambridge on the Spree," p. 347. Here Walter Gropius, visiting the exhibition, met Paul Bonatz for the first time, with such diverse personalities as Rudolf Wolters and Werner Hebebrand looking on.

182. Johannes Göderitz, "Hausformen und Bebauungsweise," in *Amtliche Katalog der Constructa Bauausstellung 1951* (Hannover, 1951), p. 89.

183. For these projects the most valuable source is Konstanty Gutschow, "Aufbau zerstörter Wohnviertel: Untersuchung an 5 Beispielen in Hannover," 1 July 1951, in ASKG/ currently in the Hamburger Architektur Archiv (HAA). See also Hillebrecht, *Neubebauung zerstörter Wohnflächen*.

184. Cramer and Gutschow, *Bauaustellungen*, p. 221.

185. For a discussion of the Interbau, *Die Interbau wird diskutiert: Die ersten Ergebnisse* (Wiesbaden and Berlin, 1960).

186. See Cramer and Gutschow, *Bauaustellungen*, p. 226.

187. The book contains a reproduction of Hoffmann's 1957 plan for a housing project for 10,000 inhabitants for Berlin-Moabit, which foresaw 6,200 residents in single-family homes, 500 in multifamily homes, and 3,300 in high-rise apartments of 12–22 stories. There is no commentary on the high-rises, which contradict the argument of the book. Rainer's proposal for a Vienna suburb of 10,000 inhabitants in two- and three-story single-family homes in also included. Göderitz, Rainer, and Hoffmann, *Die gegliederte und aufgelockerte Stadt*, pp. 68–72, 80–81.

Chapter 6

1. The term used after the war by many planners and now by all German historians of planning for the most commonly found guiding ideas is *Leitbild*, which translates as model or ideal. Other terms used at the time were *Richtlinie* and *Richtwert*, or guideline. On the term *Leitbild*, see Durth and Gutschow, *Träume in Trümmern*, 1: 220, n. 1.

2. See Anthony Sutcliffe, *Towards the Planned City. Germany, Britain, the United States, and France, 1780–1914* (New York, 1981).

3. See Gerhard Fehl and Juan Rodriguez-Lores, eds. *Stadterweiterungen 1800–1875: von den Anfängen des modernen Städtebaues in Deutschland* (Hamburg, 1983); Rodrigues-Lores and Fehl, eds., *Städtebaureform 1865–1900. Von Licht, Luft und Ordnung in der Stadt der Gründerzeit*, 2 vols. (Hamburg, 1985); and Ladd, *Urban Planning*.

4. Peter Breitling, "The Role of the Competition in the Genesis of Urban Planning: Germany and Austria in the Nineteenth Century," in *The Rise of Modern Urban Planning, 1800–1914*, Anthony Sutcliffe, ed. (New York, 1980); Gerd Albers, "Struktur und Gestalt im Städtebau. Eine Skizze," in *Zwischen Stadtmitte und Stadtregion. Berichte und Gedanken, Rudolf Hillebrecht zum 60. Geburtstag* (Stuttgart and Bern, 1970).

5. The standard work on Stübben in Cologne is Kier, *Die Kölner Neustadt*. This work also contains over 500 photos. Commenting on the Cologne competition, Stübben remarked: "Beim Kölner Planwettbewerb des Jahres 1880 war das deutliche

Bestreben erkennbar, die französischer Art mit deutschem Geist nach örtlichen Bedürfnissen zu durchsetzen und das Pariser Pathos herabzustimmen auf eines behaglicheren Ton." Cited in Kier, p. 56. The idea of moving the train station was repeated in the 1920s by Fritz Schumacher, again in 1939 as part of Nazi plans, and by Cologne's reconstruction planners after 1945. Each time it was frustrated by the high costs involved and the resistance of the railroad authorities.

6. In 1904, the first German planning journal, *Der Städtebau*, commenced publication, with Camillo Sitte of Vienna and Theodor Goecke of Berlin as chief editors. This certainly helped establish university instruction in town planning, though students at the technical universities still enrolled in the field of architecture, since degrees in planning were not offered. Indeed, it is right around the turn of the century that virtually every technical university in Germany created a professorship in urban planning. See Guther, "Zur Geschichte der Städtebaulehre."

7. See Bergmann, *Agrarromantik und Großstadtfeindschaft*, on the ideas of the "fanatical antisemite Theodor Fritsch," whose essays began appearing 10 years before Howard's *To-Morrow* was translated into German. Heide Berndt, *Das Gesellschaftsbild bei Stadtplanern* (Stuttgart and Bern, 1968), p. 35, argues that Fritsch's antisemitism was so offensive that his ideas on garden cities were generally disregarded.

8. There is a large body of literature on the garden city movement. The key source is Ebenezer Howard, *Garden Cities of Tomorrow*, Frederic J. Osborn, ed. (Cambridge, Mass., 1965). See also Robert Fishman, *Urban Utopias in the Twentieth Century: Ebenezer Howard, Frank Lloyd Wright, and Le Corbusier* (Cambridge, Mass., 1977). The International Planning History Conference held in Bournville, England, in September 1989 was devoted to the history of the garden city; some three dozen papers were presented.

9. Marc Weiss used the term "garden metropolis" for cases where greenery is introduced into the existing city. "Developing and Financing the 'Garden Metropolis': Urban Planning and Housing Policy in Twentieth Century America," paper presented at the International Planning History Conference, Bournville, England, September 1989.

10. The most important studies are Hartmann, *Deutsche Gartenstadtbewegung*, and Franziska Bollerey, Gerhard Fehl, and Kristiana Hartmann, eds., *Im Grünen wohnen—im Blauen planen. Ein Lesebuch zur Gartenstadt mit Beiträgen und Zeitdokumenten*, Stadt, Planung, Geschichte, vol. 12 (Hamburg, 1990). See also Franziska Bollerey and Kristiana Hartmann, "A Patriarchal Utopia: The Garden City and Housing Reform in Germany at the Turn of the Century," in *The Rise of Modern Urban Planning, 1800–1914*, Anthony Sutcliffe, ed. (New York, 1980); Diefendorf, "Cities of Rubble to Cities in Greenery"; and Gerd Albers, *Entwicklungslinien im Städtebau: Ideen, Thesen, Aussagen 1875–1945: Texte und Interpretationen* (Düsseldorf, 1975), pp. 47ff.

11. See Wolfgang Voigt, "Von der eugenischen Gartenstadt zum Wiederaufbau aus volksbiologischer Sicht: Rassenhygiene und Städtebau-Ideologie im 20. Jahrhundert," *Stadtbauwelt* 92 (1986). Thinking in racial terms was not limited to the political and intellectual right; such patterns could be found in the ranks of modernists, such as Martin Wagner, whose politics were on the left.

12. In addition to the literature cited in the previous chapter, see Gerhard Fehl, "Der Verlust der 'grünen Mitte': Ein Blick auf das Frankfurter 'Niddatal-Projekt' von 1927 anläßlich der für 1989 geplanten Bundesgartenschau," *Stadtbauwelt* 92 (1986).

13. See Ursula von Petz, "Nachkriegsplanung und Wiederaufbau in Deutschland—einige Anmerkungen zur Situation im Ruhrgebiet," Institut für Raumplanung, Univer-

sität Dortmund, Working Paper 55 (Dortmund, 1987). See also Dieter Rebentisch, "Regional Planning and Its Institutional Framework: An Illustration from the Rhine-Main Area, 1890–1945," in *Shaping an Urban World*, Gordon E. Cherry, ed. (New York, 1980).

14. For planning in Hamburg in the 1920s and 1930s, see Erwin Ockert, "Der Hamburg-Preussische Landesplanungsausschuss," in *Hamburg und seine Bauten 1929–1953*, Architekten- und Ingenieur-Verein Hamburg, ed. (Hamburg, 1953).

15. It is interesting that Fritz Schumacher wrote about Hamburg's planning after 1842 in *Wie das Kunstwerk Hamburg nach dem großen Brand entstand* (Berlin, 1920).

16. Dirk Schubert, "Gesundung der Städte—Stadtsanierung in Hamburg 1933–45," pp. 62–63.

17. See Erwin Ockert, *Fritz Schumacher. Sein Schaffen als Städtebauer und Landesplaner* (Tübingen, 1950).

18. Schumacher, *Köln. Entwicklungsfrage einer Großstadt*, foreword.

19. Ibid., p. 16.

20. Ibid., pp. 18, 20.

21. Ibid., pp. 177, 191, 215, 290ff.

22. Ibid.,. p. 220.

23. Ibid., pp. 259ff.

24. Martin Kröger, "Kontinuität in der Kölner Architekturgeschichte. Ein Beitrag zu Fritz Schumachers Stadtentwicklungskonzept in den frühen 20er Jahren," *Geschichte in Köln*, no. 18 (1985). This article was written to counterbalance arguments that stressed only continuities between Nazi and postwar planning.

25. I am taking these distinctions from E. R. M. Taverne, "Ouds ontwerp voor het hofplein," *Plan* 12 (1981). I am indebted to the author for having provided me with an English translation.

26. Lane, "Architects in Power," p. 288. May was not alone. Other German planners also went to Russia, including Rudolf Wolters, who, after returning, managed Albert Speer's office throughout the war.

27. Rudolf Schwarz, "Baustelle Deutschland," *Baukunst und Werkform* 2 (1948): 55. This was first published in 1932 in *Die Schildgenossen*.

28. Total planning took its most extreme form during the war in German planning for cities in occupied and annexed territories in Poland and the Soviet Union. Huge populations were to be moved or simply eliminated, existing cities completely redone, and new towns for new German settlers founded. See Durth and Gutschow, *Träume in Trümmern*, p. 18.

29. Helas, "Die Architektur der Fünfziger Jahre in Kassel," p. 60. The street no longer exists.

30. Durth and Gutschow, *Träume in Trümmern*, p. 1021.

31. Friedrich-Wilhelm Henning, "Stadtplanerische Überlegungen in der Zwischen-kriegszeit—dargestellt anhand des Planes von Hans Bernhard Reichow für Stettin," in *Stadtwachstum, Industrialisierung, Sozialer Wandel: Beiträge zur Erforschung der Urbanisierung im 19. und 20. Jahrhundert*, Hans-Jürgen Teuteberg, ed. (Berlin, 1986), pp. 219–23.

32. Michael Bose and Elke Pahl-Weber, "Regional- und Landesplanung in Hamburger Planungsraum bis zum 'Groß-Hamburg-Gesetz' 1937," in Bose, Holtmann, Machule, Pahl-Weber, and Schubert, ". . . *ein neus Hamburg entsteht* . . . ," pp. 9–15. See also Pahl-Weber, "Das Groß-Hamburg-Gesetz von 1937 und seine landesplanerischen Folgen für Harburg," in *Harburg: von der Burg zur Industriestadt: Beiträge zur Geschichte Harburgs 1288–1938*, Jürgen Ellermeyer, ed. (Hamburg, 1988).

33. Hartmut Frank, "Pläne für Groß-Mainz," in *Deutsch-französische Beziehungen 1940–1950 und ihre Auswirkungen auf Architektur und Stadtgestalt*, Jean-Louis Cohen and Hartmut Frank, eds. (unpublished ms., Hamburg, 1989), 2:196ff. In 1938 planner Heinrich Knipping hired as his assistant Adolf Bayer, a proponent of the modernist conception of the ribbon city.

34. Feder, *Die neue Stadt*. For a summary, see Durth and Gutschow, *Träume in Trümmern*, pp. 175–77. Feder was already out of power when the book was published, and his book was not universally endorsed by the regime, though it was certainly read by all planners.

35. See Mattausch, *Siedlungsbau und Stadtneugründungen im deutschen Faschismus*, and Schneider, *Stadtgründung im Dritten Reich*.

36. There is a considerable body of literature on these planning efforts, especially on Berlin. For general studies in English see Lane, *Architecture and Politics*, and Taylor, *The Word in Stone*; in German, Teut, *Architektur im Dritten Reich*, Petsch, *Baukunst und Stadtplanung im Dritten Reich*, Thies, *Architektur der Weltherrschaft*, and Dülffer, Thies, and Henke, *Hitlers Städte*. On Berlin, see Larsson, *Die Neugestaltung der Reichshauptstadt*, Schäche, "Platz für die staatliche Macht," and Helmer, *Hitler's Berlin*. On Munich, see Rasp, *Eine Stadt für tausend Jahre*. On Hamburg, see Durth and Gutschow, *Träume in Trümmern*, and Bose, Holtmann, Machule, Pahl-Weber, and Schubert, ". . . *ein neues Hamburg entsteht* . . . ." Dülffer, Thies, and Henke list 27 cities designated for Neugestaltung, but there were others, such as Stuttgart. Wilhelmshaven sought unsuccessfully to gain official designation, but plans similar to those in other cities were drawn up nonetheless. See Durth and Gutschow, *Träume in Trümmern*, p. 1037.

37. These ideas also influenced planning in cities not officially slated to become representative cities. For example, not being an administrative capital of a Gau, Mainz had not been on the list of cities that were to build representative Nazi buildings. When the bombing began to destroy the historic center of Mainz, its planners promptly planned a thorough modernization of the area, with broader streets, opening of block interiors, and the introduction of much greenery, but later in the war the Gauleiter called for proposals for representative buildings—a tower and forum. Mainz's planners complied but still sought to avoid making these buildings the centerpiece of their planning. See Frank, "Pläne für Groß-Mainz," pp. 209–17.

38. See HASK/Plankammer/ 2/1189, and HASK/KS Kriegschronik/140/ report, 8 February 1940. Several of the plans for Cologne survived. The largest, a huge plan in a dozen pieces, covers the entire city area and shows the extent to which the old street system would have vanished. The preparatory demolitions for the east–west axis, begun before the war, were actually carried through. The city was planning an international transportation fair for 1940 and hoped to have the new axes complete by that time. See also Hagspiel, "Die Nationalsozialistische Stadtplanung in und für Köln."

39. For Stuttgart, see Durth and Gutschow, *Träume in Trümmern*, pp. 1021–23. Also Roland Müller, "Das Gesicht der Großstadt: Ein Blick über die Stadtbaugeschichte Stuttgarts," in *Stuttgart im Zweiten Weltkrieg*, 2nd ed., Marlene P. Hiller, ed. (Gerlingen, 1990).

40. Durth and Gutschow, *Träume in Trümmern*, pp. 709–15.

41. For Gutschow, see Diefendorf, "Konstanty Gutschow and the Reconstruction of Hamburg," Elke Pahl-Weber, "Konstanty Gutschow—Architekt," in Bose, Holtmann, Machule, Pahl-Weber, Schubert, ". . . *ein neues Hamburg entsteht* . . ."; Durth and Gutschow, *Träume in Trümmern*, p. 662; and Durth, *Deutsche Architekten*.

42. Schumacher moved to a cottage in Lüneburg in 1933, where he lived out the

war. His dismissal, just prior to the mandatory retirement age, gave him the aura of a martyr. It is not clear, however, that he was dismissed for ideological reasons. In June 1938, he wrote a letter to Gutschow, explicitly praising his proposals for redesigning Hamburg, and he remained in contact with Gutschow during the war, even addressing a seminar with Gutschow's coworkers in 1944. Schumacher lived only a couple of years after the war, but his advice was highly prized and he has remained a kind of cultural hero to Hamburg. See SH/Architekt Gutschow/A30: Letter from Schumacher to Gutschow, 18 June 1938, and [new collection based on private papers from HAA] Konstanty Gutschow, "Nachrichten für unsere Kameraden im Felde," published by Gutschow's office between November 1941 and February 1945. Schumacher's speech is covered in numbers 27 and 28, August and September 1944.

43. For the competition, Dirk Schubert, "Führerstadtplanung in Hamburg," in Bose, Holtmann, Machule, Pahl-Weber, and Schubert, ". . . *ein neues Hamburg entsteht* . . . ." A good survey of Gutschow's planning is found in Jürgen Lafrenz, "Planung der Neugestaltung von Hamburg 1933–1945," in *Innerstädtische Differenzierung und Prozess im 19. und 20. Jahrhundert. Geographische und historische Aspekte*, Heinz Heineberg, ed. (Cologne and Vienna, 1987).

44. Gutschow's commitment to Nazism is open to debate. In November 1946, Gutschow wrote: "Ich bin der Partei weder gezwungen noch aus opportunistischen Gründen beigetreten, sondern in der ehrlichen Überzeugung, damit einer guten Sache zu dienen. Wenn ich mich damit zum nationalsozialistischen Gedankengut bekannt habe, so habe ich hierunter vor allen einen erklärten Sozialismus, Planwirtschaft und Verehrung der Kräfte des Bodens und der Heimat verstanden. Aussenpolitische, nationalistische im Imperialismus ausartende Tendenzen habe ich immer als Deutschland unangemessene Süchte und Maßstabslosigkeiten abgelehnt." He initially joined the SA in 1933, since he did not consider it "als eine politische Partei." Party membership followed in 1937. He did not appear in uniform, did not use the normally obligatory "Heil Hitler" greeting in his office, and did not attend obligatory party meetings, even though his winning the competition led to the award of the rank of Sturmführer. In his office he never inquired about the political convictions of his employees, and in fact he employed a number of former members of the Social Democratic party who had lost their jobs elsewhere. He certainly viewed himself as basically an apolitical technocrat. Gutschow's apolitical character was attested to by 37 colleagues who wrote on Gutschow's behalf in 1946, and the same was asserted strongly in interviews with Rudolf Hillebrecht and Arthur Dähn, two former employees of Gutschow who supported the Social Democrats and who had important careers after the war. See ASKG/ folder on denazification; Gutschow, "10 Jahre Architekt 1935–1945," mimeo sent to former colleagues in memory of fallen comrades in April 1946; interviews by the author of Hillebrecht, Hannover, 8 May 1982, and of Dähn, Hamburg, 11 May 1982. On the other hand, his speeches and writing during the 1930s on the subject of urban renewal had a strongly pro-Nazi, political flavor, and the city of Hamburg signed a contract with the SS for the purchase of bricks from the Neuengamme concentration camp for use in construction of the buildings called for in Gutschow's plans for the Neugestaltung of Hamburg. A recent book on Hamburg by a group of scholars there stops short of calling Gutschow a convinced Nazi, but it also denies the apolitical character of his work. See the essays in Bose, Holtmann, Machule, Pahl-Weber, Schubert, ". . . *ein neues Hamburg entsteht* . . . ." What happened to the bricks produced at the Neuengamme concentration camp has never been clarified. In 1938 the SS created the camp at the site of a brick factory that had been closed for years. The factory was modernized and automated, and in April 1940, the contract signed be-

tween the SS and the city called for the purchase of from 20 million to 40 million bricks per year. However, Hillebrecht assured me that no Neuengamme bricks were ever used for any project directed by Gutschow's office, nor were they used in Autobahn construction. It was not so much that there was a moral objection to using the bricks; they were not hard enough and were of an off color. Perhaps they were used by the DAF, though the DAF was experimenting with concrete prefabricated housing. On this camp, Werner Johe, *Neuengamme: Zur Geschichte der Konzentrationslager in Hamburg* (Hamburg, 1982); and interview of Hillebrecht by author, 25 June 1983.

45. Gutschow met with Hitler only once, when the model for Hamburg was displayed in the Chancellery. Hitler turned against Gutschow soon thereafter, though Gutschow was defended by Speer. See ASKG/Erklärung by Rudolf Wolters, denazification folder, 2 October 1946. The Hamburg archives contain several folders of drawings for different versions of the bridge and skyscraper, for example, SH/Architekt Gutschow/A202, A347, A361, and A362. See also the printed "Erläuterungsbericht, Elbufergestaltung Hamburg" by Gutschow for the basic plans of 1939.

46. This according to Hans von Hanffstengel, who worked in Gutschow's office from 1937 to 1939 before going to Giesler's office in Munich. In October 1941, Hanffstengel told Rudolf Hillebrecht, and an alarmed Hillebrecht in turn told Gutschow. Niels Gutschow provided me with a copy of Hillebrecht's letter to Konstanty Gutschow, dated 16 October 1941. Hitler's remarks were clearly recalled by Hanffstengel in an interview by the author in Nuremburg, 31 July 1982.

47. *Hamburgisches Verordnungsblatt*, 4 May 1939. The financing of Gutschow's office and the project was rather complicated. The budget was paid out of a special city account, but the city treasury in turn received a kind of tax rebate from the Reich so that in the end the city paid for only 28% of the total cost of the Neugestaltung project and other activities of Gutschow's office. See SH/Finanzbehörde I/Report of 9 August 1948.

48. For organizational charts and personnel, see SH/Architekt Gutschow/A1 and A5.

49. See the "Generalbebauungsplan 1940," Hamburg, 1 November 1940, text and map. The plan is reproduced in color in Durth and Gutschow, *Träume in Trümmern*, p. XXII. A description of the plan is in Elke Pahl-Weber and Michael Bose, "Die Generalbebauungspläne 1940/41 und 1944," in Bose, Holtmann, Machule, Pahl-Weber, and Schubert, ". . . *ein neues Hamburg entsteht* . . . ."

50. See SH/Architekt Gutschow/vols. A122, A126, and A128 for minutes of dozens of meetings and copies of position papers submitted on the project by individuals outside Gutschow's office.

51. Elke Pahl-Weber, "Architekten/Planer und ihr Arbeitsfeld," and "Konstanty Gutschow—Architekt," in Bose, Holtmann, Machule, Pahl-Weber, and Schubert, ". . . *ein neues Hamburg entsteht* . . . ," pp. 179–85, 193; and SH/ ASKG/ *Nachrichten für unsere Kameraden im Felde*.

52. For a discussion of the plan, see Bose and Weber, "Der Generalbebauungsplan 1940/41," in idem, pp. 55ff.

53. See SH/Architekt Gutschow/A118 and A119 for "Arbeits- und Zeitpläne."

54. By 1937 Hans Bahn, the director of the Historic Preservation Office of Hamburg, had already proposed the creation of a preservation zone on the Cremoninsel (an "island" on the edge of the harbor created by a ring canal). The proposal called for a radical renovation of everything in the area except the historic buildings, and though the Reichsstatthalter had approved the idea, the fate of this area was in fact still up in the air as Gutschow's plans for the city were being formed. Indeed, between 1939 and

1942, it was reported that 21 valuable buildings in the proposed zone had been demolished because they were considered unsafe. SH/Denkmalschutzamt 32/Bahn to Witt, president of Kultur- und Schulbehörde, 10 November 1937, and 38/ 5 January 1938; H. Becker (Verwaltung für Künst- und Kulturangelegenheiten), "Denkschrift zur denkmalpflegerischen Planung und Gestaltung der Cremoninsel," Hamburg, 1942, in SH/ Wohnwirtschafts u. Siedlungsamt/29.

55. SH/Architekt Gutschow/A250: Architektenwettbewerb und weitere Planungen für die Gestaltung der Ost-West-Straße, 1939–1942; Konstanty Gutschow, "Zum Wettbewerb um die Hamburger Innenstadt."

56. SH/Architekt Gutschow/A43/C20, "Wohnplatz und Arbeitsplatz sowie die Pendelwanderung der Erwerbstätigen in Hamburg" by Dr. Ing. Winkelmann, May 1941, and critical comments by Gauobmann Rudolf Habedank, 12 August 1941 and Senator Carl Werdermann, 30 August 1941. For each block, the study described all buildings and open spaces, listed the owners, number of households and inhabitants, subrenters, the age of inhabitants, occupation and place of work, rent levels, and the value of each property in terms of the frozen 1935 value and in terms of fire insurance replacement value. There are also photos of each building. This material is to be found in SH/Architekt Gutschow/A92b and at the end of Section A.

57. See SH/Architekt Gutschow/vols. A337–341. City-owned and run housing firms administered 10,715 of the 26,535 social housing units that existed in 1940. As bombs began to rain on Hamburg, these social housing firms took over some of the responsibility for repairing damaged housing, and at least until some time in 1944, reconstruction was going on alongside the destruction. After the war ended, the social housing firms took the lead in new housing construction.

58. See SH/Architekt Gutschow/A92a-96, with a list of the parcels in A95. This list includes previous owner, purchase price, and date of purchase. A survey completed 3 May 1940 listed 108 Jewish-owned properties in or near the project area. Gutschow recommended acquisition of 67, noting that the rest "ist vom städtebaulichen Standpunkt aus uninteressant" (vol. A92a). The listed purchase price, whether the property was Jewish-owned or not, was usually the market value according to the 1935 price freeze. Needless to say, Jewish property owners did not actually receive full value for their property. See SH/Finanzbehörde I/410–15–2/3 and Finanzbehörde I/410–8/16[1], both Ablieferung 1970, for documents on compensation after the war (*Wiedergutmachung*). According to the *Hamburger Adressbuch* of 1955, at least 7 of the formerly Jewish-owned properties had city-owned social housing projects built on them by that time.

59. This is most fully discussed in Pahl-Weber, "Die Ortsgruppe als Siedlungszelle," and in Durth and Gutschow, *Träume in Trümmern*, pp. 178–86.

60. See Henning, "Stadtplanerische Überlegungen"; Durth and Gutschow, *Träume in Trümmern*, pp. 189ff; and Durth and Gutschow, "Vom Architekturraum zur Stadtlandschaft: Wandlungen städtebaulicher Leitbilder unter dem Eindruck des Luftkrieges 1942–1945," in *Massenwohnung und Eigenheim. Wohnungsbau und Wohnen in der Großstadt seit dem Ersten Weltkrieg*, Axel Schildt and Arnold Sywottek, eds. (Frankfurt and New York, 1988).

61. "Grundlagen für die Gesundung und Neugestaltung des Raumes Bremen," presented at third meeting of planning Arbeitsgemeinschaft in Bremen, 17 November 1943, in ASKG, 110282, Bremen; "Grundlagen für den Raumordnungsplan in Bremen," reprinted in part in Durth and Gutschow, *Träume in Trümmern*, pp. 371–74.

62. The following is based on Hartmut Frank, "Die Stadtlandschaft Diedenhofen," in *Deutsch-französische Beziehungen 1940–1950 und ihre Auswirkungen auf*

Architektur und Stadtgestalt, Jean-Louis Cohen and Hartmut Frank, eds. (unpublished ms., Hamburg, 1989), 3:281ff.

63. "Richtlinien für die Planung und Gestaltung der Städte in den eingegliederten deutschen Ostgebieten," Allgemeine Anordnung no. 12/II, 30 January 1942. The document is reprinted in full in Durth and Gutschow, *Träume in Trümmern*, pp. 45–50. It is not clear who actually composed these guidelines; it could have come from Ley's office or from the Labor Ministry.

64. Ibid., p. 45.

65. ASKG/17–12–55/ Pieper, "Studien zum Wiederaufbau der Altstadt Lübeck: Kritik des Bestehenden," Fall 1943, p. 3. Emphasis in original. The 1946 version of Pieper's planning (*Lübeck*) reflects in its language the fact of the lost war, the presence of refugees, and the poverty of the city, but the goals are the same as in 1943. Some of Pieper's original wartime drawings, thought to have been destroyed, were recently found in the Lübeck building administration offices.

66. For Mühlenpfordt and Gruber, see Durth and Gutschow, *Träume in Trümmern*, pp. 826–31, and also Gruber, *Die Gestalt der deutschen Stadt. Ihr Wandel aus der geistigen Ordnung der Zeiten* (Munich, 1952), which is indicative of Gruber's approach to architecture and planning.

67. Memorandum from Karl Gruber, reprinted in Durth and Gutschow, *Träume in Trümmern*, p. 853.

68. Gerhard Graubner, "Der Wehrgedanke als Grundlage der Stadtgestaltung und Stadtplanung," December 1943, reprinted in Durth and Gutschow, *Träume in Trümmern*, pp. 771–76.

69. See Niels Gutschow, "Hamburg: the 'Catastrophe' of July 1943," pp. 118–20, and Durth and Gutschow, *Träume in Trümmern*, pp. 607–8.

70. Schmitt, *Der Neuaufbau der Stadt Köln*. The citations are from pp. 13, 20, 24, 28, and 109. In 1944 Carl Oskar Jatho, a friend of Adenauer, composed a dialogue on reconstruction that contained ideas like those of Schmitt. In *Urbanität. Über die Wiederkehr einer Stadt*, published in Düsseldorf in 1946, Jatho also attacks false monumentality, the romanticism of the nineteenth century, and the primacy of traffic planning. He too wanted Cologne rebuilt on the old building lots, but with new architecture, not an imitation of the old. Already in December 1943 city conservator Hans Vogts had composed a long memorandum calling for retention of the historic street pattern and housing forms. His ideas were clearly derived from his participation in the urban renewal program around the church of Groß St. Martin in the late 1930s. See HASK/171/426/Vogts, "Vorschläge für den Wiederaufbau Kölns," 23 December 1943, sent to Lord Mayor Adenauer, 26 July 1945.

71. The most extensive discussions of the Arbeitsstab are in Durth and Gutschow, *Träume in Trümmern*, Chapter 2, Durth, *Deutsche Architekten*, and Durth, "Der programmierte Aufbau—Speers Arbeitsstab zum Wiederaufbau bombenzerstörter Städte," *Stadtbauwelt* 84 (1984). See also Diefendorf, "Konstanty Gutschow."

72. Der Reichsminister für Rüstung und Kriegsproduktion an den Gauleiter des Gaues Weser-Ems Paul Wegener, SB/4,29/1–980. The letter of December 1943 is also reproduced in Durth and Gutschow, *Träume in Trümmern*, pp. 51–52.

73. Durth and Gutschow, *Träume in Trümmern*, pp. 56–57.

74. Interview of Hanffstengel by author, Nuremberg, 31 July 1982.

75. ASKG/"Richtlinien für die Statistik und Darstellung der Schäden in den zerstörten Städten," printed 15 July 1944, and distributed with a cover letter from Gutschow 27 July. By the end of the year, some 40 cities had submitted their damage reports. Durth and Gutschow, *Träume in Trümmern*, p. 65.

76. SH/Architekt Gutschow/A44: Schriftenreihe D. Gutschow continued to work on the guidelines for some 20 years after the war, hoping to produce a definitive text on urban planning. He collected vast quantities of material for this book, and it is puzzling that this hard-driven man, dedicated to his work, never finished the manuscript to his satisfaction. The material collected and parts of the manuscript are currently in the HAA/ Nachlaß Gutschow.

77. ASKG/Briefwechsel: Gutschow to Wortmann, 9 August 1944.

78. ASKG/Wiederaufbauplanung zerstörter Städte/1. Allgemeines/8. Blaue Durch-schläge: Verteilerlist of 25 November 1944; Gutschow to Wolters, 17 January 1945. On 22 November 1945, Gutschow had also written to Ministerialdirigent Steffens in Speer's ministry to complain that the continued construction of villas and single-family homes for "Prominenten" was a wasteful diversion of resources.

79. Five meetings were held in Wriezen. Minutes exist for the last four meet-ings, in ASKG/Arbeitsstab Wiederaufbauplanung and as provided by Hans von Hanffstengel.

80. Ibid., meeting of 19–21 August 1944, pp. 18, 31–32.

81. Notes on the discussion, p. 8, written by Hans von Hanffstëngel, 24 August 1944. Carbon given by von Hanffstängel to author.

82. The Germans were fascinated by and strongly approved of the approach em-bodied in the English town planning act of 1944, which gave very broad powers to planners to do the sort of things that they themselves wanted to do in Germany. From a special department in Speer's ministry, Gutschow's Hamburg office regularly received information, including clippings from English newspapers, on developments in city planning. HAA/Nachlaß Gutschow/B7/2: Gutschow to Wilhelm Wortmann, 29 Novem-ber 1944, notice of sending a copy of a "Bericht über den Wiederaufbau Großlondons nach dem Plan des Londoner City Council," provided by the Informationsdienst Ausland des Reichsministerium Speer "Sonderdienst Wiederaufbau."

83. Third Wriezen meeting of 16–17 September 1944, p. 18.

84. The list of planners and advisers for the 42 cities is reproduced in Durth and Gutschow, *Träume in Trümmern*, pp. 113–18.

85. SH/Architekt Gutschow/A134 and A135.

86. SH/Architekt Gutschow/A44/D1, "Zu den Vorskizzen für den Generalbe-bauungsplan 1944 und Wiederaufbauplan," 10 January 1944.

87. ASKG/Hamburger Wiederaufbauplanung 1944/45/4: Auftragsbearbeitungen 1–13; and presentations published in *Nachrichten für unsere Kameraden im Felde,* the "house journal" of Gutschow's office. Many of the participants in the planning process were active city planners after the war. Many of the basic premises, such as "Auflockerung" and "Durchgrünung," were common to most planners of the 1920s and 1930s in Germany. See Gustav Oelsner, "Wandlungen der städtebaulichen Grund-sätze," in *Hamburg und seine Bauten 1929–1953*, Architekten- und-Ingenieur Verein Hamburg, ed. (Hamburg, 1953).

88. ASKG/Hamburger Wiederaufbauplanung 1944/45/ 6: Generalbebauungsplan 1944, Erste Skizze, Äusserungen der Mitarbeiter, with marginal comments by Gutschow.

89. There are two documents for this presentation: SH/Architekt Gutschow/A44/ D38: "Skizze Generalbebauungsplan 1944," July 1944 (Manuskript Plassenburg); and ASKG/"Hamburger Generalplanung," Referat im Rahmen der 3. Arbeitsbesprechung des Arbeitsstabes Wiederaufbauplanung zerstörter Städte in Wriezen am 16./17. Sep-tember 1944. For a comparison of the 1940 and 1944 plans, see Annemarie Haack, "Der Generalbebauungsplan für Hamburg 1940/41 und 1944," *Uni HH Forschung* 12 (1980).

The illustrations presented by Gutschow at Wriezen demonstrate that he viewed his planning as a continuation of that of Fritz Schumacher.

90. SH/Architekt Gutschow/A44, D34: "Verwertung von Trümmern," September 1944, and D37: "Hamburger Hauptbahnhof," 9 October 1944.

91. ASKG/E5: Verkehrsverbesserungen, 23 August 1945.

92. SH/Architekt Gutschow/A45/E9: Wiederherstellungsgebiete, September 1945.

93. Gutschow supported his call for a new building law by basing his argument on an essay by Obersenatsrat Bahnson of the Baurechtsamt dated 1 September 1945, entitled "Gesetze zur Durchführung des Wiederaufbaues." In fact the ideas presented were quite in line with the discussions of building law that had been going on within the Arbeitsstab during the war.

94. ASKG/"Wiederaufbau Hamburg"/folder 271001, "Die Arbeitsweise bei der städtebaulichen Planung," Memorandum no. 1, October 1945, by the Arbeitsausschuss Stadtplanung. Comments also to be found in ASKG/E9: Wiederherstellungsgebiete. See also the work plan in SH/Baubehörde I/B2/Wiederaufbauleitung/E9: Wiederherstellungsgebiete, 8 August 1945.

95. SH/Baubehörde I/ BI/ Abschlußbericht der Sonderabteilung "Wiederaufbauleitung," 2 October 1945.

96. For the attacks on Gutschow after the war, see Diefendorf, "Konstanty Gutschow," pp. 163–65.

97. Elkart, "Erläuterungen zu dem Neugestaltungsplan der Gauhauptstadt Hannover," 1944/45, printed in full in Durth and Gutschow, *Träume in Trümmern*, pp. 776–86, here p. 779.

98. HAA/Nachlaß Gutschow/B7/1 and 2, correspondence between Gutschow, Graubner, and Wortmann. Graubner and Gutschow wrote, among other things, about finding the best candidate for the chair in town planning at the Technical University of Hannover.

99. HAA/ Nachlaß Gutschow/B7/2, Folder W. Letters from Wortmann to Gutschow, 15 August and 13 September 1944, and Gutschow to Wortmann, 18 August 1944.

Chapter 7

1. The most thorough exploration of the careers of German architects and planners in this period is Durth, *Deutsche Architekten*, but see also the many biographical sketches in Durth and Gutschow, *Träume in Trümmern*.

2. Both Konstanty Gutschow and Wilhelm Wortmann had worked in Schumacher's Hamburg office in 1927–28. See Niels Gutschow, "Fritz Schumacher— Vordenker für den Wiederaufbau zerstörter Städte in Norddeutschland," *Stadtbauwelt* 84 (1984): 346–49.

3. Fritz Schumacher, ed. *Lesebuch für Baumeister. Äusserungen über Architektur und Städtebau* (1947; rpt. Braunschweig, 1977).

4. Fritz Schumacher, "Erkenntnisse für den Wiederaufbau zerstörter Städte," *Die Neue Stadt* 2 (1948). (Published posthumously.)

5. For the Stuttgart school, see Ulrike Pampe, ed. *Heinz Wetzel und die Geschichte der Städtebaulehre an deutschen Hochschulen* (Stuttgart, 1982), and Wolfgang Voigt, "Die Stuttgarter Schule und die Alltagsarchitektur des Dritten Reiches," in *Faschistische Architekturen: Planen und Bauen in Europa 1930 bis 1945*, Hartmut Frank, ed., Stadt, Planung, Geschichte, vol. 3 (Hamburg, 1985).

6. Durth and Gutschow, *Träume in Trümmern*, p. 224, n. 37.

7. For general biographical material on Gropius, see Sigfried Giedion, *Walter Gropius: Work and Teamwork* (Zurich, 1954); William H. Jordy, "The Aftermath of the Bauhaus in America. Gropius, Mies, and Breuer," in *The Intellectual Migration. Europe and America, 1930–1960*, Donald Fleming and Bernard Bailyn, eds. (Cambridge, Mass., 1969); and, most important, Isaacs, *Walter Gropius*. For Wagner, Klaus Wächter, "Martin Wagner," in *Handwörterbuch der Raumforschung und Raumordnung*, 2nd ed. (Hannover, 1970), pp. 3665–3671; and Kempmann, *Das Ideengut Martin Wagners*. More architects were trained by Gropius at Harvard than at the original Bauhaus. His American students include such well-known men as Edward Larrabee Barnes, John Johansen, Philip Johnson, I. M. Pei, Paul Rudolph, and Ulrich Franzen. (Of these, only Pei received a masters degree in architecture; the others received bachelors of architecture degrees. All, however, heard Gropius lecture and attended sessions evaluating projects.) For a critical view of the Bauhaus influence, see Klaus Herdig, *The Decorated Diagram: Harvard Architecture and the Failure of the Bauhaus Legacy* (Cambridge, Mass., 1983).

8. These ideas can be found in many publications, including "Cities' Renaissance," a manuscript written by Wagner and Gropius in 1942 (in HLH, Gropius Papers, bMS Ger 208 [56]; the quotes here are from p. 13); Wagner and Gropius, "The New City Pattern for the People and by the People," in *The Problem of the Cities and the Towns: Conference on Urbanism*, Harvard, 5–6 March 1942 (Cambridge, Mass., 1942); Gropius, "The Architect's Contribution to the Postwar Construction Program," *The Bay State Builder* 1, no. 12 (1943); Wagner's "American versus German City Planning," *The Journal of Land and Public Utility Economics* 22 (1946); and Wagner, "Der Neubau der City," *Baurundschau* 38 (1948). The latter is a fascinating report on a project for the total redesign of central Boston, undertaken by Wagner's master class at Harvard. Gropius always favored teamwork, whereas Wagner preferred leadership by a single individual.

9. HLH, Gropius Papers, bMS Ger 208 (1472), Scharoun to Gropius, 17 April 1948.

10. HLH, Gropius Papers, bMS Ger 208 (646), Döcker to Gropius, 6 March 1950.

11. HLH, Gropius Papers, bMS Ger 208 (1202), Meyer-Ottens to Gropius, 13 September 1947.

12. HLH, Gropius Papers, bMS Ger 208 (381), Architektenring Düsseldorf to Gropius, 11 March 1952.

13. HLH, Gropius Papers, bMS Ger 208 (1063): Kühn to Gropius, 20 April 1951.

14. HLH, Gropius Papers, bMS Ger 208 (342); only Gropius's reply to Adenauer, dated 6 October 1951, remains in the file.

15. Reported in *Die Neue Stadt* 1 (1947): 128–29.

16. Karl Bonatz, "Anmerkungen zu den Presseinterviews mit Professor Gropius und zu seinem Vortrag im Titania-Palast am 22. August 1947," and Hans Scharoun, "Gropius als Gast der Technischen Universität Berlin," both in *Neue Bauwelt* 2 (1947): 550–51, and 583.

17. Gropius, "Reconstruction: Germany," pp. 35–36. Gropius was criticizing Ernst Neufert, who as a young man had helped run Gropius's bureau in Weimar but who had later worked with the Nazi regime. See Isaacs, *Walter Gropius*, 2:957, for Gropius's feelings about Neufert. For Neufert under the Nazis, see Durth, "Der programmierte Aufbau," pp. 383–84.

18. Reported in *Die Neue Stadt* 1 (1947): 128; HLH, Gropius Papers, bMS Ger 208 (854), Gropius to Hebebrand, 19 December 1947. In fact this episode is rather unclear. Clay asked Gropius to write a highly confidential report on possible planning for

Frankfurt as a capital city for West Germany. The press did not find out about this until Gropius returned to the United States, and the news of this report made something of a stir. There is nothing in the Gropius papers to indicate that he really intended to initiate a student project on Frankfurt, though it is clear that the planners and journalists who had met with Gropius in Frankfurt were led to believe that such a planning project was in the works. Possibly Gropius raised such an idea to deflect attention from his secret assignment in that city. See Isaacs, *Walter Gropius*, 2:960–62. Hillebrecht, reporting on his meeting with Gropius in Stuttgart, wrote: "Gropius ist in seiner Seele ein Deutscher geblieben." Gropius's subsequent career suggests otherwise. See Rudolf Hillebrecht, "Gespräch mit Gropius," *Baurundschau* 38 (1948): 70.

19. Correspondence of Wagner with the Luckhardt brothers, 1946, in the manuscript collection of the Loeb Library, Harvard School of Design; and HLH, Gropius Papers, bMS Ger 208 (887), letters between Gropius and Hillebrecht, Fall 1946; in 1953 he delivered an address to the Deutscher Verband für Wohnungswesen, Städtebau und Raumplanung, in which he called for radically lowered building costs.

20. Martin Wagner, "Aufbau-Planung contra Trümmer-Planung," *Baurundschau* 38 (1948): 243ff.

21. Karl Bonatz, "Der neue Plan von Berlin," *Neue Bauwelt* 2 (1947): 759, 762. Martin Wagner proposed that instead of rebuilding a huge metropolis in an age when such cities were outdated, one would be better off to abandon the ruins of old Berlin and build new, smaller, and modern cities on new locations. Examples of Wagner's ideas, and his sharp critique of Berlin's reconstruction planning, are to be found in "Aufbau-Planung contra Trümmer-Planung," pp. 243ff; "Maßstab, Mut und Meisterschaft," *Baurundschau* 38 (1948); "Die Utopien der Realisten," *Bauen und Wohnen* 3 (1948); "Vernunft—Perspektiven im Städtebau," *Die Neue Stadt* 4 (1950): 140–43; "Wurzelprobleme der Aufbaufinanzierung," *Norddeutscher Baublatt*, no. 2 (1950); and his letter published in *Neue Bauwelt* 1 (1946): 549.

22. Martin Wagner, "Ein offener Brief Martin Wagners an Karl Bonatz," *Neue Bauwelt* 2 (1947); and reply from Bonatz, in *Neue Bauwelt* 3 (1948): 99–102; Gropius to Hillebrecht, 14 October 1948, in HLH, Gropius Papers, bMS Ger 208 (887). Alfons Leitl, "Plädoyer aus Deutschland," *Baukunst und Werkform* 4 (1951): 26, in an answer to Wagner's demand that the old bombed cities be abandoned, noted that when he first walked on the bank of the Main River across from the ruins of Frankfurt, the view reminded him that there was still too much substance, "something fundamentally characteristic" that still remained and that the inhabitants would give up only if forced to do so.

23. *Neue Bauwelt* 2 (1947): 549.

24. The letters are reproduced in Franz Rosenberg, *Vom Wiederaufbau und von der Stadterweiterung in Bremen in den Jahren 1949–1970. Ein subjektiver Bericht* (Bremen, 1981), typescript in SB.

25. Wilhelm Seidensticker, "Aufgaben des Städtebaues," *Die Neue Stadt* 5 (1951): 301–7.

26. HLH, Gropius Papers, bMS Ger 208 (887), Hillebrecht to Gropius, 9 August and 3 September 1948. Kempmann, *Das Ideengut Martin Wagners*, p. 41, notes that throughout his period of exile, Wagner's attention remained focused on Berlin, so it is quite possible that Wagner might not have accepted an appointment in Hamburg, even if it had been offered.

27. HLH, Gropius Papers, bMS Ger 208 (887), Gropius to Hillebrecht, 14 October 1948, in English. Ironically, both Hillebrecht and Wagner had, independently, savagely attacked Meyer-Ottens, Hamburg's current planner, in notes to Gropius. In

his letter of 9 August, Hillebrecht described Meyer-Ottens as "ein wilder Mann, ein richtiger Bauleitertyp mit allen Vorzügen, aber dann ist es auch aus!" When Meyer-Ottens sent Gropius a copy of a speech he delivered on planning in Hamburg, Gropius passed it on to Wagner, who wrote back that "Meyer-Ottens steht aber lange auf meiner 'Totenliste'—weil er für seinen Posten einfach nicht vor- und nicht nachgebildet ist!" This is in HLH, Gropius Papers, bMS Ger 208 (1202), attached to Meyer-Ottens "The General Town Planning Scheme 1947."

28. HLH, Gropius Papers, bMS Ger 208 (1681), letter of 8 September 1940, in English.

29. They had a bitter, if private, argument over authorship and publication of a project on "townlets" (Wagner claimed full authorship and felt that Gropius was obstructing publication) and more generally over the polemical tone of some of Wagner's recent public statements and publications. Asking Gropius to debate him openly on the merits of his ideas, Wagner wrote: "Now, Gropius, you know perfectly well that I am a Parsifal of truth and justice, and therefore I can always say everything I think in good conscience." Gropius replied by calling Wagner "egocentric" and "arrogant" in "boasting" of his "love of truth." HLH, Gropius Papers, bMS Ger 208 (1681), letters of 6 and 22 December 1948. On 27 February 1937, Wagner had written: "Kein Zweifel, lieber Gropius, dass ich meinem Führer selbst bis nach U.S.A. folgen und sogar amerikanischer Staatsbürger werden würde, wenn er es von mir verlangt." Part of Gropius's letter of 17 December 1948 is reproduced in Isaacs, *Walter Gropius*, 2:973. Wagner and his "Führer" never worked together again. In spite of the evidence of this split, Isaacs, who knew both men well, assured the author in an interview in Cambridge on 26 February 1985 that Wagner and Gropius continued to respect each other, even after their break. Theirs was a professional disagreement—serious enough—but not an actual feud.

There was no public conflict, but Wagner got in a last word—and publicly—in 1956, a year before his death. In an article published in *Baurundschau*, he denounced Gropius, Le Corbusier, and the whole CIAM movement. He argued that modern building had its origins in Berlin before the advent of the Bauhaus; hence Gropius was not the pioneer that everyone believed. Furthermore, Wagner claimed that Gropius himself was not solely or primarily responsible for any work or project, apart from his house in Lincoln, Massachusetts. By implication, whatever was creative or valuable about Gropius's work was in fact attributable not to Gropius but to his assistants and collaborators. As for the Lincoln house, Wagner found it hardly habitable, however fine its aesthetic qualities. There was not even a place where one could work! Gropius's admirers offered to defend him against this attack, but Gropius thought it best not to respond. To Werner Hebebrand Gropius wrote: "The offensive articles, which he has published everywhere, can be passed over in silence. I do not believe that there is any point in responding to them." Nothing was to be gained by a final dispute with his former friend and colleague. See Martin Wagner, "Kapazitäten oder Schwanengesang?" *Baurundschau* 46 (1956), and Isaacs, *Walter Gropius*, 2:1076.

Gropius's career and reputation suffered no damage from either his disagreements with Wagner or his disinclination to become heavily involved in German reconstruction. For Wagner's reputation, on the contrary, the consequences of his biting polemics and his attack on Gropius were serious. His work has, until quite recently, languished in comparative obscurity.

30. This collective portrait is based on the data contained in the biographical sketches scattered throughout Durth and Gutschow, *Träume in Trümmern*. The portrait fits Rudolf Hillebrecht quite well, for example, though he was born in 1910 and

was thus younger than average. In noting Hillebrecht's seventieth birthday, Gerd Albers called him the most important postwar German planner and compared him in importance with Fritz Schumacher of the previous generation. See Albers, "Rudolf Hillebrecht und drei Jahrzehnte Städtebau," *Bauwelt* 71 (1980): 432.

31. For a critical analysis of the planning profession, see Berndt, *Das Gesellschaftsbild bei Stadtplanern.*

32. The private gathering of architects and planners organized by Hillebrecht at the Constructa exhibition in 1951 was described in the chapter on housing. For meetings organized in 1947 and 1949 by Rudolf Wolters of former members of the reconstruction planning group, see Durth, *Deutsche Architekten*, pp. 265ff.

33. For example, "Liste der ständigen Ausschüße" (List of Standing Committees) as of December 1950, Deutscher Verband für Wohnungswesen, Städtebau und Raumplanung, in HSANRW/ NW72/ 783/ 42–5, dated 10 August 1951. Here one finds names of such planners as Hebebrand, Hillebrecht, Leitl, Riphahn, Schmeissner, Schönleben, Schwarz, Schwippert, Rappaport, Göderitz, Blanck, Boehm, Dittus, Wambsganz, and Elsässer.

34. As examples of this sort of interpretation, Erich Konter, "Deutsche Planer und Architekten," p. 84, makes this rather ambiguous observation: "That planning of rebuilding which in the end introduced what we now consider the 'second destruction' [of the city] was still a product of National Socialism or respectively went through it." Further, Dirk Schubert, *Stadtplanung als Ideologie. Eine theoriegeschichtliche, ideologiekritische Untersuchung der Stadt, des Städtebaus und Wohnungsbaus in Deutschland ca. 1850 bis heute* (Diss., Freie Universität, Berlin, 1981), p. 193, insists that postwar planning is no more than an extension of Nazi planning and that there was no continuity with the modernism of the 1920s. Schubert also accepts the argument that Walter Gropius and Martin Wagner were prevented from returning to Germany by the former Nazis who had driven them into exile.

35. In the three years before his death in 1947, Fritz Schumacher also sought to articulate these common planning goals. See the manuscript of December 1944, SB/ 4,29/1–487 (partly reproduced in Niels Gutschow, "Fritz Schumacher," pp. 346ff; and Schumacher, "Erkenntnisse für den Wiederaufbau zerstörter Städte."

36. Central texts here are Hans Bernhard Reichow, *Organische Stadtbaukunst. Von der Großstadt zur Stadtlandschaft* (Braunschweig, Berlin, and Vienna, 1948), and Göderitz, Rainer, and Hoffmann, *Die gegliederte und aufgelockerte Stadt.* Both were begun during the war, but their contents were already well known through articles and contacts with other planners. Durth and Gutschow, *Träume in Trümmern*, pp. 161ff, and von Beyme, *Wiederaufbau*, pp. 75ff, use the term *Leitbilder* for the guiding concepts.

37. Many German planners criticized the schematic designs heralded by some of the supporters of Le Corbusier. Typical is Philipp Rappaport, "Deutsche Städte oder Kolonialstädte?" *Wiederaufbau-Mitteilungen des Bauausschusses des Deutschen Städtetags*, no. 5 (31 March 1947): 1–2, and Rappaport, "Das Ruhrgebiet—ein Rückblick, ein Ausblick," *Der Städtetag*, new series 4 (1951): 235.

38. These goals can be found in many places. The best known is Göderitz, Rainer, and Hoffmann, *Die gegliederte und aufgelockerte Stadt.* For other examples, Philipp Rappaport, *Der Wiederaufbau der deutschen Städte* (Essen, 1946); Ludwig Neundörfer, "Auflockerung von Arbeits- und Wohnstätten," *Wiederaufbau zerstörter Städte*, no. 6 (1947); Hans Högg, "Der Neuaufbau der zerstörten Städte als zentrale Aufgabe unserer Zeit," *Abhandlungen und Vorträge*, Die Wittheit zu Bremen, vol. 18, no. 2 (Bremen, 1949); Herbert Boehm, "Wirtschaftliche Baulanderschliessung. Bebauungs- und Besiedlungsdichte," in *Amtlicher Katalog der Constructa Bauausstellung 1951* (Hannover,

1951), p. 87; W. Zinkahn, "Die gegenwärtige Situation des Baurechts in der Bundes-republik Deutschland," *Der Aufbau* 8 (1953): 358.

39. Philipp Rappaport, "Gedanken zum deutschen Städtebau," *Der Aufbau* 8 (1953): 352.

40. Göderitz, Rainer, and Hoffmann, *Die gegliederte und aufgelockerte Stadt,* p. 8. Hans Bernhard Reichow in particular created the model for such illustrations with his *Organische Stadtbaukunst.* See also Peter Lammert, "Die gegliederte und aufge-lockerte Stadt vor und nach 1945. Eine Skizze zur Planungsgeschichte," *Die alte Stadt* 14 (1987): p. 356.

41. Göderitz, Rainer, and Hoffmann, *Die gegliederte und aufgelockerte Stadt,* p. 23. See also the essays in Erich Kühn, ed., *Medizin und Städtebau,* 2 vols. (Munich, Berlin, and Vienna, 1957). Berndt, *Die Gesellschaftsbild bei Stadtplanern,* pp. 75, 81, argues that the emphasis on greenery was virtually a fetish, "an abstract counterpart to the artificiality of society."

42. Rainer, *Die Behausungsfrage,* p. 19.

43. Ursula von Petz, "Nachkriegsplanung und Wiederaufbau in Deutschland," notes that the regional planning organization of the Ruhr, the Siedlungsverband Ruhrkohlenbezirk, had too little competence to be effective, and by 1975 it had ceased to be a planning agency altogether.

44. Kevin Lynch, *A Theory of Good City Form* (Cambridge, Mass., and London, 1981), pp. 72ff.

45. Alfons Leitl, "What's Wrong with German City Planning? The Lessons of Reconstruction," *Landscape* 5 (1955–56): 29.

46. Erich Kühn, "Organische Stadtplanung," in *Amtlicher Katalog der Constructa Bauausstellung 1951* (Hannover, 1951), pp. 84–86.

47. Hubert Hoffmann, for example, had helped organize the congresses of CIAM in Amsterdam in 1931 and in Athens in 1933, and he had contributed to the formula-tion of the Charter of Athens. An abbreviated version of the charter was published in Germany in early 1948, the full text in 1949. It was defended against critics by Hoff-mann, who noted that the English had made progress in realizing its ideals during the years when the Nazis were denouncing the Charter. The first German translation of the charter was published in 1947 in Saarbrücken in the *Bau-Anzeiger.* A shortened version—which was much more widely seen—was published by Hans Martin Kampff-meyer, "Die Charta von Athen," *Die Neue Stadt* 2 (1948): 66–68. The full version was again published in *Neue Bauwelt* 4 (1949): 573–79, with a defense by Hoffmann the following month (pp. 677–78). On the publication history, Ulrich Höhns, "Stadt-planung in Saarbrücken 1940–1960," in *Neue Städte aus Ruinen. Deutscher Städtebau der Nachkriegszeit,* Klaus von Beyme, Werner Durth, Niels Gutschow, Winfried Nerdinger, and Thomas Topfstedt, eds. (Munich, 1992).

48. "Ausführungen des Architekten Blanck über die städtebauliche Planung Kölns am 11.11.1946," dated 12 November 1946, in HASK/2/137, and Rudolf Schwarz, "Bericht zu Stadtvertretung u. Stadtverwaltung über eine Studienreise durch England," in HASK/2/1315. He visited England in February and March 1949. Such visits continued in the following decade. See Gottlob Binder (president of the Deutscher Verband für Wohnungswesen, Städtebau und Raumplanung), "Eindrücke vom Wohnungs- und Städtebau in England," in HSANRW/ NW 72/ 483/ 55–8. See also Friedhelm Fischer, "German Reconstruction as an International Activity," in *Rebuilding Europe's Bombed Cities,* Jeffry M. Diefendorf, ed. (London and New York, 1990), p. 139.

49. For example, HSANRW/NW/73/ 146/ Hans Schwippert to Erich Kühn, "Pla-nungsrichtlinien," 28 July 1947, pp. 1, 20.

50. Rappaport, "Wünsche und Wirklichkeit des deutschen Wiederaufbaus," p. 9.

51. RWWA/1/23/1, Bauwesen, Allgemeines, vol. 1/Verband Rheinischer Haus- und Grundbesitzer e.V. Köln, "Hausbesitz und Wiederaufbau," 12 November 1946, p. 4.

52. HSANRW/NW 73/146/ P. Rappaport to Minister für Wiederaufbau, Gruppe Planung, 8 March 1948. This volume also contains drafts by Erich Kühn, Hans Schwippert, Dipl. Ing. Weiß, and Dr. Ing. Feuchtinger. Another version is in HSANRW/NW 72/ 520/ E. Kühn to Oberbaurat Dr. Prager, "Städtebaugrundsätze," 13 February 1948.

53. For example, Höhns, "Stadtplanung in Saarbrücken 1940–1960." The French architect Georges-Henri Pingusson proposed a vertical garden city of skyscrapers along the lines favored by Le Corbusier.

54. A distinction was sometimes made between a *Großstadt*, or metropolis, and a *Weltstadt*, or world city. Claims had been made for Berlin as a *Weltstadt* in the nineteenth century. See Joachim H. Schultze, "Die Weltstadt als Objekt geographischer Forschung" and Martin Pfannschmidt, "Probleme der Weltstadt Berlin," both in *Zum Problem der Weltstadt*, Joachim H. Schultze, ed. Deutscher Geographentag, vol. 32 (Berlin, 1959).

55. Whyte, *Bruno Taut*.

56. The most extensive study of planning in Berlin is Frank Werner, *Stadtplanung Berlin: Theorie und Realität* (Berlin, 1976). A recent survey is Harald Bodenschatz, Hans Claussen, Karolus Heil, Wolfgang Schäche, Wolfgang J. Streich, Udo Dittfurth, Elke Herden, Stefan Metz, Andreas Schleicher, and Renate Villnow, "Nach 1945: Wiederaufbau, zweite Zerstörung und neue Tendenzen," in *750 Jahre Architektur und Städtebau in Berlin*, Josef Paul Kleihues, ed. (Stuttgart, 1987).

57. "Tätigkeitsbericht des Stadtrates für Bau- und Wohnungswesen des Magistrats von Groß-Berlin von Mai–Dezember 1945," reproduced in Scharoun, *Hans Scharoun. Bauten, Entwürfe, Texte*, pp. 153, 156.

58. Scharoun, "Vortrag anlässlich der Ausstellung 'Berlin plant—erster Bericht,' gehalten am 5.9.1946," in *Hans Scharoun. Bauten, Entwürfe, Texte*, p. 158. In 1949, long after Scharoun's plan had been rejected, Ernst Stähler, an engineer for water works, submitted to the planning office a proposal for a general Berlin plan in which he also called for radical decentralization of the city and a massive relocation of the population into peripheral areas. Berlin would disappear into its surrounding region, and planning for Berlin would simultaneously be planning for Brandenburg. This would have the advantage, among others, of making Berlin a less likely target in the event of atomic war. BSBWB/ unpublished memorandum, "Berlin—Gesamtplanung," 20 June 1949.

59. Goerd Peschken, "Stadtlandschaft: Scharouns städtebauliche Vision für Berlin und ihre Provinzialisierung," in *Die Metropole. Industriekultur in Berlin im 20. Jahrhundert*, Jochen Boberg, Tilman Fichter, and Eckhart Gillen, eds. (Munich, 1986), p. 304.

60. "Professor Hans Scharoun sprach zur Eröffnung der Berliner Ausstellung," *Der Bauhelfer* 1, no. 5 (1946): 5. See also Wils Ebert, a member of Scharoun's circle, who wrote of "a zone of central functions," in "Gedanken zur Raumplanung von Berlin," *Neue Bauwelt* 3 (1948): 148.

61. Walter Moest, *Der Zehlendorfer Plan. Ein Vorschlag zum Wiederaufbau Berlins* (Berlin, 1946), pp. 14–15. See Hans Stimmann, "Die autogerechte Stadt," in *Die Metropole. Industriekultur in Berlin im 20. Jahrhundert*, Jochen Boberg, Tilman Fichter, and Eckhart Gillen, eds. (Munich, 1986), for a discussion of postwar traffic planning in Berlin.

62. Moest, *Der Zehlendorfer Plan,* pp. 11, 30.
63. Hans Josef Zechlin, "Das schönere Berlin," *Neue Bauwelt* 1, no. 16 (1946): 3–7.
64. Max Taut, "Betrachtungen zum Aufbau Berlins," *Der Bauhelfer* 1, no. 2 (1946): 5; and Taut, *Berlin im Aufbau* (Berlin, 1946), which contains large-format color drawings of Taut's vision of the new city.
65. Paul Mast, "Gedanken zum Aufbau Berlins," *Neue Bauwelt,* 1, no. 17 (1946): 8. There were other proposals that cannot be discussed here. Published essays include Wilhelm Havemann, *Berlin in der Zukunft. Die Grundlagen der städtebaulichen und wirtschaftlichen Zukunftsmöglichkeiten Berlins, gleichzeitig der Versuch einer kritischen Beleuchtung der Aufbaupläne* (Berlin, 1946); Hans Borstorff, *Stadt ohne Zentrum. Gedanken über die notwendige Wiedererrichtung der Berliner City und des Zoobereiches: Ein Beitrag zur Berlin-Planung* (Berlin, 1948). There was also a solicitation of proposals from the public as part of the exhibition "Berlin plant," but the submissions were disappointing. Material on this is in the Scharoun papers in the Akademie der Künste, Berlin.
66. Forty years after Scharoun's group drew up its plan, Wolf Jobst Siedler, a Berlin journalist and publisher who sat on the city government's planning committee during the 1950s, remarked that "whoever would make the river bed of the ice age into the guiding concept for rebuilding a destroyed city makes the Neanderthal man into the general planner." Kampffmeyer, Spengelin, and Siedler, "'Zu Beginn der 60er Jahre,' " p. 331. His criticism of the Scharoun plan would have been shared by most Berliners.
67. AdKB/Nachlaß Scharoun, Magistrat/ Mappe "Ausstellung 'Berlin Plant' "/ Erläuterung Dr. Runge, SPD, 2 September 1946.
68. Bonatz, "Der neue Plan von Berlin," p. 755.
69. Karl Bonatz, "Meine Stellungnahme zu den Planungsarbeiten für Groß-Berlin, die ich bei meinem Amtsantritt vorfand," *Neue Bauwelt* 2 (1947): 163.
70. Flächennutzungsplan, Stadtverordnetenversammlung Berlin, Drucksache 1034, II. Wahlperiode (23 September 1950), p. 2.
71. Walter Moest and Richard Ermisch, "Zum Gestaltbild der Berliner City," *Neue Bauwelt* 2 (1947): 788 and passim.
72. See *Neue Bauwelt* 3 (1948): 579–85, and 4 (1949): 109ff, 516–18, 536–37.
73. Karl Bonatz, "Rund um den Zoo," *Neue Bauwelt* 4 (1949): 639; see also Stadverordnetenversammlung Berlin, Drucksache 2443, I. Wahlperiode (31 December 1953), and the debate in *Stenographische Berichte des Abgeordnetenhauses,* 1. Wahlperiode (2 March 1954). For a brief study of the problems experienced by Bonn as it became the capital of the Federal Republic, see Dietrich Höroldt, "Von der Bürgerstadt zur Bundeshauptstadt," in *Städte nach zwei Weltkriegen,* Walter Först, ed. (Cologne, 1984). See also Heinz Heineberg, "Service Centres in East and West Berlin," in *The Socialist City. Spatial Structure and Urban Policy,* R. A. French and F. E. Ian Hamilton, eds., (Chichester, 1979).
74. There are several good studies of planning in East Berlin. Most extensive is Frank Werner, *Städtebau Berlin-Ost* (Berlin, 1969) and Thomas Topfstedt, *Grundlinien der Entwicklung von Städtebau und Architektur in der Deutschen Demokratischen Republik 1949 bis 1955* (Diss., Karl-Marx-University Leipzig, 1980). An excellent brief treatment is Christian Borngräber, "Die sozialistische Metropole. Planung und Aufbau der Stalinallee und des Zentrums in Ost-Berlin 1949–1961," in *Die Metropole. Industriekultur in Berlin im 20. Jahrhundert,* Jochen Boberg, Tilman Fichter, and Eckhart Gillen, eds. (Munich, 1986).
75. In a memorable essay, Ulbricht denounced modernist architects, saying that "in their cosmopolitan fantasies, they believe that one could put up buildings in Berlin

that would just as well be built in the South African landscape." Borngräber, "Die sozialistische Metropole," p. 331.

76. All West Berlin publications contained protests over this action. For example, see *Neue Bauwelt* 5, no. 40 (Architekturteil) (1950): 165–68.

77. Karl Bonatz, "Fortführung der Stadtplanung in Berlin im Jahre 1950," *Neue Bauwelt* 5 (1950): 23.

78. The Flächennutzungsplan was presented to the city council as Drucksache 1034, II. Wahlperiode (23 September 1950).

79. BSBWB/Protokoll über der Sitzungen des Preisgerichts zum internationalen städtebaulichen Ideenwettbewerb 'Hauptstadt Berlin,' June 1958. The jury included Herbert Jensen of Kiel, Rudolf Hillebrecht of Hannover, Werner Hebebrand of Hamburg, and Hans Stephan of Berlin. Now that the division of the city has been ended, these proposals are of some interest to current planners.

80. "Die Neugestaltung des Hansaviertels in Berlin. Ergebnisse eines Ideenwettbewerbes," *Baukunst und Werkform* 7 (1954): 31ff; *Interbau Berlin 1957. Amtlicher Katalog der Internationalen Bauausstellung* (Berlin, 1957).

81. The planning controversies in Mainz are discussed in detail in Jean-Louis Cohen and Hartmut Frank, eds. *Deutsch-französische Beziehungen 1940–1950 und ihre Auswirkungen auf Architektur und Stadtgestalt* (unpublished manuscript, 1989), 2:175–480; Durth, "Mainz: Blockierte Moderne," and Durth and Gutschow, *Träume in Trümmern*, pp. 880ff.

82. Quoted in Durth and Gutschow, *Träume in Trümmern*, p. 914.

83. See Schlippe, "Wie Freiburg wiedererstehen soll?" and Schlippe, "Der Wiederaufbau für Freiburg," *Die Neue Stadt* 1 (1947): 115ff. An often-cited example is also Freudenstadt in the Schwarzwald, but this small town falls outside the framework of this book. It is interesting that here too Paul Schmitthenner was called in by former students to support the city building office against reform measures endorsed by the state government. See Hartmut Frank, "Auf der Suche nach der alten Stadt," and Durth and Gutschow, *Träume in Trümmern*, pp. 541ff.

84. Schwarz, "Baustelle Deutschland," p. 54.

85. Rudolf Schwarz, "Das Anliegen der Baukunst," in *Mensch und Raum*, Darmstädter Gespräch, no. 2 (Darmstadt, 1952), p. 71.

86. Schwarz, "Gedanken zum Wiederaufbau von Köln," p. 8.

87. Rudolf Schwarz, "Das Unplanbare," *Baukunst und Werkform* 1 (1947): 82.

88. Ibid., 83.

89. Schwarz, "Gedanken zum Wiederaufbau von Köln," pp. 13–14.

90. Ibid., p. 15.

91. Schwarz, *Das neue Köln*, p. 8.

92. Rudolf Schwarz, "Der Wiederaufbau von Köln," 18 April 1947, in HASK/30/66.

93. Ibid., p. 14.

94. Schwarz, *Das neue Köln*, pp. 18–19, 27.

95. Ibid., pp. 23–24.

96. HASK/2/1323/ "Berichte von Prof. Dr. Schwarz und Prof. Dr. Neundörfer über die Kölner Stadtplanung in der nichtöffentlichen Sitzung der Stadtvertretung am 24 Juni 1948," pp. 24–26.

97. Schwarz, "Gedanken zum Wiederaufbau von Köln," p. 17.

98. Schwarz here echoed the earlier proposals of Karl Band, "Gedanken zum Wiederaufbau unserer Stadt," 29 June 1945, in HASK/ 2/1313. Band, who subsequently worked with Schwarz in the city's Wiederaufbaugesellschaft, wanted Cologne rebuilt as a modernized version of a medieval city.

99. Schwarz, "Gedanken zum Wiederaufbau von Köln," p. 12.

100. For an explanation of the plans for Cologne, see Schwarz, *Das neue Köln*.

101. LC, Mies van der Rohe Papers, General Office Files (1923–69), container 53, Schwarz to Mies, 9 October 1948.

102. HASK/2/1323/ 4: Schwarz to Görlinger, 25 February 1952.

103. Schwarz, "Das neue Köln," and Eduard Pecks, "Kölner Stadtplanung, Erfahrungen und Sorgen," *Baukunst und Werkform* 10 (1957): 250, 265ff. For sharp criticism of Schwarz's planning efforts, see Ernest Thomas Greene, "Planning in Post-War Cologne," *Town and Country Planning* 28 (1960).

104. See Markus Caris, "Verkehr, Verkehrspolitik und Stadtplanung in Köln 1945–1948," *Geschichte in Köln*, no. 14 (1983).

105. The best study of the rebuilding of this area is Greene, *Politics and Geography in Postwar German Planning*.

106. Werner Durth uses the phrase "hectic pragmatism" for the period after the currency reform of 1948, but the widespread complaints about slow planning suggest more plodding than hectic activity. "Utopia in Niemands-Land," p. 222.

107. Rudolf Hillebrecht, "Neuaufbau der Städte," in *Städtebau als Herausforderung. Ausgewählte Schriften und Vorträge* (Cologne, 1975), p. 40. Originally published in 1957.

108. Leo Grebler noted in his pioneering study of 1956 that the main planning themes in European reconstruction were "traffic improvements and decongestion in central areas," in *Europe's Reborn Cities*, Urban Land Institute Technical Bulletin 28 (Washington, D.C., 1956), p. 17.

109. Mulzer, *Der Wiederaufbau der Altstadt von Nürnberg*, pp. 8–9, 25, 31–33, 41.

110. SAM/Bauamt-Wiederaufbau/1095, "Statistik," I, Section III (1949); and Helmut Koenig, *München setzt Stein auf Stein* (Munich, 1958). This was an official report of the city building office.

111. Herbert Jensen, "Stadtplanung und Baupolitik der Stadt Kiel seit 1945," *Neue Bauwelt* 7 (1952): 97.

112. Herbert Boehm, "Kiels inner Neugestaltung," *Die Neue Stadt* 2 (1948): 287ff.

113. Hans Bernhard Reichow, "Organischer Aufbau der Stadt Kiel," *Die Neue Stadt* 2 (1948): 329–41.

114. See Bundesministerium für Wohnungsbau, *Aufbau Kiel Holtenauer Straße: Ein Beispiel für städtebauliche Neuordnung durch Zusammenlegung* (Bonn, n.d., but probably 1957), and Ernest Thomas Greene, "West German City Reconstruction: Two Case Studies," *Sociology Review* 7 (1959): 237ff.

115. Herbert Jensen, "Neuaufbau der Innenstadt—eine Lebensfrage für die Stadt Kiel," *Baurundschau* 40 (1950); Jensen, "Stadtplanung und Baupolitik der Stadt Kiel seit 1945," and Greene, *Politics and Geography in Postwar German City Planning*.

116. Roland Rainer, "Auferstehung einer zerstörten Stadt," *Der Aufbau* 7 (1952): 393.

117. HASK/ 5/ 673, Hans Schwippert, "Notizen zum Wiederaufbau Aachens," 12 May 1945.

118. SAA/Verwaltungsbericht der Stadt Aachen zugleich Bericht über den bisherigen Wiederaufbau, 1 December 1944 to 31 December 1946 (Aachen, 1947), p. 34; Verwaltungsbericht der Stadt Aachen für das Jahr 1948 (Aachen, 1949), p. 27; and interview with Aachen's Verwaltungsdirektor Paul Müllejans, 1 July 1982.

119. Wilhelm K. Fischer, "Die Neuplanung Aachens nach dem zweiten Weltkrieg," in *Das alte Aachen, seine Zerstörung und sein Wiederaufbau*, Bernhard Poll and Albert Huyskens, eds. (Aachen, 1953), p. 159. For other brief summaries of his

planning, see Fischer, "Probleme der Stadtplanung Aachens nach der Zerstörung," *Der Deutscher Baumeister* 16 (1955): 195–200, and Fischer, *Aachen plant: 1950–1975* (Aachen, 1975). The latter is a reprint of a pamphlet first published in conjunction with an exhibition of the plans in 1950.

120. Wilhelm Fischer, "Erläuterungsbericht der städtebauliche Neuplanung der Stadt Aachen" (mimeo, Aachen, 1952), p. 3. This document, the "Neuordnungsplan der Stadt Aachen 1950," and the "Leitbild der Stadt Aachen 1956 (Änderung und Ergänzung des Leitplans vom Jahre 1950)," the key planning documents of the 1950s, were generously made available to me by Verwaltungsdirektor Paul Müllejans. All were in the files of the Aachen city building office.

121. "Erläuterungsbericht" (1952), pp. 111–13.

122. "Neuordungsplan" (1950), pp. 19, 43.

123. "Erläuterungsbericht" (1952), p. 72.

124. Ibid., pp. 138, 141.

125. Fischer, "Die Neuplanung Aachens," pp. 168, 175.

126. "Neuordungsplan" (1950), pp. 27–30. The north–south artery was never built in the form envisaged by Fischer.

127. See, for example, the statements in Max Guther et al., "'Ich kann mich nicht herausdenken aus dem Vorgang der Geschichte.'" Also Werner Hebebrand, "Der Frankfurter Hauptstrassenwettbewerb im Rahmen der städtebaulichen Gesamtplanung," *Die Neue Stadt* 1 (1947), on Frankfurt; or the remarks of Wilhelm Seidensticker, "Aufgaben des Städtebaues."

128. Karl Josef Erbs, *Grundlagen für den Aufbau in Stadt und Land* (Berlin, 1948), pp. 14–15. "Der Herr Verkehr, ein Zwillingsbruder des Kapitalismus und Hauptvertreter des Materialismus, hat sich zu einer weltbeherrschenden Stellung aufgeschwungen, hat sich der Wissenschaft und Technik bemächtigt, ist vom Diener zum Herrn geworden. Sein Name braucht nur genannt zu werden, und alle Welt erstirbt in tiefster Devotion und macht ihm Platz, damit er ungehindert den von ihm beliebten kürzesten Weg einschlagen kann."

129. Herbert Jensen, "Krisis des planmäßigen Aufbaus," *Der Bauhelfer* 5 (1950): 30.

131. Herbert Jensen, "Der Wettlauf zwischen Verkehr und Städtebau," in *Deutsche Akademie für Städtebau und Landesplanung: Jahresversammlung* (Munich, 1953), pp. 16–18. "Knotenpunkte und Sammelpunkte des Verkehrs zu sein, d. h. dem Austausch der Güter, des Geldes, der Arbeitskräfte, der Gedanken, der Kultur zu dienen, das war doch die ursprüngliche und ist noch heute die Aufgabe der Städte. . . . Der Verkehr ist für die Stadtkörper der belebende Blutstrom, die Verkehrsstrassen bilden die Adern. . . . Wir leben im Zeitalter des Verkehrs. Verkehr ist Trumpf, wir leben gerade zu in einem Rausche, in einem Taumel des Verkehrs, und zwar des motorisierten Verkehrs."

131. See Edward Relph, *The Modern Urban Landscape* (Baltimore, Md., 1987), pp. 76ff.

132. Reichow's book was titled *Die autogerechte Stadt: Ein Weg aus dem Verkehrs-Chaos* (Ravensburg, 1959). The title subsequently became a target for critics of the traffic planning of the 1950s. In 1989 Uli Zech, a member of Munich's planning department, stated that today "one can forget the auto-ready city." Quoted in Karl-Heinz Büschemann, "Unter die Räder gekommen," *Die Zeit*, no. 42 (13 October 1989): 47.

133. Summaries of these planning proposals can be found in Konstanty Gutschow, *Stadtmitte Hannover. Beiträge zur Aufbauplanung der Innenstadt* (Hannover, 1949) and in Greene, *Politics and Geography in Postwar German City Planning*.

134. See Rudolf Hillebrecht, "Ausschreibung und Preisgerichtsverfahren für den Städtebau-Wettbewerb Hannover," *Der Bauhelfer* 4 (1949).

135. In a memo issued by the building office, it was argued that "die Trennung der Funktionen [work and housing] wirkt sich letztes Endes volkswirtschaftlich als Belastung aus." True separation would mean too much lost time and energy spent in long commutes to and from work and might well preclude the needed revitalization of the inner city. Bauverwaltung der Hauptstadt Hannover, *Erste Denkschrift: Die Innenstadt,* Text Part A (October 1949), p. 9.

136. See, for example, the report by Stuttgart's Beigeordneter Fritzsch, Technischer Referat, on his trip in the summer of 1950 to study traffic planning. "Planungen und Maßnahmen zur Bewältigung des fliessenden und ruhenden Stadtverkehrs in Frankfurt, Köln, Düsseldorf, Hannover, Bremen, Hamburg und Kiel," in SAS/ZAS 41.

137. Otto Meyer-Ottens, "Zum Aufbau der Stadt Hamburg," *Baurundschau* 37 (1947): 472 (special issue, "Hamburg im Wandel"). Similar sentiments were expressed in Meyer-Ottens, "Einführung in die Probleme des Generalbebauungsplanes," in *Stadtplanung in Hamburg: Gedanken zum Wiederaufbau,* Schriftenreihe des Bundes Deutscher Architekten, vol. 6 (Hamburg, 1948).

138. Hansestadt Hamburg, *Skizzen zum Generalbebauungsplan 1947* (Hamburg, 1948).

139. Otto Sill, "Der Verkehr," in *Hamburg und seine Bauten 1929–1953,* Architekten- und Ingenieur-Verein Hamburg, ed. (Hamburg, 1953), p. 246.

140. Niels Gutschow, "Lübeck," in *Stadtbauwelt* 84 (1984); Durth and Gutschow, *Träume in Trümmern,* pp. 832ff.

141. "Denkschrift betreffend Neuregelung der Verkehrsverhältnisse in der Innenstadt der Hansestadt Lübeck," 2 February 1943, in AHSL/Hauptamt 15u/1 (1945–1947)/ W7 (Wiederaufbau), "Starrheit der Straßenführungen."

142. Hans Pieper, "Studien zum Wiederaufbau der Altstadt Lübeck: Kritik des Bestehenden," Fall 1943, in ASKG/17–12–55.

143. Pieper, *Lübeck.*

144. "Vorschlag für eine Wiederbebauung der zerstörten Gebiete der Stadtinsel," p. 95. I used the copy in ASKG. The proposal was begun during the war for the Arbeitsstab Wiederaufbauplanung; Tamms completed and submitted it before going to Düsseldorf. Of the 101 pages of the typescript, 62 are directly devoted to questions of streets and motor traffic.

145. Ibid., p. 22.

146. Ibid., p. 93. For Steffann's ideas, see "Ein Plan zum Wiederaufbau Lübecks," *Lübeckische Nachrichten,* 31 December 1946. Steffann's architectonic view of reconstruction had considerable popular support.

147. Tessenow had been approached by Lübeck's Overbeckgesellschaft, which was concerned about the acrimonious dispute between the building administration's planners and Steffann and his supporters. See AHSL/ Hauptamt 15u/ 2–64–6/ report of 14 November 1986. Also Durth and Gutschow, *Träume in Trümmern,* pp. 860.

148. AHSL/Hauptamt 15u/2–64–16/remarks to session of new Planungsbeirat on 29 September 1949, protocol of 12 October 1949.

149. See Münter's introduction to "Verkehrsführung in der Innenstadt," February 1950, in AHSL/Hauptamt 15u/2–63–15. It is noteworthy that here Münter sees traffic itself as an economic function and not something that serves the economy.

150. For a summary of the competition, see Deckert, "Wettbewerb um die Neugestaltung des Lübecker Marktes." Interestingly there are echoes of the Lübeck

discussions in the planning history of Bremen, where Wilhelm Wortmann's main concern was to use bombed areas to create new or wider arteries to carry traffic across the old city. Both the Wiederaufbau-Gemeinschaften, which Wortmann advised, and Wortmann himself were familiar with Tessenow's cautious suggestions for Lübeck, and as a result they muted their enthusiasm for one of the proposed north–south Durchbrüche, which in fact was never built. See "Erläuterung zur Aufbauplanung der Wiederaufbau-Gemeinschaften Stadtmitte Bremen," April 1948, in SB/4.29/1–511; "Vortrag, Baudirektor a.D. Wortmann über die Aufbauplanung für die bremische Innenstadt," before the city Senate on 24 January 1949. For a useful survey of planning in Bremen, see Konrad Donat, "Stadtplanung in Bremen zwischen 1940 und 1950," typescript in SB. I used a copy in the possession of Niels Gutschow.

151. Tamms's career and planning in Düsseldorf are discussed at length by Werner Durth in "Düsseldorf," *Stadtbauwelt* 84 (1984), and in *Deutsche Architekten*, pp. 277ff, and in Durth and Gutschow, *Träume in Trümmern*, pp. 428ff.

152. Friedrich Tamms, "Planungsaufgaben in Düsseldorf," *Stadtplanung Düsseldorf. Ausstellung Ehrenhof 1.–16.10.1949.* (Düsseldorf, 1949), pp. 9–10.

153. This dispute was still appearing in print as recently as 1982. See Aloys Machtemes, "Einige Erinnerungen an die Stadtplanung in Düsseldorf 1948–1958," and Josef Lehmbrock, "Ein Stadtplanungsvorschlag des Architektenrings aus der Zeit Ende 1949 und Anfang 1950," both in *Architektur der 50er Jahre in Düsseldorf. Eine Ausstellung des Stadtmuseums und des BDA Düsseldorf* (Düsseldorf, 1982). Some of the original counterproposals to the Tamms plan are in HSANRW/NW 177/vol. 248.

154. For example, Friedrich Tamms, "'Expose' zu den dem Neuordnungsplan eingegangen städtebaulichen Anregungen und Bedenken," 15 December 1949, in HSANRW/ NW 177/260/ 22. This volume also contains reports on a number of meetings between Tamms and various groups held to discuss current town planning.

155. Tamms, "Planen und Bauen in Düsseldorf," *Kommunalpolitische Blätter* 7 (1955): 147.

156. SAS/Hauptaktei/Gruppe 6/6110–9.

157. SAS/Lageplanskizze (Draft of General Plan), 15 Juli 1947/ Gemeinderat Bd. 125/ Auszugsband 1947; see also Vietzen, *Chronik der Stadt Stuttgart 1945–1948*, pp. 375–76.

158. For the disputes, see Chapter 9.

159. SAS/ZAS 25/Letter to Hoss, 16 August 1951.

160. SAS/Hauptaktei/Gruppe 6/6110–9/memo of 2 October 1950.

161. Statement to Beirat session of 6 September 1949, in SAS/ZAS 24.

162. See Meitinger, *Das neue München.*

163. Ibid., p. 9.

164. Ibid., pp. 29–32. The largest ring improvements eventually became the Oscar v. Miller Ring, Karl Scharnagl Ring, and Thomas Wimmer Ring.

165. See Abel/Ratsitzungsprotokolle/720/1 (1947), presentation of 3 June 1947, pp. 1294–1343; and Abel, "Betrachtungen zum Wiederaufbau unserer Städte," *Die Neue Stadt* 3 (1949): 213–15.

166. SAM/Ratsitzungsprotokolle/722/16, 25 April 1949.

167. SAM/Ratsitzungsprotokolle/723/1/ session of 3 January 1950, p. 57.

168. Paul, "Der Wiederaufbau der historischen Städte in Deutschland," p. 133, finds Hillebrecht's Hannover "architectonically unlike a big city [architectonisch ungroßstädtisch]," and Hanns Adrian, who succeeded Hillebrecht as chief planner, has described the city's modern architecture as modest and unimaginative. Adrian, "Hannover heute—Das Stadbild der Nachkriegszeit," mimeo (Hannover, 1982).

169. Grebler, *Europe's Reborn Cities*, p. 33, for example.
170. Interview with author in Hannover, 25 June 1983.
171. Tamms, "Planungsaufgaben in Düsseldorf," p. 25.
172. Leipner, *Chronik der Stadt Stuttgart*, pp. 167–71. In 1990 the ratio had reached nearly one automobile for every two inhabitants, according to the *Kölner Stadt-Anzeiger*, 24–25 May 1990.
173. Report by Stadtbaurat Högg, April 1951, on five years of reconstruction, in SAM/Bauamt/Hochbauamt 1044/1; HASK/Stadt Köln, *Köln. General Verkehrsplan* mimeo (Cologne, 1956), p. 76.
174. As Hillebrecht observes in Guther et al., "'Ich kann mich nicht herausdenken aus dem Vorgang der Geschichte,' " p. 371.
175. See Peter Monheim, "Fußgängerbereiche setzen sich durch," *Der Städtetag*, new series 27 (1974), and Paulhans Peters, ed., *Fußgängerstadt. Fußgängergerechte, Stadtplanung und Stadtgestaltung* (Munich, 1977).
176. Vittorio Magnago Lampugnani, "Architektur und Stadtplanung," in *Die Bundesrepublik Deutschland*, Wolfgang Benz, ed. (Frankfurt, 1983), 3:140, 152–53.
177. Jensen, "Krisis des planmäßigen Aufbaus," pp. 29ff.
178. Rudolf Hillebrecht, "Städtebau und Aufbau der Gemeinden," in *Amtlicher Katalog der Constructa Bauausstellung 1951* (Hannover, 1951), pp. 70–71.
179. Herbert Jensen, comments in *Demokratische Stadt- und Landesplanung*, Schriftenreihe der Deutschen Akademie für Städtebau und Landesplanung, vol. 7 (Tübingen, 1955), pp. 75, 77.
180. Leitl, "What's Wrong with German City Planning?" p. 27.
181. Typical is Josef Lehmbrock, for the Düsseldorf Architektenring, to the Minister for Reconstruction of Northrhine-Westphalia, 2 February 1949, in HSANRW/ NW 177/ 248/ 87ff. On the authoritarian tendency in planning, see Berndt, *Die Gesellschaftsbild bei Stadtplanern*, pp. 89ff.
182. SH/ Denkmalschutzamt/38/Cremon Insel/ Aktennotiz by Denkmalpfleger Hopp on meeting with Meyer-Ottens, 19 March 1947.
183. Schumacher, "Erkenntnisse für den Wiederaufbau zerstörter Städte," pp. 197–98, and his letter to Konstanty Gutschow of 27 June 1947, cited by Niels Gutschow, "Fritz Schumacher," p. 349.
184. Herbert Jensen, "Zum Ergebnis des Kieler Innenstadtwettbewerbs," *Der Bauhelfer* 4 (1949): 48–49.
185. "Der Bürger und der Wiederaufbau," *Der Bauhelfer* 4 (1949): 215–16.
186. Hillebrecht, "Neuaufbau der Städte," p. 37.

Chapter 8

1. "Städtebau ist Stein gewordenes Städtebaurecht"; Zinkahn, "Die gegenwärtige Situation des Baurechts," p. 359.
2. For a summary of legal developments to 1914, see Sutcliffe, *Toward the Planned City*, pp. 11ff, and Gerald Warfsmann, *Enteignung und Eigentumsbildung im Baurecht* (Diss., Georg-August-Universität, Gottingen, 1962). See also Stefan Fisch, "Joseph Stübben in Köln und Theodor Fischer in München. Stadtplanung des späten 19. Jahrhunderts im Vergleich," *Geschichte in Köln*, no. 22 (1987): 107.
3. See Berger-Thimme, *Wohnungsfrage und Sozialstaat*, pp. 213–20.
4. Ibid., pp. 220–52; Gerd Albers, "Das Stadtplanungsrecht im 20. Jahrhundert als Niederschlag der Wandlungen im Planungsverständnis," *Stadtbauwelt* 65 (1980):

486; see also *Erfordernisse der Bau- und Bodengesetzgebung* (*Weinheimer Gutachten*), Schriftenreihe des Bundesministers für Wohnungsbau, no. 1 (Hamburg, 1952), for comparison of laws before and after 1945.

5. Schumacher, *Köln*, p. 302.

6. Wilhelm Dittus, *Baurecht im Werden* (Munich and Berlin, 1951). See Erich Kabel, *Baufreiheit und Raumordnung: die Verflechtung von Baurecht und Bauentwicklung im deutschen Städtebau* (Ravensburg, 1949), for a wartime argument for a unified building law.

7. "Vorschlag der Akademie für ein Reichsgesetz über städtebauliche Gesundungsmaßnahmen," in *Jahresbericht der Deutschen Akademie für Städtebau, Reichs- und Landesplanung* (Frankfurt, 1936). It may be recalled that under the Nazis, laws were also proposed to regulate and protect the profession of architects. See Chapter 3 above.

8. Erich Heinicke, "Grundlagen für die Neugestaltung des Bodenrechts," in *Jahresbericht der Deutschen Akademie für Städtebau, Reichs- und Landesplanung* (Frankfurt, 1936), p. 30.

9. Albers, "Das Stadtplanungsrecht," pp. 486–87.

10. Herbert Boehm, "Die Gestaltung der Baugesetzgebung," in *Jahresbericht der Deutschen Akademie für Städtebau, Reichs- und Landesplanung* (Frankfurt, 1936), pp. 48–49.

11. HAA/Nachlaß Gutschow/ B6/5: Entschädigung/Enteignung. The question of property transfers during the Third Reich remains to be researched.

12. HASK/953/66/Paul Reith, "Vorlesung im Hause der Technik, Essen," 19 June 1947.

13. "Neuordungsplan der Stadt Aachen 1950," pp. 38–41, 51. The ordinances were the *Reichsumlegungsordnung* of 16 June 1937 and the *Verordnung über Neuordnungsmaßnahmen zur Beseitigung von Kriegsfolgen* of 2 December 1940.

14. See ASKG/Bahnson, Bericht, 1 September 1945.

15. Fritz Schumacher, *Zum Wiederaufbau Hamburgs* (Hamburg, 1945), pp. 8–12.

16. [Stadtbaudirektor] Kaiser, "Die bauliche Neuordnung zerstörter Städte," *Der Bauhelfer* 2 (1947).

17. Kurt Blaum, "Neugestaltung des Bau- und Bodenrechts," *Wiederaufbau zerstörter Städte*, no. 4 (1946): 5, 12.

18. HASK/5/1201: "Entwurf eines Gesetzes über Maßnahmen zum Wiederaufbau der Stadt Frankfurt a. M.," 9 March 1946.

19. Ludwig Wambsganz, "Weg und Ziel einer Erneuerung des Baurechts," *Neue Bauwelt* 2 (1947): 404; emphasis in the original.

20. Ludwig Wambsganz and Wilhelm Dittus, "Die Erneuerung unseres Baurechts als Voraussetzung für den Wiederaufbau," *Der Bauhelfer* 3, nos. 1 and 2 (1948): 34.

21. Stephan Prager, *Die Deutsche Akademie für Städtebau und Landesplanung. Rückblick und Ausblick 1922–1955*, Schriftenreihe der Deutschen Akademie für Städtebau und Landesplanung, vol. 8 (Tübingen, 1956), pp. 91ff.

22. Deutscher Verband für Wohnungswesen, Städtebau und Landesplanung, "Die Grundsätze zur Baugesetzgebung," *Neue Bauwelt* 2 (1947); in 1950, the association's committee on land and building law included Dittus and Wambsganz. HSANRW/NW 72/ 783, Deutscher Verband für Wohnungswesen, Städtebau und Raumplanung, Liste der ständigen Ausschüsse, December 1950.

23. Werner Müller, "Betrachtungen über die künftige Städtebaugesetzgebung," *Der Bauhelfer* 2 (1947): 8. See also "Bau- und Bodenrecht," *Die Neue Stadt* 2 (1948): 382–84, reporting on a presentation on English planning law to the Deutscher Verband für Wohnungswesen, Städtebau und Landesplanung.

24. [Dr.] Lauther, "Rechtlich-Wirtschaftlich-Finanzielle Fragen des Aufbaues," in *Grundlagen für den Aufbau in Stadt und Land*, Karl Josef Erbs, ed. (Berlin, 1948), pp. 53–54; Karl Friedrich Demmer, "Zur Neugestaltung des Bodenrechts als Grundlage für Planung und Aufbau," *Der Bauhelfer* 3 (1948): 453–54.

25. A. Heilmann, "Zur baulichen Neuordnung der zerstörten Städte," *Der Bauhelfer* 2 (1947): 4.

26. Wilhelm Dittus, "Neues Baurecht für zerstörte Städte," *Der Bauhelfer* 3 (1948).

27. Wambsganz and Dittus, "Die Erneuerung unseres Baurechts," p. 3.

28. Ibid., p. 31.

29. See Dittus, "Neues Baurecht," pp. 511ff.

30. Bundesarchiv and Institut für Zeitgeschichte, eds., *Akten zur Vorgeschichte der Bundesrepublik Deutschland, 1945–1949*, vol. 1: *September 1945–Dezember 1946*, Walter Vogel and Christoph Weisz, eds. (Munich, 1976), pp. 628–29, for meetings of the Zonenbeirat of the British zone.

31. See Johannes Göderitz, ed., *Neues Städtebaurecht: Der Entwurf eines Gesetzes über den Aufbau der Deutschen Gemeinden*, Schriften des Deutschen Städtetages, no. 3 (1948): 1–2.

32. Wambsganz and Dittus, "Die Erneuerung unseres Baurechts," p. 36; Göderitz, *Neues Städtebaurecht*, pp. 5, 8–9.

33. Göderitz, *Neues Städtebaurecht*, p. 7.

34. See R. Meffert, "Betrachtung zur Aufbaugesetzgebung," *Der Bauhelfer* 4 (1949); Ernst Hamm, "Betrachtungen zur Aufbaugesetzgebung," *Der Bauhelfer* 4 (1949); and *Erfordernisse der Bau- und Bodengesetzgebung* for comparisons of the various laws. In the fall of 1948, an exhibit on building law was staged at the Technische Hochschule in Hannover, to which *Baurundschau* devoted a special issue (vol. 39, no. 3, 1 February 1949). Subsequently the governments of Schleswig-Holstein, Lower Saxony, and Northrhine-Westphalia each purchased 500 copies of that special issue to distribute to legislators and others who might be persuaded to support passage of strong building laws. See HSANRW/NW 177/205: 89–104.

35. See BHSA/ II/ MA 130 543/ Letter of Franz Fischer, Staatssek. in Innenmin. to Kanzlei, 31 January 1948, on opposition to a common law.

36. Wilhelm Dittus, "Zum Berliner Planungsgesetz und den Flächenarten seines Bebauungsplans," *Der Bauhelfer* 4 (1949); Hans Undeutsch, "Der Entwurf zu einem Baugesetz für Berlin," *Der Bauhelfer* 4 (1949): 519, praised these provisions because they came close to current English planning law.

37. SAS/ZAS 24/Beirat session of 2 September 1948; see also the memo by Hoss, the chief of ZAS, to the Technische Abteilung des Gemeinderats, 16 December 1949, in SAS/ZAS 55.

38. For Hamburg, see *Stenographische Berichte der Bürgerschaft zu Hamburg* (9 February 1949), p. 89. The quotation is from RWWA/1/237/4/Protokoll, Sitzung des Rechtsausschußes der IHK Köln, 23 April 1948, statement by the chairman, Dr. L. Menne, of the Bodenkreditbank.

39. Letter of Vereinigung der Industrie- und Handelskammern des Landes Nordrhein-Westfalen to the minister of reconstruction of that state, 9 December 1984, along with other position papers in RWWA/1/237/7.

40. For example, RWWA/1/237/7/Sollinger Aufbaukreis, "Stellungnahme zum Aufbaugesetz," 25 November 1948, pp. 2, 5.

41. HSANRW/NW 177/248/Haus- und Grundbesitzer-Verein Düsseldorf, "Denkschrift über den Neuordnungsplan der Stadt Düsseldorf," 21 November 1949.

42. Ibid., p. 3.

43. SAM/Bauamt-Wiederaufbau/1112, for both the first draft and the final draft of 11 April 1946.

44. See SAM/Bürgermeister und Rat/1969/Letter from Wiederaufbaureferat to Mayor Scharnagl, 23 January 1946.

45. SAM/Bürgermeister und Rat/1969/Der Bayerische Arbeitsminister to the Oberbürgermeister of Munich, 5 January 1946.

46. SAM/Ratsitzungsprotokolle/719/9/Geh. Sitzung, Bauunterausschuß und Finanzausschuß, 22 February 1946, pp. 12–22.

47. SAM/Bürgermeister und Rat/1969/Letter from Wiederaufbaureferat to Mayor Scharnagl, 23 January 1946.

48. SAM/Bürgermeister und Rat/1969/Letter from Scharnagl to Seifried, 25 January 1946.

49. SAM/Ratsitzungsprotokolle/719/9/Niederschrift über die Besprechung der Bürgermeister der großen bayerischen Städte und Märkte, 7 March 1946, pp. 49ff.

50. AIHKM/XII/157k, Wiederaufbau-Gesetz, 1946/Report to President Reinhard Kloepfer from Friedrich Wilhelm Kärcher and Kurt Tornier, 12 March 1946.

51. BHSA/MWi/11646/ Wolf to various agencies, 24 August 1946, with "Verordnung über die Organisation im Siedlungs- und Wohnungswesen und bei der Wiederbesiedlung."

52. See BSHA/Bayer. St. Min. d. Finanzen/ Anlage 273.79/249: II-IX 248, letter of Bayer. Arbeitsmin. Albert Rosshaupter to other ministers, 27 November 1946; and 250: II-IX 249, 8697.

53. See *Bayerischer Staatsanzeiger* 3, no. 50, (10 December 1948).

54. For an analysis of the final Bavarian draft, see Wilhelm Dittus, "Der Entwurf zu einem Bayerischen Baugesetz," *Neue Bauwelt* 5 (1950).

55. SAM/Bürgermeister und Rat/1965/Referat 10, Rechtsabteilung, "Vorarbeiten zum Entwurf eines Aufbaugesetzes," 23 November 1948. See BHSA/Bayer. St. Min. d. Finanzen/Anlage 273.79/250 II-IX 249: 8697 and 8791 for examples of opposition of various ministers to proposed law.

56. SAM/Bürgermeister und Rat/Letter of 22 August 1947; in this Hoegner agreed with the position of the Bavarian Union of Associations of House and Land Owners.

57. BHSA/MWi/11647/Dr. Lukas von Kaufmann, Note for the Archives for Min. Dr. Seidel, re meeting of Ausschuß Bauwesen im Länderrat, 28 and 29 October 1948 and 5 November 1948.

58. SAM/Bürgermeister und Rat/1970/Dr. Ludwig Mellinger to Lord Mayor Wimmer, 5 May 1949.

59. SAM/Bürgermeister und Rat/1972/Bayerische Aufbaurat, report by Fischer on 19 July 1949.

60. SAM/Bürgermeister und Rat/1972/Wimmer to Bavarian Interior and Finance Ministries, 28 November 1949.

61. BHSA/Innenmin, 79663 (5571)/ Gutachten by Decker, Senatspräsident of Bayer. Verwaltungsgerichtshof, 17 May 1950.

62. SAM/Bürgermeister und Rat/1965/Report circulated on 14 June 1950, by Dr. Herterich, chairman of the Bayerischer Städteverband, p. 12.

63. AIHKM/Letters to the Munich Chamber from Würzburg, 6 September 1950; from Nuremberg, 29 August 1950; from Augsburg, 13 September 1950; and "Stellungnahme der Bayerischen Hypotheken- und Wechsel-Bank," undated but obviously submitted to the president of the Munich Chamber as that body's evaluation of the proposed law; also BHSA/MWi/13355: cover letter, September 1949, by Gottlob Binder for summary of resolutions passed at Nürnberger Bautagung.

64. For example, see ADST/Akten: 6/00–00–5, meeting of 3 February 1950; and HASK/2 (OBM)/2291/material from 18 July 1949.

65. Jean-Louis Cohen, "Le Conseil Supérieur d'Architecture et d'Urbanisme," in *Deutsch-französische Beziehungen 1940–1950 und ihre Auswirkungen auf Architektur und Stadtgestalt*, Jean-Louis Cohen and Hartmut Frank, eds. (unpublished manuscript, Hamburg, 1989), p. 161, and Blumenfeld report.

66. Views of Max Rusch and Rappaport in Rusch, "Ein Bundesministerium für Bauwesen ist nötig!" *Neue Bauwelt* 4 (1949).

67. HSANRW/NW73–99, letters of 13 December 1949 and 3 January 1950.

68. HSANRW/NW73–99, letters of 9 and 16 January 1950.

69. HSANRW/NW73–99, letter of 21 January 1950.

70. Wilhelm Dittus, "Die Problematik des künftigen Bau- und Bodenrechts unter besonderer Berücksichtigung der Aufbaugemeinschaften," in *Aufbauförderungsgemeinschaften in deutschen Städten* (Frankfurt, 1950), p. 219.

71. *Bundesgesetzblatt*, 1950, pp. 83–88; social housing had to be modest in size—32 to 65 square meters—with a rent of DM 1 to DM 1.10 per square meter, with tenants assigned by the local housing authority.

72. SAM/Bürgermeister und Rat/1965/Report by Fischer to Hauptausschuß of Bayerischer Städteverband, 26 May 1950, pp. 6–10.

73. Dittus, "Die Problematik des künftigen Bau- und Bodenrechts," p. 219.

74. Max Rusch, "Das Baugesetz," *Neue Bauwelt* 5 (1950), and Rusch, "Inhalt des Baugesetzes: Die Planung," *Neue Bauwelt* 6 (1951).

75. Wilhelm Dittus, "Wann kommt das Bundesbaugesetz?" *Blätter für Grundstücks-, Bau- und Wohnungswesen* 2 (1953).

76. W. Zinkahn, "Das Baulandbeschaffungsgesetz ist verabschiedet," *Blätter für Grundstücks-, Bau- und Wohnungswesen* 2 (1953): 212.

77. *Aufbauförderungsgemeinschaften in deutschen Städten: Bericht über eine Arbeitstagung* (Frankfurt, 1950), pp. 77, 88.

78. *Verhandlung des Deutschen Bundestages, Stenographische Berichte*, I. Wahlperiode, vol. 3: 1928–50.

79. *Neue Bauwelt* 6 (1951): 464; and ADST/Akten: 6/01–22, speech by Klett, 16 February 1952.

80. Ludwig Wambsganz, Wilhelm Dittus, and Johannes Göderitz, "Das Planungs-, Bau- und Bodenrecht," *Neue Bauwelt* 6 (1951): 439–49; also in *Amtlicher Katalog der Constructa Bauaustellung 1951* (Hannover, 1951). See also the remarks by Rudolf Hillebrecht in Max Guther et al., "'Ich kann mich nicht herausdenken aus dem Vorgang der Geschichte,' " p. 367.

81. Carl Schweyer, "Baulandbeschaffung," in *Um die Grundlagen des sozialen Wohnungsbaues: Kundgebung der Gemeinnützigen Wohnungswirtschaft des Landes Nordrhein-Westfalen* (Essen, 1950), pp. 38–39.

82. AIHKM/ XXII/157r/Stellungnahme zum Entwurf zu einem Baugesetz für die Bundesrepublik Deutschland von Dr. Wilhelm Dittus.

83. *Erfordernisse der Bau- und Bodengesetzgebung*; other members were Herman Stroebel, a Baudirektor of Stuttgart, Georg Lindemann, Stadtdirektor of Hannover, Herbert Jensen, the city planner of Kiel, Dr. Ludwig Gebhard, Regierungspräsident of Oberfranken-Bayreuth, and Dr. Ernst Forsthoff of Heidelberg. Mayor Klett of Stuttgart tried unsuccessfully to get Hoss named to the committee instead of Stroebel. SAS/Hauptaktei Gruppe 6/6100–1, letter of 13 August 1951, to Wandersleb of Bundesministerium für Wohnungsbau.

84. Dittus, "Wann kommt das Bundesbaugesetz?"

85. *Neue Bauwelt* 6 (1951): 668–69; *Verhandlung des Deutschen Bundestages, Stenographische Berichte*, I. Wahlperiode, vol. 9: 6584.

86. W. Zinkahn, comments in *Demokratische Stadt- und Landesplanung*, Schriftenreihe der Deutschen Akademie für Städtebau und Landesplanung, vol. 7 (Tübingen, 1955), pp. 59–60; and Zinkahn, "Die gegenwärtige Situation," pp. 341–42.

87. Zinkahn, "Die gegenwärtige Situation," p. 364.

88. ADST/6/00–00–16, 16th session of Bauausschuß of Städtetag, 6–7 November 1953, E39, Hamburger Anträge of 30 December 1953.

89. Zinkahn, comments in *Demokratische Stadt- und Landesplanung*, p. 61; *Erfordernisse der Bau- und Bodengesetzgebung*, pp. 15ff.

90. *Bundesgesetzblatt* (1953), Part 1, *Baulandbeschaffungsgesetz* of 3 August 1953: 720–30; see also the commentary by W. Zinkahn, a senior official in the housing ministry, in Zinkahn, "Das Baulandbeschaffungsgesetz ist verabschiedet."

91. *Entscheidungen des Bundesverfassungsgericht* 3 (1953–54): 407–39; 4 (1954–55): 219–37; also W. Blunck, "Demokratischer Städtebau," in *Demokratische Stadt- und Landesplanung*, Schriftenreihe der Deutschen Akademie für Städtebau und Landesplanung, vol. 7 (Tübingen, 1955), pp. 54–55; Zinkahn comments in *Demokratische Stadt- und Landesplanung*, p. 62.

92. This was the case in Stuttgart. See Gustav Grauvogel, "Die rechtlichen Grundlagen beim Wiederaufbau Stuttgarts," *Kommunalpolitische Blätter* 7 (1955). Nevertheless, 42 land consolidation processes were completed between 1948 and 1955 with a total area of 87 hectares, in spite of the difficulties with the building law in Baden-Württemberg.

93. Blunck, "Demokratischer Städtebau," p. 55.

94. Jensen, comments in *Demokratische Stadt- und Landesplanung*, p. 74 (emphasis in original).

95. Guido Görres, "Aufbaugesetz. Gesetz zur Durchführung der Ortsplanung und des Aufbaues in den Gemeinden," *Baurundschau* 39 (February 1949): 3, 13 (special issue).

96. *Bundesgesetzblatt* (1960), Part 1: 341–88.

97. For example, Alexander Mitscherlich, *Die Unwirtlichkeit unserer Städte. Anstiftung zum Unfrieden* (Frankfurt, 1965).

98. Interviews by author of Rudolf Hillebrecht, 8 May 1982, in Hannover, and Helmut Prost, former manager of Privatbau, Gesellschaft zur Förderung des Wiederaufbaues, Hamburg, 27 April 1982.

Chapter 9

1. Alfons Leitl, "Die Massenhaftigkeit und die Tradition," *Baukunst und Werkform* 2 (1948): 18.

2. For example, BHSA/MWi 10169/ Protokoll, Ausschuß Bauwesen im Länderrat des amerikanischen Besatzungsgebiets, 28–29 October 1948, and BHSA/MWi 11647/ Arbeitsstab des Länderrates für Wohnungsbau, Protokoll of 21 March 1949.

3. Guther et al., " 'Ich kann mich nicht herausdenken aus dem Vorgang der Geschichte,' " pp. 356, 368.

4. Ibid., p. 356.

5. See Danièle Voldman, "Reconstructors' Tales: An Example of the Use of Oral Sources in the History of Reconstruction after the Second World War," and Rémi Baudoui, "Between Regionalism and Functionalism: French Reconstruction from

1940 to 1945," both in *Rebuilding Europe's Bombed Cities*, Jeffry M. Diefendorf, ed. (London and New York, 1990).

6. Hartmut Frank, "Pläne für Groß-Mainz," and "'Caveant Consules': Berater und Gutachter des Stadtplanungsamtes bei der Mainzer Wiederaufbauplanung," both in *Deutsch-französische Beziehungen 1940–1950 und ihre Auswirkungen auf Architektur und Stadtgestalt*, Jean-Louis Cohen and Hartmut Frank, eds. (unpublished manuscript, Hamburg, 1989), 2: 220 and 432–33; Werner Durth, "Mainz: Blockierte Moderne," and Durth and Gutschow, *Träume in Trümmern*, pp. 880ff.

7. Baudoui, "L'équipe degli urbanisti della Sarre," and Höhns, "Stadtplanung in Saarbrücken."

8. Cohen, "Le Conseil Supérieur d'Architecture et d'Urbanisme," p. 146.

9. Ibid., pp. 152–53, 163. The other German members were Adolf Abel, Hans Mehrtens, Jean Hubert Pinand, Kurt Dübbers, and Kurt Fiederling. De Jaeger also contacted Konstanty Gutschow, Max Taut, and Rudolf Schwarz about possible membership.

10. Richard Döcker, "Kommission französischer und deutscher Städtebauer in Baden-Baden," *Die Neue Stadt* 2 (1948). The council included such well-known planner/architects as Paul Bonatz, Adolf Abel, Döcker, and Marcel Lods.

11. See Greene, *Politics and Geography in Postwar German City Planning*, pp. 244–55.

12. Cohen, "Le Conseil Supérieur d'Architecture et d'Urbanisme," pp. 155–56.

13. Ibid., p. 160.

14. NA/RG 165/Civil Affairs Division/380/Box 134/ letters of 5 June and 5 July 1944.

15. Records of Harley A. Notter, Library of Congress Microfilm Division, Film T 1221, Reel 1, CAC Report 32, 17 December 1943.

16. Ibid., Reel 4, Report 247, 6 July 1944.

17. For example, in early 1948 Colonel James Kelly told Munich officials that while the Americans sympathized with the desire to rebuild in a traditional style, "it would not hurt if also a newer style were used." Indeed, "reconstruction should be undertaken in a modern sense," and it should not be obstructed in the "musty offices of the bureaucracy." Such exhortations, however, did not translate into actions by the military government in Bavaria. SAM/Bürgermeister und Rat, 1969/ meeting of 29 January 1948, with the lord mayor, and Ratsitzungsprotokolle/721/12/Besprechung über Stadtplanung, 24 February 1948.

18. NA/ RG 260/ OMGUS/ Shiplist 13 1/10, Container 5911: Information Service Division, Motion Picture Branch, Minutes of Bipartite Board of 30 April 1949. See also John H. Backer, *The Winds of History: The German Years of Lucius DuBignon Clay* (New York, 1983), 52ff, 158.

19. Gropius, "Reconstruction: Germany," p. 35. This naturally appealed to those who considered themselves to have been apolitical technocrats while working for the Nazis.

20. Ibid., p. 36.

21. Gropius to Eugen Blanck, 1 January 1951, HLH, Gropius Papers, bMS Ger 208 (470).

22. Blumenfeld report, "City Planning in Germany," NA/RG 59/ State Department Central Decimal Files/862.502/12–849/ p. 1. The conclusions of these American observers were also summarized for the German public in Zisman and Blumenfeld, "Allgemeines über Städteplanung in Deutschland." In this essay they singled out the proposals for legal reform advocated by Wilhelm Dittus and Ludwig Wambsganz, discussed in Chapter 7, above.

23. Blumenfeld report, p. 5.

24. Ibid., p. 6.

25. Ibid., p. 2.

26. For such programs generally, see Henry P. Pilgert, *The Exchange of Persons Program in Western Germany*, Historical Division, Office of the U.S. High Commissioner for Germany (Washington, D.C., 1951), and Henry J. Kellermann, *Cultural Relations as an Instrument of U.S. Foreign Policy: The Educational Exchange Program between the United States and Germany, 1945–1954*, Cultural Relations Programs of the U.S. Department of State, Historical Studies, Number 3 (Washington, D.C., 1978). These official histories cover the programs of OMGUS and the HICOG. Zisman and Blumenfeld laid the groundwork for a three-month-long visit to the United States of 10 German officials, architects, university teachers, and economists in the field of planning and a two-semester stay at an American university for a dozen or more German students in fields relating to urban reconstruction. In addition, they argued that the American government should support the visit of groups of German officials from all levels of government as well as visits by architects and individuals involved in social housing projects in order to familiarize the Germans with American approaches to housing construction. Zisman and Blumenfeld also recommended that the United States arrange for lecture tours by German-speaking American experts in the fields of town planning and housing construction. Finally, they encouraged an exchange of professional periodicals in the relevant fields between American and German publishers and professional associations.

27. The guiding spirit behind this effort was Siegfried Goetze, who acted as the spokesman for an organization variously called The National Committee to Rebuild German Cities, Inc., and American Aid to Rebuild German Cities, Inc. Between May 1949 and July 1950, Goetze and his group sought to obtain the approval of Secretary of State Dean Acheson and President Truman for their efforts. Goetze also traveled to Germany in November 1949 to try to establish the legitimacy of his committee with German officials. His efforts were brushed aside in Washington, and it took a few months for the Germans to realize that Goetze really had nothing to offer them. See NA/ RG 59/State Department Decimal Files/ 862.502/ 5–549 and 7–1449; SAM/ Bauamt- und Wiederaufbau/ 1104, contains correspondence between Goetze and the lord major and chief reconstruction official of Munich.

28. "Tätigkeitsbericht des Stadtrates für Bau- und Wohnungswesen des Magistrats von Groß-Berlin von Mai–Dezember 1945," reproduced in Scharoun, *Hans Scharoun: Bauten, Entwürfe, Texte*, pp. 153, 156.

29. See *Neue Bauwelt* 3 (1948): 579–85, and 4 (1949): 109ff, 516–18, 536–37.

30. Interview by the author with Karl Böttcher, 28 October 1981, in West Berlin. This is also mentioned in Böttcher, *Bericht über meine Arbeit*, p. 37. Böttcher was supervising the procurement of building materials for the repair and reconstruction of housing.

31. *ERP und die Stadt Berlin* (Vienna, 1961), p. 16.

32. Ibid., pp. 26–30, 39–44.

33. The Kongresshalle was the American contribution to Interbau, the 1955–57 international building exhibition. The building was designed by Hugh Stubbins, who as a young man had been Gropius's assistant when the latter first came to Harvard. See Barbara Miller Lane, "The Berlin Congress Hall 1955–57," *Perspectives in American History*, new series 1 (1984).

34. Rudolf Hillebrecht and Arthur Dähn, *Fundamente des Aufbaues. Organisatorische Grundlagen*, Schriftenreihe des Bundes deutscher Architekten, vol. 14 (Ham-

burg, 1948). The two authors sent Gutschow a copy with the inscription: "Unserem 'Führer' freundlichts überreicht von den alten Mitarbeiter."

35. ADST/6/20–01/1: Rappaport to Pünder, 14 June 1946.

36. Hermann Pünder and Philipp Rappaport, "Um ein Ministerium für Wiederaufbau und Flüchtlingswesen," *Neue Bauwelt* 4 (1949).

37. SAM/Bauamt-Wiederaufbau/1112.

38. HSANRW/ NW 73/124/ comment in meeting of Allgemeine Ausschuß of the Arbeitsgemeinschaft der für das Bau-, Wohnungs- und Siedlungswesen zuständigen Minister der Länder der Bundesrepublik Deutschland und Berlin, 18–19 April 1950, Part 1.

39. For example, see HSANRW/ NW 73/232/ meeting of Ausschuß Bauwirtschaft of the Arbeitsgemeinschaft der für das Bau-, Wohnungs- und Siedlungswesen zuständigen Minister der Länder der Bundesrepublik Deutschland und Berlin, 14 November 1949. This committee pushed for standardized construction and more efficient production of building materials.

40. HSANRW/NW 73–171/ Min. f. Wiederaufbau, Gliederung, 21 August 1947.

41. RWWA/1/237/1/VII/1, p. 99, Verteiler für bauwirtschaftliche Erlasse from Minister für Wiederaufbau.

42. For example, the discussion of plans for Hagen and Paderborn on 12 December 1948, in HSANRW/NW 177/186.

43. BHSA/Bayer. Staatskanzlei, 19 July 1976/ 75 (2653)/15826: Dr. Ankermüller to various ministries, chambers of commerce, etc., 28 July 1948.

44. BHSA/Bayer. Staatskanzlei, 19 July 1976/75 (2653): Tätigkeitsbericht, 25 September 1950; also in SAM/ Bürgermeister und Rat/ 1972.

45. Niederschrift by Hans von Hanffstangel, Tagung des Arbeitsstabes Wiederaufbauplanung zerstörter Städte, 19–21 August 1944, in Wriezen, carbon provided to the author by von Hanffstangel.

46. Hans Scharoun, "Entwicklung des Instituts für Bauwesen," in *Die Deutsche Bautagung 1949* (Leipzig, 1949); and Frank, "Trümmer," pp. 71–72. For the activities of the Institute under Scharoun's leadership, see the section "Institut für Bauwesen" in the Scharoun papers, AdKB.

47. "Die Tagung des Deutschen Verbandes für Wohnungswesen, Städtebau und Raumplanung in Frankfurt am Main," *Die Neue Stadt* 2 (1948): 240ff.

48. For membership and typical activities, see *Der Städtetag*, new series 1 (1948): 23; Barbara Steimel, "100. Sitzung des Bauausschußes des Deutschen Städtetages—Ein Rückblick," *Der Städtetag*, new series 35 (1982); Werner Kallmorgen, *Deutsche Akademie für Städtebau und Landesplanung. Erinnerungen an 18 Jahre Leben und Arbeit in ihrer Landesgruppe Hamburg und Schleswig-Holstein* (Hamburg, 1965); Prager, *Die Deutsche Akademie für Städtebau und Landesplanung*; HSANRW/ NW 72/ 482 and NW 72/ 783: 42ff.

49. See [Dr. Ing. Franz] Rosenberg and [Architect BDA] Dirichs, "Über die Einschaltung von freischaffenden Architekten bei der Stadtplanung: ein Zwiegespräch zwischen einem Behördenvertreter und einem freischaffenden Architekten," *Der Bauhelfer* 4 (1949).

50. SAM/Bürgermeister und Rat/1967/ Bund Münchner Architekten Präsident Unglehrt to Otto Roth, Berufsverband der Architekten und Bauingenieure, 16 May 1947.

51. BHSA/Bayer. Staatskanzlei, 19 July 1976/75 (2653), Denkschrift zum Bayer. Aufbaurat von Berufsverband der Architekten, 9 November 1948.

52. BHSA/Bayer. Staatskanzlei, 19 July 1976/75 (2653), Denkschrift zum Bayer. Aufbaurat von Berufsverband der Architekten, 9 November 1948.

53. BHSA/Bayer. Staatskanzlei, 19 July 1976/75 (2653), Fischer to Albert Voelter, 16 December 1948.

54. AHSL/Hauptamt 15u/2/60–0-1.

55. HASK/ 171/ nos. 30, 31.

56. See, for example, RWWA/1/237/4, for the reconstruction committee of the Cologne Industrie- und Handelskammer.

57. HASK/171, nos. 13 and 77.

58. See Krieg, "München, leuchtend und ausgebrannt," pp. 83–85.

59. Frank, "Trümmer," p. 44.

60. Breitling, "The Role of the Competition in the Genesis of Urban Planning."

61. This included such things as maps showing the degree of bomb damage, maps showing current or intended zoning, photos of important buildings, statistics about the population and economy, and information about motorized and rail traffic. City governments had to supply all competitors with this sort of information in order for the competition to be fair. See Karl Friedrich Demmer, "Leitgedanken für Wettbewerbe zum Wiederaufbau unserer Städte," *Der Bauhelfer* 2, no. 10 (1947): 1–3.

62. Alfons Leitl, "Anmerkungen zur Zeit," *Baukunst und Werkform* 2 (1948): 6–9, with quotations by Philipp Rappaport.

63. Guther et al., " 'Ich kann mich nicht herausdenken aus dem Vorgang der Geschichte,' " pp. 352, 355.

64. ASKG/Wiederaufbau Hamburg, 271001, "Die Arbeitsweise bei der städtebauliche Planung," Denkschrift no. 1, October 1945, by the Arbeitsausschuß Stadtplanung. The comments received on his proposals are in ASKG/E9: Wiederherstellungsgebiete. See also the organizational plan in SH/Baubehörde I B2/ Wiederaufbauleitung/E9 Wiederherstellungsgebiete, 8 August 1945, and SH/Baubehörde I B1, "Abschlußbericht der Sonderabteilung 'Wiederaufbauleitung,' " 2 October 1945.

65. See Hansestadt Hamburg, *Skizzen zum Generalbebauungsplan 1948*.

66. For material on these associations, see the essays in *Aufbauförderungsgemeinschaften in deutschen Städten*.

67. Greene, *Politics and Planning in Postwar Germany*, pp. 231ff.

68. See Glootz, "Wie kann der Hammerbrookplan durchgeführt werden?" and generally the 15 February 1951 special issue of the *Nordwestdeutsche Bauzeitung*.

69. The following is based on SB/4 (Senator für Bauwesen, 1933–53), 29/1–510 and 511, "Der Wiederaufbau: Mitteilungsblatt des Vereins 'Wiederaufbau-Gemeinschaften Stadtmitte Bremen,' " no. 1 (December 1947) and no. 2 (February/March 1948); 29/1–513, "Vortrag, Baudirektor a.D. Wortmann über die Aufbauplanung für die Bremenische Innenstadt," 24 January 1949; Konrad Donat, *Stadtplanung in Bremen zwischen 1940 und 1950* (typescript, Bremen, 1980, in SB) and Franz Rosenberg, *Vom Wiederaufbau und von der Stadterweiterung in Bremen*. Supplementary information was provided in letters to the author from Konrad Donat, a longtime employee of the building administration (14 April 1988), and from Franz Rosenberg (17 September 1985). Rosenberg came to Bremen as city planner in 1949 and subsequently became director of the building administration. In 1983 he became the chairman of the Aufbaugemeinschaft Bremen upon the death of its founding chairman, the merchant Gerhard Iversen. For the architects and officials in these organizations, see SB/ "Aufbaugemeinschaft Bremen, zur Stadtplanung," in the reference library.

70. Opinions about Wortmann's role differ. Konrad Donat is critical; Franz Rosenberg more positive. The latter states that "as technical advisor to the Aufbaugemeinschaft Wortmann advised many citizens and in cases of differences often

served as an honest and objective mediator. From 1949 to 1956 [when Wortmann went to Hannover], we were constantly in good contact." Letter to author, 17 September 1985.

71. See Konstanty Gutschow, *Stadtmitte Hannover*, for a description of the association and its activities; and Greene, *Politics and Geography in Postwar German Planning*, pp. 75–78.

72. See Hillebrecht, *Neubebauung zerstörter Wohnflächen*, pp. 15–17.

73. Greene, *Politics and Geography in Postwar German Planning*, pp. 76.

74. Das Kuratorium für den Aufbau der Stadt Nürnberg, "Bericht über die Tätigkeit von 1948–1955" (typescript, 1955, copy in BDST), p. 1.

75. Ibid., p. 2.

76. SAM/Bürgermeister und Rat/ 1968/ Letters between Schumacher and Scharnagl of 12 November 1945 and 2 December 1945.

77. SAM/Bürgermeister und Rat/ 1968/ Letter from Seifert to Bürgermeister Stadelmeyer, 9 November 1945.

78. SAM/Bürgermeister und Rat/ 1968/ Personalreferat Stork to Stadtrat Zink, 2 January 1946.

79. SAM/Ratsitzungsprotokolle/720/5: meeting of Personalausschuss, 23 January 1947, pp. 84ff.

80. SAM/Bürgermeister und Rat/ 1968/ Oberrechtsrat Dr. Keim to Scharnagl, 5 July 1946.

81. Otto Völkers, "Vorschlag zum blockweisen und genossenschaftlichen Wiederaufbau zerstörter Innenstädte," *Neue Bauwelt* 1 (1946).

82. SAM/Ratsitzungsprotokolle/ 719/1: public session of 14 May 1946.

83. See Chapter 7.

84. SAM/Bürgermeister und Rat/ 1968/ Scharnagl to Schumacher, 3 June 1946.

85. SAM/Bürgermeister und Rat/ 1986/ Personalreferat Dr. Seemüller to Scharnagl, 22 January 1948.

86. SAM/Ratsitzungsprotokolle/ 721/1: session of 24 February 1948, p. 394.

87. SAM/ Ratsitzungsprotokolle/721/12: Altestenausschuss, sessions of 11 August and 28 September; and the entire volume of documents devoted to this issue in Bürgermeister und Rat/ 1985.

88. SAM/Bürgermeister und Rat/ 1985/ Fischer to Lord Mayor Wimmer, 25 November 1948.

89. SAM/Bürgermeister und Rat/ 1625/ election of the new Stadtbaurat in session of the city council, 19 September 1950.

90. See Vietzen, *Chronik der Stadt Stuttgart 1945–1948*, pp. 362, 370–73.

91. For membership and activities of the Beirat, see SAS/ ZAS 24 and 25. The city also staged a competition in which members of the general public could submit proposals, but nothing was done with the results. Hence this should not be seen as evidence of a serious commitment in Stuttgart to citizen participation in the planning process. See Werner Durth and Friedemann Gschwind, "Stuttgart—Wettbewerbe um Zukunftsbilder," in *Arch+* 72 (1983): 70–74.

92. AdKB/ Nachlaß Scharoun/ Versch. 5/Döcker to Scharoun, 10 October 1947.

93. See correspondence in SAS/ZAS 58, esp. the letter by Hoss of 16 November 1948.

94. *Amtsblatt der Stadt Stuttgart*, 6 October 1949, on Gemeinderat session of 29 September 1949.

95. See SAS/ZAS 78, and Bürgerversammlungen, vols. 375, 376, 377, for these organizations and protocols of the meetings.

96. SAS/ ZAS 56/ Niederschrift über die Bürgerversammlung für den Stadtteil Mitte, 7 June 1950.

97. SAS/ZAS 56/ Stellungnahme von Professor Hoss zu der Aussprache über seinen Bericht in der ersten Bürgerversammlung Stuttgart-Mitte.

98. SAS/ ZAS 58, Auszug aus der Niederschrift über die gemeinschaftliche Sitzung der Verwaltungs- und Technischen Abteilung des Gemeinderats, 27 June 1950, closed session.

99. See Chapter 7.

100. The material concerning the founding and functioning of these organizations is to be found in HASK/953/28, 54 and 81. For the Ernst-Casel-Stiftung, 953/28/ Abschrift, Gründung der Ernst-Cassel-Stiftung, 9 August 1932, Vermerk an Suth, 17 May 1945, and Oberbürgermeister an die Planungsgesellschaft G.m.b.H. z.HD. d. Herrn Direktors Dr. Braubach, 1 April 1941.

101. HASK/953/28/ Notar Justizrat Martin Prang, Account of Notarial Negotiations, 13 February 1941, and note by Oberbürgermeister Pünder, 31 January 1946.

102. HASK/953/81: Pünder to Suth, Schwering, and others, 31 January 1946; and HASK/2/137/ report in the *Rheinische Zeitung*, 4 October 1948, on a speech by Mayor Görlinger at an SPD election rally.

103. For the staffing of the new organization, HASK/953/54/ Schweyer to Suth, 16 September 1946, and HASK/2/ 1321/131. See also Greene, *Politics and Geography in Postwar German Planning*, p. 119.

104. HASK/2/1323/ Schwarz to Görlinger, 22 June 1949. An unsigned copy of the contract between Cologne and Schwarz, dated 27 January 1947, is in Best. 953/ 58. Also HASK/953/54/ Schweyer to Suth, 16 September 1946.

105. HASK/953/61/Schweyer to Suth, 14 March 1946.

106. HASK/953/61/Pünder to Kuske, 8 February 1946.

107. HASK/953/61/see correspondence, 12 April to 22 July 1947.

108. HASK/953/61/Schweyer to Kuske, 5 August 1948.

109. HASK/5/673, report of Wissenschaftliche Abteilung, sent by Schwarz to Suth on 15 February 1946, p. 7. This is the only instance I have found in any city where someone argued for the participation of historians in reconstruction.

110. Schwarz, "Gedanken zum Wiederaufbau von Köln," p. 1; and HASK/953/66, "Über den Zweck der bauwirtschaftlichen Abteilung der Wiederaufbaugesellschaft Köln," 26 May 1947.

111. The complaints are listed in a letter from Mayor Görlinger to Schwarz, 9 June 1949. Schwarz's rebuttal of the charges against him is in two letters to Görlinger, 22 June 1949. All are in HASK/2/1323.

112. HASK/2/ 1321/7–8: Niederschrift über die Sitzung des Verwaltungsrats der Wiederaufbaugesellschaft, 11 July 1949.

113. *Verhandlungen der Stadtverordnetenversammlung, Köln,* 23 June 1947, p. 210.

114. HASK/5/ 1201.

115. See HASK/953/56, for an association of owners in the Altermarkt area; HASK/3/137, for correspondence between Dr. P.J. Bauwens, as representative of the Gesellschaft der Freunde des Wiederaufbaues von Köln, and Pünder, 20 August 1947; and HASK/5/1640, speech by Albert Wolter to the Interessengemeinschaft City Köln E.V., 6 December 1949.

116. *Aufbauförderungsgemeinschaften in deutschen Städten,* p. 64.

117. Greene, *Politics and Geography in Postwar German Planning,* pp. 146ff.

Chapter 10

1. In Bartning, ed. *Mensch und Raum*, p. 24. Also Hillebrecht, "Städtebau und Aufbau der Gemeinden," p. 70.

2. SAS/ ZAS 24/ Session of Beirat of ZAS, 7 June 1949.

3. Hillebrecht, "Neuaufbau der Städte," p. 35. The essay was first published in 1957. Also Hillebrecht, "Städtebau und Aufbau der Gemeinden," pp. 70–73.

4. Hillebrecht, "Neuaufbau der Städte," p. 75.

5. Ernst L. May, *Hat der deutsche Städtebau seine Chancen verpasst? Hat er noch eine Chance?* Schriften des Deutschen Verbandes für Wohnungswesen, Städtebau und Raumplanung, no. 19 (Cologne, 1956), pp. 16–20.

6. Herbert Jensen, "Die Stadtmitte, ihre Funktionen und ihre Gestaltung," in *Beiträge zum neuen Städtebau und Städtebaurecht*, Schriftenreihe der Deutschen Akademie für Städtebau und Landesplanung, vol. 12 (Tübingen, 1961), p. 104.

7. Meunier, "Illusion als Schicksal?" p. 26. The poem can be found in Johann Wolfgang Goethe, *Sämtliche Gedichte*, Part 2: Die Gedichte der Ausgabe letzter Hand (Munich: Deutscher Taschenbuch Verlag, 1961), pp. 242–43.

> Dummes Zeug kann man viel reden,
> Kann es auch schreiben,
> Wird weder Leib noch Seele töten,
> Es wird alles beim Alten bleiben.
> Dummes aber vors Auge gestellt
> Hat ein magisches Recht:
> Weil es die Sinne gefesselt hält,
> Bleibt der Geist ein Knecht.

8. See Kähler, "Regionalismus ist kein Stil," pp. 230–39, on the problems of architecture that tries to adapt to a local style.

9. For an interesting discussion of these problems, see Amos Rapoport, *The Meaning of the Built Environment: A Nonverbal Communication Approach* (Beverly Hills, Calif., London, and New Delhi, 1982). See also Manfred Sack, "Das ist doch technisch 'ne ganz einfache Sache: Über Bauen in Berlin, Architektur und Schmuck und die Erziehung zum ästhetischen Urteil—ein Gespräch mit Julius Posener," in *Die Zeit*, Conjunctures section, 5 January 1990, p. 36. Sack and Posener complain that tenants are insufficiently educated in the meaning of architecture and hence want to modify their homes. In contrast, Friedensreich Hundertwasser designed a social housing project in Vienna where tenants not only have the right but are encouraged to modify their surroundings. Kristina Hametner and Wilhelm Melzer, *Hundertwasser-Haus* (Vienna, 1988).

10. Kevin Lynch's 1960 book, *The Image of the City*, was influential on both sides of the Atlantic in persuading planners and architects to give much more weight to the subjective judgments of the "consumers" of urban space and less weight to supposedly objective factors such as the total space needed to park cars. Lynch's arguments formed part of the criticism directed during the 1960s against the reconstruction of the previous decade. See Werner Durth, *Die Inszenierung der Alltagswelt. Zur Kritik der Stadtgestaltung* (Braunschweig, 1977), pp. 43ff.

11. Peter Laslett, "The Quality of Life in European Cities: An Overview," in *The Quality of Life in European Cities*, Robert C. Fried and Paul M. Hohenberg, eds., Occasional Papers, Council for European Studies (Pittsburgh, Pa., 1974), p. 12.

12. Werner Durth, "Wirklicher als die Wirklichkeit: Überlegungen zur Macht der

Imaginationen," *Stadtbauwelt* 92 (1986): 1838, defines urbanity as "a cultural quality, which develops out of the ethnic, social, and political heterogeneity of the population, out of the tensions between different class situations, life forms, interest orientations, wishes, and appetites, and also out of productive discontent and calm tolerance." Two of the best-known German critics were Hans Paul Bahrdt, in "Nachbarschaft oder Urbanität" and Alexander Mitscherlich, in *Die Unwirtlichkeit unserer Städte*. Jane Jacobs was saying similar things in *The Death and Life of Great American Cities*, which appeared in German in 1963.

13. Schwarz, "Das Unplanbare."

14. Alfons Leitl and Gerhard Graubner, "Die politische Gesinnung des Architekten," *Baukunst und Werkform* 1 (1947): 94–98.

15. Alfons Leitl, "Anmerkungen zur Zeit," *Baukunst und Werkform* 2 (1948): 13.

16. Heinrich Böll, Introduction, in *Zeit der Ruinen: Köln am Ende der Diktatur*, Hans Schmitt-Rost, ed. (Cologne, 1965), p. ix.

17. Not everyone would agree, of course. Having traveled through West German cities, Danièle Sallenave, for example, finds it difficult to identify anything unique and memorable. "It is as if there is no Germany anymore." In "Mein Traum von Deutschland," *Die Zeit*, 13 October 1989, literature section, p. 1.

18. See Diefendorf, "Berlin on the Charles, Cambridge on the Spree."

19. Leitl, "What's Wrong with German City Planning?" p. 27. This was originally published in German in 1954.

Works Cited

Abel, Adolf. "Betrachtungen zum Wiederaufbau unserer Städte." *Die Neue Stadt* 3 (1949).

Adrian, Hanns. "Ideen, die überlebten." In Werner Durth and Niels Gutschow, eds., *Architektur und Städtebau der Fünfziger Jahre: Ergebnisse der Fachtagung in Hannover, 2.–4. Februar 1990. Schutz und Erhaltung von Bauten der Fünfziger Jahre.* Schriftenreihe des Deutschen Nationalkomitees für Denkmalschutz, vol. 41. Bonn, 1990.

————. "Stadtplanung und Stadterhaltung in Frankfurt." In Hiltrud Kier, ed., *Die Kunst unsere Städte zu erhalten*. Stuttgart, 1976.

Albers, Gerd. *Entwicklungslinien im Städtebau: Ideen, Thesen, Aussagen 1875–1945. Texte und Interpretationen*. Düsseldorf, 1975.

————. "Rudolf Hillebrecht und drei Jahrzehnte Städtebau." *Bauwelt* 71 (1980).

————. "Das Stadtplanungsrecht im 20. Jahrhundert als Niederschlag der Wandlungen im Planungsverständnis." *Stadtbauwelt* 65 (1980).

————. "Struktur und Gestalt im Städtebau. Eine Skizze." In *Zwischen Stadtmitte und Stadtregion. Bericht und Gedanken, Rudolf Hillebrecht zum 60. Geburtstag*. Stuttgart and Bern, 1970.

————. "Über den Rang des Historischen im Städtebau." *Die alte Stadt* 11 (1984).

Allmers, F. *Die Wohnungsbaupolitik der Gemeinnützigen Bauvereine im Rheinland von 1815–1914*. Cologne, 1925.

American Commission for the Protection and Salvage of Artistic and Historic Monuments in War Areas. *Report of the American Commission for the Protection and Salvage of Artistic and Historic Monuments in War Areas*. Washington, D.C., 1946.

Amtlicher Katalog der Constructa Bauaustellung 1951. Hannover, 1951.

Anderson, David C. *Architecture as a Means for Social Change in Germany, 1918–1933*. Diss., University of Minnesota, 1972.

Applegate, Celia. *A Nation of Provincials. The German Idea of Heimat*. Berkeley, Calif., Los Angeles, Oxford, 1990.

Architekten- und Ingenieur-Verein Hamburg, ed. *Hamburg und seine Bauten 1929–1953*. Hamburg, 1953.

————, ed. *Hamburg und seine Bauten 1954–1968*. Hamburg, 1969.

Arndt, Karl. "Die Münchener Architekturszene 1933–34 als ästhetisch-politisches Konfliktfeld." In Martin Broszat, Elke Fröhlich, and Anton Grossmann, eds., *Bayern in der NS-Zeit. Herrschaft und Gesellschaft im Konflikt*, vol. 3. Munich, 1981.

Arndt, Martin. "Wiederaufbau und Bauwirtschaft." *Wiederaufbau zerstörter Städte* no. 5 (1947).

Aufbauförderungsgemeinschaften in deutschen Städten: Bericht über eine Arbeitstagung. Frankfurt, 1950.

"Ein Aufruf: Grundsätzliche Forderungen." *Baukunst und Werkform* 1 (1947)

"Aus dem Bericht des Preisgerichts über den Constructa-Wettbewerb nr. 1." *Baurundschau* 40 (1950).

Back, Susanne, Elke Pahl, and Anne Rabenschlag. *Wohnungsbau, Wohnungsversorgung und Wohnungspolitik im 3. Reich in Hamburg*. Diplomarbeit, Hochschule für bildende Künste, Hamburg, 1977.

Backer, John H. *The Winds of History: The German Years of Lucius DuBignon Clay*. New York, 1983.

Bahrdt, Hans Paul. "Nachbarschaft oder Urbanität." *Bauwelt* 51–52 (1960).

Bartetzko, Dieter. "Versteinerte Gefühle—NS Architektur als Wunscherfüllung." *Stadtbauwelt* 92 (1986).

Bartning, Otto. "Mensch ohne Raum." *Baukunst und Werkform* 1 (1947).

———, ed. *Mensch und Raum*. Darmstädter Gespräch, no. 2. Darmstadt, 1952.

"Bau- und Bodenrecht." *Die Neue Stadt* 2 (1948).

Baudoui, Rémi. "Between Regionalism and Functionalism: French Reconstruction from 1940 to 1945." In Jeffry M. Diefendorf, ed., *Rebuilding Europe's Bombed Cities*. London and New York, 1990.

———. "L'équipe degli urbanisti della Sarre." *Casabella* 567 (April 1990).

Beck, Earl R. "The Allied Bombing of Germany, 1942–1945, and the German Response: Dilemmas of Judgment." *German Studies Review* 5 (1982).

———. *Under the Bombs: The German Home Front, 1942–1945*. Lexington, Ky., 1986.

Behrendt, W. C. "Geleitwort." *Die Form* 1 (1925).

Berger-Thimme, Dorothea. *Wohnungsfrage und Sozialstaat. Untersuchungen zu den Anfängen staatlicher Wohnungspolitik in Deutschland (1873–1948)*. Frankfurt, 1976.

Bergmann, Klaus. *Agrarromantik und Großstadtfeindschaft*. Marburger Abhandlungen zur Politischen Wissenschaft, vol. 20. Meisenheim am Glan, 1970.

Berndt, Heide. *Das Gesellschaftsbild bei Stadtplanern*. Stuttgart and Bern, 1968.

Bernt, Adolf. "Baudenkmale und Wiederaufbau. Versuch einer Ordnung." In *Aufbausonderhefte*, no. 5. Stuttgart, 1948.

Beseler, Hartwig, Niels Gutschow, and Frauke Kretschmer, eds. *Kriegsschicksale deutscher Architektur. Verluste, Schäden, Wiederaufbau. Eine Dokumentation für das Gebiet der Bundesrepublik Deutschland*. 2 vols. Neumünster, 1987.

Beule, Josef. "Der Stand der Enttrümmerung in den Westsektoren Berlins." *Neue Bauwelt* 4 (1949).

———. "Die Vereinigung Berliner Baubetriebe." *Neue Bauwelt* 1 (1946).

Beyme, Klaus von. *Der Wiederaufbau. Architektur und Städtebaupolitik in beiden deutschen Staaten*. Munich, 1987.

———, Werner Durth, Niels Gutschow, Winfried Nerdinger, and Thomas Topfstedt, eds. *Neue Städte aus Ruinen. Deutscher Städtebau der Nachkriegszeit*. Munich, 1992.

Blaum, Kurt. "Neugestaltung des Bau- und Bodenrechts." *Wiederaufbau zerstörter Städte*, no. 4 (1946).

———. "Nochmals: Das Goethehaus." *Die Neue Stadt* 2 (1948).

Blumenfeld, Hans. *The Modern Metropolis*. Cambridge, Mass., 1967.

Blumenroth, Ulrich. *Deutsche Wohnungspolitik seit der Reichsgründung: Darstellung und kritische Würdigung.* Beiträge zum Siedlungs- und Wohnungswesen und zur Raumplanung, vol. 25. Münster, 1975.

Blunck, W. "Demokratischer Städtebau." In *Demokratische Stadt- und Landesplanung.* Schriftenreihe der Deutschen Akademie für Städtebau und Landesplanung, vol. 7. Tübingen, 1955.

Bodenschatz, Harald. *Platz frei für das neue Berlin! Geschichte der Stadterneurung in der "größten Mietskasernenstadt der Welt" seit 1871.* Institut für Stadt-und Regionalplanung der Technischen Universität Berlin. Studien zur Neueren Planungsgeschichte, vol. 1. Berlin, 1987.

———. Hans Claussen, Karolus Heil, Wolfgang Schäche, Wolfgang J. Streich, Udo Dittfurth, Elke Herden, Stefan Metz, Andreas Schleicher, and Renate Villnow. "Nach 1945. Wiederaufbau, zweite Zerstörung und neue Tendenzen." In Josef Paul Kleihues, ed., *750 Jahre Architektur und Städtebau in Berlin.* Stuttgart, 1987.

Boehm, Herbert. "Die Gestaltung der Baugesetzgebung." In *Jahresbericht der Deutschen Akademie für Städtebau, Reichs- und Landesplanung.* Frankfurt, 1936.

———. "Kiels innere Neugestaltung." *Die Neue Stadt* 2 (1948).

———. "Städtebauliche Grundlegung für ein neues Frankfurt." In Max Kurz, ed., *Frankfurt baut auf.* Stuttgart, 1954.

Bofinger, Helge. "Architektur in Deutschland." In Helge Bofinger, Margret Bofinger, Jürgen Paul, and Heinrich Klotz, eds. *Architektur in Deutschland: Bundesrepublik und Westberlin.* Stuttgart, 1979.

Bohleber, Wolfgang. *Mit Marshallplan und Bundeshilfe. Wohnungsbaupolitik in Berlin 1945–1968.* Berlin, 1990.

Böll, Heinrich. *Gruppenbild mit Dame.* Cologne, 1971.

———. *Und sagte kein einziges Wort.* Frankfurt, 1966.

Bollerey, Franziska, Gerhard Fehl, and Kristiana Hartmann, eds. *Im Grünen wohnen—im Blauen planen. Ein Lesebuch zur Gartenstadt mit Beiträgen und Zeitdokumenten.* Stadt, Planung, Geschichte, vol. 12. Hamburg, 1990.

———, and Kristiana Hartmann. "A Patriarchal Utopia: The Garden City and Housing Reform in Germany at the Turn of the Century." In Anthony Sutcliffe, ed., *The Rise of Modern Urban Planning, 1800–1914.* New York, 1980.

Bonatz, Karl. "Anmerkungen zu den Presseinterviews mit Professor Gropius und zu seinem Vortrag im Titania-Palast am 22. August 1947." *Neue Bauwelt* 2 (1947).

———. "Fortführung der Stadtplanung in Berlin im Jahre 1950." *Neue Bauwelt* 5 (1950).

———. "Meine Stellungsnahme zu den Planungsarbeiten für Groß-Berlin, die ich bei meinem Amtsantritt vorfand." *Neue Bauwelt* 2 (1947).

———. "Der neue Plan von Berlin." *Neue Bauwelt* 2 (1947).

———. "Rund um den Zoo." *Neue Bauwelt* 4 (1949).

Borngräber, Christian. "Die sozialistische Metropole. Planung und Aufbau der Stalinallee und des Zentrums in Ost-Berlin 1949–1961." In Jochen Boberg, Tilman Fichter, and Eckhart Gillen, eds., *Die Metropole. Industriekultur in Berlin im 20. Jahrhundert.* Munich, 1986.

———. *Stil Novo: Design in den 50er Jahren. Phantasie und Phantastik.* Frankfurt, 1979.

Borstorff, Hans. *Stadt ohne Zentrum. Gedanken über die notwendige Wiedererrichtung der Berliner City und des Zoobereiches: ein Beitrag zu Berlin-Planung.* Berlin, 1948.

Bose, Michael, Michael Holtmann, Dittmar Machule, Elke Pahl-Weber, and Dirk Schubert. *". . . ein neues Hamburg entsteht . . .": Planen und Bauen von 1933–1945*. Beiträge zur städtebaulichen Forschung, vol. 2. Hamburg, 1986.

———, and Elke Pahl-Weber. "Regional- und Landesplanung in Hamburger Planungsraum bis zum Groß-Hamburg-Gesetz 1937." In Michael Bose, Michael Holtmann, Dittmar Machule, Elke Pahl-Weber, and Dirk Schubert, *". . . ein neues Hamburg entsteht . . .": Planen und Bauen von 1933–1945*. Beiträge zur städtebaulichen Forschung, vol. 2. Hamburg, 1986.

Böttcher, Karl. *Bericht über meine Arbeit*. Berlin, 1989.

———. "Von der Retorte zum Kunststoff-Montagehaus." *Neue Bauwelt* 1 (1946).

Brandt, Peter. "Wiederaufbau und Reform. Die Technische Universität Berlin 1945–1950." In Reinhard Rürup, ed., *Wissenschaft und Gesellschaft. Beiträge zur Geschichte der Technischen Universität Berlin 1879–1979*, vol. 1. Berlin, Heidelberg, and New York, 1979.

Breitling, Peter. "The Role of the Competition in the Genesis of Urban Planning: Germany and Austria in the Nineteenth Century." In Anthony Sutcliffe, ed., *The Rise of Modern Urban Planning, 1800–1914*. New York, 1980.

Brix, Michael. "Druck der Geschichte, Druck des Wirtschaftswunders. Der Wiederaufbau deutscher Städte: Nürnberg." *Frankfurter Allgemeine Zeitung* (23 October 1979).

———. *Lübeck. Die Altstadt als Denkmal*. Munich, 1975.

———. " 'Möge München dereinst als Kronjuwel einer friedlichen Welt erstrahlen'— Formale Leitlinien des Wiederaufbaus Innere Stadt." In Winfried Nerdinger, ed., *Aufbauzeit. Planen und Bauen München 1945–1950*. Munich, 1984.

Brunisch, Arthur. "Der Wohnungsbau in der Bundesrepublik Deutschland 1945–1955." *Der Architekt* 4 (1955).

Brunn, Gerhard. "Köln in den Jahren 1945 und 1946. Die Rahmenbedingungen des gesellschaftlichen Lebens." In Otto Dann, ed., *Köln nach dem Nationalsozialismus*. Wuppertal, 1981.

Brunswig, Hans. *Feuersturm über Hamburg. Die Luftangriffe auf Hamburg im Zweiten Weltkrieg und ihre Folgen*. Stuttgart, 1978.

Bullock, Nicholas. "Housing in Frankfurt, 1925–1931—And the New Wohnkultur." *Architectural Review* 163, no. 976 (1978).

———, and John Read. *The Movement for Housing Reform in Germany and France 1840–1914*. Cambridge, 1985.

Bundesarchiv and Institut für Zeitgeschichte, eds. *Akten zur Vorgeschichte der Bundesrepublik Deutschland, 1945–1949*. 5 vols. Munich, 1976–1981. Vol. 1: *September 1945–Dezember 1946*. Walter Vogel and Christoph Weisz, eds. Munich, 1976.

Bundesministerium für Vertriebene, Flüchtlinge und Kriegsgeschädigte. *Dokumente deutscher Kriegsschäden*. 10 vols. in 7. Bonn, 1958–1971.

Bundesministerium für Wohnungsbau. *Aufbau Kiel Holtenauer Straße. Ein Beispiel für städtebauliche Neuordnung durch Zusammenlegung*. Bonn, [1957].

Burchard, John. *The Voice of the Phoenix. Postwar Architecture in Germany*. Cambridge, Mass., 1966.

"Der Bürger und der Wiederaufbau." *Der Bauhelfer* 4 (1949).

Büschemann, Karl-Heinz. "Unter die Räder gekommen." *Die Zeit*, no. 42 (13 October 1989).

Campbell, Joan. *The German Werkbund: The Politics of Reform in the Applied Arts*. Princeton, N.J., 1978.

Caris, Markus. "Verkehr, Verkehrspolitik und Stadtplanung in Köln 1945–1948." *Geschichte in Köln*, no. 14 (1983).

Chronik der Stadt Stuttgart 1933–1945. Veröffentlichungen des Archivs der Stadt Stuttgart, vol. 30. Stuttgart, 1982.

Cohen, Jean-Louis. "Le Conseil Supérieur d'Architecture et d'Urbanisme." In Jean-Louis Cohen and Hartmut Frank, eds., *Deutsch-französische Beziehungen 1940–1950 und ihre Auswirkungen auf Architektur und Stadtgestalt.* Unpublished ms., Hamburg, 1989.

———, and Hartmut Frank, eds. *Deutsch-französische Beziehungen 1940–1950 und ihre Auswirkungen auf Architektur und Stadtgestalt.* Unpublished ms., Hamburg, 1989.

Conrads, Ulrich, ed. *Programs and Manifestoes on 20th-Century Architecture.* Michael Bullock, trans. Cambridge, Mass., 1970.

Cramer, Johannes. "Wie Wohnen? Neuer Anfang mit alten Konzepten." *Stadtbauwelt* 84 (1984).

———, and Niels Gutschow. *Bauausstellungen. Eine Architekturgeschichte des 20. Jahrhunderts.* Stuttgart, 1984.

Dähn, Arthur. "Die Entwicklung des Wohnungsbaus." In Architekten- und Ingenieur-Verein Hamburg, ed., *Hamburg und seine Bauten 1929–1953.* Hamburg, 1953.

———. "Hamburg, dicht am Ozean. Eine Gesamtschau der Aufgaben, Probleme und Leistungen." *Neue Bauwelt* 5 (1950).

———. "Die Zerstörung Hamburgs im Kriege 1939–1945." In Architekten- und Ingenieur-Verein Hamburg, ed., *Hamburg und seine Bauten 1929–1953.* Hamburg, 1953.

Dann, Otto, ed. *Köln nach dem Nationalsozialismus.* Wuppertal, 1981.

Dauber, Reinhard. "Die Anfänge der Wohnungspolitik und Bautätigkeit des Gemeinnützigen Wohnungsbau im Rheinland." *Die alte Stadt* 7 (1980).

Deckert, Hermann. "Wettbewerb um die Neugestaltung des Lübecker Marktes." *Der Bauhelfer* 5 (1950).

Demmer, Karl Friedrich. "Leitgedanken für Wettbewerbe zum Wiederaufbau unserer Städte." *Der Bauhelfer* 2 (1947).

———. "Zur Neugestaltung des Bodenrechts als Grundlage für Planung und Aufbau." *Der Bauhelfer* 3 (1948).

Deumer, Robert. "Pfandbriefaufwertung und Zwecksparen als Instrument des Investitionskredits." *Neue Wege zur Finanzierung des sozialen Wohnungsbaues.* Memmingen, 1948.

Deutsche Akademie für Städtebau, Reichs- und Landesplanung. *Vorschlag der Akademie für ein Reichsgesetz über städtebauliche Gesundungsmaßnahmen.* Frankfurt, 1936.

———, ed. *Die wirtschaftlichen und rechtlichen Grundlagen einer organischen Stadtgesundung und Stadterneuerung.* Berichte zur Raumforschung und Raumordnung, vol. 10. Leipzig, 1943.

Deutscher Städtetag. *Forderungen zum Wohnungsbau.* Cologne, 1949.

Deutscher Verband für Wohnungswesen, Städtebau und Landesplanung. "Die Grundsätze zur Baugesetzgebung." *Neue Bauwelt* 2 (1947).

Diefendorf, Jeffry M. "America and the Rebuilding of Urban Germany." In Jeffry M. Diefendorf, Axel Frohn, and Hermann-Josef Rupieper, eds., *American Policy and the Reconstruction of West Germany, 1945–1955.* Cambridge, 1993.

———. "Artery: Traffic Planning in Postwar Germany." *The Journal of Urban History* 15 (1989).

———. "Berlin on the Charles, Cambridge on the Spree: Walter Gropius, Martin Wagner and the Rebuilding of Germany." In Helmut Pfanner, ed., *Cross-Cultural Influences in Exile*. Bonn, 1986.

———. "Cities of Rubble to Cities in Greenery: Postwar Reconstruction Planning in Germany." *Planning History* 12 (1990).

———. "Konstanty Gutschow and the Reconstruction of Hamburg." *Central European History* 18 (1985).

———. "Organisationsfragen im Wiederaufbau." *Die Verwaltung* 18 (1985).

———. "Reconstruction Law and Building Law in Post-war Germany." *Planning Perspectives* 1 (1986).

———. "Stadtebauliche Tradition und der Wiederaufbau von Köln." Institut für Raumplanung, Universität Dortmund, Working Paper 70. Dortmund, 1991.

———. "Städtebauliche Traditionen und der Wiederaufbau von Köln vornehmlich nach 1945." *Rheinische Vierteljahrsblätter* 55 (1991).

———, ed. *Rebuilding Europe's Bombed Cities*. London and New York, 1990.

Dirks, Walter. "Mut zum Abschied. Zur Wiederherstellung des Frankfurter Goethehauses." *Frankfurter Hefte,* no. 8 (August 1947). Reprinted in *Baukunst und Werkform* 2 (1948), and in Hermann Glaser, Lutz von Pufendorf, and Michael Schöneich, eds. *So viel Anfang wie noch nie: Deutsche Städte 1945–1949*. Berlin, 1989.

Dittus, Wilhelm. *Baurecht im Werden*. Munich and Berlin, 1951.

———. "Der Entwurf zu einem Bayerischen Baugesetz." *Neue Bauwelt* 5 (1950).

———. "Neues Baurecht für zerstörte Städte." *Der Bauhelfer* 3 (1948).

———. "Die Problematik des künftigen Bau- und Bodenrechts unter besonderer Berücksichtigung der Aufbaugemeinschaften." In *Aufbauförderungsgemeinschaften in deutschen Städten*. Frankfurt, 1950.

———. "Wann kommt das Bundesbaugesetz?" *Blätter für Grundstücks-, Bau-und Wohnungswesen* 2 (1953).

———. "Zum Berliner Planungsgesetz und den Flächenarten seines Bebauungsplans." *Der Bauhelfer* 4 (1949).

Döcker, Richard. "Kommission französischer und deutscher Städtebauer in Baden-Baden." *Die Neue Stadt* 2 (1948).

Dölling, Regine. "Protection and Conservation of Historical Monuments in the Federal Republic of Germany." In Regine Dölling, ed., *The Conservation of Historical Monuments in the Federal Republic of Germany*. Timothy Nevill, trans. Munich, 1974.

———, ed. *The Conservation of Historical Monuments in the Federal Republic of Germany*. Timothy Nevill, trans. Munich, 1974.

Dronke, Wolfgang. "Der Wiederaufbau historischer Altstadtkerne—dargelegt am Beispiel Bremens." *Städtebauliche Aufgaben der Gegenwart mit besonderer Berücksichtigung Bremens. Der Wiederaufbau der freien Hansestadt Bremen*. Schriftenreihe der Bauverwaltung, no. 1. Bremen, 1946.

Dülffer, Jost, Jochen Thies, and Josef Henke. *Hitlers Städte. Baupolitik im Dritten Reich: Eine Dokumentation*. Cologne and Vienna, 1978.

Durth, Werner. "Architektur und Stadtplanung im Dritten Reich." In Michael Prinz and Rainer Zitelmann, eds., *Nationalsozialismus und Modernisierung*. Darmstadt, 1991.

———. *Deutsche Architekten. Biographische Verflechtungen 1900–1970*. Braunschweig and Wiesbaden, 1986.

———. "Düsseldorf." *Stadtbauwelt* 84 (1984).

———. *Die Inszenierung der Alltagswelt. Zur Kritik der Stadtgestaltung.* Braunschweig, 1977.

———. "Mainz: Blockierte Moderne." *Arch+* 67 (1983).

———. "Der programmierte Aufbau—Speers Arbeitsstab zum Wiederaufbau bombenzerstörter Städte." *Stadtbauwelt* 84 (1984).

———. "Vom Sieg der Zahlen über die Bilder: Anmerkungen zum Bedeutungswandel der Städte im Denken der Planer." *Stadtbauwelt* 88 (1985).

———. "Utopia im Niemands-Land." In Hermann Glaser, Lutz von Pufendorf, and Michael Schöneich, eds., *So viel Anfang war nie: Deutsche Städte 1945–1949.* Berlin, 1989.

———. "Wirklicher als die Wirklichkeit: Überlegungen zur Macht der Imaginationen." *Stadtbauwelt* 92 (1986).

———, and Friedemann Gschwind. "Stuttgart—Wettbewerbe um Zukunftsbilder." *Arch+* 72 (1983).

———, and Niels Gutschow. "Vom Architekturraum zur Stadtlandschaft: Wandlungen städtebaulicher Leitbilder unter dem Eindruck des Luftkrieges 1942–1945." In Axel Schildt and Arnold Sywottek, eds., *Massenwohnung und Eigenheim: Wohnungsbau und Wohnen in der Großstadt seit dem Ersten Weltkrieg.* Frankfurt and New York, 1988.

———, and Niels Gutschow. *Träume in Trümmern. Planungen zum Wiederaufbau zerstörter Städte im Westen Deutschlands 1940–1950.* Vol. 1, *Konzepte.* Vol. 2, *Städte.* Braunschweig and Wiesbaden, 1988.

———, and Niels Gutschow, eds. *Architektur und Städtebau der Fünfziger Jahre.* Schriftenreihe des Deutschen Nationalkomitees für Denkmalschutz, vol. 33. Bonn, 1987.

———, and Niels Gutschow, eds. *Architektur und Städtebau der Fünfziger Jahre: Ergebnisse der Fachtagung in Hannover, 2.–4. Februar 1990. Schutz und Erhaltung von Bauten der Fünfziger Jahre.* Schriftenreihe des Deutschen Nationalkomitees für Denkmalschutz, vol. 41. Bonn, 1990.

Ebert, Wils. "Gedanken zur Raumplanung von Berlin." *Neue Bauwelt* 3 (1948).

Ede, Günter, and Emil Möller. *Trümmerrecht unter Berücksichtigung der Ruienhypotheken.* Cologne, 1949.

Edelmann, Paul. "Mietpreisstop und Wohnungsbau." *Der Städtetag,* new series 2 (1949).

Ehrich, Helmuth. "—und von der Pflicht gegenüber unserer Stadt." *Lübeckische Blätter* 85 (1949).

Elsässer, Martin. "Fruchtbare Polarität." *Der Bauhelfer* 3 (1948).

Erbs, Karl Josef. *Grundlagen für der Aufbau in Stadt und Land.* Berlin, 1948.

Erfordernisse der Bau- und Bodengesetzgebung (Weinheimer Gutachten). Schriftenreihe des Bundesministers für Wohnungsbau, no. 1. Hamburg, 1952.

ERP und die Stadt Berlin. Vienna, 1961.

"Erstes Wohnungsbaugesetz." *Bundesgesetzblatt* (26 April 1950).

Evers, Hans Gerhard. *Tod, Macht und Raum als Bereiche der Architektur.* 1939, rpt. Munich, 1970.

Fabricius, Eugen. "Architekt BDA." *Neue Bauwelt* 2 (1947).

Feder, Gottfried. *Die neue Stadt. Versuch der Begründung einer neuen Stadtplanungskunst aus der sozialen Struktur der Bevölkerung.* Berlin, 1939.

Fehl, Gerhard. "Die Moderne unterm Hakenkreuz. Ein Versuch, die Rolle funktionalistischer Architektur im Dritten Reich zu klären." In Hartmut Frank, ed., *Faschistische Architekturen. Planen und Bauen in Europa 1930 bis 1945.* Stadt, Planung, Geschichte, vol. 3. Hamburg, 1985.

————. "Der Verlust der 'grünen Mitte': Ein Blick auf das Frankfurter 'Niddatal-Projekt' von 1927 anläßlich der für 1989 geplanten Bundesgartenschau," *Stadtbauwelt* 92 (1986).

————, and Tilman Harlander. "Hitlers Sozialer Wohnungsbau 1940 bis 1945—Bindeglied der Baupolitik und Baugestaltung zwischen Weimarer Zeit und Nachkriegszeit." *Stadtbauwelt* 84 (1984).

————, and Juan Rodriguez-Lores, eds. *Stadterweiterungen 1800–1875: von den Anfängen des modernen Städtebaues in Deutschland.* Hamburg, 1983.

Fisch, Stefan. "Joseph Stübben in Köln und Theodor Fischer in München. Stadtplanung des späten 19. Jahrhunderts im Vergleich." *Geschichte in Köln,* no. 22 (1987).

Fischer, Friedhelm. "German Reconstruction as an International Activity." In Jeffry M. Diefendorf, ed., *Rebuilding Europe's Bombed Cities.* London and New York, 1990.

Fischer, Manfred. *Fritz Schumacher, das Hamburger Stadtbild und die Denkmalpflege.* Arbeitshefte zur Denkmalpflege in Hamburg, vol. 4. Hamburg, 1977.

Fischer, Wilhelm K. *Aachen plant: 1950–1975.* Aachen, 1975.

————. "Die Neuplanung Aachens nach dem zweiten Weltkrieg." In Bernhard Pohl and Albert Huyskens, eds., *Das alte Aachen, seine Zerstörung und sein Wiederaufbau.* Aachen, 1953.

————. "Probleme der Stadtplanung Aachens nach der Zerstörung." *Der deutsche Baumeister* 16 (1955).

Fischer-Dieskau, Jürgen. "Wo kommt das Geld für den Wohnungsbau her?" In *Amtlicher Katalog der Constructa Bauausstellung 1951.* Hannover, 1951.

Fishman, Robert. *Urban Utopias in the Twentieth Century: Ebenezer Howard, Frank Lloyd Wright, and Le Corbusier.* Cambridge, Mass., 1977.

Flender, A. "Die gemeinnützige Wohnungswirtschaft in Nordrhein-Westfalen." In *Um die Grundlagen des sozialen Wohnungsbaues: Kundgebung der Gemeinnützigen Wohnungswirtschaft des Landes Nordrhein-Westfalen.* Essen, 1950.

Frampton, Kenneth. *Modern Architecture: A Critical History,* rev. ed. London, 1985.

Frank, Hartmut. "Auf der Suche nach der alten Stadt. Zur Diskussion um Heimatschutz und Stadtbaukunst beim Wiederaufbau von Freudenstadt." In H.-G. Burkhardt, H. Frank, U. Höhns, and K. Stieghorst, eds., *Stadtgestalt und Heimatgefühl. Der Wiederaufbau von Freudenstadt 1945–1954. Analysen, Vergleiche und Dokumente.* Hamburg, 1988.

————. " 'Caveant Consules': Berater und Gutachter des Stadtplanungsamtes bei der Mainzer Wiederaufbauplanung." In Jean-Louis Cohen and Hartmut Frank, eds., *Deutsch-französische Beziehungen 1940–1950 und ihre Auswirkungen auf Architektur und Stadtgestalt.* Unpublished ms., Hamburg, 1989.

————. "3 Mal Wiederaufbau." Unpublished ms, 1987.

————. "Monumentalität und Stadtlandschaft. Anmerkungen zu einer bösen Architektur mit einem Abstand von 45 Jahren." In Jürgen Harten, Hans-Werner Schmidt, and Marie Louise Syring, eds., *"Die Axt hat geblüht . . .": Europäische Konflikte der 30er Jahre in Erinnerung an die frühe Avantgarde.* Düsseldorf, 1987.

————. "Pläne für Groß-Mainz." In Jean-Louis Cohen and Hartmut Frank, eds., *Deutsch-französische Beziehungen 1940–1950 und ihre Auswirkungen auf Architektur und Stadtgestalt.* Unpublished ms., Hamburg, 1989.

————. "Die Stadtlandschaft Diedenhofen." In Jean-Louis Cohen and Hartmut Frank, eds., *Deutsch-französische Beziehungen 1940–1950 und ihre Auswirkungen auf Architektur und Stadtgestalt.* Unpublished ms., Hamburg, 1989.

———. "Trümmer: Traditionelle und moderne Architekturen in Nachkriegsdeutschland." In Bernhard Schulz, ed., *Grauzonen. Kunst und Zeitbilder. Farbwelten 1945–1955*. Berlin, 1983.

———. "Welche Sprache sprechen Steine? Zur Einführung in den Sammelband 'Faschistische Architekturen.' " In Hartmut Frank, ed., *Faschistische Architekturen. Planen und Bauen in Europa 1930 bis 1945*. Stadt, Planung, Geschichte, vol. 3. Hamburg, 1985.

———, ed. *Faschistische Architekturen: Planen und Bauen in Europa 1930 bis 1945*. Stadt, Planung, Geschichte, vol. 3. Hamburg, 1985.

Frey, Walter. "Kriegsschäden und Wiederaufbau." *Der Aufbau* 8 (1953).

Galbraith, John Kenneth. *A Life in Our Times*. Boston, 1981.

Ghirardo, Diane Y. *Building New Communities: New Deal America and Fascist Italy*. Princeton, N.J., 1989.

Giedion, Sigfried. *Walter Gropius: Work and Teamwork*. Zurich, 1954.

Gimbel, John. *A German Community under American Occupation. Marburg, 1945–1952*. Stanford, Calif., 1961.

Glaser, Hermann. *The Rubble Years. The Cultural Roots of Postwar Germany 1945–1948*. Franz Feige and Patricia Gleason, trans. New York, 1986.

———, Lutz von Pufendorf, and Michael Schöneich, eds. *So viel Anfang war nie: Deutsche Städte 1945–1949*. Berlin, 1989.

Glootz, [Oberbaurat a. D.]. "Wie kann der Hammerbrookplan durchgeführt werden?" *Nordwestdeutsche Bauzeitung* 3 (1951).

Göderitz, Johannes. "Hausformen und Bebauungsweise." In *Amtlicher Katalog der Constructa Bauausstellung 1951*. Hannover, 1951.

———, and Wilhelm Blunck. *Das Aufbaugesetz von Niedersachsen*. Göttingen, 1950.

———, Roland Rainer, and Hubert Hoffmann. *Die gegliederte und aufgelockerte Stadt*. Tübingen, 1957.

———, ed. *Neues Städtebaurecht: Der Entwurf eines Gesetzes über den Aufbau der Deutschen Gemeinden*. Schriften des Deutschen Städtetages, no. 3 (1948).

Görres, Guido. "Aufbaugesetz. Gesetz zur Durchführung der Ortsplanung und des Aufbaues in den Gemeinden." *Baurundschau* 39 (1949). Special issue.

Grabe, Thomas, Reimar Hollmann, Klaus Mlynek, and Michael Radtke. *Unter der Wolke des Todesleben . . . . Hannover im Zweiten Weltkrieg*. 2 vols. Hamburg, 1983.

Grass, Günter. *Gesammelte Gedichte*. Neuwied and Berlin, 1971.

Grauvogel, Gustav. "Die rechtlichen Grundlagen beim Wiederaufbau Stuttgarts." *Kommunalpolitische Blätter* 7 (1955).

Grebler, Leo. *Europe's Reborn Cities*. Urban Land Institute Technical Bulletin 28. Washington, D.C., 1956.

Greene, Ernest Thomas. "Planning in Post-War Cologne." *Town and Country Planning* 28 (1960).

———. *Politics and Geography in Postwar German City Planning*. Diss., Princeton University, 1958.

———. "Politics and Planning in Postwar Germany." *Urban Studies* 1 (1964)

———. "West German City Reconstruction: Two Case Studies." *Sociology Review* 7 (1959).

Gropius, Walter. "The Architect's Contribution to the Postwar Construction Program." *The Bay State Builder* 1, no. 12 (1943).

———. "Reconstruction: Germany." *Task*, no. 7–8 (1948).

———. "Walter Gropius spricht über Städtebau: Auszug aus dem Vortrag auf dem

CIAM-Kongress im September 1947 in Bridgewater" (reported by Eduard F. Sekler). *Der Aufbau* 3 (1948).

———. "Will Europe Build Cities or Shanty Towns?" *Weekend* (magazine of *Stars and Stripes*) (3 January 1948).

Gruber, Karl. *Die Gestalt der deutschen Stadt. Ihr Wandel aus der geistigen Ordnung der Zeiten.* Munich, 1952.

Grundmann, Günther. *Großstadt und Denkmalpflege. Hamburg 1945 bis 1959.* Hamburg, 1960.

Grüttner, Michael. "Soziale Hygiene und Soziale Kontrolle: Die Sanierung der Hamburger Gängeviertel, 1892–1936." In Arno Herzig, Dieter Langewiesche, and Arnold Sywottek, eds., *Arbeiter in Hamburg: Unterschichten, Arbeiter und Arbeiterbewegung seit dem ausgehenden 18. Jahrhundert.* Hamburg, 1983.

Gühlk, Otto. "Einheitlicher Berufsverband der Architekten." *Neue Bauwelt* 2 (1947).

Guther, Max. "Zur Geschichte der Städtebaulehre an deutschen Hochschulen." In Ulrike Pampe, ed., *Heinz Wetzel und die Geschichte der Städtebaulehre an deutschen Hochschulen.* Stuttgart, 1982.

———, Rudolf Hillebrecht, Heinz Schmeissner, and Walther Schmidt. " 'Ich kann mich nicht herausdenken aus dem Vorgang der Geschichte, in den ich eingebunden bin'—Erinnerungen an den Wiederaufbau der Bundesrepublik: Hintergründe, Leitbilde, Planungen." *Stadtbauwelt* 72 (1981).

Gutschow, Konstanty. *Stadtmitte Hannover. Beiträge zur Aufbauplanung der Innenstadt.* Hannover, 1949.

———. "Wettbewerb Bahnhofsviertel Münster." *Die Neue Stadt* 2 (1948).

———. "Zum Wettbewerb um die Hamburger Innenstadt." *Baurundschau* 39 (1949).

Gutschow, Niels. "Die ersehnte Katastrophe." *Die Zeit* (8 January 1988).

———. "Freudenstadt: Ein Versuch über den Freiraum von Städtebau 1945 bis 1949—fern jeder Realisierungschance." *Stadtbauwelt* 84 (1984).

———. "Fritz Schumacher—Vordenker für den Wiederaufbau zerstörter Städte in Norddeutschland." *Stadtbauwelt* 84 (1984).

———. "Hamburg—The 'Catastrophe' of July 1943." In Jeffry M. Diefendorf, ed., *The Rebuilding of Europe's Bombed Cities.* London and New York, 1989.

———. "Die historische Stadt im Städtebau der vierziger Jahre. Leitbilder der Wiederaufbauplanung und des Aufbaus 1942–1952." In Hartwig Beseler, Niels Gutschow, and Frauke Kretschmer, eds., *Kriegsschicksale deutscher Architektur. Verluste, Schäden, Wiederaufbau,* vol. 1. Neumünster, 1987.

———. "Lübeck." *Stadtbauwelt* 84 (1984).

———. "Statträume des Wiederaufbaus—Objekte der Denkmalpflege?" *Deutsche Kunst und Denkmalpflege* 43 (1985).

———. "Väter und Söhne." *Bauwelt* 75 (1980).

———, and Renate Stiemer. *Dokumentation Wiederaufbau der Stadt Münster.* Münster, 1982.

———, and Renate Stiemer. *Dokumentation Wiederaufbau Münster: Materialsammlung.* Beiträge zur Stadtforschung, Stadtentwicklung, Stadtplanung, vol. 6. Münster, 1980.

Haack, Annemarie. "Der Generalbebauungsplan für Hamburg 1940/41 und 1944." *Uni HH Forschung* 12 (1980).

Haagen, [Stadtbaurat]. "Die Gestaltung des Marktplatzes der Hildesheimer Altstadt." *Neue Bauwelt* 6 (1951).

Habel, Heinrich. "Denkmalpflege in München seit 1945." In Hiltrud Kier, ed., *Die Kunst unsere Städte zu erhalten.* Stuttgart, 1976.

Hackelsberger, Christoph. *Die aufgeschobene Moderne. Ein Versuch zur Einordnung der Architektur der Fünfziger Jahre.* Berlin, 1985.

Hagspiel, Wolfram. "Die Nationalsozialistische Stadtplanung in und für Köln." *Geschichte in Köln,* no. 9 (1981).

Haines, Gerald K. "Who Gives a Damn about Medieval Walls?" *Prologue* 8 (1976).

Hametner, Kristina, and Wilhelm Melzer. *Hundertwasser-Haus.* Vienna, 1988.

Hamm, Ernst. "Betrachtungen zur Aufbaugesetzgebung." *Der Bauhelfer* 4 (1949).

Hänsel, Sylvaine, Michael Scholz, and Christoph Bürkle. "Die Grindelhochhäuser als erste Wohnhochhäuser in Deutschland." *Zeitschrift des Vereins für Hamburgische Geschichte* 66 (1980).

Hansell, Haywood S., Jr. *The Strategic Air War against Germany and Japan: A Memoir.* Washington, D.C., 1986.

Hansestadt Hamburg. *Skizzen zum Generalbebauungsplan 1947.* Hamburg, 1948.

Harlander, Tilman, and Gerhard Fehl, eds. *Hitlers Sozialer Wohnungsbau 1940–1945. Wohnungspolitik, Baugestaltung und Siedlungsplanung.* Stadt, Planung, Geschichte, vol. 6. Hamburg, 1986.

Hartmann, Kristiana. *Deutsche Gartenstadtbewegung: Kulturpolitik und Gesellschaftsreform.* Munich, 1976.

Hartog, Rudolf. "Architektur der 50er Jahre—Erlebnisse und Erfahrungen." In *Architektur und Städtebau der Fünfziger Jahre.* Schriftenreihe des Deutschen Nationalkomitees für Denkmalschutz, vol. 36. Bonn, 1988.

Hastings, Max. *Bomber Command: The Myths and Reality of the Strategic Bombing Offensive 1939–1945.* New York, 1979.

Hatje, Gerd, Hubert Hoffmann, and Karl Kaspar. *New German Architecture.* H. J. Montague, trans. Stuttgart, London, and New York, 1956.

Havemann, Wilhelm. *Berlin in der Zukunft. Die Grundlagen der städtebaulichen und wirtschaftlichen Zukunftsmöglichkeiten Berlins, gleichzeitig der Versuch einer kritischen Beleuchtung der Aufbaupläne.* Berlin, 1946.

Hays, K. Michael. "Tessenow's Architecture as National Allegory: Critique of Capitalism or Protofascism." *Assemblage* 8 (February 1989).

Hebebrand, Werner. "Der Frankfurter Hauptstrassenwettbewerb im Rahmen der städtebaulichen Gesamtplanung." *Die Neue Stadt* 1 (1947).

Hegemann, Werner. *Das steinerne Berlin. Geschichte der größten Mietskasernenstadt der Welt.* Berlin, 1930.

Heil, Karolus. "Einige Anmerkungen zur Veranstaltung." In Erich Konter, ed., *Wendezeiten in Architektur und Stadtplanung. Kontinuität in der Entwicklung nach 1945.* Arbeitshefte des Instituts für Stadt- und Regionalplanung der Technischen Universität Berlin, no. 36. Berlin, 1986.

Heilmann, A. "Zur baulichen Neuordnung der zerstörten Städte." *Der Bauhelfer* 2 (1947).

Heineberg, Heinz. "Service Centres in East and West Berlin." In R. A. French and F. E. Ian Hamilton, eds., *The Socialist City: Spatial Structure and Urban Policy.* Chichester, 1979.

Heinicke, Erich. "Grundlagen für die Neugestaltung des Bodenrechts." In *Jahresbericht der Deutsche Akademie für Städtebau, Reichs- und Landesplanung.* Frankfurt, 1936.

Helas, Volker. "Die Architektur der Fünfziger Jahre in Kassel." In *Architektur und Städtebau der Fünfziger Jahre.* Schriftenreihe des Deutschen Nationalkomitees für Denkmalschutz, vol. 36. Bonn, 1988.

Helmer, Stephen D. *Hitler's Berlin. The Speer Plans for Reshaping the City.* Ann Arbor, Mich., 1985.

Henning, Friedrich-Wilhelm. "Stadtplanerische Überlegungen in der Zwischenkriegs-zeit—dargestellt anhand des Planes von Hans Bernhard Reichow für Stettin." In Hans-Jürgen Teuteberg, ed., *Stadtwachstum, Industrialisierung, Sozialer Wandel: Beiträge zur Erforschung der Urbanisierung im 19. und 20. Jahrhundert.* Berlin, 1986.

Herbert, Gilbert. *The Dream of the Factory-Made House: Walter Gropius and Konrad Wachsmann.* Cambridge, Mass., 1984.

Herdig, Klaus. *The Decorated Diagram: Harvard Architecture and the Failure of the Bauhaus Legacy.* Cambridge, Mass., 1983.

Herf, Jeffrey. *Reactionary Modernism: Technology, Culture, and Politics in Weimar and the Third Reich.* Cambridge, 1984.

Herzig, Arno, Dieter Langewiesche, and Arnold Sywottek, eds. *Arbeiter in Hamburg: Unterschichten, Arbeiter und Arbeiterbewegung seit dem ausgehenden 18. Jahrhundert.* Veröffentlichung des Hamburger Arbeitskreises für Regionalgeschichte. Hamburg, 1983.

Hespeler, Otto. "Der Umbau der Lübecker Altstadt." *Zeitschrift des Deutschen Akademie für Städtebau, Reichs- und Landesplanung* 33 (1938).

Hewitt, Kenneth. "Place Annihilation: Area Bombing and the Fate of Urban Places." *Annals of the Association of American Geographers* 73, no. 2 (1983).

Heyn, Erich. *Zerstörung und Aufbau der Großstadt Essen.* Bonn, 1955.

Hillebrecht, Rudolf. "Architektur und Städtebau in Ost und West." *Der Städtetag,* new series 10 (1957).

———. "Ausschreibung und Preisgerichtsverfahren für den Städtebau-Wettbewerb Hannover." *Der Bauhelfer* 4 (1949).

———. "Gespräch mit Gropius." *Baurundschau* 38 (1948).

———. "Neuaufbau der Städte." In *Städtebau als Herausforderung. Ausgewählte Schriften und Vorträge.* Cologne, 1975. Originally published in 1957.

———. *Neubebauung zerstörter Wohnflächen.* Schriftenreihe des Deutschen Verbandes für Wohnungswesen, Städtebau und Raumplanung, no. 7. Frankfurt, 1952.

———. "Neuer Wohnungsbau in England." *Gemeinnützige Wohnungswirtschaft,* no. 6 and 8 (1949). Rpt. *Stadtbauwelt* 96 (1987).

———. *Städtebau als Herausforderung. Ausgewählte Schriften und Vorträge.* Cologne, 1975.

———. "Städtebau und Aufbau der Gemeinden." In *Amtlicher Katalog der Constructa Bauausstellung 1951.* Hannover, 1951.

———. "Von Ebenezer Howard zu Jane Jacobs—oder: War alles falsch?" *Stadtbauwelt* 8 (1965).

———, and Arthur Dähn. *Fundamente des Aufbaues. Organisatorische Grundlagen.* Schriftenreihe des Bundes deutscher Architekten, vol. 14. Hamburg, 1948.

Hinz, Berthold, Hans-Ernst Mittig, Wolfgang Schäche, and Angela Schönberger, eds. *Die Dekoration der Gewalt: Kunst und Medien im Faschismus.* Gießen, 1979.

Hipp, Hermann. "Der gewöhnliche Traditionalismus: Heimat im Dritten Reich." *Der Architekt* 4 (1983).

———. "Wohnungen für Arbeiter? Zum Wohnungsbau und zur Wohnungsbaupolitik in Hamburg in den 1920er Jahren." In Arno Herzig, Dieter Langewiesche, and Arnold Sywottek, eds., *Arbeiter in Hamburg: Unterschichten, Arbeiter und Arbeiterbewegung seit dem ausgehenden 18. Jahrhundert.* Hamburg, 1983.

Hoffmann, Hubert. "Zur Charta von Athen." *Neue Bauwelt* 4 (1949).

Hoffmann-Axthelm, Dieter. "Deutschland 1945–80—Der Architekt ohne Architektur." *Arch+* 59 (1981).

Högg, Hans. "Der Neuaufbau der zerstörten Städte als zentrale Aufgabe unserer Zeit." *Abhandlungen und Vorträge.* Die Wittheit zu Bremen, vol. 18, no. 2. Bremen, 1949.

Höhns, Ulrich. " 'Neuaufbau' als Hoffnung—'Wiederaufbau' als Festschreibung der Misere. Marshallplan und Wohnungsbau in der Bundesrepublik nach dem Kriege." In Bernhard Schulz, ed., *Grauzonen. Kunst und Zeitbilder. Farbwelten 1945–1955.* Berlin, 1983.

———. "Stadtplanung in Saarbrücken 1940–1960." In Klaus von Beyme, Werner Durth, Niels Gutschow, Winfried Nerdinger, and Thomas Topfstedt, eds., *Neue Städte aus Ruinen. Deutscher Städtebau der Nachkriegszeit.* Munich, 1992.

Homann, Klaus, Martin Kieren, and Ludovica Scarpa, eds. *Martin Wagner 1885–1957: Wohnungsbau und Weltstadtplanung: Die Rationalisierung des Glücks.* Berlin, 1985.

Honhart, Michael. "Company Housing as Urban Planning in Germany, 1870–1940." *Central European History* 23 (1990).

Horn, Karl. "Steuer- und Abgabevergünstigungen im Wohnungsbau." *Der Städtetag,* new series 4 (1951).

Hörner, Ludwig. *Hannover—Heute und vor 100 Jahren.* Munich, 1982.

Höroldt, Dietrich. "Von der Bürgerstadt zur Bundeshauptstadt." In Walter Först, ed., *Städte nach zwei Weltkriegen.* Cologne, 1984.

Hoss, Walter. "Der Aufbauplan der Stadt Stuttgart." *Die Neue Stadt* 3 (1949).

Howard, Ebenezer. *Garden Cities of Tomorrow.* Frederic J. Osborn, ed. Cambridge, Mass., 1965.

Hundertwasser, Friedensreich. "Verschimmelungs-Manifest gegen den Rationalismus in der Architektur." In *Neue Architektur in Österreich, 1945–1970.* Vienna, 1969.

Iklé, Fred Charles. *The Social Impact of Bomb Destruction.* Norman, Okla., 1958.

Interbau Berlin 1957. Amtlicher Katalog der Internationalen Bauausstellung. Berlin, 1957.

Die Interbau wird diskutiert: Die ersten Ergebnisse. Wiesbaden and Berlin, 1960.

Irek, Joachim. *Mannheim in den Jahren 1945 bis 1949. Geschichte einer Stadt zwischen Diktatur und Republik.* Vol. 1, *Darstellung.* Vol. 2, *Dokumente.* Veröffentlichungen des Stadtarchivs Mannheim, vols. 9 and 10. Stuttgart, 1983.

Isaacs, Reginald. *Walter Gropius.* 2 vols. Berlin, 1983–84.

Jackson, John Brinckerhoff. *The Necessity for Ruins and Other Topics.* Amherst, Mass., 1980.

Jacobs, Jane. *The Death and Life of Great American Cities.* New York, 1961.

Janssen, Gregor. *Das Ministerium Speer: Deutschlands Rüstung im Krieg.* Berlin, 1968.

Jatho, Carl Oskar. *Urbanität. Über die Wiederkehr einer Stadt.* Düsseldorf, 1946.

Jensen, Herbert. (Comments on papers read.) *Demokratische Stadt- und Landesplanung.* Schriftenreihe der Deutschen Akademie für Städtebau und Landesplanung, vol. 7. Tübingen, 1955.

———. "Finanzierung des Wiederaufbaus." *Der Städtetag,* new series 4 (1951).

———. "Krisis des planmäßigen Aufbaus." *Der Bauhelfer* 5 (1950).

———. "Neuaufbau der Innenstadt—eine Lebensfrage für die Stadt Kiel." *Baurundschau* 40 (1950).

———. "Die Stadtmitte, ihre Funktionen und ihre Gestaltung." In *Beiträge zum neuen Städtebau und Städtebaurecht.* Schriftenreihe der Deutschen Akademie für Städtebau und Landesplanung, vol. 12. Tübingen, 1961.

———. "Stadtplanung und Baupolitik der Stadt Kiel seit 1945." *Neue Bauwelt* 7 (1952).

———. "Der Wettlauf zwischen Verkehr und Städtebau." In *Deutsche Akademie für Städtebau und Landesplanung: Jahresversammlung.* Munich, 1953.

———. "Zum Ergebnis des Kieler Innenstadtwettbewerbs." *Der Bauhelfer* 4 (1949).

Johe, Werner. *Neuengamme. Zur Geschichte der Konzentrationslager in Hamburg.* Hamburg, 1982.

Jordy, William H. "The Aftermath of the Bauhaus in America. Gropius, Mies, and Breuer." In Donald Fleming and Bernard Bailyn, eds., *The Intellectual Migration. Europe and America, 1930–1960.* Cambridge, Mass., 1969.

Jürgens, F. "Der Neubau des Hamburger Schulwesens." In Erich Lüth, ed., *Neues Hamburg. Zeugnisse von Wiederaufbau der Hansestadt,* vol. 1. Hamburg, 1947.

Kabel, Erich. *Baufreiheit und Raumordnung: die Verflechtung von Baurecht und Bauentwicklung im deutschen Städtebau.* Ravensburg, 1949.

Kähler, Gerd. "Regionalismus ist kein Stil." *Bauwelt* 76 (1986).

Kallmorgen, Werner. *Deutsche Akademie für Städtebau und Landesplanung. Erinnerungen an 18 Jahre Leben und Arbeit in ihrer Landesgruppe Hamburg und Schleswig-Holstein.* Hamburg, 1965.

Kampffmeyer, Hans Martin. "Die Charta von Athen." *Die Neue Stadt* 2 (1948).

———, Friedrich Spengelin, and Wolf Jobst Siedler. "Zu Beginn der 60er Jahre hatten wir das Gefühl: Jetzt müssen wir von Grund auf neu anfangen." *Stadtbauwelt* 88 (1985).

Kellermann, Henry J. *Cultural Relations as an Instrument of U.S. Foreign Policy: The Educational Exchange Program between the United States and Germany, 1945–1954.* Cultural Relations Programs of the U.S. Department of State, Historical Studies, Number 3. Washington, D.C., 1978.

Kempmann, Joachim. *Das Ideengut Martin Wagners.* Diss., Technische Universität, Berlin, 1968.

Kennan, George F. *Sketches from a Life.* New York, 1989.

Kier, Hiltrud. "Denkmalpflege in Köln." In Rheinischer Verein für Denkmalpflege und Landschaftsschutz, *Glanz und Elend der Denkmalpflege und Stadtplanung Cöln 1906–2006 Köln.* Cologne, 1981.

———. "Das Jahr der Romanischen Kirchen in Köln—wozu eigentlich?" *Deutscher Kunst und Denkmalpflege* 43 (1985).

———. *Die Kölner Neustadt: Planung, Entstehung, Nutzung.* Beiträge zu den Bau- und Kunstdenkmälern im Rheinland, vol. 23. Düsseldorf, 1978.

———. "Der Wiederaufbau von Köln, 1945–1975. Eine Bilanz aus kunsthistorischer Sicht." In Hiltrud Kier, ed., *Die Kunst unsere Städte zu erhalten.* Stuttgart, 1976.

———. "Die Wiederherstellung der Kölner Altstadt-Kirchen." In Rheinischer Verein für Denkmalpflege und Landschaftsschutz, *Glanz und Elend der Denkmalpflege und Stadtplanung Cöln 1906–2006 Köln.* Cologne, 1981.

———, ed. *Die Kunst unsere Städte zu erhalten.* Stuttgart, 1976.

Kirchen in Trümmern. Cologne, 1948.

Kleffner, Fritz. "Wohnungsmietstop und Wohnungsbau." *Der Städtetag,* new series 2 (1949).

Klett, Arnulf. "Aufbau und Wohnungsbau—Die Aufgabe für 1950." *Deutscher*

Städtetag, Tagungsbericht. 7th Meeting of the Main Committee, 10 and 11 March 1950.

————. "Die Bedeutung der Trümmerverwertung für die kommunale Wirtschaft." *Der Städtetag,* new series 4 (1951).

Klöcking, Johannes. "Denkmalschutz und Aufbauplan." *Lübeckische Blätter* 85 (1949).

Klotz, Heinrich, Roland Günter, and Gottfried Kiesow. *Keine Zukunft für unsere Vergangenheit: Denkmalschutz und Stadtzerstörung.* Gießen, 1975.

Knapp, Manfred. "Reconstruction and West-Integration: The Impact of the Marshall Plan on Germany." *Zeitschrift für die gesamte Staatswissenschaft* 137 (1981).

Koberg, Heinz. *Hannover 1945. Zerstörung und Wiedergeburt. Bilddokumente eines Augenzeugen.* Hannover, 1985.

Koch, Georg Friedrich. "Speer, Schinkel und der preussische Stil." In Karl Arndt, Georg Friedrich Koch, and Lars Olof Larsson. *Albert Speer, Architectektur. Arbeiten 1933–1942.* Frankfurt, 1978.

Koenig, Helmut. *Beiträge zur Soziographie Münchens.* Munich, 1949–50.

————. *München im Wiederaufbau.* Munich, 1952.

————. *München setzt Stein auf Stein.* Munich, 1958.

Köllmann, Wolfgang. "The Process of Urbanization in Germany at the Height of the Industrialization Period." *Journal of Contemporary History* 4 (1969).

Konter, Erich. "Deutsche Planer und Architekten: Selbsverständnis und 'Standes'-Politik—Neubeginn oder Kontinuität?" In Erich Konter, ed., *Wendezeiten in Architektur und Stadtplanung—Kontinuität oder Bruch in der Entwicklung nach 1945.* Arbeitshefte des Instituts für Stadt- und Regionalplanung der Technischen Universität Berlin, no. 36. Berlin, 1986.

————, ed. *Wendezeiten in Architektur und Stadtplanung—Kontinuität oder Bruch in der Entwicklung nach 1945.* Arbeitshefte des Instituts für Stadt- und Regionalplanung der Technischen Universität Berlin, no. 36. Berlin, 1986.

Koshar, Rudy J. "Altar, Stage and City: Historic Preservation and Urban Meaning in Nazi Germany." *History and Memory* 3 (1991).

Krieg, Nina A. "Denkmalpflege und Wiederaufbau." In Winfried Nerdinger, ed., *Aufbauzeit. Planen und Bauen München 1945–1950.* Munich, 1984.

————. "München, leuchtend und ausgebrannt . . . Denkmalpflege und Wiederaufbau in den Nachkriegsjahren." In Friedrich Prinz, ed., *Trümmerzeit in München. Kultur und Gesellschaft einer deutschen Großstadt im Aufbruch 1945–1949.* Munich, 1984.

Krier, Leon. "An Architecture of Desire." In Leon Krier, ed., *Albert Speer, Architecture 1932–42.* Brussels, 1985.

Kröger, Martin. "Kontinuität in der Kölner Architekturgeschichte. Ein Beitrag zu Fritz Schumachers Stadtentwicklungskonzept in den frühen 20er Jahren." *Geschichte in Köln,* no. 18 (1985).

Kühn, Erich, ed. *Medizin und Städtebau.* 2 vols. Munich, Berlin, and Vienna, 1957.

————. "Organische Stadtgliederung." In *Amtlicher Katalog der Constructa Bauausstellung 1951.* Hannover, 1951.

Kühne, Günther. "Berlin." In Hartwig Beseler, Niels Gutschow, and Frauke Kretschmer, eds., *Kriegsschicksale deutscher Architektur. Verluste, Schäden, Wiederaufbau,* vol. 1. Neumünster, 1987.

————. "Wer kann 'Architekt BDA' werden?" *Neue Bauwelt* 2 (1947).

Kunst, Hans-Jochen. "Architektur und Macht. Überlegungen zur NS-Architektur." *Arch+* 71 (1983)

Kurschat, Wilhelm. *Das Haus Friedrich und Heinrich von der Leyen in Krefeld.* Frankfurt a.M., 1933.

Ladd, Brian Kenneth. *Urban Planning and Civic Order in Germany, 1860–1914.* Cambridge, Mass., and London, 1990.

Lafrenz, Jürgen. "Planung der Neugestaltung von Hamburg 1933–1945." In Heinz Heineberg, ed., *Innerstädtische Differenzierung und Prozess im 19. und 20. Jahrhundert. Geographische und historische Aspekte.* Cologne and Vienna, 1987.

Lammert, Peter. "Die gegliederte und aufgelockerte Stadt vor und nach 1945. Eine Skizze zur Planungsgeschichte." *Die alte Stadt* 14 (1987).

Lammert, U., H. J. Kadatz, E. Collein, and H. Gericke. *Architektur und Städtebau in der DDR.* Leipzig, 1969.

Lampmann, Gustav. "Architekt und Baubehörde." *Der Städtetag,* new series 4 (1951).

Lampugnani, Vittorio Magnago. "Architektur und Stadtplanung." In Wolfgang Benz, ed., *Die Bundesrepublik Deutschland,* vol. 3, *Kultur.* Frankfurt, 1983.

Lane, Barbara Miller. "Architects in Power: Politics and Ideology in the Work of Ernst May and Albert Speer." In Robert I. Rotberg and Theodore K. Rabb, eds., *Art and History: Images and Their Meaning.* Cambridge and New York, 1988.

———. *Architecture and Politics in Germany, 1918–1945.* Cambridge, Mass., 1968, rpt. 1985.

———. "The Berlin Congress Hall 1955–57." *Perspectives in American History,* new series 1 (1984).

———. "Changing Attitudes to Monumentality." In Ingrid Hammarström and T. Hall, eds., *Growth and Transformation of the Modern City.* Stockholm, 1979.

Lang, Jon. "The Built Environment and Social Behavior: Architectural Determinism Reexamined." In Mark A. Hewitt, Benjamin Kracauer, John Massengale, and Michael McDonough, eds., *VIA: Culture and the Social Vision,* vol. 4. Philadelphia, Pa., and Cambridge, Mass., 1980.

Lange, Dieter. "Bemerkungen zu Denkmalpflege und Stadtentwicklung in Hannover." In Hiltrud Kier, ed., *Die Kunst unsere Städte zu erhalten.* Stuttgart, 1976.

Larsson, Lars Olof. "Klassizismus in der Architektur des 20. Jahrhunderts." In Karl Arndt, Georg Friedrich Koch, and Lars Olof Larsson. *Albert Speer, Architektur. Arbeiten 1933–1942.* Frankfurt, 1978.

———. *Die Neugestaltung der Reichshauptstadt: Albert Speers Generalbebauungsplan für Berlin.* Stockholm Studies in the History of Art, vol. 29. Uppsala, 1978.

Laslett, Peter. "The Quality of Life in European Cities: An Overview." In Robert C. Fried and Paul M. Hohenberg, eds., *The Quality of Life in European Cities.* Occasional Papers, Council for European Studies. Pittsburgh, Pa., 1974.

Lauther, [Dr.]. "Rechtlich-Wirtschaftlich-Finanzielle Fragen des Aufbaues." In Karl Josef Erbs, ed., *Grundlagen für den Aufbau in Stadt und Land.* Berlin, 1948.

Lees, Andrew. *Cities Perceived. Urban Society in European and American Thought, 1820–1940.* New York, 1985.

———. "Critics of Urban Society in Germany, 1854–1919." *Journal of the History of Ideas* 40 (1979).

Lehmbrock, Josef. "Ein Stadtplanungsvorschlag des Architektenrings aus der Zeit Ende 1949 und Anfang 1950." In *Architektur der 50er Jahre in Düsseldorf. Eine Ausstellung des Stadtmuseums und des BDA Düsseldorf.* Düsseldorf, 1982.

Leipner, Kurt. *Chronik der Stadt Stuttgart, 1949–1953.* Stuttgart, 1977.

Leitl, Alfons. "Anmerkungen zur Zeit." *Baukunst und Werkform* 1 (1947).

———. "Anmerkungen zur Zeit." *Baukunst und Werkform* 2 (1948).

————. "Die Massenhaftigkeit und die Tradition." *Baukunst und Werkform* 2 (1948).

————. "Plädoyer aus Deutschland." *Baukunst und Werkform* 5 (1951).

————. "Die städtebauliche Seite." *Baukunst und Werkform* 5 (1951).

————. "What's Wrong with German City Planning? The Lessons of Reconstruction." *Landscape* 5 (1955–56).

————. "Der Wiederaufbau der Paulskirche." *Baukunst und Werkform* 1 (1947)

————, and Gerhard Graubner. "Die politische Gesinnung des Architekten: Zwei Briefe, zugleich für Paul Bonatz." *Baukunst und Werkform* 1 (1947).

Lowenthal, David. *The Past Is a Foreign Country*. Cambridge, 1985.

Lynch, Kevin. *The Image of the City*. Cambridge, Mass., 1960.

————. *A Theory of Good City Form*. Cambridge, Mass., and London, 1981.

————. *What Time Is This Place?* Cambridge, Mass., and London, 1972.

MacIsaac, David, ed. *The United States Strategic Bombing Survey*. 10 vols. New York and London, 1976.

Machat, Christoph. "Der Wiederaufbau der Kölner Kirchen." *Deutscher Kunst und Denkmalpflege* 43 (1985).

————. *Der Wiederaufbau der Kölner Kirchen*. Landschaftsverband Rheinland, Working Paper 40. Pulheim, 1987.

Machtemes, Aloys. "Einige Erinnerungen an die Stadtplanung in Düsseldorf 1948–1958." In *Architektur der 50er Jahre in Düsseldorf. Eine Ausstellung des Stadtmuseums und des BDA Düsseldorf*. Düsseldorf, 1982.

Machule, Dittmar. "Die Kameradschaftssiedlung der SS in Berlin-Zehlendorf—eine idyllische Waldsiedlung." In Hartmut Frank, ed., *Faschistische Architekturen. Planen und Bauen in Europa 1930 bis 1945*. Stadt, Planung, Geschichte, vol. 3. Hamburg, 1985.

Mäding, Erhard. *Beitrag der Städte zum Wiederaufbau der deutschen Wirtschaft. Bericht über deutsche Selbstleistungen im Sinne des Marshallplans*. Typescript, submitted to Bundesminister für den Marshallplan, April 1951. Copy in Bibliothek des Deutschen Städtetags, Cologne.

Maier, Charles S. "The Two Postwar Eras and the Conditions for Stability in Twentieth-Century Western Europe." *American Historical Review* 86 (1981).

Mast, Paul. "Gedanken zum Aufbau Berlins." *Neue Bauwelt* 1 (1946).

————. "Wir Architekten fordern. . . : Der Ingenieur." *Der Bauhelfer* 2 (1947).

Mattausch, Roswitha. *Siedlungsbau und Stadtneugründungen im deutschen Faschismus*. Frankfurt, 1981.

Matthus, Hans. "Wir Architekten fordern. . . ." *Der Bauhelfer* 2 (1947).

May, Ernst L. *Hat der deutsche Städtebau seine Chancen verpasst? Hat er noch eine Chance?* Schriften des Deutschen Verbandes für Wohnungswesen, Städtebau und Raumplanung, no. 19. Cologne, 1956.

Mayer, Hans K. F. "Strömungen in der heutigen deutschen Architektur." *Der Aufbau* 8 (1953).

Meffert, R. "Betrachtung zur Aufbaugesetzgebung." *Der Bauhelfer* 4 (1949).

Meier, Bettina. "Goethe in Trümmern—Vor vierzig Jahren: der Streit um den Wiederaufbau des Goethehauses in Frankfurt." *Germanic Review* 63 (1988).

Meitinger, Karl. *Das neue München*. Munich, 1946.

Merritt, Anna J., and Richard L. Merritt. *Public Opinion in Occupied Germany. The OMGUS Surveys, 1945–1949*. Urbana and Chicago, 1970.

Messenger, Charles. *"Bomber" Harris and the Strategic Bombing Offensive, 1939–1945*. New York, 1984.

Meunier, Franz. "Illusion als Schicksal? Die deutschen gebildeten Stände und der

Wiederaufbau. Ein notwendiger Nachtrag zur Goethe-Haus." *Baukunst und Werkform* 2 (1948).

Meyer-Ottens, Otto. "Einführung in die Probleme des Generalbebauungsplanes." In *Stadtplanung in Hamburg. Gedanken zum Wiederaufbau.* Schriftenreihe des Bundes Deutscher Architekten, vol. 6. Hamburg, 1948.

———. "Zum Aufbau der Stadt Hamburg." *Baurundschau* 37 (1947). Special issue "Hamburg im Wandel."

Michel, Elga. *Die Altstadt von Köln und ihr Wiedererwachen nach der Zerstörung.* Forschungen zur deutschen Landeskunde, vol. 90. Remagen, 1955.

Middlebrook, Martin. *The Battle of Hamburg: Allied Bomber Forces against a German City in 1943.* London, 1980.

Mielke, Friedrich. *Die Zukunft der Vergangenheit. Grundsätze, Probleme und Möglichkeiten der Denkmalpflege.* Stuttgart, 1975.

———, and Klaus Brügelmann. "Denkmalpflege." In Wolfgang Pehnt, ed., *Die Stadt in der Bundesrepublik Deutschland.* Stuttgart, 1974.

Mierzejweski, Alfred C. *The Collapse of the German War Economy, 1944–1945: Allied Air Power and the German National Railway.* Chapel Hill, N.C., and London, 1988.

Mitscherlich, Alexander. *Die Unwirtlichkeit unserer Städte. Anstiftung zum Unfrieden.* Frankfurt, 1965.

Moest, Walter. *Der Zehlendorfer Plan. Ein Vorschlag zum Wiederaufbau Berlins.* Berlin, 1946.

———, and Richard Ermisch. "Zum Gestaltbild der Berliner City." *Neue Bauwelt* 2 (1947).

Mohr, Christoph. "Architektur der 50er Jahre ohne Namen—Erfahrungen aus der Provinz. Ein Bericht über Erfassung, Bewertung und Auswahl in Hessen." In Werner Durth and Niels Gutschow, eds., *Architektur und Städtebau der Fünfziger Jahre: Ergebnisse der Fachtagung in Hannover, 2.–4. Februar 1990. Schutz und Erhaltung von Bauten der Fünfziger Jahre.* Schriftenreihe des Deutschen Nationalkomitees für Denkmalschutz, vol. 41. Bonn, 1990.

———. "Überlegungen zum Denkmalbegriff der Nachkriegsarchitektur." In *Architektur und Städtebau der Fünfziger Jahre.* Schriftenreihe des Deutschen Nationalkomitees für Denkmalschutz, vol. 36. Bonn, 1988.

Monheim, Peter. "Fußgängerbereiche setzen sich durch." *Der Städtetag*, new series, 27 (1974).

Müller, Roland. "Das Gesicht der Großstadt: Ein Blick über die Stadtbaugeschichte Stuttgarts." In Marlene P. Hiller, ed., *Stuttgart im Zweiten Weltkrieg*, 2nd ed. Gerlingen, 1990.

Müller, Werner. "Betrachtungen über die künftige Städtebaugesetzgebung." *Der Bauhelfer* 2 (1947).

Mullin, John Robert. "City Planning in Frankfurt, Germany, 1925–1932. A Study in Practical Utopianism." *Journal of Urban History* 4 (1977).

———. "Ideology, Planning Theory and the German City in the Inter-war Years." *Town Planning Review* 53 (1982).

Mulzer, Erich. *Der Wiederaufbau der Altstadt von Nürnberg 1945 bis 1970.* Erlangen, 1972.

Muthesius, Stefan. "The Origins of the German Conservation Movement." In Roger Kain, ed., *Planning for Conservation.* New York, 1981.

Nedden, Felix zur. *Hannover. Ehemals, gestern und heute. Stadt im Wandel zwischen Bewahren und Erneuern.* Stuttgart, 1984.

Nerdinger, Winfried, ed. *Aufbauzeit. Planen und Bauen München 1945–1950.* Munich, 1984.

——. "Materialästhetik und Rasterbauweise—Zum Charakter der Architktur der 50er Jahre." In Werner Durth and Niels Gutschow, eds., *Architektur und Städtebau der Fünfziger Jahre: Ergebnisse der Fachtagung in Hannover, 2.–4. Februar 1990. Schutz und Erhaltung von Bauten der Fünfziger Jahre.* Schriftenreihe des Deutschen Nationalkomitees für Denkmalschutz, vol. 41. Bonn, 1990.

——. "Versuchung und Dilemma der Avantgarde im Spiegel der Architekturwettbewerbe 1933–35." In Hartmut Frank, ed., *Faschistische Architekturen: Planen und Bauen in Europa 1930 bis 1945.* Stadt, Planung, Geschichte, vol. 3. Hamburg, 1985.

——. "Walter Gropius—totale Architektur für eine demokratische Gesellschaft." *Jahrbuch des Zentralinstituts für Kunstgeschichte* 1 (1985).

——. "Wiederaufbau oder Neubau?" In Winfried Nerdinger, ed., *Aufbauzeit. Planen und Bauen München 1945–1950.* Munich, 1984.

Der Neuaufbau unsere Städte. Deutscher Städtetag, Conference Reports, 7th Meeting of Main Committee. Berlin, 1950.

Neufert, Ernst. *Bauordnungslehre.* Berlin, 1943.

——. "Müssen Industriebauten häßlich sein?" In *Amtlicher Katalog der Constructa Bauausstellung 1951.* Hannover, 1951.

"Die Neugestaltung des Hansaviertels in Berlin. Ergebnisse eines Ideenwettbewerbes." *Baukunst und Werkform* 7 (1954).

Neumann, Michael. "Ängstliche Gedanken über den Kirchenbau der 50er Jahre." In *Architektur und Städtebau der Fünfziger Jahre.* Schriftenreihe des Deutschen Nationalkomitees für Denkmalschutz, vol. 36. Bonn, 1988.

Neundörfer, Ludwig. "Auflockerung von Arbeits- und Wohnstätten." *Wiederaufbau zerstörter Städte,* no. 6 (1947).

——. "Inventar des Zusammenbruchs." *Baukunst und Werkform* 1 (1947).

Nicklitz, Walter. "Die soziale Lage der Bauarbeiter." *Berlin. Planung und Aufbau der Stadt.* Berlin, 1948.

Niethammer, Lutz. "Die deutsche Stadt im Umbruch: 1945 als Forschungsproblem." *Die alte Stadt* 5 (1978).

——. "Some Elements of the Housing Reform Debate in Nineteenth-Century Europe: Or, On the Making of a New Paradigm of Social Control." In Bruce M. Stave, ed., *Modern Industrial Cities. History, Policy, and Survival.* Beverly Hills, Calif., and London, 1981.

Ockert, Erwin. "Der Hamburg-Preussische Landesplanungsausschuss." In Architekten- und Ingenieur-Verein Hamburg, ed., *Hamburg und seine Bauten 1929–1953.* Hamburg, 1953.

——. *Fritz Schumacher. Sein Schaffen als Städtebauer und Landesplanner.* Tübingen, 1950.

Oelsner, Gustav. "Wandlungen der städtebaulichen Grundsätze." In Architekten- und Ingenieur-Verein Hamburg, ed., *Hamburg und seine Bauten 1929–1953.* Hamburg, 1953.

Otto, Christian F. "Modern Environment and Historical Continuity: The Heimatschutz Discourse in Germany." *Art Journal* 43, no. 2 (1983).

Pahl-Weber, Elke. "Architekten/Planer und ihr Arbeitsfeld." In Michael Bose, Michael Holtmann, Dittmar Machule, Elke Pahl-Weber, and Dirk Schubert, *". . . ein neues Hamburg entsteht . . .": Planen und Bauen von 1933–1945.* Beiträge zur städtebaulichen Forschung, vol. 2. Hamburg, 1986.

———. "Das Groß-Hamburg-Gesetz von 1937 und seine landesplanerischen Folgen für Harburg." In Jürgen Ellermeyer, ed., *Harburg: von der Burg zur Industriestadt: Beiträge zur Geschichte Harburgs 1288–1938.* Hamburg, 1988.

———. "Im fließenden Raum. Wohnungsgrundrisse nach 1945." In Bernhard Schulz, ed., *Grauzonen. Kunst und Zeitbilder. Farbwelten 1945–1955.* Berlin, 1983.

———. "Konstanty Gutschow—Architekt." In Michael Bose, Michael Holtmann, Dittmar Machule, Elke Pahl-Weber, and Dirk Schubert, *". . . ein neues Hamburg entsteht . . .": Planen und Bauen von 1933–1945.* Beiträge zur städtebaulichen Forschung, vol. 2. Hamburg, 1986.

———. "Die Ortsgruppe als Siedlungszelle: Ein Vorschlag zur Methodik der großstädtischen Staderweiterung von 1940." In Hartmut Frank, ed., *Faschistische Architekturen: Planen und Bauen in Europa 1930 bis 1945.* Stadt, Planung, Geschichte, vol. 3. Hamburg, 1985.

———, and Michael Bose. "Die Generalbebauungspläne 1940/41 und 1944." In Michael Bose, Michael Holtmann, Dittmar Machule, Elke Pahl-Weber, and Dirk Schubert, *". . . ein neues Hamburg entsteht . . .": Planen und Bauen von 1933–1945.* Beiträge zur städtebaulichen Forschung, vol. 2. Hamburg, 1986.

———, Michael Holtmann, and Michael Bose, "Der Wohnungs- und Siedlungsbau in Hamburg." In Michael Bose, Michael Holtmann, Dittmar Machule, Elke Pahl-Weber, and Dirk Schubert, *". . . ein neues Hamburg entsteht . . .": Planen und Bauen von 1933–1945.* Beiträge zur städtebaulichen Forschung, vol. 2. Hamburg, 1986.

Pampe, Ulrike, ed. *Heinz Wetzel und die Geschichte der Städtebaulehre an deutschen Hochschulen.* Stuttgart, 1982.

Paul, Jürgen. "Die kulturelle Grundsatzdebatte über den Wiederaufbau der historischen Städte nach dem Zweiten Weltkrieg in Deutschland." *Politische Studien* 2 (1988). Special issue, "Denkmalpflege: Andenken und Auftrag."

———. "Kulturgeschichtliche Betrachtungen zur deutschen Nachkriegsarchitektur." In Helge Bofinger, Margret Bofinger, Jürgen Paul, and Heinrich Klotz, eds., *Architektur in Deutschland: Bundesrepublik und Westberlin.* Stuttgart, 1979.

———. "Der Wiederaufbau der historischen Städte in Deutschland nach dem zweiten Weltkrieg." In Cord Meckseper and Harald Siebenmorgen, eds., *Die alte Stadt: Denkmal oder Lebensraum?* Göttingen, 1985.

———. "Der Wiederaufbau des Kornhauses in Freiburg i.B. und einige Betrachtungen über Architektur und Geschichtsverständnis." *Archithese* 11 (1974).

Pawley, Martin. *Architecture versus Housing.* New York and Washington, D.C., 1971.

Pecks, Eduard. "Kölner Stadtplanung, Erfahrungen und Sorgen." *Baukunst und Werkform* 10 (1957).

Pehnt, Wolfgang. *German Architecture, 1960–1970.* New York, 1970.

Peschken, Goerd. "Stadtlandschaft. Scharouns städtebauliche Vision für Berlin und ihre Provinzialisierung." In Jochen Boberg, Tilman Fichter, and Eckhart Gillen, eds., *Die Metropole. Industriekultur in Berlin im 20. Jahrhundert.* Munich, 1986.

Peter, Konrad. "Wir Architekten fordern . . . : Der Beamtete Architekt." *Der Bauhelfer* 2, no. 16 (1947)

Peters, Paulhans, ed. *Fußgängerstadt. Fußgängerrechte, Stadtplanung und Stadtgestaltung.* Munich, 1977.

Petsch, Joachim. *Architektur und Gesellschaft. Zur Geschichte der deutschen Architektur im 19. und 20. Jahrhundert.* Cologne and Vienna, 1973.

———. "Architektur und Städtebau in den 50er Jahren." In Eckhard Siepmann, ed., *Bikini. Die fünfziger Jahre: Kalter Krieg und Capri-Sonne.* Berlin, 1981.

————. *Baukunst und Stadtplanung im Dritten Reich*. Munich, 1976.

————. " 'Neues Bauen' und konservative Architektur der 20er und 30er Jahre." *Der Architekt* 4 (1983).

————. "Zum Problem der Kontinuität nationalsozialistischer Architektur in den Fünfziger Jahren am Beispiel der Zeitschrift *Baumeister*." In Berthold Hinz, Hans-Ernst Mittig, Wolfgang Schäche, and Angela Schönberger, eds., *Die Dekoration der Gewalt. Kunst und Medien im Faschismus*. Gießen, 1979.

Petsch, Wiltrud, and Joachim Petsch. "Die Bauhaus-Rezeption in der Bundesrepublik in den 50er Jahren." In Wiltrud Petsch and Joachim Petsch, eds., *Bundesrepublik eine neue Heimat? Städtebau und Architektur nach '45*. Berlin, 1983.

————. "Neuaufbau statt Wiederaufbau. Architektur und Städtebau in Nordrhein-Westfalen 1945–1952." In Klaus Honnef und Hans M. Schmidt, eds., *Aus den Trümmern. Kunst und Kultur im Rheinland und Westfalen 1945–1952. Neubeginn und Kontinuität*. Cologne and Bonn, 1985.

Petz, Ursula von. "Nachkriegsplanung und Wiederaufbau in Deutschland—einige Anmerkungen zur Situation im Ruhrgebiet." Institut für Raumplanung, Universität Dortmund, Working Paper 55. Dortmund, 1987.

————. *Stadtsanierung im Dritten Reich*. Dortmunder Beiträge zur Raumplanung, vol. 45. Dortmund, 1987.

Pfannschmidt, Martin. "Probleme der Weltstadt Berlin." In Joachim H. Schultze, ed., *Zum Problem der Weltstadt*. Deutscher Geographentag, vol. 32. Berlin, 1959.

Pfister, Rudolf. "Hitler's 'Baukunst.' " *Baumeister* 43, no. 2 (July/August 1946).

Pieper, Hans. "Lübeck als Gegenstand der Denkmalpflege." *Lübeckische Angelegenheiten*. Supplement to *Lübecker General-Anzeiger,* no. 14 (17 January 1936).

————. *Lübeck. Städtebauliche Studien zum Wiederaufbau einer historischen deutschen Stadt*. Hamburg, 1946.

Pilgert, Henry P. *The Exchange of Persons Program in Western Germany*. Historical Division, Office of the U.S. High Commissioner for Germany. Washington, D.C., 1951.

"Planer, werdet hart." *Der Spiegel* 6, no. 1 (2 January 1952).

Pohl, Manfred. *Wiederaufbau. Kunst und Technik der Finanzierung 1947–1953. Die ersten Jahre der Kreditanstalt für Wiederaufbau*. Frankfurt, 1973.

Pommer, Richard. "The Flat Roof: A Modernist Controversy in Germany." *Art Journal* 43, no. 2 (1983).

————, and Christian F. Otto, *Weissenhof 1927 and the Modern Movement in Architecture*. Chicago, 1990.

Prager, Stephan. *Die Deutsche Akademie für Städtebau und Landesplanung: Rückblick und Ausblick 1922–1955*. Schriftenreihe der Deutschen Akademie für Städtebau und Landesplanung, vol. 8. Tübingen, 1956.

Preis, Kurt. *München unterm Hakenkreuz: Die Hauptstadt der Bewegung: Zwischen Pracht und Trümmern*. Munich, 1980.

Protokoll über die Sitzung des Preisgerichts zum internationalen städtebaulichen Ideenwettbewerb "Hauptstadt Berlin." Typescript, Berlin, 1958. In Bibliothek des Senators für Bau- und Wohnungwesen, Berlin.

Pünder, Hermann, and Philipp Rappaport. "Um ein Ministerium für Wiederaufbau und Flüchtlingswesen." *Neue Bauwelt* 4 (1949).

Rabeler, Gerhard. *Wiederaufbau und Expansion westdeutscher Städte 1945–1960 im Spannungsfeld von Reformideen und Wirklichkeit*. Schriftenreihe des Deutschen Nationalkomitees für Denkmalschutz, vol. 39. Bonn, 1990.

Rainer, Roland. "Auferstehung einer zerstörten Stadt. Städtebaupraxis in Kiel." *Der Aufbau* 7 (1952).

———. *Die Behausungsfrage*. Vienna and Zurich, 1947.

———. *Städtebauliche Prosa: Praktische Grundlagen für den Aufbau der Städte*. Innsbruck, 1948.

———. *Die zweckmässigste Hausform für Erweiterung, Neugrundung und Wiederaufbau von Städten*. Denkschrift der Akademie für Städtebau. Breslau, 1944.

Ramm, Hans. "Aufräumung." In Architekten- und Ingenieur-Verein Hamburg, ed., *Hamburg und seine Bauten 1929–1953*. Hamburg, 1953.

Randzio, Ernst. *Unterirdischer Städtebau: besonders mit Beispielen am Groß Berlin*. Bremen, 1951.

Rapoport, Amos. *The Meaning of the Built Environment: A Nonverbal Communication Approach*. Beverly Hills, Calif., London, and New Delhi, 1982.

Rappaport, Philipp. "Deutsche Städte oder Kolonialstädte?" *Wiederaufbau-Mitteilungen des Bauausschusses des Deutschen Städtetags*, no. 5 (31 March 1947).

———. "Gedanken zum deutschen Städtebau." *Der Aufbau* 8 (1953).

———. "Das Ruhrgebiet—ein Rückblick, ein Ausblick." *Der Städtetag,* new series 4 (1951).

———. *Der Wiederaufbau der deutschen Städte*. Essen, 1946.

———. *Wünsche und Wirklichkeit des deutschen Wiederaufbaus*. Schriften des Deutschen Verbandes für Wohnungswesen, Städtebau und Raumplanung, no. 4. Frankfurt, 1949.

Rasp, Hans-Peter. *Eine Stadt für tausend Jahre. München—Bauten und Projekte für die Hauptstadt der Bewegung*. Munich, 1981.

Rebentisch, Dieter. "Regional Planning and Its Institutional Framework: An Illustration from the Rhine-Main Area, 1890–1945." In Gordon E. Cherry, ed., *Shaping an Urban World*. New York, 1980.

Reichow, Hans Bernhard. *Die autogerechte Stadt: Ein Weg aus dem Verkehrs-Chaos*. Ravensburg, 1959.

———. *Organische Stadtbaukunst. Von der Großstadt zur Stadtlandschaft*. Braunschweig, Berlin, and Vienna, 1948.

———. "Organischer Aufbau der Stadt Kiel." *Die Neue Stadt* 2 (1948).

Relph, Edward. *The Modern Urban Landscape*. Baltimore, Md., 1987.

Reulecke, Jürgen. *Die deutsche Stadt im Industriezeitalter*. Wuppertal, 1978.

———. *Geschichte der Urbanisierung in Deutschland*. Frankfurt, 1985.

Rheinischer Verein für Denkmalpflege und Landschaftsschutz. *Glanz und Elend der Denkmalpflege und Stadtplanung Cöln 1906–2006 Köln*. Cologne, 1981.

Richter, Hans Werner. "Literatur im Interregnum." *Der Ruf,* no. 15 (1947). Reprinted in Hermann Glaser, Lutz von Pufendorf, and Michael Schöneich, eds., *So viel Anfang war nie: Deutsche Städte 1945–1949*. Berlin, 1989.

Rodriguez-Lores, Juan, and Gerhard Fehl, eds. *Städtebaureform 1865–1900. Von Licht, Luft und Ordnung in der Stadt der Gründerzeit*. 2 vols. Hamburg, 1985.

Rosenberg, Franz. *Vom Wiederaufbau und von der Stadterweiterung in Bremen in den Jahren 1949–1970. Ein subjektiver Bericht*. Typescript, Staatsarchiv Bremen. Bremen, 1981.

Rosenberg, [Dr. Ing. Franz], and [Architekt BDA] Dirichs. "Über die Einschaltung von freischaffenden Architekten bei der Stadtplanung: ein Zwiegespräch zwischen einem Behördenvertreter und einem freischaffenden Architeken." *Der Bauhelfer* 4 (1949).

Rostow, W. W. *Pre-Invasion Bombing Strategy: General Eisenhower's Decision of March 25, 1944*. Austin, Tex., 1981.

Rumpf, Hans. *The Bombing of Germany*. E. Holt Fitzgerald, trans. New York, 1962.

Runge, Ernst. "Vorschläge zur Finanzierung des Wohnungsbaues." *Der Bauhelfer* 1 (1946).

Rusch, Max. "Das Baugesetz." *Neue Bauwelt* 5 (1950).

———. "Ein Bundesministerium für Bauwesen ist nötig!" *Neue Bauwelt* 4 (1949).

———. "Inhalt des Baugesetzes: Die Planung." *Neue Bauwelt* 6 (1951).

Sack, Manfred. "It's Real Counterfeit Architecture." *The German Tribune,* 25 December 1983.

Salin, Edgar. "Urbanität." In *Erneurung unserer Städte*. Neue Schriften des deutschen Städtetages, no. 6. Stuttgart and Cologne, 1960.

Sallenave, Danièle. "Mein Traum von Deutschland." *Die Zeit,* 13 October 1989, literature section.

Schäche, Wolfgang. "Platz für die staatliche Macht." In Jochen Boberg, Tilman Fichter, and Eckhart Gillen, eds., *Die Metropole. Industriekultur in Berlin im 20. Jahrhundert*. Munich, 1986.

———. "Von der Stunde Null und der Legende des Wiederaufbaues." In Erich Konter, ed., *Wendezeiten in Architektur und Stadtplanung—Kontinuität oder Bruch in der Entwicklung nach 1945*. Arbeitshefte des Instituts für Stadt- und Regionalplanung der Technischen Universität Berlin, no. 36. Berlin, 1986.

Schaffer, Ronald. "American Military Ethics in World War II: The Bombing of German Civilians." *Journal of American History* 67 (1980).

———. *Wings of Judgment. American Bombing in World War II*. New York, 1985.

Scharoun, Hans. "Berlin." *Baukunst und Werkform* 1 (1947).

———. "Entwicklung des Instituts für Bauwesen." In *Die Deutsche Bautagung 1949*. Leipzig, 1949.

———. "Gropius als Gast der Technischen Universität Berlin." *Neue Bauwelt* 2 (1947).

———. *Hans Scharoun. Bauten, Entwürfe, Texte*. Peter Pfankuch, ed. Schriftenreihe der Akademie der Künste, vol. 10. Berlin, 1974.

———. "Zur Ausstellung 'Berlin plant.' " *Neue Bauwelt* 1 (1946).

Schildt, Axel. *Die Grindelhochhäuser. Eine Sozialgeschichte der ersten deutschen Wohnhochhausanlage*. Hamburg, 1988.

———, and Arnold Sywottek. " 'Wiederaufbau' und 'Modernisierung': Zur westdeutschen Gesellschaftsgeschichte in den fünfziger Jahren." *Aus Politik und Zeitgeschichte B* 6–7 (1989).

Schlandt, Joachim. "Die Kruppsiedlungen—Wohnungsbau im Interesse eines Industriekonzerns." In Hans G. Helms and Jörg Janssen, eds., *Kapitalistischer Städtebau*. Neuwied and Berlin, 1970.

Schleich, Erwin. *Die zweite Zerstörung Münchens*. Neue Schriftenreihe des Stadtarchivs München, vol. 100. Stuttgart, 1978.

Schlippe, Joseph. "Freiburgs Baudenkmäler und ihre Wiederherstellung." In Walter Vetter, ed., *Freiburg in Trümmern 1944–1952*, vol. 1. Freiburg, 1982.

———. "Wie Freiburg wiedererstehen soll?" In Walter Vetter, ed., *Freiburg in Trümmern 1944–1952*, vol. 1. Freiburg, 1982.

———. "Der Wiederaufbauplan für Freiburg." *Die Neue Stadt* 1 (1947).

Schmitt, Hans. *Der Neuaufbau der Stadt Köln*. Cologne, 1946.

Schmitthenner, Paul. "Das sanfte Gesetz in der Kunst, in Sonderheit in der Baukunst." Reprinted in part in *Stadtbauwelt* 84 (1984).

Schmitt-Rost, Hans, ed., with introduction by Heinrich Böll. *Zeit der Ruinen: Köln am Ende der Diktatur*. Cologne, 1965.

Schneider, Christian. *Stadtgründung im Dritten Reich. Wolfsburg und Salzgitter*. Munich, 1978.

Schubert, Dirk. "Führerstadtplanungen in Hamburg." In Michael Bose, Michael Holtmann, Dittmar Machule, Elke Pahl-Weber, and Dirk Schubert, *". . . ein neues Hamburg entsteht . . .": Planen und Bauen von 1933–1945*. Beiträge zur städtebaulichen Forschung, vol. 2. Hamburg, 1986.

———. "Gesundung der Städte—Stadtsanierung in Hamburg 1933–45." In Michael Bose, Michael Holtmann, Dittmar Machule, Elke Pahl-Weber, and Dirk Schubert, *". . . ein neues Hamburg entsteht . . .": Planen und Bauen von 1933–1945*. Beiträge zur städtebaulichen Forschung, vol. 2. Hamburg, 1986.

———. *Stadtplanung als Ideologie. Eine theoriegeschichtliche, ideologiekritische Untersuchung der Stadt, des Städtebaus und Wohnungsbaus in Deutschland von ca. 1850 bis heute*. Diss., Freie Universität, Berlin, 1981.

Schultze, Joachim H. "Die Weltstadt als Objekt geographischer Forschung." In Joachim H. Schultze, ed., *Zum Problem der Weltstadt*. Deutscher Geographentag, vol. 32. Berlin, 1959.

Schulz, Bernhard, ed. *Grauzonen. Kunst und Zeitbilder. Farbwelten 1945–1955*. Berlin, 1983.

Schulz, Günter. "Eigenheimpolitik und Eigenheimförderung im ersten Jahrzehnt nach dem Zweiten Weltkrieg." In Axel Schildt and Arnold Sywottek, eds., *Massenwohnungen und Eigenheim. Wohnungsbau und Wohnen in der Großstadt seit dem Ersten Weltkrieg*. Frankfurt and New York, 1988.

Schumacher, Fritz. "Erkenntnisse für den Wiederaufbau zerstörter Städte." *Die Neue Stadt* 2 (1948).

———. *Köln. Entwicklungsfragen einer Großstadt*. Munich, 1923.

———. *Lesebuch für Baumeister. Äusserungen über Architektur und Städtebau*. Braunschweig, 1977. (Reprint of 1947 ed.)

———. *Probleme der Großstadt vor und nach dem Kriege*. Cologne, 1946.

———. *Wie das Kunstwerk Hamburg nach dem großen Brand entstand*. Berlin, 1920.

———. *Zum Wiederaufbau Hamburgs*. Hamburg, 1945.

Schütz, Heinrich. "Die Frankfurter Aufbau-AG im Wiederaufbau unserer Stadt." In Max Kurz, ed., *Frankfurt baut auf*. Stuttgart, 1954.

Schwarz, Rudolf. "Das Anliegen der Baukunst." In *Mensch und Raum*. Darmstädter Gespräch, no. 2. Darmstadt, 1952.

———. "Baustelle Deutschland." *Baukunst und Werkform* 2 (1948). (Reprint of 1932 essay)

———. "Brief über Ronchamp." *Baukunst und Werkform* 10 (1956). Reprinted in Christian Borngräber, *Stil Novo: Design in den 50er Jahren. Phantasie und Phantastik*. Frankfurt, 1979.

———. "Gedanken zum Wiederaufbau von Köln." *Aufbau* 2. Stuttgart, 1947. Special issue, *Grundfragen des Aufbaus in Stadt und Land*.

———. "Das neue Köln." *Baukunst und Werkform* 10 (1957). Special issue, "Köln."

———. *Das neue Köln—Ein Vorentwurf*. Cologne, 1950.

———. "Das Unplanbare." *Baukunst und Werkform* 1 (1947).

Schweyer, Carl. "Baulandbeschaffung." In *Um die Grundlagen des sozialen Wohnungsbaues: Kundgebung der Gemeinnützigen Wohnungswirtschaft des Landes Nordrhein-Westfalen*. Essen, 1950.

Seidensticker, Wilhelm. "Aufgaben des Städtebaues." *Die Neue Stadt* 5 (1951).

Sherry, Michael S. *The Rise of American Air Power. The Creation of Armageddon.* New Haven, Conn., and London, 1987.

Siemens, Edgar. "Die Wohnungsbaufinanzierung im Spiegel der Währungsreform." *Neue Wege zur Finanzierung des sozialen Wohnungsbaues.* Memmingen, 1948.

Sill, Otto. "Der Durchführungsplan Hammerbrook." *Nordwestdeutsche Bauzeitung* 3 (1951).

———. "Der Verkehr." In Architekten- und Ingenieur-Verein Hamburg, ed., *Hamburg und seine Bauten 1929–1953.* Hamburg, 1953.

Sommer, Karl. "Der Wohnungsbau nach dem Kriege." In *Wohnungsbau in Hamburg.* Hamburg, 1953.

Sorge, Martin K. *The Other Price of Hitler's War. German Military and Civilian Losses Resulting from World War II.* New York, 1986.

Speck, Albert. "Das Dritte Reich, Krieg, Inflation, Währungsreform, Wirtschaftsbau: Wege, Um- und Schleichwege, Pannen von 1934–1948 und danach." Privately printed, Cologne, 1988.

Speer, Albert. *Inside the Third Reich: Memoirs.* Richard and Clara Winston, trans. New York, 1970.

———, and Wolfgang Pehnt. "Die Manipulation des Menschen." *Der Architekt* 4 (1983).

Speier, Hans. *From the Ashes of Disgrace. A Journal from Germany 1945–1955.* Amherst, Mass., 1981.

Spree, Reinhard. *Soziale Ungleichheit vor Krankheit und Tod. Zur Sozialgeschichte des Gesundheitsbereichs im Deutschen Kaiserreich.* Göttingen, 1981.

Stauch, Michaela. "Die Freunde des Neuen Bauens." In Winfried Nerdinger, ed., *Aufbauzeit. Planen und Bauen München 1945–1950.* Munich, 1984.

Steffann, Emil. "Ein Plan zum Wiederaufbau Lübecks." *Lübeckische Nachrichten,* 31 December 1946.

Steimel, Barbara. "100. Sitzung des Bauausschußes des Deutschen Städtetages—Ein Rückblick." *Der Städtetag,* new series 35 (1982).

Stimmann, Hans. "Die autogerechte Stadt." In Jochen Boberg, Tilman Fichter, and Eckhart Gillen, eds., *Die Metropole. Industriekultur in Berlin im 20. Jahrhundert.* Munich, 1986.

Strölin, Karl. *Stuttgart im Endstadium des Krieges.* Stuttgart, 1950.

Sutcliffe, Anthony. *Towards the Planned City: Germany, Britain, the United States, and France: 1780–1914.* New York, 1981.

———, ed. *The Rise of Modern Urban Planning, 1800–1914.* New York, 1980.

"Die Tagung des deutschen Verbandes für Wohnungswesen, Städtebau und Raumplanung in Frankfurt am Main." *Die Neue Stadt* 2 (1948).

Tamms, Friedrich. "Das Große in der Baukunst." Reprinted in Tamms, *Von Menschen, Städten und Brücken* (Düsseldorf, 1974), and in *Stadtbauwelt* 84 (1984).

———. "Planen und Bauen in Düsseldorf." *Kommunalpolitische Blätter* 7 (1955).

———. "Planungsaufgaben in Düsseldorf." *Stadtplanung Düsseldorf. Ausstellung Ehrenhof 1.–16.10.1949.* Düsseldorf, 1949.

Taut, Max. *Berlin im Aufbau.* Berlin, 1946.

———. "Betrachtungen zum Aufbau Berlins." *Der Bauhelfer* 1 (1946).

Taverne, E. R. M. "Ouds ontwerp voor het hofplein" ("Clarity in Town Planning: J. J. P. Oud's project for the Hofplein in Rotterdam 1942"). *Plan* 12 (1981).

Taylor, Robert R. *The Word in Stone. The Role of Architecture in the National Socialist Ideology.* Berkeley, Calif., 1974.

Teut, Anna. *Architektur im Dritten Reich, 1933–1945.* Berlin, Frankfurt, and Vienna, 1967

Thies, Jochen. *Architekt der Weltherrschaft. Die "Endziele" Hitlers.* Düsseldorf, 1976.

——. "Hitler's European Building Programme." *Journal of Contemporary History* 13 (1978).

——. "Nationalsozialistische Städteplanung: die Führerstädte." *Die alte Stadt* 5 (1978).

Tiedemann, Lotte, and Emmy Bonhöffer. "ECA-Entwicklungsbauten—von ihren Bewohnern und von Frauen gesehen." In Hermann Wandersleb and Georg Günthert, eds., *Neue Wohnbau*, vol. 2, *Durchführung von Versuchssiedlungen. Ergebnisse und Erkentnisse für heute und morgen. Von ECA bis Interbau.* Ravensburg, 1958.

Topfstedt, Thomas. *Grundlinien der Entwicklung von Städtebau und Architektur in der Deutschen Demokratischen Republik 1949 bis 1955.* Diss., Karl-Marx-Universität Leipzig, 1980.

Undeutsch, Hans. "Der Entwurf zu einem Baugesetz für Berlin." *Der Bauhelfer* 4 (1949).

Unglehrt, Max. " 'BDA' oder 'bda' oder Großberufsverband?" *Neue Bauwelt* 2 (1947).

United States Department of State. "A Housing Development Program for Western Germany." *The Record* 8, no. 2 (March–April 1952).

United States Strategic Bombing Survey. *The Effects of Strategic Bombing on the German War Economy.* n.p., October 1945.

Vetter, Walter, ed. *Freiburg in Trümmern. 1944–1952. Bild- und Textdokumentation.* 2 vols. Freiburg, 1982, 1984.

Vietzen, Hermann. *Chronik der Stadt Stuttgart 1945–1948.* Stuttgart, 1972.

Voigt, Wolfgang. "Von der eugenischen Gartenstadt zum Wiederaufbau aus volksbiologischer Sicht: Rassenhygiene und Städtebau-Ideologie im 20. Jahrhundert." *Stadtbauwelt* 92 (1986).

Völckers, Otto. "Der Streit um das Goethehaus." *Die Neue Stadt* 1 (1947).

——. "Vorschlag zum blockweisen und genossenschaftlichen Wiederaufbau zerstörter Innenstädte." *Neue Bauwelt* 1 (1946).

Voldman, Danièle. "Reconstructors' Tales: An Example of the Use of Oral Sources in the History of Reconstruction after the Second World War." In Jeffry M. Diefendorf, ed., *Rebuilding Europe's Bombed Cities.* London and New York, 1990.

Vorhoelzer, Robert. "Stimmen zum Neuaufbau deutscher Städte." *Baukunst und Werkform* 1 (1947).

Wächter, Klaus. "Martin Wagner." In *Handwörterbuch der Raumforschung und Raumordnung*, 2nd ed. Hannover, 1970.

Wagenmann, E. "Grundlagen zum Deutschen Wohnungsbauprogramm 1945–1980." *Neue Bauwelt* 4 (1949).

Wagner, Bernard. *Martin Wagner 1885–1957: Leben und Werk. Eine biographische Erzählung.* Hamburg, 1985.

——. "More Homes for Germans." *Information Bulletin of the Office of the US High Commissioner for Germany* (December 1951).

Wagner, Martin. "American versus German City Planning." *The Journal of Land and Public Utility Economics* 22 (1946).

——. "Aufbau-Planung contra Trümmer-Planung." *Baurundschau* 38 (1948).

——. "Kapazitäten oder Schwanengesang?" *Baurundschau* 46 (1956).

——. "Maßstab, Mut und Meisterschaft." *Baurundschau* 38 (1948).

———. "Der Neubau der City." *Baurundschau* 38 (1948).

———. "Das neue Berlin." Typescript, Berlin, 1932. (Copy in Bibliothek des Senators für Bau- und Wohnungswesen, Berlin.)

———. "Ein offener Brief Martin Wagners an Karl Bonatz." *Neue Bauwelt* 2 (1947).

———. "Städtebauliche Probleme in amerikanischen Städten und ihre Rückwirkung auf den deutschen Städtebau." Originally published in a special issue of *Der Deutsche Bauzeitung* in 1929, reprinted in part in *Stadtbauwelt* 96 (1987).

———. "Die Utopien der Realisten." *Bauen und Wohnen* 3 (1948).

———. "Vernunft—Perspektiven im Städtebau." *Die Neue Stadt* 4 (1950).

———. "Wurzelprobleme der Aufbaufinanzierung." *Norddeutscher Baublatt*, no. 2 (1950).

———, and Walter Gropius, "The New City Pattern for the People and by the People." In *The Problem of the Cities and the Towns: Conference on Urbanism, Harvard, 5–6 March, 1942*. Cambridge, Mass., 1942.

Walz, Manfred. *Wohnungsbau- und Industrieansiedlungspolitik in Deutschland 1933– 1939*. Frankfurt and New York, 1979.

Wambsganz, Ludwig. "Weg und Ziel einer Erneuerung des Baurechts." *Neue Bauwelt* 2 (1947).

———, and Wilhelm Dittus. "Die Erneuerung unseres Baurechts als Voraussetzung für den Wiederaufbau." *Der Bauhelfer* 3, no. 1 and 2 (1948).

———, Wilhelm Dittus, and Johannes Göderitz. "Das Planungs-, Bau- und Bodenrecht." *Neue Bauwelt* 6 (1951); also in *Amtlicher Katalog der Constructa Bauausstellung 1951*. Hannover, 1951.

Wandersleb, Hermann, and Georg Günthert, eds. *Neue Wohnbau*, vol. 2, *Durchführung von Versuchssiedlungen. Ergebnisse und Erkentnisse für heute und morgen. Von ECA bis Interbau*. Ravensburg, 1958.

Wandersleb, Hermann, and Hans Schoszberger, eds. *Neue Wohnbau*, vol. 1, *Bauplanung*. Ravensburg, 1952.

Wangerin, Gerda, and Gerhard Weiss. *Heinrich Tessenow. Ein Baumeister 1876–1950*. Essen, 1976.

Warfsmann, Gerald. *Enteignung und Eigentumsbildung im Baurecht*. Diss., Georg-August-Universität, Göttingen, 1962.

Webster, Charles, and Noble Frankland, eds. *The Strategic Air Offensive against Germany, 1939–1945*, vol. 4, *Annexes and Appendices*. London, 1961.

Weiss, Marc. "Developing and Financing the 'Garden Metropolis': Urban Planning and Housing Policy in Twentieth Century America." Paper presented at the International Planning History Conference, Bournville, England, September 1989.

Weisser, Gerhard. *Wünsche und Wirklichkeit des sozialen Wohnungsbaues in Westdeutschland*. Schriften des Deutschen Verbandes für Wohnungswesen, Städtebau und Raumplanung, no. 3 (1949).

Werner, Frank. *Stadtplanung Berlin. Theorie und Realität*. Berlin, 1976.

———. *Städtebau Berlin-Ost*. Berlin, 1969.

Westecker, Wilhelm. *Die Wiedergeburt der deutschen Städte*. Düsseldorf, 1962.

Whyte, Iain Boyd. *Bruno Taut and the Architecture of Activism*. Cambridge, 1982.

Wiedenhoeft, Ronald. *Berlin's Housing Revolution. German Reform in the 1920s*. Ann Arbor, Mich., 1985.

———. "Workers' Housing as Social Politics." In Mark A. Hewitt, Benjamin Kracauer, John Massengale, and Michael McDonough, eds., *VIA: Culture and the Social Vision*, vol. 4. Philadelphia, Pa., and Cambridge, Mass., 1980.

Wildermuth, Eberhard. "Begrüßungsansprachen." In *Um die Grundlagen des sozialen Wohnungsbaues: Kundgebung der Gemeinnützigen Wohnungswirtschaft des Landes Nordrhein-Westfalen*. Essen, 1950.

Willrich, Otto. "Ein Beitrag zum Wiederaufbau alter Städte: an dem Beispiel der Stadt Lübeck." *Die Kunstpflege* 2 (1948).

Zechlin, Hans Josef. "Das 'schönere' Berlin." *Neue Bauwelt* 1 (1946).

Zimmermann, H. K. "Der Wiederaufbau der Altstadt in Frankfurt am Main." *Deutsche Kunst- und Denkmalpflege* 11 (1953).

Zinkahn, W. "Das Baulandbeschaffungsgesetz ist verabschiedet." *Blätter für Grundstücks-, Bau- und Wohnungswesen* 2 (1953).

———. "Die gegenwärtige Situation des Baurechts in der Bundesrepublik Deutschland." *Der Aufbau* 8 (1953).

———. (comments on papers read). *Demokratische Stadt- und Landesplanung*. Schriftenreihe der Deutschen Akademie für Städtebau und Landesplanung, vol. 7. Tübingen, 1955.

Zisman, S. B., and Hans Blumenfeld. "Allgemeines über Städteplanung in Deutschland." *Neue Bauwelt* 5 (1950).

Index

Aachen, 61, 157, 191, 202–05, 225
 reconstruction plans, 203–05
 rubble in, 15
 Technical University, 191, 203
Abel, Adolf, 52, 60, 213
Academy of Fine Arts (Berlin), 192
Adenauer, Konrad, 96, 154, 183, 271, 272
Adenauer, Hanna, 96
Adickes, Franz, 222
Adrian, Hanns, 63
Aegidien church (Hannover) as war memorial, 79
Agrippina Insurance Company, 35, 36
Alexanderplatz (Berlin), 194, 195
Allied occupation forces, 9, 14, 22, 32, 41, 42, 54,
  63, 110, 181, 190, 245, 252, 256,
 and Berlin, 191–92, 249
 deindustrialization policy, 190, 202, 244
 denazification policy, 68, 83, 270, 272
 and housing policy, 128, 130, 131, 140
 and organization of reconstruction, 244–51
 use of German construction laborers, 22, 37
 use of undamaged buildings, 16
Alsace-Lorraine, 270
Altona, 162, 164, 208
Altstadt, 67, 73, 77, 88, 92, 95, 97, 126, 156, 197,
  202, 214, 273, 278
 reconstruction plans in Cologne, 198–201
 reconstruction plans in Nuremberg, 83–86
 and traffic planning, 207–10
Altstadt-Wiederaufbaugesellschaft (Cologne), 273
American Commission for the Protection and
  Salvage of Artistic
 and Historic Monuments in Europe, 8
American military government
 and the reconstruction of Munich, 94
 supervision of construction, 39
American occupation zone, 22, 30, 31, 34–35, 248
 damage to architectural monuments, 70
 organization of reconstruction, 246–51
Amt für kriegswichtigen Einsatz (AKE). See
  Hamburg, Amt für kriegswichtigen Einsatz
Ankara, 182

Arbeitsrat für Kunst, 45
Arbeitsstab Wiederaufbauplanung bombenzerstörter
  Städte (Working Staff for the Reconstruction
  Planning of Bombed Cities), 120–22, 170, 172–
  76, 179, 181, 187, 190, 211, 246, 253, 258, 271
Architect, title of, 57
Architects. See also Association of German
  Architects
 licensing of by Allied occupation forces, 57
 organizations, 51, 57
Architectural ideas imported from America, Britain,
  Scandinavia, 56
Architectural monuments, damage to, 70
Architecture
 modern, 45–47
 and politics, 43, 66, 68
 representative, 52
 standardized, 61
 traditional, 48–50
Architektenring Düsseldorf, 211
Area bombing, 7
Arnold, Mack, 143, 325 n. 142
Association of Chambers of Industry and Commerce
  of Northrhine-Westphalia, 31
Association of German Architects, 51, 57, 58, 63,
  102, 142, 255, 257
Association of House and Property Owners
  (Düsseldorf), 232
Aufbaugemeinschaft Bremen, 262
Aufbaugemeinschaft Hannover, 207, 263
Aufbaugenossenschaft Kiel Holtenauer Strasse, 261
Augsburg, 128, 234, 235
Augsburg Chamber of Commerce, 235
Autobahns, 161, 164, 173, 177, 182, 207, 264

Bad-Canstatt, 212
Baden, 126, 231
Baden-Baden, 246
Baden-Württemberg, 143, 183
Bahn, Hans, 74
Bahnhof Zoo (Berlin), 194
Bahnson, Wilhelm, 225

Bährle AG, 35
Bamberg, 290 *n.* 19
Band, Karl, 95, 99, 272, 287 *n.* 3, 305 *n.* 72
Bank for Reconstruction, 284
Barmbeck-Nord (Hamburg), 177
Baroque architecture and planning, 45, 48, 49, 69,
    71, 73, 78, 88, 94, 100, 152, 189, 195
Bartmann, Heinrich, 88, 89, 187, 252
Bartning, Otto, 52, 58, 60, 63, 112, 142
Basic Law, 238
Bauentwurfslehre, 119
Bauer, Carl, 305 *n.* 74
Bauhaus, 45–47, 50, 51, 56, 60, 62, 111, 112, 118,
    123, 183, 300 *n.* 9
Der Bauhelfer, 226
Baukunst und Werkform, 56, 60, 68, 168, 243
Baukunstbeirat (Nuremberg), 84
Baulenkungsgesetz, 41
Baulücken, 283
Der Baumeister, 54, 60
Bauordnungslehre, 119
Bavaria, 21, 39, 57, 58, 74
    building materials, 31–36
    historic preservation, 91, 94
    housing in, 126, 128, 132, 136, 143
    law, 222, 231, 232, 234, 235, 242
    reconstruction organizations, 252, 253, 255, 266
Bavarian Cities Association (Bayerischer
    Städteverband), 233, 235
Bavarian Labor Ministry, 233, 234
Bavarian Mortgage and Exchange Bank (Bayerische
    Hypotheken- und Wechselbank), 234, 237
Bavarian Office for the Administration of State
    Palaces, Gardens, and Lakes, 73
Bavarian Reconstruction Council, 132, 235, 252,
    253, 355
Bavarian State Office for Historic Preservation,
    71
Bayenturm (Cologne), 283
Bayer, Adolf, 196
Bayerischer Aufbaurat. *See* Bavarian
    Reconstruction Council
BDA. *See* Association of German Architects
Behelfsheime. *See* Housing, temporary
Behrens, Peter, 46, 52
Benteler, Heinrich, 89
Berlage, Hans, 259
Berlin, xiii, xv, xvii, xviii, 4, 8, 19, 38, 41, 46, 47, 51,
    53, 54, 63, 66, 72, 117, 122, 124, 142, 149–50,
    152, 154, 162, 163, 167, 181–187, 222, 224, 226,
    229, 231, 234, 236, 237, 246, 274
    Hauptamt für Aufbau/Durchführung, 250
    historic preservation, 74–8
    housing in, 62, 108, 109, 111, 112, 113, 126, 129,
        139, 147, 149–50, 250–51
    planning, 1933–1945, 158–60, 174
    postwar planning, 60, 149–50, 184, 185, 191–95,
        197, 205
    reconstruction organizations, 248, 249, 254
    reconstruction plans, 191–95
    rubble, 14, 15, 22–28

Soviet sector of, 75, 250
    Technical University, 22, 159
    town planning exhibitions, 154, 250
Berlin blockade, 193
    impact on town planning, 250
Berlin Kreuzberg, 109
Berlin Schöneberg, 112
Berliner Allee (Düsseldorf), 206, 211
Beyme, Klaus von, xvii, 55
Birmingham, 199
Bizonia, 33
Black market, 30, 34–36, 41, 131, 250. *See also*
    Building materials
Blanck, Eugen, 77, 190, 272
Blaum, Kurt, 77, 225
Block group of architects, 47
Blumenfeld, Hans, 140, 248, 249, 324 *n.* 130
Blunck, Wilhelm, 240
Blut und Boden (Blood and Soil), 113, 158
Bochum, 11
Boehm, Herbert, 77, 187, 224, 237, 254
Bogner, Walter, 142
Böhm, Dominikus, 305 *n.* 72
Böll, Heinrich, 126, 281
Bolz, Lothar, 194
Bombing campaign agsinst cities, 4–16
    American campaign, 7, 8
    area bombing, 5
    British campaign, 5–7
    casualties, 9, 11
    impressions of bombed cities, xv
    precision bombing, 7
    theory of, 4, 5
    tonnage of bombs dropped, 8
Bonatz, Karl, 41, 184–86, 193–95, 250
Bonatz, Paul, 45–47, 50, 79, 161, 162, 182, 193, 212,
    213, 246, 306 *n.* 84
Bonn, 64, 128
Bormann, Martin, 265
Boston, 183, 186
Böttcher, Karl, 250
Brandenburg Gate (Berlin), 194–95
Braunschweig, 28, 70, 113, 116, 124, 158, 187, 230,
    254, 262
    Technical University, 124
Bremen, 127, 166, 179, 182, 186, 187, 219, 261–63
    housing in, 126, 142, 147
    planning, 1933–1945, 167–68
    rubble, 15, 28
British planning and German reconstruction
    planning, 190, 254
British occupation zone, 31–32, 70, 77, 147, 230,
    245, 251, 274
Building law and illegal building, 41
Building materials, 30–36
    apportionment of in Bizonia, 33
    appropriations by American occupation forces,
        31, 32
    in Berlin, 250
    distribution in Düsseldorf, 40
    production of, 31–33

salvage of, 26–28, 35
shortages of, 30
Building permits and illegal building, 38–41
Bund Deutscher Architekten (BDA). *See*
    Association of German Architects
Bund für Heimatschutz, 49
Bundesrat, 238–39
Bundestag, 237–39
Butler, James, 142, 144, 325 *n.* 142

Center Party, 131
Central Labor Office (Zentralamt für Arbeit), 230, 251
Central Office for the Rebuilding of the City of
    Stuttgart (Zentrale für den Aufbau der Stadt
    Stuttgart, or ZAS), 270–71
Central place planning concepts, 199
Champs Élysées (Paris), 174
Charlottenburg Palace (Berlin), 75, 195
Charter of Athens, 60, 145, 157, 190, 195, 206, 245
Christian Democratic Party, 131
Churches, Catholic and Protestant
    as patrons of architecture, 61
    and the reconstruction of religious buildings, 74
CIAM (International Congresses for Modern
    Architecture), 47, 123, 190
City building offices, 256–58
"City" as planning concept, 92, 172, 176, 192–94,
    197, 212, 250
"City crown," 188, 191
Clay, Lucius, 184, 247, 248
Clemen, Paul, 67, 68
Coal, shortages and production of, 32, 35–36
Coblenz, 246
Coelsfeld, 187
Cologne, xiii, 6, 9, 31, 35–36, 39, 40, 48, 58, 61, 63,
    74, 168, 186, 187, 190, 225, 237, 278, 283
    destruction of, xv
    historic churches, xvii, 96
    historic preservation, 69, 90, 94–100
    historic preservation office, 94
    housing in, 126–30
    Marienburg, 128
    modernization and preservation in, 90, 94–100
    motor vehicle density, 217
    planning by Fritz Schumacher, 154–57
    planning, 1933–1945, 113–15, 160, 171–72
    planning by Joseph Stübben, 155–57
    Planning Corporation (Planungsgesellschaft
        G.m.b.H.), 271
    postwar planning, 197–201, 205, 206, 216, 217
    reconstruction of Catholic churches, xvii, 96
    reconstruction organizations, 256–58, 270–73
    renewal of area around Groß St. Martin's church,
        114–15
    rubble in, xv, 13, 15, 16, 21, 23, 27, 29, 35–36
    Städtebaukonferenz, 256
    Stadtplanungsausschuss, 257
Cologne Chamber of Commerce and Industry, 31
Communist Party, 273
Compensation trading, 35, 36

Competitions
    architectural, 257
    planning, 152, 257
Conseil supérieur d'architecture et d'urbanisme, 246
Consolidation of private property. *See* Private
    property, consolidation of
Constructa Building Exhibition, 62, 147–50, 186,
    237, 263
Construction bans, 227, 231, 232
Construction firms
    in Berlin, 38
    size of, 38
Constructivism, 45
Continental Rubber building (Hannover), 78
Continuities in German urban history, 49, 67, 68, 72,
    90, 91, 99, 147, 216, 221, 244, 256, 259, 274, 280
Cooperative housing, 110–13, 118, 120, 125
Corsten, Hermann, 272
Cramer, Johannes, 64
Cremoninsel (Hamburg), historic preservation of,
    74–75, 79
Curatorium for the Rebuilding of the City of
    Nuremberg, 84, 264
Currency reform, 41, 131, 134
Czechoslovakia, 281

DAF. *See* German Labor Front
Dähn, Arthur, 145, 251
Danzig, 162, 272
Darmstadt, 16, 60, 89, 111, 128, 147, 148, 170, 187,
    275
    Technical University, 89
Darmstadt Exhibition of 1901, 111, 148
Darré, Richard Walter, 51
De Stijl group (Netherlands), 45
Deckert, Hermann, 70, 102
Decongestion of inner cities, 202, 204
Dehio, Georg, 49
Die Dekoration der Gewalt, 44
Denkmalpflege und Heimatschutz, 50
Dessau, 47, 124
Deutsche Akademie für Städtebau, Reichs- und
    Landesplanung, 223
Deutsche Studiengesellschaft für
    Trümmerverwertung, 27
Deutscher Städtetag. *See* German Cities Association
Deutscher Werkbund, xv, 45, 47, 49, 51, 61, 77, 111,
    148, 154
Diedenhofen (Lorraine), 168
Dirks, Walter, 72
Dittus, Wilhelm, 223, 226, 228–31, 234, 236–38,
    240, 241, 254
Döcker, Richard, 60, 61, 71, 83, 168, 183, 246, 270
Dortmund, 14, 15, 126, 127
Douglas, Air Vice-Marshal W. S., 5
Douhet, Guilio, 5
Dresden, 8, 11, 14, 50, 109, 154
Dulsberg (Hamburg), 177
Düren, 126
Durth, Werner, xvi

Düsseldorf, xiii, xviii, 60, 61, 174, 183, 187, 216,
    232, 278
  housing in, 113
  planning, 1933–1945, 175
  postwar planning, 206, 207, 211–12
  rubble, 15, 19, 28
Dustmann, Hanns, 173, 211

East Berlin, 75, 76, 194, 195, 250
East Prussia, reconstruction during World War I, 49,
    119
Eberlein, H. G., 28
Economic Cooperation Administration (ECA), 141–
    44, 249, 326 *n.* 153
Economic Council (Wirtschaftsrat) of Bizonia, 77
Economic Miracle, xviii, 106
Eiermann, Egon, 60, 75, 76, 194
Elbe River, 26, 74, 162–65, 176, 177, 208
Elkart, Karl, 161, 178, 179, 207
Elsässer, Martin, 52, 61, 302 *n.* 42, 306 *n.* 84
Emergency Construction Law (Aufbaunotgesetz),
    232
English town planning law, 227
Equalization of burdens, 136, 282
Erbs, Karl Josef, 205
Erdmannsdorffer, Robert, 83
Erhard, Ludwig, 42
Ermisch, Richard, 193
Ernst-Cassel Foundation (Cologne), 271
ERP (European Recovery Program), 140–42
Essen, 15, 27, 29, 126, 127, 240
Esterer, Rudolf, 50, 73, 91
Europa Center (Berlin), 194
European Recovery Program (ERP), 140–42
Evers, Hans Gerhard, 64
Ewers, Hans, 101
Exhibitions, architectural and planning, 28, 35, 47,
    53, 61–63, 111, 113, 119, 147–49, 154, 186, 192,
    195, 211, 237, 250, 263
Expropriation. *See* Private property, expropriation
    of
Extension planning, 154

Feder, Gottfried, 51, 116, 120, 159, 165, 166
Federal Housing Law of 24 April 1950, 132, 134,
    140, 141, 236–37
Federal Housing Ministry, 134, 140, 143, 251, 252
Federal Republic as patron of architecture, 64
Fegers, Hans, 212
Fehl, Gerhard, 65
Fischer, Helmut, 92, 93, 132, 144, 214, 235, 237,
    252–55, 266, 268–70, 274
Fischer, Wilhelm, 203–05
Fleischer, Michael, 186, 272
Fluchtliniengesetz of 1875 (Prussia), 152
Fluchtliniengesetze, 222
Forbat, Fred, 56
Forced mortgages (Zwangshypothek), 227
Frank, Hartmut, 66, 68
Frankfurt, xv, 17, 21, 47, 60, 61, 64, 74, 94, 123, 154,

    157, 158, 182, 187, 196, 222, 224–26, 237, 249,
    254, 272, 284
  historic preservation, 71, 76, 77–78
  housing in, 111–13, 128
  postwar planning, 184
  rubble, 20, 26, 28, 29
Frauenkirche (Munich), 92, 93
  reconstruction of, 69
Frederickan Forum (Berlin), 194
Free Democratic Party, 131
Freiburg, xviii, 74, 83, 90, 107, 181, 197, 205, 246,
    258, 281
French occupation forces, 197
French occupation zone, 274
  and organization of reconstruction, 245–46
Freudenstadt, 68, 182, 281
Freymuth, Emil, 305 *n.* 72
"Friends of the Old City" (Frankfurt), 78
Friends of the Residenz (Munich), 91
Führer's Decree for the Preparation of German
    Housing Construction after the War (1940), 117
Führerprinzip and town planning, 224
Functionalism, 47, 60–62

Gardens and Garden City Movement, 48, 83, 93,
    109, 111, 112, 120, 123, 124, 149, 152–56, 159,
    165, 166, 190, 198, 199, 202, 223
Garden suburbs, 120
Gedächtniskirche (Berlin). *See* Kaiser Wilhelm
    Memorial Church
Die gegliederte und aufgelockerte Stadt, 123, 149
Gemeinnützige Aktiengesellschaft für Wohnungsbau
    (Cologne), 271
Gemeinnützige Gesellschaft für Trümmerverwertung
    und -beseitigung, 26
Gemeinnützige Heimstätten-Aktiengesellschaft
    (Gehag), 112
Gemeinnützige Wohnungsbau. *See* Cooperative
    housing
Gendarmenmarkt (Berlin), 194
Generalbevollmächtigter für die Regelung der
    Bauwirtschaft (Plenipotentiary for the
    Regulation of the Building Industry), 117–18
Gerling company (Cologne), 58, 129
Gerling, Hans, 128
German Academy for Town and Regional Planning
    (Deutsche Akademie für Städtebau und
    Landesplanung), 73, 205, 226, 229, 240, 254,
    255, 262
German Academy for Town, Reich and Regional
    Planning, 123
German Academy of Building (Deutsche
    Bauakademie), 254
German Academy of Sciences, 248
German Association for Housing, Town and
    Regional Planning (Deutscher Verband für
    Wohnungswesen, Städtebau und
    Landesplanung), 226, 236, 249, 254
German Cities Association (Deutscher Städtetag),
    129, 230, 235, 236, 251, 254

German Democratic Republic, xiii, xix, 195, 281, 283, 284
German Labor Front (Deutsche Arbeitsfront, or DAF), 51–52, 116, 117, 181
architectural projects, 52, 117–19
German national assembly of 1848, 76
Gesellschaft zur Förderung des Wiederaufbaus m.b.H. (Hamburg), 261
Giesler, Hermann, 54, 160, 162, 167, 173, 186, 265
Gilly, Friedrich, 53
Göderitz, Johannes, 123, 124, 148–50, 187, 189, 190, 229, 230, 234, 237, 240, 254, 302 *n*. 42
Goethe house (Frankfurt), reconstruction of, 71–72, 310 *n*. 22
Goethe, Johann Wolfgang von, 276
Goetze, Siegfried, 358 *n*. 27
Görres, Guido, 240
Grapengeter, Andrew, 230, 238
Graubner, Gerhard, 171, 172, 179, 279
Great Depression, 51, 77, 113, 157
Griechenmarkt quarter (Cologne), 199, 201, 273
Grindelhochhäuser (Hamburg), 147
Gropius, Walter, 45–47, 52, 60, 111, 112, 119, 139, 142, 182–86, 211, 248, 284, 305 *n*. 72, 341 *n*. 29
Gropiusstadt (Berlin), 186
Groß St. Martin's church (Cologne), 95, 97, 156
Gruber, Karl, 170, 171
Grund, Peter, 275
Grund-und-Boden Gesellschaft (Cologne), 271
Gürzenich hall (Cologne), 99
Guther, Max, 258
Gutschow, Konstanty, xiii, xiv, xvi, 64, 100, 113, 117, 130, 142, 145, 167–69, 182, 186, 187, 203, 207, 211, 261, 263, 274
and the Arbeitsstab Wiederaufbauplanung bombenzerstörter Städte, 119–23
and the Constructa Building Exhibition, 148–49
and the Neugestaltung plans for Hamburg, 162–66
organizational ideas for Hamburg, 258–60
reconstruction plans for Hamburg, 175–78
Gutschow, Niels, xiii, xiv, 64

Hackelsberger, Christoph, 55, 65
Haering, Kurt, 262
Hagen, 187
Hamburg, xiii, xvi, 3, 37, 48, 53, 78, 79, 91, 100, 101, 107, 109, 148, 154, 155, 162–67, 182–84, 186, 187, 219, 222, 238, 241, 249, 251, 263, 274, 278
air raids on, 6, 7, 10, 11
Amt für kriegswichtigen Einsatz (AKE), 10, 19, 175
building office, 259
historic preservation, 49, 74, 75
housing in, 109, 111–14, 116, 117, 119–22, 126–28, 130, 131, 133, 135, 139, 145, 146, 147
law, 225, 230, 231
planning, 1933–1945, 158–60, 160–62, 171–79
postwar planning, 206–08, 214–21
reconstruction organizations, 258–61

rubble, 13–17, 19, 21, 24, 26, 28
wartime reconstruction planning, 175
wartime repairs and rubble clearance, 19
Hamburg-Dulsberg, rebuilt social housing, 146
Hamburg-Eilbeck, rebuilt social housing, 133
Hamburg-Hamm, 177
Hamburg-Horn, 177
Hamburg-Jarrestadt, 177
Hamburg-Wandsbek, 162
Hamm, Ernst, 246
Hammerbrook (Hamburg), 27, 261
Hanffstengel, Hans von, 173
Hannover, 57, 74, 184, 186, 187, 216, 219, 237, 240, 241, 245, 254, 265, 268, 270, 273, 278
Ballhof theater, 79
historic preservation, 78–80, 83, 101
historic preservation district, 79–80
housing in, 62, 147–49
modernizing reconstruction, 78
planning, 1933–1945, 161, 171, 172, 178–79
postwar planning, 207, 208
reconstruction organizations, 258, 261, 263
Technical University, 171, 207
Hannover Trade Fair, 263
Hansa Viertel (Berlin), xviii, 195
Hansische Hochschule für bildende Künste, 164
Häring, Hugo, 112
Hartog, Rudolf, 60
Haus der Deutschen Kunst, 54
Haussmann, Baron Georges-Eugène, 152, 158, 172
Hauszinssteuer, 111, 113, 136
Hebebrand, Werner, 61, 77, 78, 142, 148, 184, 187
Heilmann, A., 227–28
Heimatschutz, 46, 48–50, 67–69, 73, 100, 101, 107, 121, 122
Hellerau suburb (Dresden), 109, 154
Henrici, Karl, 205
Henselmann, Hermann, 195
Hentrich, Helmut, 187, 305 *n*. 72
Hermann-Göring Works, 168
Hermann-Göring-Stadt, 186
Hermkes, Bernhard, 305 *n*. 72
Hess, Rudolf, 265
Hesse, 231
Hettlage, Karl Maria, 253
Hetzelt, Friedrich, 173, 187
Heuser, Hans, 187
Heuss, Theodor, 148, 150, 309 *n*. 3
High Commission for Germany, 140, 141, 325 *n*. 137
High Commissioner for Germany. *See* McCloy, John
Hilbersheimer, Ludwig, 60
Hildesheim, 13
Hillebrecht, Rudolf, 179, 186, 187, 201, 211, 216, 218, 219, 245, 251, 254, 268, 274, 275
as planner in Hamburg, 19, 122, 163
as planner in Hannover, 148–50, 207–208, 258, 263
Himmler, Heinrich, 95, 168, 174, 265
Historic buildings, new functions for, 69
Historic inner cities. *See* Altstadt

Historic monuments, arguments for restoration or reconstruction of, 69
Historic preservation. *See* Chapter 4
  and the Heimatschutz movement, 73
  laws, 48, 70
  movement, 48
  principles of, 70–74
Historic street patterns in reconstruction planning, 197, 200, 204, 214
Hitler, Adolf, xiv, xvi, 3, 4, 6, 44, 50, 64, 65, 72, 83, 117, 125, 130, 139, 158, 166, 172, 174, 185, 191, 208, 223, 224
  architectural theories, 52–54
  and the Representative Cities Program, 160–63, 212, 213, 225
  "Hochstadt" as planning concept, 199–200
Hoegner, Wilhelm, 93, 234
Hoeltje, Walter, 305 *n.* 72
Hoffmann, Hubert, 55, 123, 124, 149, 189, 190
Hoffmann-Axthelm, Dieter, 55
Högg, Emil, 50
Högg, Hans, 93, 207, 268
Hohenzollern Palace (Berlin), 75, 192, 195, 250
Holtenauer Straße (Kiel), 203, 261
Hoover, Herbert, 247
Hopp, Bernhard, 75
Horse-Shoe Settlement (Berlin-Britz), 112
Hoss, Walter, 58, 168, 187, 212, 213, 270, 271, 274, 306 *n.* 84
House of German Art (Haus der Kunst) (Munich), 53, 94
Housing. *See* Chapter 5; *see also* Social housing
  Bauhaus ideas on, 111
  biological theory of, 123–24, 149
  by modern architects in 1920s, 111
  competition sponsored by ECA/ERP, 141–43
  confiscated by Allied occupation forces, 128
  construction and repair in wartime, 19
  construction by concentration camp inmates, 119
  construction using industrial techniques, 145, 148
  damage to, 108, 125, 126
  financing of, 111, 113, 134–40, 326 *n.* 153
  for miners, 142–43
  in damaged buildings, 130
  modesty in, 149
  National Socialist policy on, 113–25
  and Nazi social engineering, 118
  and the Neugestaltung plans for Hamburg, 165
  and postwar reconstruction planning, 188
  prefabricated, 139
  priorities in assigning occupants to, 129
  repair of damaged units, 121, 130, 134
  shortages after 1945, 130, 132
  standardized, 111, 116, 142, 148
  suburban, 109, 144, 145, 147
  temporary, 119–22, 129, 130–31
  and town planning, 123
  traditional styles, 112–13
  and urban renewal, 109, 110
Howard, Ebenezer, 153, 165, 166

Hull, Cordell, 246
Hundertwasser, Friedensreich, 363 *n.* 9

Illegal building, 37–41
  attempts to prohibit, 40–42
Inflation, 1922–1924, 111
Institute for Building in the Germany Academy of Sciences (Institut für Bauwesen, Deutschen Akademie der Wissenschaften), 248, 254
Interbau. *See* International Building Exhibition
International Association for Housing and City Planning, 254
International Building Exhibition (Interbau), 62, 149, 186, 195
International Congresses for Modern Architecture (CIAM), 47, 123, 190
International Federation for Housing and Town Planning, 249
Internationale Bauausstellung Wiederaufbau Hansaviertel. *See* International Building Exhibition (Interbau)

Jacobs, Jane, xvii
Jaeger, Albert de, 246
Jatho, Carl Oskar, 95, 272, 336 *n.* 70
Jensen, Herbert, 181, 202, 203, 205, 218, 219, 240, 254, 258, 261, 274, 275
Joint Chiefs of Staff Directive 1067, 247–48
Jörg, Richard, 196, 197
Jugendstil movement, 45

Kaiser Wilhelm Memorial Church (Berlin), 75–76, 194, 250
Kameradschaftssiedlung (Berlin-Zehlendorf), 113
Kampfbund deutscher Architekten und Ingenieure, 51, 52, 116
Kärcher, F. W., 237
Karlsruhe, 152, 196
Kärntner Straße (Vienna), 174
Kassel, 15, 158, 175, 179, 309 *n.* 14
Kaufmann, Karl, 159, 163
Kennan, George, 4
Keuerleber, Hugo, 231, 275
Kiel, 28, 29, 181, 202–03, 205, 240, 254, 258, 261, 265
  reconstruction planning, 202–03
Klett, Arnulf, 28, 65, 254, 271
Knipping, Heinrich, 186–87
Koenig, Pierre, 246
Kohlmarkt (Lübeck), 102
Kolb, Walter, 77
Kollektivplan (Berlin), 192–93, 197
Koller, Peter, 159
Kongresshalle (Berlin), 251
Königsallee (Düsseldorf), 174, 211
Königsbau (Stuttgart), 79
Königsplatz (Munich), 94
Konrad-Adenauer-Straße-Neckar Straße (Stuttgart), 212, 216
Kraemer, Friedrich Wilhelm, 149
Kraft, Alfons, 246

Kraus, Emil, 196
Krefeld, 187
Kreuzkirche (Hannover), 78, 79, 149
Krier, Leon, 44, 299 *n.* 5
Kronprinzenpalais (Stuttgart), 82, 83, 212
Kühn, Erich, 183, 191, 230, 252
Kulturbaufond (Munich), 93, 94
Kunstakademie Düsseldorf, 60
Kuphal, Erich, 272
Kurfürstendamm (Berlin), 194
Kuske, Bruno, 272

Labor supply, 36–38
  and illegal building projects, 37
  for construction, 21
  for rubble clearance, 21
  former Nazis, 23
  in the countryside, 37
Lampugnani, Vittorio, 218
Land Procurement Law, 1953
  (Baulandbeschaffungsgesetz), 237, 239–41
Länderrat, 41
Landshut, 128
Lane, Barbara Miller, 43, 46, 47
Langmaack, Gerhard, 260
Laslett, Peter, 277
Lauterburg (Alsace), 68
Law. *See* Chapter 8; *see also* planning law, building
  law, reconstruction law
Law for the Redesign (Neugestaltung) of the
  German Cities, 224
Le Corbusier, Charles Edouard, 47, 60, 182, 189,
  193, 195, 245
Leine Palace (Hannover), 79, 178
Leitenstorfer, Hermann, 91–93, 214, 266, 268
Leitl, Alfons, 71, 168, 190, 219, 243, 257, 279, 284
Lemgo, 230
Lemgo draft. *See* Planning law, Lemgo draft
Leonhardt, Fritz, 305 *n.* 72
Letchworth, 153
Lex Adickes, 222, 226
Ley, Robert, 117–23, 168, 265
Leyden, Karl van der, 203, 204
Liberal party. *See* Free Democratic Party
Liddell Hart, Basil H., 5
Liebknecht, Kurt, 254
Lill, Georg, 71, 91
Linz, 53, 160
Lock, Max, 254
Lods, Marcel, 60, 195–97, 199, 245
London School for Planning Research for Regional
  Development, 254
Lorraine, 168, 198
Lower Saxony, 208, 231, 249
  state government buildings in Hannover, 78
  state theater of, 79
Lübbecke, Friedrich, 78
Lübeck, xv, xvi, 7, 74, 90, 94, 168, 175, 181, 182
  air raid on, 7
  historic preservation, 100–07
  planning, 1933–1945, 170, 171

postwar planning, 207, 208–11
  reconstruction organizations, 256
  reconstruction proposals for, 90, 100–07
  traditional architecture, 100
Lübeckische Nachrichten, 102
Luckhardt, Hans, 52, 148
Luckhardt, Wassili, 52, 148, 305 *n.* 72
Lynch, Kevin, 189

Mäckler, Hermann, 60
Magdeburg, 123, 229
Magnetogorsk, 157
Mahler, Karl, 149
Maier, Charles, 144
Mainz, xiv, 60, 68, 159, 182, 186, 191, 195–97, 205,
  245, 246
  reconstruction planning, 195–97
Mannheim, 5, 128
March, Werner, 162
Marienburg, 199
Marienkirche (Lübeck), 100, 103, 105
Marienplatz (Munich). *See* Munich, Marienplatz
Marktgasse (Kassel), 158
Marktkirche (Hannover), 78, 79, 178
Marshall Plan, xi, xii, xviii, 5, 31, 55, 57, 137–41,
  143, 144, 147, 250, 251
Mast, Paul, 193
May, Ernst, 77, 78, 111, 119, 123, 154, 157, 158, 166,
  182, 275, 302 *n.* 42
McCloy, John, 249
Meffert, Otto, 207
Meitinger, Karl, 92, 187, 213, 214, 265, 266
Merken, Theo, 95
Mertz, Eugen, 270
Metallgesellschaft A.G., 26
Meunier, Franz, 72, 276
Meyer-Ottens, Otto, 75, 183, 184, 208, 219, 260, 261
Michaeliskirche (Hamburg), 214, 215
Mies van der Rohe, Ludwig, 47, 52, 60, 61, 63, 142,
  200
Mietskasernen, xv, 108, 109, 145, 152, 156, 276
Mitchell, Billy, 5
Mitscherlich, Alexander, 241
Modernism, 45, 47, 50–52, 55, 56, 60, 61, 63, 65, 66,
  77, 117, 125, 142, 148, 168, 200
Modernist architecture
  political and social content of, 46
  and reconstruction, 55–66
Modesty in architecture, 63
Moest, Walter, 187, 192, 193
Mönchengladbach, 5
Monson, Donald, 325 *n.* 142
Morgenthau plan, 244
Motor vehicle densities, 204, 216, 217
Mühlenpfordt, Carl, 170–71
Münchner Aufbau G.m.b.H. (MAG), 268
Munich, xi, xii, xiii, 11, 31, 34, 37, 39, 41, 53, 54, 57,
  60, 66, 98, 121, 144, 152, 173, 184, 217, 225,
  237, 257, 284
  construction workers, 37
  historic preservation, 74, 83, 87–90, 107

Munich (*continued*)
  housing in, 113, 126, 128, 132, 134–36, 143
  Friends of the Residenz, 257
  law, 232–35
  Marienplatz, xi, xii, 92, 93, 213, 214
  modernization and preservation in, 90–94
  organizational plan for reconstruction, 267
  planning, 1933–1945, 158, 160, 167
  postwar planning, 206, 207, 213–14, 217
  reconstruction department, organizational plan, 269
  reconstruction of Chinese pagoda in English Garden, 93
  reconstruction organizations, 251–55, 257, 264–70
  rubble, 13–16, 19, 22–24, 26, 27, 29
  Technical University, 213, 268
  traffic planning, 92
Munich Association of German Architects (BDA), 255
Munich Chamber of Commerce, 132, 234, 235, 237
Münster, xiii, 8, 16, 20, 21, 39, 40, 127, 187, 252
  historic preservation, 74, 83, 87–90, 107
  housing in, 126
  postwar planning, 197
  rubble, 23, 27
Münter, Georg, 102, 210
Mustersiedlung Ramersdorf (Munich), 113
Muthesius, Hermann, 153, 154
Muths, Jobst-Hans, 89
Myth of the Twentieth Century, 167

Nachbarschaften (neighborhoods) as planning concept, 177
National Socialism
  housing settlements, 113, 117
  impact on modernist architects and planners, 51
National Socialist architecture, 43, 44, 50–54
Neoclassicism, 44, 50, 53, 54, 58, 63, 64, 66, 163, 206, 279
Neue Bauwelt, 60, 226
Neue Heimat, 182
Die neue Stadt, 159, 165, 226
Neufert, Ernst, 61, 62, 119–22, 148, 173
Neugestaltung plans for Nazi cities, 46, 116, 117, 119–21, 160, 162–65, 167, 170–73, 176, 177, 178, 224, 225
Neumayer, Fritz, 239
Neundörfer, Ludwig, xv
New cities founded by Nazis, 116
"New objectivity," 47
New Palace (Stuttgart), 79
New York City, 284
Niemeyer, Reinhold, 123, 173, 175
Nissen huts. *See* Housing, temporary
Nonn, Konrad, 50–51
Nord-Süd-Fahrt (Cologne), 206, 216
Norddeutsche Echo, 102
Northrhine-Westphalia, 41
Northrhine-Westphalian Ministry for Reconstruction, 252

Nuremberg, xv, 17, 53, 74, 89, 90, 128, 186, 187, 197, 202, 235, 254, 281
  historic preservation, 83–87, 107
  planning, 1933–1945, 160
  reconstruction organizations, 263–65
  rubble, 28
Nuremberg Chamber of Commerce, 235

Oberhausen, 187
Obersalzburg, 265
Offenbach, 197
Old Palace (Stuttgart), 79
Olympic stadium (Berlin), 66
Ordinance concerning measures for clearance of war damage, 20
Organicism in housing and city planning, xv, xviii, 101, 111, 155, 159, 166, 168, 169, 188–90, 199, 203, 206, 219, 226, 239, 275, 279
Organisation Todt, 35, 95, 116, 247, 264
Ortsgruppe (local Nazi party chapter), 166
Ortsgruppe als Siedlungszelle (settlement cell), 120, 165, 166, 179
Ost-West-Straße (Hamburg), 206, 216
Ostermann, Hans, 88
Ostermeyer, Friedrich, 260
Overbeckgesellschaft (Lübeck), 102

Palace of the Republic (Berlin), 195
Paul, Jürgen, 67, 90, 107
Paulick, Richard, 195
Pecks, Eduard, 201
Pedestrian streets or zones, 158, 172, 208
Pehnt, Wolfgang, 55
People's Party, 131
Pepler, George Lionel, 254
Peterskirche (Munich), 92, 93
Petsch, Joachim, 44, 55
Petsch, Wiltrud, 55
Petzold, Erich, 196, 245
Pfister, Rudolf, 54
Pforzheim, 26, 225
Philipp Holzmann A.G., 26
Pieper, Hans, xv, 100–02, 170, 175, 181, 209, 210
Pieper, Klaus, 101
Pingusson, Georges-Henri, 60
Pirath, Carl, 212
Planners, postwar, 182–88
Planning law
  and democracy, 240
  Lemgo draft, 230–32, 234
Planungsgesellschaft (Cologne), 272
Poelzig, Hans, 46, 142, 148, 302 *n.* 42
Poland, 281
Population movements, 11, 16, 127, 134
  and housing, 127, 128
Portsmouth, 254
Preis, Karl Sebastian, 93, 214, 232–35, 251, 265–67
Preservation and Museum Council of Northwest Germany, 70
Prinzipalmarkt (Münster), 88–89
Private property, 152, 194, 202, 203, 212, 216, 229, 238

consolidation of, 225, 227, 263
expropriation of, 223, 227, 230
Prussia, 48, 49, 63, 76, 119, 154, 191
Prussian housing law of 1918, 110, 222
Pünder, Hermann, 96, 271
Putlizt, Erich zu, 162

Quonset huts, 130, 131, 133. *See also* Housing,
    temporary

Railroad construction, 37
Rainer, Roland, 123, 124, 148, 149, 189, 190, 203
Randzio, Ernst, 16, 19
Rappaport, Philipp, 190, 191, 230, 236, 251, 252,
    254, 257
Rave, Wilhelm, 88
Reconstruction
    continuities in, xv, xvi, xvii
    judgment of, 276–78
    as opportunity for renewal, xv
Reconstruction Association Sögestraße (Bremen),
    262
Reconstruction Corporation (Wiederaufbau
    G.m.b.H.) (Cologne), 271–73
Reconstruction law, 225, 231
    of Saxon-Anhalt, 227
Reconstruction planning
    and British models, 190
    in wartime, 167–80
Refugee camps, 130
Refugees, 202, 281
    and housing, 108, 127–28, 134, 246
Regensburg, 33, 34, 128, 290 *n.* 19
Regional planning, 73, 123, 152, 154, 155, 158, 159,
    167, 169, 171, 173, 175, 183, 189–91, 205, 226,
    229, 230, 236, 240, 245, 246, 249, 254, 255, 262
Reich Labor Ministry (Reichsarbeitsministerium),
    117, 223, 226, 229
Reich Office for Regional Planning, 159
Reichow, Hans Bernhard, 142, 159, 166, 169, 178,
    187, 189, 199, 203, 206
Reichsforschungsgesellschaft für Wirtschaftlichkeit
    im Bau- und Wohnungswesen, 119
Reichskammer der bildenden Künste, 56–57
Reichskommissar für den sozialen Wohnungsbau
    (Reich Commissioner for Social Housing), 117,
    118
Reichskommissar für die Festigung deutschen
    Volkstums, 168
Reichskulturkammer, 51, 52
Reichslandschaftsanwalt des Generalinspektors für
    das deutsche Strassenwesen, 264
Reichsleistungsgesetz, 20
Reichsstelle für Raumordnung, 175
Remscheid, 11
Rental barracks. *See* Mietskasernen
Representative architecture, 63, 64
Representative Cities Program, 160–66
Residential suburbs, 188
Residenz (Munich), 69, 91
Retzki, Horst, 305 *n.* 72

Rhein-Beton, 35, 36
Rhine, 48, 61, 160, 196, 198, 204, 211
Rhineland-Pfalz, 231
Ribbon city, 60, 168, 196, 197, 198, 200, 201, 204
Richter, Hans Werner, 13
Riefenstahl, Leni, 83
Riemerschmidt, Richard, 154
Rimpl, Herbert, 52, 142, 159, 168, 173, 186
Ring group of architects, 47, 51, 77, 111
Riphahn, Wilhelm, 52, 272
Roberts Commission, 8
Roberts, Owen, 8
Römer complex (Frankfurt), 77
Rosenberg, Alfred, 167
Rosenberg, Franz, 185, 187, 262
Rostock, 182
Rothenburg ob der Tauber, 310 *n.* 18
Royal Air Force, 9
Rubble, xi, xii, xiv, xvi, xix, xx, 3, 4, 7, 9, 11–16, 34,
    35, 36–38, 43, 65, 71, 72, 130, 144, 147, 169,
    177, 178, 181, 185, 189, 202, 225, 227, 232, 233,
    243, 244, 251, 252, 254, 256, 259, 266, 276, 280,
    282, 283
Rubble clearance, 18–30. *See also* Building
    materials, salvage of
    by former Nazis, 13, 18, 23
    by specially created firms, 26
    by voluntary workers, 23, 24
    by women, 22
Ruhr, 31, 32, 71, 142, 154, 155, 191, 230, 251
Ruins, romanticization of, 3, 4

Saarbrücken, 60, 168, 191, 245
Salzgitter, 159, 186
Saxony, 222
Scharf, Edmund, 88, 89
Scharnagl, Karl, 233, 264, 266
Scharoun, Hans, xv, 49, 60, 112, 142, 147, 183, 184,
    191–94, 197, 199, 248, 249, 250, 254, 270, 302 *n.*
    72, 309 *n.* 3
Schelkes, Willi, 173, 174
Schelling, Erich, 305 *n.* 72
Schinkel, Karl Friedrich, 53
Schleich, Erwin, 94
Schleicher, Gustav, 176
Schleswig-Holstein, 202, 231, 261
    reconstruction law of, 102
Schlippe, Joseph, xviii, 90, 181, 197, 258
Schlüter, Andreas, 75
Schmeissner, Heinz, 83, 84, 90, 186, 187, 254
Schmitt, Hans, 63, 95, 171
Schmitthenner, Paul, 47, 50, 51, 68, 154, 162, 182,
    183, 187, 196, 246, 308 *n.* 3
Schöfer, R. von, 203
Schulte-Frohlinde, Julius, 121, 183, 187
Schultze-Naumburg, Paul, 46–51
Schumacher, Fritz, 52, 68, 71, 75, 119, 159, 162–64,
    166, 182, 219, 223, 225, 264, 266, 332–33 *n.* 42
    planning in Cologne, 48, 155–57, 258
    planning in Hamburg, 112, 162

Schwarz, Rudolf, 58, 60–62, 77, 96, 98, 99, 157, 168, 187, 190, 198, 199, 200, 201, 211, 272–74, 279, 300 *n.* 17, 305 *n.* 72
Schwarz, Max, 171, 172
Schweizer, Otto Ernst, 196, 246
Schweyer, Carl, 272
Schwippert, Hans, 52, 60, 61, 64, 71, 191, 203, 300 *n.* 17
Seidensticker, Wilhelm, 186
Seifert, Alwin, 187, 264, 265
Seifried (Bavarian Labor Minister), 233
Siedlungsverband Ruhrkohlenbezirk, 154, 230, 236, 240
Siedlungszellen (residential settlements), 167
Siemensstadt (Berlin), 112, 183, 191
Sill, Otto, 208
Slum clearance. *See* urban renewal
Social Darwinism and town planning, 153
Social Democratic Party, 110, 131, 132, 229, 230, 273
Social housing, xix, 36, 51, 57, 61, 63, 117–20, 125, 131–36, 139, 141, 146, 147, 150, 165, 182, 202, 237, 264, 271, 280, 281, 283
Social market economy, 42
Soviet occupation zone, 14, 42, 209, 227, 237
Soviet Union, 77, 157, 247
Der Soziale Wohnungsbau in Deutschland, 119
SPD. *See* Social Democratic Party
Speck, Albert 35–36, 297 *n.* 85
Speer, Albert, xiv, 3, 9, 19, 44, 53, 54, 61, 64, 65, 68, 95, 117, 119–22, 148, 160, 162, 167, 170, 172, 173, 175, 181, 186, 192, 211, 224, 228, 271, 274, 289 *n.* 3
Speier, Hans, 14
Spengelin, Friedrich, 56, 106
St. Alban's church (Cologne), 99
St. Paul's Church (Frankfurt) 60, 72, 77
Staaken, 154
Stadt der Reichswerke Hermann Göring AG (City of the Herman Göring Works) (Salzgitter), 116, 159
Stadt des KdF-Wagens (Wolfsburg), 116, 159
Der Städtebau, 153
Stadtlandschaft, 165–67, 171, 178, 188, 192, 203
Stadtweinhaus (Münster), 88–89
Staffelbauordnung, 222
Stähler, Ernst, 344 *n.* 58
Stalinallee (East Berlin), 149, 194, 195
Standardization, 61, 111, 112, 116, 118–22, 125, 143, 148, 254
Standardized housing, 111
Steffann, Emil, 101, 102, 168, 209, 210
Steinhoff (Northrhine-Westphalia Reconstruction Minister), 236
Stephan, Hans, 122, 173, 187
Stettin, 160, 166
Stiftskirche (Stuttgart), 79
Stimson, Henry, 247
Strauss, Gerhard, 72
Strength Through Joy (Kraft-durch-Freude) movement, 116
Strölin, Karl, 114

Stübben, Joseph, 152, 153, 155, 157, 200
Stunde Null, concept of, 65
Stuttgart, xiii, 14, 16, 20, 39, 47, 50, 61, 65, 111, 162, 168, 182–84, 187, 231, 240, 254, 273, 275, 278
    historic preservation, 74, 79, 81–83
    housing in, 113, 114, 130, 144
    planning, 1933–1945, 159, 161, 171, 175
    postwar planning, 206, 207, 212–13, 216
    reconstruction organizations, 270–71
    rubble, 23, 26, 28, 29
    Technical University, 182, 212, 231, 270
    town hall, 58, 59
Suburban Housing Law (Wohnsiedlungsgesetz), 223–24
Süddeutsche Zeitung, 34
Suppert, Fritz, 148
Supreme Constitutional Court, 238, 240, 241

Tamms, Friedrich, 54, 173, 175, 187, 209–11, 216
Taut, Bruno, 45–47, 60, 112, 154, 191, 302 *n.* 42
Taut, Max, 63, 192
Tegeler, Wilhelm, 120
Tessenow, Heinrich, 45, 46, 48, 49, 56, 68, 71, 102, 113, 148, 154, 182, 210, 279, 303 *n.* 53
Thoma, Fritz, 246
Thuringia, 222
Thurn and Taxis Palace, 128
Thurn and Taxis Palace, 128
Tippel, Klaus, 261–62
Todt, Fritz, 116, 117, 264
Town extension planning, 152
Town planning. *See also* Reconstruction planning; Traffic planning
    before 1933, 152–58
    and democracy, 219, 275, 284
    and the Führerprinzip, 224, 237
    guidelines, 168–69, 173–74, 191
    for Nazi occupied Poland, 169
    postwar planning models, 188–90
    Representative Cities Program, 160–66
    and Social Darwinism, 166
    socialist model of, 194–95
    in wartime, 167–69
Traditionalism, 45, 47, 49, 50, 60, 65, 68, 119, 125, 148
Traffic, xi, 70, 73, 75, 78, 79, 84, 88, 96, 100–02, 105, 106, 157, 161, 169, 175, 177, 178, 190, 193, 196–201, 226, 242, 250, 254, 255, 262, 276–78, 280
Traffic planning, 172, 173, 188, 192, 194, 196–201, 204, 205–18
    in Hamburg, 163–64
    in Munich, 92–93
Train stations, 27, 78, 79, 153, 156, 160, 163, 172, 176–79, 200, 201, 203, 206, 208, 212, 213
Tranchard, Lord Hugh, 6
Trier, 246
Triumph of the Will, 83
Troost, Paul Ludwig, 53, 54
Truman, Harry, 247
Trümmer-Verwertungs-Gesellschaft m.b.H., 26

Turkey, 182
Tyrwhitt, Jacqueline, 254

Ulbricht, Walter, 194
Ulm, 258
Umlegungsgesetze, 222
Underground capital, 19
United States policy on housing in Germany, 141
United States 8th Air Force, 9
United States Strategic Bombing Survey, 9
United States, cities in, 284
Unter den Linden (Berlin), 174, 195
Unwin, Raymond, 111, 154
Urban renewal, 109, 113, 114, 116, 152, 155, 158
"Utilitarian building," 55

Vaterstädtische Vereinigung Lübeck, 103
Verein 'Wiederaufbau-Gemeinschaften Stadtmitte
    Bremen', 262
Vereinigung Nordrhein-Westfälischer
    Arbeitgeberverbände, 236
Verhoelzer, Robert, 91
Verordnung über Neuordnungsmaßnahmen zur
    Beseitigung von Kriegsfolgen, 20
Vichy France, 245
Vienna, 76, 123, 124, 152, 174
Vierling (Dr.), 234
Vogts, Hans, 95, 96, 272
Völckers, Otto, 72
Volhoelzer, Robert, 71, 302 *n*. 42
Völkers, Otto, 265
Volkswohnungen, 118

Wagner, Martin, 46, 52, 62, 139, 142, 143, 158, 211,
    222, 284, 302 *n*. 42, 341 *n*. 29
    ideas on reconstruction, 182–86
    as planner in Berlin, 46, 112, 154, 222
Wagner, Bernard, 55, 142, 325 *n*. 142
Wagner, Hans, 118
Wambsganz, Ludwig, 223, 226, 228–30, 234, 237
Wandersleb, Hermann, 143
Warburg, Eric, 290 *n*. 19
Weber, Clemens, 168
Wedler, B., 27
Weimar Republic, 43–44, 46, 58, 65, 68, 110, 117,
119, 131, 136, 144, 145, 147, 151, 158, 182, 227,
    228, 282
    private property and the constitution, 223
Weimar, 45, 51, 72, 160
Weise, E., 101, 209
Weissenhof Siedlung, 47, 50, 111
Welwyn, 153
Werkbund. *See* Deutscher Werkbund
West Berlin, xvii, xviii, 74, 75, 124, 126, 193–95, 250
Wetzel, Heinz, 164, 182
Weyss & Freytag A.G., 26
Wiederherstellungsgebiete (designated
    reconstruction areas), 177
Wiesbaden, 186
Wildermuth, Eberhard, 132, 148, 236, 238, 239
Wilhelmshaven, 175, 179
Wittausch, William, 325 *n*. 142
Wimmer, Thomas, 235
Der Wohnungsbau in Deutschland, 119
Wolfsburg, 159, 164
Wolters, Rudolf, 121, 122, 172–74, 187
Working Association for City Planning
    (Arbeitsgemeinschaft für Stadtplanung)
    (Bremen), 262
Working Staff for Reconstruction Planning of
    Destroyed Cities. *See* Arbeitsstab
    Wiederaufbauplanung bombenzerstörter Städte
Wortmann, Wilhelm, 148, 166, 167, 169, 174, 178,
    179, 182, 186, 187, 261–63, 274
Wriezen, 122, 174, 175
Wuppertal, 11, 187
Württemberg, 231
    state policy on modernization of Stuttgart, 79
Würzburg, xiii, 11, 39, 126, 235
Würzburg Chamber of Commerce, 235

ZAS. *See* Central Office for the Rebuilding of the
    City of Stuttgart
Zechlin, Hans Josef, 192
Zehlendorf plan (Berlin), 192–93
Ziebill, Otto, 263
Zinsser, Ernst, 176
Zisman, Samuel, 140, 248, 249
Zonenbeirat, 230